6.50

D1266564

EPISTEMOLOGY

NYACK COLLEGE MANHATTAN

Christian Wisdom Series

EDITORIAL BOARD

Vernon J. Bourke, *Chairman*
Professor of Philosophy, St. Louis University

Anton C. Pegis, F.R.S.C.
Professor, Pontifical Institute of Mediaeval Studies, Toronto, Canada

Gerald B. Phelan, F.R.S.C.
Professor of Philosophy, St. Michael's College, Toronto, Canada

Gerard Smith, S.J.
Director of the Department of Philosophy, Marquette University

ETHICS—*A Textbook in Moral Philosophy*
by VERNON J. BOURKE

. .
.

NATURAL THEOLOGY—*Metaphysics II*
by GERARD SMITH, S.J.

. .
.

EPISTEMOLOGY
by L.M. RÉGIS, O.P.
translated by Imelda Choquette Byrne

. .
.

NCMC

BD
162
.R413

EPISTEMOLOGY

L.M. RÉGIS, O.P.

University of Montreal

Translated by Imelda Choquette Byrne

NEW YORK

The Macmillan Company

NYACK COLLEGE MANHATTAN

598650

NIHIL OBSTAT:

    Albert-Marie Landry, O.P.

    Louis-Bertrand Geiger, O.P.

IMPRIMI POTEST:

    Thomas-Marie Rondeau, O.P.,

      PROVINCIAL, PROVINCE OF SAINT DOMINIC.

IMPRIMATUR:

    Paul Touchette, P.A.,

      VICAR GENERAL, ARCHDIOCESE OF MONTREAL.

DATED DECEMBER 18, 1958.

© THE MACMILLAN COMPANY 1959

All rights reserved—no part of this book may be reproduced in any form without permission in writing from the publisher, except by a reviewer who wishes to quote brief passages in connection with a review written for inclusion in magazine or newspaper.

First Printing

Library of Congress catalog card number: 59-5099

The Macmillan Company, New York
Brett-Macmillan Ltd., Galt, Ontario

PRINTED IN THE UNITED STATES OF AMERICA

ACKNOWLEDGMENTS

Aquinas, St. Thomas, *The Division and Methods of the Sciences* (Questions V and VI of his "Commentary on the *De Trinitate* of Boethius), translated by Armand Maurer, C.S.B. (Toronto, The Pontifical Institute of Mediaeval Studies, 1953). Courtesy The Pontifical Institute of Mediaeval Studies.

———, *Truth,* translated by Robert W. Mulligan, S.J., James V. McGlynn, S.J., and Robert W. Schmidt, S.J. (Chicago, Henry Regnery Company, 1952–54), 3 vols. Copyright 1952–54 by Henry Regnery Company. Courtesy Henry Regnery Company, Publishers.

Eddington, Sir Arthur, *New Pathways in Science* (Cambridge, University Press, 1935). Courtesy the University Press.

———, *The Philosophy of Physical Science* (Cambridge, University Press, 1939). Courtesy the University Press.

Jeans, Sir James, *Physics and Philosophy* (Cambridge, University Press, 1942). Courtesy the University Press.

Kant, Emmanuel, *Critique of Pure Reason* (London, Macmillan, Ltd., 1902), edited by Norman Kemp Smith. Courtesy St. Martin's Press, Incorporated, N. Y.

Pegis, Anton C., F.R.S.C., *The Basic Writings of St. Thomas* (New York, Random House, 1948), 2 vols. Copyright 1945 by Random House, Inc. Courtesy the author and publisher.

FOREWORD

The purpose of this volume is to provide students of philosophy and their teachers with a monograph on the epistemological problem and its solution in the synthesis of St. Thomas Aquinas that will treat the subject as fully as possible. Its internal organization is dictated by the difficulties peculiar to this area of philosophy, as well as by the pedagogical obstacles encountered by teachers in presenting such a thorny problem to their students. We perceive clearly and not without trepidation the dangers involved in such an undertaking, which would seem to be seeking to reconcile the irreconcilable. A textbook is designed for students and should be concise and diagrammatic, since their time is limited by the other subjects they must master. But the problem whose study we are undertaking requires a detailed and comprehensive analysis of the doctrines involved; it eschews those artificial simplifications and shortcuts which tend to give only an outline of non-Scholastic systems, an outline that drains them of doctrinal substance and reduces them to a collection of contradictories easily refutable by a polysyllogism in *barbara*, giving the impression that the thinkers refuted are not only wrong but have I.Q.'s well below average. We have tried to avoid this pitfall, but no one is more conscious than the author of the imperfect nature of the result. It is the author's twenty years of long and painful experience as a student, older student, and then teacher, as well as the hope of making a contribution toward the presentation of Thomistic epistemology, that have encouraged him to offer this work, despite its lacunae, to the student public now, rather than indulge his desire to go on indefinitely trying to perfect it.

The plan of the book is simple: it flows from the internal exigencies of the subject. Epistemology is that part of philosophy which studies the mystery of knowledge and the properties proceeding therefrom: namely, truth and its characteristics of infallibility or probability.[1] For more than three hundred years philosophical thought has emphasized this problem. For over one hundred years Scholastic philosophy has made it the object of innumerable discussions, of infinite and irreducible controversies whose net result is complete ignorance of the meaning and nature of an epistemological treatise in Thomistic philosophy. Here is the verdict with which a historian of this problem concludes a long and detailed analysis of the works that have appeared on the subject since 1846: "Today, after one hundred years of effort, we have acquired a genuine historical knowledge of St. Thomas . . . we have a logic, a metaphysics, a cosmology, a psychology, and an ethics. . . . But there remains one discipline whose status has not yet been established. This is epistemology. . . . *Today we are still discussing its object and its methods, the problems it entails, and its place in a systematic philosophy; even its name is not universally accepted.*"[2] This judgment makes clear the chaotic situation of the subject we are going to explore, and the absolute impossibility of starting to deal with the position and solution of the epistemological problem without a preliminary and precise statement of the exact meaning of the question we must answer. An answer is always governed by the content of the question asked.

The first part of this book will therefore be entirely concerned with an elucidation of the epistemological problem itself, according to the different philosophical contexts in which it has been stated. This part will have a cathartic function: to rid the mind of the confusion that presently envelopes the whole field of epistemology and prevents us from seeing its true nature and its rightful place within a philosophical synthesis. Once the problem has been stated and understood, we shall study the solution given by St. Thomas in the ensemble of his works; this will be the subject matter of the three succeeding parts. Their general approach will not be that of an apologetic for the Thomistic noetic, but an attempt at the clearest possible exposition of a synthesis whose admirable unity, depth of analysis, and probity of observation leave nothing to be envied in the methods of Descartes and Kant.

Such is the plan of the work. Its material is arranged so as to make easier the work of both student and teacher. The main text is primarily meant for students and is intended to be complete in itself, by means of numerous explicit quotations in the reader's own language and the explanations accompanying these texts. The numerous references to sources and works upon the subjects in question are directed especially toward teachers, to help them give more depth to their treatment and to substantiate the points of view adopted or criticized.

L.M. Régis, O.P.

TABLE OF CONTENTS

xi

Part Four

WHAT IS THE KNOWLEDGE OF INFALLIBLE TRUTH?

EPISTEMOLOGY

Part One

THE EPISTEMOLOGICAL PROBLEM

PROLOGUE

The history of philosophy is often compared to a great cemetery in which tombstones succeed each other in awful continuity and, with their *Hic jacet*, write the many chapters of a sad encyclopedia —an encyclopedia of man's repeated but always insufficient efforts to attain truth. Instead of this pessimistic simile, I prefer that of a maternity ward wherein the intellect, always in gestation, is periodically delivered of a theory which to all outer appearances is newborn, but whose internal structure reveals a heredity that makes it contemporaneous with the very origins of philosophical speculation. That is why the history of philosophy is much more a history of birth and rebirth than one of death—a genealogy more than a necrology. Our intellect needs time in which to progress, and time, bearer of old age and death to material life, becomes an agent of rejuvenation to the life of the mind.[1]

The problem that we are now about to tackle is a brilliant confirmation of the thesis just stated. Officially, its birth is dated 1637, at the printing shop of Jean Maire in Leyden; its father is René Descartes, who gave it the name *Discourse on Method* and assigned it a very definite vocation—to teach man "to reason well and to seek for truth in the sciences." Unofficially, our problem is much older than the published date of its birth would lead us to suspect, and the baptismal name given it by Descartes is only one of the many terms applied to it by thinkers of all ages. We might even say that its name is Legion and that the history of its pseudonyms would furnish material for a large volume.[2] Not only is its name legion, but so are the guises under which it appears; its art of camouflage, of being visible or invisible, of revealing itself or escaping notice, would fill the wiliest chameleon with envy.

All these considerations should serve to fill us with the greatest circumspection about approaching this offspring of the human intellect, offspring that so clearly reveals its parent's poverty, for it is truly poverty's child and proof of our indigence. However, like Cinderella in the fairy story, this poor child, born of an intellect dependent upon the senses, can sometimes appear to us richly clad and ruling over all of the other offspring of our intellect, graciously granting or disdainfully refusing their claims to legitimacy on the pretext of its being officially commissioned to keep an eye on the intellect's integrity and to make note of any infidelities of which she might be guilty in procreating her various types of knowledge.

To grasp the true nature of this bizarre and capricious character, therefore, we must never lose sight of it, must observe each of its successive births, must from the outset expose its high and mighty airs, in order for us not to be imposed upon by the increasingly dictatorial bearing that it assumes in the course of its evolution. Otherwise, we are in danger of confusing that which makes up the wealth of our intellectual life with the proofs of its poverty, and of deposing wisdom only to place epistemology upon the throne of truth.[3]

Now, the only infallible way to remove every possibility of evasion and dissimulation from this subtle individual is to examine it as a problem before trying to find out what characterizes it as epistemological. For just as we cannot strictly define *a* being without previously having the notion of *being as being*, so the notion of *this problem* that is epistemology cannot truly be understood unless we first know what constitutes a problem *as such*.

The initial chapter of this first part will therefore be devoted to studying what a problem is as problem, the laws governing its birth in our mind, and the psychological reaction to which it inevitably gives rise. Once we know the characteristics common to every problem as such, we can then study one of its concretions, i.e., the characteristics peculiar to an epistemological problem. This will be the subject matter of the next three chapters. The second chapter will treat of the modern epistemological problem, since the modern age officially gave it birth. In the third chapter we shall consider that curious phenomenon, the Neo-Scholastic problem, which plunges roots deep into idealist methods, yet which finds its completion in the realistic metaphysics of St. Thomas.

Once we have seen the difficulties raised by the modern and Neo-Scholastic problem, it will be that much easier for us to grasp the philosophical method suited to the Thomistic synthesis, because we will have a deeper appreciation of the different aspects hidden behind the expression "epistemological problem." The study of the Thomistic method will be the subject of a fourth chapter, which will bring this first part to a close and give us the necessary equipment to study and understand the solution brought to the problem by St. Thomas—a solution to which the three remaining parts of this book will be devoted.

I · THE GENESIS OF A PROBLEM

[handwritten notes: - Birth of it] - REACTIONS in the SOUL {Wonder... Shock... fear of Ignorance...}

The aim of this chapter is to discover the circumstances that surround the creation of a problem and inevitably condition its birth and development. To help us in carrying out this investigation, we have at our disposal the immensely rich material provided by Western thought in the realm of philosophy and science. We will continually draw upon this treasure, choosing the situations that most typically reveal the nature of a problem as such. Despite the necessarily sketchy and selective character of such an analysis, we hope that the factors essential to the birth and development of a problem will progressively emerge and give us the sole fundamental datum absolutely necessary for understanding the epistemological problem we are going to study in the next three chapters. This first chapter divides naturally into the two aspects that every problem presents: a first section will deal with the universal laws governing the problem's birth; the second will analyze what goes on in the human soul when a problem germinates and develops there, in order to discover the structure of the psychological reactions common to every human being faced with a problem.

Section I: The Birth of a Problem and the Conditions of Its Existence *[handwritten: 2 stories]*

As a conscious being I am involved in a story. The perceiving part of my mind tells me a story of a world around me. The story tells of familiar objects. It tells of colours, sounds, scents belonging to these objects; of boundless space in which they have their existence, and of an over-rolling stream of time bringing change and incident. . . .

As a scientist I have become mistrustful of this story. In many instances it has become clear that things are not what they seem to be. According to the story teller I have now in front of me a substantial desk; but I have learned from physics that the desk is not at all the continuous substance that it is supposed to be in the story. It is a host of tiny electric charges darting hither and thither with inconceivable velocity. Instead of being solid substance my desk is more like a swarm of gnats. . . .

At one time there was no profound difference between the two versions. The scientist accepted the familiar story in its main outline; only he corrected a few facts here and there, and elaborated a few details. But latterly the familiar story and the scientific story have diverged more and more widely—until it has become hard to recognize that they have anything in common.[1]

Once it has been divested of its particularizing characteristics, that is, the popular and scientific character of the two storytellers, this text of Sir Arthur Eddington clearly reveals the universal law governing the existence of every problem. In the mind there must be two storytellers, who must each tell different stories about the same fact or the same universe. As long as there is but one narrator there is no problem. Neither is there a real problem when there are several storytellers whose stories agree.[2] Only when there is a coexistence in the mind of two storytellers giving divergent accounts does a problem develop. Suppress the duality of the mind's contents and the divergence of their stories, and the problem disappears.

The history of Western thought reveals a great deal about this subject. We will be content to glean some samples, here and there, of the best-known problems, so that we may judge for ourselves the truth of this statement: the emergence of a problem is inevitably conditioned by the coexistence in one soul of a duality of stories that seem contradictory. We may begin our rapid inquiry at the very cradle of Western thought, with the Greeks. We see that as long as there exists in the Greek mind only the theogonic and cosmogonic universe described by Homer and Hesiod[3] there is no problem. This universe is made up of different, juxtaposed parts. Its origin is mysterious, it is loved, feared, admired, adored, but accepted as given, and its enchanting poetry sometimes makes us forget that for centuries it was a real world for a multitude of human beings who never perceived its inherent contradictions, because they had no other universe with which to compare or oppose it. There was only one storyteller and a single story. But as soon as keen-minded thinkers start to reflect, as soon as they try to explain the three outstanding facts in this universe of immediate perception —namely, motion, the multiplicity that motion implies, and order among the different phenomena—as soon as they attempt to give a cosmological explanation of reality and try to bring into it the first law of the mind, its need for unity, then a universe other than that of the cosmogonies springs up in the human consciousness. There are now two storytellers in the human mind and two different stories. From this opposition arises the first philosophical problem, attested by the fragments we possess of the writings of Heraclitus and Parmenides: How can one same cosmos be accounted for in terms of stability and instability, immutability and mutability, temporality and eternity?[4]

Some six centuries pass and an analogous experience is repeated in a wholly different order but under similar conditions. With the advent of Christianity, which introduces the biblical universe into the Graeco-Roman world, Christian thinkers are faced with two stories so opposed as to seem irreconcilable. The Greek storyteller confronts the intellect with a universe that is necessary, immutable in its structure, eternal in its existence, and closed upon itself, because divinity has nothing to do with such a universe.[5] The Christian narrator, on the contrary, tells of a created world, whose structure and existence are totally dependent upon the liberty of its Creator, Who is simultaneously its Father and its Providence, and with Whom the storyteller maintains constant relations, since he came from Him and will return to Him. Such are the two stories the intellect continually hears, one told by Christian Wisdom, the other by pagan or Hellenic Wisdom, which are the source of the intellect's question: Are both of these universes true? Can the universe of reason be different from that of faith? Is there a double truth? This is the hard and thorny problem of the relations between reason and faith that Augustinian thought and the medieval Augustinians tried ceaselessly to resolve.[6]

A thousand years pass, during which the Christian world becomes the universe of Christianized Europe. The essential data of this universe have become part of the common heritage, as much in its philosophical as in its theological aspects. Everyone is part of it in varying degrees, the educated as well as the uneducated, to such an extent that it seems to have become the universe of immediate perception, or, as we would say today, the universe of common sense. But now science is reaching maturity, it develops new methods of observation, it invents instruments of verification and avidly sets out to examine the secrets of nature. Slowly there comes into existence a scientific universe whose nature and laws seem wholly opposed to the substantial and qualitative structures of the Christian world, which are now replaced by mechanistic or dynamic relationships within a cosmos dominated by the laws of quantity. For a third time two storytellers confront each other in the human soul, two divergent stories beget the modern problem of the relations among science, philosophy, and Christian faith.[7]

Approximately two hundred years after this encounter between the universe of philosophy and that of science, the latter (which, until then, had ruled as undisputed master in its domain) suddenly witnesses the rise of another scientific universe whose structure and laws seem contradictory to its own. According to the teller of the classical story, the universe has the three geometrical dimensions of Euclid, is measured by the arithmetic of Pythagoras, organized in the absolute space and time of Newton and according to an absolutely determined causal mechanism.[8] Against this classical universe, contemporary science sets up another that discards all these fundamental data and for them substitutes Riemann's geometry, quantic or non-Pythagorean number, and the indeterminism of Bohr. Newton's cosmos is displaced by that of Einstein.[9] Thus, the scientist himself is confronted with two far-from-homogeneous accounts. This in turn becomes the contemporary scientific problem: Which of these two universes is the true one? Are they both true?[10]

Were we to fill in all the details of this outline, we could call the result "The History of Western Thought from the Fifth Century B.C. to 1950 A.D." But despite its abridgment, so impoverishing to the life of ideas, this outline suffices to show that the genesis of a problem in any field whatsoever must entail a conflict within the human mind, a conflict that exists whenever the universe gives two seemingly irreconcilable accounts of itself, or, to say the same thing in another way, when our mind tells itself two stories pretending to apply to the same physical universe, but which are so divergent that the mind feels momentarily impotent to reconcile them or to judge their truth or falsity. Such, in very general terms, is the description of the laws governing the genesis of a problem as problem.

Section II: The Structure of Psychological Reactions

The first phase of our inquiry has shown us the objective factors that give rise to a problem in the soul. However, it has told us nothing about its psychological nature, because to note that the intellect cannot tolerate the coexistence within itself of two contradictory accounts tells us nothing about what happens in our mind, or the reason why we cannot abide contradictories. We must therefore pursue the analysis further and seek out the nature of the psychological reactions caused by the genesis of a problem; therein we shall discover its true nature. Two questions naturally occur to the mind once the general laws governing the genesis of a problem have been established. The first may be formulated as follows: What attitude does a man adopt when he is confronted with two contradictory narratives; what are his spontaneous psychological reactions? Once this question has been answered, a second necessarily arises: Why does man react in this way? What inner structural laws make contradiction intolerable to him and beget a whole train of steps to get rid of it? The answer to these two questions will reveal the true nature of a problem as such. Then we shall be able to apply this knowledge to the particular problem that gives rise to epistemology.

A. WHAT PSYCHOLOGICAL REACTIONS ARE CAUSED BY CONTRADICTORY STORIES?

The psychological reactions of a man confronted with two contradictory universes are comparable to the shock felt by the host who, having extended hospitality to two of his best friends, discovers that from the moment of their arrival his guests annoy each other, call each other liar and ignoramus, and bitterly reproach him for forcing them to eat the same foods when their tastes are different, to live under the same roof when they find the very sight of each other offensive and their stories mutually antinomic. Not expecting any such wrangling, their host can only be astounded and hurt by their attitude, and his first concern would be an attempt to pacify them; he would try to re-establish harmony between his two friends. Failing this, he would agree to the departure of one or the other of his guests, or to the departure of both if they prove unbearable. Now, that is exactly the soul's situation in the presence of a problem, of contradiction between the accounts that reality gives of itself. Its first reaction is one of shocked surprise, and this shock produces an active effort to reconcile these divergent stories, if possible. Philosophers and scientists have given to this psychological shock the name *wonder*, and to the act of endeavoring to dispel this shock, the terms *inquiry*, *research*, *investigation*, and other similar names. We shall now study the two aspects of this psychological reaction.

¶ *1. Shock or Wonder: First Psychological Reaction.* Plato is the first to give a name to this human attitude when, in the *Theaetetus*,[11] he states that "the feeling of wonder belongs peculiarly to philosophers; philosophy has no other source." When Aristotle takes up his teacher's theme and develops it, he assigns to it the value of a universal principle for explaining the origins of philosophical speculation and its progress through the ages: "It is wonder which attracted the first, as well as today's, thinkers to philosophical speculation. At first, the most obvious difficulties aroused their wonder, but soon the difficulties became greater and so did their wonder. . . .

Now to see a difficulty and to wonder at it, is to admit one's ignorance."[12] Similar statements are to be found in Christian thinkers, in the theologians of the Middle Ages, and especially St. Thomas.[13] Modern thinkers, who agree so rarely with the ancients, do not hesitate to make wonder the "soul of philosophy," as Descartes says,[14] or the "most important factor in the progress of the sciences."[15]

Since, according to thinkers, wonder is so fruitful and describes the soul's state in the presence of a real problem, it merits close examination; for it provides us with the first subjective or psychological characteristic of the reality we are investigating. Furthermore, because wonder seems to have affinities with *doubt* and thereby appears wholly modern, it should be examined all the more closely. Therefore, we shall study the word used by different philosophers to describe wonder, and the notions these words contain, in order to acquire a precise idea of the reality they express.

The word wonder *and its Greek and Latin equivalents.* Derived from auditory experience, from the frightening noise we call thunder (*F. tonnerre*),[16] the French word for wonder (*étonnement*) is an exact translation of the Latin *admiratio*[17] and the Greek *thaumadzein,* and it has kept their general meaning of psychological tension in the face of the extraordinary, the prodigious, the unusual.[18] It expresses an emotive reaction consequent upon an unusual or unaccustomed object of knowledge. Thus, it signifies that man is no longer listening to his familiar narrator, that another has replaced him, and that what he narrates is of the order of the marvelous.

The notion of wonder. By a simple definition of words, we have just seen that wonder, when analyzed, has a twofold aspect: the extraordinary or unusual character of the thing known, and man's emotive reaction in his awareness of this object. In other words, there are the *wonderful* and *wonder.* How is the wonderful analyzed by philosophers?

The wonderful, admirabile, *or* mirum. The *wonderful* displays an interesting gnosiological duality: it is composed of *knowledge* and *ignorance.*[19] Let us try to relive Parmenides' state of mind when, in a flash of intuition, he perceived the absolute necessity of the unity of being. He already had in his mind the universe of his childhood, the everyday universe filled with movement, instability, and multiplicity that he experienced daily. But now, while this universe remained in his mind, there sprang up another, opposed in every way to the former. Thus, he had experimental knowledge of the coexistence of these two universes in his soul, but he did not know how or if they could be reconciled. Whence the many questions, he had to ask himself: Where does this duality come from? What is its source, myself or reality?

Similarly, when Augustine considers the Greek Neo-Platonic world that he has studied, whose harmony he has admired, and at the same time this same world that his Faith has told him is bruised by sin, plunged into the contingency of creation, but on the other hand is bound to God by His ineffable love, he can only ask himself: Whence comes this Greek universe discovered by human wisdom and so unlike the universe revealed by divine Wisdom? He knows that the world of faith is true, but he does not know whether this truth can be reconciled with the truth of the Greek world. And when the Christian Averroists of the thirteenth century, accustomed to the Neo-Platonic world Christianized by St. Augustine, were confronted with the Aristotelian universe of which God knows nothing and to which He is wholly indifferent, their knowledge of these two worlds and their ignorance of how to reconcile them led them to invent the famous theory of the double truth,[20] the one fed by faith, the other nourished by reason. It is evident how, in these thinkers, wonder corresponds to a mixture of knowledge and ignorance.

When Descartes perceives that scientific truth is evident and that philosophical constructs are not, he wonders at this duality, because he does not know why there coexists in the soul this double image of reality, one aspect of which is true, the other false. The same is the case for Kant (as we shall see at length in the next chapter) and contemporary scientists.

The wonderful can therefore be defined or described as *a dual image or idea of a reality that is given as one, and ignorance of the source of this duality*. Thus, there is, in the wonderful, a marriage of intelligibility and unintelligibility, the intelligibility having to do with the existential opposition between two narratives and the evidence on which they rest, and the unintelligibility being concerned with the *cause* or *reason* of this opposition—which escapes us.

Wonder or admiratio. What is the nature of this psychological state? Does it belong to the order of knowledge or to the order of emotivity? We would be inclined to attribute it to knowledge, since it is by and in knowledge that it comes into being. But we must not forget that the emotive order depends upon cognitive experience, and that it is not contradictory that wonder belong to the emotive order even if it should enter through knowledge. St. Thomas and Descartes describe it as a passion.[21] Now, even though the classical arrangement of the eleven passions divided into two groups (six concupiscible and five irascible[22]) is no longer integrally accepted by modern psychology, yet the latter admits the existence of two complementary emotive aspects, love and aggressiveness, whose general characteristics are equivalent to the Scholastic division. In which division does wonder belong?

St. Thomas classifies it as irascible, for it is *fear*[23] and therefore a psychological reaction of revulsion in the presence of evil,[24] and an evil difficult to avoid. This evil that wonder fears can only be ignorance, which is one of the constitutive elements of the *admirabile;* it is the unintelligibility necessarily accompanying every contradiction that the mind cannot dispel either by excluding one of the divergent narratives or by discovering the reason why these accounts diverge.

Ignorance, the proper object of this fear that is wonder, is not *nescientia*, because nescience is unconscious[25] since it consists in a complete absence of knowledge and can consequently be neither experienced nor the cause of an emotive reaction. The ignorance connected with fear is partial—the intellect's inability to see why two accounts are incompossible when each of them seems to be comprehensible and to contain elements of truth. The narrator familiar to Parmenides, describing a world given over to motion and multiplicity, told of a plausible universe; but, along with this plausible story, Parmenides could hear another, contradicting the first and offering as much or even more plausibility. Yet, he could not perceive any point of contact between these two accounts, or under-

stand why they were opposed. He did not know, he feared this ignorance or absence of truth as one fears evil.

➤ ¶ *2. Wonder, or* Admiratio, *as Principle of Research or Inquiry.* Despair is a paralyzing and passive suffering, and the
suffering entailed by anger is blind and vengeful,[26] but fear is filled
with the hope[27] of ridding itself of the evil causing it to suffer in
order to replace it by the good of which this evil is the privation.
Since wonder is fear and suffers through the presence of ignorance,
it immediately begets an effort to put an end to this evil, therefore to
dispel ignorance. This is what Plato, Aristotle, Descartes, and others
mean when they describe wonder as a source of inquiry or investigation and the most effective factor for progress.[28] This inquiry
normally starts with the cause of wonder, that is, with the *wonderful*
or *admirabile,* inasmuch as it is simultaneously made up of intelligibility and unintelligibility. What is the intellect's attitude toward
these two accounts?

Going back to our analogy of the host and his two quarreling
guests,[29] there are three possible solutions: 1) If the host is really
fond of both guests, he will first try to reconcile and pacify them:
he will try to find some common ground for agreement; 2) If this
first attempt fails, he can put out the guest who seems more particularly insolent and unjust; 3) If he can neither re-establish harmony
nor discern which guest is right, the radical solution is to put them
both out of the house. Very well, the history of philosophy shows
us that these three alternatives have been successively experienced by
humanity through the ages, and that wonder has always been the
principle of quests for harmony, which, when successful, have endowed humanity with the admirable syntheses we call Platonism,
Aristotelianism, Augustinism in its various forms, and Thomism.
When no accord has been reached between the two contradictory
narratives, thinkers have put one of them out, and we have the
unilateral systems of Heraclitus, Parmenides, Euclid, the Megarics,
Antisthenes,[30] Descartes, Kant, and the most representative among
our contemporaries, the panmathematicism of Léon Brunschvicg.[31]
Finally, if man can accept neither of the accounts as valid, he can
remain in expectancy and wait for the light to dawn, and this is

doubt. Or he can lose all hope of ever finding the reason for their opposition, and this is skepticism, which is nothing but intellectual despair in regard to the problem of truth.

Since there is a certain order in man's attitude toward a problem, that is to say, in the fight against the ignorance that enters into wonder, since his first step is a conciliatory attempt to discover common ground or distinct, but noncontradictory, points of view, and since this step precedes all others that follow only if the first attempt fails, we should take a quick look at the way in which the quest for peace of mind is organized.

Inquiry's point of departure is wonder, that is, the coexistence in the soul of two universes known to be opposed to each other, both of which claim to refer to the same reality. How is this inquiry possible? There is only one way to solve the difficulty, and that is to inquire into the structure of the two universes *as known* and into that of the *real* universe, in order to discover whether the first two can be correlated. It will be objected that the real universe escapes experience and can only enter by means of knowledge into the parallel to be set up, and that this constitutes a sort of vicious circle! There certainly is a circle here, but that it is vicious is a statement standing in need of proof, for a circle is vicious only if it results from an intellectual fraud, from a latent or overt sophism. Now, there is a world of difference between the universe *as known* and the real universe *when known*. In the first case the universe is considered with the characteristics it derives from the very fact that it exists in the soul, whereas in the second case the universe is considered with its own characteristics, which it possesses independently of knowledge, but which we became aware of in knowledge. Thus, a human being *as known* is universal; that is a characteristic acquired from the fact of his existence in the soul, whereas his existential characteristic is to be an individual. That I can perceive his individuality only in and by an act of knowledge is a truism known to all. What is not a truism, and what many thinkers do not see, is that the universe's aspect *as known* and the characteristics belonging to this same universe as known *in its real existence* can be completely different.

Therefore, to resolve the wonderful, to discover the reason why the two universes *as known* are contradictory, we must examine the latter as such and compare them with the *real universe* of which they claim to be the exact reproduction. Now, if there are several ways of knowing, there may also be several universes *as known*; and if reality has several real aspects, it will be knowable in its very diversity and will justify the existence of a double synthesis in man. Thus, this justification will be possible precisely insofar as there is a plurality of cognitive means and a plurality of realities to be known. As long as this plurality has not been established, there is no possibility of agreement. Let us try to illustrate these brief remarks by the inquiries consequent upon the four epistemological shocks already mentioned.

√ Parmenides was confronted with two known universes; he was aware of this duality and of the contradictory properties that these two universes possessed as known. He also knew that he had all he needed to explain their subjective existence, for at this point in the development of philosophical thought, the distinction between sensation and intellection had already been recognized.[32] Therefore, he could account for the subjective duality of these two universes, but his analysis of reality was too primitive to enable him to see in each of them, as known, an aspect of reality that would verify and warrant their claim to represent that which is. Having perceived only the unity of reality, he denied that sensation had any value for knowledge. Thus, he threw out the storyteller who told of multiplicity in the universe and entertained only the one whose geometric story seemed to him to explain what is. His solution was not sufficiently developed to satisfy the human mind.

2√ The two centuries of speculation that follow witness a renewal of the problem by an analysis of reality. The theory of the atomists is a first attempt to conciliate the two quarreling guests of the human mind, by recognizing a certain multiplicity[33] in the universe. Platonism has no aim other than to account for this dual human experience: the affirmation of eternal matter, which is the principle of becoming, corruption, and instability, explains the existence of sensation (without ascribing any truth to it, because truth implies stability); while the world of forms accounts for the universe to which the intellect attests.[34] Aristotle takes up the same question[35] and seeks to reconcile the two universes we are aware of. His solution differs from Plato's, but it is nevertheless a solution to the very same problem that beset Parmenides: how to explain the coexistence of two universes in the soul. The method, too, is identical in each case, without its always attaining the same success: the analysis of the knower and the reality to be known, whose marriage, if real, authenticates the stories told by the soul and, if unreal, renders the intellect's narratives illegitimate and illusory.

3/ The constant use of this same "confronting" procedure could be traced right through the philosophical thought of the Middle Ages. However, let it suffice us to rediscover this procedure as the most characteristic factor in contemporary scientific methodology.[36] We know that modern physics is dominated by mathematics, and we often hear the remark: "In Physics, God made the mathematics, and man made the rest."[37] The mathematician works with symbols; he stays in the realm of the possible, of that which implies no contradiction.[38] He can give as many accounts of reality as he likes, provided they do not contravene the rules of the game. Nevertheless, if these accounts are to be taken seriously, they must be controlled by observation and experience; external reality must objectify the formal theory developed by the mathematician before any scientific problem can arise. Here is a typical case: Up to the end of the eighteenth century, all geometricians affirmed that the parallels of Euclid existed, because everyday experience had legitimized this notion both directly and indirectly. But about 1830 there appeared on the scene mathematicians who claimed that this mathematical truth was not demonstrated; they constructed all sorts of theories to explain how parallels could be replaced by the geodetical line or curved surface, whose properties were very similar to Euclidean parallels except that they could limit space. These statements were not taken seriously until 1866, when Beltrami discovered the *pseudosphere* and proved that the nonparallel line plays exactly the same role on unlimited surfaces that the Euclidean parallel does in limited space.[39] Then the problem became: Why does the line that had universal value for

Euclid seem to have concrete existence only within a curved surface? Research in this field led to the curious observation that "the essence of a mathematical idea is measured by the possible distortions which permit the extension of the application of this idea."[40] In other words, the truth of mathematical ideas must be modified in accordance with the objects known, which only experience and observation provide. Here again the comparison between the stories told by the mathematical intellect and by exterior reality is what produces harmony or discord. Thus, inquiry must deal with these two terms if the wonderful is truly to be the principle of progress, regardless of the field.

Confronting the immanent or known world with the exterior world is therefore the first law of any inquiry aiming either to pacify opponents or to exclude one in favor of the other. In the latter case, the first wonder may give way to a second, sometimes even more mysterious than the first. We have a typical case of such a succession in the modern epistemological problem, considered solely as a problem. By confronting the immanent universe with the physical universe, Descartes and Kant did not successfully explain the coexistence of the metaphysical universe of the ancients with the scientific universe. Therefore, they excluded the first and kept the second. However, a new problem then arose, and their wonder fell upon the mind's capacity to recount contradictory stories when there seems to be nothing in reality capable of explaining this dual account. They placed the *mirabile* in the narrator's own ability to tell a story; and this second wonder, to which only the knowing subject contributed, was the source of those long and detailed investigations retold in the *Discourse on Method* and the *Critique of Pure Reason*.[41]

Such is the nature of the psychological shock caused by the birth of a problem in the human soul, and of the inquiries it initiates. Descartes was right in saying that admiration, which we call wonder, is the very soul of philosophy, and Plato and Aristotle, too, were justified in attributing to it that power of progress and discovery which they identified with human knowledge wherever it is exercised. At the end of this second phase of our investigation we know the universal rule conditioning the birth of every problem, a rule that can be formulated in terms of awareness of an immanent and unintelligible dualism. We have also seen the spontaneous psychological reaction of the soul when confronted with this duality: a reaction of wonder or fear of ignorance, and an exertion of all the cognitive powers to dispel this ignorance and come to truth. Finally, we know the soul's natural attitudes in its attempt to resolve the dualism immanent in every problem: an attempt to harmonize the duality by discovering a basis for agreement; exclusion of the duality by rejecting one of the accounts, when conciliation is impossible; doubt's replacing discovery when neither of the first two attitudes is possible and the inquiry is completely unsuccessful; and doubt's becoming skepticism when doubt assumes permanency and falls upon the very power of the intellect to discover truth.

¶ 3. *Wonder, Doubt, Skepticism.* Before terminating this study of the psychological aspect of the problem as such, and before going on to the second question, concerning the *why* of wonder and the inquiry that springs from it,[42] we must study a historical aspect of wonder that relates it to doubt. The fact that this relationship already existed, at least lexicographically, in Aristotle and St. Thomas would be enough to oblige us to clarify the situation; but since Descartes assigned so much importance to doubt in his search for truth, and since Neo-Scholastics have used certain Aristotelian and Thomistic texts in such a way as to give them the meaning of Cartesian doubt, this question must necessarily be cleared up. Therefore, this third section will deal with the natural relations existing between wonder and doubt. A brief study of the vocabulary used by philosophers, and of the ideas expressed therein, will show us why a certain identification was made between the doubtful and the wonderful, but at the same time it will show us the absolute impossibility of considering the psychological attitude characterized by wonder as interchangeable with that characterizing doubt.

(a) Aporia-dubitabile *or the doubtful.* The Greek word *aporia* is a term composed of a privative particle, *a-*, and a substantive, *poros*, that means a way out, an opening. Therefore, the general sense of the recomposed word is: that which has no opening, provides no way out, an obstacle, a hindrance.[43] Upon this etymological meaning Plato and Aristotle grafted a whole series of nuances all of which have the general sense of hindrance, obstacle, but depend for their exact meaning upon the application of the word to the various fields of human activity. In the context of social life *aporia* signifies difficulties caused by lack of wealth or by poverty. In the order of action it means indecision, hesitation resulting from perplexity in the choice of means toward some definite end. In the order of speculative or theoretical knowledge—the only order of direct interest to us here—*aporia* is synonymous with objective difficulties, with problems that may spring from reality itself, or from our lack of intellectual acuity, or, yet, from the competence of a specialist, when this competence destroys evidence that seems to be part of the common heritage.[44] An example of these three sources of *aporia* will help us grasp exactly what it means. When Aristotle tells us that philosophers, in studying the heavenly bodies, considered as an *aporia* the curious behavior of the moon, which appears, disappears, or appears in whole or in part, this is an *aporia* with an objective source.[45] In the matter of grasping the secret heart of things, when Aristotle compares our intellect with the eye of a night bird, he is pointing to the knowing subject itself as the source of the difficulty or *aporia*.[46] Finally, when he states, as an *aporia*, the fact that his predecessors held a theory contrary to his own, their competence is the source of the difficulty.[47] To this category would belong all the statements of modern science concerning the nonexistence of colors, sounds, of extensive quantity, etc. These are *aporiai* arising from the competence of scientists whose statements contradict what is universally held as evident. The whole third book of Aristotle's *Metaphysics* is filled with these three kinds of *aporiai*, which he proposes to solve in the succeeding books.[48]

The Latin word *dubitabile* comes from *dubius*, the origin of our word *doubt*. Its root is *duo*, whose etymological meaning suggests that which is divided, which bifurcates, which lacks determination or unity.[49] By means of a different imagery, the Latin *dubitabile* has exactly the same fundamental meaning as the Greek *aporia*. The latter, as we have seen, signifies the impossibility of proceeding because there is *no* way out; the former signifies the impossibility of proceeding because there are *too many ways* out, or, in other words, there are many ways, but we do not know which is the right one to take. To this primary sense the Latins also added various nuances according to the way the word is applied to the various fields of human activity. When something is to be done, some decision to be taken, the *dubitabile* is the reason for hesitation, indecision[50]; in the order of knowledge, it means a problem, a question, a difficulty, that may have the same trinity of origin as has the *aporia*.[51]

(b) Dubitabile *and* mirabile. It is a fact that Plato,[52] Aristotle,[53] and St. Thomas seem to hold for a strict synonymity between the *dubitabile* and the *mirabile*, for they use them indiscriminately as the object of both wonder and doubt and attribute to them the same origin, ignorance.[54] There is nothing abnormal in this synonymous use of *dubitabile* and *admirabile*, for both words have the same meaning: both refer to what modern terminology calls a *problem*. Now we have just seen that every problem is the very object of wonder, whence it springs, and that it is a mixture of intelligibility and unintelligibility,[55] which is also the precise definition of the Aristotelian *dubitabile* or *aporia* when conceived as the principle of inquiry or the object of wonder:

The Stagirite declares that the *aporia* of the intellect points to a knot in the object (*pragma*). He seems to view the thing itself as somehow binding the intellect. The *knot* would seem to be something in the thing or arising from the thing. It binds the understanding until it is located and untied. . . . This state seems to coincide with the initial attitude of *wonder* described in Book A with the help of the *aporia* term. Being in a state of *wonder* and in a state of *aporia* were there regarded as synonymous. *Aporia* seems merely a more explicit notion of the initial wonder.[56]

This *objective* sense of *aporia* is found again in the Thomist *dubitabile*, and we shall study it in more detail in the third chapter of this book.[57] All we need note here is that the two words *dubitabile* and *admirabile* are used interchangeably by the ancient philosophers, for the simple reason that they refer to one and the same reality, a problem that besets the intellect.

We could easily justify this usage by the conventional character of language and simply say that the *dubitabile* is synonymous with the *admirabile* because thinkers have said so. This would be an easy solution, but it would not shed much light upon the relations between doubt and wonder. Let us therefore look at the case of *mirabile* and *dubitabile* from another angle. It may be a fact that these two words are used interchangeably, but it is not true of *mirum* and *dubium*, which, at first glance, would seem entitled to enjoy the same interchangeability. Why this difference? The reason lies in the very form of the words. Words ending in *ibilis* always refer to a potency, something that can be or not be, that can act or not act; while words ending in *um* indicate a state of fact, an actuality. Therefore, the *dubitabile* may become, but is not actually, a *dubium;* just as a *mirabile* may become, but is not necessarily a *mirum.*

Thus, a radio is an extraordinary thing, a *mirum* for anyone who knows nothing about modern physical science. Before being a *mirum*, it had the power to evoke admiration or wonder in the mind of anyone ignorant of electricity; it was a *mirabile* for the ignorant, but not for the scientist. Consequently, the *mirabile* and the *dubitabile* have a *relative* character: they can cause wonder or doubt but do not necessarily do so.

Now if we return to the notion of problem, which we have defined as the wonderful or the object of wonder, it is easy for us to explain this apparently untechnical use of such diverse terms. In effect, we have seen that from the beginning of the wonderful or the object of wonder, man was inquiring or investigating in order to solve the problem or the contradiction in the stories confronting him. This inquiry may end in the discovery of the cause of the opposition and its conciliation, or in the rejection of one of the stories, which puts an end to the problem, or in the impossibility of either discovering grounds for agreement or of rejecting one narrator in favor of the other. This latter hypothesis begets what we have called *doubt* or the intellect's despair when it is faced with two equally valid possibilities and cannot choose between them. Considering the end or outcome of the inquiry in relation to its starting point, i.e., the wonderful or *mirum*, we must admit that the *mirum* can result in doubt if the inquiry it initiates comes to no decisive conclusion. Thus, the *mirum* is a *dubitabile*, or a potential cause of doubt, at the same time that it is actually a *mirum* or wonderful.

Therefore, at the starting point of all reflection there is a problem whose proper name is *mirum* when considered in its *actual role vis-à-vis* the human soul. But because this *mirum* can be extremely difficult and because the inquiry, whose starting point it is, is not infallibly successful, this *mirum* may be called *mirabile* insofar as the difficulty it brings up is insoluble, either absolutely or for the inquiring intellect. It is not by pure caprice, then, that philosophers have used *mirabile* and *dubitabile* indistinctly to refer to the problem from which philosophical or scientific reflection springs. On the contrary, this usage rests upon a very deep insight into the laws of the intellect, of its real incapacities and of the mystery in things, a mystery we cannot always penetrate.

Such, then, are the relations between the *mirabile* and the *dubitabile*: As a starting point for inquiry the two are identical, but they are completely different when this starting point is considered not in itself but in its possible repercussions upon the intellect at the *term* or outcome of its inquiry. If this outcome is positive, leading to the discovery of truth, the *mirabile* is positive, fruitful, and the source of hope. If this outcome is negative and fails, if the inquiry has led to doubt or intellectual despair, then the *mirabile* becomes the *dubitabile*, and the fear of ignorance becomes fear of an even greater evil, the fear of error or falsity.

(c) *Doubt and wonder.* What we have just seen about the definition of the *dubitabile*, and its comparison with the *mirabile*, indicates that wonder is not doubt. Let us pursue our investigation further and try to discover the deep reason for their difference.

Their is an initial opposition between doubt and wonder that results from their *subjectum*, or the part of the soul in which they are respectively rooted. Wonder, as we have seen, belongs to the affective part; it is a passion of the soul, a fear of the evil that is ignorance, an active fear that, to dispel this ignorance, sets into motion every human resource. Doubt, on the contrary, does not belong to affectivity but is a characteristic of the mind, a *state of mind*. In other words, just as we speak of nonvolition to mean the attitude of the will that cannot do this or that, so doubt is a *non-intellection*, an inability to see that springs, not from a nonvolition[58] or a will not to see, but from a lack of luminosity on the part of things or a lack of light on the part of our intellect.

Since difficulty also can be accounted for in two ways, its cause may exist not in the objects of our study but in ourselves: just as it is with bats' eyes in respect of daylight, so it is with our mental intelligence in respect of those things which are by nature most obvious.[59]

When Aristotle wants to define *aporia* technically, not as a synonym of *mirabile*, but as a characteristic of the intellect during some of its activities, he defines it as a *state of mind* caused by the existence in the intellect of two contrary *proofs* enjoying equal evidence and therefore canceling each other out.[60] In the same way, St. Thomas defines doubt as the impossibility of deciding upon one contradictory, as a mind vacillating between two alternatives, one of which destroys the other, and refusing its assent though fear of error.[61]

While it is true that doubt and wonder differ because of the power of the soul in which they are found, the first belonging to our cognitive power, the second to the affective, they also differ in the ignorance from which they spring.[62] The ignorance at the root of wonder is directly concerned with things; its object is the complex aspects of the same reality, a complexity that seems disordered and therefore unintelligible.[63] The ignorance that is the wellspring of doubt is not concerned with things but bears directly upon the proofs of our causal knowledge of things. It has as its object the *explanation* or vindication of the truths we possess.

It is not every lack of knowledge that causes doubt; but that in which a person cannot see the reason[64] for what he is investigating, and in which contrary reasons seem to apply. . . . Doubt occurs as a result of a lack of a sufficient means[65] for the discovery of truth, and so it arises from a deficiency of knowledge.[66]

Any ignorance can beget wonder, as is evinced by the infinite number of "why's" asked by children, who wonder at everything because they know nothing, and also by the wonder besetting us throughout our lives whenever we embark upon a field of research new to us. But doubt is more exacting than wonder, for, unlike the latter, it is not an inevitable effect of the bonds existing between our powers of knowledge and those of appetite. It only concerns intellectual activity considered, not in its totality, but in the more specialized field of truth, of the one *mediate and necessary* truth. Doubt is not concerned with things, or with primary evidence, or with the immediate knowledge of contingent things, but solely with *concluded* truth whose cause is not evident when it should be. Strictly speaking, doubt is the contrary of science, when the latter is taken in the formal sense of a conclusion known through the causality of the premises. It lacks everything science has: that is, perception of the truth of what it knows, and indefectible assent to this truth or certitude. And since there is even a science concerning opposites,[67] doubt can only be described in relation to the science of which it is the total absence; whereas wonder, the starting point of the inquiry that seeks science as its end, can be defined in relation to all kinds of ignorance or to a complete absence of knowledge, whatever its nature. The number of *mira* or objects of wonder is therefore equivalent to the infinite multiplicity of our ignorance, while the number of *dubia* or real doubts equals the number of our unsuccessful attempts to perceive the truth of our conclusions scientifically.

(d) *Doubt and skepticism.* Every skeptic is a doubter, but every doubter is not necessarily a skeptic. This statement is easily verified, for if doubt is synonymous with the absence of scientific truth, it can deal only with a certain field of human knowledge, namely that of truths begotten by immediate evidence. Thus, our doubts can be quite numerous without thereby begetting skepticism. The latter exists only in that precise case wherein man, disillusioned by the many errors he perceives and by the infinite multiplicity of contradictory explanations of our universe, definitely loses confidence in the intellect as a faculty capable of attaining truth and gives up further inquiry because it is foredoomed to failure. Skepticism is absolute intellectual pessimism, and the skeptic, despairing of knowledge, *commits intellectual suicide,* since he renounces intellectual life wherever it involves contemplation of the truth.

Doubt is an absence of certitude or assent as a defense against error, the foremost evil for the intellect. Thus, it betokens a sane mind, that is somehow vaccinated against the disease of error, a mind taking the hygienic measures necessary to every intellect that not possessing the ensemble of truths for which it is made, patiently and persistently seeks these truths until they come to enlighten and enrich it. Skepticism is a disease fatal to the mind, because, under the pretense of avoiding error, the skeptic condemns himself to death or to the total inactivity that is a sign of death. It is not only error but total error, since in advance it foregoes the contemplation of truth wherein lies man's very beatitude. Consequently, when Descartes adopts doubt as a method of discovering truth, his doubt is not skepticism; it is not even a doubt but a *dubitabile* or an *admirabile,* a *mirabile* caused by an experimental establishment of the fact that error exists in man alongside truth, a *mirabile* from which proceeds a quest for a single cause to account for the presence of error in the human soul.

What we have inevitably seen about the relations between the wonderful and the doubtful, between wonder and doubt, between doubt and skepticism, has shown us that wonder is really the only psychological reaction that is both the principle of inquiry and the source of truth. And since every problem is the object of wonder, since it begets wonder and explains its nature, the definition of a problem involves two aspects; one relating to the object in which are wedded intelligibility and unintelligibility, the other dependent upon the subject wherein dwell both the fear of ignorance and a flight from this same evil, born of the desire to dispel ignorance and to replace it by true knowledge. Therefore, every problem is essentially constituted of two combined imperfections, one issuing from the defective luminosity of the real, the other from the knower's deficient power of vision. Wherever one or the other of these conditions fails, wherever reality is perfectly luminous and the intellect's vision is completely clear, the problem disappears to make way for integral perception of the totality of being and beings. Such, then, is a problem and the nature of the psychological reactions of which it is the immediate cause whenever it occurs in the human mind.

B. PRIMARY SOURCE OF MAN'S PSYCHOLOGICAL RE-ACTIONS WHEN FACED WITH A PROBLEM

We have seen that the contradiction existing between the accounts given us by our storytellers begets in us, first of all, a reaction of fear whose name is wonder, and that this fear is induced by an evil called ignorance. We have also seen that the fear of this evil that is ignorance is the principle of a whole series of inquiries, of more or less difficult and complicated steps whose sole aim is to resolve the contradiction between these two accounts and thus suppress wonder or the fear of ignorance. When this suppression is impossible, wonder gives way to doubt, that state of mind which avoids decision through fear of an evil greater than ignorance, through fear of error or falsity. Thus, a last question besets the epistemologist: What is it, in man, that seems to force him to flee ignorance and error at any price? What inner power constantly constrains him to seek tirelessly and never to rest until he possess truth? How explain that this horror of ignorance and error are so great that the human mind deliberately accepts the death of the intellect, or skepticism, rather than be exposed to the danger of error, which seems to be a personal and deeply hated enemy, as St. Thomas so admirably expresses it: "Deception and error constitute a great part of unhappiness; in fact, that is what all men naturally avoid."[68]

The answer to this question will give us the secret to the existence of every problem and to its true nature, for it will help us to understand what a problem is, not only in its observed psychological effects, but in the primary cause that explains the laws of its birth, progress, and solution. It will thereby reveal to us the origins and fundamental laws governing the birth and nature of an epistemological problem, since this latter is only a particular problem in a precise subject-matter: namely, that which human knowledge presents to the mind that reflects upon its own most characteristic activity—its activity of knowing as such.

Why does man, from the moment he is aware of their presence, feel this constraint to avoid ignorance and error as though they were the greatest of evils? If we did not detest ignorance and error, the contradictory accounts given by our two storytellers would leave us completely indifferent. Their tales would interest us as curiosities, just as novels or detective stories amuse us; but no one takes the trouble to find out why two stories about the same crime disagree, or why two novelists describe imaginary facts in opposite ways! Why then is there this difference as soon as the universe we live in appears to be involved in contradiction? Why can we not remain *neutral*, why must we always take sides? Here is one scientist's answer, which we quote because it is unaffected by either Thomistic or philosophical preconceptions.

The first question asked about scientific facts and theories such as we have been discussing in this book, is: "Are they true?" I would emphasise that even more significant than the scientific conclusions themselves is the fact that this question so urgently arises about them. The question "Is it true?" changes the complexion of the world of experience—not because it is asked *about* the world, but because it is asked *in* the world. When we go right back to the beginning, the first thing we must recognise in the world of experience is something intent on truth—something to which it matters intensely that beliefs should be true. . . . *We are that which asks the question.* Whatever else there may be in our nature, *responsibility towards truth in one of its attributes.* This side of our nature is aloof from the scrutiny of the physicist.[69]

This answer, which the physicist cannot give, must be found by the metaphysician, and its discovery gives us the sole fundamental and absolutely primary reason that is at the source of all human activities, regardless of the field. That problems or questions exist is a fact. Another fact is that these problems cause wonder and that wonder is the source of our inquiries. But the analysis of wonder reveals a fear of ignorance and an inquiry that seem to be a flight from this same ignorance. Now, this fear of ignorance and this flight explain nothing if they are but fear and flight. They must be exterior symptoms of a reality much more dynamic than the simple presence of evil, for evil has never produced anything. It is by nature an absence of act, an imperfection like the nothingness that in some manner it prefigures. We flee evil only with reference to a thing we love, desire, and whose possession gives us a certain happiness. The reality that positively animates our fear of ignorance and error is truth. To wonder or to flee ignorance, to doubt or to fear error, is to desire and seek truth. The inevitable character of wonder and doubt is only the negative aspect of the nature of our mind, which is made to know truth. To possess the world insofar as the latter is the sole source of the truths we can acquire, that is man's end, that is the secret motive we find at the source of every problem as such. This secret motive explains the genesis of a problem, accounts for its psychological structure, is the true first cause explaining the success of our inquiries, the joy of discovery accompanying them when they succeed, and the sorrow resulting from our failures—a sorrow whose peak is found in the skeptical attitude wherein despair is so great that it causes suicide in the order of the knowledge of truth.

Made for truth, we find rest only when we are sated with it, and this satiation does not provoke disgust but constitutes our happiness.[70] This is the meaning of a problem as such. Thus defined, it is independent of its subject-matter and also above the historical contingencies conditioning its birth or leading to its solution. Therefore, when in the course of this study we meet the epistemological problem clad in different formulae, dependent upon the particular turn of mind of the thinkers who pose it, or upon the epoch in which it appears or reappears, we must always remember that, beneath the diversity of formulae, the multiplicity of aspects, and the pressure of necessity, the epistemological problem is first and foremost *a problem* and obeys the universal laws that govern every problem as such:

(1) It springs from contradictory evidence, the experience of which begets wonder or the fear of ignorance.

(2) This fear of ignorance is the principle of inquiry or of the flight from ignorance.

(3) This flight from ignorance is but the negative aspect of the pursuit of truth for which man is made and which he is incapable of not loving and desiring.

Wonder or the genesis of a problem can be summarized, then, in the following formula: *The fear of ignorance is the beginning of wisdom.*

II · THE MODERN EPISTEMOLOGICAL PROBLEM

[handwritten annotations]

Our purpose in the first chapter was to define the nature of a problem as such, under the two complementary and chronologically distinct aspects that it presents to reflection: first, that of its genesis in the soul, a birth symbolized by the contradictory accounts of two storytellers, the familiar and the extraordinary; and second, that of its development through inquiry, whose immediate source is wonder or the fear of ignorance, and whose secret motive is that invincible love of truth which essentially characterizes the human intellect and governs all its activity. Now we are going to apply this natural methodology to the study of the epistemological problem, according to the various modes in which this problem has presented itself through the ages. Since the modern aspect is *officially* the first-born, we shall follow the official genealogy and begin with the modern epistemological problem.

In the philosophy of ideas, the modern epistemological problem has the appearance of a *two-faced Janus;* it has two faces that, externally, are totally dissimilar, but whose community of origin is such that they really constitute one single individual who unifies them without destroying their distinction. The first face has the features of the opposition between *science and philosophy*, or truth and error, a face created principally by Descartes and Kant. The second face of the modern epistemological problem, quite different from the first, no longer has the features of an opposition between science and philosophy, or truth and error, but has the aspect of a conflict between *science and science*, of contemporary physics dethroning classical physics and giving it an old-fashioned and antiquated look that forecasts its early demise. The mere formulation of these two aspects of the modern epistemological problem helps us to see the difference in their points of view. However, we must not dwell only upon their diversity, because they have this in common: Contemporary science is no more favorably disposed toward metaphysics than was its ancestor, and although Cartesianism and Kantianism are no longer gods to contemporary scientists, the latter's science is nevertheless unintelligible without reference to the methods of Descartes and Kant.

This chapter will be divided according to these two aspects of the modern epistemological problem. The first section will study the Cartesian and Kantian problem, while the second section will deal with the contemporary problem.

Section I: The Cartesian and Kantian Problem

We already have the framework we shall use to study this aspect of the modern epistemological problem, for every problem must first be born in order to beget in the soul the psychological reactions that are at the root of its development. This section will therefore be divided into two subsections, the first of which will try to reconstruct the particular conditions attending the birth of the epistemological problem, first in the thought of Descartes and then in the thought of Kant. By a brief analysis of the works in which they set forth their respective points of view, the second section will examine the psychological reactions caused by this problem in the soul of each of these thinkers.

A. THE BIRTH OF THE MODERN PROBLEM

¶ 1. *The Birth of the Cartesian Problem.* Three factors contributed to the birth of the Cartesian epistemological problem. The first has a universal character and is identical with the deep instinct that causes human nature to abhor ignorance and its acute form,

skepticism, because it was made for truth.[1] Descartes grew up in
the moralizing and anti-intellectualist atmosphere of the Renaissance.
He read those extremely subtle works extolling ignorance as the
only way to happiness on earth, such as Petrarch's *De sui ipsius et
multorum ignorantia*, Nicholas of Cusa's *De docta ignorantia*,
Sanchez' *Quod nil scitur*, and Montaigne, whose *Essays*, vaunt the
wisdom that has successfully freed itself of learning and its pretensions.[2] Descartes was deeply influenced by these thinkers, who
were the foremost writers of that day. He himself had an attack of
skepticism,[3] which he considered the worst illness that humanity
could suffer.[4] That is why he resolved to seek a serum with which
to immunize humanity permanently against this cancer of the soul,
skepticism.[5] But hatred of skepticism and the desire to cure humanity
of it are not enough; an infallible elixir must be found in order to
immunize the intellect, and this elixir will be discovered only when
the *cause of doubt is known*. Only this knowledge will infallibly
effect the cure and prevent the disease.[6] Such is the first factor in the
Cartesian problem.

Besides this first universal factor, there is a second, more particular
factor consequent upon Descartes' historical milieu. Mathematical
science had advanced considerably since Scholasticism had lost its
hold upon scientists. The latter had shaken off its tyrannical protec-
tion and become masters of their own affairs. Descartes had per-
sonally experienced the liberty of mathematical knowledge; it had
given him the opportunity to contribute to the progress of this
science and to bestow upon it a unity[7] it had never known before.
Now, the most striking feature of mathematical knowledge is its
interior evidence and the absence of dissension between mathematicians,[8] which proves its evidential character and therefore its
truth.[9] Therefore, if evident knowledge is necessarily true knowledge,
true knowledge is necessarily evident: evidence and truth are interchangeable. Where there is no evidence, there is error. But Scholastic
philosophy is filled with dissension[10]; therefore, it lacks evidence and
is erroneous—it feeds upon the probable. To identify the probable
with the true is precisely to open the door to error and skepticism,
since neither truth nor science can beget it. The second factor in the

genesis of the Cartesian problem is thus the identification of probability with error, and of error with the source of doubt and skepticism.

The third and last factor of the Cartesian problem consists in identifying the nature of the philosophical knowledge of the ancients with that of popular or nonscientific knowledge, which in everyday language is called common sense. According to Descartes, these two types of knowledge are radically identical, and both are the result of educational prejudices.[11] They are nourished by an illusion of truth, and through them doubt and skepticism come into the world.

Knowing these three factors helps us to understand the laws governing the birth of the Cartesian problem, because they introduce us to the two opposed storytellers we have found presiding at the birth of every problem.[12] In Descartes' soul we discover two universes; the first of which is that of Descartes, the child and pupil of the Jesuits. This universe is composed of substantial forms, sensible qualities, generations, corruptions, etc. In this universe, sensation perceives its intended objects, and the intellect discovers the intelligible, natures, and a whole hierarchy of beings. Such is the story told by the familiar narrator. But keeping him company for several years is the mathematician-narrator, and the story he tells wholly contradicts that told by the familiar storyteller. His universe contains neither substantial forms, colors, sounds, nor substantial transformations. It is a universe of pure forms, interconnected only by local motion.[13] These two universes are obviously opposed, and, as we have seen, the evidence of this opposition constitutes the very existence of an intellectual problem.

Although this juxtaposition of universes may be sufficient to pose a problem, it does not suffice to constitute an epistemological problem, at least not for Descartes. The Cartesian problem is not the coexistence in the mind of two contradictory narratives told by two storytellers, but *the fact that there are two tellers.* For truth is one and must be one in the telling; reason, our only narrator is also one and is essentially made for truth, and therefore for unity. This is Descartes' situation; he knows by mathematical experience that reason is one and infallible in its grasp of truth. He also knows that reason is made for truth, that therein lies its good and its end, the source of all its aspirations, all of which is proved by the way reason looks upon skepticism as the intellect's most dangerous disease, because at the source it dries up all our desire for truth. His problem is this: How can reason, which by its very unity infallibly begets truth in science, infallibly generate error in philosophy?[14] This is the initial contradiction seen by Descartes; this is his epistemological problem, his *mirabile;* and these are the factors that brought it into existence.

¶ 2. *The Birth of the Kantian Problem.* One hundred and fifty years after the publication of the *Discourse on Method,* whose author had proposed to discover the first cause of error and thus make skepticism impossible, a German philosopher gave us a picture of the intellectual status of the thinkers of his day. This description seems to be merely an intensified reproduction of the state of affairs in the time of Descartes.

Metaphysics has accordingly lapsed back into the ancient timeworn dogmatism, and so again suffers that depreciation from which it was to have been rescued. And now, after all methods, so it is believed, have been tried and found wanting, the prevailing mood is that of weariness and complete indifferentism, the mother, in all sciences, of chaos and night.[15]

This state of affairs inspired him, too, with the desire once and for all, to cure humanity of its skepticism, for we are made to know truth: "But it is idle to feign indifference to such inquiries, the object of which can never be indifferent to human nature."[16] Here we see again the first factor in the birth of the Cartesian problem, the universal factor of the fear of ignorance and error, which is only the negative way of expressing man's natural tendency toward truth. But to desire to heal is not in itself to cure; the cause of this disease must be found.

What then is the reason why, in this field, the sure road to science has not hitherto been found? Is it perhaps impossible of discovery . . . ? Or if it be only that we have thus far failed to find the true path, are there any indications to justify the hope that by renewed efforts we may have better fortune than has fallen to our predecessors?[17]

The second element contributing to the genesis of the Kantian problem is also peculiar to it and dependent upon the historical circumstances that conditioned the development of the Königsberg philosopher's thought. At this time the physical sciences, as well as the mathematical sciences, had progressed considerably and their success was the surest criterion of their truth: "Their success should incline us to imitate their procedure, at least by way of experiment."[18] The criterion of the truth of science springs from the unanimity of scientists, since truth is evident and can be but one.

Whether the treatment of such knowledge as lies within the province of reason does or does not follow the secure path of science, is easily to be determined from the outcome. For, if after elaborate preparations, frequently renewed, it is brought to a stop immediately it nears its goal; if often it is compelled to retrace its steps and strike into some new line of approach; or again, if the participants are unable to agree in any common plan of procedure, then we may rest assured that it is very far from having entered upon the secure path of science, and is indeed a merely random groping.[19]

Thus, the second factor is to be found in the identification of scientific evidence with evidence *simpliciter* and of scientific truth with *the truth*.

Finally, the third and last factor in the birth of the Kantian problem consists in the identification of metaphysics with common or popular knowledge.

For human reason, without being moved merely by the idle desire for extent and variety of knowledge, proceeds, impetuously, driven on by an inward need, to questions such as cannot be answered by any empirical employment of reason, or by principles thence derived. Thus *in all men*, as soon as their reason has become ripe for speculation, *there has always existed and will always continue to exist some kind of metaphysics*.[20]

Now we can easily reconstruct the Kantian *mirabile* and define his epistemological problem. Like Descartes, Kant saw that in his mind there were two storytellers (although different from those of Descartes) telling him two totally dissimilar stories. The first narrator, innate to reason, shows him a universe of things in themselves, of physical and metaphysical causality, and leads him into the arcana of the soul and of God. The second narrator is infinitely more modest, for he is content to feed the reason with the essentially changing, the becoming of things, their mobility—change, mobility, and becoming that reason frames and mobilizes, but which are the only aspects of the universe that we know. For Kant, as for Descartes, the problem springs not so much from the contradiction between two accounts as from the fact that there can be *only one narrator*, the human reason. How can one single teller infallibly recount two contradictory stories? It is understandable that two narrators tell contradictory stories, but that one single narrator tell us, simultaneously, two entirely contradictory accounts, that is the Kantian *mirabile*. It may be formulated as follows: *How is it possible that reason, which is one, be naturally the source of scientific truth and of metaphysical illusion?*

¶ *3. Conclusion on the Birth of the Modern Epistemological Problem.* The two preceding analyses have shown us that the characteristics of the modern epistemological problem do not spring from any difference of procedure in the birth of this problem. On the contrary, its birth follows the classical laws for the genesis of any problem, which laws we noted in our first chapter: namely, that there are two stories with contradiction between them. The characteristics peculiar to the modern problem, to its *mirabile*, result from its general context, which determines the very nature of the wonderful. Now this general context is a context of skepticism or error, and not a context of knowledge of the truth. What causes the wonder of Descartes and Kant is that error exists, although our mind is one. The second characteristic mark of the modern *mirabile* is its notion of truth and error: *a*) That is true which is recognized as such by the universality of thinkers in a particular field of knowledge; *b*) that is false which is incapable of unifying thinkers, of producing that harmony in methods and convergence of results which characterize successful knowledge, the pure sciences. Finally, a third distinctive mark of the modern *mirabile* is the importance assumed by the subject or *Ego*, even in its genesis. We have seen, in effect, that what causes Descartes and Kant to wonder is not directly the duality of accounts, or their contradictory aspect, but the fact that *one narrator* has the natural capacity to recount two irreconcilable stories, to be simultaneously the infallible source of truth and error.

These three marks truly characterize the modern problem; they stamp it with its own individuality and enable us to spot it wherever it is found, despite the diversity of the contexts and the variability of the formulae by which it reveals itself. In any given system, or in the elaboration of a theory, whenever the birth of particular problems gives priority to error over truth,[21] to scientific truth over truth *simpliciter*, and gives primacy to the *Ego* over the object, we may be assured that the context of this system or theory is modern, and that it obeys the laws which Descartes and Kant invented and then imposed on their successors in every field of thought.

B. PSYCHOLOGICAL STRUCTURE OF THE MODERN PROBLEM

Every problem, we have seen,[22] provokes various psychological reactions in the knower, the first of which is wonder or fear of ignorance, and the second, an inquiring effort directed toward the removal of that ignorance and to its replacement by truth. Hence, we are going to apply these distinctions to the two aspects of the modern problem, by making an analysis of the psychological reactions that have followed the birth of their moment of wonder, first, in the case of Descartes, and then in the case of Kant. Such is the plan of this subsection.

¶ *1. The Psychological Structure of the Cartesian Problem.* Whenever he is faced with a problem, the first aspect of a man's psychological reaction is wonder, whose nature is determined by the wonderful or *mirable*. Every *mirabile* is composed of two elements, one intelligible and understood, the other unintelligible and somewhat mysterious to the knowing mind.[23] If it is granted that the Cartesian *mirabile* is composed of two distinctive elements—science or infallible truth as the intelligible and understood element, and error or popular knowledge and philosophy as its element of unintelligibility—its wonder will center upon the coexistence of these two elements, and the fear betokened by wonder will be the fear of error, or of popular and philosophical knowledge as conceived and constructed by the ancients.

Since all wonder is at the source of an inquiry aiming to dispel unintelligibility, Descartes' efforts could have but one direction: to explain the error or the popular knowledge and philosophy of the ancients. There is no question here (as there was in the consideration of the problem as such) of attempting to reconcile science with popular and philosophical knowledge, since the latter is erroneous and must at all cost be expelled from the soul. In the face of such a *mirabile*, the only reasonable alternative is to safeguard the possession of truth and to immunize the mind against every possible inroad of error under its popular and philosophical form.

We have seen that the Cartesian *mirabile* did not center so much upon the duality of contradictory accounts as upon the mystery of mind, for the mind's unity would seem to make it impossible that the mind could be the source of two divergent stories, one of which is infallibly true and the other quite as infallibly false. Since the mind is the sole narrator, it is the mind that we must examine to discover the causes of our errors, i.e., the source of popular knowledge and Scholastic philosophy. It was inevitable that Cartesian inquiry center upon the *Ego*, since the *Ego* is the teller of the two contradictory stories and, despite its unity, must contain the reason for its twofold capacity to create truth and error. Thus, the Cartesian method will primarily be a method of analyzing the subject or *Ego* in order to discover the latter's nature and, once its nature is known, to discover the law of the *Ego's* natural functioning, which will give us the key to its infallibility and enable us to discern the heterogeneous elements that might slip into the natural dynamism of our mind when we become unmindful of its true structure.

First of all, the *Ego* must be discovered.[24] This quest would be extraordinarily difficult if it started from zero in knowledge or truth. But that is not the case with Descartes, for his mathematical experience gave him a definition of truth, namely, a clear and evident idea compelling the adherence of the will.[25] To discover the nature of the mind or thought, then, we must arrive at such a truth about the mind that its clarity and evidence are absolute. But in pursuing this investigation, we are continually checkmated by childhood prejudices[26] and the warping that results from a system of education seemingly directed toward satisfying our need for dialectical debate rather than toward the possession of truth.[27] Therefore, into our thought we must introduce a vaccine as powerful as our childhood and educational prejudices, and this radical vaccine, cathartic for the functioning of thought, is doubt, which, since Descartes, has been called universal or methodic doubt.[28]

Armed with this twofold instrument—consisting of clear and evident ideas as criteria of truth and doubt as the scourge to purify the mind of its preconceptions—Descartes set to work. Doubt begins by expelling as nonevident, therefore false, all sensations and images, for they do not possess the clarity and evidence necessary for truth. Then it rejects all thoughts and even geometrical demonstrations as illusions and dreams caused by an evil genius.[29] Having thus despoiled the mind of all objective content by means of doubt, Descartes finds himself face to face with the thinking, pure *Ego,* and we have the famous *Cogito ergo sum,*[30] so evident that the most convinced skeptic cannot deny it.[31] This is the first existential truth in Cartesianism, because it is the first truth discovered by Descartes that contains no other object than the subject itself: whence its simplicity and its absolute immediacy. In analyzing the *cogito,* we see that the mind producing this act of knowledge is none other than—

a substance whose whole essence or nature consists only in thinking, and which, that it may exist, has no need of place, nor dependence upon any material thing. So that "I", that is to say the mind[32] by which I am what I am, is wholly distinct from the body, and is even more easily known than the latter, and is such that although the latter were not, it would still continue to be all that it is.[33]

Since our soul is a thinking substance, entirely independent of the senses, it does not depend upon the body either to think or to acquire its ideas. Since it is a pure spirit, it is a light for the mind and completely intelligible, possessing from its inception the totality of ideas or truths it will think during its life. To attribute such a nature to the human soul is to attribute infallibility to it, so that the mind could never, by itself, explain the existence of error. Consequently, the source of popular knowledge and vulgar or Scholastic philosophy must be sought in the soul's union to the body. Here is one of the most explicit texts on the subject:

Nor, indeed, have I asserted without reason that the human soul is *always thinking*, wherever it is, even in its mother's womb: for what greater certainty or evidence could be desired for this proposition than what I have offered in proof of its nature consisting in this, that it thinks, just as the essence of the body consists in the fact that it is extended. And of course, it is impossible for anything ever to be deprived of its proper essence . . . nothing is more reasonable than for us to think that the mind of an infant which has recently been united to its body is occupied with the confused perceiving or sensing of precisely those ideas of pain, tickling, heat, cold, and the like, which stems from this union and mixture, as it were. Nor is it any the less endowed with the ideas of God, of itself, and of all those truths which are called self-evident, which adult men have, even when they pay no attention to them; indeed, it does not acquire them later, as it grows older; nor do I doubt that, if it were freed from its bonds with the body, these ideas would still be found in it.[34]

If the mind is light and always present to itself, if it is, furthermore, the reservoir of all first and immutable truths, then it is the sole source of all the sciences, metaphysical as well as physical. The reason and source of the truths we possess must therefore be sought in the mind and not in things.

For since the sciences taken all together are identical with human wisdom, which always remains one and the same, however applied to different subjects, and suffers no more differentiation proceeding from them than the light of the sun experiences from the variety of things which it illumines. . . .[35]

If the mind is light and the sole source of all infallible truth, *it cannot be, as such, the source of error.* The sole source of all erroneous knowledge, thus of common-sense knowledge and scholastic philosophy, must be sought in the union of soul to body and the importance of corporeal needs in childhood, which have accustomed our minds to project into reality the impressions we felt because of our union to the body. Here is the source of all our errors:

It is here that the first and principal of our errors is to be found. For in the first years of life the mind was so closely allied to body that it applied itself to nothing but those thoughts alone by which it was aware of the things which affected the body; nor were these as yet referred to anything existing outside itself, but the fact was merely that pain was felt when the body was hurt, or pleasure experienced when the body received some good, or else if the body was so (slightly) affected that no great good nor evil was experienced, such sensations were encountered as we call tastes, smells, sound, heat, cold light, colours, etc., which in truth represent nothing to us outside of our mind, but which vary in accordance with the diversities of the parts and modes in which the body is affected. The mind at the same time also perceived magnitudes, figures, movements and the like, which were exhibited to it not as sensations but as things or the modes of things existing, or at least capable of existing outside thought, although it did not yet observe this distinction between the two. And afterwards when the machine of the body which has been so constituted by nature that it can of its own inherent power turn here and there, by turning fortuitously this way and the other, followed after what was useful and avoided what was harmful, the mind which was closely allied to it, reflecting on the things which it followed after or avoided, re-marked first of all that they existed outside itself, and attributed to them not alone magnitudes, figures, movements, and other such properties which it apprehended as things or modes of things, but also tastes, smells, and the like, the sensations of which it perceived that these things caused in it. And as all other things were only considered in as far as they served for the use of the body in which it was immersed, mind judged that there was more or less reality in each body, according as the impressions made on body were more or less strong. . . . And we have in this way been imbued with a thousand other such prejudices from infancy, which in later youth we quite forgot we had accepted without sufficient examina-tion, admitting them as though they were of perfect truth and certainty, and as if they had been known by means of our senses or implanted in us by nature.[36]

Descartes therefore discovered the root of all possible and imagi-nable errors: it is sensation and its organization in sympathy with corporeal requirements. We objectify these sensations and needs in early childhood and, when we grow up, continue to consider them as having really external objects, because we forget their originally subjective character and attribute them to exterior nature when they are actually our creations. The union to the body, the pragmatic action, caused by our appetites, of the body upon the mind during childhood, the spontaneous forgetting of the distorting action of our body and our appetites, the exploitation of this forgetfulness and of our preconceptions by our teachers, such are the sole sources of error, doubt, and the skepticism that finally crowns so many errors and doubts.[37]

With this conclusion, the Cartesian *mirabile* disappears, for having reached it, we know why man can create a system of infallible truths and another system of infallible errors. He creates a system of infallible truths *as mind*, and a system of errors *insofar as this mind uses its body and organism as instruments of knowledge*. Actually, we will recall that the Cartesian *mirabile* like every other *mirabile*, contains an intelligible element, the truth of the account narrated by mathematical science, and an unintelligible element, the erroneous account given by popular knowledge and vulgar or Scholastic philosophy.[38] His *mirabile* centers upon the impossibility that one single narrator could simultaneously tell these two stories. But now we know that this narrator is not absolutely alone, for the mind is united to a body. Therefore, it is no wonder that this union of a pure spirit to a body could be the source of confusion, of approximations, of probabilities, whenever the mind does not distrust this proximity. Before Descartes, no one had discovered the secret of the mind in the infallibility of its nature, or that of its fallibility in its constant proximity to the body it inhabits. As long as this secret remained undiscovered, contradiction struck to the very heart of human knowledge. But now all that is over, the secret is out, and every man who wants "to conduct his reason rightly and seek truth in the sciences"[39] has only to start with the soul as thinking substance, use the cathartic of doubt, follow the four precepts given in the *Discourse*, and the thing is done. No more error, no more skepticism, only infallible truth becomes inevitably the mind's food, since the mind contains in itself the seeds of all truth.[40]

Descartes could have ended his *Discourse on Method* with the discovery of the nature of the mind and the four precepts for rightly conducting the reason, because once the *mirabile* disappeared, the inquiry of which it was the starting point necessarily came to an end. What followed this discovery, that is, the metaphysics of God and the organization of a physics, adds nothing further to the solution of the problem; it merely confirms the efficiency and ease of the discovered method by applying[41] it to metaphysical and physical problems. This part of the *Discourse* deals with applied method and nothing more. The true significance of the *Discourse* should not be sought in the application of the method Descartes discovered, but in the discovery of the method itself. Therefore, if we want to grasp the exact meaning of the Cartesian problem and the psychological reactions it causes, we shall have to concentrate our attention upon the method itself, that is, upon the parts where Descartes reveals to us the different factors that contributed to the birth of the problem and to its solution.

In the title of his work Descartes himself shows us the exact meaning of his problem and of the method he invented: *Discourse on the Method of rightly conducting the reason and seeking truth in the sciences.*[42] "Rightly conducting the reason" and "seeking *truth in the sciences*," that is what the *Discourse* aims to do. "Rightly conducting the reason" is an art everyone can learn,[43] but it must be learned; and to be learned, it must exist. Therefore, Descartes proposes to create this art, to put it at everyone's disposal. We have seen the essential elements of this art in the preceding pages. Now we should hear a word about the aim of this Cartesian art, "seeking truth in the sciences." At first it would appear that this is a pleonasm, for Descartes' definition of truth seems to be the same as his definition of scientific truth.[44] But this is not quite true, for genuine Cartesian science is wisdom, the synthesis of all knowledge. Furthermore, science is, above all, the discovery of truth, and the discovery of truth starting from immediate evidence.[45] Thus, scientific truth is not identical with truth *simpliciter*. There are two kinds of Cartesian truth: that seen by intuition, and that arrived at by deduction.[46]

However, if science is perfectly science only when it is wisdom or the synthesis of all knowledge, then, evidently, only deduction can make this unity real, and scientific truth will be distinguished from intuited truth as the conclusion is distinguished from its principle. Once this distinction between primary truth, or principle, and deduced truth is granted, it is true to say that Cartesian method is essentially oriented toward the possession of necessary or infallible truth and excludes, by definition, all knowledge not characterized by necessity and infallibility. This means that, for Descartes, only infallible truth exists, that there is *identity between truth and infallible truth, and identity between knowledge and infallible knowledge of truth.*

To reduce knowledge to knowledge of truth, and knowledge of truth to infallible knowledge, is to make an extraordinary simplification of the problem of human knowledge and to deal oneself an unbeatable hand. However, that is not all, because infallible truth could include totally different types of truth, which would somewhat complicate a method trying to teach man how to grasp different types of truth. But Descartes reduced all infallible truths to one single type—the only one that he, with his own preconceptions, had experienced—the infallibility of mathematical truth.[47] This second simplification explains how in forty pages (the first four parts of the *Discourse*, the only ones important to his method) Descartes could give us his life's history, describe the particular circumstances attendant upon his discoveries, and teach us the art of "rightly conducting the reason and seeking truth in the sciences."

How can this rather extraordinary simplification of the problem of human knowledge be explained? A brief examination of the factors that begot the Cartesian *mirabile* will help us to understand why Descartes had to simplify the problems of knowledge in this way. This backward glance enables us to grasp the true meaning of the Cartesian problem and to conclude our study of its nature.

The starting point for the Cartesian *mirabile* is the existence of skepticism, considered as the mind's worst disease, and the desire to cure the mind by discovering the cause of its illness, erroneous knowledge. This cause cannot be science, for science is certain, evident, and begets the union of minds, not skepticism. This cause must then be found in knowledge other than scientific; but there are only two other types: popular knowledge, and another type greatly resembling it, Scholastic philosophy. Thus, the error begetting skepticism must have its origin there; in fact, history proves that skepticism does

result from the philosophers' endless discussions concerning all problems, possible and impossible. This being so, we must conclude that,
since popular knowledge and philosophic knowledge are lacking in
evidence, they are also lacking in truth and therefore are false.

Having come to this conclusion, Descartes had to discover the
cause of these errors by taking as criterion the only notion of infallible
truth that he recognized, namely, mathematical truth, and he had
to ask the *Ego* to account for the errors originating in it. Now, if
we examine the *Ego* by taking mathematical evidence as criterion of
truth, the only truths we will discover in it will be those whose
evidence is of a mathematical type. That is just what Descartes did,
and that is why his method is so simple, and why it simplifies human
knowledge to such a degree that it is no longer human but becomes
angelic. That, too, is the reason that Descartes' discoveries in mathematics have endured and his physics and metaphysics have lasted
exactly as long as the life of their inventor.

The Cartesian *mirabile* was born of an equivocation: identification
of human knowledge and mathematical evidence, and the identification of error with everything that is not mathematically evident, or
whose evidence is not mathematical in type. His method of inquiry
was centered entirely upon the solution of this equivocal *mirabile*. It
succeeded perfectly in resolving the *mirabile*, but it never touched
the real epistemological problem, whose fundamental formulation
must be made, not in terms of mathematical truth, but in these terms:
What does it mean "to know?"

¶ 2. *Psychological Structure of the Kantian Problem.* We
have already witnessed the birth of the Kantian problem under the
pressure of three factors: the first being the desire to discover the
cause of the skepticism from which man suffers; the second, the
identification of the cause of skepticism with error or nonevident
knowledge; the third, the identification of error or nonevident knowledge with metaphysical knowledge.[48] Kant's *mirabile* can be expressed
as follows: How can reason, which is one, be simultaneously the
cause of infallible truth and of metaphysical error? Since every
problem begets wonder, and since wonder is the source of the
inquiry that seeks to dispel it, we shall now study the psychological

structure of Kantian wonder and of the Kantian inquiry into the epistemological problem thus conceived.

Kant's wonder centers upon the fact that man has long since discovered the laws governing the acquisition of scientific truth, but is still groping and deceiving himself in the field of philosophical thought. What is the origin of this state of affairs?

What then is the reason why, in this field, the sure road to science has not hitherto been found? Is it perhaps impossible of discovery? Why in that case should nature have visited our reason with the restless endeavour whereby it is ever searching for such a path, as if this were one of its most important concerns? Nay, more, *how little cause have we to place trust in our reason,* if in one of the most important domains of which we would fain have knowledge, it does not merely fail us, but lures us on by deceitful promises, *and in the end betrays us?*[49]

Since Kantian wonder conceives reason, in its metaphysical aspirations, as a Circe who bewitches travelers and lures them to their destruction, the fear expressed by this wonder is the fear of reason as a natural source of error. The inquiry set in motion by this wonder will necessarily be directed toward knowing this natural cause of error, that is, to an analysis of reason or the thinking subject.

Kant does not open his investigation of reason or the *Ego* from zero-knowledge, or from complete ignorance of the mind and its activities, any more than did Descartes; for scientific knowledge exists and can teach us the methods used by reason to arrive at knowledge of truth.

The example of mathematics and natural science, which by a single and sudden revolution have become what they now are, seem to me sufficiently remarkable to suggest our considering what may have been the essential features in the changed point of view by which they have so greatly benefited. *Their success should incline us, at least by way of experiment, to imitate their way of procedure,* so far as the analogy which, as species of rational knowledge, they bear to metaphysics.

Hitherto it has been *assumed* that all our knowledge must conform to *objects.* But all attempts to extend our knowledge of objects by establishing something in regard to them *a priori,* by means of concepts, have, on this assumption, ended in failure. We must therefore make trial whether we may not have more success in the tasks of metaphysics, *if we suppose that objects must conform to our knowledge.*[50]

The lesson Kant wants to learn from science is an experimental lesson in the procedures by which science becomes fruitful, since the success of science is the criterion of its truth. But science is fruitful when, instead of blindly following nature, it appoints reason to guide its knowledge of nature.

They [i.e. the scientists] learned that reason has insight only into that which it produces after a plan of its own, and that it must not allow itself to be kept, as it were, in nature's leading strings, but must itself show the way with principles of judgment based upon fixed laws, constraining nature to give answer to questions of reason's own determining. . . . Reason, holding in one hand its equivalent to laws, and in the other hand the experiment which it has devised in conformity with these principles, must approach nature in order to be taught by it. It must not, however, do so in the character of a pupil who listens to everything that the teacher chooses to say, *but of an appointed judge who compels* the witnesses to answer questions which he has himself formulated. . . . It is thus that the study of nature has entered on the secure path of a science, after having for so many centuries been nothing but a process of merely random groping.[51]

This method that has succeeded so well in physics must be tried in metaphysics, which still is and has been for centuries at the groping stage where physics suffered so long. Since reason explains the success of the sciences, let us ask it to explain metaphysics' lack of success. Let us start proceedings against reason, bring it into court.

It is a call to reason to undertake anew the most difficult of all its tasks namely, that of self-knowledge, and to institute a tribunal which will grant to reason its lawful claims, and dismiss all groundless pretensions, not by despotic decrees, but in accordance with its own eternal and unalterable laws. *This tribunal is no other than the Critique of pure reason.*[52]

This action can be brought against reason only if there is an innocent and a guilty party; i.e., if reason is both the source of truth (therein lies its innocence) and the source of error (wherein lies its guilt). Now, proceedings are always instituted by the innocent against the guilty. The Critique of pure reason, as tribunal, will therefore ask the reason that is innocent or capable of scientific truth to accuse the guilty reason of producing metaphysical error. Since metaphysical error is as old as humanity, Kant will indict all the metaphysics of which reason is guilty, including that of Descartes.[53]

Obviously we cannot here follow every document adduced in proof at reason's trial. We shall have to be content with considering the starting point, or the fact that scientific truth exists, the essential theme of innocence and guilt, or the subject-object relations, and the point of arrival, or metaphysics as a transcendental illusion. Under these three aspects, we shall try to grasp the essence of the Kantian inquiry, which sprang from his wonder at the epistemological *mirabile*. In this simplified study, we shall let Kant do the talking as often as possible, for he knows better than anyone else what he wants to say and how to say it.

(a) *The inquiry's starting point.* The starting point in this inquiry is naturally the content of the Kantian *mirabile* in its paradoxical aspect of the coexistence of two systems of knowledge, one of which is true, the other false.

In the solution of the above problem, we are at the same time deciding as to the possibility of the employment of pure reason in establishing and developing all those sciences which contain *theoretical a priori knowledge of objects,* and have therefore to answer the questions:

> How is pure mathematics possible?
> How is pure science of nature possible?

Since these sciences actually exist, it is quite proper to ask *how they are possible*; for that they must be possible is *proved* by the fact that they exist. But the poor progress which has hitherto been made in metaphysics and the fact that no system yet propounded can, in view of the essential purpose of metaphysics, be said really to exist, leaves everyone sufficient ground for doubting as to its possibility.

Yet, in a certain sense, this kind of knowledge is to be looked upon as given, that is to say, metaphysics actually exists, *if not as science, yet still as a natural disposition.* . . . And so we have the question:

> How is metaphysics, as natural disposition, possible? that is,
> how from the nature of universal reason do those questions arise
> which pure reason propounds to itself, and which it is impelled
> by its own need to answer as best it can?

But . . . we cannot rest satisfied with the mere natural disposition to metaphysics. . . . It must be possible for reason to attain to certainty *whether we know or do not know the objects of metaphysics,* that is to come to a decision either in regard to the objects of its inquiries or in regard to the capacity or incapacity of reason to pass any judgment upon them. . . . This last question which arises out of the previous general problem, may, rightly stated, take the form:

> *How is metaphysics, as science, possible?*[54]

It is interesting to note, first of all, that the *Critique of Pure Reason* does not propose the problem of the existence of truth as the point of departure for the Critique of knowledge; rather, since the fact of the existence of truth has been experienced, it asks the question: *How is it possible?* Comparing this starting point with that of Descartes, we find a striking difference: Descartes was seeking the *existence* of evident and indisputable truth, *starting from doubt,* whereas Kant starts from existing truths and looks for the conditions of their possibility. Doubt is not a component factor in Kantian method. Why? Because Kant could historically perceive the ravages that this method had wrought within philosophical thought and the woeful results to which it had led—the metaphysics and physics of Descartes.[55] Furthermore, Kant admits the evidence of physical reality as initial datum; therefore, he had no need to seek in the *Cogito* the first certitude in the existential order. That the mathematical and physical sciences give us an account of our physical universe is a fact. What he asks of the mind is that it tell us why this is a fact.

The case of metaphysics is different, for its truth does not yet exist, which is a reason for doubting its possibility. On the other hand, this type of knowledge does exist as a natural disposition, and because of this fact, we can state the problem concerning the conditions, or the why, of this existence as a natural disposition. Here, again, the method goes from the *quia est* to the *propter quid,* to use Aristotelian and Scholastic terminology.[56] But to give the why of metaphysics as a natural disposition does not explain its existence as science, which brings us to the third question: Does metaphysical truth exist? This is the only question concerned with the existence of truth, and it is restricted to metaphysical truth alone. In the latter case the problem is reversed, as we shall see, for Kant will prove that metaphysical truth does not exist, because the very nature of the mind makes it impossible.

Thus, there are two very different aspects to the starting point of the quest to solve the Kantian *mirabile*, because this *mirabile* includes two heterogeneous elements whose heterogeneity, strictly speaking, constitutes the problem of critique: Why does reason produce truth (science) and error (metaphysics)? The fact of truth must be explained; we must find the why of this truth. The fact of error, too, must be explained; we must also find its "why." Now, *the fact of error coincides with the fact of the existence of metaphysics as a natural disposition*. To seek the why of error is equivalent to seeking the why of metaphysics as a natural disposition, but it is not equivalent to establishing the existence of metaphysics as a science, or the existence of metaphysical truth. Since this latter does not yet exist, we cannot start from the fact of its existence, of its *quia est*, to seek its *propter quid*. The only remaining alternative is to examine the mind to try to discover therein the conditions of the possibility or impossibility of metaphysical truth. From this angle, the *quid sit* of metaphysical truth is prior to its *an sit*. The Kantian *mirabile* thus contains three distinct aspects of the same problem, namely, the problem of truth and error. The first aspect concerns *the why of the existence* of scientific truth; the second deals with *the why of the existence* of error, or of metaphysics as a natural disposition; the third with the possibility or impossibility of the existence of metaphysical truth, considering the very nature of this truth.

(b) *The essential theme of critique: subject versus object.* Since the Critique is a tribunal before which the mind must appear to justify the truth it possesses and the error it begets, we must discover the reasons for its innocence and its guilt, for they cannot be identical. We must therefore start the inquiry by asking the mind by what means it *knows*.

By way of introduction or anticipation we need only say that there are two stems of human knowledge, namely, *sensibility* and *understanding*, which perhaps spring from a common, but to us unknown, root. Through the former, objects are given to us; through the latter, they are thought.[57]

The structure of the mind is thus characterized by a dualism whose source is unknown but whose existence is an undeniable fact. All human knowledge springs from this double origin. What is the specific contribution of each factor? Sensibility, says Kant, gives us the object, while understanding enables us to think these objects. Here is how he describes the operations belonging properly to each of these factors and their interdependence:

If the *receptivity* of our mind . . . is to be entitled *sensibility*, then the mind's power of producing representations from itself, the *spontaneity* of knowledge, should be called *the understanding*. Our nature is so constituted that our *intuition* can never be other than sensible; that is, it contains only the *mode* in which we are affected by objects. The faculty, on the other hand, which enables us *to think* the object of sensible intuition is the understanding. To neither of these powers may a preference be given over the other. Without sensibility no object would be given to us, without understanding no object would be thought. Thoughts without content are empty, intuitions without concepts are blind. It is therefore just as necessary to make our concepts sensible, that is to add the object to them in intuition, as to make our intuitions intelligible, that is to bring them under concepts. These two powers or capacities cannot exchange their functions. The understanding can *intuit* nothing, the senses can *think* nothing. Only through their union can knowledge arise.[58]

This description of human knowledge as the absolutely indissoluble marriage of the receptive part of our mind, whose name is sensibility, with the spontaneous part of this same mind, whose name is understanding, strikes a very anti-Cartesian and, on the contrary, a very Aristotelian note. That this definition of human knowledge is anti-Cartesian needs hardly to be said, since Kant never recognized either Descartes' *cogito* or his notion of the *Ego* as a thinking substance possessing innate ideas and immediately evident truths from the first moment of its existence.[59] But that this definition strikes an Aristotelian note cannot but be surprising, since the result of the Critique is the destruction of realist metaphysics in the Aristotelian sense of the word. Consequently, we must ask Kant to explain the proper role of sensibility in receiving objects, and that of the understanding as a spontaneous power capable of thinking these same objects. His explanation will give us the key both to his Critique and to the relations existing between *subject and object*, or between the *a priori* and the *given;* for the Kantian notion of object includes the subject, and the *a priori* includes the given.

The effect of an object upon the faculty of representation, so far as we are affected by it, is *sensation*. That *intuition* which is in relation to the object through sensation, is entitled *empirical*. The undetermined object of an empirical intuition is entitled *appearance*.[60]

In this statement we witness the *first* phase in the Kantian genesis of the object, which he calls *phenomenon*.[61] The phenomenon comes into contact with the thinking subject through its causal action upon our sensibility, a causality that modifies the state of the subject itself. Grasping the subjective modifications caused by a phenomenon constitutes sensation. Sensation does not grasp the phenomenon as object but receives it passively.[62] In and by sensation, empirical intuition (the act of sensibility) grasps the phenomenon, no longer as passively received by the subject, but as unified in space and time, that is, as exterior and immanent to the knower. Thus, the matter of a phenomenon, pure becoming and multiplicity, is represented in the *exterior* unity that we term *space* and in the *interior* unity called *time*.[63] This unification, accomplished by intuition according to the aforementioned modes, is the form of the phenomenon, because it allows its matter to be present to the mind as other than the subject and as its principle of objective determination.[64] The phenomenon as object is therefore made up of two elements. One, grasped by sensation, is essentially immersed in becoming and change, and the other, grasped by intuition, fixes this multiplicity in space and time. Are these two aspects of the phenomenon related, and what is their origin?

That in the appearance which corresponds to sensation I term its *matter;* but *that* which so determines the manifold of appearance that it allows of being ordered in certain relations, I term the *form* of appearance . . . ; while the matter of all appearances is given to us *a posteriori only*, its form must lie ready for the sensations *a priori* in the mind.[65]

The matter of the phenomenon, or the *a posteriori given*, is therefore the element in the object which makes that object heterogeneous to the knowing subject, but this heterogeneity is not knowable or objective as long as it is not empirically intuited within the two *a priori* forms of sensibility, space and time. Only then does the phenomenon exist formally as phenomenon. In the last analysis, intuition of the given is possible only by means of the formal *a priori* conditions of space and time. The *a priori* enters into the constitution of the phenomenon, thus of the object undetermined as such.[66]

What characterizes the *a priori* is that it is pure or purified of every sensory element and does not therefore belong to the given as such. It proceeds entirely from the nature of sensibility itself, which provides the given with whatever perceptibility it has. It is therefore the subject, in and by its *a priori* forms, that makes the given knowable and thus constitutes it formally as object of sensibility.[67] The Kantian phenomenon as object cannot be conceived without the *a priori* forms of sensibility, or ever be considered as an exterior reality measuring a subject that passively submits to its causality. Contrary to the Thomistic explanation, Kantian reality supplies only the matter of the sensibly known object; the subject gives to this object its form, therefore, its perceptibility, by giving it a unity without which this absolute becoming would wholly escape knowledge.[68]

This description of the material and formal components of the phenomenon is only the first step in the constitution of an object according to Kant, for we must make our intuitions intelligible,[69] if human knowledge is truly to be exercised.

If I remove from empirical knowledge [intuition] all thought (through categories), *no knowledge of any object remains.* For through mere intuition nothing at all is thought, and the fact that this affection of sensibility is in me does not by itself amount to a relation of such representation to any object. . . .[70]

If each representation[71] were completely foreign to every other, standing apart in isolation, no such thing as knowledge would ever arise. *For knowledge is essentially a whole in which representations stand compared and connected.* As sense contains a manifold in its intuition, I ascribe to it a *synopsis.* But to such synopsis a synthesis must always correspond; receptivity [i.e., sensibility] can make knowledge possible only when combined with spontaneity [i.e., understanding]. Now this spontaneity is

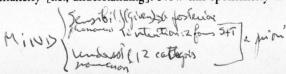

the ground of a threefold synthesis which must necessarily be found in all knowledge; namely, *the apprehension of representations* as modifications of the mind in intuition, their *reproduction in imagination,* and their *recognition* in a concept.[72]

Nothing is knowable except it be unified. The multiplicity of sensory matter is informed by the formal unity of intuition, but intuitions themselves are multiple, as are the sensations they inform. Therefore, a unifying principle superior to sensibility must be found, and this principle is the transcendental unity of the thinking subject expressed in "I think," the necessary accompaniment of all possible and imaginable representations. Without "I think," no activity of the understanding would be possible, because there would be no principle unifying all the representations of sensibility.[73] This unity of apperception synthesizes the multiple data of empirical intuition, which would be impossible were it not for the categories whose precise function is to unify the multiplicity of a given intuition.[74] Unless the *a priori* forms of the understanding (the concept or category) *be joined* to the *a priori* forms of sensibility, there can be no knowledge of the object or phenomenon.[75]

To summarize what has just been said about the conditions necessary for the existence of an object as such, we must in every *object as such* distinguish the following:

(1) The matter of the phenomenon or datum that causes sensation; it is heterogeneous to the subject.

(2) The form of the phenomenon, or intuition of sensory matter by space and time, the two unifying *modes* of the given's multiplicity. These are *a priori* forms and therefore distinct from the matter which they make knowable and thus make into an object or complete phenomenon. But since the *a priori* forms of sensibility give us a *particular object* or phenomenon, and phenomena are multiple, we need some other factor to make this particular object into *this* phenomenon, into an object in general, or an object as such. Whence the necessity for a third component to constitute the object.

(3) The *a priori* forms of understanding, or the categories, which make this phenomenon or its intuition intelligible.

Thus, the Kantian object is not the exterior reality taken in its concrete existence, but rather the appearances or phenomena of external realities *as informed by the a priori modes of sensibility and understanding*. Objective knowledge does not receive exterior objects fully constituted; it contacts external reality, not in itself, but in its appearances (sensation) and gives to these appearances the forms of the cognitional powers themselves, the forms of sensibility and understanding. There is *no objective knowledge unless there be a given*, that is, unless a phenomenon act upon the knowing subject; but the datum cannot be an object or knowable without the subjects's *a priori* forms. Therefore, the *a priori* forms of the subject formally constitute the object, while the given supplies only the material element. Without a given, knowledge has no objectivity, but without the *a priori* forms, there is no knowledge.

The essential theme of the Critique is therefore the notion of the object as such, for without it Critique is impossible, since there is no knowledge. On the other hand, the *notion* of the object is itself the judge in the tribunal of Critique,[76] since the notion of the object reveals the contribution made by the subject in every act of knowledge, and the contribution made by reality in all objective knowledge. If the knower attributes to the given the properties that the subject itself contributes to knowledge, he is guilty of error; if, on the other hand, he does not make this misattribution, he is innocent, he possesses truth. Such are the essential notions in the *Critique of Pure Reason*. Equipped with this Kantian notion of the object, we can now consider the aim or term of *Critique*, or *why metaphysics as a science is impossible*.

(c) *The aim of the* Critique: *metaphysics as a transcendental illusion*. During the analysis of the Kantian object we have seen that the *a priori* or formal element, originating in the very nature of our knowing faculties, before any act of knowledge, is independent of the given. This *a priori* element, without which the given cannot be known, is knowable without the given. Thus, it is possible to know pure forms without matter (or the given) by sensible intuition as well as by the concept. That for Kant is what characterizes reason and is the great discovery made by the *Critique*. This knowledge of pure forms is, strictly speaking, transcendental knowledge and reveals the structure of the thinking subject as such; it constitutes the difference between "I think" and "I know."[77] It establishes the superiority of the *Critique* over the *Discourse on Method*, for Kant really analyzed the *thinking subject*, whereas Descartes went no further than the *knowing subject*.

While it is possible *to think without knowing*, it is impossible to know without thinking. Therefore, all the laws governing the sensible as well as the intelligible *a priori* forms are functions of knowledge and of empirical knowledge. This is the only kind of knowledge we can have, because thoughts without intuitions, thus without sensory data, are thoughts without content. They are not objective since one of the elements essential to objective knowledge, matter, is missing. If thought were also knowledge, we would have to have intellectual intuition, and reality in itself would have to be the object of this intuition.[78] The *noumenon* would not only have to be, it would have to be knowable or intelligible for us; but this is not the case, for our power of intuition is not *originarius* but *derivatus*.[79]

Consequently, the pure sciences are a utilization of the *a priori* of sensibility and understanding and their fullest completion by empirical knowledge. This completion is what gives to these sciences their truth and infallibility. Now, the objects of metaphysics, considered as a natural tendency, are all objects that elude sensible intuition, inasmuch as they are all necessary and universal, whereas empirical knowledge is concerned with the particular and contingent.[80] Therefore, since the mind has no intellectual intuition, it cannot come into contact with necessary and universal datum, and when it does have such an object, it confuses the *a priori modes* of sensibility and understanding with the empirical datum measured by these modes. It creates a fictitious object; it lives in illusion. The history of metaphysics, past, present, and future, is the history of transcendentally illusory knowledge.[81] Such is the verdict brought down at the tribunal of reason that is the *Critique of Pure Reason*.

Accordingly, fruitless as are all these endeavours of speculative reason, we have none the less found it necessary to follow them up to their primary sources. And since the dialectical illusion does not merely deceive us in our judgements, but also, because of the interest which we take in these judgements, has a certain *natural attraction* which it will always continue to possess, we have thought it advisable, with a view to the prevention of such errors in the future, to draw up in full detail what we may describe as being *the records of this lawsuit* and to deposit them in the archives of human reason.[82]

This is the outcome of the *Critique of Pure Reason*, the goal of this long and painstaking inquiry that sprang from the Kantian *mirabile*. Having arrived at this term, this *mirabile* disappears, for we know now: 1) *why truth is possible*, 2) why error is possible, 3) why metaphysics is impossible. Reason has vindicated the paradoxical character of its narratives, both the infallibly true narrative and the infallibly false.

¶ 3. *Conclusion on the Nature of the Modern Epistemological Problem*. This study of the nature of the Cartesian and Kantian problem can be concluded by a comparison of the Cartesian *mirabile* with the Kantian and the consequences derived therefrom. This comparison can be outlined in four conclusions showing the diversity of the results obtained by the *Discourse* and the *Critique*:

First conclusion:

(a) For Descartes, reason is infallible as soon as it quarantines sensation, eliminates the object of knowledge.

(b) For Kant, reason is infallible insofar as it depends upon sensation, for the given is an essential component of the object.

Second conclusion:

(a) For Descartes, infallible reason possesses, from the first moment of existence, the seed of all future truths about God, the *Ego* and physical nature.

(b) For Kant, this infallible reason, in its relation to empirical intuition, possesses in its very structure every possibility of illusion or error about God, the self and the physical universe.

Third conclusion:

(a) For Descartes, truth is always experienced through intellectual intuition or by deduction and analysis.

(b) For Kant, truth is always dependent upon sensory intuition, since we have no intellectual intuition, and synthesis is the central factor in our experience of truth.

Fourth conclusion:
(a) For Descartes, metaphysics is not only possible but upon its existence depends the basic foundation of all truth.
(b) For Kant, metaphysics could never be anything but a transcendental illusion, and scientific truth is possible only insofar as reason realizes that it has this power of creating illusions.

How could such different conclusions follow from a *mirabile* whose genesis and nature seem to be identical?[83] The reason is that truth and falsity, the two components of their *mirabile*, are not defined in the same way by these two thinkers. Cartesian truth is defined by the *being* of things and falsity by their *appearances*, which are creations of the senses. Kantian truth is defined by the *appearance* of things, or phenomena, whereas falsity is caused by their *being*, or noumena, whose objectivity is the creation of speculative reason. Thus, when Descartes and Kant find it a source of wonder that the unity of reason could be the simultaneous source of truth and error and hold an inquest or trial of reason, they do not ask it to vindicate the same truth, or the same error. It is therefore not surprising that their answers are so different, for answers always depend upon the meaning of the questions asked.

What is the absolute truth value of these two answers? In the author's opinion they contain this truth that should never be forgotten: Every epistemological problem stated in terms of the opposition between truth and error is badly stated and therefore insoluble. Every epistemological problem must first be stated in terms of *knowledge* and *ignorance;* this is its first instance or moment. Once this question has been answered, we can ask what truth our knowledge gives us. With this question answered, we can go on to a third: Is this truth infallible? Because Descartes and Kant started with the third question before asking the second and first, whose solutions are presupposed, they were never able satisfactorily and objectively to solve their own problem. This is the truth that may be gleaned from analysis of the Cartesian and Kantian problem, a truth which the contemporary or scientific aspect of the epistemological problem will only confirm.

Section II: The Contemporary Epistemological Problem

We have said[84] that the modern problem is like a *two-faced Janus*, one of whose faces is represented by Descartes and Kant, the other by contemporary science. The study of this latter aspect of the modern epistemological problem is doubly interesting: initially, because of its dissimilarities that create a distinctive *mirabile* composed, not of the coexistence of truth and error, but of the coexistence of two scientific systems; then, because of certain characteristic attitudes that reveal its Cartesian and Kantian heredity, such as distrust of sensation and a pragmatic orientation toward knowledge.[85] In this, as in the preceding section, we shall follow the natural approach we discovered when we considered the nature of every problem. There will be a first subsection in which we shall witness the birth of the contemporary problem, and a second wherein we shall study its particular nature and its relations to Cartesianism and Kantianism. We shall also follow the same procedure in stating the problem, letting the thinkers involved explain their own position in order to avoid any distortion of their thought.

A. THE BIRTH OF THE CONTEMPORARY EPISTEMOLOGICAL PROBLEM

For two hundred and fifty years, until the end of the nineteenth century, modern science was based upon the mathematical principles of Euclid and Pythagoras, applied by Newton to explain our universe.[86] This universe has three dimensions, is measured by absolute space and time, and is composed of particles of matter at rest or in motion, while its whole dynamism is governed by the three mechanical laws of mass, force, and reaction. Scientific knowledge of this universe has an ideal of necessity and universality that make it almost divine. Here is a description of this scientific ideal:

We ought then to regard the present state of the universe as the *effect* of its antecedent state and the *cause* of the state that is to follow. An intelligence, who for a given instant should be acquainted with all the forces by which nature is animated and with the several positions of the entities composing it, if further his intellect were vast enough to submit those data to analysis, would include in one and the same formula the movements of the largest bodies in the universe and those of the lightest atom. *Nothing would be uncertain for him; the future, as well as the past, would be present to his eyes.* The human mind, in the perfection it has been able to give to astronomy, affords a feeble outline of such an intelligence. . . . All its efforts in the search for truth tend to approximate without limit to the intelligence we have just imagined.[87]

This harmonious, classical universe, in which chance and indeterminism have no place, and whose ideal of knowledge copies the divine in the way it joins past and future in the present—this universe has been superseded by another whose dimensions are vast enough to appear infinite, and whose interior structures are so incorporeal that they have no dimensions and are therefore unimaginable. In this universe, wherein the infinitely large jostles the infinitely small, there is no longer any absolute space and time, mass, or causal determinism. Groupings and fields of relation have become the essential factors to be explained. Principles of explanation no longer have the necessity, or the evidence of classical science but are indeterminate and relative, assigning a major role to chance. Knowledge by probabilities has succeeded classical science's ideal of quasi-divine certitude; Euclidean geometry has given way to that of Riemann and Einstein.[88] Even Pythagorean number has been replaced by cosmic number.[89]

This opposition between universes has all the elements of a *mirabile*, and the opposition between these explanatory theories has inevitably given rise to an epistemological *mirabile*. The consequences of this situation were quickly perceived, and since the beginning of the twentieth century, epistemological works have been produced in increasing acceleration, whereas the two preceding centuries were practically sterile in this field. This epistemological renascence in science has covered all the aspects of the contemporary problem: its source, mathematical knowledge; its methods, analysis, induction, deduction, logic, logistic; its objects; the macroscopic universe, this man-sized universe, and the microscopic universe; and finally the nature of actual physical knowledge; its truth, the degrees of certitude of this truth, its necessity, its hypothetical character, etc.[90]

This wealth of works on scientific epistemology, once again, confirms the solidity of the universal law presiding over the birth of every problem, a law whose existence we noted in studying the problem as such.[91] In order for a problem to exist, there must be two narrators telling divergent stories. For over two hundred years classical science was absolute mistress in its field. According to scientists, the Cartesian method and the Kantian Critique had definitely classed philosophical knowledge as pseudoscience, to which they no longer needed to pay any heed, and had bequeathed them a method and an ideal of knowledge that they had only to put into effect. Since conflicts between philosophy and science were done away with once and for all, since the methods and the ideal of science were one, there was no longer any possibility of duality in the stories or of any really important differences between the narrators. Descartes and Kant were the gods of the scientists, and the scientists were their prophets. The few isolated thinkers who dared stray from the beaten path were considered to be dreamers and were termed "philosophers," with all the insulting insinuations of the word. However, advances in technical knowledge and the invention of increasingly accurate instruments of control brought the day when these instruments seemed to confirm the preposterous hypotheses of a few mathematical or physical geniuses, and a second storyteller has appeared whose account of the universe is to be taken seriously. Thus, the contemporary *mirabile* is born.

The original character and the epistemological value of the contemporary problem are that, hitherto, the *mirabile* always sprang from opposition between two different types of knowledge, either between popular knowledge and philosophical knowledge, or between the latter and science or theology. But in the twentieth century a *mirabile* has appeared whose two divergent factors are scientific: mathematical evidence opposes other mathematical evidence; controlled physical observations are opposed by other equally controlled experiments. How is it possible to explain that one science can be thus opposed to another science? Are they both true? Is their opposition owing to the mind or to things? Must one of them be rejected in favor of the other? Such is the contemporary *mirabile*, whose psychological structure we will now study briefly.

B. THE PSYCHOLOGICAL STRUCTURE OF THE CONTEMPORARY PROBLEM   3 laws p 68

Every problem or *mirabile* causes a shock or wonder in the soul, wonder that begets an inquiry aiming to dispel the ignorance at the source of this wonder. We have seen that this inquiry assumes very different forms, depending upon the psychological attitude of the inquirer toward the factors of his *mirabile*. If he considers one of these components radically true and the other synonymous with error, his inquiry will be a lawsuit brought against error in the name of truth. This is characteristic of modern methods.[92] But if both components are given equal footing, if they are considered capable of being equally true, then the investigation will be made in a conciliatory spirit, by distinguishing the different objects or the points of view that may be had about reality, and the different aspects of this same reality. Contemporary epistemology has taken this direction, in the opinion of those who have dealt with the problem.

Elaborate studies made with instrumental aid have shown that the phenomena of the *world of the electron* do not in any way form a replica on a minute scale of the *world of the nebulae*. As we leave the *man-sized world* behind us, and proceed either towards the infinitely great in one direction or towards the infinitely small in the other, the laws of nature seems at first sight to change, not only in detail but in their whole essence. More careful scrutiny discloses that the apparent change is illusory; actually the same laws prevail throughout the range, but different features of these laws become of preponderating importance in different parts of the range . . . all objects are governed by the universal laws of physics, but one aspect of these laws is all-important for the electron, another for man-sized objects, and yet a third for the movements of the nebulae.[93]

The contemporary *mirabile* does not incline the epistemologist to put reason on trial in the name of a uniform and rigid criterion of truth, because reason confronts him with three universes, of which only one is true and the other two false. But it does urge him to find out what it is in man and the knowable universe that makes this trinity of knowledge possible. We have just seen that the first area of agreement is on the side of the object, since three different aspects of our physical universe are distinguishable: the infinitely large, the infinitely small, and the man-sized universe between them.

The definition of knowledge provides another basis for agreement. The principle governing contemporary epistemology is no longer the Cartesian and Kantian identification of knowledge with truth and of truth with infallible and absolutely certain truth; it is a much more flexible notion and more extensible to the different modes of human knowledge.

Some writers restrict the term *knowledge* to things we are quite certain of; others recognize knowledge of varying degrees of uncertainty. . . . I . . . prefer the broader meaning; and my own usage will recognize *uncertain knowledge*. Anything which would be knowledge if we were assured of its truth, is still counted as knowledge if we are not assured; . . . usually a reasonable degree of *certainty or probability* is attributed to the knowledge we shall have occasion to discuss. But the assessment of certainty is to be regarded *as separate from the nature of knowledge*.[94]

Such a statement would make Descartes and Kant bristle with indignation, and here is another, even more revolutionary definition to terrify the inventors of the modern method, for it is directed against the distinction and separation of method from science:

Formally we may still recognize a distinction between science as treating the *content* of knowledge, and scientific epistemology as treating the *nature* of knowledge of the physical universe. *But it is no longer a practical* partition: and to conform to the present situation, scientific epistemology *should be included* in science.[95]

Sir James Jeans is even more explicit about the inefficiency of any method that examines the mind in order to explain the truth of things, and that neglects things themselves as if they played no part in the explanation of truth! At the end of a chapter entitled, "How Do We Know?" in which he gives an historical account of idealist positions concerning the problem of knowledge, he concludes:

Our discussion seems to bring us back to the age-old conclusion that if we wish to discover truth about nature, the pattern of events in the universe we inhabit, the only sound method is to go out into the world and question nature directly, and this is the long-established and well-tried method of science. Questioning our own mind is of no use. Just as questioning nature can tell us truths only about nature, so questioning our own minds will tell us only truths about our own minds.

The general recognition of this has brought philosophy into closer relations with science and this approach has coincided with a change of view as to the proper aims of philosophy. . . . The tools of science are observation and experiment; the tools of philosophy are discussion and contemplation. It is still for science to try to discover the pattern of events and for philosophy to try to interpret it when found.[96]

This new orientation of epistemology, which makes it an integral part of the science whose method it is, obtains not only for physics but even for mathematics, which must have a certain realism in order truly to be a science.

To be too quick to condemn *mathematical realism* is to be seduced by the magnificent extension of formal epistemology; that is to say, by a sort of functioning in the void on the part of mathematical notions. But if no abstraction is made from the psychological approach of the mathematician, it does not take long to see that there is more to mathematical activity than a formal organization of diagrams, and that every pure idea has its counterpart in a psychological application, in an example which takes the place of reality. By meditating upon the work of the mathematician, we perceive *that it always results from an extension of knowledge drawn from reality*, and that even in mathematics, reality reveals itself in its essential function: i.e. to make us think. . . . There, as everywhere else, appears the dualism of the subjective and the objective.[97]

Contemporary epistemology has an increasing tendency to free itself from the tyrannical laws of the subjective method invented by

Descartes and Kant, and to ask reality, and the object, to vindicate its explanation of scientific truth. Thus, wonder caused by the actual epistemological *mirabile* does not orient inquiry solely toward the *Ego* but toward the two elements essential to all truth: man and the universe he knows. Nor does this wonder look upon the opposition of scientific theories as a sign of falsity or error, but rather as a symptom of the complexity of our universe, the depths of whose unity are revealed in different ways, depending upon the more or less primitive, or more or less evolved, character of the matter being studied.

Such is the nature of the psychological reaction characterizing the contemporary *mirabile*. To go back to the comparison we used at the beginning of our first chapter, it resembles the host who tries to find grounds for agreement between his two quarreling guests in order that he may continue to extend them his hospitality and enjoy their presence. What will be the nature of the investigations and methods of inquiry destined to dispel the contemporary epistemological *mirabile?* We know that the starting point of an investigation governs it and organizes its procedure.[98] We also know that the *mirabile* is the true starting point for inquiry, at the same time that it characterizes the inquiry, because it is the question that the inquiry seeks to answer. Now the question was this: Can two sciences dealing with the physical universe give different explanations of that universe and still be true? If the word *truth* has only one meaning and depends only upon the structure of the mind, this question must necessarily be answered in the negative. But if the word *truth* has several meanings, and the multiplicity of the aspects of the universe enters into its definition, then the question may be answered affirmatively. We shall perceive the nature of contemporary scientific truth, its criteria of existence and objectivity, by comparing it with the Cartesian and Kantian notion of the criteria for truth.

These criteria are three: 1) In order that knowledge be true, it must be *evident* or intuited; 2) It must be *necessary* and thus absolutely determined in its object, admitting of no exception; 3) It must be *certain* or infallible, never subject to change. *Intuition, objective determination, certitude* or *subjective determination,* these are the three characteristics of modern scientific truth. Let us see the characteristics of contemporary scientific truth.

All contemporary science is governed by three laws, which are the counterparts of the three characteristics of the Cartesian and Kantian scientific ideal:

(1) *The law of choice* counters intuition.

(2) *The law of indeterminacy* counters objective necessity.

(3) *The law of probability* counters certitude or subjective necessity.

¶ *1.   The Law of Choice.*   According to Descartes and Kant,[99] where there is no intuition there is no truth, for otherwise there is no contact between the mind and reality. Practically all the realities that are the object of contemporary science fall outside Descartes' category of clear ideas and escape the domination of the Kantian *a priori* forms, because these realities are measurable neither by Euclidean space nor by absolute time, which were necessary for the intuition of Descartes and Kant. Intuition has been replaced by the axiom of choice, whose various and somewhat capricious character is more suited to dealing with actual scientific realities. Here is an explanation of this axiom or law:

When two hypotheses are possible, we provisionally *choose* that which our minds adjudge to be the simpler, on the supposition that this is the more likely to lead in the direction of the truth. There can be, of course, no absolute criterion as to which of the two hypotheses is the simpler; in the last resort this must be a matter of private judgment.[100]

And here is a more detailed description of this law and its relation to intuition:

The new scientific spirit has turned the whole problem of intuition topsy-turvy. For this intuition can no longer be primary, it is preceded by a discursive study revealing a sort of fundamental duality. All basic notions can in some way be divided into two; they are all duplicated by complementary notions. *Henceforward every intuition will proceed from a choice:* there will be a kind of ambiguity basic to scientific description, affecting the immediate character of Cartesian intuition. . . . Nothing is more anti-Cartesian than the gradual modifications of the mind necessitated by the successive approximations reached by experimentation, especially when the farthest reaching of these experiments reveal previously-unknown organic wealth. Such is the case, we repeat, with the Einsteinian concept, whose richness and complex value suddenly reveal the poverty of the Newtonian concept. Such is the case, too, for the wave mechanics of Louis de Broglie which, in the full sense of the word, completes classical mechanics and even relativistic mechanics itself.[101]

The law of choice does not obtain only in physics; it plays an important role within mathematics. In a work on the nature of mathematical judgment, a philosopher, who is also a great mathematician, defends the legitimacy of this axiom against Léon Brunschvicg, who doubts its usefulness.

The axiom of choice is much more than a non-absurdity, a "pass" issued to the mind; its elegance speaks in its favor wherever hitherto unknown results are obtained by its means. The reason a better economy ensues upon its use is that it very probably penetrates deeply enough into the nature of things and expresses an aptitude thereof which is none the less real, although eluding explanation. It would be analogous in mathematics to a judgment of possibility, possibility meaning here a being in tendency that somehow escapes absolute necessity. . . . The fact remains that the axiom of choice and the judgments depending on it, more generally all those dealing with the transfinite, must be excluded from mathematics if the sole rule admitted is univocal necessity. This ostracism seems altogether illegitimate.[102]

This first law is obviously diametrically opposite to the intuitive evidence that Descartes and Kant required in order to qualify a truth as such and to make it scientific. It is hard to see what role Cartesian innatism or the Kantian *a priori* would play with respect to such an axiom; as a matter of fact, they play no role whatsoever.

¶ 2. *The Law or Principle of Indeterminacy.* Cartesian innatism accounted for the necessary structure of things, and the Kantian *a priori* imposed upon phenomena the immutable and necessary forms of the mind. With such ideas and informing power, it was inevitable that the truths found in nature by the human mind enjoy an absolute objective necessity and that it be contradictory to think of a world other than that given by science.[103] With the appearance of the quantum theory and the theory of relativity the

causal links between things disappeared from science, because individual things gave way to groupings, to groups of relations or
relative beings. Time and space having been replaced by their essentially correlative value, the knowledge we can have of the position
of beings and of the bonds uniting them becomes extremely pre-
carious, the more so because the speed at which they travel is unimaginable.[104] Therefore, some principle had to be found to state
intelligibly the lack of objective determination that characterizes
reality with regard to its exact position and the speed at which it
moves. Heisenberg discovered this principle,[105] called the principle
of uncertainty, which may be described as follows: an algebraic
formula proposing to tell the future position of an object exactly,
but in a formula of which precisely half the symbols represent
knowable quantities and *the other half unknowable quantities.*[106]

This principle of uncertainty rests entirely upon the character
peculiar to the objectivity of scientific truth. This *objectivity is
essentially relative* to an incalculable number of points or to a group
of entities that are themselves mobile. The relation objectifying
scientific knowledge must thus be of the same nature as the mobility
of the beings constituting its object; it must therefore have indetermination identical with theirs if it is to be exact, that is to say, true.[107]
Therein lies the meaning of the principle of indeterminacy, which
exactly measures the inexactitude or indetermination of the groups
that are the object of scientific knowledge. When an object's absolute has given way to its position in a group measured by correlative
time and space, the absolute of the necessity of the truth must also
give way to a certain indetermination, the exact knowing of which
constitutes the very truth of knowledge.

¶ *3. The Law of Probability.* The certitude or necessity of
Cartesian and Kantian truth springs from its immutable measure,
which is either the idea or the *a priori*. Since modern science is
measured by an essentially mutable reality, whose only stability
proceeds from the constancy of the relations between beings, because
of their prodigious multitude, the stability or certitude of scientific
knowledge must follow the laws of its measurement. In other words,
when the object is determined because it enters into an essentially

determined physical causality, certitude is possible. But when causal determinism is replaced by an ensemble of relations whose relative values are essentially mobile, all we can ask of such knowledge is that it possess the relative stability of these objects and that their stability be expressed in a law of probability defining scientific truth.

Whilst striving to perfect a system of law that would predict what *certainly* will happen, physicists also became interested in a system which predicts what *probably* will happen. Alongside the super-intelligence imagined by Laplace [see above, note 87] for whom "nothing would be uncertain" was placed an intelligence for whom *nothing would be certain but something would be exceedingly probable*. . . . Generally speaking, his predictions never approach certainty unless they refer to an average of a very large number of individual entities. Thus the aim of science to approximate to this latter intelligence is by no means equivalent to Laplace's aim. I shall call the aim defined by Laplace the *primary* aim, and the new aim introduced in the science of thermodynamics the *secondary* aim. . . .[108] Measured by advance towards Laplace's aim its progress is just *nil*. . . .[109] The physicist might continue to profess allegiance to primary law but he has ceased to use it. Primary law was the gold stored in the vaults; secondary law was the paper currency actually used. But everyone still adhered to the traditional view that paper currency needs to be backed by gold. . . . But I think it is clear that . . . present-day physics is *off the gold standard*.[110]

We have seen that efforts to discover the true nature of reality are necessarily doomed to failure, so that if we are to progress further it must be by taking some other objective and utilising some new philosophical principles of which we have not yet made use. Two such suggest themselves. The first is the principle of what Leibnitz described as probable reasoning. *We must give up the quest for certain knowledge* and concentrate on that one of the various alternatives before us which seems to be most probably true.[111]

The law of probability refers simultaneously to a property grafted on to realities because of their great number and to an attribute of our knowledge. Just as it designates a property of things *that does not make them known in themselves but known by reason of their number* and of the relations existing between the individuals of a group, so is our knowledge of them concerned with the number and relations of the individuals in a group. That is why it is opposed to causality or determinism in its objective sense and to the certitude or subjective necessity of knowledge. Sir James Jeans has admirably formulated this imperfect or noncertain character of probability in the following text:

> The wave picture does not show the future as following inexorably from the present, but the *imperfections* of our future knowledge following inexorably from the *imperfections* of our present knowledge.[112]

¶ *Conclusion on the Contemporary Epistemological Problem.* We have seen that the contemporary *mirabile* consists in the co-existence of two sciences, one of which tells of a finite, perfectly ordered universe wherein events follow one another in exact order, while the other tells us of a confused universe, unimaginable and unobservable in itself,[113] whose only unity consists in a system of relations between entities the number and mobility of which defy the imagination, but which are the object of mathematical calculations. Contemporary epistemology could have rejected the confused image and kept the clear and precise account, under the pretext that truth must be clear and precise. It did not do so because the two images correspond to facts. Therefore, it has organized its inquiry so as to explain both of these narratives; it has found a solution for their diversity. The clear image corresponds to the man-sized universe, to the universe corresponding to our lived and imagined experience; the other corresponds to the astronomical and microscopic universe. Each of these parts of the universe obeys its own aspect of the laws of nature and never becomes confused with the other. But these three universes are not separate. There is a harmony among the three aspects of a single universe. Hierarchy, not anarchy, exists among them, for the quantum theory and the theory of relativity exchange laws and explanatory procedures and govern the man-sized world without destroying its individuality.[114]

However, to achieve this harmony between the two narrators, the unilateral meaning of the formulae in each narration had to be done away with; that is, the realities expressed by the words *truth, knowledge, science* must be granted a diversity that Descartes and Kant always refused them. By conceiving knowledge as something other than the infallible intuition of an absolute, contemporary scientists have resolved their *mirabile* and have added to classical science this marvelous instrument of discovery and utilization of the forces of nature that is science today. This way of conceiving and solving the *mirabile* is a sign of great wisdom, but it also indicates that the *Discourse on Method* and the *Critique of Pure Reason* are not infallible and immutable codes in which science must seek the principles of its investigations and the criteria of its discoveries. The "gold standard" of evidence and certitude, which they claim to have discovered in the name of the eternal structure of our reason, has been rejected by science as sterile and humanly useless to the explanation of the physical universe.

Rejected by science, will this "gold standard" be adopted by philosophy and become the sole criterion of philosophical knowledge worthy of the name? Such is the problem we shall study in the next chapter.

Van Riet's history of the past one hundred years of "research into the problem of knowledge in the Thomistic school"[1] reminds us of the nightmare of a realist who suddenly discovers in his dream that he has been stripped of the garment of truth by idealist critique and is exposed, in this state of nudity, to the ridicule of other thinkers. The sleeper's first reaction is sane; he considers this nightmare a bad dream from which he will awake. But as the nightmare persists, he ends by taking it seriously; he feels immodest, indecent, and can no longer bear the shame of strolling around publicly *in naturalibus*. To cover his nakedness, he tries, furtively at first and then with an audacity to which shame lends guile, to dress himself in the only decent suits among the fashions exhibited in the philosophical market place, the idealist uniform. At first he feels a bit shy in this outfit, because it is not made to his order and must make him look odd. However, with the help of habit and the thought that it is better to be dressed in the truth of others than to be a nudist,[2] he decrees that all philosophy not togged out in the same uniform that he is wearing will henceforth be considered naïve or popular and will not truly deserve the name of philosophy. This realist's dream has lasted more than one hundred years. During the first fifty years he accepted his nakedness; since then he has been making periodic visits to the idealist tailor. Every time he comes out he looks more and more like the original he is trying to copy.

We shall try to analyze this nightmare. The method we use will be familiar, for we shall witness its birth, and then watch its development under the pressure of the psychological reactions that the dream causes in the sleeper. We shall then try to discover its causes. Is it the product of an Oedipus complex, because metaphysics has become too attached to being, its father, at the expense of its mother, the intellect? Or is it simply the result of the tyranny of style, which strikes morbid fear to the heart of all weaklings and drives them to every sacrifice, even to the sacrifice of their being and truth, in order to be up-to-date and *like* others?

The plan of this chapter will follow the general rules for studying any epistemological problem: witness its birth, see it in action and developing. This is the only way to grasp its total nature. In the first section we will attend at the birth of the Neo-Scholastic problem; in the second we will follow the different psychological reactions occasioned by this birth among the Neo-Scholastics, and the results of these reactions.

Section I: Birth of the Neo-Scholastic Problem

What factors contributed to the birth of this new problem? The first factor, chronologically, and the most important because it conditioned all the others, was the awareness on the part of Christian thinkers that their realist metaphysics had become a museum piece, dusty, mummified, interesting only to mental archaeologists and to some authors of textbooks; whereas idealism was having a golden age in the great systems of Fichte, Schelling, and Hegel. Philosophical skepticism had replaced classical metaphysics by a vague appeal to *belief* in an exterior world under the impulse of *common sense*. Descartes had affirmed the nonexistence of realist metaphysics because of its lack of evidence; Kant had decreed its character to be eternally illusory and false; the thinkers of the nineteenth century established experimentally that it no longer exists and is replaced by complete disorder in all fields of speculation except that of the experimental sciences dominated by mathematics. Add to this already black picture the progressive de-Christianization of all European thought, and you have every factor capable of shocking the Christian soul and waking it from its philosophical lethargy.

Balmès was the first to feel the shock of the nonexistence of realist philosophy with sufficient violence to try to revive it. This he did in his *Filosofía Fondamental,* a work in four volumes, in which he takes up, successively, certitude, sensation, extension and space, ideas, being, unity and number, time, the infinite, substance, necessity, and causality. This first attempt at philosophical reconstruction was the wellspring of a multitude of other works, and the impulse it gave to Christian philosophy has lasted to our day.

However, realist philosophy could not be reborn without meeting along its return route the idealist philosophy that had led it to the grave. One might even think that realist philosophy had been sufficiently impressed by the vigor of its executioner to believe it immortal; thus, upon waking from its lethargic sleep, its first battle was waged for immediate knowledge against the mediatism of Descartes.[3] It did not realize that, as a philosophical doctrine, Cartesianism was dead, that the eternally true metaphysics, which Cartesian method claimed to have conceived, was stillborn.[4] This illusion about the perennial value of Cartesianism exists only in the mind of Neo-Scholastics, for even science, in whose name Cartesian method was devised, has completely abandoned it, as we have seen. All the philosophers who have carried on Balmès' work have continued to cherish this illusion that, complemented by a similar illusion about Kantianism,[5] has given birth to the contemporary Neo-Scholastic problem.

This general factor, which we have just briefly described, conditions the birth of the Neo-Scholastic problem but does not constitute it without the addition of other, more particular factors that are peculiarly characteristic of this problem. Once revived, realist metaphysics had to try to regain its place in the sun, to try once more to represent philosophy itself in Western thought. To do this, it had to have indisputable letters of credit; its foundations had to be beyond all doubt and discussion. Whence the metaphysical or epistemological aspect of all Neo-Scholastic thought, whose avowed aim was to make nefarious undertakings, such as the *Discourse on Method* and the *Critique of Pure Reason,* impossible in the future, and to make impregnable the metaphysical stronghold called "Thomistic Realism."

The following statements clearly show that this is the distinctive character of the Neo-Scholastic problem: "The mediaeval mentality was fundamentally foreign to all the preoccupations of critique. . . . It did not occur to them to be continually examining the foundations to see if the building was well grounded. Hence the complete contrast with the methodic approach whose essence was first grasped by Descartes, and *of which we feel the need today*."[6] Father Roland-Gosselin repeats the same theme in significant terms: "The confidence placed in the mind establishing science and metaphysics always leaves room . . . for *anxiety* which neither science nor metaphysics can allay."[7] The Neo-Scholastics feel anxious about their realism; they feel the need to heed Kant's and Descartes' teaching that "*there is no good metaphysics without critical prolegomena.*"[8]

To formulate this anxiety, this need for critical prolegomena, in the terms we have been using to describe the genesis of an epistemological problem, to reduce it to the story told by Eddington,[9] we may say that the Neo-Scholastic mind is confronted by two storytellers. One, the familiar narrator, is realist metaphysics telling of a universe of existents whose evidence is beyond doubt; the other narrator tells an entirely different story, the one we have met in studying the modern problem and which is completely contrary to that of the realist narrator—nothing in the exterior world is evident to the mind; it is for the mind to illumine the universe, not for the universe to illumine the mind. Here, in other words, is the dialogue in which the Neo-Scholastic philosopher takes part: Thomistic metaphysics says, "I exist and I know that my knowledge is true, because I have analyzed my object, *being as being*." The idealist answers, "You do not exist, and you do not even know that you do not exist, because you have never analyzed or criticized the thinking subject as thinking subject." Thus the Neo-Scholastic soul is faced with the problem of *the existence of metaphysics*. This is the true problem, and to place it elsewhere is to falsify it completely.

If we grant that this existence is the object of two divergent accounts—one of which would have this existence to be possible *only after analysis of the subject*, whereas the realist narrator asserts that it is possible *upon analysis of the object*—we are confronted with a genuine *mirabile* in the strict sense of the word, for the three factors we have discerned in every *admirabile* are present here:

(1) There is a single theme under discussion: the existence of meta-physics.
(2) There are two versions of the same theme: the idealist version and the realist.
(3) These two accounts are divergent and known to be so by Neo-Scholasticism, which is caught in an impasse, for to admit the idealist narrator's version is to deny the existence of Thomistic metaphysics, and to accept the realist account is to deny the claims of critique.

Now we have to study the psychological reactions of the Neo-Scholastic thinkers faced with this problem, that is, the nature of the *wonder* which this problem begets and the direction of the inquiries of which it is the origin.[10] This will be the subject of the second section of this chapter.

Section II: The Nature of the Neo-Scholastic Problem

The contradiction found in the purport of these realist and idealist narratives concerning the very existence of metaphysics causes wonder, i.e., the fear of ignorance; for although the Neo-Scholastic perceives the opposition between the two accounts, *he does not see* how they can both be true at the same time. And since ignorance is an evil, the fear of this evil begets inquiry, which aims to discover truth by dispelling contradiction. This inquiry may have one of three positions as its starting point:

(1) The acceptance of both narratives in the hope of their both containing complementary fragments of truth, to be confirmed or denied by the inquiry.
(2) The acceptance of one of the accounts as true and the rejection of the other as false, with the inquiry demonstrating the falsity of the rejected narrative.

(3) The rejection of both accounts as nonevident or false, with the inquiry consisting in the discovery of another way of revealing the existence of metaphysics.

What direction will Neo-Scholastic philosophy take, which of the three alternatives will it adopt? This is the beginning of the nightmare, related in Van Riet's book, whose plot was given at the beginning of this chapter.[11] All Neo-Scholastics are realists, and realists in the Thomistic sense of the word. They all recognize the truth of St. Thomas' metaphysics and, therefore, its existence as metaphysics. It would seem that the only possible attitude for a Neo-Scholastic would be the second alternative mentioned above, i.e., the rejection of the idealist position in favor of the realist position, followed by an inquiry showing the falsity of the idealist method, be it Cartesian or Kantian. The only contemporary philosophers to adopt this solution (the only logical one in view of the terms in which the neo-Thomist problem is stated) are Professors Maritain and Gilson[12] and a historian of philosophy, Professor H. Gouhier.[13] On the other hand, this logical position has been opposed by almost all Neo-Scholastic epistemologists who consider it a naïve realism, hardly more vital than common-sense realism. This realism is on the same footing with that of the forerunners and initiators of Neo-Scholastic epistemology.[14]

Consequently, Neo-Scholastic epistemology must be considered in relation to the two remaining alternatives: either acceptance of both narratives in the hope of seeing some complementary accord between them, or rejection of both narratives, in which case a third account begins to take shape, whose tenor will be completely distinct from the two conflicting stories themselves. Actually, the Neo-Scholastics chose the first attitude, conciliation, but it is by no means certain that their investigations and attempts to solve the conflict have not led them to a third account that is neither idealist nor Thomist. It is this that gives this chapter in metaphysical speculation its hallucinatory quality and calls forth the comparison with a nightmare.

Let us study the nature of the Neo-Scholastic problem as an inquiry aiming to conciliate two divergent stories about the existence of metaphysics, the idealist story and the Thomist. Of all the works on so-called Thomist epistemology, filling the 659 pages of Van Riet's book—excluding the sections dealing with the position of Etienne Gilson and Jacques Maritain[15]—only two attempts have really come to grips with the problem: those of Monsignor Noël and Father Maréchal.[16] All the other works treat of one or another aspect of the epistemological problem—the problems of certitude, evidence, immediate realism, etc.—but they do not attempt to reconcile the Thomist and the idealist accounts. They adopt one point or other of the idealist story and show that it cannot destroy the realism of Thomistic metaphysics, which is quite another problem from that of *reconciling* the dialogue that goes on between Thomist metaphysics and idealism:[17] "I exist and I know that I have truth because I have analyzed my object, being as being. . . . You do not exist because you have not criticized the thinking subject as thinking subject." This is the sole problem of neo-Thomist epistemology, and only Noël and Maréchal have tried to solve it. We shall briefly examine their efforts and the results to which they led.

A. MONSIGNOR NOËL: CARTESIAN METHOD AND THOMIST METAPHYSICS

Monsignor Noël was too good a philosopher and too good a Thomist to cheat on the problem arising from the antithetically opposed statements just mentioned. He therefore adheres more particularly to the Cartesian approach of analyzing the subject as a preliminary condition for the existence of a realist metaphysics: "For a systematic philosophy, the mind is not simply one possible starting point among many others. It seems to me to be the only legitimate starting point."[18] Thus, he accepts the Cartesian method. But he also accepts the objective metaphysics of St. Thomas, although he knows he is altering it somewhat: "When St. Thomas invites us to reflect upon our intellectual experience and to realize that we have truth within us, he does not think that this reflection must necessarily *precede* all philosophical certitude. The question is *whether it is opportune and whether it is possible* . . . to transfer the reflection he recommends to the threshold of philosophy."[19] The aim of this transposition of Thomistic reflection to the threshold of philosophy is to vindicate the universe of common sense.[20]

The problem Monsignor Noël sets himself is very clear: to determine whether the elements of the Cartesian method cannot be found, at least implicitly, within the Thomistic method, which would make Thomistic metaphysics critical in the Cartesian sense of the word, since it would fulfill the requirements of Descartes' method. The latter has two principle characteristics: *methodic doubt* and the *cogito*. By the first he excludes from knowledge everything that is not unquestionably evident in order to arrive at a truth principle so evident that no one can deny it; by the second he discovers all other truths of which philosophy is the synthesis. Therefore, it becomes a question of finding two factors in the Thomistic method to correspond, point by point, to these two characteristics of the Cartesian method. Monsignor Noël claims to have discovered them in the *dubitatio universalis*—found in St. Thomas' commentaries on the *Metaphysics* of Aristotle[21] and in the *reflexio* described in a personal work of the holy Doctor[22]—by which the intellect "turns back upon itself and grasps its own act: this is indeed the *cogito* and the starting point of critique."[23] Since all epistemology can be constructed within the framework of this *reflexio*, of which the *cogito* is but a distant echo,[24] Thomistic realism is a critical, not a naïve, realism, depending implicitly but consciously upon an immediatist epistemology, and is therefore a *justified* realism.[25]

Monsignor Noël's purpose, continued by the school of Louvain,[26] was essentially to effect the complete conciliation of the Neo-Scholastic *mirabile* by showing that actually the opposition formulated at the beginning of this chapter is only a verbal opposition, for Thomism, like idealism, bases its metaphysics upon a preliminary analysis of the thinking subject. The reason that everyone has been deceived upon this point is that this critique of the thinking subject is not explicitly brought out by St. Thomas, whereas Descartes pinpoints it and makes it the explicit starting point for all true metaphysics.

Since every inquiry is governed by the *mirabile* that is its starting point, and since the *mirabile* on which Monsignor Noël bases his inquiry centers upon the apparent opposition between the conditions necessary for the existence of metaphysics in Cartesianism and in Thomism, Monsignor Noël bends his whole effort to show that this opposition does not exist. He carries out this demonstration by a comparative analysis of the Cartesian *dubitatio* with the Thomistic *dubitatio universalis* and of the *cogito* with the *reflexio*. We shall examine each of these pairs of terms and the proofs he gives of their identity.

¶ *1. Cartesian Doubt versus Universal Doubt.* To make sure that this comparison is both easily comprehensible and perfectly complete, we shall divide it under three headings, successively treating all the essential aspects of this psychology of the *dubitatio*. We shall examine (a) the origin of the *dubitatio*, (b) its object and context, and (c) its term.

(a) *Origin of the* dubitatio. Liberty is the primary source of the existence of Cartesian doubt, and that is why Descartes states that doubt is the pre-eminent type of free act. How, actually, could we push doubt far enough to suppose that the very Author of our nature deceives us, leads us into error, if we were not truly free?[27] To ask Descartes why he attributes doubt to a free act, therefore to voluntary activity, is to bring his whole psychology of knowledge into play. What characterizes this psychology is that each and every judgment is a voluntary act and, as such, essentially free,[28] except in the presence of a truth so clear that the will cannot refuse its assent, which happens only for the truth of the *cogito* and the truths derived from it.[29] Since it is the will that assents to the act of understanding, it can refuse to do so every time this act lacks *actual* evidence; in which case the will's assent would be precipitate and therefore wrong.[30]

Thus, liberty makes possible the existence of doubt; but there must be a special, concrete reason to explain the use Descartes makes of this psychological liberty, and this is the *origin of the* dubitatio *as a philosophic method*. This origin is twofold. It arises primarily from Cartesian pessimism about the relations of body and soul and the activities proceeding therefrom, the relations between sensation and intellection. According to Descartes, the body is an obstacle to knowledge, because sensations, originating in the body, are essentially organized in view of our needs and are fabricators; that is, they create objects that have no exterior existence and convince the intellect that they do exist extramentally.[31] The second immediate source of the concrete use of doubt as a method is another pessimism, which Descartes professes about all men in their quest for truth: namely, that there are very few men who have sense enough to attain to truth, a fact attested by the innumerable errors with which popular knowledge and Scholastic philosophy abound.[32] As a counterpart of this second pessimism, and basic to methodic doubt, is Descartes' absolute confidence in his own intellect, a confidence that allowed him to throw out everything that had been said before him, being convinced of his ability to rediscover by himself, untaught by any other, the whole ensemble of truths to which the intellect can attain.[33]

These are the origins of Cartesian *doubt* and the use Descartes made of it as method to discover the first principle of all metaphysics.

For St. Thomas, doubt is a *state of mind* and not an act of will[34]; unlike the will, the intellect is not *free* in face of evidence. Evidence forces the intellect's assent, and assent is an activity proceeding solely from the intellect.

Being moved from outside is not contrary to the essential character of the intellect, as it is to the will . . . instead, the working of the intellect can be against the inclination of man, which inclination is the will. For instance, some opinion may appeal to a person, yet he may be induced to assent to the contrary through his intellect.[35]

The primary origin of doubt for St. Thomas is therefore not a decision made by the will but a lack of evidence in our knowledge of things. This lack of evidence serves only to reveal the structure of our intellect: made for truth and for all truths, the intellect cannot resist truth's attraction, and that is why it is not free to refuse to see the truth or free to deny its assent to it. The mind is therefore not free to doubt. Lack of evidence and the nature of our intellect are the roots of the Thomistic *dubitatio*.

By examining the immediate origins of the use of *dubitatio uni-*

versalis as a philosophical method, we can see that none of the reasons that impelled Descartes to use his methodic doubt is applicable to *dubitatio universalis* as a philosophical method.

In the first place, St. Thomas is in no way pessimistic about the relations of body and soul; for without the body, the soul on earth is completely helpless,[36] and would be just as helpless after death, if by substitution God did not provide what the soul would normally receive from the body.[37] The body is entirely the soul's instrument, an instrument it needs for all its operations, even those that are purely spiritual. This unpessimistic view of the peaceful and fruitful co-habitation of body and soul inevitably begets total optimism about the relations between sensation and intellection. Sensation is necessary not only as a starting point for all intellectual activity, but its presence is also necessary to explain the extent of its duration. There is no conflict between the sensible and the intelligible, but rather absolutely necessary harmony and cooperation. If pre-established harmony exists anywhere, it is certainly in the indissoluble marriage of sensibility and intelligibility, whose complementary character is essential to the very existence of human knowledge.[38] And that is why, when St. Thomas makes use of *dubitatio universalis* as a principle of philosophical inquiry, he does not use it synonymously with Cartesian doubt, but as a synonym of the ignorance that begets *admiratio*, whose nature is entirely different from *haesitatio*, which is connected with voluntary activity and not with an act of vision.[39]

There is no pessimism about the union of body and soul and the cooperation between sensation and intellection; neither is there pessimism about humanity as a whole in its quest for truth. *Dubitatio universalis*, far from being the result of Cartesian pessimism, springs from St. Thomas' *confidence* in the intelligence of other men and in their competence to deal with subjects that they have long studied.[40] As a counterpart to this social optimism, we find, not pessimism about individual intelligence, but a deep humility that leads St. Thomas to avow the poverty of the human intellect, a poverty preventing it from coming by itself to full bloom, to that euphoria of sapience which is the fruit of intellectual riches accumulated and pooled through the ages. St. Thomas would have considered it a sin of presumption, the mother of error, to use *dubitatio universalis* as equivalent to Descartes' methodic doubt.

Another benefit stems from revelation—the repression of presumption which is the mother of error. For there are people who presume so much on their own mental ability that they consider themselves capable of measuring the whole nature of things by their own intellects, being convinced that what appears so to them is entirely true, while what is not apparent to them is false.[41]

Therefore, in the psychological origin of doubt and its use, we have found no reason to identify methodic doubt with *dubitatio universalis*. On the contrary, considering only the *origin* of these two doubts, we have found the nature and use of *dubitatio universalis* to have origins so completely different from those of Cartesian doubt that we must conclude that such an identification is impossible.

(b) *Object and context of the* dubitatio. Far from providing a possible basis for identification, the origins of methodic doubt and of *dubitatio universalis* show them to be irreconcilably opposed. Let us see whether their respective objects and contexts give more favorable grounds for establishing a similarity between them.

The first object of Cartesian doubt was the probable or conjectural, that is, everything depending upon dialectical and non-demonstrative arguments,[42] to which must be added all judgments concerned with sensible reality as such, since we can in no way trust the senses.[43] But when Descartes decided to use doubt as the cathartic factor in his method, then the object of doubt came to be all existing human knowledge, even mathematical knowledge,[44] since an evil genius or great deceiver could exist who might force us to err.[45] Ultimately, therefore, doubt bears on the existence of all truth, since it applies to the very existence of things: "Here the chief concern is with the existing thing, does it exist?"[46] Only one truth escapes doubt, the truth of the *cogito*, because to deny it would be to affirm it.

The context of such doubt is necessarily prescientific and *pre-philosophic*, since its aim is to discover the first principle of all philosophy and all science,[47] and since method must precede the science of which it is the method.[48] The complete title of the *Dis-*

course clearly reveals the prescientific character of its method and, therefore, of the doubt that characterizes it: *Discourse on Method in Order Rightly to Conduct the Reason and to Seek Truth in the Sciences.*

It would take a sleight-of-hand artist to identify the object of *dubitatio universalis* with the object of Cartesian doubt. Here is the text used in support of this identification:

Other sciences consider truth in some particular way, hence it is their special function to exercise doubt on individual points; but this science [metaphysics] makes a universal study of truth, and so a *universal doubt* concerning truth pertains to it, hence it makes use of a doubt which is not particularized but universalized in all its aspects.[49]

The difficulty in this passage centers upon the meaning of the word *truth*: Does it mean the truth of *things*, or of the *mind*? Is St. Thomas talking about the *nature*, or about the *existence*, of the truth of things or of the mind?

The truth which is the object of *dubitatio universalis* could not be the truth of the intellect, either in its existence or in its nature, for its existence is a *per se notum* that the mind cannot deny, and the nature of primary truth is such as to make discussion possible even with God. Furthermore, the nature of truth is the object of logic,[50] whereas the truth discussed in this extract is the object of metaphysics.

Therefore, the truth that is the object of *dubitatio universalis* is the *truth of things*, which is proved by many other explicit statements made by St. Thomas in the very same place from which this passage is taken. Here are some of them:

First philosophy considers the universal *truth of things*. . . .[51] The word *truth* is not the exclusive characteristic of any species but is applicable in common to *all beings*. . . . Hence, if we add to this deduction the fact that first philosophy considers causes, it follows, as we saw previously, that it considers the things that are most true. Hence it is in a special way the science of truth. . . .[52] And Aristotle first proceeds to show by way of disputation the points capable of being doubted concerning the truth of things. . . . So he states initially that, in the case of this science in which we seek first principles and the universal truth of things, we must first attack the matters to be doubted before truth may be determined.[53]

If the truth discussed in the above text is the truth of things and not of the mind, the *dubitatio* in question is neither Cartesian doubt nor Thomistic doubt in the strict sense of the word; rather, it simply means the *mirabile* and should be translated by the words *problem, question, aporia, inquiry, investigation*.[54] What this extract is discussing is the importance of asking the questions that should be asked when we are constructing a science, for the statement of the problems is central to the inquiry and even to the discovery of the mind's truth.

If the object of methodic doubt cannot be identified with the object of *dubitatio universalis*, neither can their *context*, for the context of Cartesian doubt is prescientific and prephilosophic, whereas the context of the Thomistic *dubitatio* is necessarily metaphysical. Let us go back to the text we quoted above.[55] St. Thomas is contrasting the problems that any particular science sets itself with the questions metaphysics asks itself: the former are particular, whereas the latter are universal or common to all beings as such. The context is indeed metaphysical, not only because this text is from a commentary on Aristotle's *Metaphysics*, but because its very content requires a metaphysical context, for only metaphysics can consider being as being and resolve the problems or questions that an object sets before the mind.

There is in Thomism, as we shall see,[56] an art of *bene dubitare*, an art of asking questions, of studying problems; for *every problem is the object of a science*, and problems vary according to the science.[57] A science can ask questions only about the conclusions possible in this science and not about its principles, for each science receives its questions from metaphysics, whose function it is to determine which are the difficulties peculiar to each science: *De illis enim a sapientibus determinandum est de quibus dubitatio est*.[58] Consequently, only metaphysics has the right to ask the most universal questions, that is, to inquire into the nature of being as being, to state all the difficulties that hinder the understanding of so difficult a truth. In this context the above quotation should be translated as follows:[59] "It belongs to this science, which deals with all aspects of being as such, to consider the universal problems which such an object entails." Such are the object and context of the Thomistic *dubitatio universalis*. They give us no reason to identify it with methodic doubt but again stress the diversity that we have already seen in studying the origin of these doubts.

(c) *The aim or end of the* dubitatio. For Descartes, doubt has a twofold purpose. First of all, it is a mental *ascesis* aiming to disincarnate the mind, to free it from sensory deceptions,[60] and thus to display a radical sincerity in face of the problem of truth.[61] But especially, it is a method to discover the first principle of philosophy, not a principle for *distinguishing* truth from error, but for *discovering* truth that is not yet known and substituting it for error.[62] If this first principle is not discovered, no truth can ever exist, since truth and science are identical, and since all science depends upon the discovery of a first, unconditioned principle so unshakable that the wildest suppositions, even those of an evil genius or a deceiving God, could never impair it.[63] What Cartesian doubt is seeking to establish as its end or aim is the very existence of truth and the possibility of the existence of all philosophy, for Cartesian science is linear and geometric. All its truths are homogeneous,[64] and in order to exist, it must borrow evidence from the *cogito*, the sole source of evidence.

The end or aim of the Thomistic *dubitatio universalis* is neither a catharsis of the soul, for the soul must keep its sensory powers in order to know, nor the discovery of the first principle, for the first principle of human knowledge is not the object of inquiry or study but is immediately perceived as soon as being is present to the intellect.[65] St. Thomas is not looking for a first principle in order to construct science or metaphysics, but, having seen it, he uses it to construct sciences and metaphysics. Were a skeptic or a Cartesian-type doubter to doubt the truth of this first principle, here is the answer St. Thomas would give him, after first remarking upon the doubter's lack of knowledge and discipline.[66]

Some people have said that it is possible for the same thing both to be and not be, in the same sense—and that it is possible to be convinced of this. Indeed this view is used by many natural philosophers, as will appear later. However, we now take as basic the truth of the principle which we have mentioned, namely that it is impossible for the same thing to be and not to be; in fact, from its truth we can show that it is most certain.[67]

The end sought by *dubitatio universalis* is therefore in no way similar to the aim of methodic doubt. To discover its aim, we have to look on the side of the object and things, not on the side of the *cogito*.

The man who wishes to find a right answer must continue looking for a solution until there is no more room for doubt . . . in all our efforts to solve difficulties, it seems to be customary to confine our inquiry to the refutation of opposing views rather than to the investigation of reality. . . . But this is not enough. When a man wants to discover a true answer, he must not be satisfied with facing all available objections, he must diligently seek out the causes. . . . This result is achieved when a man takes into consideration all the differences of things, on the basis of which the question may be answered.[68]

Such is the radical sincerity required by the Thomistic *dubitatio*. This sincerity concerns things, because in Thomism it is things that bestow their truth upon man, and not man who endows things with truth. A Thomist's first duty toward truth is to respect the nature of things and to extend them complete hospitality. When, by diligent inquiry, he has besought all the aspects of the nature of things to come into his soul, the Thomist possesses truth. This is the end of the *dubitatio universalis:* to ask questions about the nature of being *ut sic* in order to possess all truth about beings as being.

The conclusion of this study of the *dubitatio* is obvious. If Monsignor Noël hopes to solve his *mirabile* by reconciling two philosophic methods through the identification of methodic doubt with *dubitatio universalis de veritate*, this reconciliation is impossible. Not in their origins, their objects, their contexts, or their ends do Cartesian methodic doubt and Thomistic *dubitatio universalis* resemble one another. Far from resembling each other, they oppose and destroy each other.

¶ *2. Cartesian* Cogito *versus Thomistic* Reflexio. The second factor that, according to Monsignor Noël, makes Thomistic realism a critical philosophy is the analytical function of the *reflexio*, which plays a role analogous to that of the Cartesian *cogito:*

There is a celebrated passage which, from the depth of the Middle Ages, seems to echo modern critique. . . . Coming back upon its act, the mind in reflecting becomes aware of the proportion between its act and things. What else is this but the critical reflection we were speaking of a while ago? The intellect turns back upon itself, it grasps its own act; this is indeed the *cogito* and the starting point of critique.[69]

To facilitate this comparison between the *cogito* and reflection, we shall study their respective *functions* in the construction of a philosophy and their nature, i.e., the object they treat.

(a) *The function of the* cogito *and of the* reflexio. The *cogito* has a very precise function in Cartesianism. It is the first principle of science and philosophy; it is the sole source of all our certitudes. Every truth that does not spring from the *cogito* and does not hark back to it is not truth but probability and conjecture.[70] Thus, it is a principle both as *starting point* of philosophical knowledge and as *generative source* of all human truths that we can acquire, for it is the sole rule by which all must be measured.[71]

Reflexio, Monsignor Noël tells us, can play the same role, for it is a judgment objectified by the *esse* of some reality, a judgment that can be used to define the formal conditions of truth at the same time that it reveals truth's existence to us. This judgment is a natural certitude, the affirmation of an existence. It is a question of verifying this affirmation by an analysis that will discover in it both a self and a nonself and the law governing their relationship—the law by which the self tends toward the nonself,[72] which is the very nature of truth. *Reflexio* gives us the definition of truth, and that is why it is the *foundation* of philosophy.

According to Monsignor Noël, this analysis of the *reflexio* should stand at the threshold of philosophy, since the latter presupposes it. It should normally be a part of logic, since logic precedes philosophy, of which it is the instrument, and defines the nature of truth and falsity.[73] *But logic is not the foundation of philosophy*, and although it defines the nature of truth, it does not defend the nature of truth when attacked. The problem of critique is a problem of verification and of defending the very nature of truth; it is a matter of discovering the first principle of Thomistic philosophy and not of discussing the formal conditions of truth. Here is how St. Thomas solves such a problem:

The metaphysician ought to dispute against those who deny the principles of the special sciences, since all principles are founded on this principle: that affirmation and negation are not simultaneously true, and that there is no middle position between them. . . . Now, the true and the false belong properly to the thinking of the logician. . . . However, error concerning the true and the false is a consequence of error concerning being and non-being (*circa esse et non esse*): for the true and the false are defined in terms of to be and not to be. . . . Therefore, if we have destroyed the errors concerning to be and not to be, we have as a consequence destroyed those connected with the true and the false.[74]

If the *reflexio* of which Monsignor Noël speaks is a logical analysis whose function it is to reveal the nature of truth, and if the nature of truth is challenged by an adversary, it will not be up to logic to verify the truth, to vindicate it; this is uniquely the privilege of the metaphysician. In Thomism it is not the *reflexio* that lays the foundations of metaphysics and vindicates it; rather it is metaphysics that founds and vindicates *reflexio*. For St. Thomas, the realism of knowledge is neither established nor proved at the threshold of metaphysics; the office of doorkeeper given to *reflexio* is performed in his philosophical synthesis by the principle of contradiction.

To give to *reflexio* the importance the *cogito* has in Cartesianism, to make it play the role of first principle and sole source of human knowledge, is to transform this *reflexio* in such a way that it is no longer Thomistic but becomes the Cartesian *cogito*.

(b) *The nature or object of the* cogito *and of reflection.* The object of the Cartesian *cogito* is the self, and because it deals with the self, it has an existential truth value possessed by no other judgment: "Since I cannot think unless I exist, I cannot doubt unless I exist," etc. The distinctive nature of the *cogito*'s truth is owing to thought's not needing to go outside the thinking self in order to discover an existence. The fact of thought itself implies and makes evident the existence of the Ego, the only existence over which error has no hold.

Compare this object of the *cogito* with that of *reflexio*, or the term to which it leads. The *other* to which analysis of *reflection* leads is the first subject Aristotle speaks of in his *Categories*, and its independent presence dominates us.[75] Now, supposing that analysis of *reflexio*, transformed into the *cogito*, really could lead us to the individual substance that confronts the knowing subject and is its object, could we say that this knowledge is only common-sense knowledge? In Thomism, it is not common-sense realism that forms the foundation of philosophical realism; rather, it is the latter that vindicates common-sense realism.[76] Common-sense realism deals with being as sensible, therefore with a mode of being; whereas the object of metaphysics is being as being and thus includes all beings and all modes of being. And being as being is not vindicated by appealing to the existence of material substance, but by vertical ascent to the sole and necessary cause of all being, God as Creator.[77]

Descartes can ascend to God by starting from the *cogito*, because in this *cogito* he finds existing an idea of perfection of which he himself could not be the cause.[78] St. Thomas ascends to God by starting with an imperfect being, and metaphysics reveals to him the imperfection of being and the reason for this imperfection. To start from *reflexio* in order to arrive at the first subject mentioned by Aristotle in his *Categories*, and to claim that metaphysics is based upon this primary knowledge, is to turn Thomism upside down.

¶ *Conclusion on Monsignor Noël's Attempt.* Monsignor Noël's attempt to reconcile Cartesianism and Thomism did not meet with much success. Comparison upon two essential points, methodic doubt and the *cogito*, has shown them to be antinomic. The more they are studied, the more irreconcilable they are seen to be. Far from disappearing, the *mirabile* with which Monsignor Noël began his inquiry became progressively more dense as analysis of *dubitatio universalis* and *reflexio* revealed their contents and functions to be repugnant to the contents and functions of the methodic doubt and *cogito* of Descartes. Monsignor Noël has to give a tendentious interpretation of *dubitatio universalis* in order to make it play the role of doubt,[79] and he is obliged to change the nature of the Cartesian *cogito* in order to compare it with the *reflexio* of St. Thomas. He has to use the *cogito* of the *Meditations* as point of comparison, not that of the *Discourse*, for the latter is *closed*, whereas the former is open; that is, besides the mind, there is the object, there is *esse*.[80]

He also has to transfer to the threshold of philosophy a *reflexio* that, in Thomism, in no way smacks of an introduction to philosophy.

The pre-occupations of critique were fundamentally foreign to the mediaeval mind. . . . When St. Thomas asks us to reflect upon our intellectual experience and to account for the truth that is in us, he is not thinking that this *reflection must necessarily precede all philosophical certitude*. So the question is . . . is it possible, without so distorting the Master's teaching as to essentially falsify it, is it possible, I say, to transfer to the threshold of philosophy the reflection he prescribes?[81]

Therefore, if the Thomistic *dubitatio* is in no way Cartesian, if the *reflexio* is not a philosophical threshold and can never become one without presupposing the philosophy whose threshold it is held to be, what do Cartesian critique and Thomistic realism have in common? Only the forced and untenable similarities that Monsignor Noël has traced between the two doctrines. This attempted reconciliation has had the concrete result of turning the Cartesian *cogito* into a *cognosco*, which is anti-Cartesian, and of turning Thomism into pseudo-Cartesianism. A third account has replaced the other two without having the internal coherence of the narratives it has distorted in order to substitute itself for them.

B. FATHER MARÉCHAL: THOMISTIC CRITIQUE AND KANTIAN CRITIQUE

We have seen that the attempt to reconcile the metaphysical position of St. Thomas with the Cartesian position came to naught. Instead of revealing their supposed identity of nature behind the diversity in their points of view, a comparison of components produced the opposite result. This second attempt is just as vigorous and honest as the first, and at an even more difficult level, because it involves the *Critique of Pure Reason* on the one hand and the whole of Thomistic metaphysics on the other. The works in which Father Maréchal's thought is to be found are *Le point de départ de la métaphysique* (especially Cahier V, *Le thomisme devant la philosophie critique*) and three articles that appeared successively in the *Revue néoscolastique de philosophie*.[82]

The following extract amply shows that Father Maréchal's aim was to reconcile the two contrary positions concerning the existence of metaphysics and is therefore the first hypothesis described above.

> Followed through, these two critical methods, which approach the same total object from *complementary angles,* come finally to identical conclusions; for the old critique starts off by postulating the ontological Object, which includes the transcendental Subject, and modern Critique posits the transcendental Subject whose postulate is the ontological Object.[83]

Like Monsignor Noël, Father Maréchal wanted to transfer to the threshold of metaphysics that which, in Thomism, is actually at its heart, or, again, to "transpose the Thomistic critique of knowledge to the transcendental mode." To transpose an ontological mode to a transcendental mode and to harmonize them is a work requiring an inspired orchestrator, and Father Maréchal brought to the task all his talent as a philosopher and his profound knowledge of both the doctrines he was trying to reconcile.

Here, briefly, are the general outlines of this orchestration, which, being governed by the nature of the problem of critique itself, must have its starting point in analysis or reflection, a psychological attitude toward this starting point, and critique in the strict sense of the word, whose two essential phases are transcendental analysis and transcendental deduction. Agreement between the two critical methods must be established, therefore, upon the three following points:

(1) The starting point of critique in experience of the object according to Kant and according to St. Thomas.

(2) The attitude of Kant and of St. Thomas at the starting point.
(3) Transcendental critique of the subject and of the object.

Let us try to see, by comparing these three aspects of critique, how, according to Father Maréchal, *the ontological Object includes the transcendental Subject, and the transcendental Subject postulates the ontological Object.*

¶ *1. The Starting Point: Experience of the Object.* That experience is the starting point for every critical analysis of knowledge presents no difficulty to the philosopher, for only that which consciously exists in the knower can be analyzed or criticized, and the object must necessarily be immanent to the analyst and critic. A few passages will show us how this position is common to both philosophers whose doctrines we are examining here.

There can be no doubt that all our knowledge begins with experience. For how should our faculty of knowledge be awakened into action did not objects affecting our senses, partly of themselves produce representations, partly arouse the activity of our understanding to compare these representations, and by combining or separating them, work up the raw material of the sensible impressions into that knowledge of objects which is entitled experience. In the order of time therefore, we have no knowledge antecedent to experience, and with experience all our knowledge begins.[84]

That the object awakens our knowing powers and puts them into action is, we might say, the fundamental theme of all Thomist epistemology, for our powers exist, *as knowing,*[85] only insofar as the object is present: "A potency must first be brought to bear on an object before it can be directed to its own act; indeed the act of a potency must be understood before one grasps its reflection on that act."[86]

But is Kantian experience the same as Thomistic experience? Thomistic experience depends entirely upon sensibility for its existence, both in its principle or starting point and in its term or point of arrival. Even when experience deals with nonsensible realities, there must be sensation, to prevent experience from staying at the image level, by negation of this image itself.[87] In a certain sense, Thomistic experience is always empirical, even experience of God, for it is always the result of the *immediate presence* of an existent, whether the existence is its own or that of another. Kantian experience, too, is always empirical, but it is not convertible with human knowledge, for some knowledge has nothing to do with experience. Experience is the source of *a posteriori* knowledge, but *a priori* knowledge is completely independent of experience, not only of actual experience of an exterior reality, but of every previous experience that could have produced in our mind a universal knowledge drawn from actual experience. Here are a few significant quotations from the introduction to the *Critique of Pure Reason.* "But though all our knowledge begins with experience, it does not follow that it all *arises out of experience.* For it may well be that even our empirical knowledge is made up of *what we receive* through impressions and of *what our own faculty of knowledge supplies for itself.*"[88] If this knowledge, purely the product of our intellectual faculty, exists, it is distinct from that knowledge we receive from sensible impressions. This latter is called "empirical, which has its sources *a posteriori,* that is in experience," whereas the other type of knowledge, called *a priori,* is "not knowledge independent of this or that experience, but knowledge absolutely independent of *all* experience."[89]

What is the criterion for these two types of knowledge, one of which is empirical, or results from experience, and the other *a priori,* from which experience is completely excluded: "Experience teaches us that *a thing is so and so,* but not that it cannot be otherwise."[90] Thus, it lacks necessity and universality. Even if it can attain to a certain universality by induction, this universality always implies possible exceptions; whereas, "Necessity and strict universality are sure criteria of *a priori* knowledge, and are inseparable of one another."[91] Consequently, we can conclude that all knowledge characterized by strict universality and necessity does not come from experience, that it is therefore not empirical knowledge but purely a product of the mind—it is *a priori* knowledge. Notice that this purely mental product is not the result of abstraction from sensible impressions but is consequent upon the very nature of our understanding itself, a creative spontaneity that, *upon the occasion* of sensible impressions, produces *a priori* knowledge from itself.[92]

Let us compare a typical case of this kind of knowledge in Kan-

tianism and in Thomism. Our knowledge of the principle of contradiction is certainly characterized by strict universality and necessity,
both for St. Thomas and for Kant. For St. Thomas it is the
first principle par excellence,[93] for Kant, "the highest principle of
all analytic judgements."[94] Without worrying, for the moment,
about the function of the two principles in these two doctrines, let
us examine only their origin. According to Kant, this principle
cannot originate in sensation, since it is pre-eminently the analytical
principle of all *a priori* knowledge. According to St. Thomas, its
origin is in experience, for it can be drawn from no other source.[95]
The principle of contradiction is evidently not identical with sensation or with processes that go from sensation to principle by means
of imagination and memory of experience. It surpasses sensation by
the full height of the intellect, but it is not produced by a spontaneous intellective activity occasioned by sensation, for it is in and
by sensation that it exists. And while it is the effect of an act of our
intellective power, it is not purely a creation of this power, but the
consequence of its working upon a sense datum.

It must therefore be concluded that although experience is necessarily the starting point for every critique of human knowledge, it
is not identical for St. Thomas and for Kant. According to the latter,
experience is only an occasional point of departure, whereas for the
former it is the sole and total starting point of all human knowledge,
be it singular or universal, contingent or necessary. The following
passage, which is repeated many times by St. Thomas, is enough to
establish the fundamental opposition between Thomism and Kantianism: "It is impossible for a perfect judgment to be made concerning any item of knowledge without reducing it to the principle
whence it sprang. . . . But since every item of intellectual knowledge
arises from sensation, there can be no right judgment without a reduction to sensation."[96] This does not mean a corporeal dependence
upon sensation, but a dependence upon it as upon a measure: ". . . intellectual judgment does not depend on sense because this act is
performed through a sense organ; sensation is required as an ultimate
limit to which a reduction can be made."[97]

Where do these diverse conceptions of experience come from?

From their notion of the object. For Kant, the only objects are appearances or phenomenal objects,[98] therefore, those which are given over to absolute becoming and can be present to us only under the forms of unstable, intemporal, and a-spatial impressions. But such an object cannot explain the stable and permanent element either in sensible intuition or in thought. Thus, when necessity and universality are found in our knowledge, this knowledge cannot be empirical, i.e., begotten by experience or sensation. It must come from elsewhere, and this elsewhere can only be the subject and its transcendental *a priori* laws.[99] Thomistic experience of the object is the simultaneous experience of a *noumenal* and *phenomenal* object, whereas Kant's experience of the object is, and can only be, *phenomenal*. Why does Kant exclude the noumenon from the objects of experience? Because he was awakened from his dogmatic slumber by Hume, who ascribed to *belief* everything that depends upon substance and deemed only brute facts to be true knowledge. By this exclusion, Hume destroyed metaphysical truth as scientific truth, and this was the starting point for Kantian critique. The object of metaphysics does not exist because we do not *know* it; but we do *believe* it:[100] "The holding of a thing to be true, or the subjective validity of the judgement . . . if it be only subjectively sufficient, and is at the same time taken as being *objectively insufficient*, we have what is termed *believing*; . . . when the holding of a thing to be true is sufficient *both* objectively and subjectively, it is *knowledge*."

Can it be said that this starting point is the same for the two critiques in question? Yes, if the starting point is restricted to a *cogito*, i.e., to the experience of a phenomenon of knowledge without reference to its content. But neither Kant nor St. Thomas takes knowledge without content as a point of departure for his reflection; for on Father Maréchal's own admission, Kantian experience has a phenomenal content, while Thomistic experience contains both phenomenon and noumenon.[101] Consequently, we must conclude that the starting point differs for these two philosophers and that, in this respect at least, their critiques of knowledge cannot be reconciled.

¶ 2. *The Kantian and Thomistic Psychological Attitude at*

the Starting Point of Critique. "A critique does not necessarily veto metaphysics; a critique does not prejudge the absolute value of its object."[102] What we have just seen concerning experience of the object in these two definitions of experience can but leave us skeptical about the possibility of the absolute neutrality of Kant and St. Thomas with respect to metaphysical truth. Let us see whether this neutrality exists on either side. What is the psychological attitude of Kant and of St. Thomas toward truth, since this is the matter in question?

Now the proper problem of pure reason is contained in the question: How are a priori synthetic judgements possible? . . . In the solution of the problem, we are at the same time deciding as to the possibility of the employment of pure reason in establishing and developing all those sciences which contain a theoretical a priori knowledge of objects, and have therefore to answer the questions:

> How is pure mathematics possible?
> How is pure science of nature possible?

Since these sciences actually exist, it is quite proper to ask *how* they are possible; for that they must be possible is proved by the fact that they exist. But the poor progress which has hitherto been made in metaphysics, and the fact that no system yet propounded can, in view of the essential purpose of metaphysics, be said really to exist, leaves everyone sufficient ground for doubting as to its possibility.[103]

Therefore, Kantian critique does not start from zero; it does not start from universal doubt; nor does it question the existence of truth. Its distinctive problem is not, What is truth? Instead, since the existence of scientific truth is a fact, Kant asks: *How is this possible?* This question concerning the possibility of scientific truth is normally asked only about already existing truths: "Since these sciences [mathematics and physics] exist, it is quite proper to ask how are they possible."[104] But metaphysical truth does not exist. How then can it be the object of Critique? Solely because we have a natural disposition to ask questions that go beyond our experience, i.e., necessary and universal questions. What we should ask ourselves is: How is metaphysics *as a natural disposition possible?* But this natural disposition to ask questions that go beyond experience has,

NYACK COLLEGE MANHATTAN

up to now, found no satisfaction, because all the solutions given are contradictory. Thus, we must find out scientifically, once and for all, whether this natural disposition corresponds to a real object and whether reason can or cannot grasp it. This in turn leads to critique's ultimate question: How is metaphysics as a science possible?[105]

Psychologically, Kant begins his inquiry into how *scientific* truth is possible certain that he will discover how mathematical science and pure physics are possible, certain, too, that he will discover how metaphysics is possible *as a natural disposition*, since it exists necessarily. But he also begins assured that the only metaphysical science we can have is a transcendental illusion, since he excludes from human experience the very object of metaphysics, the noumenon.[106] Let us see whether, according to Father Maréchal, this attitude corresponds to the attitude St. Thomas would have had on the same subject.

It is rather surprising to find that Father Maréchal attributes to St. Thomas a psychological attitude very different from the one we have just noted in Kant's own words. According to Father Maréchal, St. Thomas would have started his critique by decreeing that "at the risk of being incurably dogmatic, metaphysics must begin with a general critique of knowledge; that is, by deliberate and unprejudiced examination of the spontaneous movement that draws the mind towards what we call the true."[107] He would have adopted a negative and expectant attitude, a universal methodic doubt toward the existence of the true, in order to experiment with its logical possibility or impossibility.[108] If it were supposed that St. Thomas' attitude at the beginning of his metaphysics[109] really was that of universal methodic doubt, his starting point would still be undeniably different from Kant's, since the latter starts with the existence of scientific truth in order to ask himself *how* and not *if* it is possible. We must therefore conclude that, on this second aspect of critique, there is no agreement between these two thinkers.

¶ *3. Transcendental Analysis of the Subject and the Object.* Kant insists rather curiously that his work is not a "*system* of pure reason, not a *doctrine*,"[110] but a *propaedeutic* to a system or doctrine of pure reason, a propaedeutic whose name is "critique" and whose function "ought only to be negative, not to extend but only to clarify our reason and keep it free from errors."[111] The proper object of critique is therefore not the analysis of the object of knowledge but "the *mode* of our knowledge of objects *in so far as this mode of knowledge is to be possible a priori.*"[112] This mode of knowledge is twofold: it is "pure intuition . . . contains only the form under which something is intuited; the pure concept is only the form of the thought of an object in general."[113] This analysis of the modes of our knowledge and not of its objects or content is accomplished by transcendental logic, which has nothing to do with empirical principles and borrows nothing from psychology. This transcendental logic is divided into two parts, of which the "Analytics" studies the concepts and principles of understanding *insofar as they make possible scientific knowledge of phenomena*, i.e., mathematics and physics.[114] The "Dialectics" studies the concepts and principles of *pure reason* insofar as they are the known but inevitable source of metaphysical illusion.[115]

In Thomism we are accustomed to hearing the words *concept* and *principles*, and to defining them in terms of object and objective knowledge. This is never the case with Kant, for a transcendental critique does not analyze the concept by dissecting its content in order to make it more clear, more distinct, etc., but consists in a "*dissection of the faculty of understanding itself*, in order to investigate the possibility of concepts a priori by looking for them in the understanding alone as their birth place, and by analyzing the pure use of this faculty. . . . We shall therefore follow up the pure concepts to their first seeds and dispositions in the human understanding in which they lie prepared, until *on the occasion of* experience they are developed and by the same understanding are exhibited in their purity, freed from the empirical conditions attaching to them."[116]

It is hard to imagine a Thomist whose analysis of concepts would be an analysis of pure form, even in formal logic. For, in Thomism, concepts, judgments, reasonings are all considered in their universality, particularity, or individuality, thus in their subjective condition, in the mode of existence they have as known, but with a reference, at least implicit, to reality considered in its concrete existence; otherwise, the words *universality, particularity, individuality* would have no meaning. Even in formal logic, forms, *modi intelligendi*, refer to experience, to empirical knowledge. Thomistic concepts may be transcendentally analyzed in the sense that they are in reference to *an absolute of being*, but this dynamic reference exists only because all these realities, despite their subjective or intentional existence, have an ontological *content* that explains their requirements as absolute or as being.

The Thomistic concept may indeed be considered as a pure possible[117]; the noumenon or formal object of metaphysics may be considered to be "perfectly universal being and also, since the logical properties of universality and necessity are correlative, a being that is unconditionally necessary as being—in a word, the absolute of being."[118] This makes it adaptable, perhaps, to a metaphysics constructed upon a transcendental mode, but unfortunately it in no way corresponds to Thomistic being as being, or to the Thomistic concept of it.[119] Furthermore, it does not turn it into a Kantian *a priori* concept.

The *a priori* may also be defined as the formal object of the ontological faculties and not only as a logical function,[120] but to make this addition is completely to forsake the Kantian point of view for a realist point of view. And to identify the formal object with the faculty itself, with its first act, as if it were a hollow prefiguration of the general form of the object that will be its natural complement,[121] is to transform into Kantian or subjective realities that which, for St. Thomas, characterizes exterior realities. Moreover, it is to transform these characteristics of the transcendental subject by giving them a window to the real, which Kant does not give them. For the opening of the Kantian *a priori* to an objective world of noumena is a glance at a world that is illusory by definition.

For here we have to do with a natural and inevitable illusion, which rests on *subjective* principles, and foists them upon us as *objective*. . . . There exists, then, a natural and unavoidable dialectic of pure reason . . . one inseparable from human reason and which, even after its deceptiveness has been exposed, will not cease to play tricks with reason and continually entrap it into momentary aberrations ever and again calling for correction.[122]

Conclusion to Chapter III

We do not need to seek out the causes that led Father Maréchal to attempt a reconciliation of Kant's transcendental critique with the ontological critique of St. Thomas. That would make a stimulating chapter in the history of epistemology, constituting a special *mirabile* whose solution would be highly interesting and full of surprises. But in our context, that is, in classifying Father Maréchal's work as an attempt to conciliate the Kantian conceptions of the critique of knowledge with the Thomistic, we are obliged to conclude that his work, whose aim was to reveal the complementary aspects of the two epistemologies, ends in a complete *rejection* of both the *Critique of Pure Reason* and Thomistic metaphysics. The contents of Father Maréchal's Cahier V, and of the articles cited, are neither Thomistic nor Kantian; the Neo-Scholastic philosopher is narrating a third story, a story that replaces the original dialogue between St. Thomas and Kant about metaphysical truth, and rejects them both. We are faced with a *Maréchalist* epistemology, as completely foreign to the *Critique of Pure Reason* as it is to a Thomistic position on the problem of human knowledge.

Being a Thomist and therefore a realist, this Neo-Scholastic philosopher realized that he was caught in a vicious circle. He had to renounce either the metaphysics he professed or the scientific character of this philosophy. Such, as we have seen, is the true epistemological problem facing contemporary Thomistic philosophers. We have seen the nightmare caused by this situation and the progressive feeling of guilt that developed among realist philosophers as they perceived their "critical" nudity. We have noted their numerous visits to that fashionable tailor, idealism. These prolonged fittings at the idealist clothier were supposed to put Thomists right in style, but they have emerged wearing Nessian tunics that have deprived them of all freedom of motion. This new uniform has become the

Thomist's prison, and every attempt to escape has accentuated his nudity the more, for he is now minus both Thomistic truth and the garment of idealism. Let us try to investigate the causes of this awful dream, whose incidents Van Riet has so scrupulously reported, and the frightful confusions they have sown in contemporary Thomistic philosophy.

A. THE CAUSES OF THOMISTIC CONFUSION

Descartes' identification of Scholastic philosophy with popular knowledge, or so-called common sense, produced among Neo-Scholastic thinkers a sort of abscessed fixation, which they have been unable to heal. They fear this identification, but they accept it. How else explain the importance they attach to the realism of popular knowledge, whose vindication would make their philosophy critical in the Cartesian or Kantian sense of the word?[123] To show that popular knowledge is realist is like breaking down a door already open, for neither Descartes, nor Kant, nor modern scientists deny it; it has even been established that all science has this realism as its starting point.[124] But to admit the realism of popular knowledge is not to prove its scientific character. That is why everyone, beginning with Aristotle and St. Thomas,[125] grants its realism and denies that it is scientific. To say that popular knowledge is scientific knowledge is to destroy the essential constituent of classical epistemology, namely, that to know scientifically is to know by causes. The fascination generated by the Cartesian identification of realist philosophy with popular knowledge must be shaken off, and our philosophy must be shown to be a wisdom. That is the aim of epistemology.

The second source of confusion among Neo-Scholastic epistemologists is that they have forgotten the very sources of idealism. Idealism sprang from the postulate that metaphysics does not exist because it has always begotten skepticism.[126] A method starting from the nonexistence of metaphysical truth, by reason of this truth's lack of unity, and seeking the causes of this nonexistence in the name of either a mathematical or physical criterion can only construct an epistemology that vindicates mathematics and physics and makes metaphysics impossible. For the possible applications of a method are exactly correlative to the evidence that is its starting point: everything that is unknowable by means of this evidential principle is unknowable by this method.

B. THE CONSEQUENCES OF THIS CONFUSION

If "they shall sow wind, and reap a whirlwind," he who sows confusion harvests even greater confusion. That is the verdict concluding Van Riet's exhaustive investigations into our subject.

But there remains one discipline whose status has not yet been established. . . . This is epistemology. . . . Today we are still discussing its *object* and its *method*, the problems it entails and its place in a systematic philosophy: even its name is not universally accepted.[127]

Here is a list of the different confusions existing among Neo-Scholastic epistemologists.

¶ *1. Confusion About the Name.* This treatise is variously called: *logica major, materialis, critica,* epistemology, criteriology, gnosiology, theory of knowledge, immediate realism that is precritical, critical, methodic, philosophical, metaphysical, natural. Thirteen names for a single reality!

¶ *2. Confusion About the Place of this Treatise in Philosophy.* It is a part of logic, of psychology, or is in the orbit of metaphysics, of which it is the threshold, the first, the second, or the last part; or else it is identical with metaphysics of which it is either the reverse side or the continual and perpetual verification. Eight different topographies for a single treatise!

¶ *3. Confusion About the Objects or Problems of Epistemology.* These are: the certitude value and the reality value of *all types* of human knowledge, of human knowledge *in general,* of *an act* of human knowledge, of that of first principles; the reality value, but *not* the certitude, of human knowledge *in general.* Four objects for one same discipline!

¶ *4. Confusion About the Method.* The method is apologetic, methodic or reflective, critical, transcendental.[128]

Van Riet explains the chaotic state of Neo-Scholastic epistemology by its overexclusive attachment to history:

> From the very birth of the Neo-Scholastic movement, but especially today, the philosophical character of epistemology has been compromised by *the ever increasing importance it assigns to history.* . . . On the one hand, epistemology tends to look for its *problems* in non-Thomist philosophies, as if its sole object were to refute them. But on the other hand, and for the same reason, it cannot be interested exclusively in the doctrine of St. Thomas. . . . *Thomist* epistemology can no more expect the texts of St. Thomas alone to supply it with questions, or to indicate the answers it must give, than it can seek the exclusive sources of its problems in non-Thomistic systems. A philosophical discipline, it must free itself of historical contingencies whatever they may be.[129]

This explanation seems to explain nothing. If the epistemology in question exists neither in the writings nor in the thought of St. Thomas,[130] why call it Thomistic? If it is Thomistic, it will naturally look for its problems and answers where Thomism has the best chance of existing, that is, in the works of St. Thomas, and will naturally combat and refute the born enemies of this doctrine. It cannot be disinterested in history. With all due respect to Professor Van Riet, the incoherencies plaguing Neo-Scholastic epistemology have been produced, not by history, but by its own deficiencies in philosophy, which should be pointed out in this conclusion.

By its history, epistemology is necessarily linked to the problem of infallible truth. The problem of truth is always complex, for to be intelligible, it requires a self, an *interior* nonself, and an *exterior* nonself. (This may be jargon, but it is the terminology preferred by the Neo-Scholastics.) The problem is always stated by the subject or the self, so the self always comes into the picture. Furthermore, the self can state a problem only by virtue of a certain duality in the self, therefore, by means of a duplication of self that exists simultaneously as experience and as object. This duality poses no problem, because it is the very evidence of the *cogito,* of ideas, i.e., of the real nonself. The problem concerns the nonself and can be stated in four ways:

(i) How can we know that the nonself or the other-in-me really and actually corresponds to an exterior nonself? This question generates criteriologies or the quest for evidential criteria. A whole series of Neo-Scholastic epistemologies have asked this problem and have tried to solve it. It is, moreover, a genuine problem.

(ii) The second possible question is: In how many ways can the nonself exist in me? This real problem of the multiplicity of truths, of their evidence and certitude, has been the object of several epistemologists.

(iii) The third can be stated as follows: What is the relationship between the interior nonself and the exterior nonself? This again is a real problem, concerning not the evidence or certitude of truth, for they are properties of truth, but the very *nature* of truth, its *quodquid est*. This might be said to be the most important problem of epistemology, for the other two problems presuppose it to be solved, since the properties or qualities of a reality flow from this reality and presuppose it.

(iv) The fourth and last question: Is the self made for the nonself, or does truth exist? To ask this question is to cease philosophizing, for it indicates that by dint of disillusionment and many quests for truth that ended in error, one has become a skeptic. Skeptics have asked this question, as have several Neo-Scholastics, but it was never asked by Descartes or by Kant. Descartes started from an existing truth whose nature he used as criterion for discovering the first principles of metaphysics: he started from mathematical truth.[131] Kant started from two existing truths to construct his critique: mathematical truth, and the truth of pure physics.[132] When, by virtue of the principle of a radical pseudosincerity, St. Thomas is considered a universal, even a methodic, doubter, he is also considered an imbecile who disobeys his own first law concerning the questions the human intellect can and cannot ask.[133] For what is unknown has never been a problem to anyone, and truth is knowable only insofar as it exists, for it exists only in the human soul. Knowing that certain truths exist, we can ask ourselves whether they are scientific, whether they are philosophical, whether they are popular, etc., but we cannot ask whether truth exists before we have experienced truth, that is, before it exists. Therefore, this is not a genuine question.

It is chiefly because it has asked itself this fourth question that Neo-Scholastic epistemology has descended into a chaos reminiscent of the one described in Genesis, but without the "Spirit of God moving over the waters." Neither history, idealism, nor Thomism has prevented this discipline from finding its place, its name, its object and method, but rather the fact that it starts by asking a question that makes no philosophical sense. It has been said that idealism has taught Thomism a great deal! One thing it has not taught many neo-Thomist epistemologists is how to ask a question. Let us see what Kant has to say about this, if what St. Thomas teaches us is not enough. The question is to be asked, not about the existence of truth, but about its nature:

The question, famed of old, by which logicians were supposed to be driven into a corner, obliged either to have recourse to a pitiful sophism, or to confess their ignorance and consequently the emptiness of their whole art, is the question: What is truth? . . . To know what questions may reasonably be asked is already a great and necessary proof of sagacity and insight. For if a question is absured in itself and calls for an answer where none is required, it not only brings shame on the propounder of the question, but may betray an incautious listener into absurd answers, thus presenting, as the ancients said, the ludicrous spectacle of one man milking a he-goat and the other holding a sieve underneath.[134]

The spectacle of our contemporary philosophy is just as ridiculous as the incident Kant alludes to, for it will never be able to extract from idealism the milk of philosophical method, nor will its Thomism ever be able to hold a sieve to this method. Our nightmare has already lasted too long; it is time that we came out of it, unless we want to justify the idealists and skeptics of all times, for whom our metaphysics has always been a transcendental illusion. Let us ask St. Thomas, the angel of metaphysical genius, to show us the true philosophic method.

IV · THE ANGELIC DOCTOR'S METHOD

The rational principles of the syllogism and of definition play the same role in defining and syllogizing that the artistic standards, to which the artist must look, do in the art process. Now the artist who makes a knife does not produce the standard which governs his work; rather, he examines whether the knife is well made in accord with the standard which he has in mind.[1]

Before attempting a study of the philosophic method used by St. Thomas in constructing his synthesis, we should briefly review what we have learned from the three preceding analyses, since each of these analyses deals with the nature of a problem and with the basic attitudes of the human mind in search of truth.

In the first chapter we learned three universal laws governing all our cognitive activities. The first is the incoercible desire for truth, a desire that haunts our soul and is expressed by our instinctive flight from ignorance and error the moment we become aware of their presence. The second law governs the activities consequent upon this desire for truth; it organizes the steps we take in discovering knowledge, steps that are normally a continual reflective interchange between the universe we know and the universe that is, in order to reconcile the different accounts reality gives of itself when we are its guests. The third law has to do with the results of our steps toward knowledge. If these results are positive—if man succeeds in resolving the contradiction between these accounts, dissolves their differences, and discovers a new truth, a truth more complete than those preceding it—then confidence in our intellectual powers increases, its methods of research improve, and there results one of those magnificent syntheses that have nourished the human mind for centuries.

If, however, his search for truth fails, if man cannot see where truth is to be found in the discordant stories he hears, then he doubts; that is, he refuses to take sides with either one or the other narrator in order to avoid error, which is a greater evil than the ignorance of which doubt is an admission. Therefore, doubt is not synonymous with error, but with a *vaccine* against error. If doubt accumulates, if man fails repeatedly in his search for truth, then he may become disillusioned, for his incoercible and seemingly unsatisfiable desire for truth becomes absurd to him. This disillusionment is called "skepticism," which is a disease of the mind, and error par excellence, since it makes a man lose the taste for truth, in the same sense that we say a man loses the taste for food; he dies in the disinterested quest of that for which we are made.

The modern epistemological experiment teaches us a second lesson and shows us what not to do if we wish to discover philosophical truth; it gives us the rules for *how not to philosophize.* The first rule is as follows: To identify doubt with error is to identify the fear of error with error, the vaccine with the disease. The second rule flows from the first: To inoculate oneself with doubt is not to cure the disease but to contract it. Disease is an evil and not a cure; therefore, doubt as a method, instead of being an infallible cure for skepticism, only makes it worse, as the history of Cartesianism has decisively proved. The third rule: When doubt is identified with error, and when what is doubtful *to me* is considered equal to what is doubtful *in itself*, no criterion of truth and error remains but *my mind*, which thus becomes *the* rule of truth, and the *cogito* remains the only logical position from which to construct a philosophy. Fourth rule: If my mind is the only source of truth, it is also the only source of error.[2] Consequently, it must be put on trial to defend itself, that is, to account for the existence of error. In such a context, every philosophic method becomes an analysis of our capacity to err and not an analysis of our power to attain to truth. The fifth rule deals with the results of the suit brought against the mind by method. The verdict may be not guilty, once the human soul is considered as a pure spirit, endowed with ideas and truths from the first moment of its existence: In this case, error is imputed to the body and education. The verdict may be guilty, when the soul is defined, not as a pure spirit filled with ideas, but as a Platonic Demiurgos whose creative power can draw from its spontaneity all ideas and forms, but not the matter these forms animate, which must be supplied by sensibility. This creator of *a priori* forms keeps on creating even in the absence of matter, and these creations are transcendental illusions: it creates errors. The life of a pure spirit entombed in a deceitful body, the life of a Demiurgos condemned to transcendental illusion, such is the life of a Cartesian and Kantian man, such is the philosophy born of their method.

The third and last lesson is drawn from the Neo-Scholastic experiment. Here are its essential points: Adherents of a philosophy that conceives man to be neither angel nor Demiurgos, a philosophy wherein what is doubtful *to me* is in no way synomymous with what is doubtful *in itself*, are supremely illogical in adopting a philosophic method consisting essentially in criticism of the angel or Demiurge for the constant disillusionment (skepticism) that it causes the human soul. For any such adherent, philosophic method should normally be conceived in relation to man proceeding toward truth. If there is a trial, it will be a trial of human truths, not of the disillusions caused by an angelic spirit or a demiurgic creator of *a priori* forms.

It is in the light of these lessons that we shall approach the study of the epistemological problem as St. Thomas saw and solved it. Our procedure in this chapter will be the same as that in the three preceding chapters. A first section will deal with the genesis of the problem caused by the opposition between the familiar account given by Augustinian theology and the surprising narrative told by Aristotelian cosmology; the second section will study the Thomistic *mirabile* and the methods of inquiry flowing from it.

Section I: Birth of the Thomistic Problem

(handwritten margin note: Familiar Story-Day Per / Arist-Thom)

A. THE FAMILIAR STORYTELLER

The ideological context in which the Thomistic synthesis was born and developed was a context of Christian faith immanent to a Neo-Platonic mode of thought.[3] Faith taught St. Thomas that the universe is created, that he was himself a part of this universe, but it gave him a definition neither of creatures nor of man. The definitions that faith did not provide, Augustinian theology undertook to supply. We shall let the last and most perfect storyteller of the Augustinian medieval universe tell us this story of a *universe-on-a-trip*. Its itinerary is mapped out from all eternity, for the way it must follow is called the "Word of God." Let us listen to St. Bonaventure describe the three steps in the itinerary that creation follows in coming forth from God, and that is its destiny to retrace.[4]

(handwritten margin note: St Bonaventure)

¶ *First Stage: Creation or the Multiple Comes from the One.* Multiplicity is an experienced fact; its divine origin is a revealed fact; its description fills the first pages of the Bible. Here is St. Bonaventure's description of this coming forth. God, Who is Being, Essence, the Immutable, and infinitely rich, freely willed creation. Whatever is necessary for creating He possesses, for, being omnipotent and an artist of infinite resource, He is filled with ideas or imitabilities.[5] Despite His simplicity, His artistic ingenuity succeeded in the feat of creating composite beings, for every creature, even the spiritual, is composed of matter and form.[6] This composition starts from the depth of *entis* and *esse* to find completion in matter and form, to which are added genus and difference, substance and accidents.[7] This is the first stage in the composition of creatures. With man is added the composition of spiritual and corporeal nature, as well as the composition belonging to every corporeal nature, that of homogeneous and heterogeneous parts.[8]

The chronological series of creatures started with the empyrean heaven, was continued by the angels, the matter of the elements, and the first measure of every creature, time. From three corporeal creatures flowed all the others, which are legion.[9] The Bonaventurian universe is finally crowned by a last creature, wholly different from the rest—grace, a creature that permits sin and with it decreation. All these creatures are one, i.e., undivided in themselves and divided from all others. We are confronted with the most incredible multiplicity that could ever come from a single artist, God.

¶ *Second Stage: Unity Immanent in Multiplicity or Exemplarity.* It might seem that the divine art hurled beings into time and space, that it dispersed them one by one without the slightest possibility of unity between creatures and themselves or the divine simplicity. However, this is not at all the case. The Divine Artist is present to each and every one of His works through His conserving activity and as their model, for they are but copies of divine ideas. This artistic aspect of things is not added to their nature; it constitutes it: "A creature is nothing but a copy of Wisdom."[10] "To be the image of God is not accidental to man, but rather substantial: just as to be a vestige is not accidental to any creature."[11]

Bound to the Divine Artist as copies, creatures are linked to each other by two ontological bonds, of which the first is prime matter, the universal appetite for forms, which supports the weakest as well as the most noble of these.[12] The second ontological bond is the fellowship of forms, which, far from being mutually exclusive, band together and abide in the same thing.[13] This second phase of the universe-on-a-trip consists in a pooling of the divine exemplarity that measures all created things and unifies them in their model, and a pooling of their poverty (prime matter) with their wealth (their substantial form). Thus unified, the universe is ready to embark upon the third and last stage of its journey, the return to God.

¶ *Third Stage: Return to God by Dynamism and Finality.* This third stage is made up of two very distinct phases. First, the material universe progresses toward man, which is to say that everything active or passive in the material world is inclined toward formation by the highest of forms, the human soul.[14] This inferior causality is not fortuitous or contingent, for God moves material things like puppets; all their movements, taken as a whole or singly, are ordered from all eternity by the providence of God. Furthermore, this causality does not consist in producing other beings, for this privilege is reserved to God alone. (By the production of being, Bonaventure understands the production of forms or essences both substantial and accidental.[15] The causality of infrahuman creatures is thus dispositive. It causes a being to pass from one mode of being to another (for example, it causes the bud to become a rose), but it can do no more than that, since God created everything from the principle of the seminal reasons that are contained in matter and that await the time foreseen for their blossoming.[16]

So much for the return of the material universe to God through man. But once in man, what will man do with it? He will make it continue on the way to its final beatitude by means of knowledge and love, which constitute the causality proper to spiritual creatures. The second phase in the itinerary is a voyage whose medium is truth and love, for to know is to possess truth, and God alone is truth. He alone is truly undivided and indivisible, whereas all creatures, being composite, are divisible and therefore lack truth just as they lack being.[17] But how can man cause truth, since truth and being are identical and only God can cause being?

In order to be equated with being by means of the intellect, which is the definition of truth,[18] the two terms of the equation must be immutable; but neither created intellects nor created things are immutable. Therefore, to explain the production of truth, we must have recourse to divine causality, just as recourse to it was necessary to explain the appearance of new beings. Just as *seminal reasons* account for new beings (created causality influencing only appearances), so Augustinian *memory*[19] contains eternal reasons, eternally deposited therein by divine illumination. To know truth is not really to produce it, but to reveal it where it already existed by means of illumination, the human intellect's true motive power.[20] The *ratio movens* that is illumination is active at every stage in the acquisition of truth: in the grasping of vestiges by sensation and the conservation of their image by sensible memory, in the grasping of natures by simple apprehension, of their truth by judgment, and of the necessary bonds between different truths by reasoning.[21] Always more completely and intensely to actualize truths already existing in the soul, by means of the constant cooperation of illumination, until the very moment when, face to face with Truth, its journey will be over—such is the itinerary of the human soul and its proper role. This is the metaphysical explanation of the Bonaventurian universe.

The epistemology of St. Bonaventure, his "Discourse on Method," is patterned exactly after the reality to be known and the nature of knowledge. Since the metaphysical structure of the universe belongs to the order of history, since it is a sort of theogonic drama whose impresario is God, truth consists in the ability to read this divine scenario, to follow the trilogy of efficiency, exemplarity, and finnality. The method of knowing it is a *method of reading*.[22] Now faith has already given us another book, the Bible, and we know that the rules by which it should be read are four, according to the four meanings of the divine text. And the same is true of the divine book that is the universe: the only correct method of reading it is the exegetical method. This method consists in beginning with the literal meaning, then grasping the allegorical sense, to which is added the tropological meaning, which is crowned by the anagogical sense. Let us see how Bonaventure applies this exegetical method.

(a) *The literal meaning.* The universe is a book written by God, and this book obeys the general laws of writing: there are letters, the primary elements of which every creature is composed; there are syllables and words, the syntheses of these elements, constituting the natures of things; there are dynamic bonds between these natures that make up sentences and chapters. Speculative grammar, which discovers the laws of morphology and syntax of this book, is *science*, and Aristotle has excelled all others in studying the literal meaning of the book of the universe. But although grammar gives us the elements and laws for composing a book, it can tell us nothing of its meaning and truth. Aristotelian science alone does not therefore grasp the meaning of the book, and if it asserts that everything is found in grammar, it is false.[23]

(b) *The allegorical meaning.* To understand the meaning of the signs studied through grammar is to grasp what really constitutes them; it is to grasp truth. To do this we must penetrate to the soul of the writer, discern his intentions and the ideas he used as models in composing his book. That was Plato's work; his interest was not centered in the physical aspect of things, but in their character as copies or images of separated forms, the only realities that truly are and are really true. This kind of knowledge is called *Wisdom*, for it sees the whole lower world under the mark of the exemplarity and unity of its artist or author.

(c) *The tropological meaning.* Platonic wisdom rightly discerned the spiritual meaning of the universe and its participated character, but it never understood the meaning of this participation, because it never knew the *locus* of forms—the Word of God. Grace puts us into contact with the Holy Trinity, the true *locus* of forms, and *theology* explains the tropological meaning of the universe by showing us that it comes forth from God by creative activity and returns to Him through Christ and the Christological activity of the sacraments. Without this new knowledge, Platonic wisdom is false, for it does not truly explain the meaning of the universe, which must lead to the Trinity or be false.

(d) *The anagogical meaning.* Once we have understood that the universe is a copy made by an artist who is at first unkown (Platonic wisdom) and then known (Theology), we might think that truth has finally been won and that we have reached our goal. But we are still far from it, and woe to him who is satisfied with a reading of the book of creation that leaves us plunged in time and space, even though it be in the presence of the Trinity. We are not made to live in time but in eternity, not made to live in faith but in glory. A final meaning must be added to the first three. This is the anagogical sense given us by the gifts of the Holy Spirit, the consciously savored presence of the Three Persons in the soul, a foretaste of the glorious vision of eternity. *Mystical* knowledge gives us this final way of reading the universe by which we may taste God and everything in God. It is truth in its totality, and, as far as Bonaventure is concerned, it characterizes the only genuine metaphysician.[24] The successive stages in the acquisition of metaphysical truth are given to us in a very enlightening passage: "*Among philosophers*, Plato was given wisdom, Aristotle science. The former looked most to the higher things, the latter to the lower. But *through the Holy Spirit* both wisdom and science were given to Augustine . . . it was present in a more excellent way in Paul and Moses . . . in the most excellent manner in Christ."[25]

There is the story told by Bonaventure, and Thomas Aquinas was perfectly familiar with it. In its broad outlines this narrative is to be found in St. Augustine, but Bonaventure embellished it with borrowings from Scotus Erigena,[26] Gilbert de la Porrée,[27] Avicenna,[28] and William of Auvergne.[29] Such an account of the universe could not but cause the Christian soul to rejoice, for the treasures of the interior life, whose importance is primary in Christianity, could only be increased and exalted by the place assigned to them in this doctrine. In fact, they had exclusive claim to truth, a sort of universal copyright on the ensemble of God's works. In such a synthesis, reason is not the handmaiden of faith but its slave, and every attempt to be independent necessarily dooms reason to the depths of error and jeopardizes its chance to attain truth.

At the very same time that Bonaventure was telling this familiar story to the medieval soul, another story, which had already been circulating undercover for twenty years, began to be made public and provoked very violent reactions among theologians of that epoch. It was the story, so scandalous to the Neo-Platonic mind, told by the physics and metaphysics of Aristotle. Every story that scandalized the supporters of the Augustinian synthesis was bound to be scandalous to the Christian faith that had for eight centuries been theologically formulated in Augustinian terms. Thomas had already heard this narrative from his master, Albert. He had read it in the poor Latin translations of Arabic texts, and he was soon to read it again in a new translation made directly from the Greek text. How was this story opposed to the one we have just heard from Bonaventure?

B. THE ARISTOTELIAN STORY

Aristotle did not come into conflict with the Augustinian universe by his notion of being, composed of potency and act, substance and accidents, because potency was necessary to the distinction between creature and creator, who alone was simple. The scandal began with the unicity of substantial form,[30] with the introduction of real causality into the world of becoming and of a causality affecting forms.[31] In the Aristotelian universe there were real generations and corruptions, and the cause of these generations and corruptions was not God acting through the mediation of seminal reasons primordially latent in prime matter, for prime matter was pure potency. It was the causality of creatures that accounted for forms, both substantial and accidental. For Bonaventure, the realm of forms was identical with that of being; it was taboo for created causality, which could at most work toward the flowering of a form, never toward its production.[32]

The second scandalous feature in the Aristotelian story (it was in fact heretical) was the eternity and necessity of his physical universe: only individuals were born and died; structurally the universe had always been and would always be what it was. There was neither progress nor regress, only a fundamental identity underlying perpetual new beginnings in the eternal story of an eternal world.[33]

Even more heretical, if possible, was the divinity that presided over these eternal changes and their order. Instead of one God, there were more than forty[34]; instead of a providential God, these forty divinities presided imperturbably over earthly and celestial events that they did not even know about, since they did not produce them.[35] Sources of universal motivity, they attracted this world of mobility and change by means of their very immobility, their impassibility which the physical universe tried to imitate by the eternity of species, which somewhat corrected the instability of individuals.[36]

Into this world without a destiny, without progression or regression, governed by divinities who did not know what was going on in it and who would have been debased by taking an interest in it, Aristotle plunged the human soul, whose substance consisted in being the form of a body on which it depended for its subsistence and for all its activities. There was no Platonic reminiscence; much less was there Augustinian memory, where in advance eternal *reasons* had inscribed all the truths of which the soul was capable. Neither was there divine illumination to establish contact between the being of God, source of all truth, and this human intellect "which is as a blank sheet of paper upon which nothing has been written." There was a divine element, a *theion ti*, called the separate intellect, but it did not seem to belong to every man's soul.[37] The soul was really in a state of complete desolation; its only hope came from sensation, which was much better equipped to attain its object than was the intellect. A soul that was not immortal,[38] that had no personal contact with a God who did not even know it existed, a soul whose whole beatitude lay in perceiving the imperfect order of a world without a destiny, and thus without divine significance—such was the final scandal in the Aristotelian narrative. If a totally pagan and a-religious universe exists, it is certainly Aristotle's, and we can easily imagine the instinctive repulsion that a Christian and mystically Christian soul would feel when confronted by such an account, which contradicts both Christian faith and the theology explaining and exploring the data of faith. This was the second narrative that Thomas could read in the philosopher's text. The accompanying commentaries of Averroës, whose refined rationalism further emphasized these purely pagan constructs, only served to increase its scandalous character. Thus was born the Thomistic *mirabile*. Let us see what was the object of his wonder and the inquiries it initiated. In so doing we shall discover his method.

Section II: Nature of the Thomistic Problem

It is not enough to witness the birth of the Thomistic *mirabile* and the growing awareness of the basic conflict between medieval Augustinism as synthesized by Bonaventure and Aristotelianism. We must also determine the exact points upon which this opposition is based, for only the conflict whose cause is unknown gives rise to a problem. Among the antithetical statements in the Augustinian and Aristotelian syntheses, some can be explained by the presence of the Christian faith in Augustinianism and its absence in Aristotelianism.[39] These points of conflict do not constitute a problem for St. Thomas,

since he knows their cause: faith's enabling man to perceive truths
whose content wholly escapes the human reason, which is incapable
of even suspecting their existence.[40] As for that group of truths
called *revelabilia*,[41] which do not fall completely outside the range
of reason, and knowledge of which is necessary for salvation, St.
Thomas finds them in Aristotle, or at least interprets Aristotelian
texts in accord with these truths.[42] The real Thomistic *mirabile* is
not to be found at the level of relations between faith and reason,
but at the level of reason itself, in the contrary accounts that
Augustinian Platonism and Aristotelianism give of the physical universe, its organization, its causality, and the relations that this universe
and everything in it have with its first cause, God. The *mirabile* of
St. Thomas must therefore be formulated in terms of *Neo-Platonism
versus Aristotelianism*. We shall try to describe this *mirabile* precisely, before considering the psychological reactions it brought
about.

A. THE NATURE OF THE THOMISTIC MIRABILE

Since the real source of dissension between Augustinianism and
Aristotelianism does not lie in revealed or revealable truth,[43] the
basic elements of the Thomistic problem must be sought elsewhere.
Stripped of its theological and theologal content, Augustinianism
consists in a Neo-Platonic view of the universe. In that universe, the
physical is not being, but only appearances, shadows of forms or
essences whose origins and nature can easily be described in a
mythology or a theology of the six days of creation,[44] but which
cannot be the object of a philosophical cosmology. Inasmuch as a
universe so constituted cannot lead to a *physica* or philosophy of
nature,[45] we can know it only through a definition referring to the
essence or exemplary cause of which it is the effect or sign. Actually,
this is one of the characteristics of Augustinian thought, as we have
seen in the mystical synthesis of Bonaventure,[46] wherein science
without wisdom is false knowledge. In Aristotelianism the procedure is just the opposite. The philosophy of nature necessarily

precedes metaphysics, whose very name indicates that it comes after the physics which it presupposes and needs in order to exist, i.e., in order to discover its object, the intelligible or *separabile* and the *separatum*.

If the Thomistic *mirabile* is to be determined, this is the context in which it must be done, and in the following terms: Why is it that Platonism has only a mythical cosmology, whereas Aristotelianism gives us true knowledge of the physical universe and the beings in it? St. Thomas himself took pains to stress Aristotle's originality in organizing philosophical knowledge upon a properly physical or sensible basis. One of the many passages pointing out this originality[47] is to be found in the very same part of the commentary on the *Metaphysics* wherein he explains the method of first philosophy and speaks of the *dubitatio universalis de veritate*, so renowned among Neo-Scholastic epistemologists.[48] In this text, St. Thomas, after commenting on Aristotle's justification of his metaphysical method, adds a second reason to Aristotle's. This second justification hits precisely upon the nature of the Thomistic *mirabile:*

He [i.e., Aristotle] does not proceed in the same way as other philosophers in seeking truth. For he starts from the sensible and appearances and proceeds to the separate, as may be seen below, in the seventh book. But the other philosophers wanted to apply the intelligible and the abstract to the sensible.[49]

What struck St. Thomas was the opposite character of the procedures by which Platonism and Aristotelianism seek truth: *Non autem eodem ordine ipse procedit ad inquisitionem veritatis.* In Platonism the intelligible is an *a priori quoad se* and *quoad nos*,[50] and the sensible is an *a posteriori*, since we construct it, starting from the intelligible.[51]

That the Thomistic *mirabile* is primarily concerned with the conflict between the Aristotelian and Platonic *methods*[52] is clearly attested by St. Thomas' absolute liberty as regards the *contents* of the two philosophies and his fidelity to the Aristotelian *method*. We are sometimes surprised to see St. Thomas abandon some Platonic or Neo-Platonic tenets and substitute Aristotelian doctrines, or, on the contrary, reinforce the Aristotelian synthesis with Platonic or Neo-Platonic doctrines.[53] Also, we are likely to conclude that his synthesis is only a syncretism or, again, a baptized Aristotelianism. However, neither of these suppositions is wholly true, although both of them contain elements of truth, for Thomism takes its truth where it finds it and integrates it within a completely original synthesis.[54] But the philosophic method of St. Thomas is entirely borrowed from Aristotelianism, hence the Aristotelian characteristics of his doctrine even where Aristotelianism is excluded or entirely surpassed.[55]

Having adopted the Aristotelian method, the Angelic Doctor was constrained to criticize Platonic and Neo-Platonic procedures or methods. This he does continually in dealing with the texts of Augustine,[56] Boethius, and Dionysius,[57] and in defining philosophic style as compared with the Platonic or Neo-Platonic style,[58] which belongs properly to poetry and to the Bible,[59] but is antiphilosophic because it lacks unity and conciseness.[60]

It would be easy to give historical proof that St. Thomas completely accepted the Aristotelian philosophic method, simply by considering his continual quotations of the Stagirite's methodological texts.[61] An even more direct argument is to be found in his interest in Aristotle's purely logical works and in the precision of his commentaries upon those parts of logic that deal explicitly with scientific or philosophic knowledge. We must never forget that St. Thomas professed but one vocation, that of a Christian doctor whose sole goal is to know God and make Him known.[62] Now, Aristotelian texts speak little of God and center upon natural realities.[63] How then explain that a Christian doctor devoted so many years of his short life to examining the teachings of a pagan entirely dedicated to the study of physical beings? St. Thomas himself has given us the reason for his interest in Aristotle's works by establishing the necessary bonds that exist between knowledge of creatures and knowledge of the Creator,[64] as well as the methodological difference between philosophical knowledge and theological knowledge.[65] The description of the difference between philosophical method and theological method is a portrait of oppositions among Aristotelianism, Platonism, and all its medieval derivatives.

Moreover, St. Thomas accepts the methodological doctrine of Aristotle and the latter's criticisms of Platonic separatism[66]; he makes the conclusions of these criticisms his own. In short, if we observe that, in his commentaries on Aristotle, St. Thomas follows the literal formula and does not paraphrase him,[67] that these analyses of Aristotle's texts are models of their kind, and that they are continually strewn with value judgments about the force and fruitfulness of Aristotle's arguments,[68] we cannot but conclude that, for St. Thomas, Aristotelian method was *philosophic method* in all its purity.[69] For him Aristotle personified natural wisdom, which he had so organized that it was absurd to pretend to find defects of method in it[70] or errors in anything that touched upon the area of rational truth. From this conviction sprang the many battles he fought against Averroistic interpretations of Aristotelianism and the biting remarks, from such a peaceful man, that he levels at the Commentator "who was not so much a Peripatetic as a debaser of peripatetic philosophy.[71] This conviction is also the cause of his frequent recourse to the *intentio auctoris* to justify certain arguments[72] and the subtleties he attributes to the Philosopher when the latter's proofs seem to him to be frivolous or sophistic.

It could be said that in these discussions the Philosopher uses not only probable but sophistical arguments, adducing reasons which he has borrowed from others. But it does not seem reasonable that in so important a matter, so great a philosopher would adduce so frivolous and trivial an argument.[73]

We could go on indefinitely, accumulating examples of this kind to show that, although Aquinas rejected some of Aristotle's doctrines, he never criticized his method but, rather, defended it on every occasion and brought it to its highest possible fruition by transposing it to regions that the Stagirite would never have dreamed could be studied by means of the methodological instruments that he himself had perfected. But these general remarks suffice to conclude that the Thomistic *mirabile* is concerned much more with the conflict between Aristotelian and Neo-Platonic *methods* than with the divergent *contents* of these two philosophies. What struck him was the fact that Aristotelianism takes all human experience as its

starting point and, neglecting none of its aspects, tries to put hierarchy into its components rather than to mutilate it. By following a
sure and irrefutable path, starting from the earth, Aristotelianism
succeeds in discovering a God who is the Thought of thoughts;
whereas Platonism despises everything in human experience that
depends upon sensibility, mutilates man by transforming him into
a spirit, mutilates reality by reconstructing it after the model of
abstract ideas, and, with the help of examples and metaphors, ends
up with a God who is beyond being and therefore absolutely unknowable.

The real Thomistic *mirabile* has as its starting point the fact that
Aristotle constructed a cosmology and a cosmogony, a physics that
permits of a metaphysics and is its substratum; whereas Platonism
and all its Arabian and Christian offshoots were never really able
to explain the physical character of the universe, except in terms of
symbols. This *mirabile* may be formulated as follows: What is the
principle whose presence enables Aristotelianism successfully to
explain the universe and whose absence sterilizes Platonism and transforms it into a mythology of the physical universe? We know that
this conflict springs from their *respective methods,* and we shall see
St. Thomas ask Aristotle for the secret of this fruitfulness by a deep
and painstaking study of that which constitutes Aristotle's greatest
originality; his philosophical method.

B. ANALYSIS OF THE ARISTOTELIAN MIRABILE
OR METHOD

We are now acquainted with the two storytellers to whom St.
Thomas, as a young student, listened at length. We know the particular attention he gave to the divergence of these stories and
especially to the *conflict between their methods:* the Platonic story
always starting in heaven and ending on earth, with the Aristotelian
accounts always departing from earthly things and rising gradually
to contemplate heavenly realities.[74] Now we must more closely
examine the philosophical method adopted by St. Thomas and see

how he used and deepened it in organizing his synthesis. As a Christian scholar, St. Thomas' only concern was to enlist philosophy in the service of faith and thus to integrate the whole field of natural truth within revealed truth, so as to unify human knowledge and facilitate our understanding of supernatural mysteries.[75] But the ancillary character of philosophy differs very greatly in Thomism and Augustinianism. Within the framework of Augustinian thought, which Bonaventure most faithfully and perfectly represents, philosophy is a *servant-slave* and theology a matriarch and despot; philosophy is allowed neither liberty nor autonomy; philosophy must *believe* in order truly to be philosophy, that is in order to be true knowledge.[76] In Thomism, philosophy is queen in the realm of natural truth; it dons a servant's uniform only when undertaking a task beyond its capacities, when it attempts to study the intimate mysteries of God and of deified man, for then it is blinded by that surpassing light and must be guided by faith.

Leaving aside the problem of the relationship of philosophy and theology, let us consider only the properly philosophic aspects of St. Thomas' inquiry into the procedures by which reason, without the intervention of faith, grasps truths that are at its level. The inquiry deals necessarily with the two methods under discussion; it will terminate in the rejection of the Platonic *a prioris* and the acceptance of Aristotelian experimentalism. The spirit in which this criticism and rejection are made appears in the following text:

But because, in accepting or rejecting opinions, a man should not be affected by love or hate of *those introducing* the opinion, but rather by the *certitude of truth*, he says that we should love both those whose opinion we follow and those whose opinion we reject. For both were looking for truth and helped us, in so doing. Nevertheless we should follow the opinion of him who has more certainly arrived at truth.[77]

St. Thomas always rejects his adversaries gently, or, rather, he never wholly rejects their stories, only what is false in them, because he has but one criterion of choice, and this criterion is not based upon the thinkers, but upon the truth of their thought, "for the study of philosophy is not intended to tell us what men have thought but what is really the truth in the matter."[78] Absalom of St. Victor said, "The spirit of Christ does not reign where rules the spirit of Aristotle."[79] St. Thomas maintains the opposite and proclaims that the spirit of Christ reigns wherever truth is found, for He is Truth. This is the sympathetic and understanding attitude with which he approaches the study and formulation of a philosophic method completely independent of the scriptural and theological method. In this, Aristotle is his only master.

Aristotle conceives the apprenticeship of philosophical knowledge as a constant and protracted dialogue between man and the universe, but, unlike Descartes, the apprentice philosopher is neither isolated from his milieu nor able to discover all truth by himself. His dialogue is made up of all previous inquiries, of all previously given answers. It is, by the mediation of one man, all humanity that carries on this dialogue with reality. Aristotle would certainly agree with Bernard of Chartres that "we see farther than did our ancestors; we are dwarfs standing upon the shoulders of giants."[80] This Aristotelian method (which accounts for the long historical introductions forming the first books of his major works) is commended by St. Thomas as an essential element in the virtue of prudence and, therefore, of the human activity that is the acquisition of knowledge:

As in the case of the other parts of prudence, docility indeed stems from natural aptitude; but human effort contributes a great deal to its development, provided man carefully, frequently and reverently applies his mind to the writings of his predecessors, neither neglecting them because of laziness, nor holding them in contempt because of pride.[81]

Aristotelian and Thomistic inquiry into the problem of knowledge is utterly different from a *Discourse on Method* or a *Critique of Pure Reason*. There is none of the pride and intellectual presumption characteristic of the inventors of the modern method; instead, there are a humility and a social sense that explain the extraordinary results of these inquiries.[82]

In order that this dialogue between humanity and the universe be fruitful, we must possess the science of asking questions, the technique of asking the questions the human mind must ask the universe if it would lay bare the latter's secrets and discover its mysteries.

Otherwise, there is the inevitable risk of asking ridiculous or disordered questions to which the interrogated universe would no
longer know what to answer. Kant had true insight into the method
of science when, in his preface to the second edition of the *Critique*,
he compared this method with an interrogation of the universe by
man.[83] But his questioning is of the type to which a judge subjects
a witness, whereas that of Aristotle and St. Thomas corresponds to
the respectful but avid questions a pupil asks his teacher.

Aristotle invented the technique of questioning; he even invented
two such techniques. One is for the purpose of discussing knowledge
that is already possessed with other philosophers and with his own
mind, in order to classify and set it in order, to defend it against
opponents, to expose sophisms in argumentation, to dispose of adversaries whose contentions are irrational and contradictory. This
first technique is called "dialectics" and is set forth in the *Topics*, as
are its three functions concerning properly philosophical knowledge.[84] The other technique is the very backbone of scientific and
philosophical knowledge and consists in the direct interrogation of
reality by the intellect, an interrogation made up of a precise number
of questions to be answered by the universe under the threat of
remaining obscured by a heavy veil, hiding it from the intellect and
leaving visible only its outer contours. This questionnaire is fully set
forth, along with its vindication, in the second book of the *Analytics*.
St. Thomas clearly recognized the distinction between these two
techniques, as well as the good or bad uses to which they might be
put. The following text proves this:

The man who wishes to find a right answer must continue looking for a
solution until there is no more room for doubt: and that is what these
people fail to do. Including himself among those criticized, in order to
avoid pride, Aristotle gives the reason for this defect: in all our efforts
to solve difficulties, it seems to be customary to confine our inquiry to the
refutation of opposing views rather than to the investigation of reality—
that is, not to go as far as the nature of the thing requires but only to
the point at which the adversary offers no further opposition. He even
remarks on this in his own case, when he is in doubt on some point he
inquires within himself only until he finds that he has no further objections at hand. But this is not enough. When a man wants to discover a

true answer, he must not be satisfied with facing all available objections, he must diligently seek out the causes. For this reason, as Aristotle adds, the successful investigator of truth must be ready to face both his own difficulties and those of other men, not sophistical objections but ones that are real and reasonably pertinent, that is to say, appropriate to the matter under investigation. This result is achieved when a man takes into consideration all the differences of things, on the basis of which the question may be answered.[85]

This art of philosophical dialogue, whose needs are imposed not by the arbitrariness of the mind or its belligerence, but rather by the profundity of the real itself. *Quousque natura rei requirit*, this art was studied subtly and at length by St. Thomas in his commentary upon those eleven pages of the *Analytics*[86] in which Aristotle expounds his teaching on the acquisition of scientific truth by means of exact and exhaustive determination of the questions that the human intellect can present to reality, as well as the correct order of these questions. We shall limit ourselves, here, to analyzing the most important passages, but the reader is strongly advised to study this whole commentary, whose depth and literalness make it a model of its type.[87]

C. INQUIRY INTO THE PHILOSOPHICAL QUESTIONNAIRE

As soon as we begin to study the philosophical questionnaire, we are in familiar territory, for Aristotle and St. Thomas define the *quaestio* in the very terms that we used to describe the nature of a problem and its psychological effects: wonder and the desire for knowledge, of which wonder is the sign.[88] We have seen that a problem and the wonder consequent upon it are the result of the marriage of knowledge and ignorance. Here is a description of a *quaestio:*

In every question there must be something known and something sought which we do not know.[89] No question is asked concerning immediately evident matters—which though true involve no mediate knowledge; truths of this kind, *since they are evident, do not submit to questioning.*[90]

Since evidence excludes a *quaestio* or problem, and since in the latter there is a mixture of evidence and lack of evidence, the statement of every problem must begin with what is evident or known. There are two possible combinations of evidence and lack of evidence. In the first the *nature* of a being is known, but its actual *existence* is not, and, vice versa, the thing's existence is known, but its nature is not. In this first combination there are two possible questions. If the nature is known, the question asked is, *An est?* If the existence is known, the question becomes, *Quid est?* In the second combination the question does not simply concern nature and existence, but substance and its accidents. In this case, the subject being known, we can ask whether this or that accident inheres in it; this question is, *Quia?* Or, on the contrary, the accident being known to inhere in a given subject, we can ask why it inheres, and this question becomes, *Propter quid?* Thus, four questions are possible, but, actually, only two of them can exist; for if the existence is known, only the *quid est* remains, and once the fact of inherence is established, the only remaining problem concerns the reason for this inherence.

We have said that this art of questioning belongs properly to philosophy or science in the ancient sense of this word. Here is how St. Thomas explains the nature of this interrogation and its relations with knowledge in the strict sense:

Aristotle states that there is an equal number of questions and of things that can be known demonstratively. The reason for this is that science is knowledge acquired through demonstration. Now, the things which have to be known by means of demonstration are those which were previously unknown. These are the things we ask questions about, for we do not know them. Consequently, the things that are questioned are equal in number to the things that are known demonstratively. Now there are four kinds of questions: is it a fact, for what reason, does it exist, and what is it (*quia, propter quid, si est, et quid est*). Whatever is capable of being asked or known may be reduced to these four queries.[91]

To understand this point, we ought to consider the fact that, since there can only be scientific knowledge of the true, and since the true is expressed only in the enunciation, of necessity it is the enunciation alone that is knowable and consequently subject to questioning. Now, as is stated in the second book *On Interpretation*, the enunciation is formed in two ways. One way combines a noun and a verb, for instance in the statement, *man is;* the second way involves a third item which is attributed, as in the statement, *man is white.* Thus, a question may be formed so as to refer either to the first mode of enunciation, and in this case it will be a somewhat simple question—or, to refer to the second mode, and in this case it will be a rather complex question . . . for, it will be asked about the composition of two items.

Concerning this kind of complex enunciation, two questions can be asked. One is whether this statement is true . . . for example, we may ask whether the sun wanes as a result of an eclipse, or not, and whether man is an animal, or not. In such cases, we are said to ask: is it a fact? The question is not whether I express the question with a certain word (*quia*) or in a certain form of interrogation, but rather we ask the question in order to ascertain, *is it so.*[92]

After we know that it is so, we ask, *for what reason is it* so. For example, when we know that the sun disappears as a result of an eclipse, and that the earth is moved during an earthquake, we then ask for the reason why the sun wanes, or why the earth is so moved.[93]

Next Aristotle indicates two other questions which do not figure in the original enumeration, though they are simple. He says that we ask some questions in a different way from the previous questions, that is to say, apart from the original four questions. For example, we may ask whether a centaur exists or not. Here, we are simply asking about the centaur, does it exist—the question is not whether the centaur is this individual, say this white thing, or not. And in the case where we know that this thing is of a certain kind, we have asked the question, why is it?— so also, when we know about a thing that it is simply so, we then ask, what is this thing?—for example, what is God, or what is a man. And so, these are as many questions as we can ask; when we find their answers, we are said to know.[94]

Since the analysis of philosophical questioning interests us here only insofar as it will help us state the epistemological problem, we shall study its essential structure briefly, in order to observe the method that St. Thomas borrowed from Aristotle and used constantly in his works. The progressive steps of this philosophical methodolgy are as follows:

¶ *1. Formulation and Number of Questions.* First of all, we are dealing with scientific or philosophical knowledge, therefore, with knowledge by causes. Knowledge by causes can be of two types, because there are two modes of causality, intrinsic and extrinsic. The *intrinsic* mode is subdivided into matter and form in material things considered in the abstract, and into potency and act when these same things are considered as being.[95] The *extrinsic* mode is subdivided into efficiency and finality. Knowledge that grasps reality in its intrinsic causes is knowledge by apprehension; whereas the grasp of extrinsic causes depends upon reasoning, a complex act whose object includes the complexity of relations between cause and effect.

Second, every *quaestio* is conceived by an act of judgment and formulated in an enunciation:

(a) Simple or existential enunciation has only two terms: the subject and the verb, or predicate,[96] as when we say, "Socrates exists," "God exists."

(b) Complex enunciation has three terms: the subject, the predicate, and the sign of their composition, the verb,[97] as when we affirm, "God is eternal," "Socrates is white."

Third, since every enunciation is made up of several terms, the *quaestio* may deal with the subject, the predicate, or the bond uniting predicate to subject. Whence are derived four questions:

(a) Two are for simple or existential enunciation:
    One deals with the predicate of the act of existing: "Does God exist?" (*An sit?*)
    The other deals with the nature of the subject: "Who is God?" (*Quid sit?*)

(b) Two are for complex enunciation:
    One deals with the existence of an accident in a substance or subject: "Is God eternal?" (*Quia est?*)
    The other is concerned with the bond between accident and substance: "Why is God eternal?" (*Propter quid?*)[98]

¶ 2. *The Object of Each of These Four Questions.* The first of the four questions, *An sit?*, can only be asked when the existence of the thing escapes our immediate powers of perception, that is, either our external senses or our intellect. Thus, only the causes and effects of immediately sensible and immediately intelligible things are the object of the question, *An sit?* Consequently, everything studied by macroscopic and microscopic physics (which deals with sensibly perceived movements) can be the object of the question, *An sit?*, as well as God, spiritual realities other than the soul, and the causes of the immanent acts of the soul:

Likewise, our intellect knows *whether a thing is,* in three ways. We know in one way, because the answer falls within the range of sensation. In a second way, we know *from the cause-effect relationship* of things within the range of sensation, as in the case of knowing fire as result of the perception of smoke. Thirdly, we know that a thing is in itself, as a result of a tendency that it has toward certain acts, and we know this inclination from reflection on our own actions, being aware that they are going on.[99]

But for everything that is the immediate object of sensible or intellectual perception, the question of existence cannot be asked except dialectically, and that no longer falls within the properly philosophical questionnaire.[100] Furthermore, the question of existence presupposes an at least nominal knowledge of the thing about which the question is asked.[101]

The second question, *Quid sit?*, is the most important of all, since it corresponds to the natural object of the human intellect made to apprehend natures. But it is also the most difficult question to answer, because we grasp natures only by means of their accidents,[102] and accidents do not, strictly speaking, have a nature.[103] Thus, the proper objects of this second question are substances or natures, and every time its object is an accident, it is so by reference to the substance whose accident it is.[104] The reason substance has such exclusive rights over definition, in the proper sense, is that the definition, as its name indicates, implies strict unity (i.e., indivision in itself and division from everything else), and only substance has a sufficiently rich mode of being to possess the unity that makes it intelligible.[105] When the question *Quid?* is asked about nonsubstantial beings, it assumes a derivative and relative meaning,[106] which must be clearly recognized if we would avoid impasses or pseudoproblems. We shall see this when we take up the subject of human knowledge.[107] Here is a text summing up Thomistic doctrine on the knowledge of natures:

What a thing is, may be known when its quiddity is comprehended. Now sense does not grasp this quiddity, but only sensible accidents; nor does imagination, but only the images of bodies; instead, it is the *proper object of the intellect.* . . . Our intellect comprehends the essence of a thing, in three ways. First of all, it comprehends the essences of *things falling within the range of sensation,* by abstracting from all the individuating characteristics which accompany these essences in sensation and imagination, for the resultant will be the pure essence of the thing, for instance of man, which consists of those factors belonging to man as man. Secondly, we know the essences of *things which we do not see,* through their causes or proportionate effects which are sensible. Of course, if the effects are not in due proportion with their cause, they will not enable us to know *what* the cause is but only *that* it is, as is clear in the case of God. Thirdly, we know the essences of *artificial objects that have never been seen,* by investigating the requisites of such an artifact in terms of its proportioned relation to its end.[108]

Such is the object of the second question and the procedures used by the intellect to answer the question asked. It is important to note that everything relating to knowledge *as an immanent activity* enters into the third category of things, which can be defined only in the third way mentioned in the text above, since we are dealing here with realities essentially ordered to the grasping of exterior sensible things and spiritual realities within our range.

In the third question, *Quia ita est?*, we are again dealing with a problem of existence, but accidental existence or nonexistence of a form or accident in a substance or subsisting nature, as in the examples: Is Socrates white? Is Socrates an animal? But here we are no longer concerned with the substantial *actuality* of the subject of the enunciation, but with the actuality of the forms constituting the subject or added to its substantial actuality. The object of this question is therefore the properties of subsisting beings, and this object is as vast as the field of predication, both universal and analogical.[109] In this third question, as in the first, the knowledge of nonexistence is either attained by sensible or intellectual intuition (in which case this knowledge is immediate and poses no problem), or else the nonexistence eludes sensible and intellectual perception, whereupon the question *Quia ita est?* is asked. This question could be formulated as follows: Is this so?; or by concrete problems: Is the soul immortal, is being one or multiple, is knowledge true or false, is Descartes an idealist?

The fourth and last question in the philosophical questionnaire, *Propter quid ita sit?*, is the most important question in the order of demonstrative knowledge, because it is the very soul of demonstration.[110] Once accidents or multiple forms are known to inhere in a substance, we ask *what bond* exists between the subject and the accidents inhering in it: Is it a necessary bond? Is it contingent? To answer this question it is not enough to say that this bond is necessary (or contingent) because this accident of this form always accompanies this substance; we must also know the *cause* of this inherence, for it is only upon this condition that the necessity (or contingence) of the bond will truly be known, because we know the *propter quid*. The *propter quid* that is the object of this last question is nothing but the *quid* of the second question, not in that it constitutes the nature of the thing, but that it *causes* this nature's properties, as efficient cause, final cause, or, again, as material cause *in qua*.[111] A perfect example of this search for the *propter quid* is provided by the demonstration of the attributes of God.

St. Thomas constructs this demonstration by starting from the existence of these attributes as described in Scripture and links them all to the *quid* of God known negatively, i.e., to the pure act of existing, which constitutes the intimate nature of divinity, to the *Ego sum Qui sum*. Thus, starting with the *quid*, he eliminates from the Divine Nature all predicates implying the slightest imperfection, because they go against the nature of the *Ipsum esse subsistens*.[112]

The unity of the *propter quid* determines the unity of the properties or *propriae passiones*. This unity can be either absolute or relative,[113] and consequently so can the *propriae passiones*. Thus, when the *propter quid* of the unity, multiplicity, truth, and goodness of beings is discovered in the constitution of being as being, since this latter is only a unity of order, the transcendental properties flowing from it will also be one with a unity of order. This means that each being is one, true, and good in *its own way* because it is a *being in its own way*.

There is one last remark to be made; the question *Propter quid?*

is never asked about substances as such. The objects of this question are the accidents of substances or substantial realities *as effects* of higher causes.[114] We must never ask why man is man, why nature is nature, why a brute animal is a brute animal, but why man is quantified, qualified, living, intelligent, etc. We can therefore say that the first two questions account for the absolute unity of a being considered as an existing nature, whereas the last two questions explain the multiplicity existing either in a being (substance and accidents) or in the universe, the diversity of whose beings is explicable by the unity of a sole first cause's making intelligible this ensemble of beings and their activities.

¶ *3. The Order of These Four Questions.* We have seen the number of questions that man must ask the universe; taken together, the answers to these questions make up philosophical knowledge. But since the latter is knowledge of order, the philosophical questionnaire must proceed according to an *ordinata interrogatio*,[115] which is to say that it must conform to the needs of both being and the human intellect, and not to the caprices of the questioner. The following text explains the necessary order existing among these questions:

Sometimes (1) we know *that* a thing is so (*quia*), and we still may ask why it is (*propter quid*); at other times (2) the answers to both questions are at once apparent to us; but (3) the third variation is impossible, namely that one should know why a thing is before he knows that it is. The same is true of knowing the quiddity (*quod quid erat esse*): (1) for sometimes we know that a thing is but do not know perfectly what it is; (2) sometimes we know both; (3) but the third variation is impossible, that is, for us to know what it is, when we are ignorant as to whether it is.[116]

The first paragraph of this passage tells us three things about the third and fourth question: first, that there is no question if the existence of the effect and the nature of the cause are known; second, that there can be no question about the nature of the cause as long as the existence of the effect is unknown; and, finally, that when the existence of an effect is known, the only question that can be asked is *Propter quid?* The second paragraph follows the same order concerning the first two questions: As long as the existence of a being is not known (*An sit?*), the problem of its nature (*Quid sit?*) is unintelligible; when the existence and the nature of a being are known simultaneously, there is no question. Finally, the question *Quid est?* presupposes that the existence of this being is known.

Therefore, the normal and complete order of the four questions is as follows: The existence of a thing must be evident before we can ask questions about its nature; then, we must have evidence of the existence of accidents or effects in order to ask questions about the cause of these effects. The immediate conclusion to be drawn from these statements is that, chronologically speaking, the first object of the philosophical questionnaire is a being whose existence is immediately known by the human intellect, i.e., material things in their concrete and physical existence.[117] If this existential starting point is not accepted, there can be no philosophy, since the questions *Quid?* and *Propter quid?* can never be asked.

To conclude this overly brief study of the philosophical questionnaire, we must note St. Thomas' insistent warnings against identifying problems or questions with the reality that is their object. Thus, the *quid*, or definition, is not the thing's nature, but the intelligible and intellected sign expressing that nature.[118] Also, the *propter quid* or the *medium* of demonstration is not the cause of effects, but is the known sign, the intelligible expression of this cause whose existence and nature have been intellectually apprehended.[119] The same is true of the *an sit* and of the *quia ita est* designating the *esse* of the enunciation, which *signifies* the existence of things but is not that existence.[120] We must not ask knowledge to provide replicas or material images of the things we know. It is enough for our knowledge to signify these realities adequately, for it to make these realities present to our soul, in order that questions and answers about them become legitimate. It is because we know the existence and natures of things that we ask these questions and arrive at these answers. The philosophical questionnaire is not merely a grammar of discourse, as Léon Brunschvicg would have it,[121] but is the grammer of cognitive being itself, since it is a book whose printer, reality, makes a microcosm of our soul.[122]

Such is the philosophical questionnaire that Aristotle invented and

St. Thomas adopted, not because of its Aristotelian origin, but because it expresses the twofold law of being and knowledge of which being is the measure. We must now consider the dialogue between the intellect and things as it applies to the problem of knowledge, so as to bring into this problem the order without which knowledge remains an insoluble puzzle for philosophical reflection.

D. APPLICATION OF THE QUESTIONNAIRE TO THE EPISTEMOLOGICAL PROBLEM

Now that we know the philosophical method which St. Thomas borrowed from Aristotle and used constantly in his works,[123] let us see how it applies to the epistemological problem. Can we and should we ask, about knowledge, the four questions circumscribing and explaining a reality under all the aspects from which it can be grasped by our mind? If so, our questionnaire will be as follows:

(1) Does knowledge exist (*An sit*)?
(2) What is knowledge (*Quid sit*)?
(3) What are its properties (*Quia ita est*)?
(4) Why does it have these properties or characteristics (*Proper quid*)?

Of these four questions, the first is impossible, for the existence of knowledge is immediate evidence which serves as starting point for all the problems arising about knowledge but which cannot itself be questioned. Thus, three problems remain. The first concerns the nature of knowledge, the second, its accidents or properties, and the third, the reason why these properties seem to characterize the existence of knowledge. Let us briefly examine the meaning of these three questions and the order existing among them.

Starting from common experience, which is nothing but interior evidence of the existence of knowledge, we must first ask what the nature of this mysterious phenomenon is. This is the problem of its definition, i.e., its intelligible unification. But to define knowledge, we must know whether it is a substance or an accident, for the processes of unifying or defining differ greatly according to whether the thing to be defined is substantial or accidental. If the thing is a substance, it must be conceived as an absolute, a thing-in-itself, an *indivisum in se et divisum ab aliis*; if it is an accident, it must be defined in relation to the subject in which it inheres. Experience shows us knowledge as an indefinite variety of human activities that have no existence other than that given them by man. Consequently, man is included in the definition of knowledge as the subject of this accident, as its efficient principle, and, in a certain respect, as its end.[124] It is therefore impossible to conceive the nature of knowledge without an immediate reference to man, its source. But, what characterizes the particular accident that is knowledge and makes it heterogeneous to all other accidents of man is that we are aware of it as being the presence of another; we are aware that we are ourselves *plus* something other than ourselves. Thus, it is impossible to define knowledge without constant reference, first, to man, its cause, and then to the object characterizing it.

Once knowledge has been defined by its twofold reference to the knower and the reality, we must ask what its characteristics are; and then we shall discover that it is necessarily either true or false. Therefore, we must study truth and falsity as a double *existential* property of human knowledge, a sort of Dr. Jekyll and Mr. Hyde who never meet but are nevertheless the two faces with which one and the same human knowledge exists and presents itself to reflection.

Finally, these characteristics of truth or falsity necessarily accompanying human knowledge also have properties or characteristics, for the truth and falsity of our knowledge are marked by either necessity or contingence, characteristics usually translated by the words *certitudo* and *probabilitas*.[125] We must ask *why* truths have this certitude and probability, and with this last question, the cycle of the epistemological problem is complete.

Let us look at these three epistemological questions and try to see how they give birth to one another, the first conditioning the existence of the second, the second conditioning the third. This order and conditioning will be more evident if we reverse our questionnaire and start with the third question: *Why is truth necessarily cer-*

tain or probable? To account for the certitude or probability of truth we must know *what truth is,* for the properties of truth are explained by the nature of truth (the nature of truth explains the properties flowing from it). The second question therefore has priority over the third, which is unintelligible without it. But this second question itself, *What is truth?,* remains impossible to answer as long as we do not know *what knowledge is,* since truth is an accident of human knowledge and flows from its nature. Thus, the first question conditions the second, as the second does the third; and this conditioning is such that the intelligibility of these questions depends upon it.

Now it is easy to understand the defects in the modern way of stating the epistemological problem. Descartes and Kant asked the *third question* without having previously asked the second and first. They asked: "Why is our reason the source of infallible truth and error?"[126] To state the problem in this way is to identify the nature of knowledge with the nature of truth, and the nature of truth with that of certitude or infallibility. But this identification is impossible, for knowledge is to truth as cause is to effect, truth is to certitude as cause is to effect, and a cause cannot be identified with its effect since, by definition, they are opposites.[127] It is therefore not surprising that, starting from such an identification, neither the *Discourse on Method* nor the *Critique of Pure Reason* could truly state and solve the problem of knowledge. Descartes and Kant made the same mistake in epistemology as was made in metaphysics by Parmenides, who, having indentified being with one of its properties, *immutability,*[128] was constrained to refuse the name of being to everything that was not genuinely immutable. Similarly, the inventors of the critique identified knowledge with one of its properties, *infallibility,* and were thus obliged to refuse the name of knowledge to everything that did not present this identification card to the intellect. Not knowing how to ask questions, they could not answer them, and for three hundred years we have been suffering from the disorder they introduced into this philosophical problem, which epistemology must solve.

In order to impress our minds deeply with the different aspects of the epistemological problem, let us repeat again that, to solve this problem, we must ask three questions, which must follow a rigid order for the following reasons: In order to answer the question, *What is knowledge?*, we must know that knowledge is an accident of man which begets a duality in him, and that consequently it must be defined in relation to both man and the duality it introduces, i.e., the object. To answer the question, *What is truth?*, we must know that truth is an accident of knowledge, that it must be defined in terms of the constituents of knowledge, the subject and the object. Finally, to answer the question, *What is infallible or certain truth?* (or its contrary, probable or fallible truth), we must know that infallibility is an accident of truth, and that truth must be included in its definition, as it must be in the definition of its contrary, probability. It is impossible to define infallibility without having previously defined truth, since the latter is the former's *propter quid*. It is impossible to grasp the nature of truth without first having defined knowledge, since knowledge is the *propter quid* of truth. Finally, it is impossible to define knowledge without referring to the nature of man and the object, since these are the *propter quid* of knowledge.

With these three questions and the order obtaining among them, we are far removed from the epistemological exegesis that characterized medieval thought before St. Thomas.[129] The exegete has ceded to the philosopher, the symbol has been replaced by things having ontological value. Secondary causality takes its true place within the universe and, under the constant efficacy of primary causality, fulfills its vocation as creature and part of a perfectly harmonized whole.[130]

E. THOMISTIC CONTEXT OF THE EPISTEMOLOGICAL PROBLEM

What we have just seen about the number and order of the questions that must be asked if we would find an adequate answer to the epistemological problem enables us to determine the philosophical context in which St. Thomas situated this problem and organized its solution. Since knowledge is an accident and must be defined in relation to that whose accident it is, the being of man is necessarily the center from which must start and toward which must converge all the different aspects of the problem under study. Sören Kierkegaard forcefully expressed the necessity of this human context when he said: "Supposing that we knew *what a man is*. Then we would have the criterion of truth which was sought, doubted, postulated or fruitfully exploited by all Greek philosophy."[131] But the Angelic Doctor did not have *to suppose that he knew what a man is;* his faith and his metaphysical inquiries had given him the answer for all time. To be a man is primarily to be a creature, therefore a beggar for existence. Because he is but *one* being, man is perfectly imperfect, since the very fact of his oneness excludes all other beings outside him and therefore the perfection that these beings represent. But a creature, despite its radical imperfection, tends toward the perfection of the principle whose image it is, which obliges the creature constantly to imitate divinity.[132] To be correctly understood, the problem of knowledge in Thomism must be situated in this context of imitation on the side of the creature and exemplarity on the side of God.[133] Exactly what does this imitation consist in, when we use our cognitive powers? St. Thomas has told us in an admirable text that can serve as prologue to the whole of his epistemology:

A thing is found perfect in two ways: the first is in terms of the perfection of its act of being (*esse*) which belongs to it in virtue of its proper species. But since the specific *esse* of one thing is distinct from the specific *esse* of another, therefore every created thing, in terms of the perfection possessed by any type of thing, lacks precisely that amount of perfection which is more perfectly present in other species. Thus the perfection of any given thing, considered in itself, is imperfect—for it is but a part of the perfection of the whole universe which results from the combination of the perfections of singular things. Hence, in order that there might be a remedy for this imperfection, we find a second type of perfection among created things, inasmuch as the perfection appropriate to one thing may be found in another. Now, this is the *perfection characteristic of the knower as knower*. . . . And thus it is said that the human soul is, in a way, all things, for it is naturally able to know all things. So, this is the ultimate perfection achievable by the soul, according to the philosophers—the order of the entire universe and of its causes may be inscribed within it.[134]

This passage expresses the true nature of created being, which is to be perfect inasmuch as it is, but radically imperfect too, since it is only itself. At the same time, it expresses the true nature of created knowledge. It is a *remedy* for the radical imperfection flowing from the limitation of *esse* by a particular nature and from the exclusion of every other *esse* but its own, since every nature is closed in upon itself; it is an *aliquid*. There is but one possible way to overcome these ontological limitations without violating the creature's structure, and that is to be able to be *everything* in a way different from that in which one is one's self. The philosopher's stone that changes a limited creature, locked within his own being, into a library of the universe, that turns a creature, unable ever to be more than a pale reflection of divinity, into all creation, since in him the whole of God's work may be reconstructed "so that in him may be found the order of the whole universe and its causes," that which makes possible this miracle is—knowledge.

This passage makes the doctrinal situation of Thomist epistemology perfectly clear. It is an epistemology of creatures; it rests upon the very nature of created being as such; but, at the same time, what a horizon it opens to man! He is no longer the prisoner of his own nature, or, rather, this nature holds within its limitations the key to his prison. This nature can come out at any time, or, more precisely, it can open the door to its prison and invite in the totality of creatures and God, their cause. Every creature can come and write the secret of its being upon the soul, and not only its own secret, but those of all other creatures to which it is related. When each and every being has thus revealed its mystery, the human soul will be like to God, to His infinity, because that which His creative power has produced, our receptive power will have assimilated.

This first kind of imitation, characterizing the doctrinal context in which Thomistic epistemology is situated, springs from a metaphysical axiom underlying the whole doctrine of created activity: *operatio sequitur esse*.[135] For just as "everything is by virtue of its act of existing,"[136] and as the *esse* of a creature likens it to God,[137] so also are the activities following upon this *esse*[138] all assimilations of creative causality.[139] But the activity of knowing is the most perfect of assimilative activities,[140] and by it, especially, are all creatures arranged in relation to God. To be a creature is to possess a certain perfection, but this perfection falls short of each and every perfection existing outside it; thus, every creature is perfectly imperfect. There is but one remedy for *having* being and not *being* being, and that is to become what we are not. Knowledge is the art by which our soul can capitalize upon all the reflections of the infinite perfection of God.

To know what man is as a creature gives Thomistic epistemology its metaphysical context; but this context is not sufficient, for man is a particular creature and his imitation of God depends upon his own nature, since nature determines *esse*.[141] But our nature is hyle-morphic. Therefore, when we say *operatio sequitur esse,* the *esse* we are talking about belongs to a creature that is *nature* in the Aristo-telian sense of the word. The immediate context of Thomist epis-temology is thus a *philosophy of nature*.[142] Every nature is a complex but unified reality, at the same time that it is predestined or predeter-mined to an end.[143] Man answers to this definition, since he is es-sentially complex and his imitation as a creature orients him toward God. To actualize his predestination to his end, man, like every nature, needs a natural motion, an activity that is simultaneously a march toward and a taking possession of the end that is his. This natural movement will have the same complexity and enjoy the same unity as the being to which it belongs: *operatio sequitur esse.* Since our nature is not composed of *two* natures, one of which would be body and the other soul, but of a hierarchy of two principles, one of which is matter and the other form,[144] so also will our natural motion, i.e., human knowledge, not consist of two processes, one of which would be sensation and the other intellection, but of a sort of epistemological hylemorphism wherein sensation plays the role of matter and intellection that of form.[145]

In such a context, the Cartesian hypothesis of sensibility antag-onistic to intellect is absurd,[146] and a cathartic ascesis purporting to purify knowledge of the deceptive elements surreptitiously in-troduced into it by sensibility is an impossibility that contradicts Divine Wisdom itself, for *proprie loquendo, actiones naturales sunt*

Dei instituentis naturam.[147] Sensation and intellection are two *principles* of knowledge conditioning each other, just as body and soul are two principles of being that condition each other, and cannot exist without one another. As soon as man knows as man, as soon as he is in possession of all his natural means for attaining the divine imitation that is the very end of his knowledge, neither *pure* sensation nor *pure* intellection exists within him. The body is not human except in union with the soul, and the soul is human only in its relation to the body. Also, sensation cannot be the human principle of knowledge except in union with intellection, and intellection is human only in and by its necessary union with sensation.[148]

A knower who is not God but creature receives both his being and his knowledge; a creature that is neither Demiurgos nor pure spirit, but the spiritual form of corporeal matter, receives its knowledge and being according to the twofold spiritual and material law of its being. Superior in nature to all other beings in the physical universe, man seeks God in a way superior to all other physical beings, but this way *imitates* the physical nature of which it is a part. The physical universe is characterized by *motion*,[149] through a continual reciprocation between diverse realities by means of mutual exchanges and aids. The same is true of human knowledge, which is enriched by a certain metaphysical motion leading it to the very threshold of immobile Divine Perfection by means of the wisdom that is its crown. To forget this context of the philosophy of nature in stating the problem of human knowledge is to make it impossible even to state this problem; it also renders unintelligible numerous passages in St. Thomas' works, because it cuts them off from the only doctrinal context that saw them take life and gives them their full significance.

CONCLUSION OF PART ONE

This first part of our study has had but one purpose: to prepare us to grasp the Thomistic statement of the epistemological problem so that, in the three parts to follow, we may freely devote our minds to understanding the solution to this problem without continual interference from the critical positions and solutions of the moderns. We undertook this thankless task, not for the pleasure of criticizing thinkers whom we respect, whose works we admire, and to whom we are obliged for a keener awareness of the difficulties involved in the problem of knowledge, but because we think that their positions are, in themselves, erroneous and likely to beget endless confusion in the formulation of a truly philosophical epistemology. We have tried, in all sincerity, to bring out the source of their errors, which a concatenation of historical circumstances seems to have made inevitable.

In order to achieve this end, we have adopted a method that seems to us to be the simplest and least likely to create constant misunderstandings. Our first chapter analyzed the nature of a problem as such, the laws governing its birth, progress, and solution, the objective and psychological factors it necessarily involves, independently of the epochs in which it appeared and the matter of which it treats. More than any other, this starting point seemed to us sufficiently universal and impersonal to guarantee impartiality and realism. With the help of this impersonal criterion, we studied the epistemological problem as stated by Descartes, Kant, contemporary scientists, and the Neo-Scholastics,[1] in order to determine to what degree they fulfill the conditions characteristic of every problem that is not a pseudoproblem, or badly stated and therefore insoluble. In our imperfect but objective sketch we presented the epistemological problems of the last three centuries and their fundamental and characteristic defects.

We then tried to locate the epistemological problem exactly as St. Thomas saw it, seeking to learn from him the secret of his philosophical method, which we applied to the epistemological problem in the Thomistic framework and according to the spirit of the Thomistic questionnaire and the Thomistic synthesis. A survey of the philosophical questionnaire, although too brief, gave us a glance at the diverse aspects presented by the problem of human knowledge, its doctrinal context, and the hierarchical order of its different parts. From man to knowledge, from knowledge to its property, truth, from truth to its characteristics of certitude and probability—this is the inevitable procedure in a Thomistic epistemology.

Now we shall see this method of the dialogue between man and his knowledge in action; we shall watch St. Thomas build the noetic synthesis that his genius constructed and that our neglect has left dormant in his writings. The Angelic Doctor himself will show us the nature of human knowledge, its accompanying truth, and the conditions necessary for the infallibility or probability of this truth. My role here is perfectly described in a sentence from a modern poet: "If this indeed be the Hour in which I lift up my lantern, *it is not my flame that shall burn therein.*"[2] The light and flame of Thomistic doctrine will lead us to the heart of the mystery of knowledge, without reducing it to those impoverishing outlines in which our reason tends to substitute its own light and arrogant power for the omnipotence of Him who simultaneously created both being and knowledge. With St. Thomas as our guide, we shall penetrate deep into the realm of epistemology, in order to examine its wealth and its poverty. We shall enter by stages, as befits the poor travelers we are. There will, in fact, be three stages. The first will lead us into the holy of holies of human knowledge, where the latter appears as an accident of man and things. The second will answer the question: What is knowledge? In this second stage we shall see an immanent universe live with the intellect's own life, through the intellect's dynamic spontaneities that bring a beginning of unity and beauty into a discontinuous and bondless immanent world. Our third part will answer the question: What does it mean to know truth? This third and final stage will present us with a completely unified universe, whose order and harmony reflect the art of its Creator and Exemplary Cause. Then shall we come to the very throne of God by means of philosophical wisdom,[3] the last and most perfect of citizens in the kingdom of knowledge. The fourth part will answer the question: What does it mean to know infallible truth? Such will be our plan in the pages to follow.

Part Two

WHAT DOES IT MEAN TO KNOW?

PROLOGUE

A listener's understanding becomes confused, if a person uses a word with many possible meanings and fails to make these meanings distinct. For, when a person uses an ambiguous term without distinguishing the meanings, it is not clear as to what meaning gives rise to his conclusion.[1]

During the last three centuries Western thought has tended constantly toward unifying the meaning of the word *knowledge*. According to this trend, the word should not have several meanings, and the methods used to achieve this unity have become more and more radical. In philosophy the mutilation of the different meanings of the word *knowledge* started with Descartes, was continued by Kant, and completed by the theorist Leon Brunschvicg, who denies the word every meaning except that of judicative activity, the prototype of which is mathematical judgment.[2] Contemporary science is no less demanding in its requirements for unity; its process of progressive elimination resembles surgical intervention designed to mutilate human nature more than it does methods of thought oriented toward the unification of human knowledge. Here is a significant text:

When we have eliminated all superfluous senses, what have we left? We can do without taste, smell, hearing, and even touch. We must keep our eyes or rather one eye, for there is no need to use our faculty of stereoscopic vision. The eye need not have the power of measuring or graduating light and shade; I think it is sufficient if it can just discriminate two shades so as to detect whether an opaque object is in a certain position or not.

With this reduced equipment we can still recognize geometrical form and size. We can recognize that one object appears round and another square, or that one is apparently larger than the other. . . . By limiting the sensory equipment of our observers we do a great deal to stop their quarreling. . . . But it was found that the observers were still quarreling even when they had only form and size to quarrel over. So, in 1915 Einstein made another raid on their sensory equipment. He removed all the retina of the eye except one small patch. The observer could no longer recognize form or extension in the external world, but he could tell whether two things were in apparent coincidence or not. . . . Since we have so mutilated him, he cannot make the experiment himself. We perform the experiments, and let him keep watch. . . . *The point is that all our knowledge of the external world as it is conceived today in physics can be demonstrated to him. If we cannot convince him we have no right to assert it.*[3]

It would be difficult to discover a more Draconian method of reducing the meanings of the word knowledge than this elimination of the very sources of our knowledge; for if man thus obtains knowledge that has but *one meaning*, he pays for this unity with his whole natural endowment of sensorial equipment. The ancient philosophers had a much more flexible and human method; instead of surgically mutilating man's cognitive powers, *they distinguished in order to unite.* They invented theories of *formal objects* and of *analogy*, which safeguarded both the diversity of the types of knowledge and the unity of meaning of the word knowledge, a unity without which the word becomes unintelligible.[4]

The interesting thing about this absolute univocity of the word knowledge and the brutality of the methods leading to it is that both are symptoms of an antinatural and antiphilosophical mentality. Nature itself does not actually tend toward homogeneous unification of reality by suppression of diversity. It is, on the contrary, an unfailing source of differentiation; it has created and continues to produce the most varied types of things in every domain. In nature nothing goes to waste, nothing is self-creating, everything is put to use. Nature has no junk heaps, it casts nothing into the sewer; in it there is no rubbish, no refuse, no left-overs, no filth. Whatever remains from one being becomes a principle of fecundity for another. If we compare the incredible pragmatism of the universe of nature with the pragmatism of our industrial universe, we discover that the latter does not know what pragmatism is; for the immense cemeteries of scrap iron, of junk, of all kinds of refuse surrounding our cities indicate that, compared with nature, we are extremely limited in our sense of the useful and the serviceable. Scientific method follows the laws of the technology whose child it is; it throws almost all our senses on the junk heap, because they are the source of countless obstacles in our comprehension of the physical universe. The insights into reality that the senses give us are too rich, too qualitative, and, since instruments do not record qualities, science has no *objective norm* for bringing harmony among them. Therefore, the simplest way out is to get rid of them.

In view of its extremely precise and impoverished goal, science is probably right in proceeding in this way; for what modern science seeks is to comprehend the universe as it was on the first day of creation, when everything was "formless and bare," before Divine Wisdom *educated* and matured the physical universe, i.e., filled it with extremely diversified natures linked to each other by bonds of harmony, cooperation, and love. To reconstruct this primitive state and to rediscover the physical universe's most imperfect state, modern science is obliged to *diseducate* creation, to bring it back to its childhood,[5] in order to do a sort of psychoanalysis of the basic laws obeyed by all purely physical phenomena.[6] And since man is the product of the sixth day of creation and came into being when the physical universe was already educated and mature, his sensorial equipment is made to know the universe in its perfect state and not to grasp it in its primitive imperfection. Whence the modern scientist's driving need to replace the senses by an instrument and to throw the senses onto the junk heap of popular knowledge and ancient philosophy.

However, philosophy does not aim to deconstruct the physical universe *in order to measure and use it,* to diseducate it in order better to dominate it,[7] but aims rather to be measured by it.[8] It takes the universe as it is. Philosophical epistemology takes the universe of knowledge *as it is* and is measured by it. Like nature, epistemology does not discard any of the various instruments with which man is armed[9] to undertake the arduous task of imitating divinity, the ultimate goal and only truly explanatory cause of all the aspects of human knowledge. Unlike science, it does not consider the world of sensation as useless and harmful; it does not turn this world into a cemetery of illusions, but, like the poor man in the Gospel, it accepts with humility and gratitude the smallest crumbs of reality granted it through sensory channels, because they are a fragmentary but true reflection of the infinite perfection of God. In the universe of knowledge, every time we meet a process that seems to destroy or discard some component element of being and knowledge (such as abstraction, the *via negationis, resolutio*), we must interpret it in a positive context of harmonization and unification by distinction, never in the sense of mutilation as practiced by science. Epistemology imitates God whose wisdom destroys nothing but disposes all "according to number, weight, and measure."[10]

In the prologue to his treatise on human knowledge, St. Thomas approaches this problem in a very characteristic way, which is, furthermore, the only way: "How the soul united to a body understands?"[11] This is the only way really to begin an epistemology seeking a definition of knowledge, for to answer this question is to define knowledge and therefore to unify it, since every definition is a vision of unity. We have just seen that while the need for unification is as essential to philosophic knowledge as it is to scientific knowledge, the former's methods are more natural and respect the whole ensemble of data more than do those of the latter. What do we want to define? Human knowledge in its totality. Now, we experience knowledge as an extraordinary multiplicity of immanent activities, therefore of *accidents*, added to human nature already constituted. At the same time that we experience it as an overflowing interior activity, knowledge appears to us as an invasion and occupation of our soul by an incredibly large army of realities other than ourselves. This awareness of *the other* enters into noetic experience to such a degree that the first philosophers concluded that the soul must be intrinsically constituted by the principles of all beings, since it discovers them all within itself.[12]

If our first contact with noetic experience impresses us with the incredible multiplicity of activities by which other things penetrate within us, a less superficial reflection shows us that this diversity tends entirely toward the unity of an operation and an object: the intellectual operation and its object, intelligible being.[13] Therefore, we shall try to account for all the data given us by the experience of knowing, without neglecting any. Since these data are complex, we shall study them in their complexity, beginning with what is most characteristic in the activity of knowledge, its immanence (Chapter V). Then we shall proceed to a study of the object as *principle* of intellection and sensation (Chapter VI), continue with the study of the object as *term* or end of these two operations, and conclude with the unification of all these objects of knowledge in the comprehension of being as being (Chapter VII).

V · KNOWING AS A MULTITUDE OF IMMANENT ACTIVITIES

[handwritten marginal notes: 1. Life + movement / physical / immanent 3; 2. Soul + powers; 3. multiplicity of phenomena]

The experience of knowing confronts us with a multitude of interior activities that are additions to the human being and consequently are accidents of his substance.[1] As accidents, these activities of knowledge can be defined only with constant reference to the human being who is their source and end.[2] Let us try to determine, from without, a first general context in which the reality we want to define is found.

In Thomism the activities of knowledge are designated by the words *actio, operatio.* The origin of these two words belongs to the material and temporal realm:

This word, act, which is used to signify entelechy and perfection, that is to say, the form and other items of this sort such as any kind of operations, gets its meaning chiefly from physical motions, as far as the origin of the term is concerned. Since words are the signs of intellectual conceptions, we first assign names to the things which we first understand, even though these things are posterior in the order of nature. Now among various other acts, motion is best known and most apparent to us, for it is observed through sensation. So, the name, act, was first assigned to it and then it was transferred from motion to other things.[3]

How the notion of act and operation, which are synonymous with perfection, was drawn from physical movement, the most imperfect of realities, is explained in the following text:

Therefore action, in the primary meaning of the term, denotes the origin of motion. Just as motion, in the sense that it is present in a thing moved by another, is called passion—so also the same motion, in the sense of originating from another thing and ending in the thing moved, is called action. So, without motion, action has no other meaning than that of a relation to an origin.[4]

This passage shows us the sensible origin of the notion *actio*, and at the same time, by defining it in terms of the idea of *origin* actively considered, it indicates how we should distinguish this notion from its material origins. Considered in this way, *actio* simply means the perfection of a cause or principle as such, and this is the meaning of the act of knowing, "as proceeding from a subsistent person."[5] The following extract explains this:

No action of a cognitive faculty can be described as flowing or passing over, as are the acts of physical powers which proceed from agent to patient; cognition is not called a flowing out from the knower to the thing known, as happens in the actions of physical things; rather, it is called the existence of the known thing in the knower.[6]

Cognitive activity, then, is contrasted with *physical* or *natural* activities that occur in time and place and imply movement in the strict sense. This does not mean that knowledge is unnatural to man, for it is part of his nature. Instead, this opposition simply marks the difference that obtains between the workings of inanimate beings and those of living beings.

The action of the soul transcends the action of nature in the workings of inanimate things; but this occurs in two ways, namely, in regard to the manner of acting, and in regard to what is done. As for the manner of acting, every action of the soul must transcend the operation or action of inanimate nature, and since the action of the soul is a vital action, and a vital being is one which moves itself in its operating, it must be that every operation of the soul goes on by virtue of an intrinsic agency.[7]

The whole field of knowledge escapes the laws of nature in that the latter is physical, in the modern sense of the word, because knowledge depends upon the laws of life and possesses properties of immanence and interiority of which physical movement cannot give us the slightest inkling. Therefore, it is impossible to define or precisely to describe all these phenomena of knowledge, whose existence we perceive within us, without constantly referring to the nature of life itself and to our own life. Furthermore, since the first objects of human knowledge belong to the category of material and physical beings, as experience shows, and since it is with these first objects that we begin to grasp spiritual objects progressively, our comprehension of what life is will obey the laws governing the evolution of human knowledge and will start with a comparison of the similarities and differences between the characteristics of living and non-living beings in their respective activities. That is the argumentation of the three texts just quoted. In the first, St. Thomas stresses the sensible origin of our notion of action and the derivative character of this notion when it designates some reality other than motion. The second explains how this derivation is made: by leaving aside the successive or temporal character of *actio* and keeping only the original idea of source or cause. In the third text the nature of this origin or cause is described by comparing it with nature or with the inanimate, as an *intrinsic agent* is compared with a cause that affects things extrinsically. We shall deepen the notion of life by a brief study of its relation to physical movement.

A. LIFE AND MOVEMENT

For the human intellect, the distinction between the living and the physical is by no means a primary notion. On the contrary, the primitive mentality tends to identify them by attributing to the material universe the same interior dynamism it perceives in man. This explains the "cosmogonic romances" of Hesiod, Pindar, Anaximander, and Pherycides, who sang of the successive transformations of the physical universe as the troubadours of the Middle Ages sang of the different phases in the love of their lady.[8] Eighteenth- and nineteenth-century science conceived life after the model of physical movement, whereas contemporary scientists find matter and motion so fluid that they tend to identify them with the mind and its laws[9] and to destroy the secular dualism of matter and spirit. The distinction between the living and the physical depends, therefore, upon a philosophical explanation from experience, and this experience has a common starting point, the existence of movement.

Since Aristotle, philosophers have commonly defined life as a sort of movement, a motion with an interior principle, as contrasted to physical motion whose cause is extrinsic. Here is what St. Thomas thinks about the origin of the definition of life:

That thing is said to have life which *through itself* possesses the power of nourishment, increase and decrease. It should be understood, however, that this explanation is more on the level of exemplification than of definition.[10]

Now, every explanation by means of examples is dialectical and not scientific. It does not give the *quod quid est* of the things known,[11] and that is why everything whose motive principle is hidden can be called living: "By analogy, we say that those things are living whose motive principle is not perceived by the ordinary person."[12] What is the similarity between vital activity and physical motion that makes possible their comparison? Here is a preliminary explanation:

As is stated in Metaphysics, action is twofold. Actions of one kind pass out to external matter, as to eat or to cut, while actions of the other kind remain in the agent, as to understand, to sense and to will. The difference between them is this, that the former action is the perfection not of the agent that moves, but of the thing moved; whereas the latter action is the perfection of the agent. Hence, because movement is an act of the thing in movement, the latter action insofar as it is the act of the operator, is called its movement, *on the basis of similitude* that as movement is an act of the thing moved so an action of this kind is an act of the agent.[13]

That life is termed movement springs, therefore, from the following proportionality—*vivere* : *agens* : : *motus* : *patiens*. Both of them are act or perfection. We shall have to see, now, whether this proportionality is analogical or metaphorical; for if it is analogical, movement will really enter into the notion of life, but if it is metaphorical, we shall have to purify this similarity between motion and life in order to perceive their difference. As a matter of fact, this similarity is only metaphorical[14]; therefore, we shall have to analyze physical and vital motion more closely in order to understand their nature. For by grasping the differences between things, we deepen our understanding of their real nature:

Indeed we know each thing more perfectly to the extent that we more fully contemplate its differences from other things, for each thing has within itself its own act of being (*esse*) which is distinct from all others. So, in the case of things whose definitions we know, we first place them in a genus through which we know in a general way what it is, then we add the differences by which it is distinguished from other things—and in this way the knowledge of the complete substance of a thing is perfected.[15]

But neither physical movement nor vital activity is a substance; therefore, neither is definable in the strict sense of the word definition. They are known in and by reference to their subject and term. Since physical motion is better known than vital activity, it serves as a starting point[16] for understanding vital operation, not in itself, but in its function of perfecting the thing moved. Thus, we shall compare the perfection that is movement with this other perfection that is life and knowledge, in order to discover their differences and, consequently, their analogical nature.

¶ *1. Physical Movement.* In every physical movement three factors must be distinguished:

(1) The *movens*, or agent, which is always extrinsic to, or other than, the *motum* or thing moved.
(2) The *motus*, or motion, which is always exterior to the agent, since it springs from and is always intrinsic to the thing moved, since it is its perfecton.
(3) The *motum*, that which is moved, is by definition the subject, therefore potency in relation to movement.

Therefore, to define movement as *actus imperfecti* (the act of the imperfect) or the "act of being in potency inasmuch as it is in potency,"[17] is to define it formally; that is, it is to define it with reference to that which is moved or to the imperfect whose perfection it is, and by contrast with the act of the *movens*, which gives it existence and whose effect it is. Considered in this way, motion is seen to have three characteristics that always and everywhere accompany it, whether it be local motion, alteration, or increase. These three characteristics are:

(1) *Exteriority* of agent and recipient; for it is impossible to move and be moved at the same time and in the same respect.[18]

(2) *Imperfection*, or the essentially potential character of the recipient or the moved; for we can only receive or become what we are not, and we cannot give ourselves that which we do not have.[19]

(3) *Destruction or transformation* necessarily accompanying every movement; for a thing cannot be moved in place without changing place; it cannot increase or decrease without losing the quantity it had; and the same is true for motions resulting in alteration.

These are the essential components of physical motion as such. If we go back to the source of these characteristics, we always find matter.[20] In fact, matter is the principle of *exteriority*, since it is the foundation of quantity, the principle of *extension*, which is defined as the *exteriority* of the physical parts of the continuum, and the principle of number, which is defined as discontinuous quantity and is therefore exterior to another quantity.[21] Quantity is also the immediate subject of motion; it makes possible time and place, two extrinsic measures of physical reality.[22] Matter is also the principle of *imperfection* since it is by nature an appetite for all forms and is determined by none in particular. Finally, since it cannot exist simultaneously under two forms, it is also the principle of *destruction* or transformation, because it cannot become the subject of a form without losing the one it had before.[23] Inasmuch as there can be no motion without quantity and the latter is rooted in matter, it is basically matter that makes physical motion possible and explains its distinctive characteristics.

¶ *2. Vital or Immanent Movement.* To characterize vital activity by immanence is immediately to oppose it to physical movement, which is essentially exterior or extrinsic. Deeper study of immanence will therefore be necessary for us to have a more distinct perception of the fundamental opposition between life and motion and a better understanding of the superior vital activity that we call knowledge. Exactly what does *sese movere*, "self-move-ment," mean?

It must be considered that since a thing is said to live insofar as it operates of itself and not as moved by another, the more perfectly this power is found in anything, the more perfect is the life of that thing.

In things that move and are moved three things are distinguished in order. In the first place, *the end moves the agent;* and the principal agent is that which acts through its own form; sometimes it does so through some *instrument* that acts by virtue, not of its own form, but of the principal agent, and does no more than execute the action.

Accordingly, there are things that *move themselves,* not in relation to any form or end *naturally inherent* in them, but only with relation to the *execution* of the movement. The form by which they act and the *end* of the action are determined by their nature. Of this kind are plants, which *move themselves* according to their inherent nature, with regard only to executing the movements of growth and decay.

Other things have self-movement in a higher degree, that is, not only with relation to the execution of the movement, but even with relation to the *form which* is the principle of the movement, which they acquire by themselves. Of this kind are animals, in which the principle of move-ment is not a *naturally implanted form,* but one received through sense. Hence the more perfect their sense the more perfect is their power of self-movement. Such as have only the sense of touch, as shell-fish, move only with the motion of expansion and contraction; and thus their movements hardly exceed that of plants. Whereas such as have the power of sense in perfection, so as to recognize not only what is joined to them or touches them, but also objects apart from themselves, can move them-selves to a distance by progressive movement.

Yet although animals of the latter kind receive through sense the form that is the principle of their movement, nevertheless they cannot of themselves propose to themselves the *end of their operation* or their movement, for this has been implanted in them by nature; and by natural instinct they are moved to any action through the form apprehended by sense. Hence such animals as *move themselves in relation to an end that they themselves propose* are superior to these. This can be done only by intellect and reason, whose province it is to know the proportion between the end and the means to that end, and duly co-ordinate them. Hence a more perfect degree of life is that of intelligent beings, for their power of self-movement is more perfect. This is shown by the fact that in one and the same man the intellectual power moves the sensitive powers; and these, by their command, move the organs of movement.[24]

The immanence discussed in this passage is the immanence of the *principles* of real *physical* movement. This discussion explains what *sese movere* means: *sese* refers to the interiority of the instrumental, principal, and even final agent, and *movere* refers to local motion whose immanent principle is the soul. However, the passage does not explain the *nature* of the singular movement it calls vital or immanent,[25] for local motion is not immanent, even if its principles are. It is an *actus imperfecti*, even if the living thing moves *itself*, for the soul is the immanent principle of this movement, but the body is its subject and therefore that which is moved in the strict sense of the word.[26] The immanence of the principles of local movement distinguishes the living from the nonliving but does not tell us exactly wherein vital operation is distinguished from physical movement.[27] Therefore, we shall have to discover, in these immanent principles of which St. Thomas has just spoken, a distinctive activity that will be unlike physical movement and will thereby define life as an immanent operation. St. Thomas has already alluded to this characteristic activity in the above quotation,[28] when he refers to vital operation by the word *movement*. It is also implied in the whole discussion we have just read about self-movement as a distinctive sign of life, for movement executed by an immanent instrumental cause implies that this cause has its own *proper activity* that is the principle of local movement and not confused with it. *A fortiori* when both the principal cause and the end are immanent, these causes have completely characteristic operations, of which physical movement is an *exterior sign* but does not indicate their nature. This distinctive activity is the act of a living thing as such; it does not proceed into another, a recipient, but perfects the agent. Thus, to eat, grow, sense, understand, will, are all activities *of* the living *in* the living, and *for* the living. Were they really movements, the agent and the recipient would be identical, which is contradictory, for the agent is in act through its perfection and the recipient is in potency by this same perfection. But it is impossible that the same thing be both in potency and in act under the same aspect.[29]

In a passage too long to quote,[30] St. Thomas returns to the theme of life as an immanent operation and studies it, not as principal, instrumental, and final agent, but as the *term,* or jurisdiction, of the vital operation itself. From this point of view, vital operation is distinguished from movement insofar as the latter *proceeds into exterior matter* (*transit in exteriorem materiam*) whereas the former remains in the agent (*manet in agente*). This passage paints a masterly picture of created, as well as uncreated, causality, a picture wherein the absence or presence of immanence and its degrees of perfections is taken as criterion for the hierarchy among these different causalities: *Quanto aliqua natura est altior, tanto id quod ex ea emanat, magis est ei intimum.*[31]

At the lowest rung of beings are inanimate bodies, because their emanation or action is in no way immanent but is found in the recipient. At the next level come the plants, whose acts of self-nourishment and growth are immanent, but whose most perfect vital act, that of generation, terminates in another. After plants come animals, whose cognitive acts have an immanent term, but by means of the multiplication of potencies. Lastly come intelligent beings whose immanence is complete, although this total immanence admits of different degrees according to the levels of intelligence.

Analysis of the different texts in which St. Thomas describes the activity peculiar to living things indicates that vital operations have characteristics contrary to those which we have seen to be peculiar to movement.[32] Vital operation is, in fact, interiority, perfection, and self-construction.

It is interior, since life must *at least* possess the instrumental principle of all its movements[33] and be the source of activities that remain in the living thing. Moreover, the degrees of life depend upon the degrees of immanence of the different principles of operation, and the inwardness (*magis ei est intimum*) of the term of this operation itself. Psychological awareness is both the sign of this immanence and its effect; liberty is its result.

It is also perfect, for the very definition of vital operation is that it is an act and therefore the perfection of the agent. But the agent does not act because it is imperfect but *because it is perfect: Est actus perfecti.*

And although movement is an act of the imperfect, that is, of what is in potentiality, this kind of action is *an act of the perfect,* that is to say, of what is in act, as is stated in *De Anima.*[34]

We must note this characteristic of life: Its operations signify a perfection that is already possessed, since a living being is the cause of its acts and every agent is an agent only to the extent that it is in act through the perfection it bequeaths; to live is to give oneself a perfection in that one is perfect; it is to give oneself in a second act that which one already possesses in a first act,[35] for operation follows being.

Everything acts insofar as it is in act. For to act is nothing other than to *communicate,* as far as possible, *that through which the agent is in act.*[36]

Vital operation is self-constructing. We have seen that every movement implies the disappearance or corruption of a form, quantity, or place, and generation or appearance of a new form, quantity, or place. Mobile being can acquire nothing without losing something. In the activity of living beings the contrary is true, for the living lose nothing but acquire something; vital activity is a gift that a living being gives itself from its own wealth. This wealth is the actuality of the soul itself and of its powers.

These, briefly, are the characteristics of life, and just as some of its properties are contrary to those of physical movement, so also is the root or sole source of these properties contrary to the root of the properties of physical movement. The root of physical movement, as we have seen, is matter. At the source of every vital operation, then, there is a certain immateriality[37] to be found in every soul; thus, the soul is entirely present in each of its parts,[38] because it is not subject to the laws of the continuum whose principle is matter. Also, vital activities are accompanied by a certain awareness, which, in plants, consists in a power of adaptability instilled by God into the very being of plants, rendering them able to meet the requirements of self-preservation. In animals this awareness is governed by instinct, and in man it consists in man's presence to himself, in and by his operations. In God, self-awareness is pure and total because He is spirit and His life is His being.[39]

This comparison between physical movement and vital activity has shown us both why movement enters into the definition of life and the inexactitude of this definition, since movement is but an equivocal sign[40] of the reality that is life. Furthermore, studying the immanence of the principles of cognitive operation and of its term has given us some insight into the mystery of knowledge *insofar as it is an accident* of man. We must not forget that our starting point, in this part of our investigation into the nature of knowledge, was to establish the dependence of knowledge upon its originating principles. One of those principles is man as a knowing substance. We know now that it is as living that man is the source of the particular activity called knowledge, and that *his soul,* his immaterial component, explains the immanence of knowledge and makes this accident heterogeneous to all the other accidents of man. The principle of knowledge is man, body and soul, since operation follows being,[41] but it is the presence of the soul that explains knowledge's characteristics of interiority, perfection, and self-construction.[42] The soul is the only source of all immanent activity in the order of knowledge. Now we must seek the reason for the multiple activities we observe in experiencing the world of knowledge.

B. THE SOUL AND ITS MULTIPLE ACTIVITIES: THE SOUL AND ITS POWERS

The soul is man's only substantial form. This is one of the doctrinal points in which St. Thomas departed from medieval Augustinianism and, for metaphysical reasons, sided with Aristotle.[43] The multiplicity of the soul's activities cannot be explained by the presence of several forms as their immediate principle. Moreover, the soul is a substantial principle, a first act in the order of substance, whereas all vital activities are accidents, second acts, or perfections of the first act. But it is impossible that a substantial act be the immediate principle of any perfection except a substantial perfection, and that is the function of the soul in relation to the body, which receives its substantial act of existing through the soul, which in turn receives its own existence directly from God.[44] Therefore, the reason for the diversity of immanent operations must be sought in an immediate principle other than the soul; and this consists in the powers of the soul.

It is impossible to admit that the power of the soul is its essence, although some have maintained it. For the present purpose this may be proved in two ways. First because, since potency and act divide being and every kind of being, we must refer potency and its act to the same genus. Therefore, if the act be not in the genus of substance, the potency which is mentioned in relation to the act cannot be in the genus of substance. Now, the operation of the soul is not in the genus of substance, for this belongs to God alone, whose operation is his own substance. Therefore the divine potency or power which is the principle of his operation is the divine essence itself. This cannot be true either of the soul or of any creature, as we have said above when speaking of the angels.

Secondly, this may also be shown to be impossible in the soul. For the soul by its very essence is an act. Therefore if the very essence of the soul were the immediate principle of operation, whatever has a soul *would always have actual vital actions,* as that which has a soul *is always an actually living thing.* For, as a form the soul is not an act ordained to a further act; it is rather the ultimate term of generation. Therefore, for it to be in potentiality to another act does not belong to it according to its essence as a form, but to its power. So the soul itself, as the subject of its power, is called the first act, with a further relation to the second act. . . . Therefore it follows that the essence of the soul is not its power; for *nothing is in potentiality by reason of an act, as act.*[45]

Thus, all vital or immanent activities proceed radically from the soul by means of an immediate principle of operation called a "power." However, were there only one power, there would be only one type of activity, since a power is a principle of self-construction or acquisition of *one* determined perfection, because it is the principle of a particular activity:

A power as such is directed to an act. Therefore we must derive the nature of a power from the act to which it is directed; and consequently the nature of a power is *diversified according as the nature of the act* is diversified.[46]

Now, vital activities are extremely diversified. There are acts of vegetative life, of sensible life, and of intellectual life, and since there is but one soul to account for this diversity and it cannot explain it directly in and by its substantial unity, the powers of the soul must be multiplied in accordance with the diversity of these activities. The reason for the multiplicity of powers that explain the diversity of our vital operations is given by St. Thomas in a metaphysical context dealing with order in the universe and that imitation of the divine which we spoke of above.[47]

Of necessity we must place several powers in the soul. To make this evident, we observe that, as the Philosopher says, the lowest order of things cannot acquire perfect goodness, but they acquire a *certain imperfect goodness*, by few movements. Those which belong to a higher order acquire *perfect goodness by many movements*. Those higher yet acquire *perfect* goodness by *few* movements, and the highest perfection is found in those things which acquire perfect goodness *without* any movements whatever. . . . We conclude, therefore, that things which are below man acquire a certain limited goodness, and so have a few determinate operations and powers. But *man can acquire universal and perfect goodness*, because he can acquire beatitude.[48] Yet he is in the lowest degree, according to his nature, of those to whom beatitude is possible; and therefore the human soul requires many and various operations and powers. But for angels a smaller variety of powers is sufficient. In God, there is no power or action beyond His own Essence.

There is yet another reason why the human soul abounds in variety of powers: it is on the confines of spiritual and corporeal creatures, and *therefore the powers of both meet* together in the soul.[49]

Consequently, it is in the soul that the diversity of vital acts is to be found, but we must look outside it, or we must at least consider it as a part of the universe, to discover the primary reason for this diversity and its metaphysical meaning. The diversity of powers, required by the multiplicity of vital operations, is ordered to the absolute perfection of the soul, to the beatitude it can achieve only in its likeness to God, which is owing to knowledge by which the soul becomes a microcosm and thus participates in the fullness of the Divine Being whose created reflections are mirrored within it.[50]

It is in terms of a continual reciprocation between concrete experience of the different aspects of human knowledge and this metaphysical and theocentric vision of man as a part of the universe that St. Thomas builds his epistemology. He explains the integral immanence of the world of knowledge by the number and nature of the powers that are its immediate source. Psychology enumerates these powers and explains their functioning[51]; epistemology, as the wisdom of noetic activity, must confirm this number and nature by the finality of each of these powers, its role in this progressive imitation of God by man, imitation that pushes man beyond his limitations as creature and hylemorphic creature and, as far as possible, enables him to be all creation.

C. MULTIPLICITY OF THE SOUL'S POWERS AND THEIR IMMANENCE OR INTERIORITY

The human mind, in its dependence upon phantasms and the local and temporal properties accompanying them, tends to conceive this multiplicity of powers and their activities as separate entities, subsisting beside each other like players in an encyclopedic drama, whose entrances and exits are carefully calculated, whose actions and speeches never coincide, and who must leave the stage as soon as they have spoken their lines. Nothing could be further from gnosiological reality than this artificial arrangement of our powers and their operations, for their nature and activities obey the laws of interiority, perfection, and self-construction by which life is defined. The acts of powers are not exterior to the powers themselves, and the latter are not exterior to one another,[52] or to the soul that is their source and end. We are not here dealing with a being in which matter separates, localizes, and sets up oppositions, but with a being whose immateriality permits of identity in distinction and of multiplicity in a unity of origin and hierarchy, all of which we find hard to conceive because we cannot imagine it.[53] The diversity of powers and their acts is not explained by the phenomena of transmutation, generation, and corruption, but by a sort of emanation, of gushing from within, that has nothing to do with quantitative juxtaposition.[54] St. Thomas establishes this truth by comparing substantial form, the subject it actuates, and the accidental forms that are the soul's powers and their acts with the subject they actuate, i.e., with the soul itself:

Substantial and the accidental forms partly agree and partly differ. They agree in this, that *each is an act*, and that by *each of them some-*

thing is in some way actual. They differ however in two respects. First, because the substantial form makes a thing to be absolutely, and its subject is only potentially a being. But the accidental form does not make a thing to be absolutely, but to be such, or so great, or in some particular condition, for its subject is an actual being. Hence it is clear that *actuality is found in substantial form prior to its being found in its subject; and since that which is first in a genus is the cause in that genus, the substantial form causes actual being in its subject.* On the other hand, *actuality is found in the subject of the accidental form prior to its being found in the accidental form; and therefore the actuality of the accidental form is caused by the actuality of the subject.* So the subject, in as much as it is in potentiality, is *receptive* of the accidental form; but inasmuch as it is in act, it produces it. . . . Secondly, substantial and accidental forms differ, because, since that which is the less principal exists for the sake of that which is more principal, matter exists for the sake of the substantial form; while, on the contrary, *the accidental form exists for the sake of the completeness of the subject.*

Now, it is clear from what has been said, that either the subject of the soul's powers is the soul itself alone . . . or else this subject is the composite. *But the composite is actual by the soul.* Whence it is clear that all the powers of the soul, whether their subject be the soul alone or the composite, *flow from the essence of the soul as from their principle. . . .*[55]

The subject is both *the final cause* and in a way the *active cause* of its proper accident. It is also as it were the material cause *inasmuch as it is receptive* of the accident. From this we may gather that the essence of the soul is the cause of all its powers, *as their end, and as their active principle,* and of some, as receptive of them.[56]

A living thing is thus simultaneously the recipient, the agent, and the end of all vital accidents; it produces these accidents *for itself,* not to enrich anything outside itself, but *for its own self-completion.* So egocentric is the realm of vital immanence that the soul cannot produce anything by which it does not profit and become enriched. Unlike the field of moral action, where the intention makes the act good or evil, psychological activity, from the very fact that it is the subject's act, is the subject's perfection, independently of any moral intention, for it is superbeing that the subject gives itself. Thus, every psychological act is added to a pre-existing wealth from which it results and which it enriches the more by the increased awareness it brings. It is the act of an act and, as such, excludes every imperfection, every impoverishment. This perfection, which it signifies and makes explicit, can be of greater or less degree according to the nobility of the power or soul from which it springs; but this relative hierarchy, this greater or less degree, does not alter the fact that every power of the soul, and every one of its activities, has an absolute *value* before comparison with another value gives it a relative aspect.

Consequently, the soul is *present* to each and every one of its powers. More than this, because the soul's powers are present to each other, each of the higher powers governs and directs the inferior powers, and the latter prepare the activity of the former.

In things which proceed from one according to a natural order, just as the first is the cause of all, so that which is nearer to the first is, in a way, cause of those which are more remote. Now it has been shown that among the powers of the soul there are several kinds of order, therefore one power of the soul proceeds from the essence of the soul by the medium of another. But since the essence of the soul is compared to the powers both as active and final principle, and as a receptive principle, either separately by itself, or together with the body; and since the agent and the end are more perfect, while the receptive principle as such, is less perfect, it follows that those powers of the soul which precede the others in *the order of perfection and nature* are the principle of the others after the manner of an end and of an active principle. For we see that *sense* is for the sake of the intellect, and not the other way about. Sense, moreover, is a certain imperfect participation of the intellect, and therefore, according to its natural origin, *it proceeds from the intellect* as the imperfect from the perfect.

But considered as *receptive principle*, the more imperfect powers are principles with regard to the others; and thus the soul, according as it has the sensitive power, is considered as the subject, and as somewhat material in relation to the intellect. On this account, the more imperfect powers precede the others *in the order of generation*, for the animal is generated before the man. . . .[57]

As the power of the soul flows from the essence, *not by a transmutation,* but by a certain natural resultance, and is with the soul, so is it in the case of one power as regards another. . . .[58]

The powers of the soul are opposed to one another as perfect and imperfect; as also are numbers and figures. But this opposition does not prevent the *origin* of one from another, because imperfect things naturally proceed from perfect things.[59]

One might think that this trinity of presences—the presence of the soul's powers to the soul, of the soul to its powers, and of the powers to each other—would suffice to describe immanence and explain all vital activities. But this presence must be pursued even further, for the acts of the different powers themselves can be immanent to one another. Thus, all the acts of the external senses are immanent to the activity of the *sensus communis*, or sensible awareness. The activity of the latter is immanent to that of the imagination, which is itself present to the activity of the memory. All these sensory riches are immanent to the *sensus cogitativus*, which enlists them in the service of intellect and will.[60] Finally, this whole ensemble of sensible operations is immanent or present to the intellect by means of the agent intellect acting upon the phantasm, and the activity of the agent intellect itself becomes present to the intellect possible through the production of the species and its specifying function.[61]

Lastly, analysis of the activities of our intellect, with its three categories of acts—apprehension, judgment, and reasoning—shows that apprehension is present to judgment, since it provides the matter for its act,[62] and that judgment completes it by giving it truth.[63] Judgment is both the principle and the end of reasoning, for it is in judgment that reasoning begins and towards judgment that it is directed and finds its term.[64]

CONCLUSION ON THE IMMANENCE OF KNOWLEDGE

This chapter has attempted[65] to define knowledge as an accident[66] of the subsistent being, man, an accident extraordinarily varied in appearance and characterized by immanence to the soul or knower whose act it is. We know now, at least partially, what knowledge is as an accident, for we have discovered its *propter quid*. It is a vital act unlike physical movement in that its efficient and final principles are interior to the knower. Its term also remains interior to the act that begets it. Not only do we know that it is immanent, but we also know that what makes possible this presence of act to agent is the very immateriality of the agent itself, its capacity to act in defiance of the laws of matter and quantity, to unify without homogenizing, to safeguard the distinction and the actuality proper to each aspect of the real without dividing or destroying it. Finally, when we ask how far this power of interiority goes, we come to the nature of the soul as act, as act begetting other acts called powers, and begetting them without their becoming exterior and without the powers' being extrinsic to each other. These powers generate acts in their turn, and far from being opposed to or destroying each other, these acts further this cooperation to the point of integrating themselves in an incredible, vital synthesis called "human knowledge," a synthesis in which the myriads of immanent accidents are so ordered that, without losing their distinction, they combine and harmonize to constitute but one act of knowledge.

In succeeding chapters we shall have to come back to this aspect of knowledge as an immanent accident. Right here, however, it is important to note the unintelligible character of the problem of truth, error, science, or wisdom, when we state this problem without first knowing that knowledge is an accident of man, and that its intelligibility must be learned from man. When we ask man to tell us about the intelligibility of knowledge, he will describe it as an immanent operation, something emanating from the soul without becoming exterior to it, emanating from the soul by the mediation of numerous and distinct powers, whose multiplicity and distinction are *not numbered* in the mathematical sense of the word number.[67] Their acts are not numbered either, in the mathematical sense of the word, but are coordinated and cooperate in a concatenation impossible to imagine, whose existence is established through the very experience of knowledge that every act of reflection reveals.

The unity of the soul and the knower, the diversity of the soul's powers and their operations, a unity and diversity that depend upon life and not upon anything physical, upon the immaterial and not upon the quantitative, a unity and diversity that are not exterior to each other but are very intimately present in a continuous hierarchy of cause and effect, of remote cause and proximate cause[68]—such is the first aspect of the nature of knowledge as immanent activity.

VI · KNOWLEDGE AS THE PRESENCE OF OTHER THINGS

A Section I nature of object
B Section II External reality 'sensible': cause
Intellectible: cause of intellection
Conclusion p 248

This immanent universe of knowledge, with its ordered diversity of powers and the myriad acts of which the soul is simultaneously the theatre, source, and end, everywhere bears an imprint that seems sharply opposed to immanence, because this imprint is the sign of otherness, of an exteriority hard to reconcile with the extraordinary interiority observed in the relations between the soul and its powers and between the powers and their activities. This immanent activity bears the imprint of the object, a stranger who invades and takes possession of the soul to such a degree that the soul can rediscover itself only in and by this stranger.[1]

This is the second observation the epistemologist must make if he would state the problem of human knowledge in terms of an integral experience of its essential character: It is a world of immanent activities, therefore a world of interior acts, but these acts are all controlled, governed, and determined by a universe seemingly heterogeneous to the soul and its life, namely a *universe of multiple objects*. How can we reconcile the immanence of cognitive activity, wholly concerned with the soul that is its center and end, with the duality and heterogeneity incontestably characterizing the object as such and tending to organize this immanent activity in function of something other than the soul? For, while cognitive activity is egocentric because of its essential interiority, the object invading this activity is eccentric and seems to take the soul outside itself. The solution of this second aspect, essential to all human cognitive activity, is prerequisite to understanding the particular problems posed by truth and its infallibility. This duality, which knowledge sets up and observes, between knower and known has, in modern parlance, become the opposition between subject, or ego, and object, or nonego.

This opposition between self and nonself has become so primary for modern thought that it has brought about the famous *problem of the bridge:*[2] the distance that must be bridged between self and nonself in order to vindicate the truth of our knowledge. This quantification of epistemological data has to account for the interiority that essentially characterizes vital activity, and only a new notion of the nature of the object and nonego will make this possible. Let us ask St. Thomas to reteach us what the object of human knowledge is, its unity and its multiplicity.

Section I: Description of the Nature of the Object

Among the words that St. Thomas uses constantly in constructing his doctrinal synthesis, none is used more frequently or more variously than *object*. It is the source of the distinction between the powers of the soul, between *habitus* and their acts. It is by virtue of the object, that the natural and the supernatural are not confused, that knowledge is divided into the speculative, the practical, and the artistic, that appetite and the different appetites differ from the phenomenon of knowledge, that sensibility is opposed to the spiritual, that faith, grace, and theology have their respective functions in the order of salvation, and that all human science is integrated in theology without rupturing the latter from within. Remove the word *object* and its substitutes from St. Thomas' writings, and you suppress one-third of his works. Misunderstand the extremely flexible and varied meanings of this word, and his synthesis turns into an encyclopedia of the writings of his predecessors but loses all its intelligibility and originality only to become a puzzle or cryptogram, the joy of subtle and argumentative minds, and the torment of historians. Restore this notion to its true place in his philosophical and theological synthesis, and you will immediately observe the inspired power of this mind, no longer a sphinx but truly a *Doctor* again, he who teaches truth. A cryptogram can be decoded only by studying the repetition of signs revealing the cipher that is the key to understanding its contents. The object and its constant repetition is truly the cipher by which Thomism can be decoded and its epistemology given the nature and role that its author assigned it. We shall analyze some of the innumerable texts that St. Thomas wrote upon the nature and different aspects of the object, so that we may be able to perceive its primary role in Thomistic epistemology.

A. SUBJECT-OBJECT AND THEIR CORRELATION

First, let us look at some texts where the nature of the object is described with a sort of universality, without its being related to any definite field:

A thing is called the object of the soul because of some relation that it has to the soul. . . . Now a thing may have two kinds of relations to the soul: first, the thing may be in the soul according to the mode of the soul and not according to the thing's own mode; second, the soul may be brought into relation with the thing in its own existing being (*esse*). And thus a thing is an object of the soul in two ways: in one way, as it is naturally adapted to be in the soul, not according to the thing's *esse* but according to the mode of the soul, which is spiritually—and this is the formal character of the knowable thing as knowable; in a second way, a thing may be the object of the soul as the soul is inclined and ordered to it, in accord with the mode of the thing as it exists in itself—and this is the formal notion of the thing as an object of appetition, as desirable.[3]

The object is not a thing taken as an absolute, nor the soul taken as another absolute, but a *habitudo* between things and the soul and vice versa. This *habitudo*, whose precise nature we shall study, is first stated by St. Thomas as an established fact, *invenitur duplicem habitudinem habere*, then as a fact to be explained, not by chance circumstance or the whims of things and the soul, but by the very nature of soul and things, *in quantum* natum est *esse in anima . . . spiritualiter . . .* secundum quod anima ad ipsum inclinatur et ordinatur. The object is the thing inasmuch as it is made *to exist in the soul* according to the being of the soul, and it is properly called the *knowable*. The object is also the thing in that it is the existential

term of an inclination or immanent ordination to the soul, and it is
called the *object of appetition*.

What modern parlance has agreed to define as nonselves cannot
therefore be defined in Thomism except by reference to the self,
the subject. Instead of being heterogeneous, the subject and object
are intelligible in the world of knowledge only *in and by* correlative
reference. There is no problem of the *bridge* in Thomistic epistemology any more than there is when we speak of father and son,
for father has no meaning without son, or vice versa. To pick out
some father and then to look for a son to prove the father's existence
is nonsense as long as words mean anything, and if words have no
meaning, they are nonsensical in themselves and do not merit discussion. Thus, the subject is included in the definition of the object,
and the object is included in the definition of the subject. They
neither exist nor are intelligible except simultaneously. To suppress
one of the terms, soul or *res*, is to suppress the object.

One might think that this correlation of subject and object would
oblige us to conclude that there are as many objects as there are
things or distinct *res*. But this conclusion would run counter to the
very nature of the object as described in the preceding passage, for
it is not necessarily in itself, in its totality and indivision, that a
thing is an object, but in its relation to the soul. There are cases in
which a single thing could be said to be a multitude of objects in
accordance with the multitude of its relations to the different activities of the soul; or, on the contrary, a multitude of things could
be just one object, according as they enter into a single relation
with a certain activity of the soul:

The formal notion of an object is understood according to a proportion
of the thing (to which an operation, habitus or potency is directed) to
the act of the soul in which the habitus or potencies are present. Now,
since things which are combined and most unified in reality are sometimes divided by the operation of the soul, it is possible that there be
various formal notions of an object, when there is only one thing present.[4]

One single thing, Socrates for example, is simultaneously the object
of sight as colored, the object of hearing as speaking or making
sounds, the object of the imagination as absent, the object of the

intellect as possessing human nature, as philosopher, etc., and the object of the will as lovable. Things cannot therefore be multiplied at the rate of objects. Neither can we conclude upon the unity of the thing from the unity of the object. Thus, common sense and imagination can know as one the sensible qualities that the external senses differentiate; the intellect can know as *one* the whole ensemble of beings, inasmuch as it knows them as being. In the case of imagination and intellect there is a unity of object but an incredible diversity of real things.[5]

Here, in the nature of the object, we find the flexibility and immateriality that we have observed in studying the immanence of our noetic activities. With the nature of the object we are at the very heart of the nature of knowledge as a vital act, an act in which knowing subject and exterior thing are united in a unity which we cannot imagine but which experience forces upon our observation. Now, it is experimentally observable that the objects of different powers are interior to each other, as are the soul's powers and their acts. St. Thomas speaks of this immanence or interiority of objects in discussing the hierarchy of objects, their greater or less universality and their priority of nature or time in the structural functions performed by them in epistemology:

The higher power, of itself, regards *a more universal formality* in its objects than the lower power; because the higher a power is, to a greater number of things does it extend. Therefore many things are combined in the *one formality* of the object which the higher power considers of itself, while they differ in the formalities regarded by the lower powers of themselves. Thus it is that various objects belong to various lower powers, which objects, however, are subject to one higher power. . . .[6]

Nothing prevents inferior powers or habits from being diversified by objects which yet agree with one another in coming together under a higher power or habit because the higher power or habit regards its own object under a more universal formality. Thus the object of the *common sense* is the sensible thing, including, therefore, whatever is visible or audible. Hence the *common sense*, although one power extends to all the powers of the five senses.[7]

In this correlation of man and his powers as source of his cognitive activity, with the thing-object as principle of this same activity, there is a concrete application of those laws of immateriality that we have seen to be essential to the exercise of every vital act, and particularly to the exercise of the superior vital energy that is knowledge.[8] The more perfectly immanent the principles and terms of knowledge, the more universal and common will be its objects, and the greater the number of external things these objects will include. Once more we can see the marvelous harmony between reality and man, harmony resulting from the pre-established plan of the Creator-Artist who made all things for man and man for the real universe of which he is a part. Man is made in the image of the universe because the universe is made after the image of God and because man was created to imitate God through the mediation of the universe.[9]

The general notion of what an object is consists in a careful sifting of reality by knowledge, and this screening can, in a way, be described by the analogy that Sir Arthur Eddington uses to explain scientific method:

Let us suppose that an ichthyologist is exploring the life of the ocean. He casts a net into the water and brings up a fishy assortment. Surveying his catch, he proceeds in the usual manner of the scientist to systematise what it reveals. He arrives at two conclusions: (1) no sea creature is less than two inches long; (2) all sea creatures have gills.

An onlooker may object that the first generalization is wrong: "There are plenty of sea creatures under two inches long, only your net is not adapted to catch them." The ichthyologist dismisses this objection contemptuously. . . . What my net can't catch is not fish.[10]

Our knowing is very much like a continual fishing trip during which our soul, armed with this multitude of more or less specialized nets that are its powers and *habitus*, snares different aspects of reality, which it then systematizes with the help of the notion of *object*. The latter is a generalization made by our intellect, which simultaneously takes into account the net used, i.e., the nature of the power, and its catch, i.e., the aspect of reality seized; for the net, or power, is constructed to the exact measurement of the object to be seized: net and fish are correlative. Nevertheless, an abyss separates the ichthyologist from the knower, for the former *con-*

structs his nets with the express purpose of catching fish two inches long and having gills. Everything not meeting these conditions is to be thrown out: "What my net can't catch is not fish." But the knower is equipped with a great number of nets whose successive catches are added to each other, just as the nets fit into each other. Furthermore, the knower's nets have not been made by man, but have been given to him by nature; they are the powers whose existence we discussed in analyzing knowledge as an immanent activity.[11] The fisher of objects, who is man-as-knower, knows that no one net can catch all that is to be caught, that what it does not catch is not rubbish but other objects that higher powers will undertake to bring into the soul.

Continuing this comparison of knowledge and fishing-with-a-special-net, we can *a priori* determine the number and nature of our powers by the number and nature of objects, since they are correlative, or, on the contrary, we can enumerate and define objects in accordance with the number and nature of powers. Actually, only the first alternative is legitimate in the world of knowledge, for the existence of our powers is perceived in and by grasping their objects, just as the existence of the soul itself can be perceived only in the activity it originates.

And just as through the soul itself we know that the soul *is*, inasmuch as we perceive its acts, and seek by a study of its acts and their objects to know *what it is* . . . so too, concerning those things that are in our soul, namely its *powers and habits*, we know indeed that they are, inasmuch as we perceive their acts, but what they are we gather from the nature of these same acts.[12]

Therefore, as perceived or present in the soul, objects reveal the existence of powers or *habitus*, and as analyzed by reflection, they reveal the nature of these powers, for they not only signify but cause the activity of our powers or *habitus*. The fish we catch tell us the number and nature of our nets, and we cannot, *a priori*, decide the number and quality of our knowing powers; only the experience of our acts and their terms will give us this knowledge. The following text synthesizes all we have just seen about the nature of the object, its correlation with the soul, and the function by which it determines the number and nature of the soul's powers in the order of vital operation:

Now the powers of the soul are *distinguished* generically by their *objects*. For the higher a power is, the more universal is the object to which it extends, as we have said above. But the object of the soul's operation may be considered in a triple order. (1) For in the soul there is a power *whose object is only the body that is united to that soul*: and the powers of this genus are called *vegetative*, for the vegetative power acts only on the body to which the soul is united. (2) There is another genus in the powers of the soul which regards a more universal object, namely, *every sensible body*, and not only the body to which the soul is united. (3) And there is yet another genus of powers of the soul which regards a still more universal object—namely, not only the sensible body, but *universally all being*. Therefore it is evident that the latter two genera of the soul's powers have an operation in regard not merely to that which is united to them, but also to something *extrinsic*. Now, since whatever operates must in some way be united to the object in relation to which it operates, it follows of necessity that this something extrinsic, which is the object of the soul's operation, must be related to the soul in a twofold manner. First, inasmuch *as this something extrinsic has a natural aptitude to be united to the soul, and to be by its likeness in the soul.* In this way there are two kinds of powers—namely the sensitive in regard to the *less common object*, the sensible body; and the intellectual, in regard to the *most common object*, universal being.[13]

In summarizing the results of our investigation into the nature of the object and its relations with the knowing subject, three very clearly defined aspects stand out:

1. The object is an exterior thing, more or less particular, in that *it is able to exist in the soul* according to the being of the soul and, consequently, in that the latter has what is necessary to receive it. Thus, the object is a kind of predestination of things to dwell in the soul, and a predestination of the soul to serve as their dwelling. The object is not intelligible without reference to the soul, and the soul's activity is unintelligible without reference to the object.

2. The object, or the knowable, enumerates and defines our cognitive powers, whose existence and nature we perceive by means of the object, which makes us aware of what we are and of our interior riches. In Thomism, the existence of the knowing subject is always

the term of an activity of knowing that reveals it to us in and by an objective influence, and never the principle of determination of an exterior reality. The self-awareness of the subject as such results from awareness of the object as such.

3. Finally, there are two kinds of objects determining two kinds of powers: the *sensibile* and the *intelligibile* designating two different modes or aptitudes of reality that permit it to exist in our soul. Later, in the course of a more searching analysis of the nature of the object, we shall see the exact meaning of the words *sensibile* and *intelligibile*. For the moment it will suffice to remember that these two terms do not refer to reality in its absolute existence but in its association with human activity.

B. HYLEMORPHISM OF THE OBJECT

St. Thomas did not content himself with this general description of the nature of the object. With critical discernment that might seem surprising in a thinker whose works antedate the invention of critique by four centuries, he pursued his inquiry until the object revealed to him all the complex aspects of its nature. Here are two characteristic texts in which he sets forth the different aspects of the object:

It is possible to consider three things in the object of any power: that which is *formal, material* and *accidental.* This is obvious in the case of the object of sight, for light is formal in it because it makes color actually visible, then the color which is potentially visible is material, while the quantity and other such concomitants of color are accidental. . . .[14]

The object of every cognitive habit includes two things: first, that which is known materially, and is the material object, so to speak, and secondly, that whereby it is known, which is the formal aspect of the object. Thus in the science of geometry, the conclusions are what is known materially, while the formal aspect of the science consists in the means of demonstration, through which the conclusions are known.[15]

This analysis of the object in its three aspects, formal, material, and accidental, must not lead us astray about its real nature. What we are dealing with here is an analogical treatment of a reality in the order of knowledge, therefore an accident, and the three expressions used—*that which is formal, that which is material,* and *that which is accidental in an object*—must be interpreted in relation to the thing perceived, not as an absolute, but in its association with the activity of knowing. We must keep in mind that the object is the thing, or reality, inasmuch as it maintains a *habitudo* with the soul and is able to exist in the soul in accordance with the latter's being[16]; therefore, the thing is being dealt with *as relative.* Now, the ontological structure of the relative as such is altogether different from other accidental realities, and to grasp it requires a quite special intellectual effort. To understand the description that St. Thomas has just given us of the object, we must first know what constitutes the relative, for this description is but an application of the notion of relation to the thing as object. Let us briefly examine the nature of the relative and its different realizations in order to be able to understand the object's three elements.

¶ *1. The Object as Relative.* The special difficulties associated with understanding the nature of the relative, difficulties springing from its lack of being,[17] oblige St. Thomas to describe the nature of relation first by comparing it with better-known accidents. Once these similarities have been noted, he proceeds to describe the structure proper to the relative as such:

We must consider that in each of the nine genera of accidents there are two points for remark. One is the nature belonging to each one of them *considered as an accident,* and this is, in the case of all of them, that *their being is to inhere in a subject;* for the being of an accident is to inhere. The other point of remark is the *proper nature* of each one of these genera. In the genera apart from that of relation, as in quantity and quality, even the *true notion* of the genus itself is derived from comparison to the subject; for quantity is defined as the measure of substance, and quality is the disposition of substance. But the true notion of *relation* is not taken from its respect to *that in which it is,* but from its respect *to something outside.*[18]

This passage explains one of the expressions used by St. Thomas to describe the object, the *id quod est accidentale,* which is none other than the *subject* of the relation. We have just seen, in fact, that relation is not strictly defined by reference to the subject in which it inheres, but by an *opening up* to something extrinsic to the subject. Thus, the relationship of paternity implies a personal biological activity inhering in the begetter, but this activity, considered only in its inherence, does not constitute the relation, for it can exist without the existence of paternity. In order that this activity be considered as relative, it must terminate in something other than the generative substance; it must result in a son. This is easily verified, for as soon as the term disappears, as soon as the son dies, the relationship of paternity dies with him. Again, we say of a man that he *was* a father, but our use of the past tense indicates precisely that the relation no longer exists. Using this example of paternity to further our analysis of the nature of relation, we perceive the following factors:

(1) First, there is the man who begets; considered as man, he is entirely extrinsic to the relation of paternity, but he is its subject.

(2) Then there is the procreative activity of this same man; that is the *basis* of the relation of paternity, insofar as this activity terminates in a son.

(3) Finally, there is the term of the activity, the being which is begotten.

Of these three factors, the first is extrinsic to the *propria ratio* (true notion) of relation; it is not included in the definition of relation and therefore can be said to be accidental in the sense that it is not essential to, or constitutive of, the nature of the relation of paternity. But the *id quod est accidentale in objecto*, of which St. Thomas speaks in the above-quoted text, is precisely the *subject* in which are found color and light, that is, the *id quod est formale et materiale in objecto*. This aspect of the thing is not therefore essential to the object, which must be defined only by the two *material* and *formal* factors. To what aspects of the relative do these two factors of the object correspond?

If we eliminate the *subject* from the definition of relation, two other factors remain, the cause or basis of the relation and its term.

Of these two factors, the cause or basis is more typical, for it gives specific unity to the relation.

Since a thing has being (*esse*) and unity from the same principle, therefore the real unity of a relation must depend on the very foundation or cause of the relation. Thus, since there is one quantity through which one is equal to others, so in my case there is but one real relation of equality having respect to several other persons; likewise, since I was generated in one nativity stemming from my father and mother, I am called the son of both of them by one real filiation, although the references (*respectus*) are pluralized.[19]

The thing is said to be relative to the soul; that is, it is said to be an object of knowledge, insofar as it contains a basis or cause permitting it to exist in the soul according to the soul's mode of existence. The expressions *id quod est materiale et formale in objecto* refer precisely to that in the thing which permits it to come into the soul and make the soul to its image and likeness, for they refer to the totality of the knowable object, therefore, to that which is the basis and cause of knowledge: "Now the object is to the act of a passive power *as the principle and moving cause*, for color is the principle of vision inasmuch as it moves the sight."[20]

Since the thing is an object insofar as it is a *principle and moving cause*, and since, on the other hand, this capacity that it has results from several factors which are to each other as potency-act or matter-form, we shall have to define the nature of the object in terms of all the factors constituting it as a principle or cause of cognitive activity: "The *sufficient*[21] *mover* of a power is none other than that object that in every respect possesses the nature of the mover of that power. If, on the other hand, it is lacking in any respect, it will not move of necessity, as was stated above."[22] Now, this is exactly the case with the object of human knowledge at every level. In order to exist as object, it needs a sort of hylemorphic composition without which it cannot exercise the particular causality on which rests the whole specific character of the thing as knowable:

There are two items to consider in the object of any power: namely, what is material, and what formally perfects the notion of the object. For instance, in the case of sight the color is what is visible *in potency,* and it does not become visible *in act* except through the act of the light. . . .[23]

Now two items concur in the object of any act: one is present materially as it were, and the other as a rather formal aspect perfecting the notion of the object—as color and light concur in constituting the visible object.[24]

The *visibile,* proper object of sight, is thus the thing as capable of moving our visual power, therefore, as able to cause the relation of object, which it can do only in the synthesis of two factors, color and the luminosity of this color by the action of light. Regardless of the scientific theories that may exist concerning the interdependence of color and light, it is a fact that we always see an illuminated color or a colored light, and that the coexistence of these two factors is essential to the act of seeing. Therefore, they are the specifying data of the object of sight; they constitute the latter as formally relative to our visual power. As for the analogical words *materiale* and *formale,* which we use to designate the thing considered as cause or object, they can be explained by the laws of language, which, themselves, rest upon the laws of human knowledge. The first known of these laws pertains to material reality, which serves as starting point for knowledge and for the naming of everything else:

Increase, like other things pertaining to quantity, is transferred from bodily quantities to spiritual and intellectual realities *because* of the natural connection of the human intellect with corporeal things, which come under the imagination.[25]

In physical reality, matter appears as the element of indetermination, both in the order of being and of causality, whereas form is determination, act, and perfection. Whence our natural tendency to refer, in everything we know, to what is incomplete, but on its way to completion, by the word *material,* whereas we use the word *formal* to mean that which actuates, perfects, makes to exist and act. Thus, we must beware of literally interpreting the formulas referring to the nature of the object as if the latter were composed of matter and form. In these expressions we must always see the analogical functions of the object's essential elements in their causal role vis-à-vis the cognitive powers. Before examining the nature of this causality (which will be analyzed in the second section of this chapter), we must more closely examine the relative mode to which the object belongs, for by determining the object's relative mode, we shall be better able to understand the proper structure of its causality.

¶ 2. *The Different Kinds of Relation and the Mode to Which the Object Belongs.* Since the essence of the relative springs from what founds or causes its opening up to something other than itself, there will be as many different types of relation as there is diversity in the bases or causes of the ordering of one thing to another. These bases are three in number:

Since a relation which is present in things consists of an ordering of one thing to another, relations of this kind must exist in as many modes as there may be ways in which *one thing can be ordered to another.* Now a thing is ordered to another, either according to being (*esse*), in the sense that the *being of one thing depends on another* . . . or according to active and passive power, in the sense that *one thing receives something from another or confers something on another* . . . or according as the quantity of one thing *may be measured* by another.[26]

To which of these three relative modes does the object belong? The relation based on quantity, which is of the spatial and temporal order, can be immediately rejected, for the single reason that the object belongs to the order of knowledge and, therefore, is bound up with a higher vital activity, escaping the dominion of matter and quantity.[27] The object's independence with reference to the laws of matter and quantity is evinced by the expressions that St. Thomas uses in defining the object, when he opposes *esse proprium rei* to *esse animae, modus rei* to *modus animae,* or, again, *esse naturale* to *esse intentionale, immateriale, spirituale.*[28]

Since quantity as such cannot cause the object relation, does the latter depend upon action and passion? Considering only the expressions used by St. Thomas, it would seem that the object belongs to this mode of relation, for the activity of knowing is generally described in terms of passivity on the part of the knower and activity on the part of the object. Nevertheless, we must note that these expressions are never used in the strict meaning, which would make them synonymous with physical movement, but always in an analogical and improper context.

In a less proper sense, movement is found in the workings of the sensitive soul. Movement is present in these, not according to physical but spiritual being. This is clear in the case of sight, for instance, its operation is not in the area of physical being but of the spiritual, for it occurs by virtue of sensible species that are received into the eye according to spiritual being. . . . Of course, movement is not properly attributed to operations unless they be directed toward physical being. . . . But it is in the least proper sense, indeed simply by way of *metaphor*, that movement is found in the intellect . . . for its operation is the act of an already perfected power, whereas movement is the act of the imperfect.[29]

The object relation cannot therefore be based upon a physical activity of the thing, to which would correspond a physical passivity in the soul's powers. Consequently, to define the object as relative, only the third mode remains, that mode resting upon dependence in being or upon the relation of measure to measurable:

The third mode has to do with the relation of the measurable and the measure. In this case, measure and measurable are not taken quantitatively . . . but in accord with the measuring of being and truth. In fact, the truth of a science is measured in terms of the knowable object . . . and the same is so of sense and its object.[30]

This text places the object as a relative in the third mode, since the *scibile* and *sensibile* are objects of the intellect and senses respectively. But the relation of measure to measured is distinctive in that, unlike all other relations, it is not correlative, which is to say that it is real only in the measured and not in the measure:

This third mode differs from the previous ones in the fact that they cover cases in which a thing is called relative because it is referred to another, not because another thing is referred to it: thus two-to-one is a reciprocal relation, and likewise the father-son relation is mutual. But in this third mode, a thing is called relative, solely from the fact that something else is referred to it; for instance, the sense object and the knowable or intelligible object are called relative because other things are referred to them. Indeed a thing is called a knowable object because knowledge may be possessed concerning it; similarly, a thing is an object of sense because it can be sensed. Hence, the designation as relative is not due to anything on their side, like quantity, quality, action or passion, as happened in the previous relations, but it is only because of the actions of other beings—even though these actions do not affect these objects as terms. . . .[31]

There is a threefold diversity of related things. One type implies a relation which does not exist in reality but in reason only. . . . A second type implies a real relation, as in the case of father and son. But a third type implies on one side a real relation, and on the other side a mere relation of reason, as in the case of knowledge and its object. The explanation of this diversity is found in that on which the relation is founded: sometimes this is found in the other thing only, and sometimes it is found in both things. For instance, the relation of knowledge and its object is based on apprehension according to a spiritual mode of being. Now, this spiritual being, on which the relation of knowledge is founded, exists only in the knower and not in the knowable object, where the form of the thing is present according to physical being: so, the relation is real on the side of the knowledge but not on the side of the knowable object.[32]

It is very important that this doctrine about the object as relative or measure of knowledge be perfectly understood, for by a super-ficial understanding of it we risk falling into imaginative projections that could destroy the immanence of knowledge, as well as its realism. Therefore, we shall briefly paraphrase the preceding texts in order to extract their exact meaning, which can be stated in three propositions.

(a) The thing, as object, would enter into a real relation with the cognitive powers, were there in it a real basis or cause relating it to the soul; that is, if quantity, or physical action and passion, consti-tuted the object. But none of these three physical aspects of the thing constitutes the object relation, since the latter belongs to the order of relations that exist between the measured and its measure. Therefore, the object does not refer to a real relation or to any real inter-dependence between a thing and our cognitive powers.

(b) However, the activities of our knowing powers do enter into a real relation with the thing as object because the latter is the measure of our activities, just as the essence measures the act of existing, determines it, and enlists it in a given genus.[33]

(c) Although the object thing does not enter into a real relation with the knower, it enters necessarily into a logical relation, or relation of reason, with cognitive activity, as its different names indicate. Why should we call a physical thing *visible, audible, odorous, sensible, imaginable, intelligible*, if we did not consider it to be the *term* of an activity of our different faculties? Were our acts of knowing not immanent, if they terminated really in an object as in a recipient which they transformed by that very fact, then the thing would become physically correlative to our knowledge of it. Actually, it is we who create the relation of things to our souls by knowing them as measures of our acts, and that is why we call this a logical relation, or a relation of reason—to stress its subjective and nonexistential origin.[34] To close this analysis of the object as relative, we have a synthetic text wherein we find all the factors analyzed in the foregoing pages:

We should understand that, since a relation needs two extremes, there are three conditions that make a relation to be real or logical.

(1) Sometimes both extremes are ideas only, as when a mutual order or relation can be between things only because they are apprehended; as when we say that *the same is the same itself*. For the reason, by apprehending one thing twice, regards it as two; and thus it apprehends a certain relation of a thing to itself. And the same applies to relations between *being* and *non-being*, formed by reason, inasmuch as it apprehends nonbeing as an extreme. The same is true of those relations that follow upon an act of reason, as genus and species and the like.

(2) Now there are other relations which are realities as *regards both extremes*, as when a relation exists between two things according to some reality that belongs to both. This is clear of all relations consequent upon *quantity*, as great and small, double and half, and the like; for there is quantity in both extremes. The same applies to relations consequent upon *action* and *passion*, as motive power and the movable thing, father and son, and the like.

(3) Again, sometimes a relation in one extreme may be a reality, while in the other extreme it is only an idea. This happens whenever *two extremes are not of one order*, as sense and science refer, respectively, to sensible things and to knowable things: which, inasmuch as they are realities existing in nature, *are outside the order of sensible and intelligible existence*. Therefore, in science and in sense a real relation exists, because they are *ordered* to the knowledge or to the sensible perceptions of things;

whereas the things looked at in themselves are outside this order. Hence in them there is no real relation, *but only an idea*, inasmuch as the intellect *apprehends them as terms of the relation of science and sense*. Hence the Philosopher says that they are called relative, not because they are related to other things but because others are related to them.[35]

CONCLUSION ON THE DESCRIPTION OF THE NATURE OF THE OBJECT

What conclusions can be drawn from this study of the nature of the object as seen in its common characteristics? First of all, that it is an essential part of Thomistic gnosiology and that knowledge of its real nature is not only a *sine qua non* condition for understanding the true structure of immanent activity, but is its soul. Its suppression takes away all distinction and therefore all hierarchy between cognitive acts and powers and gives the world of knowledge over to the anarchy of a phenomenology of subjective states, more interested in discovering what is going on than in perceiving what is, more concerned with description than explanation. But the purpose of philosophical epistemology is not to describe our activity in the world of knowledge, but to explain or to inquire into the causes of this activity. Since the object is the specifying cause of all our acts of knowing, it is therefore essential to the organization of an epistemological treatise.

As described by St. Thomas, the nature of the object helps us further to penetrate the mystery of that immanence which is the act of knowing. For outer reality enters into logical relation with the act of knowing only because this act is wholly interior to the knower; it is his own wealth that he can give to things. Unlike the other dynamisms originating in man and transforming material and institutional realities,[36] the pure act of knowledge is wholly for the sake of the knower who builds and transforms himself by means of the objects that Divine Wisdom has put at his disposal. This constant use that man makes of the treasures of the universe in no way impoverishes the universe, since the universe gives itself to us without losing anything of what it is.

Such is the mystery of the object of knowledge as revealed by this first glimpse into its nature. We shall now examine the equally mysterious character of its causality in the two orders in which it acts: that of sensation and that of intellection. This will be the subject of the second section of this chapter on knowledge as the immanent presence of *the other*, or the effect things have upon us.

Section II: External Reality as Cause of Our Knowledge

We have just seen the totally immanent character of the object of knowledge and the physical independence of exterior things in relation to our act of knowing. In this context, how is it possible to conceive any causality on the part of external reality? Indeed, it is by definition absolutely indifferent to the fact of being known or unknown, since it is foreign to the order of knowledge: "Inasmuch as they are realities existing in nature, [things] are *outside* the order of sensible and intelligible existence."[37] How can St. Thomas say that on one hand our knowledge is totally *dependent* on the object and that, on the other hand, the object is totally *independent* of any knowledge we may have of it? This problem has been discussed ever since the very beginnings of Western thought, and its solution, in one way or another, gives to philosophy its realist or idealist character, since the nature of knowledge, its truth and its certitude, depends upon the existential relations between the soul and things. The importance of this problem explains why it is so often treated in the works of St. Thomas. The pages he devotes to it are models of a philosophical treatise upon the history of ideas. Here is one of the texts in which he explains the fundamental principle prerequisite to all knowledge as well as the interpretation that thinkers have given it:

The ancient philosophers held that the soul knows bodies through its essence. For it was universally admitted that *like is known by like*. But they thought that the form of the thing known is in the knower in the same way as in the thing known. The Platonists however were of a contrary opinion. For Plato, having observed that the intellectual soul has an immaterial nature, and an immaterial mode of knowing, held that the forms of the things known subsist immaterially.[38]

Like is known by like. This epistemological principle of the *syntonization* of the soul and reality, from which results our experience of knowledge as a possession of the other, as the existing of the object in our soul, has given rise to two opposed theories about the nature of the object. The ancient physicists concluded that the soul was *physically* all material things and that its knowledge of the outer world resulted from its physical identity with it. Plato, on the contrary, observing the immaterial character of human knowledge, concluded that outer reality, the object of this knowledge, must necessarily be immaterial too. Both these theories interpreted the principle of identity of knower and known as an *identity of nature.*

The early natural philosophers, observing that the things known are corporal and material, held that they must exist materially even in the soul that knows them. And therefore, in order to ascribe to the soul the knowledge of all things, they held that it has *the same nature* in common with all. And because the nature of an effect is determined by its principle, they ascribe to the soul the nature of a principle. Hence it is that those who thought fire to be the principle of all, held that the soul had the nature of fire, and like manner as to air and water. . . .[39]

Plato, as we have said, held that the forms of sensible things subsist by themselves without matter. . . . He said therefore that the forms are participated both by our soul and by corporal matter; by our soul for knowledge and by corporal matter for being; so that, just as corporal matter by participating the idea of stone becomes an individual stone, so our intellect, by participating the idea of a stone is made to understand a stone.[40]

St. Thomas rejects this identity of nature between object and knower as incapable of explaining human knowledge. First, he refutes the theory of the early physicists:

But this opinion will not hold . . . because if it were necessary for the thing known to exist *materially* in the knower, there would be no reason why things which have a material existence outside the soul *should be devoid of knowledge;* why for instance, if by fire the soul knows fire, that fire also which is outside the soul should not have knowledge of fire.

We must conclude therefore, that the material things known must need exist in the knower, not materially but rather immaterially. The reason for this is that the act of knowledge extends to things outside the knower; *for we know even the things that are outside us.* Now by matter the form of a thing is determined to some *one* thing. Therefore it is clear that *knowledge is in inverse ratio to materiality.*[41]

Here now is his refutation of Platonic innatism, which results from the pre-existence in the soul of the objects of our knowledge by participation of both the soul and things in separated forms:

But in this opinion *no sufficient reason can be assigned for the soul being united to the body.* For it cannot be said that the intellectual soul is united to the body for the sake of the body, since neither is form for the sake of matter, nor is the mover for the sake of the thing moved, but rather the reverse. Especially does the body seem necessary to the intellectual soul for the latter's proper operation, which is to understand; since as to its being the soul does not depend upon the body. But if the soul by its very nature had an inborn aptitude for receiving intelligible species through the influence of certain *separate* principles and not to receive them from the senses, it would not need the body in order to understand. Hence it would be united to the body for no purpose.

But if it be said that our soul needs the senses in order to understand, in that it is in some way awakened by them to the consideration of those things whose intelligible species it receives from the separate principles, even this seems *an insufficient explanation.* For this awakening does not seem necessary to the soul, except in as far as it is overcome by sleep, as the Platonists express it, and by forgetfulness, through its union with the body; and thus the senses would be of no use to the intellectual soul *except for removing the obstacle* which the soul encounters through its union with the body. Consequently, the reason for the union of the soul with the body still remains unexplained.[42]

This double refutation of the explanation of knowledge by means of *identity of nature* between the soul and its objects rests upon two completely different proofs. The refutation of the ancient physicists is based upon the nature of knowledge *as such.* As such, the nature of knowledge requires a certain immateriality on the part of the knower and must therefore call on something other than physical identity between soul and things to be known: "knowledge is in inverse ratio to materiality."[43]

The refutation of Platonism and the medieval Platonists, on the contrary, rests upon the nature of *human* knowledge, on the natural and necessary dependence of intellectual knowledge upon organic

and sensory powers, as well as on the dependence of these latter
upon outer reality. It is a universal observation of experience that
man depends upon the outside world for both sensible and intellectual knowledge; it is another that knowledge is the interior presence
of the object, and presence of such a kind that the knower is really
the thing known. These two experiences have been and are still the
starting point for all philosophical epistemology; from them St.
Thomas argues the necessity of the causal action of things on the
soul and, by that fact, destroys all innatism:

Since *form is the principle of action,* a thing must be related to the form
which is the principle of an action in the same way as it is related to
that action. . . . Now, we observe that man sometimes is only a *potential
knower,* both as to sense and as to intellect; and he is reduced from such
potentiality to act: (1) to the act of sensation *through the action* of the
sensible object on his senses; (2) to the act of understanding by instruction or discovery. Therefore we must say that the cognitive soul is in
potentiality *both to the likenesses* which are the principles of sensing and
to the *likenesses* which are the principles of understanding. For this
reason Aristotle held that the intellect by which the soul understands has
no innate species, but is at first in potentiality to all such species.

But since that which actually has a form is sometimes unable to act
according to that form because of some hindrance . . . for this reason
Plato held that man's intellect is naturally filled with all intelligible species,
but that by being united to the body, it is hindered from the realization
of its act. But this seems to be unreasonable. First, because, if the soul
has a natural knowledge of all things, it seems impossible for the soul
so far to forget the existence of such knowledge as not to know itself to
be possessed of it. . . . And specially unreasonable does this seem if we
suppose that it is natural to the soul to be united to the body, as we
have established above; for it is *unreasonable that the natural operation of
a thing be totally hindered by that which belongs to it naturally.* Secondly,
the falseness of this opinion is clearly proved from the fact that if a sense
be wanting, the knowledge of what is apprehended through that sense
is also wanting. For instance, a man who is born blind can have no knowledge of colors. This would not be the case if the soul had innate likeness
of all intelligible things.[44]

Since the soul is not physically all things, since it is not filled with
forms by participation in things in themselves, exterior things must
inevitably exert a certain causality upon our knowing powers; other-

wise, knowledge, as the immanent presence of another to the subject, remains unintelligible. The causality of outer reality can nevertheless be exercised at two very different levels. Thus, Kant admits that the physical universe must play a role in human knowledge, but, in constituting the object, this universe has only the function of *id quod est accidentale* to the object in Thomism[45]; the *a priori* of sensation furnishes *id quod est materiale* and the *a priori* of the understanding provides *id quod est formale*. Of the three factors that constitute the object as knowable or imaginable, the thing furnishes only pure matter, unknowable in itself, whereas the subject provides intelligibility or particular objectivity through the spatial or temporal *a priori*, and universal objectivity through the categories.[46] The Kantian object results from the simultaneous cooperation of reality and the soul, but the soul plays only the role of a Platonic Demiurgos, of a *dator formarum* stabilizing an essentially changing matter and making it capable of fulfilling its objective function. All the objects of Kantian man are made to his image and likeness; he is the architect, and the *a prioris*, sensible as well as intelligible, are the inevitable models to which reality must conform. This is the price it must pay for its knowability.

In Thomism the roles are reversed, for the physical universe plays the part of *dator formarum* with respect to the extraordinary plasticity of the powers of the soul. This theme is continually being developed in the works of St. Thomas under the double heading of the passivity of the powers of knowledge and the activity of objects. However, since this general theme of the causality of things as objects is applicable in two very different ways, depending upon how we deal with sensation or intellection, we shall successively examine the causality of the object of sensation and that of the object of intellection, always keeping in mind this text, which expresses the fundamental idea of Thomistic epistemology:

The soul is given man in place of all forms, so that man may be, in a sense, the entirety of being: to the extent that he is, as it were, all things by virtue of his soul, because his soul is *receptive of all forms*. Indeed the intellect is a potency *receptive* of all intelligible forms, and the sense power is a potency *receptive* of all sensible forms.[47]

A. THE SENSIBLE AS CAUSE OF SENSATION

From the outset of this analysis of the object's causality, we must keep in mind that our procedure will follow the chronological order, and not the order of nature or perfection. Were we to follow the natural order, our analysis of intellectual activity would have to precede that of sensation, since upon the former ultimately depend the laws of sensible knowledge:

For we see that sense is for the sake of the intellect, and not the other way about. *Sense, moreover, is a certain imperfect participation of the intellect, and* therefore, according to its natural origin, it proceeds from the intellect as the imperfect from the perfect. But considered as *receptive principles,* the more imperfect powers are principles with regards to the others; and thus the soul, according as it has the sensitive powers, is considered as the subject and as something material in relation to the intellect. On this account, the more imperfect powers *precede the others in the order of generation.*[48]

The causality of physical things as sensible chronologically precedes the causality of these same things as intelligible, although by nature and finality it is the soul that, as spiritual or intelligent, is at the source of our sensory activity and determines and completes its inner structure. Imperfect participations of the intellect, the senses draw from it their origin and work for its good. Thus, sensory causality is both a function of the senses it affects and of the intellect that completes it. Let us try to discern its nature by studying these two factors together, the passivity of sensory powers and the active character of their objects.

❡ *Passive Powers.* We must first eliminate a certain misunderstanding concerning the expression *passive power* as it is used to designate the immediate principles of all human knowledge. Actually, passivity means a capacity to receive and belongs on the side of matter, but to conceive the powers of knowledge as pure receivers of forms without any activity on their part is to reduce knowledge to a static state and to make absurd its definition as an immanent activity.[49] Therefore, in order to avoid confusion, we must carefully define the meaning of the word *passive* when it refers to cognitive powers.

Active and passive potency are not distinguished by the fact that only one has an operation, for, since there is an operation for every potency of the soul both active and passive, every potency would then be active. The distinction is known by the way the potency is related to its object: for, if the object stands in relation to the potency as the patient and as the thing that is changed, this will be a case of active potency; however, if conversely it stands as agent and mover, this will be a case of passive potency.[50]

Since the passivity of our sensory powers of knowledge cannot be interpreted to mean inefficacy in the order of operation but only dependence upon its object, the passivity of our senses must be understood only in the order of formal causality:

The object is on a different footing in an immanent and transient action. In a transient action, the object or matter into which the action passes is something *separate* from the agent, as the thing heated from what gave it heat, and the building from the builder. But in an immanent action, for the action to proceed, *the object must be united with the agent;* just as the sensible object must be united with the sense in order that the sense may acually perceive. And the *object* which is united to a power bears the same relation to actions of this kind *as does the form* which is the principle of action in other agents; for as heat is the *formal principle* of heating in the fire, so the species of the thing seen is the formal principle of sight in the eye.[51]

Every cognitive power is therefore operative by nature; what makes it passive is its indetermination or neutrality with respect to a specific act.[52] This amounts to saying that every power is actual in the order of operation or exercise, but that in the order of specification,[53] when there is no specifying principle precisely determining the operation, a power must receive *before* being able to exercise its energy in a given direction, and that is what entitles it to the name *passive:*

It must however be borne in mind that this likeness of the object exists sometimes only potentially. So in order that there may be actual knowledge, it is required that the power of knowledge *be reduced to an actual possession of the species.* But if it always possesses the species, it does thereby have actual knowledge without any preceding change or reception. From this it is evident that *to be moved by the object is not of the nature of the knower as such, but as only knowing in potentiality*.[54]

To understand the nature of the passivity by which St. Thomas characterizes our cognitive powers, we must keep in mind his teaching on knowledge as an immanent activity. To know, the knower must *be* the object; but knowledge does not consist in this ontological possession of the object, it is an effect thereof. Because the power *is* the object, it can live it, which is to say that psychologically, it can give itself what it already possesses ontologically. However, it cannot live it *before* having received it, and it is in this phase, prior to the vital act, properly so called, that we can speak of *actio-passio*, activity on the part of the object and passivity on the part of the power.[55] If we could use the Kantian vocabulary to designate the passivity of our senses toward their objects, we would say that the latter are *a priori forms* with which our powers must be informed in order that they may be able to elicit a determinate act of knowledge. Their passivity is an objective indetermination, not a subjective or dynamic one, since it is of the very nature of a power to operate. That, moreover, is what explains the quasi-infinite amplitude of our cognoscitive powers: *a priori* forms or objects can be indefinitely multiplied[56]; numerically identical, dynamically the same, and subjectively unchanged, the same sense is always there to receive these *a priori* forms and, having received them, to live them or give them to the immanent life of the knowing subject.[57]

¶ *The Causality of the Object.* We have distinguished, within cognitive activity, the act of knowing that springs from the dynamism of the power, from its interior wealth, and the *preparation* for this activity in the case of a power lacking the formal or objective element that determines its operation. The question that comes up immediately is this: Whence comes the form to specify the passive or indeterminate power; how is this communication between the efficient principle and the formal principle of this efficiency effected? St. Thomas answers: Outer reality provides the form and the communication takes place through a singularly penetrating osmosis, in the course of which the thing gives its inner wealth and the knowing power gives its existence to the wealth that exterior things have brought it. The synthesis of these two gifts constitutes the dynamic being that is the knower as such.

Since whatever operates must in some way be united to the object in relation to which it operates, it follows of necessity that *this something extrinsic which is the object of the soul's operation,* must be related to the soul in a twofold manner. First inasmuch as this something extrinsic has a natural aptitude to be united to the soul and *to be by its likeness in the soul.* In this way there are two kinds of powers . . . namely the sensitive in regard to the less common object, the sensible body; and the intellectual, in regard to the most common object, universal being.[58]

Thus, the factors in the causality of the object are, on the one hand, reality's aptitude to be united to the soul, which presupposes the soul's own aptitude to enter into this union, an aptitude whose proper name is passive power. On the other hand, there is the capacity to contract this union, *to be by its likeness in the soul.* We shall examine this communication of outer reality to the soul, first in its natural aptitude for communicating itself, and then in the mode of communication itself.

¶ *Reality's Aptitude to Give or Communicate Iself.* To understand the different texts affirming outer reality's capacity to fecundate the human soul, we must go back to the most fundamental principles in the metaphysics of being, for *operation follows being,* and the causality of the object is a part of the dynamism of being.[59] In Thomism, being is act, it is even act par excellence. Only by reference to being do the complex components of the real deserve the title of act.[60] Now, it is of the *very nature of act to communicate itself,* and therein lies the metaphysical explanation of the axiom, *unumquodque agens agit secundum quod in actu est.*[61] In order to communicate itself, a thing must be. But by their forms, things have a limited act; therefore, it is by their form that they communicate themselves in a determinate way to our passive powers, from which communication knowledge results, for every form is, of itself, communicable because it is act.[62] It is not, to use J. de Finance's apt phrase, "energy being deployed but perfection being communicated."[63] And this self-giving to which form tends naturally cannot be done except insofar as the form is, for to exist is form's act, just as form is the act of matter.[64] Exterior things can exercise their causality upon the soul only to the degree that they exist and according to the mode of their existence. Since their existence is determined by their form or quiddity, things exert their causality only within the limits of their formal actuality, i.e., accordng to the form that makes them to be what they are, which determines them within a particular category of being. Because things *are*, they are causes and can therefore become objects. Because they are *sensible*, they are sensibly causes; therefore, they can become the object of sensation. Such is the ontological background for the causality of the object.

¶ *The Mode of Communication of the Object as Sensible.*   In order that the human soul be perfectly equipped to live or know, it must first be things. If these things are not present, then they must be made present to the soul, they must communicate themselves to the soul. How will this be done on the part of the being that exercises its causality or gives itself to the soul? This being is actually *physical* and actually *sensible;* therefore, it will have a double causal action upon man: one in the physical order through the intermediation of an *actio* in the physical sense, a transitive action, the other in the spiritual order by a sort of formal measurement of organic power by the likeness of the thing-object.

It is to be noted that a body has two kinds of action: one is in accord with what is proper to a body, that is it acts *through movement* (for this is appropriate to a body, as a moved thing it moves and acts); but it has another action, according as it touches upon the order of immaterial substances and participates somewhat of their mode—just as it is customary for inferior natures to participate something of the property of a higher nature, for instance certain animals participate in something like prudence which is proper to humans. Now, this second kind of action is not for the purpose of changing matter but is directed to the *diffusion of a likeness of the form* . . . and it is received from the thing into sense or intellect.[65]

This Thomistic theory of the twofold activity of corporeal things makes many philosophers, even Scholastics,[66] smile, and it obviously seems utterly ridiculous to all idealist philosophers and to modern scientists who tend more and more to identify the physical with the

mental universe.[67] When physical reality is defined exclusively by
the framework of instrumental experimentation, it clearly excludes
all that is not due to action-passion, or physical movement, and the
world of sensation becomes *primitive frames of thought* that the
scientist cannot reject but whose inanity is obvious to him.[68] It even
excludes every concept of the individual and every concept of
existence having any meaning other than a mathematical one.[69]

When a scientist, in the name of his science and its formal limitations, rejects aspects of the real that cannot come within the orbit
of his investigation, we can only respect his honesty and vigorous
regard for objects. But a philosopher is not, in the modern sense of
the word, a scientist, and if he wants to accept the conclusions of
modern science, he can do so only to the precise degree that these
conclusions can come within another experience: philosophical experience: which is in no way instrumental. Philosophical experience
establishes the existence of physically subsisting things that have
two wholly different actions upon us, physical and psychological.
These two actions of physical reality are experiential facts, the
first of which is instrumentally verifiable, and the second can be
verified by self-awareness and reflection. Let us try to see how St.
Thomas makes use of this twofold action of things to show the
outer world's objective causality upon our sensibility:

Now, immutation is of two kinds, one *natural*, the other *spiritual*. Natural
immutation takes place when the form of that which causes the immutation is received according to its *natural* being into the thing immutated,
as heat is received into the thing heated. But spiritual immutation takes
place when the form of what causes the immutation is received according
to a *spiritual* mode of being into the thing immuted, as the form of color
is received into the pupil which does not thereby become colored.[70]

Our body is therefore the object of this double causality exerted
by the outer world of which the body is itself a part. As physical,
it is subject to the laws of the energy of matter and its resulting
mutations. As *sensitized* physical, it has the natural aptitude to receive
this second causality, belonging to the spiritual or intentional order,
which bodies exert in virtue of their participation in and submission
to spiritual forces that organize the physical world and explain its

harmonious motion. Do all senses undergo this double *immutatio*, and is physical immutation the necessary condition of intentional immutation? St. Thomas holds that it is not, for reasons springing from the experimental physics of his day.[71] Today scientists tell us that every sensory act is necessarily accompanied by a physical mutation of the organism on the part of exterior reality. However, this universalization of physical mutation in every sensation only adds vigor to the Thomistic theory of the *duplex immutatio*, for if physical movement accompanies every sensation, it is not its cause but only its condition, just as respiration conditions human life but does not cause it.[72] The true cause of sensation is the *mutatio spiritualis:*

Now, for the operation of the senses, *a spiritual immutation is required,* whereby an intention of the sensible form is effected *in the sensible organ.* Otherwise, if a natural immutation alone sufficed for the sense's action, all natural bodies would have sensation when they undergo alteration.[73]

¶ *Physical Causality of the Object.* There is no need for us to linger over the empirical explanation of the mode of physical causality that St. Thomas borrowed from Aristotle, or on the role of light, media, and physical constitution of the organism. All that relates to experimental science and varies in relation to the instruments for measurement, discovered through the ages. What we must observe is the fact of physical or organic causality, man's only point of contact with the physical world around him, assuring his knowledge the physical and ontological realism that distinguishes it from all idealisms, gives it its properly human value, and prevents it from becoming epistemological angelism. The individual physical existent is the real cause of sensory knowledge in philosophy, whereas it is one of the first castoffs of scientific knowledge,[74] because it is unknowable as such. Philosophical experience of the singular is basic to all other experience and to our way of speaking about it:

Since sense has a sure apprehension of its proper sensible object, it is a common usage of speech, when we understand something for certain, to say that we *sense* it. And hence it is that we use the word *sententia.* . . . For we have experience when we know *singulars* through the senses.[75]

. . . The senses indeed do not know being, except under the condition of *here* and *now*.[76]

The sense grasps the singular in this way because the latter exerts on it a physical causality that bears with it a psychological or intentional causality.[77]

Thus, the physical individual acts on our organic powers because it exists. But this action is determined just as its act of existing is determined; the same interior principle of determination determining the singular's act of existing determines the causality of the singular. Since this principle of determination is substantial form or total essence, the action of physical things is, in short, limited by the limitation of the singular existent's own nature. Since, on the other hand, no substance is immediately operative but acts only through the intermediation of its powers, the physical thing acts upon human beings through the immediate causality of its accidents:

Action belongs to the composite, as does being; for to act belongs to what exists. Now the composite has being substantially through the substantial form; and it *operates by the power which results from the substantial form*. Hence an active accidental form is to the substantial form of the agent as the power of the soul is to the soul. . . .[78]

That the accidental form is a principle of action is due to the substantial form. Therefore the substantial form is the *first principle of action, but not the proximate principle*.[79]

Therefore, between the knower and the physical thing there are correlative contacts of action and passion, establishing between them relations of the second mode, real relations in the order of movement[80] by which the knower is a recipient (*patiens*) in the full sense of the word. So rigorous is this starting point for all sensation, in Thomism, that we could truthfully say, "I sense, therefore outer reality exists," just as Descartes was obliged to affirm his existence in the very exercise of his thought. These physical relations between the knower and the outside world are set up through the intermediation of the human organism on the one side, and through that of the accidents of physical things on the other. What are these accidents that have the power of physical mutation on the human organism?

Not every accident has in itself a power of immutation, but only qualities of the third species, according to which there can be alteration. Therefore only such qualities are the object of the senses, because *the senses are affected by the same things whereby inanimate bodies are affected*.[81]

In this passage St. Thomas definitely separates his conception of the physical and our knowledge of it from the whole modern scientific theory, for which quantity is the formal principle of measure. In Thomism the entire field of sensation is given over to the causality of *quality;* every sensation is qualitative because its cause is quality, even in the purely physical order. And it is St. Thomas' metaphysics of the act, not, as is often believed, the experimental science of his day, that compels him to give to the individual, as physical cause of sensation, a formal and qualitative aspect. Only act causes, and only form or quality is act, apart from the act of existing that completes it:

Every form, as such, is the principle of action like to itself; hence, since color is a certain form, it possesses of itself the capacity to cause its likeness in a medium.[82]

What is said of color is equally true of all sensible qualities or qualities of the third type, which are the formal structure of physical causality, whereas quantity conditions this causality but does not constitute it. However, St. Thomas in no way neglects the influence of quantity upon the causality of physical qualities. He synthesizes his teaching in his theory of the *sensibilia communia*, whose importance is primary for the complete objectivity of sensation, particularly for that which is furnished us by the internal senses. Here is a rather complete text in which he sets forth the essential of this complementary aspect of *quantity* in the physical causality that things have on our organic powers:

Size, shape and the like, which are called *common sensibles* are midway between *accidental* sensibles and *proper* sensibles, which are the object of the senses. For the proper sensibles first, and of their very nature, affect the senses since they are the qualities that cause alteration. But the *common sensibles are all reducible to quantity.* As to *size* and *number* it is clear that they are species of quantity. Shape is a quality about quantity, since the nature of shape consists in fixing the bounds of magnitude.

Movement and *rest* are sensed according as the subject is affected in one or more ways, in the magnitude of the object or of its local distance, as in the movement of growth or of locomotion, or again, according as it is affected in some sensible qualities, as in the movement of alteration; and thus to sense movement and rest is, in a way, to sense one thing and many.

Now, quantity is the proximate subject of the qualities that cause alteration, as surface is of color. Therefore the common sensibles *do not move the sense first and of their own nature*, but by reason of sensible quality; as the surface by reason of color. Yet they are not accidental sensibles, for *they produce a certain diversity in the immutation of the senses*. For sense is immuted differently by a large and by a small surface.[83]

Physical qualities are thus the immediate principles of the real's causal action upon us. However, since these qualities exist only in quantity, the latter conditions the qualities' efficacy by modifying their action according to circumstances of place, dimension, aspect, motion, or rest—circumstances that depend upon the very nature of concrete quantity.[84] The quantified and qualified individual thing exerts its causality upon the human organism by the totality of its accidents that modify its action according as the thing-cause is itself conditioned by extension, distance, number, exterior appearance, rest, and mobility. Existing substance is always the cause, but its causality is exercised in relation to the quantitative and qualitative *dispositions* that (by quantity and exterior figure) reveal the stable elements of its inner nature[85] as well as its dynamic and formal aspect (by the qualities characterizing it).

This *physical* union of the human being and the physical thing through the instrumentality of quantified qualities is a first step in the preparation of sense knowledge. By this union, man and that which is other than he no longer constitute two separate realities extrinsic to one another, but are respectively implied in a causal motion that in some way identifies them, since *action is in the recipient* and constitutes its perfection as recipient.[86]

In this first physical and physiological aspect of the union of man and exterior things—an aspect preliminary to the immanent act of sensing—sensation falls under scientific analysis, which must take into acount the laws of motion, action, and reaction ruling the relations of the exterior world with our organism.[87] The action of exterior reality upon the recipient organ occurs in space, subject to the conditions set by concrete quantity, which divides or separates man from his object; the only point of contact is the motion in which the action of the thing blends with the passion of the organism. From this flows the multiplicity of the senses, whose number is equal to the possibilities of specific action by the exterior real upon the physiological living being. From this also flows the limitations of each sense, for if the exterior thing is not powerful enough to act upon the sense, and if the sense is not capable of receiving the action of that thing, then contact between the two is impossible and there is no sensation.[88]

¶ *Intentional Causality of the Object.* This physical action of the object upon human physiology by means of qualitative and local movement is not sufficient to explain sensation, for it is only its material aspect, a sort of excitant for the vital act, a *sine qua non* condition instrumental to another causality, the causality that St. Thomas calls *immutatio spiritualis:*

Now for the operation of the senses, a spiritual immutation is required whereby an *intention* of the sensible form is effected in the sensible organ.[89]

Just what is this *immutatio spiritualis* which the object causes and of which our organic powers are the beneficiaries? To understand the accuracy and necessity of this bit of Thomistic epistemology, whose existence seems so strange to our modern minds, we must recall what has been said about the nature of knowledge itself, its immanent character.[90] At the same time, we must not forget the passive character of our sensory powers.[91] To know is to live the real *because one is the real!* Granting that we are not naturally this real that we live (a fact attested by our absolute ignorance at birth), we are constrained by each cognitive experience to conclude that *we have become* that which we were not, since one must be in order to know. The word *immutatio* translates this becoming that is a necessary presupposition about knowledge. Since, however, this *being-the-object* prior to knowledge can in no way be identified with our physical or material being (which hinders and does not cause knowledge), this *mutatio* can only be described in terms other than physical transformation, and that is why we speak of a *mutatio spiritualis:*

Knowing beings are distinguished from non-knowing beings in that the latter possess only their own form, whereas the knowing being is naturally adapted to have also the form of some other thing, *for the species of the thing known is in the knower.* It is manifest that the nature of a non-knowing being is more contracted and limited; whereas the nature of a knowing being has a greater amplitude and extension. . . . Now the contraction of a form comes through the matter. . . . Therefore it is clear that the immateriality of a thing is the reason why it is cognitive, and that according to the mode of immateriality is the mode of cognition. Hence it is said in *De Anima* that plants do not know because of their materiality. But sense is cognitive *because it can receive species free from matter.*[92]

From the aspect of *immutatio spiritualis*, the object's causality does not *transform* the knowing subject but *informs* it, gives it an existence higher than its own, opens it to another form, to a nature other than its own. It breaks its ontological bonds not "by a desperate leap outside its own form,"[93] a leap by which the knower would lose himself in another, but by enriching the knower with everything it is not, by a sort of mysterious osmosis, a transfusion during which the object becomes a donor of its own form, the sensible and intelligible capital that constitutes all it has.

Spiritual immutation is thus opposed to physical immutation as immanent action is opposed to transitive action,[94] as a spiritual agent to a physical agent, and as an imperfect being is opposed to the perfect. By this spiritual immutation or becoming, exterior things exercise on our cognitive powers a causality of exemplary type; it becomes the measure of the power's activity, the form participated by this power, the form by which everything issuing from this cognitive power will be completely specified. The least inadequate parallel we can draw between the nature of spiritual immutation and physical immutation is the one St. Thomas sets up between creation and change as production of a new being. Just as creative activity produces all being without any becoming, that is, in an absolute

simultaneity of beginning and end without any sort of time interven-
ing between the start and term of the act, so is it in the order of
production by the intentional form:

In things which are made *without motion,* to become and to be already
made are simultaneous, whether such making is the term of motion, as
illumination, or whether it is not the term of motion as the concept *is
being made in the mind and is made* at the same time. In things of this
kind, what is being made, is; but when we speak of *their being made,* we
mean that they are from another, and that previously they did not exist.[95]

Just as creation is not an action but a relation, so intentional
mutation does not belong to the efficient order, or to the predica-
ment of action-passion, but to the order of the relation of measure
to measured:

Creation posits something in the created thing *only according to creation:* for what is created is not made by motion or change. . . .[96]

Indeed creation is not a change but is the very dependence of the existing
being of a created thing on the principle by which it is established. So it is
in the genus of relation.[97]

When we were studying the notion of object, we saw that the
latter belongs precisely to the third mode of relation, the relation
of dependence.[98] Its causality is exemplar in type, just as is the
causality of Divine Knowledge in creation. The object is a measure
immanent to the cognitive power, which makes the latter really
dependent upon exterior reality but leaves exterior reality supremely
indifferent to the knower, to whom it gives its soul or form.[99]

¶ The Nature of the Intentional Species, or the Thing's Gift to the Soul

Knowing beings are distinguished from non-knowing beings in that the
latter possess only their own form; whereas the knowing being is naturally
adapted to have also the form of some other thing, *for the species of the
thing known is in the knower.*[100]

Every knower as such is *multiform;* self-awareness of cognitive
activity reveals this secret to every human being. We must now
explain the nature of this multiformity that seems to contradict one
of the fundamental laws of being, which is that every being is one,

i.e., itself and no other, and is opposed to everything that is not itself. But knowledge consists precisely in being oneself *plus the other*, without any fusion or transformation of self or other. It requires an unimaginable unity within an absolute distinction. What is this unity and this distinction, and what must be the nature of this unifying reality that informs but does not transform? This is the particular mystery of the *species intentionalis*, the keystone to the arch of Thomistic epistemology, without which neither the distinctive immanence of the cognitive act nor its objectivity can be explained.

In order to conceive (not *imagine*) the mysterious nature of the *species intentionalis*, we must first have an exact notion of the role it plays in cognitive activity. We must remember that knowledge is an immanent act, therefore wholly interior to the being that is its principle.[101] Neither must we forget that our powers are passive and need to be fecundated by the object before they can exercise their immanent activity.[102] Finally, we must keep well in mind the absolute necessity of our borrowing their riches from exterior things without impoverishing them or changing their natural being. In short, in order that there be an act of knowledge, we must first *be* what we will know.

The knower and the thing known are not related as agent and patient . . . but as two items out of which there develops *one principle of cognition*; and so, contact between the knower and the knowable thing does not suffice for knowledge, instead, the knowable thing must be united as a form with the knower, either through the essence of the object or through its likeness.[103]

But we must be it in such a way that the physical thing's existence in us in no way alters the nature of that thing:

A thing is known in the way in which it is *represented* in the knower and *not* as it *exists* in the knower. The likeness existing in the power of the knower is a principle by which a thing is known but not according to the *esse* it has in the knower. . . .[104]

The exterior thing does not therefore become an object or knowable in that it borrows our existence, but in that this borrowing of our existence is not detrimental to its function of *representing* the other, that it does not prevent it from being a *likeness* of a thing which is opposed to what we are by the very fact of its opposition. St. Thomas illustrates this teaching by an ingenious comparison:

If there were one corporeal statue representing many men, it is evident that the image or species in the statue would have singular and proper being as it exists in this matter; but it would have a *ratio* of community, by means of which it would represent many in a general manner.[105]

The *species intentionalis* (sensible as well as intellectual) thus has singular existence from the fact that it is ours, that it informs our power; it is a psychological accident. But as *similitudo* or *imago* of an exterior thing, it has only one function, that of representing, of making us to be the other without ceasing to be ourselves. To bring it about that the knower and the known be *one on condition that they remain identical with themselves* is the mysterious secret defining the nature of the *species intentionalis* and governing its structure. To understand this structure on which depends the existence of knowledge and its objectivity, we shall very briefly consider three notions used continually by St. Thomas to explain the possibility and nature of sensible and intellectual knowledge.

 ¶ *The Species Is an Intentional Being.* The existence of intentional being is a metaphysical necessity for every realist philosophy. In Thomism, intentional being plays such an important a role that to suppress it is tantamount to completely suppressing the Angelic Doctor's doctrinal synthesis. Here is the opening paragraph of a work on intentional being:[106] "The theory of intentionality plays an essential role in realist metaphysics. It alone makes possible a coherent explanation of the world's exteriority and man's knowledge of it; ultimately, too, it makes possible a coherent explanation of God's transcendence and how it is that a finite intellect knows Him."

Again, here is how one of the most profound commentators upon the thought of St. Thomas propounds the necessity for the existence of intentional being:

There are two kinds of beings. Some are created primarily in order to exist, though perhaps secondarily they may represent others: these we call things (*res*). Others are primarily created in order to represent others: we call these intentions of things, and species—either sensible or intelligible. Now the necessity for granting these two genera of realities lies in the fact that the knowing nature must be not only itself but other things, and the intellective nature must be all things. . . . Nor can the natures of things in themselves exist in the knowing power (for a stone does not exist in the soul); nor can the knowing power itself, in its solitary and finite substance, be of such great excellence that it possess within itself the means whereby the natures of knowable things in their proper *rationes* may be assimilated to it. Hence the conclusion remains, since neither the being of the knowing nature is the *ratio* of the knowable things, nor is the natural being of the knowable things present in itself in the cognitive power, therefore it was necessary for nature to create intentional being, whereby the cognitive power might be its objects.[107]

In this commentary upon Thomistic doctrine we revert to the general context in which we stated the epistemological problem.[108] Knowledge, we said, was invented by the Creator to remedy the finite and limited character of certain creatures and to permit them to imitate divine infinity. Since this infinity could not occur in the order of *esse naturae*, the Creator had to invent another mode of being, which is *esse intentionale*. The existence of intentional being is metaphysically necessary to account for the universe of knowledge, of which it is, as it were, the objective reverse, whereas the cognitive powers are the right side:

The cognitive and the intentional are not distinguished as two orders but rather as concurring in the perfection of one order, that of cognitive natures: because the intentional is the intrinsic complement of the cognitive.[109]

Intentional being is not a sort of logical being invented by human reason, a sort of hypothesis to account for facts. It is a creature of God, intended to expand the limited being of some of His creatures so that they might, without being God (which would be absurd), become the whole universe, or one or another of its aspects.[110]

Although a *species* is an intentional being, not every intentional being is a species, for intentionality is necessary not only in the order of representation, to make the exterior world present to the soul, but also in the efficient and final order, to make present the motivating and attracting cause. This is why St. Thomas often uses the word *intentio* to mean the act that the principal efficient cause produces in the instrumental cause, as well as the *a priori* act that the good or end sows in the complete being in order to set it off, by a series of activities, toward the possession of that which will perfect it.[111] These two other aspects of intentional being accompany the species or external thing that has become immanent to the soul; they enable it to play its role of representing, but do not constitute it. Therefore, we must penetrate the nature of intentional being more deeply in order to discover its inner structure.

¶ *The Species Is an Intentional Being-Image.* We have just seen that the typical function of the species is to *represent*, to educe a new presence. The exterior thing present in the physical world, without losing its physical mode, acquires another type of presence in the soul it informs, and this new mode of presence is called representation. However, there are different ways of representing, for some representations are but traces, whereas others are images.

Every effect, in some degree represents its cause, but diversely. For some effects represent only the causality of the cause (its existence), but not its form; as smoke represents fire. Such a representation is called a *trace;* for a trace shows that someone has passed by, but not who it is. Other effects represent the cause in terms of *a likeness of its form* . . . as a statue of Mercury represents Mercury; and this is called the representation of *image*.[112]

One of these modes of representing leaves us completely ignorant of the nature it represents, whereas the other reveals its likeness. Since species is always defined in terms of formal or natural likeness, it belongs to the second way of representing, the one that St. Thomas calls *imago* and describes in the following text:

The idea of image includes likeness. Still, not any kind of likeness suffices for the nature of image, but only likeness of *species*, or at least of some specific sign. For we see that the species of different animals are of different figures, but not of different colors. Hence if the color of anything is depicted on a wall, this is not called an image unless the figure is likewise depicted. But neither the likeness of species nor that of figure is enough for an image, for it requires also the *idea of origin*. . . . Therefore, for a true image it is required that (a) one thing *proceed* from another (b) be *like* to it (c) in species, or at least in specific sign.[113]

According to this description, the image has three characteristics: *a*) it originates in another, *b*) it imitates or copies this other, *c*) this imitation of its model or exemplar must copy the model's formal elements or at least its specific appearance. This third characteristic gives rise to two kinds of image, perfect and imperfect. *A perfect image* imitates both the true specific nature and the appearance of its original, as a son resembles his father. *An imperfect image* imitates the outer appearance of its model without copying its real nature. Such is the case, for example, in works of art reproducing only outer appearance, "as the image of the king in a silver coin."[114]

To terminate this inquiry into the notion of *image*, we must establish the necessary connection between this notion and that of *species*. The latter is an image if it naturally possesses the three characteristics of an image; that is, *a*) if it springs from a principle or cause that is its exemplar, *b*) if it is a likeness of this cause, *c*) if this likeness belongs to the specific or essential order. Does the *species sensibilis* have these three notes with respect to the thing it presents to the soul so that the latter may perform a sensory act?

¶ *The* Species Sensibilis *Is an Image Because It is Caused by the Thing.* The problem of the origin of the *species sensibilis* has not been so controversial as has that of the intelligible species, which crops up every time the existence of the nature of the agent intellect is discussed.[115] Yet it entails particular difficulties by reason of the alteration that the physical action of material things entails, for which the materiality of things cannot account. That is why, as soon as man discerned the distinction between physical alteration and intentional activity,[116] the problem of the original cause of this activity arose. Some explained it in terms of the organism's vital reaction to the physical action of things, by virtue of the principle, *quidquid recipitur ad modum recipientis recipitur*[117]; others had recourse to a *sensus agens* whose function was to produce a sensible species through the physical action of things upon our organism.

Neither of these solutions was accepted by St. Thomas, for they deprive human knowledge of the only experimental contact possible

between it and the physical universe by which it is nourished; they
destroy not only the objectivity of sensation but the objectivity of
all intellectual knowledge, which, in the final analysis, depends upon
the determining realism of our every sensation.[118] There remains but
one alternative, that the physical thing be the cause of the *species
sensibilis,* and that the external sense have no part in its production
but play a purely receptive role in this respect.[119] We need not
speak again of the mode of this causality, since that has already been
discussed; suffice it to say that in the doctrine of Thomas Aquinas
the sensible species has the first note essential to its function as image
of external reality—*it originates in it.*

¶ *The Sensible Species Is an Image Because It Is a Likeness of
the Thing.* Likeness is an inferior form of identity. By identity
a thing is one, that is, undivided in itself; if there are other entities,
identity makes this thing distinct from all that it is not, opposes it to
everything that is not it. If we suppose that this unity of identity is
accompanied by poverty, that it stamps a being's nature with an
indelible seal but, by that very fact, deprives it of all other riches
existing outside itself, how then can that being escape this poverty
and borrow from the riches of the things surrounding it? Only one
strategy is possible, which is to imitate the diverse riches of outer
things by copying them more or less faithfully either by means of
the thing's own resources or by borrowing from another being, by
forcing it in some way to give, not what it is in itself (for that would
destroy it), but to give some aspects of its nature, possession of which
would set up between the recipient and donor a certain relation of
unity. *This unity is called similitude or likeness.*[120] This notion of
likeness is the key to the arch of Thomistic metaphysics, for by its
means is made possible the unity of the universe without the destruction of the diversity of things; by it God can create without identifying Himself with creatures, and divine immanence and transcendence can be simultaneously affirmed without contradiction.[121] Key
to the metaphysical arch, likeness is also key to the arch of epistemology, since to know is to be the other without losing one's identity
or destroying the identity of the other in any way.

The *sensible species* is precisely this gift which the physical thing
makes to our soul, a gift by which the species penetrates within us

because it is a likeness representing the donor. If the latter is singular, so is its likeness; if it is spiritual, its gift is of like nature:

The knowledge of every knower is measured by the mode of the form which is the principle of knowledge. For the sensible species in the sense is the *likeness* of only one individual thing, and can give the knowledge of only one individual. But the intelligible species in our intellect is the *likeness* of the thing as regards its specific nature which is participable by infinite particulars . . . the intelligible species of our intellect is the *likeness* of man, not as to the individual principles, but as to the principle of the species.[122]

It must nevertheless be noted that this likeness, which the thing gives to the soul, is not a likeness in the order of physical or natural existence, but in the order of intentional form, an order that escapes the transforming and therefore destructive laws of quantified matter:

The *likeness of nature* is not a sufficient principle of knowledge. Otherwise, what Empedocles said could be true, that the soul needs to have the nature of all in order to know all. But knowledge requires that the likeness of the thing known be in the knower as a kind of form in the knower. . . .[123]

The *likeness* through which we understand is the *species* of the thing known in the knower. Hence, a thing is prior in being known, not according to the *likeness of its nature* to the knowing power, but according to its agreement with the proper object of this power.[124]

Since the likeness or representative character of the sensible species enters into the very nature itself,[125] we must therefore conclude that it has the second note essential to an image as such. We need only establish that this likeness is specific to be able to identify species and image.

⁋ *The Species Is an Image Because It Is a Specific Likeness of the Sensible Real.* From the lexicographical point of view, the word *species* reveals the answer to this question, for the word *specific* comes from species and means that which is most fundamental in a thing.[126] However, we do not need this linguistic prop to establish our proof, for every description of species, sensible as well as intelligible, presents it as a formal aspect of reality, a specific representation whether of an aspect or of the whole thing. To have their true meaning, these passages must be read in the epistemological context proper to St. Thomas, that of a knowledge-cure for the ontological limits characterizing every created being.

By these limits every creature is and can be only itself. If it wishes to imitate God, it must be able to destroy its own specific and individual frontiers without destroying itself, or becoming God. Only Divine Wisdom could invent an ersatz for His infinity which enables His creatures to imitate divinity while it respects the intangible laws separating His being and ours. Intentional being, on one hand, and the very nature of our cognitive powers, on the other, constitute this ersatz.[127] In this context the function of intentional species is to burst through the creature's own limits by introducing into it that which characterizes things other than itself. But what characterizes a being is its nature, for by it the thing is itself and distinct from every other thing. Thus, the role of the species is to bring into the knower the nature of things other than himself and thereby to enrich the knower's own poverty. To fulfill its role as substitute, the species must therefore faithfully reproduce the nature of the thing it represents. If the species is not an image, the knowledge resulting from it could never remedy created finitude, never be instrumental in imitating the infinite amplitude of Uncreated Being.

Creationist metaphysics makes all reality dependent upon God, nothing escapes divine causality. Matter, physical energy, the quantitative and qualitative properties of the beings composing our universe, all these are created by God and, in a certain respect, represent one aspect of His perfection.[128] The consequence of such a doctrine is that even sensible knowledge is divine imitation, and the role of the sensible species is to re-create, in the human soul, the most common or most imperfect of the imitations that came forth from God, but which are nevertheless a vestige of the Creator's unlimited magnificence. Progressively to capture these traces of divine exemplarity and to integrate them into the finite being which is man so that he may reconstitute the world of substances from their specific accidents—such is the final purpose of sense knowledge and the mensural unit to which every sensible species must conform if it would not be unfaithful to its nature and to the intention of the Divine Artisan.

But the specific accidents of material things are grasped in their existential individuality[129] by the ensemble of our sensory powers and therefore constitute the structure of the intentional species itself. Since specific accidents all belong to the order of quality, and sensible quality is always the quality of a determined quantity whose act and form it is, there exists a sort of hylemorphism in the world of accidents as exists in the order of physical substance. This accidental hylemorphism is, moreover, the proper effect of substantial hylemorphism[130] and the only natural path leading man to the comprehension of the nature of a thing. Therefore, to the exact degree that specific accidents are simultaneously grasped in their qualitative and quantitative aspects, they will also be exterior images of the reality hidden beneath sensible appearances, a sort of shadow theatre projected into the soul by the dynamism of sensible things and serving as a starting point from which the human intellect can proceed to the heart of the substance of beings. Such is the content of the species of our different sensory powers; the species gives this content to our senses by vivifying them in some way through this form image of exterior appearances, an image whose role is to enrich an ontological poverty, whose only *raison d'être* is to beg for the treasure the image brings it.[131] The sensible species is an *image* precisely in this sphere of the physical universe, since its role is to start human knowledge off and, so to speak, to sow the soul with the seeds of things that are specific accidents[132] so that they may germinate and, like the grain of mustard seed, become the mighty trees of the substance of things, trees whose progressive accumulation will produce that great forest of things living with the life of the human intellect because they were first lived by the Creative Intelligence.[133]

❡ *Conclusion on the Causality of the Sensible Object.* It would be interesting immediately to examine the effect produced in our powers of sense knowledge by this causality and by the thing in its exterior accidents, but this would involve an analysis of the act of knowledge itself, whereas our purpose in this chapter is to study what is prerequisite to the object for the existence of sensation and intellection as immanent activities. Before examining the intelligible object and its informative causality with respect to the passivity of our intellect, let us summarize the results of our metaphysical inquiry into the causality exercised by the physical real upon our sensorial powers.

(1) We know by experience that man is born absolutely destitute of the objects necessary for a sensory act. This destitution is called ignorance, and this ignorance is complete for each and every one of our sensory powers.[134]

(2) It is another fact of experience that we need the presence of physical things and a minimum of organic health in order to use these same sensorial powers. If the thing were not present to us, or the organism defective, sensation would be impossible.

(3) Now, by comparing these two facts with our inner experience of the act of knowledge itself, we observe that there is a sort of contradiction between this activity's immanent character and our total dependence upon an exterior object. For to know, one must *be* the known; but we are born destitute of every object. Therefore, to fill this void, objects must exercise a presential causality upon our soul, and the soul must be able to receive this causality. These two consequences follow inevitably from the three above-mentioned experiences: the fact of our ignorance, the need for the presence of exterior objects, and the inward character of the act of sensation. These two causalities are developed in the two philosophical theses we have just been studying: *the passivity of our cognitive powers*, and *the causality of objects*.

(4) The passivity of our sensorial powers and the causality of objects are correlative; that is, they cannot exist without one another, and the mode or modes of passivity of our sensorial powers govern the mode or modes of objective causality. Since our sensorial powers are at once physical and psychical, they have a double passivity; consequently, the causality of the object must be exercised in a double mode: that of *physical action*, experimentally observable and measurable by appropriate instruments,[135] and that of *intentional diffusion*, a sort of exemplar causality that things exert upon the soul, writing their signature on it as in an autograph album huge enough to collect and indefinitely preserve the most diverse signatures. It belongs to the sensible species to exercise this intentional causality, because it is, itself, an intentional being, because it is the

authentic autograph that the diverse sensible aspects of the thing inscribe upon the different external senses, so that they may gradually penetrate to the very depths of the soul, complementing each other and reconstituting all the aspects of the physical substance that will become the field for intellectual activity.

(5) The sensible species is a mode of participation in physical being, and through it knowledge is no longer an absurdity but becomes a mysterious blossoming or self-extension of the knower as such. That is why the contemporary incomprehension of the nature and necessary function of intentional reality has deprived sense knowledge of all real objectivity and has reduced it to no more than a series of subjective phenomena, pragmatic in character and possessing an emotional value only.[136] The first goal of philosophical epistemology is therefore to restore intentional causality to the physical universe, to revivify the metaphysics of the sensible species shrouded in three centuries of derision and grotesque caricature. But this revaluation of the world of sensible qualities is impossible in a scientific context whose every effort is bent toward the quantification of physical energy, toward an instrumental unity of measurement in which diverse phenomena can be identified and exchange their diversity for statistical anonymity. Philosophical knowledge, on the contrary, seeks not the anonymity of a being but its originality, that which makes it to be itself and distinct from everything else. Conserving the diverse aspects of reality is as essential to the ideal of philosophical knowledge as the vision of unity or order of hierarchy in this multiplicity. But the sensible species are precisely the *singular* presence of physical things in the human soul, a singular presence multiplied according to the varying needs of the thing, because it is the proper effect of the thing's actuality, giving itself to the sense powers, which are made to receive it, just as it is made to give itself to them.

B. THE INTELLIGIBLE AS CAUSE OF INTELLECTION

We have seen in the first section of this chapter[137] that the object is not the thing considered as an absolute but as *relative* to the human soul, and that the particular character of this relation is to measure cognitive activity without being really modified by this measuring. We have also seen that the object's activity, or causality, of measurement is necessitated by the character of our knowing powers, which are wholly passive, that is, naturally devoid of the things that they were made to know,[138] so that knowledge can be begotten only after the fecundation of the powers by their object. Having examined the thing as measure of sensation, we shall now have to study it as *object or cause* of intellection. Here are the questions we shall try to answer:

(1) Can a material or physical thing be the object of intellection, that is, can it so measure our intellect inwardly as to enable it to produce its cognitive act?

(2) If the physical thing cannot, by itself, explain its causality upon the intellect, what factor must be present in the soul to account for noetic experience, and what is its role in constituting the material thing as an actual object, capable of measuring the intellect and fecundating it by this very mensuration?

¶ *Can Physical Reality Be the Measure of the Intellect?* Every man who is not a skeptic is convinced that he knows the outer world, therefore, that he is this outer world, since to know is first and foremost to be the object of one's knowledge. However, inasmuch as we are not naturally the physical universe that we purport to know, we must become it; it must give itself to us, be bountiful, nurture us, so to speak, with its body and soul. In analyzing the *sensibile*, the object of sensation, we observed that the exterior real lavishes its appearances upon us through its exterior causality upon each of our sensorial powers. Now, we shall inquire about how it can saturate us with its soul, that is, with its substance, by becoming the object of our intellectual knowledge.

Sense does not apprehend the essences of things, but only their outward accidents. In like manner neither does the imagination, for it apprehends only the likenesses of bodies. The intellect alone apprehends the essences of things. Hence it is said that the object of the intellect is *what a thing is*, regarding which it does not err.[139]

The object of the intellect is the nature of material things, of their accidents as well as of their substance; it is this nature that must somehow penetrate to the heart of our intellectual power and enrich it with everything the intellect does not itself possess. But how can a material thing be sufficiently penetrating to act upon an entirely spiritual power, since the agent must be nobler than the recipient and the degree of nobility is proportionate to the degree of spirituality.[140] If then the physical does not belong to the spiritual order, it cannot act upon it, or be its object, since, by definition, the object of a passive power is that which by nature moves and actualizes it.[141]

The metaphysical necessity of a natural correlation between the object of knowledge and the power of knowing is so evident to real thinkers that it gave birth to all the realist epistemologies of the ancients, particularly those of Plato and Aristotle, which were the source of all others, even the modern.[142] Here is a summary of this position concerning the relations between the intellect and its object:

Plato supposed that the forms of natural things subsisted apart from matter and consequently that they are intelligible: for a thing is actually intelligible from the very fact that it is immaterial. And he called such forms species or ideas. From a participation in these, he said that even corporal matter was formed, in order that individuals might be naturally established in their proper genera and species, and also that our intellect was *formed by such participation* in order to have knowledge of the genera and the species of things. But since Aristotle did not allow that the forms of sensible things exist apart from matter, and since forms existing in matter are not actually intelligible, it follows that the natures or forms of the sensible things which we understand *are not actually intelligible*. Now nothing is reduced from potentiality to act except by something in act, as the senses are made actual by what is *actually* sensible.[143]

Since actual intelligibility is denied to material things as such, we might think that they acquire it through intentional existence in our sensory powers, especially through existence in the imagination; here is St. Thomas' answer to this hypothesis:

Colors, as being in individual corporal matter, have the same mode of being as the power of sight, and therefore they can impress their own image on the eye. But phantasms, since they are the images of individuals and exist in corporal organs, have not the power, of themselves, to make an impression on the possible intellect.[144]

We are therefore faced with a dilemma: The proper object of the human intellect is the substance or nature of material things, and without this object all truly human knowledge is impossible.[145] But we have just seen that this object is not *actual*, which is to say that it is not actually intelligible and consequently cannot cause intellection because it does not have what it needs to exist in the soul *secundum esse animae* (which is the definition of the object as such).[146] Thus, we must either forego knowledge of the physical universe because it is not, in its concrete existence, intelligible or actually able to communicate itself to us, or else we must discover among the powers that nature has given us a source of intelligibility capable of acting as spiritual complement to physical reality and making it intelligible in act, i.e., actually able to inform our intellect with all its own riches. Such is the epistemological dilemma facing every philosopher who analyzes man's total noetic experience in trying to discover the causes that, to make it possible, necessarily pre-exist the fact of knowledge.

To summarize our argumentation so far: In order that human knowledge be a fact, two coprinciples are necessary—a power able to exercise this immanent activity and an object *actually* determining its operation. But our intellectual power does not possess any of the objects for which it is made, as is proved by the complete ignorance in which we are born. Therefore, previous to cognitive activity, the object must fecundate our knowing power and determine it to a definite act. In order that this fecundation take place, the object as such must exist, that is, it must be actually intelligible or immaterial. Such, however, is not the case, since none of the things in the physical universe, which are the proper object of the human intellect, enjoys any actual immateriality; therefore, they are actually unintelligible. Since we do experience the fact of intellectual knowledge, it must be that *that which was not intelligible became intelligible*. What, then, is able to superelevate physical reality to the immaterial order, and by what transforming activity is this superelevation accomplished?

¶ The Agent Intellect and the Constitution of the Intelligible in Act. The problem of the agent intellect is one of the essential articulations of realist philosophy, and the innumerable discussions to which it has given rise during two thousand years bear witness to the central position it holds in every epistemology based upon the metaphysics of causality. With Descartes and Kant the agent intellect disappears from philosophical discussions, to be replaced by speculations about innatism or the man-angel and about the *a priori* understanding or demiurgic man, *dator formarum.*[147] As soon as we reject Descartes' simplistic optimism and Kant's metaphysical pessimism in order to rediscover man—no longer as a caricature of an angel or a Demiurgos, but as a natural being who comes from God and must return to Him—we discern in man all that he needs to find his way to God, his beatitude.[148] In this context St. Thomas' principle is seen in its full worth: "The small intellectual light that is connatural to us suffices for our act of understanding."[149]

Here is what this principle means: Man does not create the things he knows, because he is neither God nor Demiurgos. Neither is he born completely equipped with the knowledge he will become aware of during his lifetime, for he is not a pure spirit. However, he does possess intellectual equipment, the most imperfect of all, yet sharing sufficiently in the divine intellect to understand the latter's work and through this work to come to some knowledge of its Author. The divine factor—connatural to the human soul and enabling it to transpose to a spiritual level the physical thing made immanent by the ensemble of sense powers—is the agent intellect.[150] Ours, the most imperfect of intellects, is created in a state of absolute indigence, but it is created with such mendicant power that the whole physical universe becomes a sort of welfare bureau, where the agent intellect collects the riches accumulated for us by the Creative Intellect in order to give them to the possible intellect, whose appetite is insatiable and whose assimilative capacity is infinite.

There is no other way to understand the need for the agent intellect and its noetic function than to study its nature as a spiritual power. Since it is revealed to us only in a distinctive activity that is intelligible only in relation to an object, we shall try to group the essential teachings concerning this mysterious factor of the human soul around three principal points: the *object*, the *operation*, and the *nature* of the agent intellect.

¶ *The Object of the Agent Intellect.* *The object of the agent intellect is the fruit of its own activity.* We have intellectual knowledge, that is, knowledge that surpasses the singular as such and grasps material things spiritually or immaterially without deforming them. But this experience of universality cannot be explained either by the nature of our intellect or possible intellect (a passive power devoid of its objects) or by the activity of its object, which does not exist since the intelligible, immaterial, or universal does not actually exist in things.[151] We have just seen that the agent intellect is the causal factor linking our intellect, devoid of its objects, with reality that, by itself, is incapable of being an object or intelligible. Consequently, *its object must be the term* of the productive activity of the intelligible as such; its object is *the fruit and not the cause* of its act, as was said of our cognitive powers.[152]

The necessity for admitting an agent intellect is due to this, that the natures of material things which we know are not immaterial and actually intelligible outside the soul. Consequently *it is necessary that there should be some power capable of rendering such* natures actually intelligible, and this power in us is called the agent intellect.[153]

What does it mean to make actually intelligible or immaterial the natures of material things that are already present in the soul through their accidents? First, let us rid our minds of any imagery tending to represent this transfer of natures as a sort of physical transformation, or, as an X-ray photograph leaving aside the accidents of material things to show us a skeletal residue of the natures of things. There can be no question of a transformation here, for as soon as natures are altered they disappear, that is, are replaced by another thing.[154] Neither is the X-ray comparison acceptable, for the residue of reality captured by the X-ray belongs to the same order as that which was left aside and pre-existed the work of the light waves; whereas the effect or object of the agent intellect's activity is a being belonging to a new order. It is *spiritual instead of material, intelligible instead of sensible*, and its name is *species* or *similitudo intelligibilis*.[155]

To grasp less inadequately the nature of the object of the agent intellect, we must first recall that the latter is an *active* power, unlike the possible intellect, which is a passive power. The distinction between these two kinds of powers can be explained in two different ways, first by the diversity of their end, which St. Thomas expresses in a simple formula whose meaning is profoundly analogical: "An active power is for action, while a passive power is for being."[156] The second difference stems from the object: The object of a passive power is its cause and exemplar, whereas the object of an active power is an effect, an *ens factum*,[157] a reality measured by the power that produces it and, therefore, resembling that power— which means that the intelligible species, fruit of the agent intellect, is spiritual and immaterial like its cause. Nevertheless, the similarity between species and agent intellect is far from being complete; otherwise, the species would be the intellect, since the intellect is the cause of the species. But the agent intellect's causality does not aim to produce an intellect inferior to itself but an intelligible in act, that is, a *way of being present* by which exterior things may fecundate the possible intellect and make it identical with what they are so that it may know them. Thus, like every nondivine active power, the agent intellect does not create the intelligible species out of nothing, but starts from pre-existing matter, which provides it with the diverse elements of things that our sensory powers have introduced into the soul and that have been synthesized in and by the phantasm.

The object of the agent intellect, the intelligible species, is thus the offspring of a marriage between the exterior thing, immanent to the soul by sense knowledge, and the superelevating activity of the spiritual faculty, which is conventionally called the agent intellect. Our only image, and a very deficient one it is, of this kind of causality is taken from vegetative life, from the phenomenon called nutrition, by which physical and chemical factors act as matter for a vital activity causing them to pass from a mode of physical existence to a biological mode. However, this phenomenon is a transformation and therefore obeys natural or physical laws,[158] whereas the procreation of the *species intelligibilis* from the phantasms is not a transformation of the phantasm or a transfer of the nature of things in the phantasm into the intellect, but the production of another likeness, a spiritual likeness of the exterior thing:

> But through the power of the agent intellect, there results in the possible intellect a certain *likeness* produced by the turning of the agent intellect towards the phantasms. This likeness *represents what is in the phantasms,* but includes only the specific nature. It is thus that the intelligible species is said to be abstracted from the phantasms: *not* that the identical form which previously was in the phantasm is subsequently in the possible intellect, as a body transferred from one place to another.[159]

¶ *The Nature of the Object of the Agent Intellect or of the Intelligible Species.* The nature of the intelligible species is determined by its final end, as is that of the sensible species. In order to represent exterior things authentically, it must have the characteristics essential to this kind of representation; that is, it must be an *intentional likeness* of the things it would make us know,[160] for we know intellectually to the same precise degree that things are present in our soul by their specific images, their intelligible species. Made to exercise specifying causality upon the activity of the possible intellect, whose natural vacuity or indetermination requires fecundation before producing its fruits, the intelligible species must be of the same nature as the intellect and the reality of which it is the likeness.

By the fact that the intelligible species, which is the form of the intellect and the principle of understanding, is the likeness of the external thing, it follows that the intellect may form an intention like that thing: for every thing produces operations of like nature with itself.[161]

We have seen that the intelligible species is the effect or fruit of the agent intellect, which explains why it is spiritual like the possible intellect to which it gives form. But how shall we explain that this fruit or effect of the agent intellect is an authentic likeness of the exterior thing? To solve this problem—which is a key problem, since the whole objectivity of human intellectual activity depends upon its solution—we must study the operation of the agent intellect, the matter upon which it works, and the typical determinations this matter imposes upon the activity of our intellectual light. This will be the object of our second paragraph, concerning the production of the intelligible in act by the agent intellect.

¶ *The Operation of the Agent Intellect.*   Everywhere in the works of St. Thomas we find him using two technical words for the causality proper to the agent intellect; these words are *abstrahere* and *illuminare*.[162] The first term, *abstrahere*, designates the dematerializing or spiritualizing action of the agent intellect with respect to things already pre-existing in phantasms, where they are actually sensible through their exterior accidents. The second word, *illuminare*, refers to the agent intellect's simultaneous causality upon phantasms and upon the intelligible species that informs our intellect and whose participated luminosity makes possible the whole ensemble of our intellectual operations.[163] A brief analysis of these two aspects of the agent intellect's causality will help us better to understand the nature of the agent intellect.

¶ *The Agent Intellect Abstracts Natures in the Phantasms.* The following description of the agent intellect's operations must be seen and experienced in the metaphysical context of human nature, which is composed of an organized body and spiritual soul, whence results the human person, the principle of each and every one of our activities. The *experience* of this composition and this unity is the starting point from which St. Thomas formulates his theory of the abstractive activity of the agent intellect:

In the opinion of Plato, immaterial substances are not only understood by us, but also the *objects* we understand first of all. . . . But in Aristotle's opinion, *which experience corroborates*, our intellect in its present state of life has a natural relation to the natures of material things; and therefore it can understand only by turning to the phantasms, as we have said above.[164]

Thus, the metaphysical bases upon which Creative Wisdom willed human epistemology to rest are the natural and necessary relations between man and the physical universe surrounding him, and, in man, the continual exchange that goes on between the sensory and spiritual powers of knowledge. The abstraction effected by the agent intellect is one of the privileged aspects of this exchange whose mystery is rooted in the mystery of the essential relations between flesh and spirit. Let us try to situate, in the ensemble of elements that go to make up human knowledge, the why and how of this association of the intellect and sensory powers, so that we may better understand the nature of the intelligible species, the joint product of the agent intellect and our sensibility. Here is a first description of the abstractive activity answering the needs peculiar to our human nature:

The object of knowledge is proportionate to the power of knowledge. Now there are three grades of cognitive powers. For one cognitive power, namely the sense, is the act of a corporal organ. And therefore the *object* of every sensitive power *is a form as existing in corporal matter;* and since such matter is the principle of individuation, therefore every power of the sensitive part can have knowledge only of particulars.

There is another grade of cognitive power which is neither the act of a corporal organ, nor in anyway connected with corporal matter. Such is the angelic intellect, the *object* of whose cognitive power is therefore *a form existing apart* from matter. . . .

But the human intellect holds a middle place; for it is not the act of an organ, and yet it is a power of the soul which is the form of the body. . . . And therefore *it is proper to it to know a form existing individually* in corporal matter, but *not as existing in this individual matter.*

But to know what is in individual matter, yet not as existing in such matter *is to abstract the form* from individual matter which is represented by the phantasms. Therefore we must need say that our intellect understands material things by abstracting from phantasms.[165]

This description is based upon noetic experience of and metaphysical insight into man's place in the universe. For, as a matter of fact, we do experience a twofold mode of knowledge, one of which puts us into the presence of individual things *as individual,* and the other presents us with the same things in an *abstract or immaterial* mode. What must be explained is how a single exterior thing is known in two different ways, since epistemology, as a philosophical discipline, must discover the causes of our twofold noetic experience. Although individual natures account for our knowledge of the singular, as we saw in analyzing the object of sensation,[166] they cannot explain the immaterial and abstract mode of our intellectual knowledge of the singular. Thus, there is the necessity for a spiritual cause whose action is, on the one hand, abstractive or spiritualizing, to enable material natures to fecundate the intellect, and whose activity, on the other hand, remains in direct contact with the individual existence of these same natures. This is the twofold aspect of the agent intellect's operation that St. Thomas described in the above-quoted text. The result of this operation is the *species intelligibilis*, a spiritual reality because it is the fruit of a spiritual power, and an intentional reality because it is the immaterial but authentic image of the thing's nature with all its essential notes. We shall have to examine the *how* of this abstractive causality that, without deforming the thing, gives it a mode of existing much superior to the one which it has outside the soul and in the cognitive powers of our sensibility, and which nevertheless needs phantasms to authenticate its operation.[167] In other words, what is the nature of this cooperation between the agent intellect and the phantasm for the production of the *species intelligibilis* resulting from abstraction?[168]

Here are the expressions St. Thomas uses to describe the abstraction performed by the agent intellect: *Facere intelligibilia in potentia esse intelligibilia in actu . . . facere objecta in actu . . . causare universale . . . facere phantasmata intelligibilia in actu.*[169] Obviously the first and the last of these four expressions are synonymous, since the phantasm is defined as an intelligible in potency, whereas the other two refer more immediately to the dematerializing effect of the agent intellect, that is, to the object of our knowledge insofar as it is intelligible, abstract, or made universal, and, as such, capable of formally *causing* the subsequent activity of the possible intellect. In short, the meaning of all four of these formulae is this: The agent intellect works with actually sensible matter and gives it the *form of intelligibility*, by means of which the content of the phantasm can actualize our intellect and enable it to produce its cognitional activity.[170] However, the problem still remains untouched concerning the proper and positive activity of the agent intellect and the specific contribution that the ensemble of our sensory powers, whose phantasm synthesizes the activity, provides to the agent intellect. The study of the second causality, designated by the word *illuminare*, will make, not more evident, but more intelligible the function of agent intellect and sensibility in the formation[171] of the object as *motivum seu causa movens* of the human intellect.

¶ *The Illuminative Function of the Agent Intellect.* Let us not forget that the purpose of this section of our work is to discover what the object of our intellect is; that is, what intentional form representing a material thing will make this thing actually *present* to the intellect and enable it to produce its act, since knowledge is the joint immanent effect of our cognitive power and its object.[172] But the object and the power it fecundates must belong to the same order, and since the intellect is spiritual or immaterial, its object must be so too. Now, such an object does not exist in the physical world that we are made to know, yet it is a fact that we do know physical things spiritually. Therefore, in the course of its travels through our soul, the exterior thing must have taken on a spirituality it did not have at the outset.[173] This progressive spiritualization of a physical thing during its deeper and deeper penetration into our soul culminates when this thing must prepare to espouse our intellect and father its children.[174] This ultimate preparation or spiritualization is the agent intellect's effect upon the thing as present in the phantasm; it is the characteristic working of this power of our soul and the source of its name:

The distinction of agent and possible intellect in us is in relation to phantasms, which are compared to the possible intellect as colors to sight, but to the agent intellect as *colors to light*.[175]

Interpreting this text literally, we have to say that our intellect is called active because it illumines the phantasm as light illumines color, which, in an objective context, means that just as color is actually a motive cause of our visual power only because it is illumined by light, so the phantasm can move the possible intellect only insofar as it is illumined by the light of the agent intellect.[176] This is such that the total object or integral motive cause of our possible intellect is the phantasm *plus* the light of the agent intellect. We have already seen that the object of our intellect is the intelligible species,[177] which results from the activity of the agent intellect working on the phantasm, and whose content represents the

content of the phantasm without its individual accidents.[178] Therefore, we now have to state more precisely what is this illumination
whose source is the agent intellect and what is its action upon the
phantasm, as well as the proper causality of the phantasm in the
production of the intelligible species (the term of the agent intellect's
activity and the motive object of the possible intellect).

We shall center our explanations of the phantasm's cooperation
with the illuminative action of the agent intellect around the following text, which not only establishes the link between the abstractive
and illuminative function of the intellect, but also stresses the role
of the phantasm in the production of the intelligible in act, that is,
of the *species intelligibilis* as form of our possible intellect and
specifying principle of its conceptual operation.

Not only does the agent intellect *illumine* phantasms, it does more: by its
power intelligible species are abstracted *from* phantasms. It *illumines*
phantasms because, just as the sensitive part acquires a greater power by
its conjunction with the intellectual part, so through the power of the
agent intellect *phantasms are made more fit for the abstraction of intelligible intentions from them.*[179]

This passage can only be interpreted in the light of two complementary teachings of St. Thomas: the hylemorphic nature of man, and
the dynamic order existing between sensory powers and spiritual
powers.[180] The human spirit is embodied in flesh because it is
created in complete poverty and must beg its spiritual food from
the material things composing the universe in which it lives.[181] The
whole mystery of the joint activity of agent intellect and phantasm
is nothing but the inevitable consequence of this substantial union of
soul and body: *operation follows being.* Now, the phantasm's illumination by the agent intellect, and the intelligible in act resulting
from the conjunction of these two factors, one of which is material
and the other spiritual, is only a repetition in the dynamic order of
the mystery of man's unity despite the natural opposition of his two
component factors.

Hence it is as natural for the soul to understand by turning to the
phantasms, as it is for it to be joined to the body. But to be separated
from the body is not in accordance to its nature, and likewise to under-

stand without turning to phantasms is not natural to it. That is why it is united to the body, in order that it may have a mode of being and operation suitable to its nature.[182]

The intelligible in act, the *species intelligibilis*, results therefore from the composition of two factors, one of which is spiritual, the other material, just as man is made of flesh and spirit.

The intelligible species receives its *formal* element, that by which it is intelligible in act, from the agent intellect which is a power superior to the possible intellect; but that which is *material* in it is abstracted from the phantasm.[183]

This definition of the intelligible in act in terms of matter and form should not disturb us, for the hylemorphism of the intelligible species is not a substantial hylemorphism, like that of man, but is the *hylemorphism of an object*, therefore, of a *measure* of our act of intellectual knowledge. As we have already seen, the object is not the thing taken as an absolute, but as existing in the soul in accordance with the being of the soul, and one thing can be different objects according to its different aptitudes for existing in the soul in compliance with the latter's requirements.[184] Thus, a single apple can be nine different objects inasmuch as it is tangible, odorous, visible, savory, audible, sensible, imaginable, memorable, and useful, because it is able to exist in the soul according to these nine different modes.

Thus, when St. Thomas describes the intelligible in act as being constituted of two factors, one of which, material, is drawn from the phantasm, and the other, spiritual, comes from the agent intellect, he is trying to clarify the inner structure of this reality called intelligible species, whose proper function and *raison d'être* consists entirely in measuring our intellect by giving it the nature of exterior things. But measure and measured must be of the same nature and order, just as we observe in everyday life where the unit of measure varies according to whether length, surface, or time is being measured. Also, the object measure of sense knowledge belongs to an order other than that of the object measure of intellectual knowledge, because the former is characterized by singularity, whereas the latter is characterized by universality. We should note in passing

that the question here is not that of providing human knowledge with
two realities as object, but of giving it one reality capable of existing
in the soul under two different modes: the singular mode dependent
on matter, and the universal mode depending on immateriality.[185]

The object measure of our intellect must therefore belong to the
same order as the intellect, which is to say that it must be immaterial.
Furthermore, it must make the exterior thing present to the intellect,
since the object is nothing but the exterior thing as existing in the
soul in accordance with the being of the soul.[186] The whole problem
of collaboration between phantasm and agent intellect and their
respective roles—a problem that has been discussed for centuries[187]
—is none other than the problem of conciliating the requirements for
immateriality and objectivity on the part of the intelligible species,
which is both the only object or *causa movens* of the possible intellect and the only object term of the agent intellect cooperating with
the phantasm.[188]

Thus, the intelligible species is simultaneously object measure of
the agent intellect and object motor of the possible intellect, because
the former is an active power and the latter is a passive power: "Now,
the object is to the act of a passive power *as the principle and moving
cause.* . . . On the other hand, to the act of an active power the
object is a *term* and an *end.*"[189]

Let us consider the intelligible species as the object of the agent
intellect, i.e., as its fruit, the result of its activity. Like every created
active power, the agent intellect needs a pre-existing reality in order
to be able to act,[190] and this reality is always called *matter,* whatever
its nature may be.[191] Now, the reality on which the agent intellect
acts consists in things themselves, but things as immanent to the
soul, what tradition calls phantasms.[192] When the Angelic Doctor,
in the text quoted above,[193] speaks of the illumination of the phantasm by the agent intellect, he describes the latter's proper activity
upon its matter as an activity that makes phantasms "more fit for
the abstraction of intelligible intentions from them." What does that
expression mean? Does it mean a superelevation of the phantasm,
a sort of vocation to immateriality under the illuminative action of
the agent intellect, which would make the phantasm *objectively*

intelligible without making it *formally* spiritual?[194] Or, on the contrary, does it mean a docility, a plasticity (we might almost say an obediential power) of the phantasm to illumination, peculiar to human sensibility because of its completion by the intellect, to which it is subject?[195] Finally, is illumination of the phantasm simply a metaphor by which St. Thomas expresses the instrumental character of the images through which flows the power of the agent intellect, that these images may become capable of determining the intelligible species *objectively*?[196]

Of these three explanations—the work of the most famous commentator upon the Thomistic doctrine of the illumination of the phantasm by the agent intellect—the last seems most to conform to the generic theory of the cooperation of diverse subordinate causes, as well as to the particular nature of the object's causality, which of itself is not an efficient cause of the act of knowing, but a formal measure of the power eliciting this act.[197] Here, in brief, is an explanation of this difficult point of doctrine according to the texts of St. Thomas himself.

First, since the phantasm is neither a power nor a *habitus*, it can in no way be an efficient, or even an instrumental, cause of the intelligible species.

Secondly, since the agent intellect is by nature an active power, it is not strange that it should really be the sole efficient cause of its object, which is the very reality of the intelligible species, a spiritual quality informing the possible intellect as an accident informs its proper subject.

Thirdly, since the intelligible species is the joint effect of the agent intellect and the phantasm, and since, on the other hand, the latter has no efficient causality with respect to the former, what causality is possible to the phantasm and how can it, being sensory, contribute to the production of a spiritual effect?

In the actualization of our possible intellect by the natures of things which it receives from phantasms, the latter play the role of *instrumental and secondary agent*, whereas the agent intellect's role is that of *first and principal agent*: so the effect produced in the possible intellect bears the mark of both these causalities and not of one only. That is why the possible intellect receives species that are on the one hand intelligible in act through the activity of the agent intellect, and are on the other hand likenesses of things determined by means of phantasms. Consequently intelligible forms really exist neither in the imagination nor the agent intellect, but only in the possible intellect.[198]

This text is related to and further explains the text we quoted above,[199] and it helps us understand what St. Thomas meant by the *formal* and *material* elements in intelligible species. The formal element of the species is nothing other than the *intelligible actuality* given it by the agent intellect; the material element of the same species is defined by its likeness to the phantasms from which it was drawn or abstracted. We could express the Doctor's thought through the following analogy:

$$\frac{\text{effect of the agent intellect}}{\text{effect of the phantasm}} : \frac{\text{being of nature}}{\text{intentional being}} : \frac{\text{immaterial}}{\text{likeness}} : \frac{\text{form}}{\text{matter}}$$

This series of proportions sets forth the double causality of the agent intellect and the phantasm, the nature of their respective causality, and the complex but single effect resulting therefrom. In actual fact, the agent intellect *efficiently* causes the object, i.e., the intelligible in act or the intelligible species, but its causality is not that of object or measure. The phantasm, on the contrary, has no efficient causality whatsoever; its causality is that of object or measuring presence. Being sensible, it cannot, by itself, be the measure of an immaterial power, so it receives from the agent intellect's illumination an *intentio fluens*, a sort of fluid and motive power that makes it into the agent intellect's instrument,[200] not to produce the spirituality of the species, but to determine it objectively so that it may represent this nature instead of some other. Here is how St. Thomas explains the causality of the agent intellect, as contrasted with that of the object:

If the relation of the agent intellect to the possible intellect were that of an *active object* to a power (as for instance of the visible in act to the sight), it would follow that we could understand all things instantly, since the agent intellect is that which makes all things in act. But the agent intellect *is not an object, rather it is that whereby the objects are made to be in act:* and for this, besides the presence of the agent intellect, we require the presence of phantasms, the good disposition of the sensitive powers and practice in this sort of operation.[201]

And here is a description of the causality of the phantasm as something extrinsic, a sort of limitation or objective specification:

> Although our soul is endowed with agent intellect and possible intellect, an extrinsic factor is needed to make possible the act of intellection. First of all there must be phantasms received from sensible things whose function is to make the likenesses of determinate things present to the intellect. For the agent intellect is not an actuality from which we can receive the determinate species of all things in order to know them, any more than light can determine vision to see definite colors unless distinct colors pre-exist its action. . . .[202]
> Our possible intellect is in potency to the intelligible just as the indeterminate is in potency to the determinate, for it does not positively possess the nature of any sensible thing. . . . *But, with respect to these same sensible natures, the agent intellect is not in act either.* For did it possess in itself the natures of all intelligibles, the possible intellect would have no need of phantasms, since it would receive all intelligibles from the agent intellect itself, which would then no longer be compared to intelligibles as the artisan to his work, but as identical with these same intelligibles. So, the agent intellect is likened to an act with respect to intelligibles insofar as its nature as an immaterial active power enables it to bring forth likenesses of itself, i.e. immaterial realities, and thus intelligibles in act.[203]

To understand these different texts of St. Thomas, we must give the comparisons he uses their full analogical sense. The analogy he ordinarily uses to compare the agent intellect's causality with that of phantasms is the analogy of light and color. Therefore, we must always keep in mind his theory of light and color (irrespective of this theory's scientific value) in order to understand the metaphysical meaning of his statements.

We can only speak of intellectual light by referring to what we know of corporeal light. Now corporeal light is *that by which* we see, and serves our vision in two ways. Firstly, light makes that which was only potentially visible to be actually visible, and secondly, by its very nature, light helps our sense of sight to see better. So we can attribute the same power to intellectual light, namely of being the very vigor of the intellect in its act of intellection and of being the source of the knowability of its objects.[204]

Thus, light is never *that which* is seen but always that *by which* we see. It enables us to see because it gives visibility and strengthens our power of sight itself. Let us apply that teaching to the light of our agent intellect.

The light of our intellect enables us to see by making visible the object of our possible intellect. This object is the *nature of material things*, which in their outer physical existence and in their immanent intentional existence are actually unintelligible because they are material. The agent intellect makes them luminous by giving them a higher, that is, an immaterial, mode of existence. This intelligibility of material natures is to natures themselves what visibility is to colors.[205] Going back to our analysis of the essential factors in the object of knowledge, we will recall that these factors are two, the *material* element and the *formal* element. Applying these two elements to the object of sight, we get the following hylemorphic pairing-off:[206]

$$\frac{light}{color} : \frac{form}{matter}$$

Since the agent intellect gives luminosity, or intelligible being, and the phantasm furnishes the natures to the intellect, or—what amounts to the same thing—since the natures presented by the phantasms are intelligible only insofar as they are illumined by the agent intellect, we must conclude that the formal element in the intelligible species is given by the agent intellect, whereas the material factor, i.e., the nature of things, is provided by the phantasm.[207]

One last confusion remains to be cleared up in order that we may correctly conceive this collaboration between the agent intellect and the phantasm, as well as their interdependence. While it is true that the effect of the agent intellect is inevitable, that the intelligible species terminating its action is always spiritual and therefore intelligible in act, since it is an activity of nature and thus infallible, we do not have the same certainty about the content of the species, i.e., the distinct natures represented in and by the phantasm. For the phantasms on which the intellect works are not necessarily the automatic fruits of the activities of our external senses; otherwise, dating from our first sensory experiences after birth, we should have, serving as matter, a certain fund of images that the agent intellect, always in act, could illumine and from which it could abstract an intelligible in act. But such is not the case, for experience shows us that years of preparation are needed before a child produces a genuine intellectual act, and that this first act is far from providing precise knowledge of the nature of material things.

In children the acts of the external senses are accurate, but the acts of their imagination are confused, which leads to confusion in their intellectual activity; for the intellect receives directly *from the internal senses* and not from the external senses. . . .[208]
  Phantasms are to the intellect as colors are to sight. Consequently just as from a confusion of colors there follows indetermination and confusion in the act of seeing, so, from a confusion of phantasms flows a certain lack of precision in the intellect's act. That is why at first children have only a very confused vision of some objects; but with time they acquire a very distinct knowledge of these same objects.[209]

We must therefore rid ourselves of the illusion of an abstractive illumination of the intellect, comparable to a flash that suddenly would make visible to the intellect the nature of things automatically inscribed in our phantasms by the exterior senses, while leaving obscure the individual characteristics of these natures! The precision and richness of content of our intelligible species is in exact proportion to the precision and richness of our phantasms. Here is what can be found in our imagination:

In the imagination the forms of sensible things exist not only in the original order in which they were received from sensation but also in an order that has been recast in several different ways, either under the influence of corporeal transmutations, as for example in men who are sleeping or violently insane, or again at the command of reason disposing phantasms in view of intellectual ends.
  Just as the same letters, arranged in different orders, have different meanings, so, according to the different order in which phantasms are arranged, there result different intelligible species in the intellect.[210]

Given this correlation between the phantasms' organization or lack of organization and the precision or imprecision in the content of intelligible species, on which the acuteness of our intellectual knowledge depends, we can easily see the primary importance of a sort of education for our internal senses, a training added to their natural finality as instruments of intellection[211] and enabling them to offer to the agent intellect's activity an orderly synthesis of the exterior accidents of natures, a synthesis permitting instantaneous illumination of those natures' specific notes.[212] Now we shall briefly explain the sensible factors contributing to the elaboration of *phantasmata* which make them better able to provide well-prepared matter for illumination. Here is the general formula St. Thomas uses to express this function of sensibility in the elaboration of intelligible species:

But the agent intellect is not an object, rather it is that whereby the objects are made to be in act. And for this, besides the presence of the agent intellect, *we require* the presence of *phantasms*, the *good disposition of the sensitive powers*, and *practice in this sort of operation*.[213]

Analysis of this text will enable us to make a final restatement of the relations of objective dependence between the agent intellect and sensibility taken in its entirety. This analysis will deal with three factors: *phantasms, good disposition*, and *practice in this sort of operation*.

¶ *Phantasms*. We know that this word (practically always used in the plural to mean the matter illumined by the intellect) can mean very different things. First of all, it can mean all the images presented to the imagination by the activity of exterior things affecting our different sensorial powers, therefore, tactile images, olfactory, gustatory, auditory, and visual, and this to an indefinite number. *Phantasmata* also means, as we have seen above, a certain natural order linking different images to each other, e.g., a unity accruing to them from a definite area and time that serve as focal points for different sensations. This natural order can be replaced by disorder brought on by sleep or illness,[214] also by an order set up under the supervision of the intellect itself,[215] or even by a particular action of God and angels.[216] Therefore, when we say that phantasms provide the agent intellect with material from which to produce intelligible species, we must remember that this material can vary in quality and quantity, and that consequently the agent intellect's fruit will be modified with respect to the quality of its content, if not to its spiritual nature.

¶ *Good Disposition of the Sensitive Powers.*   This is the second factor necessary for the production of the intelligible in act. The term *dispositio* has a technical meaning in St. Thomas' vocabulary. Following Aristotle, he generally defines it as *the order existing between the parts of a composite being,*[217] an order applicable to the continuum, to place, or to dynamic factors in the finalized things.[218] That the latter meaning is the one implied in the thought of St. Thomas is shown by his little metaphorical treatise on the Divine Artist's ordering of the different parts of the soul as the best *disposition* of this instrument in view of the soul's ends,[219] and also by the following text:

A *disposition* may be related in three ways to that to which it disposes . . . sometimes it is neither the same thing nor in the same subject, as in those things which are *ordered* to one another in such a way that we can arrive at one through the other, as for example *goodness of the imagination is a disposition to science*, which is in the intellect.[220]

This *bonitas imaginationis* as a disposition to science is found at two different degrees. First of all, at the natural level the imagination, like other sensory powers and because of its being rooted in a spiritual substance, has a sort of participation in the spiritual faculties.

For we see that sense is for the sake of the intellect and not the other way about. Sense moreover, is a certain participation of the intellect, and therefore *according to its natural origin*, it proceeds from the intellect as the imperfect from the perfect.[221]

To its power of preserving forms received through sensation, the human imagination's natural participation in a sort of spiritual spontaneity adds the power to take the initiative in composing or dividing these forms, therefore, of organizing them according to some order other than that in which they entered the soul.[222] It is precisely this reorganization of images that St. Thomas always calls *phantasmata*, and he attributes this reorganization not only to the imagination but to the memory and the cogitative power that works with it to synthesize the images from which the agent intellect draws its species.

For its intellective act the soul needs powers to prepare phantasms to become intelligible in act, that is, the cogitative power and the memory. . . .[223]

As long as the soul is united to the body, it cannot understand without phantasms, nor remember without the *cogitative power and the memory, by which the phantasms are prepared.*[224]

In the next chapter we shall see how the internal senses work together with the external senses to organize the perfect matter on which the agent intellect works to produce the intelligible in act. For the present it is enough to note that the internal senses are those *vires sensitivae* of which the best organization is essential for the production of phantasms and therefore for intellectual illumination and abstraction.

The good disposition of sensory powers does not exist at the natural level alone; it also exists at the individual level, from which result the intellectual inequalities found among individuals.

But in respect of the *individual nature*, a habit of knowledge is natural as to its beginning, in so far as one man, from the *disposition* of his organs of sense, is more apt than another to understand well; since we need the sensitive powers for the operation of the intellect.[225]

It would be impossible to overemphasize the existential or personalist character of the intellectual function, which, without in the least affecting the objectivity and realism of human knowledge, gives it such an analogical character that there are as many degrees of intellectual activity as there are individuals. It remains true that all sensibility is organized so as to present to the intellect exterior reality with all its accidents and significant appearances. But it is no less certain that this universal realism of human sensibility is far from democratizing and equalizing human knowledge. There are privileged beings in this order, a sort of oligarchy arising not from birth, wealth, or social position, but from the sense organism that fate (pagan synonym for Providence) predestined for this or that man.[226] Therefore, we may conclude that although the precision and wealth of the intelligible species, product of the agent intellect, depends upon the quality of phantasms, and although the quality of phantasms depends first and foremost upon the *good disposition of the sensitive powers,* i.e., on the natural health and keenness of our sensory powers, especially our internal powers, it is obviously impossible to consider the operation of the agent intellect as if it were patterned after a standard model and infallibly produced identical results in all men.

One may understand the same thing better than someone else, through having a greater power of understanding; just as one man may see a thing better with his bodily sight, whose power is greater and whose sight is more perfect. *The same applies to the intellect in two ways.* First as regards the intellect itself which is more perfect. For it is plain that the better the *disposition* of the body, the better the soul alloted to it . . . and thus because some men have bodies of better *disposition,* their souls have a greater power of understanding. . . . Secondly, this occurs in regard to lower powers of which the intellect needs its operation; *for those in whom the imaginative, cogitative and memorative powers are of better disposition,* are better disposed to understand.[227]

¶ *Practice in this Sort of Operation.* This is the third factor that prepares the way for the agent intellect's illuminative and abstractive activity, by providing it with material that is better organized, that is, more representative of individual natures. This factor is not given us by nature but consists in actualizing interior powers independently of their native perfection or imperfection. Here the thing is to put to work the capital, great or small, with which we have been endowed by nature, so that it will bring in a 100 per cent return. And the disparity in capital, or in the natural value of the sensory organism, does not necessarily beget any inequality in the value of the intellectual knowledge dependent on the smooth functioning of this organism. An excellent organism that is out of order, for reasons peculiar to the individual or to his milieu, can actually provide very poor nourishment for the agent intellect's activity, whereas a less delicate sensibility can offer it richer material, more suited to its proper ends. The importance attached to the use of our internal senses is owing to their subjection to human liberty, which commands and directs their activity in the work of preparing phantasms, a subjection that makes them docile and quickly responsive to the needs of the spiritual powers they serve. The role of *practice in this sort of operation* is therefore to create, within sensibility, a sort of sublimation of its natural instinct, resulting in eager diligence to comply with every demand of the soul:

The sensitive powers can be considered in two ways: first according as they act from *natural instinct;* secondly, according as they act *at the command of reason.* . . . But according as they act at the command of reason, they can be ordained to various things. And thus there can be habits in them, by which they are well or ill disposed in regard to something. . . .

And yet even in the interior powers of sensitive apprehension we may admit of certain habits whereby man has a *facility of memory, cogitation or imagination.* . . . The reason for this is that these powers also are moved to act at the command of the reason.[228]

How is practice in this sort of operation acquired? In two ways, corresponding to the two ways of acquiring intellectual knowledge. St. Thomas calls them *ordo inventionis* and *ordo disciplinae.* The first way, more difficult and less used, consists in discovering the art of abstraction by means of unaided personal effort, which is the art of organizing precise and complete phantasms by means of more than ordinary control over the three sensory powers whose teamwork produces these phantasms. The second way, more normal for human beings, consists in a sort of training by instruction of our whole internal sensory equipment. If training can give a sort of docility surpassing their natural capacity to the memorative, imaginative, and estimative powers of animals,[229] it is with much greater reason that education can succeed in helping the child and adolescent to acquire a certain discipline over his internal senses, a discipline achieving "facility of memory, cogitation, and imagination," without which is impossible that acquisition of intelligibles which are the perfect likeness of exterior things and on which our whole knowledge of truth depends.[230] In training the internal senses to serve the agent intellect efficiently, the role of language, as *sign* of exterior realities, is of the utmost importance, for language is the sensible sign of an intelligible reality. This sensible sign of an intelligible in act is much more able than are phantasms of extramental things to provide the agent intellect with matter from which to abstract distinct and plenteous species.

In the pupil's soul the intelligible forms, of which knowledge learned from a teacher consists, are immediately transcribed by the agent intellect and mediately by the teacher. For the latter proposes signs of intelligible things, from which the agent intellect *gathers intelligible forms and transcribes them into the possible intellect.* That is why the heard or read words of the teacher have the same type of causality in producing knowledge in the intellect as have exterior things; for from these two sources the intellect gathers intelligible forms; with this difference however, that the teacher's words are more immediately able to cause knowledge than are exterior things, because they are the signs of intelligible likenesses.[231]

The role of teacher to pupil belongs even more especially to parents in relation to their children, for children should receive not only their bodily life from their procreators but also formation of their soul.[232] Since the agent intellect's operation depends for its rich effectiveness upon the value of our phantasms, and since, on the other hand, phantasms depend on the good functioning of our internal senses, on their organization according to the ends of intellectual knowledge, who more than educators can facilitate the birth and development of the intellect? They have in their hands the whole of the child's sensibility and can influence it as much by the objects with which they surround their children as by what they say to them. From this combination of objects and words proportioned to the child's capacities result, little by little, increasingly well-constructed phantasms, containing more and more potential intelligibility, making more substantial the motive cause of our possible intellect, i.e., this species, this intelligible in act upon whose existence our whole intellectual knowledge entirely depends.

¶ *The Nature of the Agent Intellect.* What we have just seen about the agent intellect's object and the different aspects of its operations makes it easier to understand its nature. This nature is spiritual and always in act; therein lies its grandeur, for our agent intellect really imitates the actuality of the divine intelligence of which it is, in us, the participation.

For the intellectual light itself, which is in us, is nothing else than *a participated likeness of the uncreated light,* in which are contained the eternal exemplars. . . .[233]

The material sun sheds its light outside us, but the intelligible Sun, Who is God, shines within us. Hence the natural light bestowed upon the soul *is God's illumination,* whereby we are illumined to see what pertains to natural knowledge.[234]

Being a participation of the divine intellect, the agent intellect is nobler than the possible intellect, for it is light whereas the latter is illumined.[235] It does not create things, as does the divine light, but it causes their intelligibility and plays the same role in our knowledge of natural truth as does the divine light in the grasping of supernatural truths.[236] Like this divine light, the light of the agent intellect is infallible with respect to the object and the truth proportioned to it, which are the natures of physical things and that primary evidence which springs spontaneously from the very first apprehensions of the real as being. Thus, do we really share in the nature of spirits; that is our claim to glory and the root of our intellectuality: *"By the seal of the divine light in us,* all things are made known to us."[237]

We must not forget, however, that although we do belong to the family of spirits, we are the last-born of this family, and our portion in its heritage is that which falls to the youngest of a large family. Our part of the heritage of intellectual light is not enough to make us shareholders in the spiritual order; we have to depend upon constant hard work to earn our intellect's daily bread, its share of truth. Let us finish this study of the agent intellect's preparation of the intelligible by meditating on a last text in which St. Thomas shows us the littleness and misery of our intellectual light compared with the angelic and the divine intellect; it will remind us of our human condition and make us better epistemologists.

We must consider that while it is true that in itself it is nobler to understand by turning to something higher than by turning to phantasms, nevertheless such a higher mode of understanding would be less perfect for the soul, if we consider her power. This will appear if we consider that every intellectual substance possesses intellective power by the influence of the divine light. This light is one and simple in its First Principle, and the farther off intellectual creatures are from the First Principle, so much the more is the light divided and diversified. . . . Hence it is that God by His essence understands all things, while the superior intellectual substances understand by means of a number of species . . . but inferior intellectual natures possess a greater number of species, which are also less universal, and bestow a lower degree of comprehension, in proportion as they recede from the intellectual power of the higher intellectual substances. If therefore, inferior substances received species in the same degree of universality as the superior substances, since they are not so strong in understanding, the knowledge which they would derive through these species *would be imperfect*, and of general and confused nature. . . . Now it is clear that, in the order of nature, human souls hold the *lowest place among intellectual substances*. . . . If therefore, God had willed human souls to understand in the same way as separate substances, it would follow that human knowledge, so far from being perfect, would be confused and general. Therefore, to make it possible for human souls to *possess a perfect and proper knowledge of things, they were so made that their nature required to be joined to their bodies*, and *thus receive a proper knowledge of sensible things from the sensible things themselves*. So, too, we see in the case of uneducated men that they have to be taught by sensible examples. It is clear then that it was for the soul's good that it was united to a body, and that it understands *by turning to the phantasms*.[238]

Such is the wealth and poverty of our agent intellect, such is the mode connatural to man for acquiring intellectual knowledge and using it.

Conclusion on Knowledge as the Presence of Other Things

In this chapter we have studied the role of physical things in this dynamic world that is immanent in the human soul and is the universe of knowledge. The role of outer reality can and should be summarized in one phrase, *to provide the object*. For it is not because they *are* that exterior things have such an influence on cognitive

activity, but *because they are objects*. Now, to be and to be an object
are two quite distinct aspects of the physical world; their being in no
way depends upon our knowledge of them, whereas their being an
object depends entirely on the knower, *for a thing is an object or
knowable only insofar as it exists in the soul in accordance with the
being of the soul*.[239] The current habit of opposing object and subject as if they were two contrary and mutually exclusive entities
directly contradicts the Thomistic doctrine which teaches that the
object and the subject, or the knowable and the knower, are correlative factors that can exist *as such* only in their correlation. Using
the technical vocabulary of Thomas Aquinas, we shall try to summarize in a few paragraphs the epistemological doctrine on the
object as principle of our knowledge, leaving to the next chapter a
more detailed account of the *object as term* of this same knowledge.

(1) To know we must pre-exist what we know; the object as
principle or measure is therefore nothing but the extramental thing
as it exists in my soul according to the being of the soul, that is, as an
intentional species and not with its own natural existence. This
superexistence of things in me, prior to any cognitive activity on my
part, is not one of my natural *innate* endowments; I have to receive
it from things themselves, which can become objects or actually
knowable only insofar as they invade my soul and inhabit it more
or less permanently. Things must *live above* themselves in me so that
I may live them, i.e., know them. This power to conquer, to superexist, which makes an object out of a physical thing, is exactly proportioned to the thing's natural wealth. The gift that things make of
themselves to our cognitive powers, a gift by means of which they
enter the realm of objects by penetrating the soul, has the same
stature as their natural being: the more they are poor and indeterminate (i.e., the more their form is immersed in matter), the more
restricted is their dynamism, and, consequently, the more feeble their
coefficient as object. That is why things *as object* are divided into
two great categories, *the sensible* and *the intelligible*. When the
extramental thing has very limited ability to invade or occupy the
soul, giving it a hold over only the sensory powers, it is said to be
sensible. When, on the contrary, the thing, with the help of a foreign

and much superior power to increase its actuality, has a hold on the intellect and actually conquers it, then it is called intelligible or object principle of an intellective act.

When a physical thing becomes an object because it gives itself to us in intentional superexistence, it neither enriches nor impoverishes itself, but communicates to us the actuality it has. When the agent intellect illumines phantasms and abstracts intelligibles from them, far from reducing physical natures to a sort of proletariat and ruining them for its own profit, the agent intellect overcapitalizes their original value and sets them up so prosperously that they can exchange the poor dwellings they inhabit in sensibility for the dwelling of the spirit itself. This they do by means of the intentional species, the spiritual likeness of outer reality, which makes the latter intelligible therefore knowable, hence object principle and measure of intellection.

(2) While it is true, as we have just tried to explain, that a thing becomes an object or principle of knowledge according to the actuality it possesses and communicates to us by means of intentional species, and while it can rightly be said that the natural being of things is really the cause of their object being, yet the latter, considered as an entity, is inferior to its cause; it is a lesser reality, imperfect and incomplete,[240] totally dependent upon the causality of the real. But this intentional being, whose value as being is so imperfect compared with the natural existence of its cause, becomes, *in the order of knowledge or as object, the principle and cause of all I grasp of the exterior thing*. There is a sort of palace revolution when we pass from the ontological to the epistemological order; intentional being, poor relation of the being of nature from the metaphysical point of view, becomes the form and actuality of the natural being, which is now considered particularizing and limiting.[241] This reversal of causal values between extramental being and intentional being that occurs in passing from one order to the other explains both St. Thomas' technical vocabulary in his analysis of the object and the supreme importance of intentional being (be it *species sensibilis* or *species intelligibilis*) in the immanent

structure of the universe of knowledge. Let us review the technical formulae used in analyzing the object.

The first formula defines the essence of the object as knowable: *There is a relation into which a thing enters with the soul, not according to the thing's own being of nature, but according to the being of the soul, according to intentional being.*

The second formula analyzes this relationship, set up by an intentional being, and distinguishes within it two essential elements after the model of the hylemorphic composition of natural substances. The object of every cognitive power comprises two things: *that which is knowable—the material aspect; and that by which it is knowable—the formal aspect.*

Applying these definitions of the object and of its essential elements to the material thing as object of human knowledge, both sensible and intellectual, we get the following results.

That which is knowable by sensory powers consists in material things insofar as they have external accidents; this is the *material aspect* of the object of sensibility. *That by which* this thing is knowable in its accidents is their intentional being; this is the sensible species and the *formal aspect.*

That which is knowable by the intellect consists in these same material realities insofar as they have a nature[242]; this is the *material* aspect of the intellect's object, or the intelligible. *That by which* this reality is knowable is its very nature, its intentional being; this is the intelligible species, the work of the agent intellect and the *formal aspect* of the intellect's object.

Thus, we can set up the following analogical comparisons concerning the object, that is, concerning the knowability of external things:

$$\frac{\text{intentional being } (specias)}{\text{being of nature}} : \frac{\text{that by which } (quo)}{\text{that which } (quod)} : \frac{\text{a form}}{\text{matter}} : \frac{\text{to exist}}{\text{essence}}$$

The intentional being, in a word, is the *ultimate actuality* of reality in the order of objects; it is, as St. Thomas says, *ratio cognoscibilis in quantum est cognoscibile.*[243]

Such is the ontological origin of the object in Thomism, and such is its causality in the epistemological order. Consequently, we must cast off the centuries-old prejudice that pictures man as being in pursuit of objects which he gathers capriciously here and there as he pleases, choosing his victims and disdaining the rest as trash. Integral experience of the genesis of our knowledge tells us a completely different story, an authentic story in which the role of the human soul in relation to its objects is much more analogous to the Sleeping Beauty waiting for Prince Charming to come and awaken her than it is to the role of Don Juan always pursuing new victims! Things conquer us, and to the degree that they succeed in invading us by means of intentional being, to an equal degree do they waken us to the life of knowledge, because we imitate God by becoming all things, and thus participate in His infinite actuality.[244]

VII · THE OBJECT AS TERM OF HUMAN KNOWLEDGE

By means of the physical and intentional causality of external things, human beings are, in the strong sense of the word, inhabited by the universe. Continually invaded by hordes of strangers, man offers his soul to them just as a new country opens its doors to immigrants who come from all parts of the world to adopt it as their homeland. That was our theme in the preceding chapter, under the heading of the causality of objects and the passivity of our cognitive powers. Now we must study the soul's reactions to this stimulus from without, for although our cognitive powers are passive, being innately deprived of the objects they are made to possess, they are by nature principles of operation. Once perfected by the immanent and intentional presence of things,[1] they obey their natural instincts and, as if by magic,[2] produce cognitive activity—joint effect of the specifying influence of the object and the vital energies of the soul's powers. But this act of knowing, gushing forth spontaneously from a living source, obeys the laws of life and therefore does not become exterior but remains in the knower. The following text brings out this point.

It cannot be said of any cognitive activity that it flows or issues from its principle as do physical activities which proceed from agent to recipient. For knowledge is not an emanation from agent to patient such as occurs in physical activities, but an existing of the known in the knower.[3]

However, this same act of knowledge must terminate in exterior reality since a thing is said to be an object only because it is the extrinsic measure of every act of knowledge:

253

The thing known is said to be an object of knowledge *insofar as it subsists in itself, outside the knower,* although this thing can be known only because it in some wise exists in the knower.[4]

It would therefore seem that our cognitive activity is caught between two contradictory requirements from which it cannot be freed without losing its distinctive structure. For if it terminates in external reality, it renounces its immanence and everything characterizing it as vitally dynamic; and if it gives up its exteriority to safeguard its immanence, it loses its objectivity to become purely subjective. This is the formidable paradox set by the experience of human knowledge, a paradox that may be expressed in this formula: *How can reality be the object term of our cognitive activities* when all knowledge is immanent?

The solution of this paradox is to be found in the doctrine of the Angelic Doctor. In this mystery of created life that is knowledge, he discerned the principles that retain all the interiority of knowledge without in any way prejudicing its objective realism. To facilitate our study of this point of doctrine, we shall divide this chapter into three sections. The first will look into the general conciliatory elements between the laws of immanence and of exteriority in cognitive activity. The second and third sections will study the particular mode of immanence and exteriority presented, respectively, by sensible and intellectual knowledge.

Section I: Immanence of Cognitive Activity and Exteriority of the Object

We shall not speak here of the immanent structure of the world of knowledge, since we have already devoted a whole chapter to that subject.[5] We need only recall what is necessary to explain the present paradox: how an activity that is naturally immanent, and thus does not go out of our soul, can terminate in an external thing. The solution of this paradox cannot consist in modifying the laws of immanence characterizing cognitive life, for that would be tantamount to destroying that life, but must be found in the marriage of two causalities, one wholly on the side of the subject, the other characteristic of the object. The technical formulae for this double causality are: *exercitum actus, specificatio actus*. It is by virtue of these two complementary sources of cognitive activity that the latter can integrally safeguard both its interiority and its objective exteriority. We shall first read a passage describing these two orders of causality, then we shall try to analyze the truth expressed by these formulae, in order to apply it to the problem we are trying to solve. Here is the text:

Now a power of the soul is found to be in potentiality to different things in two ways: first, with regard to acting and not acting; secondly with regard to this or that action. Thus the sight sometimes sees actually, and sometimes sees not; and sometimes it sees white, and sometimes black. It needs therefore a mover in two respects: viz., as *to the exercise* or use of the act and *as to the determination* of the act. The first of these is *on the part of the subject* which is sometimes acting, sometimes not acting; while the other is *on the part of the object*, by reason of which the act is specified.[6]

Note in this text the insistence with which St. Thomas distinguishes two aspects of every cognitive activity. On the one hand, he stresses the exercise of the activity, or the expanding of the power in a sort of inner dilation that, under the pressure of the intentional species (sensible as well as intellectual), culminates in a vital explosion, which is more or less intense, depending on the natural perfection of the knower, and is this perfection's blossoming. On the other hand, he points out the specification of this activity, because of which the exercised dynamism is never neutral or indeterminate but always has in itself a certain form that situates it, makes it to be this particular act of seeing a particular color, just as a meadow's blossoming is always determined by the specific forms and colors of the flowers growing in it. In other words, the fact of *seeing* is not identical with that of seeing *something*, although it is impossible to see without seeing something. Here is therefore a distinction of aspects in something that is indispensably and essentially complementary. But how is this distinction of aspects arrived at? The answer is clear: The *subject* exercises the act, the *object* specifies it. We need only give this answer in relation to the immanence of cognitive activity and its objective exteriority in order to resolve the paradox stated at the beginning of this chapter.

A. EXERCISE OF THE ACT OF KNOWING AND ITS IM-MANENCE

In reading Thomistic treatises on knowledge, one often gets the impression that the *causal subjective* aspect, expressed by the words *operare, exercere, elicere*,[7] is of minor importance and that our whole attention should be fixed upon realism or objective causality. This unilateral deformation of gnosiology, owing to doctrinal deformations brought on by all the successive idealisms of the past three centuries, has been admirably expressed by Kierkegaard: "Superstition attributes to objectivity the power of Medusa's head, the power of *petrifying subjectivity*; and this absence of liberty no longer permits man to break the enchantment."[8] In Thomism, causal objectivity, far from petrifying subjectivity, vivifies it; it delivers it from the paralyzing torpor that philosophical language calls the "passivity of the soul's powers"[9]; it permits the indefinite unfettering of operations and cooperations that make man such a powerful architect and his soul such a vast field that he can reconstruct the whole universe therein. But what must not be forgotten in this majestic work of re-creating the universe is man's part in it, the *exercitium actus* characterizing the knowing subject and making his activity a life, that is, an interior welling-up of which he is at once author, spectator, and recipient.

To define knowledge as life is to stress the knowing subject and his inner dynamism, a sort of spontaneous energy springing from an increased inner wealth of which it is the immanent expression. The Latin word *elicere* expresses very well, by its mysterious imagery, the surprise we should feel every time we experience an act of knowledge. The etymological origin of *elicere* takes us into a world where deceit, stratagems, and magic charms hold sway, and the verb has kept this original meaning, since it primarily signifies the act of using strategy to trick an army into leaving tactically strong positions, or to obtain the intervention of a mysterious force or person by magic.[10] Every vital activity is like a magical apparition, for it rises suddenly in the soul without our knowing exactly what mysterious presence has caused it to be where it did not previously exist. For *elicere* is characteristically an outburst of vital energy without any sort of foreign intervention nor any pressure other than that of an interior and spontaneous wealth. Here is the comparative description given by St. Thomas:

There is between to elicit and to command an act this difference, that a power or habit elicits the act it produces with regard to its object *without any intermediary*, whereas a commanded act is always the result of the intermediary activity of a power or habitus with respect to its object.[11]

Therefore, it is not natural to every cognitive power to command the act of another power, but it does belong naturally to it to produce its activity spontaneously. It is made to do this as a bird is made to fly, and such is the naturalness of this operation that its nonexistence would make the whole of creation purposeless:

Indeed, all things created would seem, in a way, to be purposeless, if they lacked an operation proper to them; since the purpose of everything is its operation. For the less perfect is always for the more perfect. Consequently, just as the matter is for the sake of the form, so the form which is the first act is for the sake of its operation, which is the second act; and thus *operation is the end of the creature*.[12]

From this passage may be seen the importance St. Thomas assigns to the *exercise of the act;* without this exercise, without this operation, created beings would lose their meaning, for they would no longer imitate their Creator, in Whom to exist and to act are the same. The theory of the distinction of powers in the substantial nature of every creature is justified only by their imperfect state and the perfective character that these powers acquire through operation. The same is true of the *habitus* of powers, which are not a function of objects but a function of powers; their purpose is to perfect the operation of the soul's powers and therefore to perfect the being that acts.[13]

Knowledge is a vital operation entirely directed to the perfecting of the subject, not the object. To know enriches the knower, but it does not give or take away anything from the thing known. Consequently, it is not surprising that the *exercise of the act*, being essentially subjective in character and destined to the subject's progressive enrichment, peculiarly favors the laws of interiority and immanence that characterize all life, but most especially the life of knowledge.[14] It is also by virtue of this subjective or immanent aspect of the exercise of the act that we may say that one man knows this or that thing more perfectly than another, is more or less intelligent, more or less learned, etc.

To say that a thing is understood more by one than by another may be taken in two senses. First, so that the word "more" be taken as determining the act of understanding *as regards the thing understood* [we have here the specification of the act]; and thus, one cannot understand the same thing more than another, because to understand it otherwise than it is, either better or worse, would be to be deceived rather than to understand. . . . In another sense, the word "more" can be taken as determining the act of understanding *on the part of the one who understands* [we have here the exercise of the act, the elicitation]. In this way, one may understand the same thing better than someone else, through having a greater power of understanding; just as a man may see a thing better with his bodily sight, whose power is greater, and whose sight is more perfect. The same applies to the intellect in two ways.[15]

We should retain from what has just been said this seemingly inescapable conclusion: If we consider the *subjective aspect* of the act of knowing (or the exercise of knowledge insofar as it is the ultimate perfection of the soul's powers and thereby of the whole knower), every cognitive activity obeys the essential laws of living: its cause is the knower and its term this same knower. It is of him, in him and, for him.

B. SPECIFICATION OF THE ACT OF KNOWING AND EXTERIORITY OF ITS TERM

Although the act of seeing is entirely immanent, *what it sees or the object of vision* is entirely external. This is the second part of the

paradox we faced at the beginning of this chapter. Fortunately, we
are equipped to solve this difficulty, inherent to the mystery of
cognitive life, thanks to the doctrine of the object as principle of
cognitive activity, which was explained in the preceding chapter.
Simply recalling the different factors of which the object is composed will suffice to dispel the apparent contradiction between an
immanent activity and the exteriority of its object.

In the text quoted above[16] we saw that the act of knowledge, like
every immanent act, is doubly dependent: subjective dependence
for its act of existing, objective dependence for its specification. The
latter dependence is thus subject to the laws ruling the nature and
role of the object as such. We have seen that the fundamental law
ruling the whole field of speculative knowledge with respect to its
object is the law of the *measured in relation to its measure*,[17] which
makes the act of knowing a real relation, and the object, its measure,
a logical correlative.

Sometimes a relation in one extreme may be a reality, while in the
other extreme it is only an idea. This happens whenever two extremes
are not of one order, as sense and science refer, respectively, to sensible
things and to knowable things, which, inasmuch as they are *realities existing in nature, are outside the order of sensible and intelligible existence.*
Therefore, in science and in sense, a real relation exists because they are
ordered to the knowledge or to the sensible perceptions of things, whereas
the things looked at in themselves are outside this order.[18]

But it is of the essence of a relation to be defined, not in reference
to its subject, but in reference to an external reality: "The true
notion of relation *is not taken from its respect to that in which it is,
but from its respect to something outside.*"[19] Therefore, when we
described knowledge as an immanent act of a power and its
spontaneous enrichment, we described it as an accident of the soul's
powers. But when we want to characterize it as relative, that is,
when we really want to define it specifically, then we must define it
with respect to the extramental or the object, since the object is
the external reality that measures and specifies knowledge.

It is easy to see, now, that the paradox presented by the immanence requisite to every cognitive act and the exteriority necessary
to its objectivity was the result of superficial reflection upon the

nature of knowledge as such. We have seen, in effect, that methodical investigation into a thing's nature demands that we first know whether the thing be substance or accident, for the answer will differ in each case.[20] To know is undoubtedly an accident of the living thing, man, and as such must be defined in relation to the subject; it must be in the subject. In our brief inquiry into the *exercitium actus* we tried to stress this character of human knowledge by bringing out its characteristic immanence. But to know is not just any accident but an accident whose proper nature indicates a relation to another: it is the presence of another within us.[21] Now, as such, knowledge is defined by this other whose presence it indicates, i.e., by the object. But it is essential that a relation as such receive its specifying notes, not from the subject in which it inheres, but from its extrinsic term. The few paragraphs in which we discussed the *specificatio actus* gave us the key to conciliating the complete exteriority of the object of human knowledge with the perfect interiority of the act by which this object is grasped. It remains only to apply these two complementary aspects of human knowledge to the two modes by which man, without going outside himself, can become the whole sensible and intelligible universe.

Section II: Immanence of Sensible Knowledge and Exteriority of the Object

It is always with fear and trembling that the epistemologist enters the labyrinth of sensory knowledge and the material universe that is its object, for during the past three centuries philosophy has tried to destroy the marvelous symposium of powers and activities organized by the ancient philosophers, while at the same time scientists have sought to annihilate the aspects of the physical universe traditionally considered as objects of this type of human knowledge. Nevertheless, it is in this sensible universe that we must find the objective principle of all our cognitive life, just as it is in and by the complexity of sensory perception that the life of the mind is assured of its object and wrings from it admittance to the gates of the

kingdom of the Absolute. To facilitate our study, we shall first consider the increasing immanence of the different operations of sensory
life, then we shall have a quick look at this life's order of specification,
i.e., at the world of its object.

A. IMMANENCE OF SENSORY LIFE AND INCREASING AWARENESS OF THE KNOWING SUBJECT

"The more perfect a being, the more what emanates from it
remains interior to that being."[22] This statement of principle prefaces
one of St. Thomas' most complete texts about the relations among
life, immanence, and self-awareness. But the operations of sensory
life are far from homogeneous with respect to their interiority, and
if one dared use a geometrical comparison in this field, which by
definition excludes all reference to the laws of quantity, one might
say that the immanence of some of these operations is like a mathematical point, without dimensions, whereas the immanence of other
operations have one, two, or three dimensions. This lack of uniformity in the degrees of immanence implies, according to the
principle stated at the beginning of this paragraph, that there exist
more or less perfect powers of operation at this level of human
knowledge.

For concrete illustrations of this universal statement, let us examine
the five types of sense knowledge formulated in the following
propositions: 1) I see; 2) I see that I see; 3) I imagine that I see;
4) I have seen; 5) It is useful that I see.

Analytical comparison of these five sensory experiences, which
are within the range of every normal being, illustrates the metaphor
we used when we spoke of nondimensional immanence, like a
point, and immanence, with one, two, and three dimensions. The
first statement (1) is entirely a function of the object, therefore of
that which is exterior to the knowing subject; the spontaneity of
the act of vision, a sort of point of immanence and enrichment of the
subject, is a conscious enrichment that loses itself in exterior reality.
This is not true of the second statement (2), wherein the subject

and object are both in the line of consciousness; here, immanence has a sort of length, of which one of the extremities consists of the act of vision and the other of the object seen. The third experience (3) is still more richly interiorized, for it cares not whether the sensed object be present or absent, but is entirely concerned with restoring a sort of autonomy to previous vital activities: immanence here has not only length but surface. With the fourth (4) and fifth (5) statements, the immanence of sensory life takes on breadth, volume; it dominates its object, the physical thing, and the act of sensation itself, since it gives them an existence that they no longer have or do not yet have. "I have seen" implies that sense life is no longer subject to the caprices and continual change of sensory acts but measures it definitely in time; whereas "it is useful that I see" is a cognitive act in which the knowing subject is taken as value criterion with respect to a future act and object. Sensory life really becomes the life of the knowing subject; it is for him, it is in him, and the object itself has taken on a certain spatial and temporal stability, thanks to a sort of progressive domination of immanence and awareness over the fluidity of objective reality.

This experience of the progressive immanence of sensible life, of the ever increasing intimacy between the knower and the term of his knowledge, of an interiority that starts from a certain point to end up in the depths of the sensory soul itself, can only be explained by the existence, in this soul, of increasingly perfect cognitive powers, increasingly completed by the intimate life of the knower and by his awareness of himself and of his needs. This is the experience that has given us the classical division of the sensory powers of knowledge into external and internal senses: the first are totally ruled by the physical reality it is their business to know, whereas the latter intensify the living being's intimacy with himself. Nothing can better help us to grasp the progressively immanent character of this ensemble of acts in the sensory life of knowledge than the following text; its frequent and careful meditation is worth volumes of explanations.[23]

As nature does not fail in necessary things, there *must needs be* as many actions of the sensible soul *as may suffice for the life of a perfect animal.*

. . . Now we must observe that for the life of a perfect animal, the animal should apprehend a thing not only at the actual time of sensation, but also when it is absent. Otherwise, since animal motion and action follow apprehension, an animal would not be moved to seek something absent; the contrary of which we may observe especially in perfect animals, which are moved by progression, for they are moved towards something apprehended and absent. Therefore, through the sensitive soul an animal must not only receive the species of sensible things, when it is actually affected by them, but it must also retain and preserve them. . . .

Again we must observe that if an animal were moved by pleasing and disagreeable things only as affecting the sense, there would be no need to suppose that an animal has a power besides the apprehension of those forms which the senses perceive, and in which the animal takes pleasure, or from which it shrinks in horror. But the animal *needs* to seek or avoid certain things not only because they are pleasing or otherwise to the senses, but also *because of other advantages and uses, or disadvantages;* just as the sheep runs away when it sees a wolf, not because of its color or shape, but as a natural enemy. Soo too a bird gathers together straws, not because they are pleasant to the senses, but because they are useful for building its nest. Animals, therefore, *need to perceive such intentions,* which the exterior sense does not perceive.

Thus, therefore, for the *reception of sensible forms,* the proper sense and the common sense are appointed. . . . But for the *retention and preservation of these forms*, the phantasy or imagination is appointed, being, as it were a storehouse of forms received through the senses. Furthermore, for the *apprehension of intentions which are not received through the senses*, the estimative (or cogitative) is appointed; and for *their preservation*, the memorative (or reminiscence) power, which is a storehouse of such intentions.[24]

Let us sum up what we have just seen about the exercise of sensory acts and the powers eliciting those acts, taking as criterion of the degree of immanence the greater or lesser fascination exerted upon these activities by exterior reality as such. With the help of this criterion we shall perceive that immanence varies from the external senses to the internal senses, and from one internal sense to another. Here is the hierarchy:

(1) All the activity of the external senses is completely at the mercy of the presence of external reality; without the latter, there can be no sensation. So great is this fascination that the external senses cannot grasp extramental things other than they are. The

ancients expressed this fascination in this way: The senses are infallible in grasping their proper object.[25] The immanence of this vital operation is reduced to the minimum, for only the act is interior; what is known, i.e., the natural being of material things, is wholly external.

(2) The common sense or sense awareness[26] is also bound to external reality, since it perceives everything grasped by the external senses; but the fascination of outer reality is no longer absolute here, for the object of the common sense implies the activity of the external senses by its very immanence and consequently implies the *sensible species*, which has informed the external sense and enables it to perform its act.[27] The immanence of the common sense's operation is therefore both that of its act and of all the aspects of its object, and this enables it to become aware of the knowing subject as such; it serves two masters, the exterior object and the knowing subject.

(3) Imagination is even freer than the common sense, for even though the exterior thing be absent, it can know its image or its intentional being, whose reservoir or treasury it has become. This function is dangerous, for this power possesses such autonomy in man, such immanence, that it can add to what it has received and must be controlled by the external senses for the sake of truth[28] and by the intellect for the needs of science.[29]

(4) With the cogitative power and memory, the subject is no longer fascinated by sensed physical things; rather, it is the subject that, in a certain way, enslaves the sensed reality within himself, depriving it of its role as measure and reducing it to the role of an instrument, either useful or detrimental to the life of the knowing subject. Here we are in a domain so interior that external senses do not even have access to it.[30] At this stage of the life of sense knowledge, the tyrannical fascination of external reality is overruled by the requirements of the living being. Psychological sense awareness, and so the immanence of sensory operations, has reached its peak.[31]

B. SENSE KNOWLEDGE AND ITS SPECIFICATION BY EXTERNAL REALITY

While the exercise of the different operations of sensory life reveals a progressive autonomy of the knowing subject and an awareness of its needs, specification of these same operations reveals a progressive ascendancy over the whole of outward reality. Fragmentarily grasped at first, outer reality is finally contrasted with a knower that is a singular whole, despite its diverse appearances. We shall try briefly to distinguish the different levels of this manifestation of the real by means of sense knowledge taken as a whole.

¶ *1. External Reality as Object Term of the External Senses.* It has been maintained, and rightly so, that in Thomism being explains knowledge, and not the reverse. All we have seen about the causality of the real in the production of the *species intentionalis*[32] has confirmed this statement, and we can make the same observation when showing that outward reality is the object known through sensation. What do we know through our senses? Only the outward accidents of things: "Sense does not apprehend the essences of things, but only their outward accidents."[33] To speak of the outward *accidents* of material things is to imply the existence of other nonvisible accidents, and especially the existence of a nature that is other than accidents and is not perceived by sensation. Thus, to describe the object of sensation in terms of accidents and by contrast to nature or substance is to presuppose a metaphysics of reality without which epistemological explanation is impossible.[34]

Exactly what are the outward accidents of things? They are the accidents we have seen to be the principles of this physical and intentional *immutatio* without which no cognitive act is possible. They are qualities called changing, active, physical,[35] or are included in the expression *materia corporalis seu sensibilis*,[36] which would mean colors, sounds, odors, tastes, and all tactile qualities, hot, cold, hard, soft, light, heavy. Only these qualities have immediate causality upon the organ of the sensorial powers, and, consequently, only they can be the proper object of sensation, for we know only that which we have first become.

Not every accident has in itself a power of immutation, but only the qualities of the third species, according to which there can be alteration. Therefore, only such qualities are *the object of the senses*, because the senses are affected by the same things whereby inanimate bodies are affected.[37]

These physical qualities, or *passiones et patibiles qualitates*, are intimately mingled with the becoming of physical things, for movement is possible only in reference to these qualities, or objects of sensation.[38] On the other hand, since physical reality is defined by becoming, to assign as object to the external senses that without which becoming is impossible is to ascribe to it direct and immediate knowledge of a world in motion, and, consequently, to consider it as essentially unstable knowledge, changeable as the reality it measures. If this be the case, we must admit that there is no permanence in sensation as such. Being bound to the physical causality of a changing being, it must have the same fluidity as its cause or become illusory, for that by which we know is the actual likeness of what we know.[39]

It is easy, now, to understand that the fascination exerted by the object of sensation—a fascination that leaves only the strict minimum of immanence to the act—is necessary for the realism of sensation. As soon as the sensory act is no longer subjugated to this changing and fluid reality, it is in peril of every deformation. This happens, for example, when the organism is ill or when the imagination of the knowing subject, governed by its prejudices or needs, organizes the world of knowledge in relation to its preconceptions or dreams. However, as long as sensation is influenced by the real, it does grasp the latter in a fragmentary and superficial way, but this is to the advantage of its objective realism, since to know is to grasp that which belongs to nature in its being.

These sensible qualities, proper objects of sensation, do not exist in a separate state, isolated from the things of which they are the qualities. They exist in quantity and are conditioned by it, that is, in number, extension, and figures, and the derivatives of these properties of quantity, motion, and rest. This quantitative conditioning does not modify the nature of qualities but rather the action they have upon the sense organ:

Sensible qualities move the sense as having extension and location. Their action is different accordingly as the body in which they exist is big or small and differs in location, i.e. whether it is far or near, unchanging or changing. And all these modifications are referable to the common sensibles.[40]

Thus, the senses grasp sensible qualities as immobile or moving, as one or multiple, as having extension and shape, all of which are aspects characterizing exterior reality considered at the human level,[41] with its appearances of continuity:

Qualities, the proper object of the senses, *exist in a continuum;* and that is why the continuum itself, as immediate and necessary subject of these qualities, must have an objectifying action upon the senses. Now everything which is called a common sensible is connected with the continuum, whether it measure it as extension, or divide it as number, or limit it as figure, or finally reveal its distance or proximity as movement.[42]

This integration of dimensive quantity into the essential object of the external senses gives objective unity to the instability and transience of physical qualities. Without this unity the universe would appear to us as a series of successive and incoherent mirages.

A world of numbered, shaped, moving, or immobile physical qualities, grasped in the very actuality of their causality upon our sensory powers—such is the total object of sensation, such is the Medusa's head that petrifies our sensory subjectivity and enslaves it in the order of specification.

¶ 2. *External Reality as Object Term of the* Sensus Communis. At this point of our inquiry into the life of sense knowledge, we should take for granted the doctrine of the correlative interiority of the different cognitive powers and their activities, for this doctrine was developed in a preceding chapter.[43] Now we shall apply it to the *sensus communis* with respect to the external senses:

The interior sense is called common not by predication, as if it were a genus, but *as the common root and principle of the exterior sense.*[44]

Since all the external senses are rooted in the sense awareness that is our *sensus communis*, and since their activities blossom there like different flowers on the same plant, it is not surprising that the different objects of the senses are grasped by the common sense.[45] Thus, all the proper sensibles and all the common sensibles are object term of this new vital power,[46] which is characterized by the fact that although it is fascinated by the ensemble of sensible objects, it is not sustained by any in particular.

The higher a thing is, the more is its power unified and far-reaching. Thus in man himself it is manifest that the common sense, although it is but one power, knows everything apprehended by the five outward senses, and some other things which no outer sense knows; for example the difference between sweet and white.[47]

This domination over the proper objects of the external senses is due to the fact that the object of the common sense is not only exterior reality in its *esse naturae* but also in its *esse intentionale*, its existence within the soul itself.

It [the common sense] perceives the mutations of the external senses and differentiates between the different sensibles. By it we perceive that we live and distinguish the object of the different senses, i.e. white from sweet.[48]

Thus, it can perceive different sensible species, distinguish them, compare them, be aware of them as entities that are distinct from the emotive accompaniments they cause, especially from the pleasure and pain concomitant with sensory acts.[49]

Because of the common sense's quasi-infinite capacity to grasp the sensible[50] in its *esse naturae*, as well as in its intentional being, this aspect of sense knowledge becomes of primary importance to our awareness of the objective character of human knowledge as a whole. For to perceive that an actually present being is distinct from our sensation of it is basic to the distinction between the universe as experienced by the soul, i.e., as existing in the soul in accordance with the being of the soul, and the exterior universe in its very exteriority.[51] It is because of this first awareness that the subsequent activity of the other internal senses and of the intellect possesses *a sort of instinct to return to the senses,* precisely in order to use the existing universe as a control.

3 The common sense has another objective function, namely, to grasp the universe as a dynamic entity whose activity possessses duration, therefore, temporal and spatial unity. The *hic et nunc* characterizing physical things cannot be grasped without the soul's intervention, without awareness of movement and of a being dominating this movement, since it endures.[52] The common sense's grasp of the *nunc fluens* or the *nunc temporis*[53] makes possible the concrete reckoning according to a before and an after from which intellectual notions of time and place are drawn.[54] By comparing the experienced sensible universe and the universe immersed in becoming (especially local motion), we grasp the latter with its dimensions of length, surface, volume, and duration.[55]

d) A last objectifying function of the common sense, without which it would be impossible for the intellect to grasp the act of existing, consists in the perception of outward things as actually moving now, at the present time. Motion is, in effect, the operation properly belonging to being in process of becoming, it is the most perfect sign of its actuality, therefore, of its act of existing. Starting from this knowledge of the actuality of movement and its duration, we understand act and, consequently, existing in act:

Since names are signs of our concepts, it is to the things first grasped by the intellect that we give names, although these things are not first in the order of nature. *But of all acts, the best known and most immediately knowable is movement* which we perceive through the senses. For it is to movement that the name of act was first given and thence applied, by derivation, to other things. And that is why we never speak of motion apart from existents.[56]

This amounts to saying that if, metaphysically speaking, operation follows being, in the epistemological order *our knowledge of being depends upon our knowledge of its operation,* not only for knowledge of its nature, but also for knowing its existence as the act of its nature.

Such is the importance of the common sense for objective knowledge of the extramental world; such are the different aspects of the world it reveals to us, aspects that the intellect needs continually in order to preserve, for their intelligibility, the existential character of its objects.[57]

¶ 3. External Reality as the Object Term of the Imagination. St. Thomas studies the imagination, and phantasms too, from two different points of view. Most often imagination signifies all internal knowledge, with inextricably intermingled contributions from the common sense, memory, and the cogitative power, in its relations with intellectual knowledge, speculative as well as practical, of external things.[58] Sometimes imagination means an internal power of specialized knowledge distinguished from all others and having its own domain. This is the limited aspect of the imagination we are studying here. Rooted in the common sense to which it, so to speak, belongs,[59] the proper function of imagination is to *preserve* whatever is perceived by the external senses and common sense:

For the reception of sensible forms, the proper sense and the common sense are appointed. . . . But *for the retention and preservation of these forms*, the phantasy or imagination is appointed, being as it were a storehouse of forms received through the senses.[60]

Left to its own initiative, this treasury of sensibility has no other function than to store the riches perceived by the external senses and experienced by the common sense in order to return them to the latter and facilitate its work upon new material or material renovated by means of previous experiences whose objects are no longer present:

A thing is known, in a second way, by a sort of secondary mutation, which is nothing but a prolongation of the mutation of the particular sense by an exterior thing. This prolonged motion remains even in the absence of exterior objects and characterizes the imagination.

Thus considered, imagination is nothing but a property of the common sense, for it follows every mutation of the sense whose principle is the proper sensible and whose term is the common sense. Whence it is apparent that extension, motion and time, as preserved by the imagination, *are understood and known by the common sense.*[61]

Considered as keeper of the proper effects of exterior sensibles, the imagination has the same objectivity that the external senses and the common sense have. It is not, as is too often stated, a purely capricious power concerned with the likenesses of physical things,[62] but a cognitive power whose activity is an effect of the causality of things upon the soul. Therefore, *in due proportion*, it enjoys the same realism as do the external senses with regard to proper sensibles, common sensibles, and accidental sensibles,[63] at least when they are present. In their absence, imagination is more subject to inner influences, i.e., to impulses that come from the will through the cogitative power, and then imagination's objective realism can be lessened or completely destroyed.[64] However, in such a case we are no longer dealing with the solitary workings of the imagination itself, but with teamwork wherein pressures other than those of exterior things are brought to bear. According to the pressures exerted on it, the imagination can either go berserk or become the most precious instrument of philosophical, artistic, mathematical, and scientific knowledge.

Left to itself, imagination brings to the objectivity of the physical world a temporal and spatial permanence independent of the actual presence of spatial and temporal things. It frees knowledge from the physical servitude to which every sensation is subject; it enables the knower to take with him the totality of the known object and thus to enjoy a certain objective ubiquity.[65]

¶ 4. *External Reality as the Object-Term of the Cogitative Power and Memory.* Just as common-sense knowledge is at the root and term of imaginative knowledge, so is it basic to the activity of the memory and cogitative power, which feed upon knowledge previously acquired by the common sense in the same way that the powers of growth and procreation use the assimilative activity of the nutritive power to further their own ends.[66] But unlike the imagination, whose proper function is to record what is already known by the external senses and the common sense in order to make them present even in the absence of sensation, the cogitative power and memory perceive aspects of things that none of the sensory powers have grasped before them. What aspects of things are these? They are neither proper sensibles nor common sensibles and therefore are nothing related to physical qualities and the quantity of physical being, since all that is the object of the senses. Nor are they quantified qualities as known, for these are the proper object of the common sense and imagination. Consequently, what real object remains for the cogitative power and memory to know? Exactly nothing, since the sensible realm has been exhausted by the preceding ways of knowing. Nor may we seek in physical things a facet of the real that might have escaped sensation and be revealed to the two internal senses in question, for by definition the object of these two senses is a sensible only accidentally, in that it falls directly into the orbit of no sense but *is apprehended by the knower upon the occasion of sensation.*[67] St. Thomas calls the object which is thus newly known by the cogitative power the *intentio* and explains the term by saying that *intentiones* imply advantage or disadvantage, usefulness or harmfulness.[68] This *intentio* is not knowledge of a new thing but new knowledge of a same thing. The same extramental being that was experienced as measure of our knowledge is now perceived *as being good or bad in relation to the knower;* the whole domain of the known as such loses the neutrality, the indifference that characterized it as a specifying measure, and acquires a value coefficient situating it in the order of good or evil; it becomes an object to be sought or avoided that involves the affective nature of the knowing subject.[69] The cogitative power does not give us more knowledge of a thing but a better-known thing, a thing *appreciated* by the knower, evaluated as giver of being. This *intentio,* which St. Thomas says is inaccessible to the external senses, the common sense, and the imagination, is the unity of the sensible thing, a unity that is no longer merely local and temporal, as grasped by the common sense and imagination, but is ontological and existential:

The cogitative power apprehends the individual existing as a particular nature . . . it knows this man as this man, and this wood as this wood. This is not true of the estimative power which grasps the individual, not as absolute, but as principle or term of an action or passion. Thus the ewe knows this lamb not as lamb but *as its nursling,* and this grass inasmuch as it is its food.[70]

This knowledge of material things as particular natures, or insofar as they are absolute as existents and relative as natures (for the word *particular* implies a division, a distinction with respect to a factor common to several beings), characterizes sensory knowledge as human, in that as sensibility is rooted in the spirit and receives from it life whereby to animate the organism.[71] Here we are in a zone of human activity where the cogitative power's order of exercise is so dominated by reason that the order of specification is, as it were, superelevated, with the result that sensibility imitates what is most characteristic of reason—grasping the relative within the absolute.[72]

The subjective and objective ascendancy of the mind over the cogitative power (its ascendancy over both the exercise of the act and its specification) is best explained by St. Thomas in texts wherein he deals with the relation between sensible appetite and liberty.

In two ways do the irascible and the concupiscible powers obey the higher part, in which are the intellect or reason, and the will. . . . They obey reason in their own acts (order of specification), because in other animals the sensitive appetite is naturally moved by the estimative power; for instance, the sheep, esteeming the wolf as an enemy, is afraid. In man the estimative power, as we have said above, is replaced by the cogitative power, which is called by some the particular reason, because it compares individual intentions. Hence, in man the sensitive appetite is naturally moved by this particular reason. But *this same particular reason is naturally guided and moved according to the universal reason.* . . . Anyone can experience this in himself; for by applying certain universal considerations, anger and fear or the like may be lessened or increased.[73]

This natural subordination of the cogitative power to the command of reason gives it an impartiality not shared by the estimative power in lower animals, for the latter works only in the subjective interest of the living being, and never in favor of the object as such; it lives the subject-object relation but does not perceive it: "Knowledge is given to animals, *not for the sake of knowledge, but for the sake of action.*"[74]

On the other hand, the cogitative power, insofar as it ceases being estimative and really becomes the instrument of a spiritual soul, perceives the real disinterestedly; it grasps it *as possessing this concrete nature,* independently of its utility or harmfulness, purely as an object of knowledge. The objectivating character of such knowledge is evident, for at this height, the object is distinct from the subject, it is experienced as distinct from it, as opposed to it, *as other than the subject.* The objectivity of its intuition—extraordinary for sense knowledge—gives the cogitative power[75] so much freedom in assessing the value coefficient of things that, unlike the estimative power of animals, it evaluates the whole field of sensory objects. For man's goods are coextensive with his needs, and his needs are as varied as the vegetative, sensible, intellectual, and supernatural life they characterize and reveal.[76] But there is a field in which the cogitative power plays a predominating epistemological role, and that is in organizing those famous *phantasmata* which St. Thomas is always talking about and which he practically never defines.[77] They are the matter on which the active intellect works, and the quality of the intelligible species produced by the active intellect is dependent upon the quality of the *phantasmata.* Now, what power will organize, unify the diverse images peopling our soul, so that these images may be useful to the intellect? The cogitative power, for it alone can grasp the bonds of utility existing between different images, by referring them to this particular existent outside the soul, which it alone knows directly and the deeper knowledge of which belongs to the intellect.

In this task of objectively knowing the singular thing and its appetible value, the cogitative power is marvelously assisted by another sensitive power, called the memory (or reminiscence if it is the human memory). The primary end of this faculty is to *preserve what the cogitative power knows and to locate it in time.*[78] It is the treasury of the cogitative power just as the imagination is the treasury of the common sense. We have seen that the cogitative power has two functions in man. On the one hand, it presents him with a physical universe composed of absolutes, of particular existents that differ from one another and are distinct and one. On the other hand, it perceives these absolutes as values, as things worthy of the knower's interest, or, on the contrary, as harmful to him. But these particular things, considered absolutely or relatively to their value, are immersed in movement and therefore change in time and place; this modifies both their being and value. Therefore, in order to preserve all the objectivity of knowledge, physical things must be *reknown,* which is to say that our present knowledge of them must in some manner be etched upon previously acquired perceptions in order to familiarize the soul with things, a familiarization that will become experience and serve as starting point for the acquisition of intellectual virtues.[79] This is where the need for memory comes in. Memory plays this role of such primary importance to our knowledge of a physical universe immersed in time, in a *nunc fluens* bound to the past and projected into the future.[80] The cogitative power, as we have seen, grasps the particular existent *as object of a future act*,[81] a thing to be sought or avoided; memory grasps it as *having already been the object* of pursuit or flight. With the *sensus communis* that seizes the *hic et nunc*, the cogitative power that projects it into future activity, and memory that locates it in the past, we have all the factors for a complete knowledge of time:

Which is nothing but the number of movement according to before and after. For since succession occurs in every movement, and one part comes after another, the fact that we reckon before and after in movement makes us apprehend time, which is nothing else but the number of before and after in movement.[82]

CONCLUSION ON IMMANENCE OF SENSIBLE KNOWLEDGE AND EXTERIORITY OF THE OBJECT

Now that we have considered sense knowledge in the immanence of its act and the exteriority of its object, what general insight do we have into the sensory process as a whole? First of all, we see it as a progressively better life, which becomes more and more immanent as the thing's causality penetrates the soul more deeply and frees it from its native passivity. Fascinated by the object to the point of being unaware of the subject, sensation is entirely and exclusively directed toward exterior things. The common sense and imagination keep their objective orientation but admit the subject into their orbit of knowledge; with the cogitative power and memory, the knowing subject becomes as well known as the object; it even assumes such importance that it subordinates, not knowledge of the object, but the being of the object to the interests of the subject; sensory life then becomes really interior.

A second general view of the sensory process reveals the progressive objectivity with which outer reality is known; first, because the aspects of things which, to begin with, were fragmentary and successive are unified in space or extension and are fixed as such by the common sense and imagination; then because they are also fixed in time by the cogitative power and memory, which gives to things in the process of becoming both a duration that determines them and a stability without which they would be unintelligible. We have not yet attained to knowledge of the physical universe as being, but we have already perceived it as *a being*.

The senses indeed do not know being, *except under the condition of here and now*, whereas the intellect apprehends being absolutely and for all time.[83]

In grasping being as particular, sense knowledge is like the porter or gatekeeper of the intellect; it leads the intellect to the contemplation of a universe that is not only composed of existents differing from each other by the individuality of their form, but united to each other by the very actuality of their act of existing.

Section III: Immanence of Intellectual Knowledge and Exteriority of the Object

The study of this last aspect of the nature of human knowledge brings us to the most bitterly discussed problem of the past two hundred years. The problem's longevity attests its difficulty but also facilitates its solution, for all its aspects have been analyzed, discussed, and reviewed from every angle. Therefore, all we have to do is to point out the meaning of the solutions given by St. Thomas, as well as their epistemological justification, which we shall do according to the plan we have followed throughout this chapter, by first considering the exercise of the act of knowledge and then its specification by exterior things.

The Act

A. IMMANENCE OF THE INTELLECT'S LIFE IN THE ORDER OF EXERCISE *5rols analogous to external sens.*

No sense knows itself or its own operation . . . for that depends on a higher power. The intellect, on the contrary, knows itself as well as its act of intellection.[84]

Intellectual knowledge is the life of the mind, and the mind is characterized by self-consciousness or the presence of a being to itself, a presence enabling it to fill two roles at once, those of observer and observed. This self-awareness varies with the being's degree of spirituality: in man, the most imperfect of spiritual beings self-awareness exists only after the stimulative action of exterior things upon the intellect, action leading man out of the unawareness that makes him a stranger to himself and enables him to know himself.

There is yet another intellect, namely the human, which is not its own act of understanding, nor is its own essence the first object of its act, for this object is *the nature of a material thing.* And therefore, that which is *first* known is an object of this kind, and that which is known *secondarily* is the act by which that object is known; and *through the act,* the intellect itself is known whose perfection is the act of understanding.[85]

Thus, our knowledge of the object is prior to our awareness of our acts, and this latter awareness makes us aware of ourselves:

We owe our actual knowledge of the existence of our own soul to the acts of the soul itself. For we perceive that we have a soul, live or exist, when we sense, understand and behave like a living being. But no one can be aware of knowing except by knowing something, *for the act of grasping the intelligible precedes the act of understanding it.* Perception of the soul's existence terminates the activity of sense and intellect concerning their objects.[86]

For us, the object therefore plays the role of a clutch with a two-gear shift, the first of which opens the soul to outward things, while the second opens the soul to itself, by the mediation of its own acts and the powers that are the principles of these acts. The immanence of the intellect's life has to do with this second aspect, during the study of which we shall see revealed the wonderful richness of intellectual activity and the infinite flexibility of its reflexivity.[87]

If we apply to the intellect's life the conditions we have seen to be essential to the perfection of sensory life,[88] then the possible intellect, the only knowing power we have in this order, must be able to fill the five following functions:

(1) It must be able to *receive* everything intelligible in the physical universe and, having received it, must know it in and by the actuality of its presence.

(2) Besides knowing the intelligible, it must be capable of *knowing* the act of intellection by which it grasps the intelligible.

(3) It must *preserve* the intelligible in act, even when the outward thing is absent, in order to be able to experience it freely.

(4) It must *perceive intentions*, the bonds between its different acts of knowing, and the concepts terminating them, in order to organize the microcosm that it becomes by means of its concepts.

(5) It must *preserve these perceived intentions* in order to use them again when the appropriate time comes.

These are the conditions essential to a perfect sensory life, conditions actualized by a minimum of five external and four internal senses. Can the possible intellect, by itself, fulfill the perfective role of all the external senses, of the common sense, of imagination, the cogitative power, and memory? If so, the immanence of the intellect's life is so superior to that of sensibility that the multiplicity of sensory powers seems like a sort of parody of intelligence.[89] But how could a single power fulfill all these seemingly diverse functions without having the quality of its activity suffer from so doing, without losing in efficiency and finish what it gains in extension? To discover the secret of the possible intellect's encyclopedic character is to penetrate its inner life and perceive its wholly immanent character in the order of exercise. Let us try to do so, by a brief consideration of each of the five points enumerated above.

The possible intellect is capable of receiving all the intelligibility of the universe and of knowing it. This point is easily established as soon as we remember what has been said about the nature of our intellectual power and its proper object, material being. Every intellect is equipped to know the being most immediately proportioned to it. The human intellect, belonging to the substantial form of a body, is immediately made to know being as corporeal,[90] to the degree that the latter is intelligible in act, that is, insofar as it is able to be in the intellect in accordance with the being of the intellect.[91] We have seen that the only reason why the agent intellect needs to exist is to give to the possible intellect its object, the intelligible in act, and that the latter is nothing but the physical thing as illumined by the agent intellect.[92] The function of the agent intellect is to make every physical being intelligible and to present it to the possible intellect, whose function it is to receive it and, having received, to know it. Therefore, it knows it, and since vital operation is immanent, this act remains within it as its property, the interior fruit of its fecundation by the intentional presence of the outward thing.[93] Thus, our possible intellect is able to *receive* the whole intelligibility of the universe and to know it.

2) *The possible intellect is able to know its act of intellection.* We have seen that, in the field of sensory life, awareness of the activity of the external senses is not due to the latter but to the common sense which knows simultaneously the objects and the acts of the external senses; and the reason this awareness is impossible is the materiality of sensory powers. However, the intellect is an immaterial power, able to reflect upon its own acts, and thus it is able to be aware of them. This is St. Thomas' answer to the objection that would deny awareness of its acts to the possible intellect by comparing it with the external senses:

The proper sense perceives by reason of the immutation in the material organ caused by the external sensible. A material thing, however, cannot immute itself, but one is immuted by another; and therefore the act of the proper sense is perceived by the common sense. The intellect, on the contrary, *does not have understanding by the material immutation of an organ,* and so there is no comparison.[94]

Therefore, thanks to its spirituality, the intellect can do everything the external senses and the common sense do, for its spiritual nature makes possible reflection and, by reflection, awareness of everything it does and all that enriches it. It knows both its act and the intentional species, effect of the agent intellect and principle of its proper operation: "Since the intellect reflects upon itself, by such reflection it understands *both its own act of understanding and the species by which it understands.*"[95]

Through this ability to reflect, our possible intellect becomes aware of the simultaneously objective and subjective principle of its act, i.e., the existence within itself of the intelligible species, and, by the latter, of its own nature as a spiritual power distinct from the soul. The object really awakens the intellect to itself and enables it to give unsuspected depth to the immanence of its operations, for by this reflexivity in knowledge we can discover not only the existence of the human soul, but also the spirituality of its nature and the infinite character of its needs and desires.

3) *The possible intellect is able to preserve the intelligible as known.* The common sense perceives the known as actually present by its action upon the external senses, but it cannot *preserve* this known as such; that function belongs to the imagination.[96] By itself, our intellect can do all the work of the imagination, for the object is not only present within it as principle of knowledge, but also as immanent term of this same act.

It must further be observed that the intellect, fecundated by the intentional species of the thing, *in exercising its fecundity begets within itself a likeness of the thing known*. . . . This must needs be so because we understand a thing equally well whether it be present or absent; in this the intellect is like the imagination. . . . But, since this likeness of the thing known terminates intellection, it differs from the intentional species which actuates the possible intellect, for the latter is at the beginning of the intellectual act; nevertheless both are likenesses of the thing understood.[97]

The concept is therefore truly the intellect's child, a child whose whole existence is interior to the power that serves as its mother, whereas the exterior thing serves as its father.

When the intellect knows something other than itself, this thing is as the father of the word conceived in the intellect, whereas the intellect is like the mother in whose womb conception takes place.[98]

But this child, or concept of the intellect and thing, is truly what the intellect first knows, for only here does being and the nature of things exist in an absolute way, without the mark of the *hic et nunc* or singularity.

The intellect has more [than the imagination] in this, that it understands the real *as separated from material conditions*, without which it does not exist in exterior things; but it could not do this without producing this likeness [or concept] of which we have spoken.[99]

Therefore, from the point of view of the exercise of intellectual activity, we are in a highly privileged position; for the intellect no longer needs the actual presence of the singular sensible, whereas it did depend on it to receive the intelligible species, the principle of its act, since, without referring to singular existents, the agent intellect would not have had a precise phantasm on which to work.[100] Furthermore, since exterior things exist in us, not only as *knowable* in act but *as known in act in and by* the concept, the latter, by its everpresent immanent presence, can itself become the object of our reflection and serve as starting point for a deeper knowledge of its content, for the discovery of bonds and characteristics of things that at first escape the intellect and then appear to it in this reflex motion. In so doing the intellect impersonates the cogitative power and memory, for it *perceives intentions*, perceives the unifying bonds between them and things, relations of conformity or nonconformity between concepts, and having perceived them, it carefully *preserves* them.

The possible intellect perceives and preserves intentions. With its assumption of functions identical to those of the cogitative power and memory, the intellect forsakes the *intuitive* character of its former procedures to adopt *rational* procedure; it becomes *collativa rationum universalium*, just as the cogitative power is *collativa rationum individualium*.[101] This new role of the intellect, which we usually conceive as exclusive to the mind's third operation, is much vaster than we imagine, for it defines the nature of our intelligence itself.

Thus it is evident that for the selfsame reason our intellect understands by discursion and by composing and dividing, namely *that in the first apprehension of anything newly apprehended it cannot at once grasp all that is virtually contained in it.* And this comes from the weakness of the intellectual light within us.[102]

It is therefore in the act of apprehension itself, an act essentially defining human knowledge, that we find the reason, or *ratio*, aspect of our intellect; it is because it belongs to the very nature of knowledge as such that the *rational* is found in those subsequent acts which reveal our knowledge's distinctive characteristic, truth, and the property of this truth, necessity.[103]

If we consider only the *immanent aspect* of the intellect's activity as *ratio*,[104] it is evident that, since the matter of this activity is the concept (i.e., the thing as actually existing in the soul as known), reason can freely compare concepts with each other. It can make a *collatio* of them,[105] collect them, and this is the group of cognitive operations that St. Thomas habitually refers to by the technical expressions *division*[106] and *abstraction*,[107] of which *definition*, another act of reason, is the result. Indeed, it is evident that all the possible intellect's abstractive activity is concerned with concepts and not with phantasms and things, and that it is wholly immanent to the intellect performing it, as the following text points out.

Abstraction by the intellect is twofold. One takes place when the universal is abstracted from the particular, as animal is abstracted from man; the other, when form is abstracted from matter, as the form of a circle is abstracted by the intellect from all sensible matter. The difference between these two abstractions consists in the fact that in the abstraction of the universal from the particular, that from which the abstraction is made does not remain; for when the difference of rationality is removed from man, the man *no longer remains in the intellect* and animal alone remains. But in abstraction in terms of matter and form, both the form and the matter *remain in the intellect*, as for instance, if we abstract the form of a circle from brass, there *remain in our intellect separately* both the understanding of a circle and the understanding of brass.[108]

This reflexive activity of the intellect can only be performed by reason, for all that results from it are those extraordinarily numerous *intentions* that people the soul; but they issue from it in an order constructed by reason itself, an order whose final perfection consists in that masterpiece of conceptual organization which is the key to Aristotle's *Topics*[109] and which, since the all-too-famous *Isagoge* of Porphyry, has been given the name of *the five predicables*. Completed by another conceptual arrangement, that of the ten predicaments and postpredicaments, these *intentions*, fruit of the intellect-reason, have nourished and still nourish logic as a rational instrument whereby the real may be better known.

Such is the function of reason insofar as it *perceives intentions* in the concepts provided and preserved by the intellect, intentions that the intellect as intuitive cannot perceive. All that intellect-memory contributes to this activity of reason is to preserve these intentions, these rational orderings collected by intellect-reason, and to re-serve them at the opportune moment, situating actual knowledge in time, which measures, not the intelligible, but the activity of the intelligent being.[110]

At the end of this study of the immanence of the intellect's life in the order of exercise, we can easily see the extraordinary superiority of intellectual knowledge over sensory knowledge. While the latter needs a multitude of powers in order for the qualified and quantified world to penetrate progressively into the soul, and while this progressive penetration always depends upon organs that are the instruments of sensorial powers and upon their state of health, the intellect's life needs but a single power, whose multiform functions terminate in results unsuspected by sensory life and with complete independence of the body in exercising its activity: "The body is necessary for the action of the intellect, *not as its organ, but on the part of the object.*"[111]

B. EXTERIORITY OF THE TERM OF THE INTELLECT'S LIFE IN THE ORDER OF SPECIFICATION

In the second aspect of its life, the intellect must from without seek the measure of its acts of knowledge and be nourished by an increasingly perfect assimilation of the riches offered it by this world.

Here the intellect is so completely dependent on the physical world, and particularly on the physical reality which is its body, that it can know absolutely nothing (in the strict sense of the word, of grasping *what is*) without the continuous help of the body and all the activity of sensory knowledge. Consequently, we must now re-examine the different activities of our possible intellect, no longer in relation to its progressive awareness of its own acts and the spiritual soul whose power it is, but from the point of view of its increasingly perfect presence to the exterior world, a presence enabling it deeply to penetrate the real, and to force that real to disclose its secret, which sensory knowledge cannot do.

Senses do not apprehend the essences of things, but only their outward accidents. Neither does the imagination, for it apprehends only the likenesses of bodies. *The intellect alone apprehends the essences of things* . . . regarding which it does not err, as neither does sense regarding its proper sensible object.[112]

Let us glance briefly at the successive stages through which the half-light that is our possible intellect must pass if it would finally succeed in grasping outward things wholly.[113]

¶ *First Stage: Apprehension of the Outward Real as Indistinct Being.* In the epistemological texts of St. Thomas this statement is constantly repeated: Being is the first aspect perceived by the intellect in its relations with things and underlies the ultimate intelligibility of the real.

In the first operation, there is a first thing conceived by the intellect, namely what I call *being;* and nothing can be conceived by this operation without conceiving being. . . .[114]

That is prior in idea which is first conceived by the intellect. Now the first thing conceived by the intellect is *being*, because everything is knowable only inasmuch as it is actually. Hence *being* is the proper object of the intellect and is thus the *first intelligible*, as sound is the first audible. . . .[115]

Now a certain order is to be found in those things which are apprehended by men. For that which *first falls under apprehension is being*, the understanding of which is included in all things whatsoever a man apprehends.[116]

But what is this being, which is the first intelligible and the first object that is understood?

The first object of our intellect, in this state of life, is not every being and everything true, but *being and true as found in material things* . . . from which it acquires knowledge of all other things.[117]

The humblest of intellects must therefore seek its first food in the universe of physical things, for there is to be found the sole object that falls within the immediate grasp of a spirit which is the form of a body.

The first thing known by the human intellect is physical being. Does the intellect apprehend it immediately and suddenly, without any previous act of reflection? Certainly, for if it were not intuitive with respect to its proper object, it would not be an intellect.[118] Nevertheless, there is a whole gamut of intellects whose perceptive acuity varies strangely. Compared with divine intellect, every created intellect is but darkness and obscurity; it is *aenigmaticus*. Compared with an angelic intellect, our own is filled with darkness and shadow (*in aenigmate vidit*), because it depends upon sensibility to receive its first and most natural object, while an angel is *deiformis*, depending only upon God to be a locus of forms.[119] Possessing a natural object whose existence is measured by duration, our intellect, in becoming aware of an object, is conditioned by this object, which is a mixture of act and potency; its knowledge, indistinct at first, is gradually actualized:

In our knowledge there are two things to be considered. *First*, that our intellectual knowledge in some degree arises from sensible knowledge. Now because sense has singular and individual things for its object, and intellect has the universal for its object, it follows that our knowledge of the former comes before our knowledge of the latter. *Secondly*, we must consider that our intellect proceeds from a state of potentiality to a state of actuality; and that every power thus proceeding from potentiality to actuality comes first to an incomplete act, which is intermediate . . . before accomplishing the perfect act. The perfect act of the intellect is complete knowledge, when the object is *distinctly and determinately known*, whereas the incomplete act is imperfect knowledge, when the object is known *indistinctly, and as it were confusedly*. A thing thus imperfectly known is known partly in act and partly in potentiality . . .

and thus to know animal indistinctly is to know it as animal, whereas
to know animal distinctly is to know it as rational or irrational, that is to
know a man or a lion. And so our intellect knows animal before it knows
man; *and the same reason holds in comparing any more universal concept with the less universal.*[120]

But the most global universal that we apprehend is precisely the
first-known being,[121] which may be described in the words St.
Thomas uses to describe the radically imperfect way in which the
Greek physicists first grasped the four causes of being:

They spoke confusedly of these causes, for although they alluded to all
of them, they did not deal thoroughly with any one of them. As when
children, in their first attempts to talk, speak imperfectly and falteringly,
so does the philosophical knowledge of the first thinkers seem to us, in
its infancy, like stammering about the principles of everything that is.[122]

The same is true of being: its existence, like that of nature, is evident
even though we do not distinctly know what constitutes it.[123] This
is the reason that it is evident in the mind's first act, and this evidence
pervades each and every one of the subsequent acts, which are but
the actualization of this first whole.

What is the content of this first universal, this first concept; to
what aspect of the thing does it correspond? We can safely answer
that the content of this first universal corresponds to the aspect of
the real that pre-exists in phantasms, since the latter play a specifying
role in the production of the intelligible species,[124] to which the
concept is related as a child to its father. But what do phantasms
contain before the intervention of reason? In them are the forms of
sensible things as rudimentarily received through sensations, therefore, quantified, localized, numbered, and moving forms, preserved
by the imagination, organized by the cogitative power and memory
in a determined place and time, and relative to the interests aroused
by the imagined thing in the knowing subject.[125] That is the state
of phantasms in the soul of a child before the first intellectual act.
What unity does this group of images present to the agent intellect?
Primarily it offers unity of the quantitative order; all these known
singulars are corporeal, therefore, have three dimensions; furthermore, they are all localized and temporal and thus are either mobile

or immobile. This lack of differentiation in quantitative unity and becoming suffices for abstration of the *first universal:*

For when several known singulars are *undifferentiated* with respect to one aspect existing in them all, *this aspect in which they are undifferentiated,* once known by the soul, *constitutes the first universal,* independent of its content, i.e. independent of whether or not this aspect belongs to the nature of the singulars.[126]

By interpreting this text, describing the genesis of the first universal, in the light of the text that describes the chronological order in which the unity of a thing is grasped, we can readily see what aspect of the real is perceived in the concept of being. The first unity that we perceive in the thing is the unity of the *continuum,* because, as St. Thomas says, apprehension of magnitude as a whole is indistinct when compared with apprehension of its parts and therefore precedes it, since imperfect knowledge precedes distinct knowledge.[127] But magnitude is one of the common sensibles accompanying all sense knowledge, because it is the first subject of sensible qualities. Thus, all singulars existing in the imagination are undifferentiated in this aspect, which can therefore serve as matter for the agent intellect's first abstraction. However, this first undifferentiated aspect, common to all singulars, is never alone, for, as we know it, magnitude is always conditioned by nearness or distance and thus has immediate reference to movement:

Movement and rest are sensed according as the sujbect is affected in one or more ways *in its magnitude* or in its local distance, as in the movement of growth and locomotion, or again, as it is affected in some sensible qualities, as in the movement of alteration.[128]

The unifying aspect of all singulars known by the imagination is therefore both magnitude and the actual state of becoming that conditions it. The expression St. Thomas always uses for this is *hic et nunc* (here and now), which refers to both place and time, measures of the movable and of movement. All singulars are *undifferentiated* because they are actualized by movement or absence of movement, two correlatives that have meaning only in coexistence; they are thus matter for abstraction insofar as *magnitude or cor-*

poreity and the movement informing it are common to each and every thing. If the agent intellect puts singularity aside to consider only the commonly held undifferentiated aspect, what remains as intelligible content? Something in process of becoming that can be verbally expressed by *quod est,* what is, or being.

It may seem surprising that we apparently identify the thing in motion with the thing in act of existing, an identification which makes possible the affirmation that since the first universal is the apprehension of an actually moving corporeal thing, it is also the apprehension of being or of the *quod est.* But what is more plausible than that an intellect whose proper object is being in process of becoming should grasp this object in what characterizes it, i.e., in its mobility, and that movement be for us like a substitute for the act of existing, since it reveals it?

Since words are signs of our concepts, we give names to the things the intellect first apprehends, although these things are not first in the order of nature. But *the most immediately knowable and evident of all acts, for us, is motion* which we perceive through the senses. Consequently the name of act has primarily been given to movement, and thence applied to other things. And that is why there can never be any question of movement outside of existents. . . . For since *to be moved* means *to be in act,* it would follow that non-existents exist, which is evidently false.[129]

Therefore, since the first universal is being and since being is *what is* (a concept we express in two words, one of which is a pronoun, the other a verb), and, furthermore, since the verb's function is to signify *action and passion,*[130] which are the two factors essential to the being of movement itself,[131] it is natural that being (which is defined in terms of becoming) be known by a concept that apprehends it simultaneously as a *quod* in *process of becoming,* therefore as a *quod est.* For the verb expresses action by mode of action, as inherent to an actually present or existing subject,[132] and the first meaning of *est* is *in actu esse,*[133] which is identical with the meaning of movement, the first analogue, in our way of conceiving, of all acts to come.

First-known being is therefore the real considered as every actually existing corporeal thing. Obviously this knowledge has extraordinary potentiality since all singulars, whatever they may be, are virtually contained in this first and most universal of all concepts. But universality of extension pays a high price in comprehension, for, because of its poverty of content, this concept is predicable of each and every singular without distinction. Being as first known is not only in potency to two species, as animal is, but contains virtually all corporeal beings, past, present, and future; it truly is, as the *Summa* text explained, imperfect and indistinct knowledge which is but a first step toward determined and perfect knowledge.[134] The imperfection of this first concept does not result from the universality of the concept itself as a medium of knowledge, but from the indetermination of the thing known, the indetermination of the exterior thing that reveals itself only by its appearance—its corporeity and becoming. This distinction between the two kinds of universality is of capital importance in differentiating this first knowledge of being from the knowledge of being as being, which we will come to at the end of this inquiry. Here is how they are distinguished:

To know anything universally can be taken in two senses. In one way, on the part of the thing known, namely, that *only the universal nature* of the thing is known. To know a thing thus is something less perfect; for he would have an imperfect knowledge of a man who only knew him to be an animal. In another way, *on the part of the medium* of such universal knowledge. In this way it is more perfect to know a thing in the universal; for the intellect, which by one universal medium *can know singulars properly*, is more perfect than one which cannot.[135]

What makes first-known being the poorest of concepts is that it contains no distinct knowledge, not only of any singular, but also of any specific nature, nor even of the nature of being as such. It is approximate evidence of physical being in the very actuality of its becoming, whence the lack of distinction and determination of its content.

¶ *Second Stage: Apprehension of Outward Reality as Distinct Being.* Since the poverty of first-known being is owing to the indistinctness of the real as presented by phantasms and abstracted by the agent intellect, all subsequent knowledge will still be acquired in terms of being, but with greater precision. In this progressive determination of the content of our concepts, universal being as first apprehended serves as a natural starting point.

In our intellect there are some concepts naturally known by all, such as the concept of being, one, good, etc., which the intellect uses as a starting point in seeking *the quiddity of each thing*, just as it seeks knowledge of conclusions starting from self-evident principles. This happens either with the help of what is perceived through the senses, as e.g. when we conceive the quiddity of a thing by means of its sensible properties; or by means of the spoken words we hear . . . or again, by means of truths revealed to us, as in faith.[136]

What order is followed in this quest for the quiddity? We know that its starting point, being as first known, is indeterminate like *quod*, since it contains virtually everything insofar as it is corporeal or has dimensions; it is also indeterminate like *est*, since we find it in movement, whether local motion, growth, or change, in that it actually inheres in and issues from this corporeal whole.

What is the goal of this quest for the quiddity? That which is *quod quid est*. We should note right here that *quod quid est* includes *quod est*, indeterminate being plus *quid*. What does this addition mean? Does it determine the *quod* or the *est*? To find out we need only put the three terms in grammatical order, and we have the following formula: *quod est quid*, or being as *quid*, as having a particular or specific nature—briefly, insofar as it is a thing or *res*. Thus, the second stage in our pursuit of the real seeks first and foremost to determine the *quod* element of being. The term, or goal, of this search is actual knowledge of the nature of existing things, knowledge of being as *res*.[137]

The poverty of first-known being is, in effect, only apparent, for beneath the very general aspects striking the intellect is hidden a wealth of determinations of which we are not yet aware, because the phantasms presenting the thing to us are themselves indeterminate:

Phantasms are to the intellect as colors to the sight. Consequently, just as a confusion of colors produces indetermination and confusion in the act of seeing, so, from the confusion of phantasms there results a certain lack of precision in the intellect's act. That is why children have at first only a confused vision of some universals, but subsequently and with time acquire a distinct knowledge of each.[138]

The theory that intellectual activity depends completely upon phantasms, a theory pronounced axiomatic and tacitly assumed in the explanation of concepts, has cost Thomism its *a posteriori* and inductive character, for which has been substituted an *a priori* and deductive skill that is more like a capricious game of concepts than a progressive apprehension of reality through what is most ontological in reality. The insistence with which St. Thomas continually returns to this thesis reveals its importance.[139] By applying it, the human intellect succeeds in grasping existing quiddities.

As the word indicates, intellect implies knowledge which attains the inward depth of things. . . . But it sometimes happens that the intellect can reach the heart of things only by passing through a series of zones that are as its approaches. Such is the human mode of apprehending; it proceeds from *knowledge of the effects and properties of things to that of their essence.* And as this cannot take place without a certain reciprocating movement, human apprehension is called *ratio* although its term is intellectual, for rational inquiry attains to the essence.[140]

Our distinct knowledge of the thing as quiddity therefore makes use of the characteristic accidents that exteriorize the inward nature of things, so as to penetrate, by their intermediation, to the very heart of things and define them in their essence. This knowledge of accidents is given us by the whole group of sensory operations:

Our intellect, which knows the essence of a thing as its proper object, is dependent on sense, of which the proper objects are external accidents. Hence it is that from *external appearances we come to the knowledge of the essence of things.*[141]

Knowledge of being as distinct, i.e., as quiddity, is acquired by a process contrary to that by which the universal concept of being is formed; for, instead of working with undifferentiated phantasms, the ensemble of images has to center upon differentiating factors that disclose the real nature of a whole category of things. Thus, the phantasms that the agent intellect uses as matter from which to abstract the quiddity of man must combine all the aspects characteristic of a multitude of human individuals: shape, form, something composed of flesh and bones, a certain inner and outer behavior, a sensibility, and a few spiritual acts. If this immense fund of images, preserved in the imagination and memory, is united in such a way as to reveal the typically human aspects of these different accidents or properties, the knowledge resulting from the abstraction of this phantasm will be the apprehension of the quiddity of man. If, on the contrary, these images are combined in such a way that interest is centered upon the secondary aspects, then this knowledge will be purely nominal.[142] For the agent intellect, the ideal sensible matter for abstraction is the unification of phantasms in an order whose principle is the specific accidents of the things apprehended, because, "just as when the same letters, arranged in different orders, have different meanings, so when phantasms are differently arranged, different intelligible species result from them in the intellect."[143] This unification of phantasms is necessary not only at the beginning but also at the end of intellectual knowledge of natures, for the intellect knows only by turning back to the phantasms that furnish the specifying element of the intelligible species.[144] It is in the phantasms that the intellect contemplates the quiddity of things.

The possible intellect, like every other substance, acts in accordance with what it is; now it is, by nature, the form of a body; so it understands immaterial things but sees them as immersed in matter. That this is necessary is attested by the use of particular examples as illustrations in the teaching of universal truths. The possible intellect, in its need for phantasms, behaves differently before and after receiving intelligible species. Before, it needs the phantasm as the source from which it will receive the species, and the phantasm's role with respect to the possible intellect is that of object-motor. But after receiving the species, the possible intellect needs the phantasm as an instrument or basis for its species; here the possible intellect behaves towards the phantasm like an efficient cause. For, *at the intellect's command there is formed in the imagination a phantasm adapted to the intellectual species in which the latter shines forth like the exemplar in a copy or image.*[145]

The first reason that this return to an organized phantasm is necessary is identical with the reason that the phantasm is necessary at the beginning of our knowledge: the imperfection of the human intellect, which can know nothing distinctly without using its body, because its proper object exists in matter, for it discovers the *quod quid est* in the same place that it discovers the *quod est* in the physical universe.

The proper object of the human intellect, which is united to a body, is the quiddity of a nature existing in corporal matter. . . . Now it belongs to such a nature to exist in some individual, and this cannot be apart from corporal matter; for instance, it belongs to the nature of a stone to be in an individual stone and to the nature of a horse to be in an individual horse, and so forth. Therefore the nature of a stone or of any material thing cannot be known *completely and truly* except in as much as it is known *as existing in the individual.* . . . And therefore, for the intellect to understand *actually* its proper object, it must of necessity turn to the phantasms in order to perceive the universal nature existing in the individual.[146]

The passage from indistinct to distinct knowledge of being takes place through determination of the *quod;* it is the nature of this corporeal whole found in the first-known being that is the object of our investigations. We scrutinize it, weigh and examine all its characteristic aspects, eliminating some to give preference to others that seem more typical; in this way, we succeed in apprehending not a vague *quod*, but a *hoc quod* in its quiddity, a corporeal whole with its distinctive elements, or a *res*. The choice of the word *res* to designate the specific nature of a category of things gives vivid emphasis to the correlations that should exist between a vocabulary and the ideas it expresses. Taken literally, *res* means the goods, or stable possessions, of a man, or of a society.[147] Every being as *this* being is the owner of a fixed and stable domain that no created force could ever take away.[148] To know a being as *res* is precisely to recognize that all these accidents, these *circumposita*[149] surrounding this being like so many suburbs, depend on it, live off it, and that by crossing through them we will come to the true owner, being as quiddity or *res*.

Nevertheless, we must not imagine that, in analyzing the *quod*, the *est* is totally eliminated, for what we are seeking is the *quod quid est*. Being, the *quod est*, is always both the starting point and the goal of our quest; but whereas in the beginning we perceived it very confusedly, from what might be called generic aspects,[150] at the end we find that it is still being though now precise and formed. To use St. Thomas' apt expression, in the first concept of being, the universality of our knowledge refers to the *thing known*, in the second, universality refers to the *mode* of knowledge and not to the thing known.[151] For the thing is apprehended in that which makes it to be itself, in the quiddity that makes it indivisible in itself and separate from everything not itself; it is known in its specific determination by the intellect and in its individual determination by sensibility, for the apprehension of natures, like that of being in general, can be perfect only in the wedding of intelligence and sensibility.[152]

¶ *Third Stage: Apprehension of External Things as Substance and Accidents.* The intellect therefore knows being as a distinct *quod*, as a nature composed of this matter and this form that it intuitively apprehends as a whole, indivisible in act, whose components can be distinguished by the mind in a subsequent act according to genus, according to specific and *individual* difference.[153] In order to apprehend the quiddity the intellect made use of the *circumposita* as visible signs obscuring this nature, but revealing it too, insofar as careful selection eliminated lesser aspects and kept only the typical characteristics capable of disclosing the quiddity of a being.

But a problem remains: What shall we do with these *circumposita*, the quiddity's entourage of accidents? Shall we consider them as refuse to be cast out by the agent intellect into the realm of non-being? In stating the problem of knowledge, we saw that, unlike science, Thomistic philosophy has no disposal unit for the left-overs of being and knowledge[154]; it loses not a crumb of either but keeps and orders them in a hierarchy of values. That is what our intellect does in the presence of quiddities and their external appearances; instead of reducing being to quiddity and the act of existing, it tries to lose nothing that the physical universe discloses; it considers this changing world according to the organic bonds revealed in distributing it into two main sections, substance and accidents.

This new information that being imparts concerning itself opens up a new field to the intellect, the field of *intentiones*, bonds uniting the different aspects of reality and apprehended as such by the intellect-reason. Our intellect's effort to deepen its knowledge of being is no longer directed toward the thing considered as an absolute quiddity, but rather as a center of convergence and radiation for a multitude of modifications that perfect natures without modifying their essence. No longer is the intellect interested in only the *quod quid est* and the *est* of the thing; now it is interested in all the ontological bonds between the *quod quid est* and its *circumpositae* which make the former a substance and the latter not only visible signs of a hidden reality but accidents, effects of substances and the instruments of their perfection: "The subject is both the final cause, and in a way the active cause of its proper accidents. It is also as it were the material cause, inasmuch as it is receptive of the accidents."[155]

In this new view that the intellect takes of distinct being, there is something similar to the way the cogitative power looks at sensible things. For, as we have seen, the knowledge acquired through the cogitative power is not knowledge of a new thing but new knowledge of the same thing, which, instead of being seen as an absolute, enters into a network of correlations wherein it is the center of attraction.[156] Now it would seem that the being which the intellect knows through outward appearances as *quod quid est* is none other than the being known as constituted by the two opposing elements, substance and accident (the latter of which is subdivided into nine irreducible categories); therefore knowledge of the thing as substance and accidents adds nothing to what we have already known. As a matter of fact, we can truthfully say that there is not more of reality in the apprehension of being as substance and accidents, but that there is new knowledge of something already known; we are pouring old wine into new bottles! The old wine is the *quod quid est* and its *circumpositae*. The new bottles are the hitherto unperceived bonds situating the thing in a wholly different context. Indeed, as long as we know being as quiddity, what matters is its interior unity, but as soon as we consider it as substance and accidents—although unity is always present and presupposed—what is most important for being is its *perfection;* for a created being is not perfect through its quiddity but through its accidents.

Since being properly signifies that something actually is, and actuality properly correlates to potentiality, a thing is, in consequence, said absolutely to have being, accordingly as it is primarily distinguished from that which is only in potentiality; and this is precisely each thing's substantial being. Hence *it is by its substantial being* that every thing is said to have being absolutely; but by any further actuality it is said to have being relatively. Thus to be white signifies being relatively, for to be white does not take a thing out of absolutely potential being, since it is added to a thing that actually has some being.

But goodness expresses perfection, which is something desirable, and hence it expresses something final. Hence that which has ultimate perfection is said to be absolutely good, but that which has not the ultimate perfection it ought to have (although, in so far as it is at all actual it has some perfection) is not said to be perfect absolutely nor good absolutely, but only relatively. In this way, therefore, viewed in its first or substantial being, a thing is said to *be absolutely* and to be *good relatively,* in so far as it has being; but viewed in its complete actuality a thing is said *to be relatively* and to be *good absolutely.* . . .[157]

Thus, created being is perfect by means of its accidents; and, since perfection is in things and is identified with the whole being,[158] to know being as perfect is not to apprehend more being but to apprehend it differently. That is exactly what knowledge of being as substance and accidents gives the intellect, for in this way the intellect apprehends being not only in itself but in all its relations with other beings about it. Thus, in giving extension to being, quantity enables it to be situated in place; qualities bestow on it a multitude of capacities for action and passion enabling it to come into contact with other things, to set up relations, to be the principle and term of movements. In other words, it is by means of its accidents that every created thing can be a part of the universal whole, can take its place and fulfill its function in this whole, and in so doing sing the glory of God, each in its own way. Accidents are really the complements of quiddity, and through them its act of existing is made fruitful. The axiom, "Every agent acts in so far as it is in act," can be applied to created substance only when this substance has all its accidents, for through them it attains to absolute actuality. Whereas the being of accidents is meaningful only with reference to quiddity, and accidents are truly beings only insofar as they inhere concretely in substance,[159] all the perfection of substance is to be found, on the contrary, by reference to its accidents. Through them it is perfect; they are in it, by it, and for it; they are the effect of its substantial being and are the means of perfection for this same substantial being.[160]

¶ *Fourth Stage: Apprehension of Exterior Reality as a Multitude of Unified Beings.* To apprehend each being distinctly as quiddity, to apprehend it distinctly as a perfect whole composed of substance and accidents, is to penetrate to the very heart of the thing and perceive its total wealth. This done, the *quid* of being is known from every angle, and each being is seen as an absolute unity distinguished from everything that is not itself and does not properly belong to it as a perfection. But what progress have we made in apprehending the *est*, which is surely an essential element of the definition of being? Has our work on the *quod*, to discover its quiddity and free it from indistinctness, made us forget the *est*?

No, we have not been able to forget it, for every quiddity, in order to be a quiddity, implies the act of existing[161]; besides, substance defined as absolute actuality and the concrete character of accident, considered as in-existent, have stressed the fact of existence. But the nature of *est*, if we may use this word, has been left obscure, and it is time to bring it to light. This is not easy, for *est* is on the side of act and act is one of those altogether primary and simple aspects that cannot be defined and can only be circumscribed inductively from within a group of proportionalities.[162] Consequently, we shall use all the material discovered in analyzing *quod est, quod quid est*, and substance and accidents, to apprehend *est* in its fundamental characteristics.

In our first perception of being, *est* is seen as an act. What intelligibility does act have at that moment? That of the first analogue or first actuality we are able to apprehend—motion.[163] By the becoming and causality of things we perceive their existence, just as by the very act of knowledge we perceive that we exist.[164] Therefore, at this initial phase of the knowledge of being, *est* designates each and every movement, those of exterior things as well as those we experience within ourselves. In one way it is *too determined*, for to identify *est* with the most knowable of its symptoms, movement, on the pretext that they both mean *in actu esse*, is certainly to impoverish the act of existing and to deprive it of the enigmatic character that has made it the despair of all philosophers.[165] This equation is valuable at the level of being indistinctly known, but it must become flexible and even disappear as soon as the word *actus* means realities that, by nature, are not mobile. When we define *res*, or the *quid* of *quod est*, as being composed of matter and form and want to know the respective functions of the matter and form whose composition constitutes the *quidditas*, we apprehend *form* as the *actus* of matter. Here, the word *act* no longer has any immediate relation to movement,[166] but merely indicates that what was indeterminate is now determined. It is the same when we define the soul as the first act of a physically organized body,[167] for there is no question of defining the soul as act in the sense of movement, since we have rejected this definition given by some Greek thinkers[168]; we are defining it, rather, as the specific or formal element of a body endowed with life. Act no longer means becoming but *that by which* a thing is what it is. The same is true of the accidents that are called *acts* of substance; the word act no longer signifies motion but *that by which* an already constituted thing is endowed with supplemental being.[169]

If, from the new perspective offered by the different meanings of the word *actus*, we look back at the *est* that enters into the definition of being, we see that it can have three meanings: becoming substantial form, or *that by which* matter is actualized; and accidental form, *that by which* a substantial being receives a new actuality. But the *est*, or act of existing, without which being is inconceivable, is not becoming: "The act of existing is the stable, immobile element in being."[170] Nor is it a substantial form, for otherwise only beings composed of matter and substantial form would exist. Furthermore, substantial form is but the first act supposing a second act other than itself; this second actuality, added to the substantial actuality given by form, has as its principle the act of existing.

The nature of material things . . . contains a twofold composition. The first is that of matter and form, from which the nature is constituted. Such a nature is not its own being but being is its act. Hence the nature itself is related to its own being *as potentiality to act*.[171]

Finally, *est* cannot, *a fortiori*, signify accidental form that exists only through the intermediation of substance: "Since being is not a genus, the *act of existing* cannot be the essence of either substance or accident."[172]

Since *est* means *actus* and none of the meanings, examined so far, of *quod quid est*, substance and accidents, can be applied to it, this act must be something completely particular, giving it a privileged place in the series of realities to which we apply the word *actus!* What then is the meaning of *est?*

To be is in itself *the most perfect* of all things, for it is compared to all things *as that which is act: for nothing has actuality except so far as it is*. Hence to be is the actuality of all things, even of forms themselves. Therefore it is not compared to other things as the receiver is to the received, but rather as the received to the receiver. When therefore I speak of the *existere* of man, or of a horse or of anything else, to be is considered as a formal principle, and as something *received,* and not as that to which it belongs to be. [173]

The act of existing is therefore that which is shared by all, but which shares in nothing.[174] Strictly speaking, it signifies neither form, nor substance, nor essence, and much less matter or subject, but *that by which* everything in reality is formally said to be and without which nothing deserves that title: "Before quiddity exists *it is nothing,* except in the creative intellect where it is not a creature but the creative essence itself."[175]

For St. Thomas, the act of existing, *est*, formally characterizes *being as being*, because in it and by it everything is opposed to nothing. Consequently, it belongs to all, without anything's being able to claim it for itself alone or to have inalienable rights over it, at least among creatures. But precisely this *communism in the act of existing* enables the human intellect to unify the multitude of distinct beings it knows as *quod quid est* and to consider each thing, with its essential complexity of matter and form, its existential complexity of substance and accidents, no longer as an isolated thing separated from everything not itself, but as constituting with each and all of the beings around it a unity, a wholly distinctive totality that we designate by the concept *being as being*. With this concept we reach the peak of our awareness of the real, for we possess the most perfect concept the human intellect is capable of originating here below.

To conclude this analysis of the specification of human knowledge by external reality, we should like briefly to describe the formation of this concept of being as being and to destroy some preconceptions branding it as the poorest offspring of the intellect; actually, it is the richest and has the most spectacular destiny, since it is the sole direct path leading our mind to the throne of God.[176] Obviously, knowledge of being as being cannot be identified with our first knowledge of being, since first-known being is the most indeterminate and potential of all the concepts constructed by the intellect in its relations with the physical world. Examination of the indetermination characterizing our concept of first-known being reveals that it deals with the *quod* and not the *est* of being, for just as *quod* is potential, since it refers to all corporeal things insofar as they have dimensions, and therefore to the whole quantified physical universe, so is *est* determined because it has to do with being in its visible substitute, movement.[177] This first determination of *est* by its identification with the first-known act, movement, disappears at the second stage of our knowledge of the real, i.e., the definition of being as quiddity or particular nature. For the notion of *actus*, instead of remaining identical with movement, broadens and refers to that aspect of things called substantial form in its function with respect to primary matter: it is the *actus* of matter. There is a third indetermination of the notion of *actus* when, in the division of being into substance and accidents, the latter are known as the perfection of substance, as a new *actus* added to the first act, form.

Reflecting upon the phenomenon just described, we arrive at this strange observation: *The greater the determination of the* quod *of being, the greater the indetermination of the meaning of* est *defined as "act."* For instead of having only the meaning of becoming, as it did at the beginning, it now has three seemingly contradictory meanings. Furthermore, we have seen that none of these three meanings was really the original meaning of *est*,[178] since becoming is being only by virtue of the actuality engendering it, and substantial form, accidental form, and essence are called acts only insofar as they are determined by the act of existing. Consequently, at the conclusion of our analysis of being, *est* or the act of existing seems to be the most undifferentiated reality we know, whereas the *quod* or *res*, on the contrary, has achieved the utmost differentiation, by the distinction of its components, matter, and form, by the distinction of its unity and perfection, substance and accidents, and finally, by the distinction of essence and existence.

Things are not distinguished from each other by their existence, for in this they are all alike. . . . Things differ in this, that they have *different natures*, by means of which they acquire existence in different ways.[179]

To infer lack of differentiation is to mean vagueness, or lack of distinction, and lack of distinction is synonymous with potentiality and confusion, therefore, with imperfection.[180] Whence the rather remarkable conclusion that the term of our knowledge of being as such would be knowledge as indeterminate and imperfect as was the principle of our knowledge! Consequently, we should be able to set up the following proportion:

$$\frac{\text{first-known being}}{\text{being as being}} \quad : \quad \frac{\text{as the indetermination of } quod}{\text{is to the indetermination of } est}$$

Can this proportion really be set up? A reading of St. Thomas' texts would seem to insist upon it, for all his expressions lean in that direction. Indeed, he expresses being as the existing by the words *commune, universale, communius, universalius*.[181] Besides, when he describes our knowledge of being as being, he does so in the following terms: *cognoscere in universali, in communi, in potentia*, as opposed to *cognoscere proprie, particulariter, actu*.[182]

However, we must not hastily conclude that common or universal knowledge of being as existing is identical with knowledge of first-known being, or that it is less perfect than our knowledge of quiddity. For in the language of St. Thomas the words *universaliter* and *communiter* can have two completely opposite meanings, depending on whether they indicate the *thing known* or the *medium* by which it is known, as we have already pointed out above.[183] The poverty of universal knowledge is owing to the confusion of its contents and not to the universality of the medium through which it is acquired. Therefore, universal knowledge of singular natures is infinitely richer than individual knowledge acquired through all or any of the senses, since universal knowledge apprehends the nature proper to each individual, whereas the senses know only the exterior accidents of these same singulars.[184] Thus, angels apprehend material things by much more universal media than ours and yet their knowledge, unlike man's, gives them distinct knowledge of the singular.[185] And in God's knowledge of singulars there is but one medium through which is apprehended everything that exists, down to the minutest detail.[186]

It is therefore to the degree that the *thing known* is indistinct and potential that the universal knowledge it begets is imperfect and potential. In concluding our inquiry into the nature of the real, can we say that *est* is indistinct? For a final answer to this question, whose solution reveals both the greatness and the littleness of our intelligence, we shall consult a text from *De Ente et Essentia*,[187] the understanding of which is essential to the notion of distinctness or lack of distinctness in a thing, and to our proper or confused knowledge of it. In this text St. Thomas is comparing the different aspects of the nature of a thing from the angle of distinctness or the lack of it, using the *quod quid est* of man as illustration. He sets forth two ways of apprehending this quiddity: concretely and abstractly. The explanation has two phases.

¶ *1. Concrete Knowledge of the Quiddity.* Man can be considered solely in what is imperfect in the totality of his nature, in which case he is apprehended as animal or sensible living thing; this presupposes the indetermination of what perfects him, namely, rationality. Man can, on the contrary, be known in his most perfect and actual aspect, i.e., his rationality, which distinguishes him from every other nature but leaves him indeterminate with respect to individuals. Man can be known as Socrates, and in this third knowledge the determinateness is not concerned with human nature but with this nature's mode of being, with the individuation it owes to matter, thus with what is unintelligible to us.

Comparison of these three aspects of human nature gives us the following result.

(a) Man, as animal, is indistinct as form or act. (b) Man, as rational, is distinct as nature, *indistinct as individual*. (c) Socrates is distinct as nature and distinct as individual. If we compare the first indistinctness, wherein man is considered as animal, with the second, in which he is considered as possessing a specific nature without its individual notes, it is obvious that the first introduces *imperfection* into our knowledge of quiddity, whereas the second brings *perfection;* for individuation by quantified matter is a sign of the imperfection of a nature that cannot subsist in itself and is obliged to borrow from without in order to become subsistent. The quidditative knowledge of man is therefore perfect knowledge of his nature's perfection, while individual knowledge is the perfect apprehension of the imperfection of this same nature that cannot exist in itself but must exist in a subject. Thus, the individual is a limitation of the perfection of human nature, whereas rationality is a limitation of the imperfection of animal nature. We can therefore set up the following proportion:

$$\frac{man}{animal} \; : \; \frac{\text{nature of man}}{\text{Socrates}} \; : \; \frac{\text{perfect}}{\text{imperfect}}$$

To know man as nature is therefore to know what is perfect in man, while to know his animality and individuality is to apprehend what is imperfect in human nature, because act is either lacking or limited.

¶ *2. Abstract Knowledge of Man's Quiddity.* If we now consider the relations between *man* and *humanity,* we perceive that *humanity* is to *man* as the determinate to the indeterminate, the distinct to the confused. Indeed, humanity is *that by which* a man is a man, it is the formal element of the subsistent man or Socrates. Consequently, it is the principle of determination and distinction of man as specific nature, whereas the subject, man, is that which is determined, actuated by humanity. Knowledge of humanity is thus knowledge of human nature purified of all that is not exclusively itself, knowledge of this nature absolute and in itself, separated from everything that can share it in one way or another.[188]

By applying these definitions of confused and distinct knowledge to being as being, known concretely and abstractly, we shall see why the lack of differentiation implied in the act of existing, or *est*, gives to our knowledge of being a perfection absent in every previous apprehension of it. All concrete knowledge of being can be reduced to perception of a *habens esse*, just as concrete knowledge of man is knowledge of a *habens humanitatem*, of a subject sharing in humanity but not possessing it totally.[189] In all concrete knowledge the *habens* is to its form, i.e., *esse* or *humanitatem*, as a determining principle of an act or form; it differentiates act and form by limiting them, just as individuality differentiates absolute nature by curtailing its actuality, which, instead of being relatively infinite,[190] is limited by the subject in which it inheres. Such limitation by composition always betokens imperfection. Abstract knowledge of being, or of a being, tends on the contrary, toward complete purification of the essence, complete purging of whatever is foreign or nonessential to the nature in order that the latter may be apprehended in its very identity, in its absolute simplicity.[191] This is determination by *distinction* and not by *limitation*, a knowledge of the real through the actual, everything potential having been eliminated.

Knowledge of being *as existere* is abstract knowledge resulting from the purification and purgation of the real by means of which the mind can get to being's absolute actuality, having eliminated everything that contracts, limits, and differentiates it by combining it with that whose act it is, with the human nature of which it is the ultimate perfection. In so doing, the human intellect reveals how it can be raised up to Him who is *Existere:*

But our intellect, or the angelic intellect, inasmuch as it is elevated above matter in its own nature, can be raised above its own nature to a higher level by grace. An indication of this is that sight cannot, in any way, know in abstraction what it knows concretely; for in no way can it perceive a nature except as this one particular nature; whereas our intellect is able to consider in abstraction what it knows in concretion. For although it knows things which have a form residing in matter, still it *resolves* the composite into both elements and considers the form *separately by itself*. Likewise also, the intellect of an angel although it naturally knows the *existere* as concreted in a nature, still it is able to separate that *existere* by its intellect, since it knows that nature is one thing and its *existere* is another. Since therefore a created intellect is naturally capable of apprehending the concreted form and the *concreted existere in abstraction by way of a certain resolution,* it can by grace be raised up to know separate subsisting substance and separate subsisting *existere.*[192]

The knowledge of being as *est* obtained by this analysis, which purifies it of everything that limits, determines, and makes it imperfect, is the most perfect apprehension we can have on earth, since it shows us being, not as an act mingled with potency, as a perfection cut to the measure of the receiving subject, but as an *absolute actuality*, the sole source of everything in the real that deserves the name of act.

Is . . . means first that which is understood after the manner of *absolute actuality*. For *is*, when it is expressed without qualification, means to be in act, and therefore it has its meaning after the manner of a verb. But since the actuality which is the principal meaning of the verb *is*, is *indifferently* the actuality of every form, either the substantial or the accidental act, hence it is that when we wish to signify that any form or act actually inheres in any subject, we signify it by this verb *is*.[193]

Knowledge of being as being, or of everything insofar as it is, constitutes *the most universal* as well as the most perfect apprehension that man can have. For this universality is not concerned *with the thing* known as indistinct or potential, since *est* denotes the absolute actuality of things, and so what is most determinate as act. Rather, this universality has to do with the *medium* or concept by which all things (substance and accidents, corporeal and spiritual beings) are properly and distinctly apprehended *insofar as they are,* and not insofar as they are *this or that*. The indeterminate in the concept of *est* is *that by which* beings are imperfect and limited, i.e., their essence or quiddity; the distinct aspect is *that by which* they are acts and perfect, thereby imitating Him whose essence is to be the Subsisting *Existere*, i.e., absolutely unlimited and therefore infinite perfect *existence*,[194] the sublime truth that is the goal or term of the earthly knowledge which man will never have of God through things.[195] For although knowledge of being as *est*, as absolute actuality, is an ultimate in our *apprehension* of the human intellect's proper object, this apprehension is the starting point for apprehending truths that we construct about realities whose essence surpasses our apprehension but whose existence we can apprehend.

CONCLUSION OF PART TWO

What is knowledge? This was the question we asked when we began this second part of our study of epistemology. We started our answer by considering the complex experience that reflection shows knowledge to be, and we immediately found that it has two apparently paradoxical aspects; the first of which is the perfect interiority of the act of knowledge, and the other, even more surprising, the continual invasion of this immanence by outer reality. We sought the causes of this interiority of knowledge by reducing the activity of knowing to a form of life characteristically autonomous in its being and operations.[1] Then we considered the other aspect of knowledge, the invasion and constant occupation of the soul by *the other*, which seems to be essential to the life of knowledge and a condition of its perfection. We called this other *the object*, which is characterized by belonging simultaneously to the exterior and interior universe; we studied it in its *causal activity* upon our cognitive powers, sensible and intellectual.[2] Having explained the fruitful presence of outward things in the soul, we had to solve the problem: How can a naturally immanent activity remain immanent while it is constantly subject to external things? We tried to show that this antinomy inherent in human knowledge could be reconciled by the distinction which must be made between the *exercise* of knowledge and its *specification*, its exercise being entirely on the side of the knowing subject, and its specification entirely on the side of the object. Applied respectively to the two complementary aspects of human knowledge, this distinction enabled us to perceive that the progressive immanence of both sensible and intellectual knowledge, far from hindering their objectivity, furthers it, and that the external thing is never more solidly entrenched in the independence of its physical existence than at the very moment in which we apprehend it in its most inward wealth, namely, being as *existere*.[3]

Having made this investigation, we should know how knowledge is defined both as immanent activity and as the existence of another in the self, since we have discovered the respective causes of immanence and objectivity. A last explanation is necessary, however, because knowledge is a dynamic *accident* of the subsisting substance, man; but no accident can be defined without reference to the substance in which it inheres.[4] Thus, it is man who sees, hears, imagines, remembers, abstracts, understands; and although we have analyzed knowledge as a series of hypostatized or subsisting operations, we must not forget that only individuals perform these operations, that one soul is at the root of all the life of man, and that in these composite beings no part is the radical principle of operation.

That which enters into composition with anything does not act primarily and essentially, but rather the composite so acts; for *the hand does not act, but the man by his hand*. . . .[5]
Hence the operation of the parts is, through each part, attributed to the whole. For we say that man sees with the eye, and feels with the hand. . . . We may therefore say that the soul understands just as the eye sees; but *it is more correct* to say that *man understands through the soul*.[6]

The unity of the many operations exercised by the ensemble of our knowing powers springs therefore from the unity of the knower, and it is not surprising that such different activities, proceeding from a single source, should beget a single act of knowledge of which man is both the origin and the end. Not only is knowledge one, considered in the order of exercise or as an accident of a knowing subject, it is also one considered from the point of view of specification, since what the senses know, what the intellect knows—all these aspects of the thing penetrating us by way of the different senses and the agent intellect's activity—is *being* and is known as such by our intellect. Such is the definition of human knowledge, such is its unity, both subjective and objective, a unity of order, and not a product of the mutilation of man and of the universe, which unity is called upon, as it were, to superexist in and through man's knowledge.

Part Three

WHAT DOES IT MEAN TO KNOW TRUTH?

PROLOGUE

Just as every other thing is said to be good because of its perfection, so the intellect is good because of its truth.[1]

If to know is to superexist reality inwardly[2] by virtue of reality's fecundating action,[3] and if, on the other hand, apprehension consists in this superexistence of each aspect of the real either by itself or unified by the act of existing,[4] it would seem that a treatise on epistemology should normally end with a study of our possession of things by the whole ensemble of the acts of apprehension since they actualize the definition of knowledge. These acts remedy the limitations of our nature by making us share in the nature of others and make each of us imitators of the fullness and limitlessness of Uncreated Being.[5] Such an ending would be suitable were it not for the extreme weakness of our intellect and its powers of assimilation, which, instead of letting reality surge into us with the entirety of its being, sift it by means of the external senses, each one grasping but a single aspect of sensible things, and by means of the agent intellect, which, being dependent upon phantasms, can only give the intelligible to us successively, bit by bit, in a multitude of intelligible species differing in number and content.[6] Thus, the outward real, whose unity is absolute, exists in our intellect dispersed into a multitude of concepts, each of which is the likeness of one or another facet of being; it exists whole and entire within us *but with a mode of existing unlike the mode it possesses outside us.*[7] If we may borrow a comparison from the world of mass production, we can say that in order to facilitate its entrance into the soul, the thing is dismantled, disassembled; each part of the whole is there, the essentials as well as the accessories, but it needs to be put back together; we need an assembly line.

God . . . knows each thing by simple intelligence, by understanding the essence of each thing; as if we, by the very fact that we understand what man is, were to understand all that can be predicated of man. This however does not happen in the case of our intellect, which proceeds from one thing to another, *since the intelligible species represents one thing in such a way as not to represent another.* Hence, when we understand what man is, we do not forthwith understand other things which belong to him, but we understand them one by one, according to a certain succession. On this account, the things we understand as separated *we must reduce to one* by way of composition and division, by forming an enunciation.[8]

And the reason for the imperfection of apprehension—an imperfection without which human knowledge would terminate in this operation—is the poverty of our agent intellect:

If the intellect in apprehending the quiddity of the subject were at once to have the knowledge of all that can be attributed to or removed from the subject, it would never understand by composing and dividing, but only by understanding the essence. . . . *And this comes from the weakness of the intellectual light within us.*[9]

In these two passages St. Thomas is explaining that the weakness of our intellectual equipment obliges us to disassemble or dismantle the thing in the act of apprehending it, but that we have a capacity for reassembling it in the act called *judgment.* In judgment we reconstruct the original unity of the thing by regrouping its different aspects according to its mode of existing outside the soul: divorce is just as unnatural in being as it is in marriage, and knowledge must not put asunder what God has created as one. However, in order not to misunderstand the true nature of the mind's second operation, we must note one thing, which is that judgment *completes* apprehension, not by taking its place, by grasping an aspect of the thing that escaped apprehension, but by bringing unity into discontinuous knowledge. In other words, judgment works with concepts, with the already known, and not with exterior reality. The latter comes in only when the work of reassembling concepts is finished, for it is the criterion determining the value of the regrouping; it is the model by which judgment's unification is measured and seen to be conforming or not, i.e., true or false.

In judgment's perfective character with relation to apprehension, we see the metaphysical law governing all creatures applied to human knowledge. Wherever the act of existing and quiddity are not identical, *being and perfection do not coincide*, for things are what they are by substantial being, whereas they are perfect by their accidental being.[10] Such, proportionately speaking, is the case with human knowledge, all of whose essential elements are present in apprehension, but whose perfection is the result of the increase in knowledge adduced by judgment. In the same way that accidents perfect substance by putting at its disposal various means of attaining its end, judgment brings to apprehension the intellect's sole means of perfecting its knowledge, that is, of possessing the truth of its knowledge, just as by apprehension it possesses the truth of things. And since the truth of knowledge can only be in the mind, judgment deals first and foremost with mental activity:

Just as every other thing is said to be good because of its perfection, so the intellect is said to be good because of its truth. Which shows that *the true and the false, being objects of knowledge*, are found in the mind.[11]

Thus, to know truth is first and foremost simultaneously to know *distinct concepts*, previously possessed[12]; it is not to apprehend an aspect of the real that has escaped apprehension. In the judgment there is no superexistence of a new thing in us, as there is in apprehension, but the unified superexistence of that which previously was multiple: *No more things are known, but the same thing is better known.*

There is a certain composition in things but it constitutes a single reality which the intellect grasps as one in a simple concept; as for the composition and division by which the intellect combines or divides its concepts, it exists in the intellect and not in things. And so, the fact that a being is true by virtue of such a composition is different from items which properly are beings really existing outside the soul, such as quiddity, substance, quality, or quantity. . . .[13]

Thus, we must insist that judgment consists not in knowing what things are, neither in their quiddity nor in their existence, for apprehension does that, but rather in regrouping the concepts by which we apprehend the quiddity and *existere* of things, in order to perfect our initial knowledge of them. To bring out more vividly the difference between apprehension and judgment (i.e., between our knowledge of things and the truth of our knowledge), St. Thomas draws a rather surprising comparison between *the true* and *accidental being,* so as to exclude them both from metaphysics. Both of them, he tells us, contain nothing more than exists in being by itself, for accidental being results from the unforseen meeting of two ontological aspects of an external thing, whereas the true consists in the meeting, in and by the mind, of the pre-existing concepts that are themselves the likeness of an outward being. That is why neither accidental being nor the true "reveals a new ontological aspect of the real, foreign to what subsisting beings are."[14]

Such is the Thomistic context for the knowledge of truth. There is the same distinction between analysis of the knowledge of truth and analysis of the nature of knowledge that exists between the apprehension of being as quiddity and that of being as perfect.[15] Consequently we can set up the following proportion:

$$\frac{\text{Knowledge of truth}}{\text{is to the nature of knowledge}} : \frac{\text{as accidents}}{\text{are to substance}}$$

$$: \frac{\text{as being } secundum \ quid}{\text{is to being } simpliciter} : \frac{\text{as the perfect}}{\text{is to the imperfect}}$$

The object of this third part of our treatise is therefore the perfection of human knowledge. To ask, "What is true knowledge?" is the same as asking what factors cause our knowledge to pass from its inevitably imperfect state at the level of apprehension to the state of perfection that is knowledge of truth. Our plan in answering this question is given us by the materials with which we are working. It is a matter of examining the immanent activity by which we *reassemble* the different concepts of the real produced by apprehension, in order to restore to known beings a unity more consistent with that outside the soul. This conceptual regrouping can no more be effected without reference to the real, the unit of measure, than a complicated machine can be reassembled without reference to a plan showing the exact interconnections of its various parts. Therefore, in Chapter VIII we shall analyze the nature and functions of this operation that perfects knowledge by substituting unity for multiplicity of concepts; then, in Chapter IX, we shall examine the consequences of this unification upon human knowledge—truth, the effect of unity. This will be the division of the Part Three.

VIII · WHAT OPERATION PERFECTS HUMAN KNOWLEDGE?

[handwritten marginalia]

Since the reality we are going to study belongs to the realm of the living and of the life of knowledge, we shall proceed to seek its nature by the method that we must inevitably adopt in order to perceive its essential aspects. Therefore, we shall follow the same plan that we used in analyzing apprehension; first we shall consider the exercise of the act, and then its specification. Hence, there will be two sections in this chapter.

Section I: Exercise of the Operation Perfecting Human Knowledge

A. ORIGINS AND SUBJECTIVE CAUSES OF THIS NEW ACT

[handwritten marginalia]

The human intellect knows through the fecundating action of the intelligible species communicating the light of the agent intellect and of the nature of things[1]; under what pressure does it know perfectly? Under the pressure of a natural desire making our intellect a natural appetite for all being[2] and, therefore, for the truth which is the perfect possession of being,[3] but especially under the action of the agent intellect, our natural light, which everywhere accompanies the operation of the possible intellect in its exercise:

The intellectual light, which exists in a subject as a permanent and perfect form, especially perfects the intellect's apprehension of the principles of the things which this light reveals. So, *by the agent intellect's light*, the intellect knows, above all, the first principles of everything it naturally understands.[4]

The action of the agent intellect, as it is described in the preceding pages, must not be imagined as something transitory which, having prepared the intelligible species and given it to the possible intellect, takes no further part in intellection. That would be a purely spatial conception of a spiritual activity and would in no way correspond to the respective immanence of the different powers and their operations.[5] When St. Thomas uses the expression *intellectual light* to mean the agent intellect, this term must be given its full analogical value. In illuminating color, physical light does not give it permanent visibility in such a way that the light may stop its action without the color's ceasing to be actually visible. Proportionately speaking, the same is true of the agent intellect's action with respect to the object and operation of our intellect. The illumination of the agent intellect must be permanent; every intellectual activity begins and proceeds through its action, which is so well put by the following text:

Because intellectual light is that which makes things intelligible purely and simply (*simpliciter*), every intellect must produce its act *by* this light it possesses.[6]

If the agent intellect functions at the beginning of knowledge because it produces the intelligible in act, it is also at the heart of knowledge in the act of apprehension itself, for it is to the act of intellection as the sun is to the act of seeing[7]; it actualizes the object and strengthens the power:

We can speak of the intellectual light only by referring to what we know of physical light. Physical light . . . does two things for vision. First, it makes actually visible that which was only potentially visible; secondly, by its very nature, it enables our visual power to see better. So we can attribute to intellectual light the same power, namely *of being the intellect's vigor* in its act of *intellecting*, as well as being the source of the knowability of its object.[8]

This vigor brought by the agent intellect to the intelligence enables it to grow to its ultimate perfection—possession of total truth. But this growth has successive stages of which the act that we are now studying is only the first. Even though St. Thomas rarely mentions it, we must never forget this necessitating role of the intellectual light in studying the mental operation by which it attains a state of perfection not possessed in apprehension, for St. Thomas' metaphysical theory of the intercausality of the two intellects is always presupposed in his explanation of human knowledge, because, as we have seen above, it is its center.

However, the completion of our knowledge by a perfective act cannot be explained merely in terms of the intellect's natural appetite for being and the agent intellect's illuminative role. There is also a sort of psychological need, that causes us deep intellectual dissatisfaction and insatiable curiosity as long as we have not reduced to unity that which is presented as multiple, for the multiple as such is unintelligible to us.[9] As we have observed, human knowledge results from a multiplication of concepts that present themselves as so many different aspects of reality. The intellect's irrepressible tendency is to unify its concepts according to an order it constructs itself, an order that, without destroying each concept's identity, situates it within a whole of which it is an integrating part. Thus, it is as parts of a whole[10] that apprehended concepts are known by this new intellectual operation, whose essential function is to perfect knowledge, because it substitutes, for the primitive multiplicity, an intelligible arrangement answering the deepest needs of our intellect's nature. Such are the subjective origins of this second mental act whose nature we must now study.

B. ANALYSIS OF THE OPERATION PERFECTING OUR KNOWLEDGE

Impelled by the forces just mentioned, the human intellect sets out to perfect its knowledge. Unlike apprehension, which is at the mercy of things and wholly dependent upon them, the soul shows a hitherto unknown initiative in this perfective activity:

In its judicative activity the soul is not at the mercy of things but, in a way, takes the initiative in its act. . . .[11]

The composition of a proposition is not a work of nature but of reason and intellect.[12]

This difference of noetic attitude between apprehension and the operation perfecting it affects the latter's structure throughout. Apprehension has an abstract mode, imposed by the agent intellect, and its act is assimilation and its term a simple likeness of the substantial or accidental quiddity of things; but the mode of the second operation is *concrete*, its act is *judgment*, and its *term* an *enunciation*, or complex concept. An explanatory word about each of these aspects will suffice to indicate the nature of this second operation of the mind.

¶ *1. Concretion or Composition as a "Mode" of Knowledge.* Whenever St. Thomas wants to describe the intellectual operation we are analyzing here, he uses the terms *componere, compositio*,[13] *Concretio*,[14] *unitio*,[15] to show that this act must be understood with reference to the intelligible whole resulting from its effort:

Since mental concepts are likenesses of things, we can always consider and name them from two different angles. First, in themselves; secondly in relation to the things of which they are the likenesses. Thus a statue of Hercules, considered in itself, is and is said to be copper; but as a likeness of Hercules it is said to be a man. Likewise, considering mental concepts *in themselves, there is always composition wherever there is truth and falsity*, because the latter can exist in the mind only insofar as the intellect compares a simple concept with another.[16]

Ex multis unum, this is the motto for this act of the intellect,[17] because it is the sole means of extending the radius of human knowledge, which is allergic to multiplicity as such[18] and, therefore, to the very situation in which it is placed by the nature of simple apprehension, a situation from which it can emerge only by substituting unity for multiplicity. This substitution is performed by the intellect upon the concepts of simple apprehension, not by transforming them, which would destroy them as likenesses of things, but by integrating them within the whole. This gives these concepts a *functional value and meaning* that entitles them to a new name, a sort of surname indicating their particular vocation in this new context of intelligibility. The surnames given to simple concepts in their quest for unity are *noun* and *verb:*

Simple words may be considered in three ways, the first . . . considers them as the absolute signs of simple concepts, the second sees them as *parts of the enunciation . . . inasmuch as they are nouns and verbs . . .* and the third studies their constitutive role in the syllogistic order as *terms.*[19]

When, therefore, the soul takes the initiative to perfect knowledge by reducing its multitudinous concepts to unity, through composition, it gives simple concepts a function foreign to them as absolute likenesses of things: *it makes them correlatives.* This means that the two simple concepts which were the material for the composition constructed by the intellect now take on a new meaning, essentially relative to their role in this whole constructed by the intellect; they become subject and predicate, the function of subject being taken over by *concept nouns* and that of predicate by *concept verbs.* We must not forget that the second operation of the mind consists in the composition of two simple concepts, and that consequently all the material used as integral parts in this composition[20] pre-exists in apprehension. Thus, apprehension must contain some concepts capable of playing the role of subject and others capable of taking over the role of predicate. What concepts are these, which can respectively fulfill such different functions?

Concept nouns are those which are likenesses of the quiddity of things, while *concept verbs* are likenesses of particular accidents springing from substance, such as action, passion, and, in a way, as "is," or *est*[21]; they express the dynamism emanating from substance or that which it receives.[22] It is interesting to note that with the notion of noun and verb, whose essential function is to work for the *perfection* of human knowledge, we again encounter the aspect of simple apprehension wherein the thing is apprehended as *perfect,* i.e., as substance and accidents.[23] The same laws apply because knowledge is of being and obeys the laws of being. In this original composition that the mind constructs from its concepts in order to have unified knowledge of them, it imitates the behavior of things as it grasped this behavior in the act of apprehension. Within this intelligible whole constructed by the intellect, concept nouns are what substance is in the extramental thing; they are the stable, permanent element remaining identical despite the attribution of a multitude of predicates.[24] This is why they are *subjects*, for what characterizes substance is precisely, as its name indicates, its support of accidents, its giving them existence. Concept verbs, on the contrary, have an entirely different role to play in the intellect's synthesis of the concepts of apprehension. Their function relative to the subject is informative, actualizing; they are its form, its acts, just as accidents are the perfective form of substance; they express action, passion, *existere*, insofar as they inhere in the subject, insofar as the subject is their source and term.[25] Since action, passion, and *existere* are always *acts* whose perfective elements, concept verbs, are always predicates par excellence, and no other concept can play the role of predicate unless the verb be present to help it perform this function, "the verb *always* signifies what is predicated."[26]

Verbs themselves are *what is predicated* before being the signs of predicates. It must be understood that the verb is the sign of the predicate because every predication, by reason of the composition it implies, is accomplished by the verb, be it essential or accidental. . . .[27]

But since the actuality which is the principal meaning of the verb *is*, is indifferently the actuality of every form, either the substantial or the accidental act, hence it is that when we wish to signify that any form or act actually inheres in any subject, we *signify* it by this verb *is*.[28]

An example will bring out the change in perspective undergone by simple concepts when they become part of the synthesis set up by the mind. Take the concepts *man* and *running;* in apprehension they express two concepts, one corresponding to human nature and the other to local motion. But these two concepts cannot be thought of *simultaneously* as long as they are considered as two absolutes, for their respective intelligibility is mutually independent. To think these concepts simultaneously we must establish a bond between them in such a way that they constitute only *one intelligibility*. This bond is the composition of two concepts, one of which becomes the subject or matter of the other, which is its act; thus, we have, *the man runs*, i.e., a certain subject actually performs a certain activity. The man and his activity are known as *one thing:*

> It is manifest that man and white are the same in subject and diverse in idea; for the idea of man is one thing and that of whiteness is another. . . . To this diversity in idea corresponds the plurality of predicate and subject, while the intellect signifies the *identity* of the thing by the *composition* itself.[29]

The mode of composition, or *concretio*, characterizing the act that perfects our knowledge is, therefore, essentially unifying, for it unites the different concepts dealing with being as such, with the essential principles of substances, and with the different accidents of these same substances[30] by means of the functional significance assumed by absolute concepts within the framework of the composition constructed by the mind. We must now examine the act of knowledge characterized by this mode of composition and the term emanating from this act.

¶ *2. Judgment and Its Term, Enunciation.* We have just seen that the mode of this intellectual act is completely different from that of apprehension, whose abstractive mode isolates concepts and multiplies them in order to model itself after the different intelligible aspects of the thing. Composition, on the contrary, unifies, sets up the subject-predicate relationship that enables it to include in one single grasp the multiple aspects of its knowledge of things. To this difference in the mode of knowledge corresponds an act in no way resembling apprehension, for whereas the latter is *assimilation*, the act of the second mental operation is *judgment*.

Borrowed from law, this term still keeps something of its origin despite the transposition it necessarily undergoes in being taken into an order so completely different from that concerned with the administration of laws governing a society.[31] All the words used by grammarians and logicians to designate the intellectual act that predicates something of a subject, or attributes an action or form to it, have a judiciary origin. Etymologically, the word attribute means *ad tribunum*, i.e., before the tribune, the Roman magistrate who dispensed justice, hence our word *tribunal*.[32] Similarly, the words *predicare*, *praedicatum*, and *judicium* come from the root *deik*, which means to show or indicate, and all belong to legal terminology.[33]

When the intellect brings before the tribunal of its reflection[34] two or more concepts, one of which, the subject, plays the accused and the others, the predicates or attributes, play the alleged crimes of the accused, the intellect hands down the verdict of guilty or not guilty. What does it judge? Does it judge the extramental real or the unification of concepts that it has just made? This is the delicate problem we must solve in order to understand the true nature of this intellectual act; for if we say that the *direct* object of the act of judgment is the extramental real, we assimilate judgment into apprehension, but if its direct object is our unified concepts, then judgment is a distinct act added to apprehension and perfecting it. If apprehension knows the quiddity of things, while judgment knows their act of existing, then both have the exterior thing as their direct object, both *apprehend* different aspects of the thing, and they are only numerically and chronologically distinct, one coming after the other. However, if the act of existing is the direct object of judgment, since judgment is the act of the passive power that is the intellect, and a passive power must receive its object before knowing it[35]—then the intellect would have to be fecundated by an intelligible species of *existere*, just as it had to be fecundated by the quiddity's intelligible species before apprehending it. All the objections that can be brought against the abstraction of *existere* remain in its apprehension by the judgment, for we know only what we are. To know is intentionally to superexist the extramental thing, and unless the thing's act of existing (*existere*) superexists intentionally in us, we will never know it! To say that the thing's *existere* is the direct object of judgment is to say that judgment is the act of apprehending this existence. It perfects knowledge just as every apprehension of a new aspect of the real perfects it, but it is not that perfection of knowledge which *corrects the analytic character* of apprehension (which has only fragmentary knowledge of the real) by regrouping concepts so that man may, in his poor fashion, imitate the comprehensive intuition that God and angels have of the real.[36] In this interpretation, judgment is still apprehension of the most perfect aspect of the real, since it apprehends the act of acts, but *it is not a more perfect state of our knowledge of the real*, the state to which knowledge is essentially destined, since the reason for the judgment's existence is precisely the naturally imperfect state of human knowledge, whose necessary mode is abstraction.

If, on the contrary, the direct object of judgment is the composition or synthesis of concepts with which simple apprehension has already enriched the intellect, then judgment's role is to perfect knowledge, to increase its wisdom and order,[37] to make it imitate the concrete and synthesized way in which things exist by correcting the fragmentation introduced by the intellect into our knowledge of the real. Judgment perfects our knowledge, not by nourishing it with more of the real, but by making more realistic its way of superexisting the real. Thus, its activity is directly concerned with our knowledge of the real, with our concepts as psychological realities. To use one of St. Thomas' comparisons' the statue of Hercules considered as having certain properties is copper, and considered as a likeness, it is a man; the same is true of concepts. They can be grouped or unified insofar as they have characteristics caused by their state of abstraction, in which case they are subjects or predicates; and they can be grouped insofar as the composition in which they are united by the intellect is, or is not, a likeness of the extramental real, and in this case they are true or false.[38] This second consideration, however, is consequent upon the first and presupposes it. In the order of exercise, which is the aspect we are examining now, judicative activity bears directly upon the composition of concepts and not upon the thing with which this synthesis is or is not equated.

It is relatively easy to prove this view by means of an example frequently used by St. Thomas. This example makes it clear that a judgment can be perfect without in any way referring to extramental existence, because it is the fruit of a perfect composition constructed by the intellect from a concept that it duplicates, not as a likeness of the real, but as an element in a synthesis made by the intellect itself. To affirm that *the man is a man*, is to judge. Is this judgment concerned with the real existence of the man or with the identity of the two terms in the synthesis constructed by the intellect? Obviously the judgment is concerned with the composition of concepts and not with human *existere* in its outward reality.

In propositions where the same thing is predicated of itself, the same rule in some way applies, inasmuch as the intellect considers as the suppositum what takes the place of the subject; and what takes the place of the predicate it considers as the nature of the form existing in the suppositum, according to the saying that predicates are taken formally, and subjects materially. To this *diversity in idea* corresponds the plurality of predicate and subject, while *the intellect signifies the identity* by the composition itself.[39]

Another proof, even more radical than the judgment of identity, destroys the illusion that judgment has to do directly with the existence of things and not with the composition of concepts. This proof is to be found in a text wherein St. Thomas explains the opposition between "is" considered as a likeness of *existere*, or the act of existing and "is" meaning the composition constructed by the intellect in a judgment of existence. Having commented upon the Aristotelian text dividing being into two modes, the first extramental, the second in the mind, St. Thomas defines the second mode as, "the *esse* and the *est* which signify the composition the mind constructs with its concepts,"[40] and then he makes a comparison that is at first rather surprising:

The act of existing of every being in nature is substantial. When we say that Socrates is and that this *est* is used in the primary sense of the word, it is a *substantial predicate,* for being is superior to each being as animal is superior to man. But taking *is* in the second meaning of the word to be, it is an *accidental predicate.*[41]

This passage brings out the essential difference between the *est* which is a likeness of the *existere* of things, and the *est* which signifies the composition made by the mind. In the first case, *est* expresses the act of the substance it perfects and from which it is distinguished. In the second, the *est* expressing composition is a predicate inhering in a subject as a form or accident; it has a functional meaning; it is a concept verb, or the part of a whole.[42]

A third and final proof that the act of judgment bears directly upon the conceptual composition and not upon the existence of things is given us by every affirmation that has God as its object. When we say, "God exists," "God is good," etc., it is impossible that the object of these judgments be the existence of God, since to apprehend His existence is no more within our intellect's grasp than is the apprehension of His essence! Consequently, all these judgments concern the composition of our concepts about God and not His existence:

To be can mean either of two things: it may mean the *act of being* or it may mean the *composition* of a proposition effected by the mind in joining the predicate to a subject. Taking *to be* in the first sense we cannot understand the to be of God, no more than his essence; but we can *in the second* sense. We know that the proposition which we form about God when we say God is, is true.[43]

We can thus conclude that the first object of judgment is the unification which it has itself constructed from apprehended concepts and that the *est* characterizing this act primarily signifies the identity of the components it unites in a relation of attribution enabling it to side with unity against multiplicity:

Nevertheless the composition of the intellect differs from the composition of things, for the components in the thing are *diverse*, whereas the composition of the intellect is a sign of the *identity* of the components.[44]

The *immanent term* of judgment, the fruit of its fertility, bears all the hereditary marks of its origin. Offspring of the intellect, it has the same spirituality and simplicity as its principle; being the result of a composition, it has the complexity of the elements that contributed to its formation, but a complexity in no way detrimental to its unity.[45] The proper name of the intellect's new child is *enunciation*. This term, too, is borrowed from legal terminology and means the official proclamation of a public decision[46]; thus, it is wholly in character with the act it terminates and whose fruit it is:

Just as in external acts we may consider the work and the work done, for instance, the work of building and the house built, so in the act of reason, we may consider the act itself of reason . . . and *something produced* by this act. With regard to the speculative reason, this is first of all the definition; secondly the enunciation.[47]

Just as the concepts of apprehension can be considered successively in themselves and as likenesses of the real[48] and, in accordance with this twofold consideration, can possess different characteristics,[49] so enunciation as concept of the second mental operation has different characteristics when considered in its intentional existence and when considered as a likeness of the mode by which things exist. We shall look briefly at the outstanding characteristics of enunciation considered as a mental reality, while leaving our examination of its characteristics as likeness of the mode of *existere* of things for the next section.

As we have seen, *ex multis unum* is the mode proper to judgment[50] this too is the nature of its immanent term or end, enunciation. Enunciation is not a term or end in the same sense that we intend when speaking of the end of a trip or the end of a nice day, but in the sense that fruit is the end or term of a whole group of biological processes from which it springs and which it crowns. Enunciation crowns the intellect's work by stabilizing its discoveries, by unifying a group of concepts that apprehension can conceive only successively. *Unity* of meaning despite complexity of its elements, this is the first property of enunciation,[51] a property that diametrically opposes it to the primary characteristics of the concepts of apprehension, namely, unity of abstraction. For the latter unity is gained at the expense of multiplicity, by not considering it, whereas enunciation's unity of meaning is achieved by *concretio*, i.e., by awareness of the multiplicity of concepts and their integration in an order reconstructed by reason.

Upon enunciation's unity of concretion are grafted two distinct properties modifying its meaning without destroying its unity. The first relates to the *subject* and begets the universal, particular, or singular character of the enunciation.[52] The second depends upon the *verb* or predicate, and therefore upon the formal element of enunciation, which makes the latter an affirmation or a negation.[53] The enunciation's affirmative or negative character is very important, for judgment's need to be either an affirmation or a negation is fundamental to all the propositions governing the intellect's functioning. Add the fact that affirmation and negation necessarily include time

—past, present, and future—and it becomes immediately evident how important this property of enunciation is in the field of singular judgments.[54]

Considered strictly from the point of view of the exercise of intellectual activity, without immediate reference to the things known through their acts, both judgment and its immanent term have as their final end the perfection of knowledge, since their sole function is to substitute, for the inevitable scattering caused among concepts by apprehension's abstractive mode, a synthesizing view and concept of which the act of apprehension is utterly incapable. Besides this synthesis of simple concepts, judgment uses the treasures of intelligibility already existing in the conceptual hierarchy of predicables and predicaments. Therefore, even from this still limited angle of the immanence of the life of knowledge, it can rightfully be said that judgment is intended to be *completivum cognitionis*.[55] Now let us examine the perfection it gives to knowledge by relating it to exterior things in the order of specification.

Section II: Exterior Reality as Term of the Knowledge of Judgment

In treating judgment as an act of knowledge in the preceding section, we denied that its direct object is *existere*, which would play for judgment the role quiddity plays for apprehension,[56] and we did this despite the popularity of this position and the textual evidence that seems to support it.[57] However, we did not intend to deny judgment all contact with extramental reality. On the contrary, we refused it this specialization with respect to *existere* in order to increase the realism of judicative activity, for judgment is made for the whole of being, essence and existence, substance and accidents. As context for studying the second mental operation of the mind, we took the distinction existing in every created thing between being and perfection and applied it to human knowledge, in which the act of simple apprehension in some way plays the role of substance, while judgment has the perfective function of accidents.[58] To illustrate this abstract situation of judgment in relation to apprehension, we compared the act of apprehending with disassembling, dismantling a thing, whereas judgment's first function is to reassemble concepts so that they may more faithfully reproduce the thing's extramental mode of existing.[59] In the preceding section we analyzed this operation of reassembling concepts as performed by the intellect, and the fruit of this work, enunciation. Now it remains for us to consider the model by which the intellect guides itself in unifying a plurality of apprehended concepts, and the characteristics the verb of the second operation acquires from the fact that it is measured by being. This section is divided according to these two aspects.

A. THE EXTERIOR TERM THAT SPECIFIES JUDGMENT

Just as the concepts of simple apprehension are likenesses of things because they are their effect and have no other purpose than to make them superexist in the soul, so enunciation[60] is a likeness of the thing because it results from the judgment's unification of apprehended concepts. But enunciation is the likeness of what? Of the *ipsum esse rei*, says St. Thomas.

The intellect has two operations. One, called the apprehension of indivisibles, by which we know the quiddity of every thing; the other which composes and divides by forming an affirmative or negative enunciation. To these two operations correspond the two real aspects of things. The first operation has to do with the nature of the thing itself; by means of it the known is situated at a certain degree of being, whether it be a complete or whole thing, or an incomplete thing like a part or accident. The second operation deals with the *very being of the thing*, which results from the composition of principles in composite things or coincides with the simplicity of nature in spiritual substances.[61]

What does St. Thomas mean by the expression *ipsum esse rei*, which he uses to distinguish simple apprehension from judgment? Should *esse* be translated by *act* of existing, or by *mode* of existing? Is this *esse* the object of judgment, as quiddity is the object of apprehension? We must answer these two questions in order to grasp the nature of the exterior term specifying judgment, as well as the relations between this exterior term and enunciation, its immanent term.

¶ *1. Should* ipsum esse rei *Be Translated as Act or as Mode of Existing?* According to our analysis, the progressive apprehension of being proceeds from the confused to the distinct in two ways, the first of which is directed toward the *res* or quiddity,[62] whereas the second is oriented toward the act of existing itself, as being what is most perfect in the real.[63] If this analysis is correct, it is highly improbable that this act of existing could be the term of judgment, for we make innumerable judgments before knowing that the *existere* of things is their highest perfection. In fact, the apprehension of this fact is the prerogative of the wise man, since by it all metaphysical knowledge is defined. If, on the other hand, the word *esse* is given the meaning of *act* as known in the first apprehension of being, then it is no longer the act of existing as such that is the object of judgment but rather a *mode of existing*, the mode that is characteriestic of being immersed in movement, the *existere* of mobile being as such.[64] Our first enunciation could thus be conceived in such terms as, "Something is running, going up, coming down," etc., and if this first enunciation is followed by another affirming that, "Something exists," it would mean, "A thing having a body exists," which amounts again to knowing *a mode of existing* and not the act of existing, which, by definition, is separate from all its modes and, furthermore, needs a judgment to be known as such.[65] In other words, since we cannot give to the *ipsum esse rei* of judgment the meaning of *act of existing* as pure actuality, the only remaining possibility is to give it the meaning of *mode of existing*. But there are ten modes of existing, one of which belongs characteristically to substance and the nine others to accidents. Consequently, if judgment is terminated in the mode of existing of things, it simply means that judgment knows the real as substance and accidents, as substance composed of essential elements, and as multiple accidents of one or another substance.

Let us examine this interpretation of *ipsum esse rei* in relation to St. Thomas' explicit teaching about the nature of judgment.

Just as there are two elements in a thing, its quiddity and its act of existing, so are there two intellectual acts corresponding to these two elements. One by which the intellect apprehends the quiddities of things . . . the other by which it understands the act of existing, by composing an affirmation, because the *existere* of a thing composed of matter and form . . . also *consists in a certain composition of form with matter or of accident with subject.*[66]

This passage is in itself sufficiently explicit to show that the *esse* in question is the whole being of the thing, its essence and its existence, and not only the substantial but also the accidental mode of existence. Here is another text further explaining the passage just quoted:

The likeness of a thing is received into the intellect according to the *mode* of the intellect, not according to the *mode* of the thing. Hence, although something on the part of the thing corresponds to the composition and division of the intellect, still it does not exist in the same way in the intellect and in the thing. . . . Now in a material thing there is a twofold composition. First, there is a composition of form with matter. *To this corresponds that composition of the intellect whereby the universal whole is predicated of its parts.* . . . The second composition is of accident with subject and to this composition *corresponds that composition* of the intellect *whereby accident is predicated of subject,* as when we say the man is white. Nevertheless the composition of the intellect differs from the composition of things; for the components in the thing are diverse, whereas the composition of the intellect is a sign of the identity of the components. . . . In other words, man is *identical in subject* with the being having whiteness. It is the same thing with the composition of form and matter. For animal signifies that which has a sensitive nature; rational, that which has an intellectual nature; man, that which has both; and Socrates, that which has all these things together with individual matter. And so, according to this kind of identity our intellect *composes* one thing with another by means of predication.[67]

Were it necessary to expound this text, we might say that there are as many modes of enunciation for the judgment as there are modes of existing for composite things. If the mode of composition is that of essence and existence, we have an enunciation with two terms or a judgment of existence, in which the *existere* itself enters into composition with the subsistent, as in "Socrates is," a judgment whose composition should logically be translated, *ens habens esse individuale per se est.* It is in this sense that St. Thomas affirms that in the judgment "Socrates is," the *is* is a *substantial* predicate; i.e., it expresses the *ipsum esse* of Socrates and therefore a *substantial mode of existing.*[68] When the mode of composition is in the very substance of things, then the enunciation designates the identity of the composite with one or the other of its essential components, as in "Socrates is an animal, or a man." Finally, when the mode of composition is that belonging to a substance and its accidents, the enunciation indicates the accidental mode of this act of existing. Furthermore, the link between the mode of existing and the mode of predicating—that is, the enunciation itself, which is nothing but a relation of attribution or predication—is dogmatically affirmed when real being is divided into its ten modes:

Being must be divided into different kinds according to differences in modes of predicating, differences derived from diversity in the modes of being; for there are as many modes of predicating something as there are modes of signifying that something is. . . . And of things predicated, some designate substance, some the qualified, others the quantified and so on, to each mode of predication must correspond an identical being; thus when we say that man is an animal, being signifies substance; when we say man is white, it signifies quality, and so for the other modes.[69]

This analysis of the extrinsic term of judgment brings us right back to our starting point, where we said that judgment is the perfection of knowledge, because it is the unification of a multitude of concepts, a unity purporting to reorganize apprehension with the existence of things as a model. Things exist according to a substantial and accidental mode, the first giving them stability and the second, perfection. Judgment gives us the thing both in its being and in its perfect being, the two aspects being simultaneously perceived in the complex but single term, enunciation. Judgment is modeled after the *mode of existing* of things, and not after that act of existing perceived as the perfection of quiddity.

¶ *2. Is* ipsum esse rei *the Object of Judgment?* In analyzing the nature of human knowledge, we saw that the object could signify two entirely different aspects of the thing. It can mean the thing as *cause* or *principle* of the act of knowledge, sensible or intellectual[70];

on the other hand, it can signify this same thing as the *term known* by the cognitive act.[71] The distinction between intelligible species and concept shows the difference between the two aspects of the object, the one being at the source of the act, the other manifesting its fruit.[72] Now, we have just seen that the *ipsum esse rei* is the object term of our judgment, since the substantial and accidental composition of things is precisely what we know through this mental operation.[73] It is a question of knowing whether it is also the object principle of our knowledge. To answer this question we need only recall the reasons necessitating the fruitful causality of sensible as well as intelligible reality, namely, the passivity of our powers, a formula that merely substitutes for an admission of ignorance or of nonpossession of the real.[74] But as soon as a passive power is fecundated by its object, it is active, it conceives, in the strictest sense of the word, that which it has become, and the concept or mental word —superexistence experienced in and by the mind—is born in complete reference to the real whose likeness it is. But at the beginning of the act of composing and dividing, the intelligible is already present; therefore, the passive phase is past.

There are two operations in the sensible part. One is limited to immutation, and thus the operation of the senses takes place when the senses are impressed by the sensible. The other is formation, inasmuch as the imagination forms for itself an image of an absent thing, or even of something never seen. Both of these operations are found in the intellect. For in the first place there is a *passion* of the possible intellect *as informed* by the intelligible species; and then the possible intellect, as thus informed, *then forms* a definition, or a division or a composition, which is expressed by language. . . . Words do not therefore signify the intelligible species themselves, but that which the intellect *forms* for itself *for the purpose of judging the external things.*[75]

This is the sense in which we can say that the intellect takes the initiative in the act of judgment and that the term of this act is a work of reason and not a work of nature, as are simple apprehension and its concept. Therefore, we cannot say that the *ipsum esse rei* causes judicative knowledge by depositing in the possible intellect an intelligible species that is its likeness and whose enunciation is a sort of image. This would be to reduce judgment to apprehension and to conceive human knowledge as an intuition of things according to their mode of existing; whereas knowledge has, by definition, an abstractive mode that breaks the thing's concrete mode of existing down into as many absolutes as there are intelligible aspects in the thing.[76] The relation of enunciation to the *ipsum esse rei* is that of measured to measure, and not of cause to its effect. Thus, it is not because a house is made up of feet and yards that it is measurable, but because it is built of materials that can be measured in feet and yards. Similarly, it is because the enunciation is made of concepts, likenesses of different aspects of a thing, that the composition it expresses can and must be measured by this extramental thing insofar as it concretely and singly contains these different aspects of which concepts are likenesses. The *ipsum esse rei* therefore is the object of judgment, not because it causes the composition of its term, enunciation, but because the *ipsum esse rei* is itself composite, thus, the intellect can compare the thing's *mode of existing* with the *mode of existing of its knowledge of things* and perceive its conformity or nonconformity with the concrete real. What the *ipsum esse rei* causes in judicative knowledge is not the composition of concepts authored by the intellect, but the truth or falsity of this composition, which is another story, to be told in the next chapter.

B. THE CHARACTERISTIC OF ENUNCIATION AS MEASURED BY THE *ipsum esse rei*

Before concluding this section on judgment and its specification by extramental reality, we should emphasize the characteristics of its immanent term considered as intentional superexistence of the thing's *mode of existing*. Enunciation, like the concept, can be considered *in itself*, that is, as an intellectual product possessing properties that are the result of its intelligible existence; but it can also be considered as a likeness of the real,[77] and then the exigencies of realism bring it new properties. Considered as a fruit of the intellect, enunciation has three characteristics, as we have already seen.[78] With reference to the mode of existing of things, it also has three characteristics depending upon whether we consider the subject, the verb or predicate, or the unified complex as representative of being and its mode. Just a word about each of these properties will be enough, for we shall meet them again in studying truth.

¶ *First Characteristic: Enunciation Is Necessary, Impossible, Possible.* The basis for these properties is the *subject* insofar as it is the likeness of a nature which needs or rejects this or that predicate, or is neutral with respect to such and such a predicate, i.e., with respect to this substantial or accidental form. Thus, the following enunciations, "Man is reasonable," "Man is an ass," "Man is white," respectively indicate the natural need, repugnance, and neutrality that human substance entertains with respect to the three predicates attributed to it.[79] This characteristic of enunciation resulting from its subject as likeness of the thing is basic to the division of predicates into substantial, accidental *per se*, and accidental properly so called.

A predicate behaves in three ways toward a subject. Firstly it signifies *what the subject is*, as in "Socrates is an animal." . . . Secondly when it signifies *what inheres* in the subject, either by itself and absolutely as flowing from the matter, and this is quantity, or as flowing from the form, and this is quality; or it signifies *what inheres* in the subject not absolutely but with reference to another, and this is relation. Thirdly the predicate signifies *what is extrinsic* to the subject.[80]

¶ *Second Characteristic: Enunciation Is Categorical or Hypothetical.* The source of this property is not the subject but the verb-predicate; for example, "Socrates is seated," "If Socrates is seated, he is not running." This characteristic of enunciation is entirely in relation to the verb, to such a degree that the subject can change indefinitely without in any way modifying the meaning of this judicative composition. That is why this category of enunciation is usually called *formal*, as opposed to the first category, called *material*, because of the analogy between the function of subject and predicate in a mental composition and the function of matter and form in a physical composite.

The predicate is the principal element in an enunciation because it is its formal and perfective part.[81]

When the intellect constructs a composition, it takes two concepts, one of which, the predicate, has a formal function toward the other insofar as it exists in it; and that is why predicates always have a formal value.[82]

Hypothetical enunciation also has to do with the verb or predicate since it is constructed of two categorical enunciations, one of which depends upon the other, as to both its existence and its truth.[83] The importance of this second characteristic of enunciation lies in the knowledge of truth, for only a categorical enunciation contains an absolute of truth that can serve as starting point for the discovery of other absolute truths.[84]

¶ *Third Characteristic: Enunciation Is True or False.* This characteristic depends upon the *whole* content of the enunciation, and therefore upon the complex unit constituted by the relation which the mind sets up between the subject and predicate. It is not the act of judging that is formally true or false, but the fruit of its activity, its enunciation:

Truth pertains to *what* the intellect says and not to the operation by which its says it. For the intellect to be true it is not necessary that the act itself be equated with the thing, since the thing is often material whereas the act is always immaterial; but *what* the intellect says and knows by its act *must* be equated with the thing, that is, the thing must be as the intellect says it is.[85]

The above remark is of primary importance to our study of truth in the next chapter; for if enunciation, the immanent fruit of the intellect, is the subject of truth, then this fruit must exist *before* truth can exist. Just as it is neither matter nor form that exists, but the composite of this matter and this form, so is it neither the subject, nor the predicate, nor the intellectual act uniting them that is truth, but the enunciation resulting from the composition of subject and predicate by the intellect.

This third property of enunciation, resulting from its unity with reference to the unity of the *ipsum esse rei*,[86] necessarily accompanies every enunciation insofar as it is measured by things. It is the soul of the concept of this second mental operation, and when this soul is defective, when the enunciation is devoid of truth, it is a *monster* in the order of intellectual procreation:

A false opinion in the order of knowledge is what a monster is in corporeal nature, for it is outside the finality of the first principles, which are as the seminal powers of knowledge, just as monsters occur despite the intention of the agent's natural causality.[87]

St. Thomas formally defines enunciation in terms of its finality, its intention to be naturally equated with the mode of existing of things, both as an intellectual concept and as the external sign of this concept:

Here is the definition of enunciation: enunciation is discourse in which exist the true and the false. . . .[88]

Of all the types of intellectual discourse, the true and the false exist only in enunciation, because only enunciation signifies absolutely the intellectual concept in which the true and false exist.[89]

We must now study the epistemological structure of this essential property of enunciation, as well as the way in which it comes into the intellect; this will be the subject of our next chapter.

IX · TRUTH AS THE EFFECT OF JUDGMENT AND OBJECT OF KNOWLEDGE

Since truth consists in a certain rectitude and commensuration, its measure must be included in its definition.[1]

Truth, as we have just seen, is an effect of judgment because it is a property of its immanent term, enunciation, inasmuch as this term refers, as to its measure, to the mode by which things exist. It is also the object of judicative knowledge, since judgment knows its verb and what measures it. Therefore, this chapter will study these two aspects of truth. In the first section we shall analyze truth as the *effect* of the act of composing and dividing; in the second we shall deal with truth as the *object* experienced by this same intellectual act.

Section I: Truth as Effect of Judgment

That *truth is in the mind* is continually affirmed by St. Thomas[2]; the frequency of this first affirmation is almost matched by a second, that truth exists properly and formally only in the second operation of the mind, judgment.[3] On the other hand, some forms of expression seem to identify truth and things, and to affirm that truth exists in the act of apprehension and even in sense knowledge.[4] Therefore, this word has several meanings, just as have the words *being* and *knowledge,* and consequently we must discover the first root meaning that will serve as the principle governing the hierarchy of secondary meanings. The word *truth* is analogous, and we must find the first analogate—what this word means first and foremost—before we are able to apply it to others extrinsically.[5] Let us therefore examine the different senses of the word *truth* and try to discover the unity or ruling principle of its different meanings.

337

A. MULTIPLICITY AND UNITY OF MEANINGS OF THE WORD TRUTH

Although the etymological origin of words tells us nothing definite about their philosophical meaning,[6] it can nevertheless help us discover the deep intuitions that have led men to fashion a new word designating a reality of the intellectual order. The etymology of the Greek word *alètheia*[7] and its Latin equivalent *veritas*, which in English we render as *truth*, is quite suggestive. The Greek *alètheia* comes from *lèthô*, ancient form of *lanthanô*, which means to escape notice, to remain invisible, concealed, and from the negative *a*, which destroys the negative sense of the original word and replaces it by a wholly positive idea, namely, that of being discovered, perceived, visible, and, therefore, luminous. According to this origin, truth would mean either the luminousness of the real, its evidence, or the mind's discovery of this luminosity. The Latin *veritas* is rooted etymologically in a wholly different primitive intuition, having to do with belief, choice[8]; thus derived, truth signifies the intellect's choice, its belief, or, again, the thing chosen or believed. So, with both Greeks and Latins there is, at the root of the word they adopted to signify the epistemological reality we call truth, the idea of an interference between the real and our powers of knowing, for discovery implies a discoverer and something to be discovered; and belief or choice is unintelligible without a subjective and objective element. In this linguistic context, truth means *what* the intellect discovers and chooses, or the *act* by which it succeeds in discovering or choosing.

Despite the insight it provides into the psychology of the inventors of the word, the etymological definition of truth cannot serve as a basis for philosophical investigation of the notion, for words have a life of their own; they are born and transformed in the course of time and take on new meanings that become popular and then the common property of mankind. Philosophical reflection must take as its starting point the nominal definition of truth, a definition that may be formulated as follows: *Truth is an agreement between thought and it object.*[9] Starting from this general notion, let us try to discover the elements necessary to make this notion of truth intelligible and place them in order according to their respective importance.

¶ *1. Truth Is an Agreement.* Politicians speak of agreement among nations, grammarians of agreement between subject and verb, musicians of agreement between notes, and moralists of agreement between conscience and acts! What these different uses of the word *agreement* have in common is the existence of a plurality of factors coincident with a certain unity or harmony. Thus, when we define truth as an agreement, we must find both the multitude and the unity, the multitude being made up of knowledge and the real, whereas the unity consists in their harmony. But what kind of harmony are we talking about? Harmony between musical notes is brought about by the musician, agreement between subject and predicate by him who writes grammatically, agreement among peoples, when it exists, by the stronger power! Is there, then, a power superior to our intellect and to the material reality that is its object, of which one function is to set up a sort of pre-established harmony whereby truth would be defined? Undoubtedly such a power exists for St. Thomas, and later we shall see what role it plays in the existence of human truth. But the mass of men are certainly not thinking about this superior power when they conceive truth as an agreement, for their outlook has neither this breadth nor this universal perspective. When men speak of agreement in defining truth, they simply mean a harmony existing between knowledge and the real. But who is the author of this agreement, the real or knowledge? That is to say, is it a question of things being in accord with knowledge or knowledge agreeing with things? Which one agrees with the other, bows to the other's needs?

This question is easy to answer after all that we have seen about the nature of knowledge—intentional assimilation of the real, therefore, essentially measured by it—and about the nature of judgment and its term. Knowledge is measured by exterior things; knowledge must agree with the real, and not vice versa.

The reason you are white is not that we truly think you are, but on the contrary, we truly think you are white because you are white.[10]

If things cause the truth of our knowledge, do they cause this truth because they are true, as a man begets a man because he himself is a man, or does a causality other than efficient causality enter here? This is the second question to be answered.

¶ 2. *Things Are the Measure of Truth.*   Here is a brief synthesis explaining the problem we have just posed—first the question, then the answer:

QUESTION: That because of which a thing is so, is itself more so. . . . But it is from the fact that a thing is or is not, that our thought or word is true or false. . . . Therefore truth resides rather in things than in the intellect.[11]

ANSWER: Although the truth of our intellect is caused by the thing, yet it is not necessary that the essence of truth should be there primarily, any more than that the essence of health should be primarily in medicine rather than in the animal: for it is the power of medicine *not its health* that is the cause of health, since the agent is not univocal. In the same way, the being of the thing, *not its truth*, is the cause of truth in the intellect. Hence the Philosopher says that an opinion or a statement is true from the fact that a thing is, *not from the fact that a thing is true*.[12]

What is the analogical causality by means of which the thing can produce that which it itself does not possess? To understand and solve this difficulty, without transgressing the laws of cognitive life and those of reality, we must call to mind everything we have seen about the nature of the object and its double causality. On the one hand, the causality that exists at the beginning of the *cognitive act*[13] and unites with the knowing power to form a total and single cause of the act and concept in the order of exercise, and, on the other hand, the causality that is *the term* of this same cognitive activity and measures it extrinsically.[14] When we say that the thing causes truth not because it is true but because it is, we are considering the thing as the specifying and extrinsic object of true knowledge, and from this aspect, truth is not in it: "That any thing be the object of a *true* affirmation of the intellect or of discourse is accidental to that thing."[15]

Now let us investigate the mode of causality according to which the being of things really causes the truth of our knowledge without formally possessing what it causes.

There are three categories of things whose names are signs. The first category, whose total and complete being is exterior to the soul, are complete realities, like man or stone. The second are in no way outside the soul, like dreams or chimaeras. The third have their *foundation* in extra-mental reality but need to be supplemented, as it were, by an *operation of the soul.* This supplement formally constitutes their definition, as e.g. in the case of the universal. *Humanity* is actually an aspect of the real but, as real, universality does not belong to it, because outside the soul there is no *humanity* common to many. But, once known by the intellect, the latter by means of an action adds a relation which makes *humanity a species.* . . . Similarly for truth, whose foundation is in the thing but whose essential supplement is provided by that operation wherein the intellect apprehends things according to their mode. . . . By means of this operation by which the intellect apprehends the being of the thing as it is, *by imitating it* the relation of adequation which defines truth is completed. We must also add that the being of the thing is the cause of truth *only insofar as it exists in the act of intellectual knowledge.*[16]

This is a capital text for the comprehension of the nature of truth and the role that extramental reality and cognitive activity unite to play in constituting its nature. First of all, the thing's mode of existing is given as that which acts as *foundation* with respect to the unity that is truth, and as a foundation which is identical with a cause, since the thing is cause of the truth of our knowledge.[17] The meaning of these two terms and their role as essential component of truth is explained in the following text.

The truth or falsity of discourse or of enunciation must be referred to the *disposition of the thing as to their cause.* When the intellect constructs a composition, it takes two concepts, one of which, the predicate, has a formal function with respect to the other, insofar as it exists in it. . . . So if such an intellectual operation must be referred to the thing as to its cause, then in composite substances the composition of matter and form or of what plays the role of matter and form, or again the composition of accident with subject, *must guarantee,* as foundation and cause of truth, *the composition which the intellect forms interiorly*, and expresses in discourse. Thus, when I say Socrates is a man, the truth of this composition is caused by the composition of the human form with individual matter which makes Socrates to be this man; and when I say that the man is white, the cause of this truth is the composition of whiteness with a subject: and the same is true in every case.[18]

For the extramental thing to be the cause and foundation of truth, then, means that it *guarantees*, justifies the intellect's composition of concepts. The composition of the thing bears witness to the composition the mind constructs; it testifies, as a model does for a copy, that the intellect's fruit conforms with the complexity of the extramental thing, that by means of this fruit the intellect superexists the thing according to the mode of unity this thing has outside the mind. The truth of knowledge is therefore the consequence of a sort of intellectual justice with respect to the thing, insofar as the latter exists in the intellect. The abstractive mode, to which everything entering the soul must submit, strips physical being of the concrete and existential unity that constitutes its wealth, by dispersing it into a multitude of fragmentary aspects which apprehension considers as absolutes. Judgment *restores* to the thing as known the unity it enjoys outside the soul, and this restoration of unity has as its necessary reward the truth of our knowledge itself.

¶ *3. Truth Exists Formally in Enunciation Alone.* Since the truth of our knowledge is not caused by the truth of the thing but by its mode of existing considered as measure of the knowledge we have of it, truth exists formally in the soul and there only. But the soul is the scene of a multitude of different operations, those of the external senses, those of the intellect, which has at least two different types, simple apprehension and judgment. Why should not truth be possessed in common by each and every one of these operations, so that knowledge and truth might be *convertible* and thus to speak of true knowledge would be a pleonasm, while to attribute falsity to knowledge would be absurd! Furthermore, this would seem necessarily to be so, since our definition of the thing as *object* of human knowledge has shown us that the only way being could really deserve the title of object is as *measure* of the act of knowledge.[19] But we have just seen that truth consists in the measurement of knowledge by being, which is the definition of knowledge itself insofar as it is a superexistence of the thing in the soul.

Not only the definition of knowledge seems to necessitate identification of knowledge and truth, but the usual formulae used by philosophers would seem to make this identification inevitable. Thus, the axiom, that being and truth are convertible,[20] certainly gives the impression that this is so; also, we habitually say that sensation is true, common sense is true, apprehension is true, etc. Unless we accuse philosophers as a whole of inexact terminology and deny everything that we have been saying about the second operation of the mind and the properties of enunciation,[21] we shall have to discover the reason which makes truth the exclusive property of the second mental operation and which at the same time warrants the character of universal predicate that seemingly belongs to it. This reason has already been mentioned: *The notion of truth is analogical.*

We have not yet spoken of analogy, the key notion of Thomistic epistemology, although we have used it constantly in analyzing knowledge, and particularly in analyzing our knowledge of being as such. The difficulties brought up by the word and concept of truth give us an opportunity to mention it here; therefore, we shall briefly explain the characteristics of analogical words and concepts. Analogy is a property belonging to certain names and concepts; it does not qualify the real[22] but qualifies our knowledge and naming of the real insofar as it is *diverse* and as its unity is reducible neither to generic nor to specific identity, nor to the identity of a subject. The univocity of knowledge corresponds to the quidditative unity of things, and analogy corresponds to unity of order or causality between many things precisely because of their multitude. "In creatures one form does not exist in several supposita *except by unity of order*, as the form of an ordered multitude. . . . For we say that many men are a college or an army or a people."[23]

Analogy is therefore an intellectual procedure by which a multitude of concepts signifying different things are united by virtue of a certain order that we discover between them and the things they signify. Analogy is an even more radical revelation of the mind's allergy to multiplicity as such,[24] for it reveals an effort, much more intense than univocity, to unify concepts so dissimilar that they can only be linked by our discovering a common bond of either dependence or functional similarity between them. The classical example used by St. Thomas is that of health applied to concepts as different as climate, complexion, animal, and mind. Obviously, these four concepts have nothing in common when taken absolutely; yet, the intellect can unify them by stressing the relations

that can be set up between them. An animal is said to be healthy
because it has a well-balanced organism, climate is said to be healthy
because it contributes to this balance, the complexion because it
indicates it, and the mind because it enjoys, intellectually and
morally, an equilibrium comparable with that of a healthy body.[25]
Therefore, the unity of an analogical concept is not based upon
identity of nature, or upon the identity of the single subject of many
accidents, but upon an order discovered by reason between concepts
that can be interrelated because the things of which they are the
likenesses are related through causality, origin, or likeness.

Thus, considering the notion of truth from the aspect of analogy,
we must try to unify the multitude of concepts and things which
this notion associates within an apparent unity. *Words are, in effect,
signs of concepts, and concepts are signs of things*[26]; to the unity of
word must correspond unity of concept, and unity of concept necessarily signifies the unity of the thing conceived. We have just seen
that the word *truth* can be used equally well to mean any kind of
human knowledge, discourse or the expression of this knowledge, and
the real that is its object. The same word seems to signify such a
diversity of concepts and things that it signifies nothing, for if we
take away a sign's unity of meaning, we take away its soul,[27] and
thus it stops being a sign; for how can it reveal to another the
speaker's thought if it has no definite meaning? In such a case, it
becomes equivocal and spreads confusion and error.[28] To avoid the
confusion inherent in a word and a notion designating a multitude,
there must be a principle of order, a first meaning on which all the
others depend.

A sign is ambiguous and fallacious when it signifies a number of things
which have no order between them. But when it signifies things that are
unified by a certain order of relationships, then it is a perfectly definite
sign.[29]

What is this first sense of the word and concept *truth*, which will
serve as rallying point for all other meanings by being an element of
their definition?

By its etymological meaning and its nominal definition, truth
implies a multiplicity of components, and a multiplicity of com-

ponents that are related to each other as cause to effect, the cause being the measure, and the effect, the measured. Thus, truth belongs to the category of relations of the third mode.[30]

The third mode has to do with the relation of the measurable to its measure. This is not a matter of measure and measurable according to quantity . . . but according to a measurement of *being and truth*. For the truth of knowledge is measured by its object. From the fact that a thing exists or does not exist, enunciation is true or false, and not inversely. The same is true of the sense and the sensible.[31]

This relation of measured to measure is usually connoted by the term *adequation*,[32] and, like every relation, it requires two distinct terms— knowledge and the real—and a unifying principle called the *foundation*, which is the very form of the relation.[33] By examining this relation of adequation that defines truth according to the essential requirements of every relation—that is, the distinction of terms and the nature of the foundation or cause uniting them—we quickly see that only in judicative activity do we find sufficient diversity between knower and known to establish a relation of equality between them.

Actually, in simple apprehension our sensory powers and our intellect *are* what they know, because apprehension's mode is one of assimilation and identification with the fragmentary aspect of the thing it receives from the extramental real.[34] To know is really to be the known, and so great is this unity of knowing power with thingss by means of intelligible species that we cannot discover in physical things a point of comparison to help us understand it; for even the composition of essence and existence does not do justice to this mysterious identity between knower and object. Apprehension, whether sensory or intellectual, does not work toward a distinction between knower and thing, but toward a certain identification between them. The relation of adequation requires that the two terms, knower and known, oppose each other and that each have its own identity distinguishing it from the other and permitting comparison and, therefore, relationship.

Truth consists essentially in the adequation of thing and intellect. Now nothing can be equated with itself, for equality implies diversity. So the essence of truth exists in the intellect at the precise moment when, for the first time, the intellect possesses something of its own, something the extra-mental thing does not have but with which it has a certain equality making possible adequation between them.

Now when the intellect expresses quiddities it possesses nothing but the likeness of the exterior thing, just as the sense does when it receives the species of the sensible thing. But when it begins to judge the thing apprehended, then judgment itself is a typical possession of the intellect which does not exist in extra-mental reality. When it is equated with what is in the exterior thing, judgment is said to be true. But the intellect judges the thing apprehended only when it says that something is or is not, and this is what the intellect does in composing and dividing. Which is is why the philosopher says that composition and division exist in the intellect and not in things.[35]

In the light of our analysis of the judgment's perfective role as an operation reassembling the concepts of apprehension, of its typical initiative, of the characteristics of the *esse* that properly express the composition it constructs[36]—in this light, it is easy to understand and interpret the meaning of the seemingly ambiguous expression, "having something of its own," the something that characterizes judgment and opposes it to the extramental real. Moreover, when St. Thomas speaks of something of its own which the thing has corresponding to the distinctive something belonging to the intellect, *sed aliquid ei correspondens*, his formulae become clear if we recall the meaning of *ipsum esse rei* and its function as measure of truth.[37] Since the mode by which things exist is complex, and since this complexity corresponds to the conceptual composition constructed by the intellect, there is a possibility of adequation because there are two distinct terms. For the complexity of the thing's mode of existing is wholly different from the composition of concepts constructed by the mind, and this complex thing's mode of unity is also entirely different from the mode of identity that the mind sets up between the subject and predicate. In the act of judgment, therefore, we have the elements necessary to the distinction of terms in the relation of adequation that is truth, whereas this distinction must be denied to the intellect and the senses in the act of apprehension. If senses and intellect had a likeness of the thing other than that which the thing causes in them, the result would be ignorance or absence of knowledge; for knowledge exists insofar as sensory or intellectual apprehension is identified with the thing, and insofar as this likeness of identity is absent, knowledge does not exist.[38] To sum up the difference between knowledge and true knowledge in their dependence upon the extramental thing, we can say that knowledge exists insofar as the thing causes knowledge and is its principle by giving it what it is through the intermediation of intentional species, consequently, insofar as the knower is identical with the thing. But knowledge is true exactly to the degree that the intellect recombines, reassembles the fragmentary identities of the thing that it is through apprehension, and this reassemblage is *guaranteed* by the unified complexity of the thing.[39] The thing measures the being of knowledge insofar as it is identical with it, but it measures the truth of knowledge insofar as knowledge by its synthesizing activity identifies a multitude of concepts with its concrete mode of existing.

Only in the operation of composing and dividing do there arise the elements essential to a relation of adequation. But is the foundation, the formal or causal component of this relation in the act or in its term? Since truth is in the intellect and not in things, the foundation for the relation of adequation must be found in the intellect, for judgment is relative to the real, and not the contrary.[40] In studying the properties of enunciation as term of the act of judgment, we say that judgment, as referred to the real, is necessarily true or false, for it (but not the act which begets it) is equated with reality.[41] Therefore, the immanent foundation of all human knowledge is enunciation, and this foundation is none other than the verb-predicate that signifies the unity of the composition constructed by the mind, therefore, that which characterizes judgment as such and makes it comparable with the mode of existing that things have outside the mind.

The following text sums up the explanations we have been giving about the nature of truth and its formal localization in the concept of the second intellectual operation:

Truth belongs to *what the intellect says and not to the operation* by which it says it. For the truth of the intellect it is not necessary that the act itself be equated with the thing, since often the thing is material whereas the act is always immaterial; but *what* the intellect says and knows by its act *must be equated with the thing.* . . . When, on the contrary, what is said and understood is incomplex, the incomplex considered in itself *is neither equated nor not-equated with the thing*, for equality and inequality imply relation; but the incomplex considered in itself implies no relation or application to the thing, so that it can neither be said to be true nor false, unlike enunciation which involves comparison of the incomplex with the thing by the sign of composition or division.[42]

When therefore, we speak of truth in the formal sense of the word, we always mean a property of enunciation considered as immanent term of the second operation of the mind, insofar as this immanent term, being distinct from the being of things, is related as measured to measure with the thing whose complex unity it expresses. However, since truth is an analogical notion, it follows the law of analogical attribution and designates multiple but ordered things.

When anything is predicated of many things univocally, it is found in each of them according to its proper nature; as animal is found in each species of animal. But when anything is predicated of many things *analogically*, it is found in *only one of them* according to its proper nature, and from this one the rest are denominated. So healthiness is predicated of animal, of urine and of medicine; not that health is not only in the animal, but from the health of the animal, medicine is called healthy insofar as it is the cause of health, and urine is called healthy insofar as it indicates health. And although health *is neither in medicine* nor in urine, yet in either there is something whereby the one causes and the other indicates health.[43]

We have seen that things are said to be true, that discourse is said to be true, and that the other operations of knowledge are called true. The truth of enunciation must therefore be what is formally true, and the rest must all be called true by denomination or reference to this equivalence.

The truth of enunciations is nothing other than the truth of the intellect, for an enunciation resides in the intellect and in speech. Now *according as it is in the intellect, it has truth in itself*, but according as it is in speech, it is called enunciable truth, according as it *signifies* some truth of the intellect and not because of any truth residing in the enunciation as though in a subject. . . . In like manner, it has been already said that *things are called true* from the truth of the intellect.[44]

B. TRUTH IS THE EFFECT OF JUDGMENT

It is now easy to understand the statement made at the beginning of this chapter, that truth is an effect of judgment. For if truth exists formally in our mind only as a property of the term of the second mental operation, the cause of this term or of enunciation is the cause of this truth's *existence* in us. Therefore, the existence of truth is really an effect of the second operation of the mind and must primarily be sought there, not in the operation causing it but in its living fruit, enunciation, whose soul is truth.[45] In every act of knowing other than judgment and the reasoning flowing from it, truth cannot be spoken of in the strict sense. The knowing *power* can be said to be true, as we say of a thing that it is true, but we cannot say that the knowledge possessed by this power is true.

Since everything is true according as it has the form proper to its nature, the intellect, as a knowing power, must be true according as it has the likeness of the thing known, which is *its form as a knowing power*. . . . Truth therefore may be in the sense or in the intellect knowing what a thing is, *as in a true thing*, but not as a thing known is in the knower, which is implied by the word truth; for the perfection of the intellect is true as known.[46]

Thus, truth exists formally in enunciation alone, in this *complexum* that is the product of the intellect; all other simple concepts make the intellect true because they are its form as knowing power, but they themselves are neither true nor false: "Although the incomplex intelligible is neither true nor false, the intellect conceiving it *is* true insofar as it is equated with the thing."[47]

We shall now consider the truth of enunciation whose existence is an effect of judgment as the *object* of our knowledge, in order to see the procedure by which the intellect, in giving existence to truth, can simultaneously be aware of it.

Section II: Truth as Object of Knowledge

Truth is the effect of judgment since it exists formally only in enunciation and is as its property. It is therefore in the mind that we must seek it as object of our knowledge, and at the term of the act called judgment. "From what we have just said it is also evident that the true and the false, as objects of knowledge, exist in the mind."[48] Like every object of knowledge, truth can be considered in two ways: in its existence and in its nature. To know the existence of an object is to perceive it in its natural being by a sort of experience or intuition; to know its quiddity is to grasp its intelligibility absolutely, independently of its particular realizations.[49] We can perceive one or more truths *because they exist* in the mind as epistemological facts, and being in possession of these facts, we can seek out the constitutive factors that define and distinguish one truth from another; this is *quiddative* knowledge of the different truths we experience.[50] But knowledge that a thing exists always precedes knowledge of its determinate nature, for it would be absurd to look for a thing's quiddity before having observed its existence.[51] We must therefore analyze the processes by which the intellect knows truths as existing within it before examining the nature of these different truths. The study of these two aspects of our knowledge of truth will be undertaken in the two following subsections.

A. HOW DO WE KNOW THAT AN ENUNCIATION IS TRUE?

It is an undeniable epistemological fact that man is aware that he knows truth and also that he knows that he is able to be in error. On this fact of the coexistence of error and truth in the human soul, all modern epistemology has been constructed.[52] But knowledge of the existence of truth and error brings up a special difficulty, because truth and error are *relations* and consequently require the apprehension of two terms, namely, what the intellect says and the mode of existing of things in its function as measure. Knowledge of the existence of truth presupposes simultaneous awareness of both the enunciation and the thing it is concerned with, which cannot be done without a certain reflection whose object is necessarily the intellect's own activity with reference to extramental things. Of what does this reflection consist?

¶ *1. Need for Reflection to Apprehend the Existence of Truth.* For some years there has been considerable discussion about the reflective aspects implied by the Thomistic theory of the knowledge of truth, either in order to answer idealist criticisms and set forth the critical character of the *philosophia perennis*,[53] or else in response to the Thomistic texts that stress the importance of reflection.[54] St. Thomas does undoubtedly state that reflection is necessary in order to perceive the existence of truth, but this is not surprising in view of his theory that the intellect first knows its object and *then* the concepts that present the object to it by reflecting on those concepts, which thus become objects of knowledge.[55] Since truth exists formally only in the concept of the second mental operation, it is not extraordinary that the intellect perceives the truth of the concept by reflecting on this same concept, inasmuch as the latter does not exist in things or, consequently, in the object of judgment.[56] The difficulty here is not the need for reflection, but its precise object; for the concept of the second mental operation, the enunciation as immanent term of judgment, can be known as true only insofar as it is referred to the thing's mode of existing, and, apparently, therefore, only insofar as its whole being is essentially projected toward the being of the thing. Thus, we might ask what use there is in reflecting on the concept if its truth or falsity is revealed only by comparing it with its exterior measure.

Let us examine the most explicit text concerning the need for reflection in grasping the existence of truth in our knowledge:

Truth is in the intellect and in the sense, but not in the same way. For it is in the intellect both as a *consequence* of its act, and as known by it; it proceeds from the intellect's operation accordingly as the latter's judgment expresses the thing as it is; *but it is known by the intellect accordingly as the intellect reflects upon its act*, not only to know it but to perceive its relation to the thing. But this relation cannot be known unless the nature of the act be known, and the latter cannot be known except the nature of its active principle be known, the intellect itself, whose whole being is to conform with things. So it is by reflecting upon itself that the intellect knows truth.[57]

First, let us divide this passage according to its content, then we shall see what meaning should be given to the reflection now being considered. To begin with, the particular context of this teaching is given by St. Thomas' purpose: to distinguish truth in the senses from that in the intellect. In the senses, truth exists only as a consequence of a sensory judgment proceeding from the common sense,[58] but it is not known by this operation because there is no reflection there. In the intellect, on the contrary, it is not only the consequence of intellectual activity, since it is a property of its immanent term, enunciation,[59] but it is the object of intellectual knowledge, and this is where reflection comes in. The description of this reflection takes up the last part of the passage and can be divided according to the following aspects:

(1) *The purpose of reflection* is to know the act of judgment and its implied relation with the real.

(2) This relation with the real cannot be known except the nature of the act be known.

(3) The nature of the act cannot be known unless that of the intellect, its principle, be also known.

(4) But the nature of the intellect is to be conformed with things.

(5) Therefore, it is by reflecting upon itself that the intellect knows truth (i.e., conformity of enunciation and thing).

In this argumentation there is an implicit syllogism marking the different analytical levels of our awareness of the existence of a true knowledge. The point of departure of this analysis is the existence of a true judgment that is the object of reflection. Here is its syllogistic formulation:

(1) To know truth is to perceive the relation between judgment and thing;
    But to see the relation between judgment and thing is to perceive its nature;
    Therefore, to know truth is to perceive the nature of judgment.

(2) But to perceive the nature of judgment is to know the nature of its active principle, the intellect;
    Therefore, to know truth is to know the nature of the intellect.

(3) But to know the nature of the intellect is to see that it is naurally made to conform with things;
Therefore, to know truth is to perceive the intellect as naturally made to conform with things.

The general idea to be derived from this syllogistic description of the reflection by which we know that our knowledge is true in no way corresponds to the usual picture we have of it. The intellect is not described here as having the strabismic power to look in two directions at once, one eye fixed on the thing and the other on the concept of the judgment! This spatial imagery, requiring the intellect to step outside itself to compare its knowledge with the physical thing it copies, is the result of a complete misunderstanding of the intellect's life and wholly destroys the immanence of the operations of knowledge: "The thing known is said to be the object of knowledge according as it subsists in itself outside the knower, although there can be no apprehension of this thing except as it exists in the knower."[60] We know things existing outside ourselves, but we know them because they exist in us. Knowledge of truth is not arrived at by comparing things as known with things as existing, for that brings up the famous problem of the bridge with which the whole history of idealism is filled, and whose solution is impossible because it is a pseudoproblem. *The intellect knows truth by reflecting upon itself*, and not by eyeing both its act and the extramental thing. Analyzing the reflection that must precede awareness that our knowledge is true has led us to this conclusion. Now let us try to define the meaning of this reflection more precisely.

¶ *2. Analysis of the Reflection by Which the Existence of Truth Is Known.* We must note, for it is important, that the starting point of this reflection is necessarily judgment, since truth is the *consequence* of judgment and this consequence is what we want to know. It is from enunciation, term of the second operation of the mind and subject of truth, that this reflection starts whose object is to find out whether enunciation is equated with the real. One might normally expect that a description aiming to discover this relation of adequation with the thing would consist in a comparison between the complexity of the thing and the complexity of the enunciation. However, this is not so, because the whole process of reflecting is directed toward the intellect and its life. St. Thomas concludes that our knowledge of the existence of truth parallels our knowledge of the nature of the intellect, and, at first glance, this appears quite paradoxical. But it is the only possible route that reflection can take, for it alone respects the nature of the pre-eminent life that is knowledge, while taking into account the nature of judgment, whose function is to perfect the life of knowledge.

Let us come back to the argumentation of the text we quoted above.[61] The major of the first step (1) is the definition of truth; its minor is nothing but the definition of judgment, since the latter is formally defined as an opening upon the mode by which things exist.[62] The conclusion is inevitable and is further confirmed by our study of truth as the effect of judgment.[63]

The starting point for the second step (2) is the conclusion of the first syllogism, identifying knowledge of truth with that of the nature of judgment; then comes the statement that to apprehend the nature of judgment implies apprehension of the nature of the intellect that is its principle. The evidence of this statement can be perceived by recalling what has been said about our intellect's natural need for totality and unification[64] and the work it does in the second operation to satisfy this essential need to reassemble and clarify the knowledge acquired through simple apprehension.[65] The human intellect takes the initiative in this second operation only because the first operation is not satisfactory since it stops halfway in its possession of being, due to the inevitable fragmentation to which the abstractive mode of simple apprehension subjects the real. Our natural need to judge and the determinate nature of this act reveal the profound finality of the active principle of this act. Thus concludes the second argumentation.

The third and last step (3) rests upon the definition of our intellect and its proper operation, knowledge. Its nature is to conform with things; that is its definition. Hesitation in accepting this definition of the intellect's nature indicates that we have either misunderstood or forgotten the explanations that have been given of the nature of knowledge. For since knowing primarily consists in *being* what we know, and since we are not naturally what we know but must become it, then the intellect, like every power of knowledge, must be essentially a capacity to conform to things. This is the whole meaning of the formula, *the intellect is a passive power*, for the nature of a passive power is to let itself be informed by its object, to become *con-formed* with it, to communicate in the same form.[66] What reflection discovers at the end of the third step is that our intellect does not make its objects but *receives* them, that they cause its knowledge in the order of specification, that its concepts are the *effects* of being's causality upon the intellect, and that the intellect is what being makes it to be. Now, if by its concepts it is a likeness of the real, and if judgment consists in composing and dividing concepts that are naturally likenesses of things, then composition and division will naturally constitute a whole that is itself a likeness of the thing. Consequently, in seeking to discover the existence of truth, reflection is naturally directed, not toward the exterior object dealt with by judgment, but toward the act and its immanent principles. For the intellect demands by nature that its knowledge be true, because to know is to be what it is, and to know perfectly what is, is the definition of judgment: Judgment is to be perfectly what is.

¶ 3. *The Term of Reflection that Makes Known the Existence of Truth.* Does reflection end with the perception of the intellect's nature and its passivity with respect to things? In the text we have just analyzed it is not pursued any further than that. But to perceive the intellect's passivity is to be aware of its dependence upon things and, therefore, upon sensation and the phantasm that serve as grooms for the thing and help it penetrate to the soul's depth, so that it may there be worked on by the agent intellect and be enabled to become the spouse of the possible intellect and the father of its concepts. Reflection must therefore continue until it apprehends the actual dependence of concepts upon phantasms, which are both the matter from which the agent intellect draws intelligible species and the copy or image in which the possible intellect contemplates its concept.[67] Reflection may even go so far as to know the singular, when the truth of our judgment depends upon certain aspects of the thing whose mode of existing varies according to the individual. For example, I cannot know that the judgment, "Socrates is running," is true without the actual help of sense knowledge. Here is a description of reflection concerned with the sensible origins of concepts that the judgment composes and divides to construct enunciation, thus true knowledge:

Sometimes the mind accidentally penetrates to singulars insofar as there is a continuity between the mind and the sensory faculties whose particulars are its object. This continuity may be established in two ways. First when sensory activity terminates in the mind, as occurs in motion going from things to the soul; and then the mind knows the singular *by means of a certain reflection* which, starting from knowledge of the object, which is a particular nature, consists in coming back upon knowledge of the act itself, and from apprehension of the act to apprehension of the species, its principle, and from knowledge of the species to knowledge of the phantasm from which it was drawn. In this way the mind has some knowledge of the singular.[68]

It is not surprising that the intellect's reflection should penetrate as far as the singular, for man knows through the intermediation of his intellectual as well as his sensory powers; he is the theatre where the drama of our knowledge of things is played, and the different personages appearing on this stage are as much his creation as they are that of things. He is therefore aware of all that is produced in the order of sensation and everything the agent intellect lays before the possible intellect, and all the universal concepts born of intellectual vitality, concepts both complex and incomplex. He is at the same time author and spectator of the whole of his knowledge and of each item in it.[69]

What points should be especially noted in this study of our knowledge of the existence of truth? First of all, that this knowledge is possible to the same extent that man is aware of the processes by which he naturally grasps exterior things, by simple apprehension as well as by the second operation of the mind. Secondly, that knowledge of the existence of truth is just as immanent an act as are the other acts of knowing, and consequently that it takes place wholly within the soul. To imagine that the intellect checks with exterior reality in order to see whether or not its judgment conforms with the existential mode of things is not only puerile but absurd, for we know only the reality that exists within us and nothing else. If we cannot control the legitimacy of the composition made by judgment without having recourse to physical reality as it exists outside the mind, then such control will always remain impossible! Knowledge of truth does not consist in going from the world of thought to that of being, but in being united with the world of being in the effects that its physical and intentional activity has caused or actually causes in our soul. Because being makes us to be itself, we can refer to the likenesses we have of it to see whether or not the composition constructed by judgment corresponds with what is.

There is a third and final point that must never be forgotten, which is that the mind's compositions vary with the concepts it uses. For concepts can have a universal or particular, an essential or accidental meaning, and, depending upon the meaning of the concepts, the reflection leading to perception of our judgments' truth or falsity goes all the way back to knowledge of the singular, or stops at phantasms. This remark brings us to the problem of the multiplicity of truths and their nature, which we shall study in the next section.

B. HOW DO WE KNOW THE HIERARCHY OF TRUTHS?

When the mind makes these two judgments, "Peter is walking," "Peter is a man," it is author of two enunciations, that are formally true, and yet no one would maintain that the truth of the first enunciation is identical with that of the second, for the former has a stability totally lacking in the latter. Now, it seems contradictory to define truth as an adequation between the composition of concepts constructed by the mind and the composition existing in things, and to admit at the same time that there is a hierarchy in the diversity of truths. For just as it is impossible that a geometrical figure be more or less a circle or a triangle, so an adequation cannot be more or less adequate: either it exists, or it does not. It would seem then that the only possible multiplicity among truths would be numerical, because numerically distinct acts of intellect are the principles of successive enunciations, just as there are numerically distinct circles because different materials have circular form. But not only are truths numerically multiple, they are diverse, and their diversity is such that it is impossible to reduce them to absolute unity; only a certain hierarchical order and unity of proportionality are possible. Thus, we must look for the cause of this hierarchy in the multiplicity of truths, whose very existence seems to destroy the nature of truth, that is, its essential need to be adequated with the real. Here is how St. Thomas states the problem and gives it a universal solution, a solution we shall have to explain carefully in order to perceive its full riches.

Since truth is defined as the adequation of intellect and thing, it cannot admit of more or less *from the point of view of equality*, because equality excludes the more and the less; consequently we cannot speak of a more or less true enunciation. But if we consider the *being of the thing which is the measure of truth*, then, as is said in the second book of the *Metaphysics*, there is the same disposition of things in being and in truth and therefore things which are more are also more true.[70]

The consequence of this doctrine is this: Every time the question of degree and hierarchy comes up between different truths, it is not the intellect's adequation that is being considered, but the *ipsum esse rei* to which enunciation must be strictly equated under penalty of not being true. Consequently, there are as many typically different truths as there are cases of *ipsum esse rei* capable of measuring the different compositions constructed by the mind and expressed in and by the complex concept that is enunciation. In other words, to use the Aristotelian adage so often repeated by St. Thomas, there are as many dispositions of *simple concepts in the compositions made by judgment* as there are *dispositions of things in being*, because truth exists formally only in the immanent term of the act of composing and dividing. We must keep in mind here that the term *dispositio* has a technical meaning in Thomism,[71] that it always implies multiplicity and order in the multiple. The same is true of the expression *ipsum esse rei*, which implies, at the minimum, the composition of essence and existence and can, and most frequently does, connote the multiplicity of substantial principles of natures as well as the accidents of these natures.[72] It seems advisable again to quote one of our Master's most explicit commentaries on the adage, "There is the same disposition of things in being and in truth."[73] This commentary defines *dispositio in esse* in terms of the composition that enunciation must imitate to be equated with what is:

Truth and falsity in discourse and enunciation must be referred to the *disposition of things as to their cause*. But when the intellect constructs a composition it takes two concepts, one of which, the predicate, has a formal function with respect to the other, insofar as it is considered as existing in it. . . . And that is why, since such an operation of the intellect must be referred to the thing as to its cause, in compound substances the composition of matter and form, or of what plays the role of matter and form, or again the composition of accident and subject, must guarantee after the fashion *of a foundation or cause of truth*, the composition which the intellect forms interiorly and expresses in discourse. So when I say: Socrates is a man, the truth of this enunciation is caused by the composition of the human form with individual matter which makes Socrates this man; and when I say: man is white, the cause of this truth is the composition of whiteness with a subject, and so for all cases. The same is true concerning division.[74]

Thus, the correct translation of the expression *dispositio rerum in esse* can only be the mode by which things exist, as we defined it above,[75] and this is what differentiates and brings hierarchy into truths.

If the composition and division of the thing is the cause of truth and falsity of enunciation in discourse, then it necessarily follows that a difference of composition and division in the being of things produces a difference of truth and falsity in enunciation and discourse.[76]

The things' mode of existing is thus the absolutely primary source of diversity in human truths. This existential mode of things can be considered from three different angles, which give rise to three different kinds of truths.

There are three possible ways of considering the nature of a thing. The first considers this nature according to the being it has in singulars, for example, the nature of stone in this stone or that. The second is concerned with the nature as it exists in the intellect. The third consideration has to do with the nature as an absolute, independent of its singular and universal existence.[77]

The singular mode of being is the measure of all existential truths, those bearing upon the individuating notes of singular things, upon all the phenomena observed by popular and scientific knowledge. These truths necessarily require control by the sense or its substitute, the instrument, since the composition that measures enunciation belongs to the singular and physical order. The intelligible or universal mode of being is the measure of all logical truths, even those concerned with nonbeing and privations, and these truths cannot be guaranteed by the individual mode of existing. For example, take the following reasoning: "Man is a species, but Peter is a man; therefore, Peter is a species." This reasoning is not valid because the first enunciation is measured by the intelligible being of man, the second by his absolute being or *quod quid est*,[78] and the third attributes to an individual that which belongs to the intelligible or universal mode of being. Consideration of natures in their absolute being, in their *quod quid est*, gives birth to all abstract truths, analogical truths concerned with being as such, as well as those concerned with natures considered in their essential elements and properties. This is the field of abstraction, total as well as formal, the abstraction of apprehension as well as that of judgment.[79] Abstraction leads us to the realm of science and wisdom, therefore, to knowledge of truth as infallible, a topic to be dealt with in the fourth and last part of this book.

To summarize this overbrief outline of the diversity of truth, let us compare this doctrine with what has just been said about the properties of enunciation:

(1) Every enunciation is true or false, therefore, equated or not equated with the existential mode of things. From this point of view, there are no multiplicities other than those of the number of truths, and all degrees or hierarchy of truths is impossible since adequation does not admit of more or less.

(2) However, if we take the measure of truth, that is, the specifying term of enunciation, then there is diversity and hierarchy among

truths, for the modes of being measuring our judicative knowledge differ because the composition constituting them is different.

(3) When composition is logical, the truths involved are logical and are called universal, particular, or singular, according to the subject's mode of signifying; they are affirmative or negative depending upon the nature of the verbal copula.

(4) When composition is physical and singular, the truths concerned are physical and contingent: "Peter exists, is white, is Paul's son," etc.

(5) When composition or division belongs to the order of absolute nature, truth is necessary because the bond between subject and predicate cannot not be, or, on the contrary, because this bond is contradictory. "Peter is a man," "Peter is not an ass." When the nature enters into composition with accidents that do not necessarily emanate from it, then the truth is contingent: "This man is white, a musician," etc.[80]

(6) When composition belongs to being as such, then all related truths are metaphysical and analogical, according to the mode of being implied.[81]

CONCLUSION OF PART THREE

In Part Three we have explored the epistemological question, *What does it mean to know truth?* The bond linking this exploration of a natural property of human knowledge to the exploration of its nature springs from two sources. On the one hand, there is the radical imperfection of our intellect whose abstractive mode obliges it to break the real up into fragments in order to enable it to come into the intellect; on the other hand is the need for unity and wholeness, without which human knowledge would always remain essentially imperfect. Truth is an effect of the perfection of human knowledge, a perfection the intellect acquires by an act whose internal structure is altogether different from that of the apprehension we studied in Part Two under the heading, "What Does It Mean to Know?" We began our study by considering the act that produces truth, since the latter exists formally only in the soul; we analyzed judgment in its subjective causes, then in the intellectual operation from which it emanates by way of composition, and finally in the immanent term of this act called enunciation, whose properties are wholly other than those of the concept terminating simple apprehension. Having completed our study of immanent activity, we sought its object term; that is, we asked ourselves, "With what aspect of the exterior real do we enter into relation by the act of judgment?" Doctrinal and textual analysis here compelled us to conclude that the object term of judgment could only be the existential mode of things, or the real taken in its totality as essence and act of existing, substance and accidents. Judgment's essential reference to exterior reality in its complexity gives to enunciation, the immanent term of judgment, an exclusive characteristic, the characteristic of being equated or not equated with the real to which its whole being refers, and it is at this moment that truth or falsity exists formally in the human intellect.[1]

Since the existence of the truth of our knowledge is a fact, it was natural for us to inquire next into the genesis of this fact, its noetic and ontological implications, and then to study the procedures by which the mind becomes aware of truth.[2] One last problem remained, namely, the multiplicity and hierarchy of human truths, a problem that has been a stumbling block for most philosophers from the Greeks to our day, and whose final solution will be found in the fourth and last part of this treatise on epistemology. As we have just seen, this problem is not tied to truth as adequation but to the *measure* of this adequation, i.e., the being-term of judicative knowledge.[3] Our intellect is in debt to the thing, since it must receive from this reality its object causes or principles. Every just debtor reimburses his creditor for what the latter has lent him, capital plus interest. By the act of judgment, the intellect settles its accounts with extramental reality, it acknowledges that it is what the real has made it to be. When this acknowledgment is complete and integral, then enunciation—which represents both the capital borrowed from the thing and the interest that the intellect's life has made it produce— then enunciation is just, i.e., true. Human truth might therefore be defined as the justice a debtor-intellect renders to things when it acknowledges its creditor as the primary possessor of all the wealth of knowledge whose use and usufruct it has. Human truth is a sort of re-cognition, in the sense that it is new knowledge of things already known and an act of gratitude toward the thing that has given itself for the intellect's nourishment, to make it grow and attain perfection: "And yet, even created truth, which resides in our intellect, is greater than the soul, not absolutely, but to the extent that it is *the perfection* of the intellect. . . ."[4]

Such is the meaning of the knowledge of truth; it is not identical with human knowledge, as Descartes and Kant would have it, but is added to knowledge as accidents are added to every created substance, to give it the second actuality without which—even while it is absolute being—it would remain imperfect and unable to reach the end for which it is made.[5] If error were to take the place of truth, then would our knowledge become a monster, because it would run counter to the nature of the intellect and its Author.[6]

Part Four

WHAT IS THE KNOWLEDGE OF INFALLIBLE (formal)
TRUTH?

(x) 1 - Enunciation (evidence)

(xi) 2 - Assent to first principles

(xii) 3 - Infallible Knowl of Mediate Truth.

PROLOGUE

As we saw in our analysis of sensible and intellectual knowledge and in our analysis of the different kinds of truth,[1] the goods of our creditor, the exterior real, do not all have the same value. Neither does the work of the intellect, increasing these goods to full worth, have equally valuable results; which is to say that the truth value of an enunciation varies according to the value of the being that is its source and term. We have just seen that we consciously apprehend very diverse truths. How shall we go about *judging* the value of these truths, and doing so infallibly? This is the last point that needs to be clarified in a complete and strictly philosophical treatise on epistemology. It is well to note that we finish just where Descartes and Kant began, because our inquiry has followed the order of a philosophical questionnaire. This order demands that we inquire into the nature of knowledge before worrying about the existence of its truth, and that the nature of truth be known before we ask questions about its necessity and immutability.[2] St. Thomas has explained his method to us, and we have followed it scrupulously; that is why our last problem is to discover an infallible criterion that will enable us to judge the different kinds of truth and to arrange them according to their value.

The leitmotiv of this last part will be truth considered as good and end of the intellect, formal truth which exists only in the intellect and which, in some ways, *is greater than the soul because it is its perfection.*[3] Our problem is to discover whether there are any immutable truths which the intellect cannot not know infallibly, and the reason for this infallibility. Once these immutable truths are infallibly known by the intellect, we must ask what use we make of them in acquiring and controlling other truths which are not equally evident and immutable, either because the being measuring them is less intelligible or because it immeasurably surpasses the being for which the human intellect is naturally made, i.e., physical reality and the human being that crowns this material universe. During this investigation, however, we must never forget the essentially reflective character which this new knowledge of truth must have; for if truth exists only in the complex concept terminating judgment, and if, on the other hand, all our concepts, simple or complex, can be known only in and by a reflex act,[4] the truth characterizing enunciation can obviously become the object of knowledge only by reflective activity upon the enunciation itself. And if there is a judgment concerned with the truth of our judicative activity, this second judgment will differ entirely from the one dealing with the real and whose effect is truth. In other words, when, in the preceding chapter, we considered knowledge of truth and the multiplicity of enunciative truths, what we were doing was taking stock of a fact, the *quia est* of the truth of our proposition. Now, however, what we want to discover is the *propter quid*, the cause of the infallibility of some of our truths, the nature of the act by which we grasp this infallibility and the functions this supplementary activity of the intellect plays in acquiring and organizing philosophy, both natural and metaphysical.

The division of this part will therefore conform to the requirements of our infallible knowledge of immutable truths. We shall first inquire, in Chapter X, why there are immutable truths that are necessarily the term of some of our judgments, inquire into their number, nature, and hierarchy.

Then, in Chapter XI, we shall study the nature of the knowledge whose object is the truth of these infallible judgments and the epistemological properties of such knowledge.

Finally, we shall analyze the epistemological procedures that enable the intellect to use these infallible truths as criteria for other truths, which analysis will be the topic of Chapter XII.

X · DISCOVERY OF THE ENUNCIATION WHOSE TRUTH IS INFALLIBLY EVIDENT

No enunciation or proposition can be neutral; it is by nature either true or false.[1] Now, personal experience and the history of ideas give evident proof that this child of the mind consorts more frequently with error than with truth, to such a degree that this disease[2] is congenital to it, and although they do not all die of it, all seem to be stricken by it:

Error seems to be even more natural to men as they actually are than knowledge. For experience proves that people easily deceive and delude themselves, whilst to come to true knowledge they need to be taught by others. Again, the soul is involved in error for a longer time than it spends in knowing truth, for to acquire this knowledge even a long course of study hardly suffices.[3]

This passage, whose pessimistic undertones, make the complaints of Descartes and Kant sound like a weak and distant echo, increases the paradox of the apparent nonexistence of a critique of error in the works of St. Thomas, for it seems to imply a complete absence of illusion and naïveté concerning our tendencies toward error and the difficulties of attaining truth. We marvel at this, we try to attribute the silence of St. Thomas to the silence of Aristotle and to the lack of contemporary controversy on the point.[4] But our surprise is merely a feeble indication of the frightful distortion that modern and contemporary philosophical thought has undergone. For three centuries we have become used to considering the philosopher either as a sort of high priest brandishing the aspergillum of doubt so that the thrice-holy water might cleanse human knowledge of all defilement from error, or as a severe and merciless judge charged with ferreting out our secret and guilty intimacies with the ghosts of truth. Indeed, error has become such an obsession with thinkers, or the abyss into which we are always ready to fall and must at all costs avoid, that we no longer have time to face and contemplate truth. Our sense of error has become hypertrophied to the same degree that our sense of truth has atrophied, just as, in the moral domain, the avoidance of sin has become more important than the doing of good.

Were a scientist asked to preface a theory of light by a long dissertation upon the nature of darkness, his answer would be a smile or a shrug of the shoulders, for it is light that gives intelligibility to darkness, just as the experience of sight enables us to understand blindness. And so it is with truth and error, two contraries and, therefore, objects of the same science.[5] If truth is the health of the intellect and error its disease, and if epistemology, by virtue of a searching analysis of the operations productive of truth, is primarily knowledge of the mind's health, then epistemology must be positively centered in truth and error must enter into it only by precaution, as a sort of preventive medicine teaching us what to avoid in order to preserve this interior equilibrium with the outer world, the equilibrium of knowledge whose proper name is truth. In this the teaching of St. Thomas is entirely contrary to that of Descartes and Kant; for them the human mind naturally seeks the illusions of the senses or of the *a prioris* of understanding and can rid itself of these illusions only by acquiring a subtle and difficult art, the fruit of free reflection. For St. Thomas, truth belongs rightfully and actually to human nature, it has priority over error, which enters into us only by imprudence, by a guilty impulsiveness for which personal liberty is partly responsible.[6] All truth is therefore not the fruit of a free apprenticeship of our knowing powers which corrects a nature of itself given to error; on the contrary, truth is the product of a nature essentially dedicated to truth, whose functioning can be corrupted by misunderstanding and free misuse of those laws whose negation engenders error. The nature of the intellect, and not the art of reasoning, gives man his first truths, by means of which he learns the art of abiding in truth.

Although no man can attain to perfect apprehension of truth, *yet no one is so completely deprived of it as not to know any at all.* The knowledge of truth is easy in this sense, that immediately evident principles, by means of which we come to truth, *are evident for all men.*[7]

Therefore, human nature, not human liberty, is at the source of this apprehension of a minimum of truth, a minimum by whose means all other truths are made accessible to us.

Of all material beings man alone escapes the determination of nature and exercises his operation freely, with the exception in each kind of activity, of the natural principle. Thus, although the conclusions of both speculative and practical sciences are the product of rational invention and not of nature, the first indemonstrable principles, whence proceed all our other knowledge, *are naturally known by us.*[8]

Hence, it is not to a dialectical investigation governed by the most absolute doubt that St. Thomas entrusts the discovery of the truth principle which serves as starting point for acquiring all other truths and as ultimate criterion for judging their value. Rather, he returns to the very sources of our acts of knowledge: the nature of man and the nature of his cognitive acts. The first step in an epistemological study of infallible truth is an inquiry into the existence of natural *judgments* whose evidence and truth are such as to enable us to discuss with God[9] of whose wisdom they are the participation.[10] The second step analyzes the causes of the evidence and infallibility of these natural judgments. Such will be the object of the two following sections.

Section I: Are There Any Natural or Necessary Judgments?

In studying the nature of a problem as such we saw that wonder, the starting point for all inquiry, is naturally rooted in the nature of our intellect, which fears ignorance as a natural evil, and that doubt, the ultimate result of fruitless inquiry, has identical origins— the fear of error, which is an evil worse than ignorance.[11] This observation leads us to conclude upon the existence of an instinct for truth by which the nature of every human intellect is defined.

Universal consent to first principles is not caused by the unicity of the possible intellect but by the likeness of our nature which makes us tend toward a same goal in the same way, as sheep unanimously consider the wolf as an enemy.[12]

We must therefore seek to find, in the ensemble of human *judgmental* activities, which judgments come from the *instinct of truth* because they are the vital reaction of the nature of man's intellect when confronted with his primary object. Now, we cannot do this without briefly recalling some notions from natural philosophy and some metaphysical notions about nature and the characteristics of its operation.

A. CHARACTERISTICS OF A NATURAL OPERATION

Modern scientists prefer to speak of *nature* rather than of *natures*, for whereas *nature* is pure matter or energy, *natures* are all *dead energy*, a sign of age or entropy. Natures are the death of nature. For a philosopher, on the contrary, natures are extremely important. The reign of the pure uniformity of matter, subject to instantaneous and universal local movement, gives way to the kingdom of diversified matter, informed by a superior creative idea of which God is the efficient, exemplar, and final cause[13] as well as the principle of its new activity.

The divine will, source of every natural movement, precedes natural operation; it is required for every natural activity. . . .[14]

Just as movement emanating from the soul to the body is the life of the latter, so the movement by which the whole universe is moved by God is as the life of this universe.[15]

Every natural operation enters into the whole called the order or good of the universe, a whole whose value is superior to each and every singular being.[16] For the co-ordination of this ensemble of particular forces, God is the source and the end. Consequently, it is not strange that we find His provident and infallible wisdom at the origin of every nature and its specific activity.

Every inclination of anything, whether natural or voluntary, is nothing but a *kind of impression from the first mover;* just as the inclination of the arrow towards a fixed point is nothing but an impulse received from the archer. Hence, every agent, whether natural or voluntary, attains to its divinely appointed end, as though of its own accord.[17]

Every nature is thus signed with the seal of Divine Wisdom, and its proper operation is only a sort of instinctive obedience to the immanent directives inscribed in it by its Creator; therefore, this operation has all the characteristics of instinct and natural appetite, namely, spontaneity, infallibility, necessity, as opposed to free operation, which is the fruit of *deliberation,* of *choice,* and is susceptible to error *by virtue of its very indetermination.*[18]

B. ARE SOME OF OUR JUDGMENTS NATURAL OPERATIONS? (by SYNDERESIS

It may readily be observed that there are natural operations in the order of knowing as such. The theory of objects as specifying principles of the acts of our noetic powers,[19] and the theory of the division of the object of sensation into *per se proprium, per se commune,* and *accidentale*[20] are but applications of this doctrine. "Each power of the soul is a form or nature, and has a natural inclination to something. Hence, each power desires, by natural appetite, *that object which is suitable to itself.*"[21] The object of a power is simply the term of a natural finality of that power, and things lose their character as object insofar as the activity of a power no longer comes within the limits of their finality.[22] As a power of apprehending being and quiddities, the intellect obeys this law of nature, and that is why acts of simple apprehension are infallible in grasping the proper and connatural object of the intellect.

Just as a thing has being by its proper form, so the knowing power has knowledge by the likeness of the thing known. Hence *as natural things do not fall short of the being that belongs to them by their form, but* may fall short of accidental or consequent qualities . . . *so the power of knowing* cannot fail in the knowledge of the thing with the likeness of which it is informed, but may fail with regard to something consequent upon that form, or accidental thereto. . . . Hence the intellect is not deceived about the essence of a thing, as neither the sense about its proper object.[23]

But does this law of nature, which holds good in the order of knowledge by simple apprehension, obtain also in the order of judgment? In other words, are there acts of composition, and of division or reassembling of concepts,[24] whose synthetic activity is stamped with the seal of Divine Wisdom and which obeys an instinct directly instilled into us by the Creator?

The intellect is always right as regards first principles, since it is not deceived about them *for the same reason* that it is not deceived about the essence of a thing. For self-known principles are such as are known as soon as the terms are understood, from the fact that the predicate is contained in the definition of the subject.[25]

In this passage, which affirms the fact of the existence of natural operations in judicative knowledge *for the same reason* that it exists in the activity of apprehension, the reason given applies only to the comprehension of terms. The subject of the composition contains the predicate, that is, lends it its intelligibility; therefore, the intellect is in practically the same situation here as it is in apprehension. Since it is a power of seeing simple intelligibles and has two such intelligibles presented to it, the intellect composes or divides with the same sureness of vision that it possesses in apprehension. This reason is evidently valid for explaining the fact, but it does not give the reason for the fact, its primary as well as secondary ontological cause. But there are other texts completing this one by showing the divine origins of this judicative knowledge and its natural character. Let us begin with some texts upon the divine origins of the judgments called first principles.

Knowledge of naturally known principles has been divinely instilled in us by God, the author of our nature. Thus these principles contain Divine Wisdom itself and what is contrary to them is equally contrary to Divine Wisdom.[26]

And in his commentary on Job, commenting on the text, St. Thomas says:

Who has put wisdom in the loins of man? By man's loins we are to understand the interior powers of the soul, i.e. the intellect and reason by which God has sown wisdom in man by giving him both the light of reason and the seeds of wisdom and science through natural knowledge of first principles.[27]

Thus, there is a twofold divine origin for the human knowledge of truth: the light of reason (or the agent intellect) that is a participation in divine intelligence,[28] and therefore a sort of instinct for truth since God is Truth, and the seeds of wisdom and science given by the natural grasp of first principles. What is the meaning of the expression, "the seeds of wisdom and science that exist in the soul by divine action?"

This refers to the particular *habitus* that are not the result of our own efforts but an infallible directive of our intellect in the order of speculative and practical truth, *habitus* that are called *intellectus* and *synderesis.*

Hence it is that human nature, insofar as it comes in contact with the angelic nature, must both in speculative and practical matters know truth *without investigation.* And this knowledge must be the principle of all the knowledge which follows, whether speculative or practical, since principles must be more stable and certain. Therefore this knowledge *must be in man naturally, since it is a kind of seed plot containing in germ all the knowledge which follows,* since there pre-exist in all natures, certain natural seeds of all the activities and effects which follow. Furthermore, this knowledge must be habitual so that it will be ready for use when needed.

Thus, just as there is a *natural habit* of the human soul through which it knows principles of the speculative sciences, which we call understanding of principles, so too there is in the soul a natural habit of first principles of action, which are the universal principles of the natural law. This habit pertains to synderesis.[29]

But *natural* habits come from God, for they are nothing but a spiritual law of our nature inscribed in us by its Author.

Natural habits exist in us because they have been divinely engraved upon us: and as conscience is the act of the natural habit called synderesis, it is attributed a divine origin in the same way as all our knowledge of truth which is said to come from *God Who engraved* in our nature the knowledge of first principles.[30]

Natural judgments therefore have all the stability of natural acts because they are doubly bound to the infallible activity of the Creator, by the intermediation of the agent intellect, immanent participation in the divine light itself,[31] and by the habit of *understanding* that is spontaneously generated from the meeting of primary notions and the illumination of the agent intellect.

In every man there is a certain principle of knowledge, namely the light of the agent intellect, through which certain universal principles of all the sciences are *naturally understood as soon as proposed to the intellect.*[32]

Here is a text summing up the factors that concur in the production of a spontaneous, indefectible, and immediately evident natural judgment:

It is in virtue of the agent intellect that first principles become manifest; they are not acquired by reasoning but from the sole fact that their terms are known. Starting from sensible objects the memory is formed, and starting from memory, experience, and from experience proceeds the knowledge of terms; once these are known, we become aware of common propositions which are the principles of the arts and sciences.[33]

Thus, we have judgments that are natural operations, because, like every natural operation, they are but an actualization of powers instilled in our souls by the Creator, namely, the illuminative power that makes the real luminous and the possible intellect not only illumined but fascinated by the light of being, a fascination that deprives it of all capacity to refuse as well as any liberty to acquiesce. Our intellect is truly determined by the luminosity of being, and it participates in the actuality of the agent intellect by means of the habit of understanding that arises in and from the very fascination which being exerts upon it.

But the possible intellect which, like prime matter is of itself undetermined, *needs a habitus* to make sure that it follows its right rule: it needs a *natural* habit to grasp determinations like first principles, determinations which are the effects of the agent intellect which is its rule; and it needs an *acquired* habit for everything which may be derived from these principles.[34]

Since they are the necessary consequences of two natural powers, one of which is essentially illuminative and the other, the possible intellect, essentially illumined (as much by the luminosity of the being it has received as by its dynamic conjunction with the pure light that is the agent intellect), first judgments possess the characteristics of natural operations; they are spontaneous, immediate, and necessary. These characteristics St. Thomas renders by the terms *subito, sine inquisitione, sine investigatione, necessaria, indemonstrabilia, absque discursu, sine studio.*[35] We shall now see what are the objective or specifying causes of those judgments of which our nature is the immediate cause and God the First Cause.

Section II: The Nature of Naturally Evident and Necessary First Judgments

In the preceding section we studied the fact of the existence of spontaneous and necessary judgments and the primary and secondary sources of their existence. We have seen that in the *order of exercise* these judgments have God and our nature as efficient causes. Now we must ascertain their specifying causality, i.e., their objects, the concepts composing them, and the essential bonds linking these concepts to each other and compelling the intellect to unite them in the synthetic act called judgment. To facilitate our explanation of this point, we shall first briefly enumerate the judgments that are given us as first, as well as the reason they are called principles; then we shall analyze their objective content in order to perceive their necessitating evidence value.

A. WHAT JUDGMENTS ARE CALLED FIRST PRINCIPLES?

It is somewhat pleonastic to speak of first principles, for the very meaning of the word *principle* implies primacy in relation to a multitude of secondary realities[36] whose hierarchy it sets, either because it is their point of departure or because it is their origin and cause in the order of existence, finality, and nature. "We call *principle* that which is *first* either in the order of being . . . or in the order of becoming . . . or in that of knowledge."[37] A first principle is, therefore, a *first among firsts* in a given order; applied to judicative knowledge, it means the initial judgment by which our cognitive life possessed its first perfective element and starting from which it continued on its way toward a more and more perfect knowledge. A judgment may thus deserve the name *primary* either because it is a sort of absolute beginning in the synthesizing activity of the intellect, or because from this absolute beginning other judgments flow as from an everpresent source, so that to suppress its existence would be tantamount to suppressing every other judicative activity. In a subsequent chapter we shall study judgment principles as the source of other judicative activities, such as philosophical science and wisdom. But here we shall limit ourselves to the analysis of those judgments as absolute beginnings, as primary intuitions from which the intellect cannot escape.

If there is a pleonasm in speaking of a *first* principle, the plurality of first principles in the order of judicative knowledge seems to imply a contradiction, for there cannot be several first in a given order. The expression *first principles* must therefore be understood to mean a group of judgments by which the intellect observes the existence of necessary bonds between several primary concepts, bonds that oblige it to identify them in affirmation or to separate them by negation. What are these primary natural judgments conceived by every man even before he knows what a judgment is, or what truth is?

Any proposition is said to be self-evident in itself, if its *predicate is contained in the notion of the subject.* . . . Hence it is that . . . certain axioms or propositions *are universally self-evident to all;* and such are the propositions whose terms are known to all, as, every whole is greater than its part, and, things equal to one and the same are equal to each other.[38]

Thus, there are as many primary, immediately evident judgments as there are syntheses made up of terms *universally known by all*, i.e., outside scientific or sapiential knowledge that is the prerogative of certain individuals. But the notions common to all, anterior to any scientific knowledge, are very universal notions, very virtual and vague, since our mind goes from the imperfect to the perfect.[39] These most primitive notions are those of being, the one and the many.

There are likewise in our intellect certain concepts naturally known to all, like the concept of being, the one, the good, and others similar to these, starting from which our intellect seeks the quiddity of each thing, in the same way as, starting from immediately evident principles, it seeks to know conclusions.[40]

The judgments resulting from the synthesis of absolutely first and universally apprehended notions are called, *dignitates, maximae propositiones, communes animi conceptiones*.[41] These primary judgments, which are so universal and vague that they include virtually all the determinations of being and knowledge, are such only because they are the effect of the meeting between the nature of the intellect and its formal object.

Since every nature is always ordained to one thing, to every power there naturally corresponds one object: to sight, color; to hearing, sound. Since the intellect is a power, it must have a determinate object which it naturally and necessarily possesses. Now this object must be the aspect under which everything is known by the intellect, just as color is the aspect under which everything is necessarily visible; this formal aspect is nothing else than being. Thus our intellect naturally knows being and its properties and in this knowledge is rooted the knowledge of first principles.[42]

One might therefore expect that the list of first principles would have to do with being and its properties, usually called transcendentals,[43] but this does not seem to correspond to facts, as the following list indicates:

(1) A thing either is or is not.[44]
(2) It is impossible that something both be and not be.[45]
(3) Everything is identical with itself.[46]
(4) We cannot both affirm and deny at the same time.[47]
(5) Every subject whatsoever must be either affirmed or denied.[48]

(6) Affirmation and negation are not simultaneously true.[49]
(7) It is impossible that contradictories be simultaneously true.[50]
(8) Whatever the subject, *either* affirmation *or* negation is true.[51]
(9) Everything that is moved is moved by another.[52]
(10) Every agent acts for an end.[53]

If we give careful consideration to this list of primary and immediately evident judgments, we will perceive that neither their content nor their formulation is identifiable. They are divisible into four groups. The first concerns being and nonbeing and notes that (1) they do not coincide and (2) absolutely cannot coincide (3) because every being is positively itself and resists all admixture. The second group is not directly interested in the opposition between being and nonbeing but rather in the opposition of mental acts whose affirmation and negation are opposed as (4) a fact and (5) a necessary fact. The third group of universal, immediately evident judgments is directly concerned neither with the opposition of being and nonbeing, nor with the opposition of acts of judgment, but with a property of the immanent terms of these judgments —their truth and falsity.[54] In this, as with the two preceding groups, the first fact observed is (6) the opposition of truth and falsity in contradictories; (7) the necessity of this fact is then affirmed, and (8) the hypothesis of an intermediary between the true and the false is eliminated by the principle of excluded middle, which reveals the truth of the negation if the affirmation is true, and vice versa. The last group does not have the same universality as do the first three; its evident principles cannot be affirmed of all being, but of that particular being which is the proper object of the human intellect and which is called being in process of becoming—being that can neither be nor be intelligible without the intervention of efficient and final causality.

Such is the list of *dignitates*, of those judgments whose necessity and evidence are universal, that is, common to every human being by virtue of the very nature of his intellect, whose dynamism and determinate object compel us to see *what is* in its opposition to *what is not*, under the epistemological sign of contradiction. We must now seek, not the proof of the evidence and truth of these first judgments, which would be absurd,[55] but the justification of their primacy and infallibility by the analysis of their terms.[56]

B. ANALYSIS OF THE JUDGMENTS CALLED FIRST PRINCIPLES

The truth and the knowledge of indemonstrable principles depend on the definition of the terms; for as soon as we know what is a whole and what is a part, we know *at once* that every whole is greater than its parts. Now to know the definition of being and non-being, of whole and part, and of other things consequent to being, which are the terms of which indemonstrable principles are constituted, is the function of wisdom, since universal being is the proper effect of the highest cause, which is God. And so wisdom makes use of indemonstrable principles, which are the object of understanding, not only by drawing conclusions from them, as other sciences do, but also by passing its judgments on them, and by vindicating them against those who deny them.[57]

Every man knows first principles by a sort of instinct of being and sees their truth by an instinct of perfection[58]; but it is up to the philosopher to disclose the cause of this evidence and truth, which compel the mind's adherence under the pressure of a natural determination. This manifestation is not a proof but a comparison between the two terms of a judgment, a comparison constraining the mind to observe their composition or their division. In analyzing these first judgments, we shall concentrate our efforts upon the most characteristic of the ten formulae enumerated above.

¶ *1. The Principle of Noncontradiction.* In analyzing first principles, we shall make use of the doctrine explained in studying judgment, the perfective act of our intellect that aims to reconstruct the unity of the real within our soul, a unity destroyed by the abstractive mode that is distinctively our own.[59] Now, the act of unifying necessarily presupposes plurality, because, being a substitute for identity, unification imitates identity in its own way by organizing multiplicity[60]; since every judgment is an affirmed or denied synthesis, it presupposes at least a duality of concepts. But to admit duality, either in things or in concepts, is to affirm the fact of opposition, for duality inevitably implies distinction, which opposes two realities or two concepts and forbids their identifications.[61] Metaphysics springs from observation of the opposition existing between being and beings—an opposition to which the doctrine of transcendentals is a first solution. The same is true of epistemology, which is born of the opposition between different concepts; the primary solution of this opposition is given us by natural or first judgments. Since the notion of opposition is so important for the explanation of the multiplicity of things and concepts, and of their reduction or non-reduction to unity, we shall briefly recall its nature and modes, leaving deeper study of this subject to metaphysics and logic.[62]

There are two major modes of opposition, one of which is characterized by *lack* or *absence*, the other by *dependence*. In the first mode there are three types:

(1) The lack or absence is absolute: everything constituting the wealth of one of the terms is denied to the other. Thus, between being and nothingness opposition is total, for nothingness is the negation of being. This opposition is called *contradiction*.

(2) The lack or absence does not circumscribe the whole reality but only one of its aspects, and an aspect it should have. Thus, between *seeing* and *being blind* opposition is not total, for being remains even though sight is absent; there is lack, deficiency, but not nothingness. This is a *privative* opposition, which does not deny the subject, but one of its aspects.

(3) Finally, the lack can have even less ontological depth and concern only a complementary or perfective aspect of the real. The fact of being *small* is opposed to being *large*, not as an absence of quantity, but as an existing quantity whose dimensions lack as much extension. In this last opposition, called *contrariety*, neither the subject nor the aspect immediately founding the opposition is denied, but two quantified modes are compared, one of which has more extension than the other.

The second mode of opposition, called relative opposition, is the weakest of oppositions because it rests upon the weakest aspect of being, relation,[63] by which a certain order is set up betwen two beings that oppose each other as agent-recipient, cause-and-effect, measure-measured.[64] Unlike the three preceding types of opposition, this last type does not result from lack or absence of being or perfection but, on the contrary, from a gift, a more or less intimate presence of one being to another. Thus, a father is opposed to his son, not by virtue of any deficiency in either one of these beings, but because he is at the origin of a generative movement and the son is the term. It is the same for the Creator-creature opposition, for the dependence of the created being constitutes its whole wealth, a wealth that is actually received, it is true, but whose very reception makes the creature to be and not to be nothing.[65]

Now, in judgment there is at least the duality of concepts compared to each other; therefore, there is a distinction between concepts and, consequently, opposition between them. Since natural judgments are made up of natural or first concepts, they are characterized by the different oppositions encountered in these concepts. But there is a natural order in the genesis of first concepts, a genetic order corresponding to being and the transcendental properties confusedly and indistinctly known by every normal human intellect, which can transform this confused and vague knowledge into actual, precise vision, by acquiring the *habitus* of philosophical wisdom.[66] Here is a description of the natural genesis of our first concepts:

It is *being* which is first understood, then, flowing from it, *non-being* and next *division* which springs from their opposition; fourthly the *one* denotes the absence of division and finally the *many* implies division excluded from unity.[67]

By comparing the genesis of first concepts with the transcendental properties of being, we immediately perceive that they follow identical orders; for first-known being is a *quod est*, a certain *res* possessing the act of existing. The negation of being or of the *quod est* in its opposition to being engenders the notion of division, whose negation gives us the notion of unity and whose affirmation gives us the notion of multitude or of *aliquid;* then comes being and its relations to the soul, engendering truth and goodness.[68] Now, all these transcendental properties indicate the same reality: being taken in its universality, or in one or the other of its particular modes.[69]

Since the first principles flow from terms that are most naturally and most universally known by all men and are the fruit of a sort of instinct of being and truth and not a deliberate act of reason,[70] they will normally follow the natural order of concepts and the opposition between concepts. And as the natural order of concepts goes from being to nonbeing, then to unity and multiplicity, the first principle will be the one whose structure is essentially constituted by the notion of being, of nonbeing, and of their opposition; and this is the principle of noncontradiction. We shall analyze the three aspects it presents to philosophical reflection: *a*) its ontological aspect, which is nothing but the opposition between being and nonbeing; *b*) its psychological aspect, or the opposition between two mental acts, affirmation and negation; *c*) finally, the epistemological aspect, or the opposition between the truth and falsity of the proposition that is the fruit and term of affirmation and negation.[71]

(a) *Ontological aspects of the principle of noncontradiction.* There are three familiar formulations of the ontological aspects of the principle of noncontradiction: being is not nonbeing; it is necessary that being not be nonbeing; it is impossible that being be nonbeing. Let us examine each of these statements in order to perceive their intelligible content distinctly.

Being is not nonbeing. This judgment contains the terms usual to every judgment: a subject, a predicate, and a (negative) verb. The being-subject, first object and first concept of the human intellect, whose genesis we sketched in a preceding chapter[72] is both the most universal and the most imperfect or indistinct of all our concepts, since it designates every thing that is in act of becoming, every body in motion.[73] Its assigned content is very vague: every subject in act. The predicate, *nonbeing*, is purely a construction of our mind that gives it existence and intelligibility.[74] This predicate is made up of a positive element, whose meaning is identical with the subject's, and the particle *non*, which nullifies this positive content and makes it wholly indeterminate; for nonbeing should not be formulated as *quod non est*, a subject deprived of existence, but as the *negation of both subject and the act of existing.* If we now try to identify this subject and this predicate in a judicative synthesis, the mind can only perceive the absolute opposition between what is and what is not, and affirm this opposition by denying their identity—being is not nonbeing.

It is necessary that being not be nonbeing. Not only can we not not-perceive the opposition between being and nothingness, but reflection upon the preceding judgment compels us to perceive the *necessity* of this opposition between being and nothingness; this is reflective awareness of a primary intuition, a judgment of judgment whose direct object is the identity or negation of identity established by the mind between two concepts by a preceding judgment. What we have here is a modal judgment, or value judgment, concerned with this whole which is the enunciation, taken as immanent term of a categorical judgment. The object of the intellect and reflection, here,[75] is the composition made by judicative activity.

It is impossible that being be nonbeing. This third formulation of the principle of noncontradiction reveals the absurdity of identifying being and nonbeing. It is awareness in terms of intelligibility, of opposition between being and nothingness; the mind sees that it must affirm its radical inability to think the absurd. This ontological aspect of the principle of noncontradiction is extremely important, for it discloses the simultaneous reversibility of being and knowledge of which Parmenides was the first to become aware: "What is not cannot be known . . . that is impossible . . . or be expressed; for it is one and the same thing to be intelligible and to be."[76] The identity of being and nothingness is absurd or unthinkable because being is the law of intelligibility. "The future, which is distinct in time, does not actually exist, and therefore is not knowable in itself; *for so far as a thing falls short of being, so far does it fall short of cognoscibility.*"[77]

Therefore, the passing of the intellect from one to the other of these statements of the principle of noncontradiction represents real progress. The first intuition is concerned with the contradictory opposition of being and nonbeing, the second with the necessity of this opposition; the third results from the awareness that the law of being is the law of knowledge and that the distinction of the one necessarily entails distinction of the other.[78] The defense of the principle of noncontradiction, given in metaphysics,[79] centers upon the twofold identification of being with the intelligible, and of nonbeing with the nonintelligible. He who denies this double identification lives in absurdity, i.e., gives up living the life of the intellect, both speculatively and practically.[80] The principle of noncontradiction might therefore be translated by a formula wherein the intellect defends being against nonbeing, because it defends the first source of its own life and progress—it is absurd to identify being and nonbeing.[81]

(b) *Psychological aspect of the principle of noncontradiction.* In analyzing the mental activity by which the principle of noncontradiction is conceived under its ontological aspect, we discover that the same law of contradictory opposition obtains between its two essential acts (affirmation and negation) that has already been seen to hold good in the relations between being and nonbeing. This is not surprising since being measures intellect and the measured is entirely subject to the measure. In the first stammerings of the intellect, to affirm is to say that it is impossible that being be nonbeing; and to deny is to state that being is not nonbeing (the human intellect does not discover and formulate these principles under this universal aspect but under views more implicit and particular, e.g., it is impossible that a same thing both be and not be under the same aspect, at the same time, etc.).[82] When the principle of noncontradiction is formulated in terms of the opposition between the two judicial acts essential to our mind, it must not be forgotten that these two acts have their own respective objects, that, in Thomism, they are cases of *knowing* and not merely of *thinking*, and that their specification has its origin in the content of the concepts that are the matter of composition and division.[83] In other words, the foundation for affirmation or negation by the mind is external being.[84] Here are some psychological statements of the principle of noncontradiction:

Affirmation and negation are never experienced simultaneously. Simultaneity of affirmation and negation is impossible.

Whatever the subject, we must opt either for affirmation *or* negation.

Our explanation will be centered in the second formula, which implies and explains the other two by its own absolute evidence.

Simultaneity of affirmation and negation is impossible. We never inwardly experience affirmation and negation simultaneously, although we can express such simultaneity in language.[85] But reflection upon this lack of experience immediately shows us its *subjective* and *objective* impossibility. The subjective impossibility springs from the fact that affirmation and negation are two opposed acts of the same intellect, which is their source and their subject. These acts are two spiritual accidents of an intellectual substance, two accidents of which one is the negation of the other, just as, for the eye, black is the negation of white; so it is impossible that they coexist simultaneously in the same subject.[86] Now, *est* is the soul of every affirmation, just as *non-est* is the soul of every negation,[87] and these two verbs are two diametrically opposed acts of our intellect. But in order that two distinct acts be able to coexist in the same subject, they must be unified, arranged in hierarchy, one must be the cause of the other; thus, the intellect is the act of the soul that is itself the act of the body, but the soul is the source of our intellective power. In the same way, a habit and the act of a habit are simultaneous acts of a power, but the power is their cause. However, affirmation is not the source of negation but is its contrary, in the sense that one expels the other, puts it out.[88] Translating affirmation and negation into the verbs they express immediately reveals their opposition. For the mind to be able to seize these two opposites simultaneously, it would have to unify *est* and *non-est*, therefore, be able to judge that *est* is *non-est*; but in this judgment the predicate is opposed to the subject just as *non-ens* is opposed to *ens* in the ontological aspect of the principle of noncontradiction.[89] Thus, simultaneity of affirmation and negation amounts to negation of the principle of noncontradiction, which we have shown to be unthinkable.

The *objective* impossibility of simultaneous affirmation and negation has a source other than the one we have just discussed, and it arises from the necessary exclusion of two contrary acts in a same subject and under the same aspect; it rests upon the respective objects of affirmation and negation, on their specification by the outer real.[90]

Let us examine the affirmation and negation of being in the two following formulae: *being is being; being is not being*. The terms of the two propositions are identical; being has the function of subject and predicate in both enunciations. Now, for the mind to be able to think affirmation and negation simultaneously it would have to be able to identify being and nonbeing. For to say that being is not being is the same as affirming that being is nonbeing, which is counter to the ontological principle of noncontradiction. Therefore, the objective impossibility of simultaneous affirmation and negation rests ultimately upon the impossibility of identifying being and nonbeing—the two hypotheses are absurd or unthinkable for the mind.

As to the third proposition, frequently called the principle of excluded middle or excluded third,[91] it is merely the logical consequence of the absurdity implied in a simultaneous *yes* and *no* about the same thing considered from the same aspect.[92] This consequence will be briefly explained in our study of the opposition between truth and falsity in contradictories, which is the topic of the following paragraph.

(c) *Epistemological aspects of the principle of noncontradiction.* In our analysis of truth we have said that truth exists formally neither in the exterior term of judicative activity, nor in the act of judgment itself, but in its immanent term, enunciation.[93] Having considered contradictory opposition in the object of knowledge or being, and then in the act of judgment, we must now consider the role of this opposition in the characteristics of enunciation as measured by being, i.e., in its truth or falsity. Two questions arise about this subject, and they may be stated as follows: Can two contradictory statements be simultaneously true or false? Or, on the contrary, must one be necessarily true if the other is false, and vice versa? The answer to these two questions constitutes the epistemological study of the princple of contradiction.

It is impossible that contradictory statements be simultaneously true. This affirmation remains obscure as long as it is not illumined by the previously explained doctrine concerning the complexity of human truth (which is a relation of measured to measure between the intellect and reality) as well as by the nature of contradictory opposition.[94] Upon the absolute comprehension of these two doctrinal points rests the evidence of the absolute incompossibility of the truth of contradictories. As we have seen, truth taken formally belongs neither to reality taken absolutely nor to the intellect considered in itself, but is the result of a bond established by judicative operation between the fragmentary aspects known about reality and the ontological unity of this same reality. There is no truth without enunciation and no enunciation without the complex act of the mind's referring to an equally complex reality by which it is admittedly measured. Therefore, when we examine a truth, our object is always made up of a mental activity and the thing which is its term and measure. But contradictory opposition between two propositions is always made up of two mental acts, *yes* and *no*, respectively concerned with the identity and nonidentity of being and nothingness. Consequently, if the identification of being and nothingness plunges the intellect into absurdity, and if simultaneity of yes and no begets the same absurdity,[95] then simultaneously true contradictories involve the same absurdity, since the truth of a proposition depends upon the mental act and the object by which it is measured.

If one contradictory is true, the other is necessarily false. We have seen that there can be no intermediary between being and nothingness because one is the absolute negation of the other; nor can there be any intermediary between yes and no, because *yes* deals with the identity of being with itself, whereas *no* denies the identification of being with nothingness. But being essentially constituted by the absolute character of yes and no, and of the being that is its object, the truth of a contradictory cannot admit an intermediary, any more than its constitutive elements can. Therefore, the principle of the excluded middle, inevitable consequence of the opposition between being and nothingness, between yes and no, also excludes with like inevitability the possibility of an intermediary between the truth and falsity of contradictories. Whence the principle so often repeated by philosophers: Whatever the subject, either its affirmation *or* its negation is true. Hence, if one of them is true, the other is inevitably false.[96]

Among our contemporaries this epistemological aspect of the principle of contradiction is most frequently called the principle of *raison d'être*, or sufficient reason,[97] an expression found in neither Aristotle nor St. Thomas, although both of them were in possession of the primary evidence hidden behind these expressions. They expressed this first evidence in terms of convertibility between being and the intelligible: *eadem est dispositio rei in esse et in veritate*.[98] If, indeed, being and the intelligible are proportional, nonbeing and the unintelligible are also. But the principle of *raison d'être*, or sufficient reason, is nothing but the thing's capacity to account for itself to human reason,[99] to reveal its luminosity, to be intelligible and understood. But truth is nothing but judicative knowledge as vindicated, guaranteed by the intelligibility or the unity of the being with which this activity is concerned.[100] Now, two contradictories are characterized by the fact that one is concerned with being and the other with its negation; therefore, one deals with the intelligible and the other with the unintelligible. However, the unintelligible has no *raison d'être*, guarantees nothing, therefore is the foundation for no truth, however small. Consequently, if one of these contradictories is true, the other must necessarily be false.

This analysis, at once too succinct and too long, has shown us the role of the primary object of the intellect in its natural acts, of which truth is the inevitable term. Being is always present under very different modalities according to the case, but it cannot not be present, for otherwise judicative activity would wholly disappear from the human soul. This activity, which composes and divides concepts, is itself subject to the law of noncontradiction, and its term, enunciation, is also determined, in its truth or falsity, by the presence or absence of being, the first and constant concern of every human intellect. Thus, the principle of noncontradiction embraces a trinity of correlative fields: that of being, of affirmation of being, and of the truth of this affirmation. Now we shall see that it underlies all other *dignitates* or first principles, which depend upon it to give the intellect immediate evidence, the object of which is more limited than its own, despite its transcendental character.

¶ 2. *The Principle of Identity.* Since the advent of Kantianism and the tyrannical rule of mathematical knowledge over contemporary science, the principle of identity has been much discussed. It has either been given primacy over the principle of noncontradiction,[101] or been reduced to nothing by emphasizing its tautological character,[102] or been denied all real value and granted only a formal value directing the mechanism of the mind completely cut off from the real. This overvaluation and devaluation of the principle of identity are both rooted in common ground, the arid and sterile ground of philosophical idealism. For, by denying that concrete and existential being is the starting point for philosophical reflection, the mind has locked itself within logical frames that have held and will hold it prisoner until the day when a right and, therefore, humble view of human nature will make it understood that we are "below the angels but above the beast," that we do not create our concepts or possess them at birth, but that neither are we condemned to an animal empiricism in the order of knowledge. In the context of realist philosophy, the principle of identity has kept its value as evidence and as concrete truth, but under the domination of the principle of noncontradiction, of which it is a sort of contraction or specialization. First, let us look at its ontological sense and then at its epistemological meaning, or the truth it conveys.

(a) *Ontological aspect of the principle of identity.* Here are the different ways of stating the principle of identity: everything is identical with itself[103]; being is being; every being is necessarily what it is[104]; being and one are convertible.[105] To see how these different formulae are equivalent, we must necessarily recall to mind the notion of identity whose strict meaning is nothing but the unity of a being with itself.[106]

Identity is unity or union: either the things which are said to be identical are many as to their existence, and their identity comes from the common possession of one element; or there really is unity as to their existence, but the intellect uses this unity as a plurality in order to conceive a certain relation; this is the case when we say that a thing is identical with itself . . . but this relation of identity is not real but is only a relation of reason, and it is according to this relation that a thing is said to be identical with itself, absolutely.[107]

Since the principle of identity is nothing but the affirmation by the intellect of the unity of being with itself, to speak of unity is to speak of the intrinsic nondivision of the real and its division from all else that is not itself.

One does not add any reality to being but only the negation of division; for *one means undivided being*. This is the very reason why *one* is convertible with being. For every being is either simple or composite. But what is simple is undivided both actually and potentially; whereas what is composite has not being while its parts are divided but only after they make up and compose it. Hence it is manifest that the being of anything consists in indivision; and hence it is that *everything guards* its unity as it guards its being.[108]

We are now in a position to understand the different formulae used to express the evidence of the principle of identity.

Everything is identical with itself. We know that being as such has five properties or general modes[109] which the mind discovers by deeper study of its nature. The first of these properties is being as *res*, i.e., as endowed with a quiddity that determines it and gives it a stability that the act of existing by itself does not possess[110]; these are, in a way, the special and stable riches[111] that everything possesses as its own because it is constituted by a nature or specific quiddity which makes it to be itself, that is, intrinsically undivided and externally divided or opposed to all that is not itself. But from the fact that being as *res* has a special type which characterizes it internally and divides it from everything that is not itself, it is *unum et aliquid*, one and something,[112] which is precisely the notion of identity.

Now let us consider the formula of the principle of identity. It is made up of the subject of a verb and a predicate. The subject is every being as quiddity or *res;* the predicate is every being as undivided in itself (*unum*) and divided from all others (*aliquid*). But it is the same reality that is *ens, res, unum,* and *aliquid,* a reality which the human intellect considers as a plurality by virtue of the weakness of its hold on the real and the fragmentary and the abstractive character of its cognitional procedure. Thus, there are many concepts but an absolute oneness of the thing designated by these concepts. In this judgment of identity the intellect does nothing but measure the multitude of its concepts of being by the concrete unity of the latter, and that is the whole ontological significance of the principle of identity. There is no tautology here but an explanation, for our intellect, of the interior and typical riches of every being, riches that make it a mirror reflecting something of the infinite opulence of the creator, while at the same time they enable it to hold a precise place among the indefinite multitude of the other beings surrounding it.

Being is being. This statement of the principle of identity, whose transposition into mathematical language seems like pure tautology, means nothing of the kind in metaphysical language, for the meaning of the being-subject is entirely different from that of the being-predicate. Indeed, the being-subject is a name expressing the substance of the being itself, therefore, of that which is composed of essence and existence; whereas the being-predicate is actually a qualifier, a determination grasped by the mind as a property of being, a determination making it to be *itself*, internally determined, undivided, and opposed to everything that is not its own substance, i.e., this essence and existential act characterizing it. This, in turn, comes back to the first formula that every being is *res, unum, aliquid,* or every being is identical with itself.

(b) *Epistemological aspect of the principle of identity.* In the preceding paragraph the human intellect perceived being and its ontological capital; here it is the truth of the enunciation, term of mental activity, that we shall analyze. Reflecting on this concept, which is the fruit of a judicative act, man cannot help observing that the bond uniting subject to predicate, i.e., being and its absolute unity, is a necessary bond whose rupture would inevitably entail loss of intelligibility to the real. Here we enter the field of the *per se* proposition, characterized by the causal link binding predicate to subject, whether this predicate be essential or accidental.[113] This doctrine of predicates *per se* as opposed to predicates *per accidens* is the basis for a division of propositions which we have already met in studying judgment.[114] Actually, this kind of proposition, called modal, is a judgment of judgment whose immediate object is not the thing but the truth of our knowledge of the thing; it is a sort of value judgment on the truth of our knowledge, a judgment expressed by the phrases, *it is impossible, it is necessary, it is possible, it is contingent.*

Reflecting upon this proposition—every being is being, or every being is identical with itself, or every being is one, i.e., interiorly undivided at the same time that it is divided from everything else—the intellect cannot fail to see that the link uniting the predicate to the subject is a necessary link, immobile, and, in a certain way, eternal, transcending time and the intellects that think it. This unification made by the mind between two concepts inseparable from each other and measured by one single and same thing considered as double by a trick of our intellect—this unification conveys an infallible truth to which we cannot not adhere. It is then that the mind utters its value judgment: it is impossible that being not be identical with itself; or, again, it is necessary that being be undivided in itself and divided from everything else; or this other affirmation—it is necessary that being and one be convertible.

In this modal judgment on the principle of identity, we perceive the same laws of our intellect's imperfection in regard to the real on which it must feed. We cannot think the truth of being without opposing it to nothingness, which is its negation; in the same way, we cannot think the truth of the identity of being with itself without conceiving it as a negation of interior division without which it neither exists nor is intelligible. This identity of being with itself and its affirmation by the mind beget a truth whose analogy is as flexible as that of the principle of contradiction, for the modes of identity of things flow from their being, whose diversity is indefinite.

By comparing the truth of the principle of contradiction with that of the principle of identity, we quickly discover that they are complementary; for—in that it is repugnant to being to be identified with nonbeing, which expresses the truth of the principle of contradiction—being must be identical with itself, which constitutes the truth of the principle of identity. It could be said that, for an intuitive intelligence, the truth of the principle of identity would precede that of the principle of contradiction, because intuitive vision of being would reveal its existential actuality determined by a positive quiddity whose interior, indivisible, and undivided riches would, in a way, exaggerate it and oppose it to everything else. But our abstractive mind, whose feeble light fragments the real and can unify it only by the intermediation of many comparisons, first grasps being as actuality in its opposition to what it is not, in order to be able, thereafter, to exploit its interior riches and to perceive it in the unity of its quiddity, whose determination limits and distinguishes it from all the other quiddities surrounding it and which it is not.[115] That is why the truth of the principle of identity can be defended by the truth of the principle of contradiction, but the inverse is not possible; he who in words would deny the principle of identity can be reduced to the absurd. Indeed, if being is not being, it is nonbeing, and if being is nonbeing, the principle of contradiction is false; but if the principle of contradiction is false, the human intellect is consigned to total absurdity, to the absolute inability to conceive anything whatsoever: every thought is unthinkable.[116]

¶ 3. *The Principle of Causality.* With this principle we have reached the last group of axioms we listed above,[117] axioms that do not have the same universality as those we have just studied, or the same function in human knowledge. For the principles of causality and of finality that make up this last group of axioms are directly concerned with being in process of becoming, which is the first and characteristic object of the human intellect, being from which, by means of these two principles, we can go right back to the existence and intelligibility of realities surpassing the usual and immediate horizons of our reason. The most general and also the most comprehensive statement of this principle is: *Everything contingent is caused.* Actually, this general statement applies to three domains: 1) that of physical motion, in which the principle is stated thus: Everything moved is moved by another; 2) that of efficiency, and the principle here is stated in this way: Every efficient action, which is a passage from potency to act, is caused; 3) that of existence, where we have the third statement: Everything that is not its own act of existing is caused.

Perception of the essential contingency of the movement, efficiency, and existence in which the proper object of our intellect is immersed—such is the springboard we use to surpass this proper object and to ascend to the invisible and transcendent causes of motion, efficiency, and existence. Such is the immense domain of the principle of causality. In analyzing it, we shall concentrate upon the notion of contingency and cause that are the key by which we may penetrate the twilight wherein dwells being in process of becoming and the pure luminosity where being abides.

(a) *Ontological aspect of the principle of causality.* Examination of the subject and predicate of the principle of causality reveals that the thing as contingent has the role of subject and the thing as cause the role of predicate. Now, even superficial reflection upon the notion of contingency compels the mind to recognize that this notion is unintelligible without the notion of cause and, consequently, that the existence of the contingent demands the existence of a cause. A word of explanation about these two notions will show us their correlation.

Being as contingent. Contingent comes from *cum-tangere*, that which touches upon,[118] whence the nautical term for landing: to touch on shore. The contingent is *what happens*, what has not always been and, consequently, what can not-be. The philosophical meaning is grafted upon this primary meaning and is expressed by the following formulae: that which can be other than it is; that which can not-exist.[119] The notion of mutability adequately expresses that of contingence, whether it be contingence of movement, substances, or existence, and is irreducibly opposed to necessity, whose etymological origins express immobility in place[120]—a local meaning to which has been added the philosophical sense of immobility or impossibility of being otherwise, unchangeable, immutable.[121]

Hence, the subject of the principle of causality is being as mutable and changing, either because it is movement or change, or because its activity can not-be, or because its existence is immersed in becoming and doomed to vanish. The contingent is not only opposed to the necessary, for there is necessity in the contingent; it is opposed to *act* inasmuch as act is autonomous, not derived, not received from another, which is to say, divine. That is why the properties of essences are filed under the heading of necessity, immutability, and a certain eternity—if that means anything—but contingency effects the existing of all these essences and their properties because what they are and what they have, they are and have because they receive it actually and without the possibility of discontinuity. This is the reason that contingency is found first and foremost in the act of existing, because its deficient and defective character distinguishes us from Him Who is His own *Existere*, from Him whose metaphysical proletariat we are, always awaiting and receiving from Him our existential salary. Until we have perceived this first root of contingency, the principle of causality remains unintelligible.

Being as caused. The etymology of the word *causa* cannot be historically determined,[122] but its philosophical meanings can be reduced to four, two of which express the thing in its intrinsic constitutive elements, matter and form, while the other two express the origin and orientation of being and its different activities, the efficient and final causes.[123] The notion basic to the idea of cause is always *dependence;* there is no cause unless there is a plurality of beings or a plurality of principles of beings between which there is a bond of dependence. The interdependence of the constitutive principles of a being constitutes the intrinsic causes when it is a question of the quiddity of a composite being, and essence and existence when it is a question of created being. The principle of causality does not apply to this type of dependence, unless the principle of sufficient reason be included within the principle of causality.[124] It is primarily in the field of efficiency and finality, therefore, in what is commonly called extrinsic causes, that the principle of causality exerts its influence and is used by the intellect to explain phenomena, proper accidents, and the contingency of things in the order of existing.

Consequently when we speak of *being as caused,* we mean the real as dependent upon something which is not itself, i.e., which does not belong to its own interior wealth, which it does not possess, but by which, we might say, it is possessed[125] and from which it continually receives, insofar as it is caused. Since causality can be exerted in the realm of physical becoming, in the realm of metaphysical becoming or of the passage from potency to act in the order of efficiency, and, finally, in the realm of existing or of the creation and

preservation of being—the principle of causality applies to all movement and mutation properly so called, to everything that is created
being and operation or efficiency.

Trying now to rethink the principle of causality with the help
of the notions of contingency and cause as we have explained them,
we see its concrete meaning thus: Every contingent thing—every
being in process of physical or metaphysical becoming and every
being that *is* not its own *existere* but *has* its *existere*—depends upon
another for its becoming and existing. Now, to depend upon
another is, in a way, to be possessed by this other, to be its property,
to share in what belongs properly to that other without having any
claim to independence within this participation. To depend on another, in a context of contingency, is to have a borrowed being and
a borrowed efficiency. But that is just the case with caused being,
movement, and efficiency. To say that everything contingent is
caused is to affirm immediate and *per se* evidence, for caused being
is intrinsically contained in contingent being; without each other
they are unintelligible. Whether contingent being is the thing in its
physical or metaphysical becoming, whether it is being according
to its created mode—this does not in any way affect the evidence
and perseity of the principle of causality, because contingency is
always fundamentally the same: every being that receives from or
participates in another neither is nor is intelligible, except in relation
to that other, i.e., to its cause.

(b) *Epistemological aspect of the principle of causality*. Like
every truth, the truth of the proposition affirming the principle of
causality depends upon the measurement of that proposition—the
concept produced by our second mental operation—by the real in
which it terminates.[126] Reflection upon the truth of the principle of
causality enables us to make a value judgment or modal judgment
qualifying the nature of the bond unifying the predicate to the
subject. As we have just seen, this bond is essential, since the notion of
contingency is defined by the fact of its causal dependence; therefore,
to try to conceive contingency outside its relation to its explanatory
cause is as ridiculous as to try to square a circle. When the mind
reflects upon the principle of causality, it cannot not see the neces-

sity of its truth, which may be stated as follows: it is necessary that everything contingent be caused; or, rather, it is impossible that everything contingent not be caused, for the contingent needs a cause just as potency needs act.

A second proof of the necessity of this truth can be made by confronting it with the truth of the principle of noncontradiction. Indeed, if the truth of the principle of causality is not necessary, then we can say: Everything contingent is not necessarily caused; but if everything contingent is not necessarily caused, what is essentially potency is not necessarily potency; but if what is potency is not necessarily potency, nonact is act, for potency is synonymous with nonact; but if nonact is act, then nonbeing is being, which is to deny the truth of the principle of noncontradiction. Thus, we must admit that to deny the necessity of the truth of the principle of causality is equivalent to denying the truth of the principle of noncontradiction, which is impossible because it is absurd and unthinkable.

¶ 4. *The Principle of Finality: Every Agent Acts for an End.* The study of this principle brings us to one of the most important aspects of philosophical thought, because it marks, in a sense, the crowning point of the order on which metaphysics feeds and the blossoming of the knowledge of order by which epistemology is defined. In positing the epistemological problem as formulated by Thomas Aquinas, we saw the importance of order and of the idea of finality.[127] It is by means of the principle of finality that the great metaphysical and epistemological theses are discovered and their solutions investigated and made evident to our reason. In a few pages we shall try to show the immediate evidence and necessity of this principle.

(a) *Ontological aspect of the principle of finality.* Translating the terms in the principle of finality into the ontological vocabulary gives us the following statement: Being as agent is finalized. We shall analyze the subject and predicate of this proposition in order to discover its precise meaning.

Being as agent. The being in question here is not being as contingency, potency, or recipient, but its correlative, being as dynamism or second act. Actually, agent being is everything *insofar as it gives*

of its superabundance, insofar as it overflows with interior riches
which it communicates to others.[128] The word *agent* must be taken
in its widest and deepest meaning, which includes not only the
efficient cause whose effect is exterior to itself, but also every immanent causality expressing and revealing its ontological superabundance by an effusion of interior fruits that are both its wealth
and the sign of its perfection. Thus understood, the word *agent*
designates not only physical causes but also and especially living
things in this psychological activity which is peculiar to them and
of which the fruits of knowledge and love are the most typical and
richest effects.[129]

Our experience of the agent being, like our experience of being as
such, shows us action (*agere*) as a quest, a desire for perfection,
a passing from potency to act, and that is, indeed, the physical and
human mode of action that we recognize as a means of acquiring a
desired and unpossessed good. However, closer analysis quickly
shows us that the agent as such excludes this imperfection, this
potentiality revealed by desire for what we are not, yet which
appears to us as our perfection.

I answer that it is in the nature of every act to communicate itself as far
as possible. Wherefor every agent acts forasmuch as it is in act: while
to act is nothing else than to communicate as far as possible that whereby
the agent is in act.[130]

In the ordinary meaning of the word, then, to be an agent is to be in
second act; but to be in second act excludes potentiality or imperfection, at least from the aspect in which the being is in second act,
i.e., insofar as it is formally an agent. Every agent, as such, is thus
perfect, and its perfection is proportional to the intensity of its act.
This is true to such a degree that the absolute agent is at the same
time absolute perfection.[131] The real definition of agent being is
therefore *being insofar as it is perfect or in second act.*

Being as finalized. The predicate of the principle of finality is the
expression, *acts for an end.* What does this mean in a metaphysical
context? Here is the Thomistic meaning:

One acts for an end in two ways: either for the end of the work or for
the end of the worker. The end of the work is that to which the agent

directs his work, and is called the why of the work. The end of the work-man is that which directs the latter's intention; which is why, whereas the end of the work can be in another, the end of the worker is always in himself. . . . But action for the end of the worker is of two modes: either by *desire* for the end, or by *love* of the end. For the object of desire is a thing not yet possessed, but the object of love is a posses-sion . . . which is the reason why every creature acts through desire of the end because every creature receives from another its good, which it does not possess by itself; whereas it belongs to God to act through love of the end, because nothing can be added to His perfection.[132]

To act for an end, the predicate of the principle of finality can thus have two meanings, one of which implies imperfection because it is synonymous with absence or lack, whereas the other is identical with absolute perfection because it means nothing but the act of giving with absolute gratuitousness and disinterestedness. However, in both cases there is a gift, the first being the effect of a received act, and the second the pure outgoing of an actuality so great that it overflows into effects that are like the explosive blossoming of an irrepressible interior fruitfulness. Therefore, we can express *action for an end* by the verb *to give oneself,* to communicate.

Reconsidering the principle of finality in light of the data we have discovered by analyzing the terms composing it, we arrive at the following formulae: every being that is perfect or in second act is self-giving; every perfect being is love, therefore, self-communicat-ing, which comes back to the formula of Dionysius; the good is self-diffusive,[133] diffusing itself either by instilling an appetite for itself in imperfect beings[134] or by producing actually participated perfec-tions, as does substance with respect to accidents, universal causes with respect to particular beings, and the Creator with regard to every creature. Such is the ontological meaning of the principle of finality.

(b) *Epistemological aspect of the principle of finality.* Like the other principles we have studied, the principle of finality is formulated epistemologically as a value judgment or a modal judg-ment bearing directly upon the truth of the proposition of finality, and indirectly upon being and its perfection. Here are some of the various ways of stating this principle, all of which have the same identical meaning despite their variety of expression, because they all reveal the immediately evident character of the truth of this principle: it is necessary that every agent act in virtue of an end; it is necessary that actuality communicate actuality; it is impossible that being as perfect communicate anything but perfection; it is impossible that perfect being act in view of a nongood or not be finalized.

Whatever formulation is adopted, the necessity of its truth is easily perceived and controlled as soon as it is reduced to the principle of noncontradiction. Indeed, to say that it is not necessary that an agent act in view of an end amounts to affirming that it is possible that being be nonbeing. As we have seen, the word *agent* means the thing as actual or perfect, and the term *end* also means the real as perfection.[135] But existing is the ultimate perfection of every being, and the degree of a being's perfection is proportionate to the degree of its existing. If, therefore, a thing is an agent insofar as it is,[136] and if a thing is an end insofar as it is being, to say that it is not necessary that an agent act for an end is the same as saying that perfect being is not perfect being, which is counter to the principle of identity, and what denies the principle of identity destroys the truth of the principle of noncontradiction. Thus, it is impossible that the truth of the principle of finality not be necessary and immediate or self-evident, as soon as its terms are perceived by the human intellect. To deny it is to accept absurdity as a law of the mind, which is impossible without knowledge of the intelligible; for the absurd is intelligible only by negation of intelligibility, just as nothingness is knowable only as a negation of being.

Conclusion on the Discovery of Enunciations

We have tried to discover the existence of certain truths which our intellect cannot not perceive, not by means of a method that is the fruit of the intellect's effort and ingenuity, but by a natural and, in some way, instinctive power that Divine Wisdom has instilled in the intellect, making it a knowing power. Having discovered these truths, we tried to list those which are within the grasp of every man without any kind of philosophical or technical preparation.[137]

Then we showed how these primary truths are resolvable into the very first notions grasped by the human intellect, those of being, quiddity, unity, truth, and goodness or perfection. We should like now to pursue our epistemological analysis, not from the point of view of the object or of the truth the intellect grasps, as we have just done, but from the point of view of the intellectual act by which these first truths are grasped, in order that we may perceive the particular nature and properties flowing from that act. This will be our goal in the next chapter.

XI · ASSENT OR VALUE JUDGMENT ABOUT THE TRUTH OF FIRST PRINCIPLES

Throughout our analysis of first principles we have distinguished between the ontological aspect of these principles, that is, the realism of the terms of which propositions are constructed, and the epistemological aspect of these same first principles, or their truth value. Now it remains for us to determine the nature of this judgment of judgment whose immediate object is the truth of the proposition, or, better, a property of our knowledge and not a property of the real.[1] Here, we are not interested in our knowledge of the *existence* of truth, which knowledge results from simple reflection upon the various steps in our discernment of the real,[2] but rather in that inner perception of truth whose fruit is an explicit or nonexplicit modal judgment proclaiming and guaranteeing that the truths whereby the intellect is enriched have a stability which neither time, space, nor circumstance can shake. In fact, our purpose here is to answer the question asked at the end of Chapter IX, "How do we know the hierarchy of truth?"[3] for the hierarchy of truth is possible only when the different modes of the *ratio veritatis* have been perceived and compared. But it is impossible to criticize the different modes of truth without studying the intellectual act that is their immanent and conscious instrument; therefore, it is necessary to study the reflex act which is concerned with the nature of truths and which judges their intrinsic value as well as their relations to each other. Since this act is called *assent* in the philosophical vocabulary of St. Thomas Aquinas, we shall examine the description he gives of it as well as the characteristics he attributes to this very distinctive mental act. This chapter will therefore be divided into two sections, the *first* analyzing the nature of the act of assent, the *second* studying its essential property, certitude.

Section I: Nature of the Act of Assent

Just as St. Thomas uses the notion of object constantly without making a separate study of it,[4] he also uses the notion of assent in his philosophical and theological treatises, in dealing with problems of knowledge, without ever elaborating upon its general theory. He is content to describe the nature of this act here and there, dividing it more or less strictly, while applying it to problems raised by the meeting of philosophy and Christian faith. Consequently, explanations of the nature of this intellectual act and its proper object must be picked up where they are scattered throughout his works. Our study of the nature and properties of this act of assent will be organized in terms of the notion of object and act that are always the axis around which turn the essential aspects of our immanent activity.[5]

A. OBJECT OF THE ACT OF ASSENT

The word *assent* is given different meanings by St. Thomas in different contexts. Sometimes he gives it the completely general and popular meaning of agreeing with someone, of sympathizing with a way of thinking, of acceding to a request[6]; but usually he gives it a definite technical sense, and then its object is the true as infallible.

The object of the intellect is the *true* whereas the object of the will is the good. Now there is a certain kind of truth which exludes even the appearance of falsity, as may be seen in the evidence of first principles which the intellect cannot escape without by that fact assenting to them. There is also a kind of falsity which excludes every appearance of truth, and to which the intellect can in no way assent.[7]

The object of assent is truth as seen by the intellect to be infallible, undeniable, and secure from every possibility of mitigation by error.

Where is such truth to be found? It can only be found in the propositions formed by the intellect, since truth exists formally only in the
concept of the second mental operation[8] and assent cannot deal with
the ontological truth of the concepts of the mind's first operation.

It is clear from what has just been said that assent is not to be found in
that operation of the understanding by which it forms the simple quiddities of things, for there is no truth or falsity there. For we are not said
to assent to anything unless we hold it as true.[9]

This determination of the proper object of assent leads to the conclusion that assent is impossible as long as its object does not exist
within us. And since truth as such exists only as the effect of the
second operation of the mind, whose concept or enunciation necessarily conveys either truth or falsity,[10] it is impossible that assent
exist without the pre-existence of a direct judgment of the intellect. Neither is it enough that intellectual judgment dealing
directly with things exist and be true in order for assent to possess
its object; the intellect must also perceive the truth of the term of
this judgment, must know the adequation of the proposition with the
being of the thing. In other words, the truth must be apprehended
as existing before assent can find its object.

Since the reason acts reflexively, hence, just as it directs the acts of
other powers, so it can direct its own act. Consequently its act can be
commanded. But we must take note that the act of reason may be considered in two ways: first as to the exercise of the act . . . secondly as
to the object,[11] in respect of which two acts of the reason have to be
noticed. One is the act whereby *it apprehends the truth about something.* . . . The other act of the reason is that by which it assents to what
it apprehends.[12]

Since assent has to do only with formal truth, it is evident that the
expression *it assents to what it apprehends* can only mean a truth
formally apprehended as existing by the intellect, a truth which becomes an object of reflection and which the intellect judges to be
true by the act of assent. Not every truth compels assent, but only
those truths whose evidence is such that the mind cannot not grasp
them, i.e., the truth of *per se* propositions.

In order that a proposition be true it suffices that the predicate agree with the subject in some way. But in order that a proposition be true *per se* the predicate must agree with the subject *by reason of the form of the subject*.[13]

Every time the human intellect is presented with a truth whose structure is such that identification or denial of identification of the predicate and the subject depends upon the essential constituents of the subject, assent is necessary and inevitable to the same measure that the terms are understood. But when this identification or denial of identification rests on an observed fact and not on essential factors, then the mind can apprehend the truth of the fact and say, "This is so," but it cannot assent or affirm, "It is necessary that this be so." The only value judgment it can bring to bear on such a truth is a possible judgment based upon the fact thus, "Since some men are white, it is possible that man be white." But only the truth of first principles and the truths whose evidence and necessity can be reduced to those of first principles enjoy this cogency and necessitate assent.

There exists a certain truth which is known by itself: this is the truth of indemonstrable principles to which the intellect must necessarily assent. There also exist truths which are not known by themselves but through other truths. This kind of truth is two-fold: some flow necessarily from principles in such wise that they cannot be false as long as the principle remains true: of this kind are the conclusions of demonstrations. To these truths the intellect cannot refuse its assent, *after* having perceived their link with first principles and not before.[14]

As for the other truths that do not flow from first principles and cannot be proved by a necessary connection with the truth of these principles, the intellect remains free to assent or dissent.

But some apprehended truths do not convince the intellect to such an extent as not to leave it free to assent or to dissent, or at least to suspend its assent or dissent because of some cause or other; and in such cases, assent or dissent is in our power, and is subject to our command.[15]

In this teaching on the object of assent we re-encounter the law of the perfection of human knowledge, whose actualization is the function of judgment.[16] The intellect's perfection is the conscious grasp of being and all its riches. But, just as apprehension enriches us with a segmented, disassembled world that is judgment's function to reconstruct in us by means of composition, so does direct judgment give us a unified and therefore true world, but a world whose truth is observed as a fact rather than perceived in its nature and stability. That is why the intellect must again analyze the truth with which its knowledge is endowed in order to discover its value and establish a certain hierarchy among the immanent riches it possesses. This is the role of the act of assent; and it is not surprising that this perfective act of human knowledge should have a critical sense sufficiently strong to discern, among the truths it has capitalized, which ones are characterized by an absolute necessity securing them from every possibility of change and thus permitting the human mind to count on an investment so safe that no revolution or depression of the market of human truths will ever affect the value of the stock it holds. In the philosophical world the gold standard of infallible truth has never been abandoned,[17] and, what is more, this gold standard has been identified with the primary truths measuring all truths whose stability merits the full confidence of the human mind. The role of the act of assent is therefore to register the intellect's approval of the truths presented to it, absolute or relative approval depending upon whether the truth in question is presented to it with guarantees of infallibility or with possibilities of bankruptcy. Also, the function of dissent is to reveal the intellect's disapproval in face of error, absolute or relative disapproval depending upon whether the error is presented as identical with the absurd[18] or may possibly be changed into truth by means of modifications in the real that measures it.

This theory of assent, in relation to its proper object, formal truth, is explicitly, albeit concisely, stated in some rare texts of Aquinas.[19] We shall quote the one that seems to us most strongly worded and shall briefly explain the passages whose conciseness might make them obscure.

The possible intellect, however, so far as its own nature is concerned, is in potency to all intelligible forms . . . Therefore, it has no intrinsic determination which necessitates joining rather than dividing concepts, or the converse. Now, everything which is indetermined with reference to two things is not limited to one of them unless by something which moves it. But only two things move the possible intellect: it's proper object which is an intelligible form, that is a quiddity . . . and the will, which moves all the other powers.[20]

In this passage St. Thomas poses the problem of assent in relation to the mental act that gives the mind its object, i.e., affirmation or negation in whose term, the proposition, truth exists.[21] But when it comes to adhering or not adhering to *yes* or *no*, our possible intellect, considered in itself, is indifferent, which is to say that it could adhere or not adhere just as well to affirmation as to negation, just as it can receive all material quiddities without preferring any one of them. Therefore, we shall have to explain what happens when our intellect loses its neutrality toward *yes* or *no* and accepts or rejects one of the two propositions, whether affirmative or negative. This fact can have only one explanation—the intervention of an agent, which for the intellect could only be its proper object or the will, whose efficacity would determine the intellect's natural indifference and make it side for *yes* against *no*, or, vice versa, would make it assent or dissent. That is the way St. Thomas poses the problem of the act of assent in the foregoing text. Now we shall see how he applies this theory to the different mental acts, to determine which are acts of assent and which are not.

In this way, then, our possible intellect is related to the extremes of a contradictory proposition differently. For, sometimes, it does not tend toward one rather than the other, either because of lack of evidence, as happens in those problems about which we have no reasons for either side, or because of an apparent equality of the proofs for both sides. This is the state of one in doubt, who wavers between the two members of a contradictory proposition. Sometimes, however, the understanding tends more to one side than the other; still that which causes the inclination does not move the understanding enough to determine it fully to one of the members. Under this influence, it accepts one member but always has doubts about the other. This is the state of one holding an opinion, who accepts one member of the contradictory proposition with some fear that the other is true.[22]

Two cases are presented in this text. In the first the agent defaults, i.e., the truth is not evident in either affirmation or negation, and since the mind has no object to adhere to, it cannot side with either one of the alternatives: it makes an act of doubt, which is precisely the negation of the act of assent and of its contrary.[23] The second case is more complicated: truth does appear to the mind in one of the two alternative contradictories, but this truth does not have all the intrinsic guarantees it should possess. There is factual evidence to show that the predicate is concretely and practically linked to the given subject, but we do not know the nature of this bond: Is it necessary or contingent? We do not know. Could this unity of subject and predicate be only accidental and therefore cease to be? Possibly. Thus, the mind opines for the truth as for a fact, but without absolutely opposing the other alternative. The intellect takes no definite stand, so there is no strict assent, because there is no compelling object or truth.

Sometimes, again, the possible intellect is so determined that it adheres to one member without reservation. This happens sometimes because of the intelligible object and sometimes because of the will. Furthermore, the intelligible object sometimes acts immediately, sometimes mediately. It acts *immediately* when the truth of the proposition is unmistakably clear to the intellect from the intelligible objects themselves. This is the state of one *who understands principles*, which are known as soon as the terms are known . . . in this case the very nature of the terms immediately determines the intellect to propositions of this sort. The intelligible object acts *mediately* however, when the understanding, when it knows the definition of the terms, is determined to one member of the contradictory proposition in virtue of first principles. This is the state of *one who has science*.[24]

This text summarizes the causality of necessary truth upon our intellect, the grasping of which truth is comparable to the grasping of quiddities, because it is, in fact, the result of comparing two quiddative notions that imply each other,[25] either immediately in the case of natural principles, or mediately in demonstrative conclusions. The text goes on to describe the special case of the assent of supernatural faith, which enters into theological epistemology but not into the philosophical epistemology that concerns us here. Therefore, we shall proceed immediately to the conclusions St. Thomas draws from this analysis of the *motor object* of our act of assent, that is, of evident and necessary truth insofar as it draws our intellect out of its neutrality with respect to the affirmation and negation making up the two parts of the contradiction.

It is clear from what has just been said that assent is not to be found in that operation of the understanding by which it forms the simple quiddities of things, for there is no truth or falsity there. For we are not said to assent to anything *unless we hold it as true.*

Likewise, one who doubts does not have assent because he does not hold to one side rather than the other. Thus also, one who has opinion does not give assent, because his acceptance of the one side is not firm. The Latin word *sententia* (judgment), as Isaac and Avicenna say, is a clear or very certain comprehension of one member of a contradictory proposition. And to assent is derived from *sententia.*

Now, one who understands gives assent, because he holds with great certainty to one member of a contradictory proposition. Such one, however, does not employ discursive thought,[26] because he fixes one side without any process of comparison.

One who has scientific knowledge, however, does use discursive thought and gives assent, but the discursus causes the assent, and the assent puts an end to it. For by the very act of relating the principles to the conclusions, he assents to the conclusion by reducing them to the principles; there the movement of the one who is thinking is halted and brought to rest. For in scientific knowledge the movement of reason begins from the understanding of the principles and ends there after it has gone through the process of reduction.[27]

In the order of pure knowledge, we may therefore include that, in abstracting from the specifying dynamism of the will—whose intervention is necessary in cases where intelligible factors are lacking[28]—the only motor whose efficacy can infallibly produce intellectual assent—can determine the intellect absolutely to one of the members of the contradiction—is immediately evident *per se* truth. Therefore, these are the first truths we analyzed and the sensible evidence that is immediately reducible to these first self-evident principles.[29]

B. THE ACT OF ASSENT

That the act of assent belongs to the second operation of the mind, nothing could be more certain, and all the texts are categorical on this subject: "In its activity of judging, the intellect has two acts: affirmation by which it adheres to the true, and negation by which it rejects adherence to error."[30] But can it be identified with every judgment in such a way as to be a constitutive factor of the second operation of the mind in its most formal aspect? This question has long been discussed, and there is no unanimity about its answer[31]; however, its solution seems relatively easy as soon as the proper object of assent is determined. We have stated that this object is the formal truth of our propositions and thus a reality which cannot exist without a previous judgment; in this context, assent obviously cannot be identified with judgment or be one of its constitutive elements, since the object of assent follows upon the existence of a direct judgment of things. However, we are not going to support our position here by an analysis of texts, because that would be a very lengthy and useless procedure. But this is how we can prove that assent must have formal truth as its object and, consequently, that it cannot be identified with the nature of judgment itself.

Let us suppose that the ontological truth of the act of apprehension is the object of the act of assent, as a result of the intellect's reflection upon its likeness and the thing measuring it, which is the way an act of judgment does take place. If this is the case, then assent is identical with judgment and to say that man is white and to adhere to the truth of this judgment is one and the same thing. However, if the ontological truth of the act of apprehension is the object of assent, the ontological falsity of this same act should be the object of the act of dissent, since the latter is concerned with the contrary of the object of assent. But, in Thomism, ontological falsity is meaningless: the intellect either apprehends the quiddity of things or does not, but it cannot err about the nature of things.[32] If the object of assent is the ontological truth of the concept of apprehension, then dissent has no object. Besides, there is a teaching essential to Thomism that makes it forever unacceptable to Cartesianism, and that is the division of truth into the necessary and the contingent.[33] If the truth that is the object of assent is the truth existing in the concept of the mind's first operation, this truth can only be necessary, since the intellect is infallible in this first operation. Where, then, do contingent truths come from? And if there are contingent truths, they cannot be the object of assent, for the latter deals only with necessary truths, just as dissent deals only with necessary error.[34] But if every judgment implies assent as an essential constituent, judgments about contingent things are impossible, and by that fact the whole field of opinion and dialectics is thrown out of the Thomistic synthesis. It is an undeniable fact that in Thomism opinion is a judgment, that contingent truth exists and is the daily and customary food of the great majority of men, and that this truth, which can exist only by and in a judgment, does not deserve the intellect's assent; not only does it not deserve it, but to bestow assent upon contingent truth is to sin against the very nature of our intellectual power.[35] Therefore, it is not possible to say that ontological truth is the motor object of assent, and, consequently, it is impossible to identify it with judgment properly so called, or to make it an essential element of its psychological structure.

Although, as we have just seen, assent is not identical with judgment, that does not prevent it from being a judgment; but what kind of judgment is it? In studying judgment as an act perfecting human knowledge, we saw that its function is to synthesize the concepts which the abstraction of the agent intellect provides to the possible intellect, and that this synthetic act must be measured by the unity of the real, which is the definition of truth itself. The existence of this judicative act is perceived in and by the act of judgment itself —which implies reflection upon the genesis of our concepts. But just as knowing a thing's existence is not the same as perceiving its nature, so awareness of the existence of truth is not identical with awareness of its nature.[36] There must be a second act of reflection whose object is the truth or falsity of our affirmation and negation; it must perceive their *quod quid est*, i.e., the value of this truth possessed by our propositions. If this value is such that it can never be shaken or obscured, then the intellect, whose end or good is knowledge of the kind of truths whose values are eternal, cannot resist it; it surrenders and submits to the object of its love,[37] and this is the definition of the act of assent itself.

But how can we judge the truth of our propositions? By analyzing the bond uniting predicate to subject. This bond can be of four kinds: either it signifies what the subject is, or what inheres in the subject by itself and absolutely as flowing from its nature, or what inheres in the subject with relation to another, or finally what is extrinsic to the subject.[38] Now, a judgment concerned with the *bond* uniting or dividing subject and predicate is a *modal judgment* whose immediate object is the necessity or impossibility of the truth of this or that proposition, or the contingency or probability of the truth and falsity of our propositions.[39] If the matter of modal judgment is necessary or impossible, it formally constitutes what St. Thomas calls assent or dissent; if its matter is contingent and possible, it constitutes what he sometimes calls probable assent or the judgment of opinion or of dialectic.[40]

Although this statement may at first glance seem strange and foreign to the philosophy and vocabulary of St. Thomas, reflection shows its expression and doctrine to be in perfect conformity with the Master's texts. For, as we have just seen, St. Thomas always relates assent to the contradictory opposition existing between affirmation and negation.[41] For him, assent consists in adherence to one member of the contradiction and complete denial of the other alternative. Now, careful examination of the way assent to the truth of the principle of contradiction is stated shows this assent to be nothing but a modal judgment: *it is impossible* that the same thing both be and not be[42]; *it is necessary* that every subject whatsoever be either affirmed or denied[43]; *it is impossible* that contradictories be simultaneously true.[44]

Here then is the exact situation of our problem. The first of all assents is stated as a modal proposition; on the other hand, all other immediate assents imply this first assent, and mediate assents can exist only insofar as they can be reduced to the principle of non-contradiction,[45] for science and opinion are differentiated by the fact that the object of the former is reducible to this principle, whereas the object of the latter is not.

Science is incompatible with opinion about the same object absolutely, for the reason that science demands that its object *should be deemed impossible to be otherwise*; whereas it is essential to opinion that its object should be deemed possible to be otherwise.[46]

Therefore, since assent bears upon the only immediate and necessary evident truth and, by its intermediation, upon necessary truths whose absolute evidence depends on their reduction to the evidence of first principles, and ultimately to the evidence of the principle of non-contradiction, since, on the other hand, the assent of contradiction is nothing but a modal judgment stated in a modal formula—we may legitimately conclude that assent, in the strict sense, is a modal judgment concerned with the nature of the formal truth of a direct judgment whose term is the being of things. It is a judgment of judgment, therefore, it is not identical with the nature of every judgment, nor can it be considered as an esssential element in every second mental operation. In fact, it designates nothing other than that group of propositions which are characterized by their adequation with the real[47] and by perception of the bond of perseity unifying predicate to subject. This is a bond that cannot be other than it is, which is what constitutes the necessity and infallibility of truth.[48] Such is the nature of the act of assent and its object.

Section II: Assent and Certitude

It may perhaps seem surprising that throughout these many pages devoted to studying the knowledge of truth, the problem of certitude has not been mentioned, whereas this problem appears to have preoccupied all thinkers from the Greek skeptics to our day.[49] It is even more surprising that an examination of the legion of texts in St. Thomas about the problem of knowledge, both natural and supernatural, reveals none whose sole object is the study of certitude. Certitude is always mentioned[50] as being part of perfect knowledge, but its function in epistemology and its constitutive elements are

never studied in themselves. "Happiness consists in a perfect operation. *Now perfect knowledge requires certitude*, and that is why we
cannot be said to know unless we know what cannot be otherwise."[51]
Perfect knowledge gives to the intellect its natural good, truth, and
perfect possession of this truth; therefore, it implies assent or modal
judgment upon the value of the truths we possess. That is why St.
Thomas, in the text quoted above, describes perfect knowledge or
certitude in terms of assent or modal judgment—*we cannot be said
to know unless what we know cannot be otherwise*—which is the
definition of the object of assent, infallible truth.[52] Certitude and
assent should therefore be identical, which would imply that where
there is no assent, there can be no certitude. However, this identity
seems difficult to affirm, as the following text proves:

> Whoever considers an element belonging to several things as belonging
> properly to one of them, is necessarily on the way to error. Now *certitude
> of adherence* does not belong properly to the act of faith; first because it
> also belongs to the intellectual virtues of science, wisdom and understand-
> ing; then because it is common to both true and false faith . . . for men
> do not adhere any the less firmly to truth than to falsity: finally because
> certitude of adherence does not always result from a habitus but may also
> result from the free willing of someone who can firmly establish his
> assent to truth and to falsity before possessing a habitus of truth.[53]

Thus, were it true that assent is always accompanied by certitude,
it would be impossible to make certitude a property of assent, since
certitude can accompany error. In order exactly to know what relations exist between assent and certitude, we must give more precision
to the meaning or meanings of this word, as it is used in St. Thomas,
and establish some kind of order among the different meanings it can
have. That is what we must do first; then we shall try to discover the
exact meaning of *certitude* when it necessarily accompanies the act
of assent.

A. THE MEANINGS OF "CERTITUDE"

The word *certitudo* is taken from the Latin word *cernere*, which
is itself drawn from the Greek *krinein*. Now, the root of this word,

krei, expresses the idea of separation, distinction, which has given to its Latin and Greek derivatives the following meanings: to sort, to distinguish, to decide, to see clearly, to be fixed.[54] Its philosophical meaning has been largely the work of Aristotle[55] and his Greek and Arabian commentators, whose translated works became the heritage of Latin Scholasticism. It was in these texts that St. Thomas found the philosophical meaning of certitude that he used constantly in his works, either keeping its first Aristotelian meaning or the meaning the Arabian thinkers had added to it, or giving it new meanings to meet the needs of the new problems brought up by revelation.

St. Thomas kept Aristotle's ontological meaning of certitude, by which it expresses the quiddative determination of being,[56] its simplicity,[57] the precise dimensions of the order of quantity.[58] He also kept the methodological function of certitude in the hierarchy of the sciences arranged according to their necessity.[59] The ontological sense of Aristotelian certitude had primacy over all the other meanings; it was its formal meaning. But in St. Thomas there was a transposition of the Aristotelian meanings and a union of the subjective determination of knowledge with the ontological determination of its object. In the Thomistic context the first and formal sense of the word *certitude* belongs to the epistemological order, whereas its derived meanings belong to the order of the object and appetite.

Certitude exists in two ways in a thing: by essence and by participation. It exists by essence *in the cognitive power* and by participation in everything which is infallibly moved towards its end by the cognitive power; which explains why we say that nature operates with certitude inasmuch as the Divine Intellect moves every being towards its end with certitude.[60]

The cause of this formal or essential certitude, whose subject is the knowing power, is more efficient the more it determines the intellect to unity:

Certitude is nothing but the determination of the intellect to unity. The degrees of certitude depend therefore upon the degree of power possessed by the determining principle. The intellect's determination to unity is accomplished in three ways, as we have said. In the understanding of principles the determination is caused by the fact that the light of the agent intellect renders the object sufficiently evident in itself. In knowl-

edge of conclusions the determination to unity is caused by the fact that
the rational conclusion is reduced to the intrinsic evidence of the principles. In faith, by the fact that the will commands the intellect.[61]

This text gives us both the definition and the division of certitude,
but it is quite curious to observe that the definition and division of
certitude are identical with the definition and divison of assent, as
given us.[62] It does not seem possible to reconcile this identification
with the group of texts describing certitude and situating it in a
very different context from that characterizing the judgment of
infallible truth which is assent. We shall try to solve this problem by
showing that, in a certain sense, certitude and assent always go together for they are essentially complementary, and that, on the
other hand, both assent and certitude can be used by St. Thomas
in wider meanings and contexts which are still legitimate but whose
precision and technical character have lost all their primary value in
order to take on another that corresponds better with our usual
way of talking.

B. THE CORRELATIVE CHARACTER OF ASSENT AND CER-
    TITUDE

To understand the apparent identification established by Thomistic
texts between the notions of assent and certitude, we must recall an
essential aspect of Thomistic epistemology: the problem of knowledge must be situated in a context of imitation of divine perfection,[63]
and the problem of the knowledge of truth must also be understood
as an essentially perfective factor of apprehension.[64] But, just as the
knowledge that consists in the apprehension of quiddities obeyed an
evolutionary process wherein confused and indistinct vision of the
real was gradually replaced by a distinct and precise grasp of it,[65] so
in the second operation of the mind there is movement from the imperfect to the perfect in awareness of truth, which we first know as
existing when we are in the act of judging the real, and then know in
its deep nature and indefectible value in the reflex and modal judgment that is assent. Now, there is a natural law by which beings tending toward their end or perfection perform a series of acts that bring

them closer and closer to their good, until a last act takes final possession of their end, and then they rest in this possession because they have attained the term for which they are made. Movement toward possession, possession of the true end, and rest or joy in the good possessed—these are the three aspects of the natural dynamism of all beings that have not but must attain their perfection. But this is precisely the case with man as intelligent: made to know all things, he is born ignorant; made to know reality as it is, he is compelled by his natural process of abstraction to fragment the real in order that it may enter into him, even though he must reconstruct its unity by judicative activity; made to be perfectly aware of the immanent reconstruction of the exterior world, which constitutes the domain of truth, this awareness occurs and illumines the intellect only gradually. Analysis of assent has shown us the human intellect exercising a natural, spontaneous, necessary act that takes possession of a natural good for which it is made, namely, infallible truth. To reflection, certitude appears as the repose in the possession of this good, a sort of partial beatitude of the intellect caused by the presence of truths, of which nothing in the world could ever deprive it.

It may seem strange in Thomistic philosophy to present the doctrine of certitude in a context of appetite, and to bring the analogy of love and delight or repose into play in the order of knowledge! And yet, nothing could agree more with the doctrine and texts of Aquinas, as soon as we see that the object of assent is formal truth and that the object of certitude is this same truth considered as its place of repose. For formal truth is immanent to our intellectual faculty and is formally the proper good of our knowing power, inasmuch as it is a natural thing.

Everything that comes from God receives from Him a certain nature by which it is related to its final end. But it is also true that every power has a natural appetite . . . with respect to its proper good . . . and with the exception of the will all the powers of the soul are necessitated by their objects.[66]

Our cognitive power therefore has a natural, necessary, and unconscious tendency toward truth, a sort of natural love that is the basis of all our acts of knowing, and it sets off a whole series of inquiries among which some cannot attain truth.

Several philosophers have let themselves be guided by truth so far as to affirm that the principles of things are contraries; which is indeed true, but they have not been impelled to this statement by a proof so much as they have been compelled to it by truth itself. *For truth is the intellect's good and the term of its natural ordination;* and just as things without knowledge are moved toward their end without knowing it, so sometimes does the human intellect by a natural inclination tend toward truth although it does not perceive its nature.[67]

Thus, the intellect's natural appetite for truth makes it discover the existence of some truths even when it does not know what truth is. This unawareness results from our ignorance and lack of reflection[68] upon the intellectual riches we possess; this is the way we apprehend the truth of first principles—we assent to them by a sort of instinct for truth. But our intellect is light and luminosity, and of this we should be aware. It is reflection that makes us relive in the light what an invincible tendency of nature has produced. Now, this reflection upon natural assent and the nature of its object demands that we conceive it as a spontaneous or immediate,[69] necessary, and infallible[70] possession of the human intellect's proper good, whose efficacity it cannot resist. This means that when the intellect meets the truth for which it is made, it grasps it; truth becomes consciously present to it. The intellect rejoices in this presence, rests in it, and this is certitude, or joy in the good possessed. "Delight which is nothing but *repose of the natural appetite* is found in every power upon its union with its object."[71] Now, this natural repose or delight of a power in the presence of its object, or end, has several aspects that throw light on the explanations given about the nature and variety of the act of assent and its certitude.

When the beloved is really *present* as much as it possibly can be, delight results as the effect of a perfectly harmonious unification; when the beloved is completely *absent*, the greatest sorrow reigns; finally when the beloved is partly present and partly absent, delight is mixed with sorrow.[72]

Let us apply this sketch of the relations between appetite and the presence of its good to the speculative data on assent and certitude considered as the possession of the intellect's good and joy or repose in this good.

(1) In intellectual assent to the truth of first principles there is awareness of the presence of necessary truths in the soul, and a grasping of the nature of their necessity, thanks to the agent intellect that makes the contradictory opposition between yes and no visible to the possible intellect. This intellectual vision or possession makes the motor good of our cognitive power actually *present* as much as it can be.[73] The result of this perfectly harmonious conjunction between our cognitive power and its good is joy or repose in the necessary truth possessed, and this is absolute intellectual certitude with no admixture of any incertitude, because this truth is totally present or perfectly evident.[74]

(2) In scientific assent, possession or presence of the intellect's good is brought about by means of analysis or resolution; therefore, reason or *cogitatio* is always in play, as long as the bond linking the concluded truth with the truth of first principles has not been established. Once this bond has been established, the intellect is *fixed and rests*.[75] And this is the definition of scientific certitude which results from the intellect's testifying to itself that that for which it is made is actually and permanently present.[76]

(3) In the assent of faith, the intellect does not possess super-natural truth, because such truth is beyond our intellect's illuminative capacities; therefore, the good is absent, and relations with it can only be established by the testimony of another, in this case, infallible divine truth. By means of this sort of *presence by proxy*, the intellect is made *captive* to the motion of the will; but since this captivity is not the effect of intrinsic evidence, the intellect is deeply dis-satisfied and restless; certitude and joy depend on the will that, being in the presence of the absolute good, divine truth, adheres to it with all its strength.[77]

This third kind of assent, accompanied by certitude that does not stem from joy in the intellect's present good but from a voluntary determination, explains why in some texts St. Thomas speaks of assent and certitude that have bearing on contingent truth and even on error. In all these cases, assent and certitude do not result from the presence of infallible truth to the intellect but are the product of voluntary pressure commanding adherence either for practical reasons of activity, or through prejudice, ignorance, rashness, or lack of reflection, which may imply lack of prudence and therefore a moral defect.[78] The assent and certitude produced by sensible evidence is in a class by itself, *experimental certitude*,[79] which has value only for the duration of the sensation and in no way increases our treasury of stable and certain truths.

Thus, we may conclude that when certitude is taken *formally* as *intellectual* repose of our power in possession of its good (necessary and self-evident truth), it always accompanies assent taken in the sense of value judgment on truth. But when certitude is taken in a participated sense—depending on the human will as free and determined to goods that are not proper or present to the intellect—then certitude, as well as assent, in no way resembles the certitude and assent we have been discussing, for these depend objectively upon the speculative intellect only and the essential laws controlling its functioning. But the certitude depending on will leads us into the domain of human liberty with its capacity for good and evil; we leave the spontaneous and autonomous structures of the intellect to enter the realm wherein will can rule intellect when the latter is no longer necessitated by its infallible mover, necessary truth, which is self-evident in itself and for us.

Some truths which are apprehended do not convince the intellect to such an extent as not to leave it free to assent or to dissent, or at least suspend its assent or dissent because of some cause or other; in such cases, assent or dissent is in our power, and is subject to our command.[80]

Such are the correlations existing between assent and certitude in the doctrine of St. Thomas, when these two words are taken to mean the natural activities of the intellect confronted by its proper good. Such also is the lack of correlation between these two words when used in a context of free will where choice exists because the intellect is not necessarily determined by the evidence and infallibility of truths, but by their value as the absolute good for man, taken as a whole or in one of his aspects. In this latter alternative, assent signifies conviction, and certitude means the practical satisfaction that the decision taken brings to action.

Conclusion on Value Judgment About the Truth of First Principles

With this chapter on assent, on the value judgment of the infalli-bility of natural human truth, we bring to a close our study of knowledge as a natural act rooted in sensibility, but gradually dis-engaging itself to evolve toward a purely spiritual possession of the universe in which we live. Spiritual and fragmentary in the act of apprehension, human knowledge is synthesized and perfected by judicative activity that enables it to reconstruct in the soul a substi-tute for the ontological unity of the things on which it is nourished. This new activity puts it into a measured-to-measure relationship with the exterior real, and from this new aspect the world of truth and error appears in the human soul.

Now, it behooves us to be aware of this world of truth and error and to possess the control instruments enabling us to know when and how truth, our health, and error, our disease, dwell in us. In this field, as in that of apprehension, we have natural instincts for truth, by which we apprehend its existence as soon as it appears in the very simple judgments called primary or immediate judgments, dealing with the most fundamental and evident notions of the human intellect. Once the existence of these truths is apprehended, we have to judge their validity, see their essential structure, and make judg-ments so as to arrange them in hierarchy and observe their quasi-eternal value. Here again we have a natural act, called assent, which is irresistibly attracted by the necessarily evident truth expressed by the first judgments. Once assent possesses this intellectual good, the intellect delights in it by and in the certitude that is nothing but our intellect's repose and quietude in the unshakable security of the treasures it possesses. Such is the progressive advance of human knowledge and its evolution toward more and more immanent and therefore perfect knowledge of the exterior universe of which man is a part, and which he must use to live the life of the mind and to attain his destiny.

XII · INFALLIBLE KNOWLEDGE OF MEDIATE TRUTH

In the two preceding chapters we studied the birth of some infallible truths, our knowledge of these truths, and our value judgments about them. But examination of these first truths shows that their content is vague and that, in the realm of truth, it corresponds to the content of being as first known in our awareness of things. Just as our first confused grasp of being is but the starting point of a long inquiry that normally leads to being as being,[1] so natural truths, grasped with absolute evidence and certitude by the intellectual *habitus*, are only the starting point for reason's long and painful pursuit of more and clearer truths that will lead it to beatific truth itself, that is, to the total truth in which reason's ultimate happiness lies.

Now it is not possible that man's ultimate happiness consist in contemplation based on the understanding of first principles, *for this is most imperfect* as being most universal, containing potentially the knowledge of things. Moreover it is the beginning and not the end of human inquiry, and comes to us from nature and not through the pursuit of truth. Nor does it consist in contemplation based on the sciences that have the lowest things for their object. . . . It follows then, that man's ultimate happiness consists in wisdom, based on the consideration of *divine things*.[2]

To this realm of truth which escapes primary evidence and assent belong all the truths called *mediate*. Their extent is as vast as the power of human reason itself.

Natural human knowledge can extend to those things which we can know under the guidance of natural reason. And there is a beginning and a term of the natural knowledge. It has its beginning in a kind of confused knowledge of all things, in so far as man naturally has within him a knowl-

edge of the general principles in which, *as in seeds,* there virtually pre-
exist all the objects of knowledge which can be known by natural reason.
This knowledge reaches its term when the things which are virtually in
the principles *are expressed in act,* as animal generation is said to reach its
term when the animal, with all its members perfect and distinct, is
developed from the seed of the animal in which all its members pre-
exist virtually.[3]

Therefore, mediate truth means everything that comes within
the perspective of science and philosophy, insofar as these intellectual disciplines have as their term of inquiry truths whose
evidence is not immediately grasped by the mind.[4] Like all truth,
this mediate truth belongs to the realm of cognitive life since it is
one of its effects.[5] It must therefore be studied according to the essential requirements of every vital activity, requirements arising,
on the one hand, from immanence and, on the other, from specification by an exterior term.[6] Furthermore, since mediate truth results
from the difficult and delicate workings of a fallible reason, we must
know the processes that ensure legitimacy and health to the gestation
and birth of this new child of the mind. Finally, since by definition
this truth has only borrowed evidence, it must be justified to the mind
and must reassure the mind of its authenticity and value. From these
three aspects of our problem result the three sections into which this
chapter is divided:

(1) The nature of the operation giving birth to mediate truth.
(2) Method or art of discovering mediate truth: analysis and synthesis.
(3) Value judgment on mediate truth: assent to conclusions.

Section I: The Nature of the Operation that Gives Birth to Mediate Truth

We have seen that judgment, the second operation of the mind,
owes its existence to two sources. The first of these is our mind's imperfection, the abstractive nature that forces it to "disassemble" the
real in order to know it. The second source is knowledge's own need

for perfection, for knowledge seeks to grasp the real as it is, therefore, to grasp it in its unity, whence the need for an assembly line, which is none other than the second operation of the mind.[7]

The third mental operation has its source in the same duality of principles, for it is, on the one hand, the result of the intellect's imperfection and, on the other, the result of our knowledge's need to grasp the real as one and integral.

As in the intellect, when reasoning, the conclusion is compared with the principle, so in the intellect composing and dividing, the predicate is compared with the subject. For if our intellect were to see at once the truth of the conclusion in the principle, it would never understand by discursion, and reasoning. In like manner, if the intellect in apprehending the quiddity of the subject were at once to have knowledge of all that can be attributed to, or removed from, the subject, it would never understand by composing and dividing, namely, that in the first apprehension of anything newly apprehended it cannot, at once, grasp all that is virtually contained in it. *And this comes from the weakness of the intellectual light within us.*[8]

We reason and discourse because our intellect is imperfect, but also that it may become perfect.

The perfection of spiritual nature lies in the cognition of truth. But there are some higher spiritual substances which immediately in the beginning receive knowledge of truth without any movement or reasoning by a sudden or simple reception. ... There are also lower spiritual substances which can arrive at *perfect knowledge of truth only through a certain movement* in which they go from one thing to another, in order to reach knowledge of things unknown through those which are known. This is proper to human souls. And this is why . . . souls are called *rational* substances.[9]

What we are looking for, then, is the nature of this cognitive activity that terminates in the discovery of truths not immediately evident and is characterized by its discursive aspect. In order to discover the essential aspects of any cognitive activity, we must first study it in its immanence, that is, in the very exercise of its activity, and then in its specification, i.e., as measured by its exterior term or object.[10] The study of these two aspects makes up the two subdivisions of this first section.

A. REASONING AS AN IMMANENT ACTIVITY

From its very beginning the study of this third mental operation shows us that if reasoning is characteristic of the human intellect's very nature, it also reveals all the complexity of that intellect. In simple apprehension we were concerned only with showing how real things come into our mind and our vital reaction to the presence of these wealth-bearing guests.[11] What we saw in judgment was a unification in which the mind takes the initiative in order to be measured by the real thing in the latter's own unity.[12] But in discourse or reasoning, what interests us is the very diversity of the unifications produced by the judgment; we want to see what bonds unite them, to set up an immanent order within the multiplicity of our truths. The complexity of this operation is not surprising since it presupposes the actuation of all the previously studied elements by an activity that has neither the passivity of apprehension nor the spontaneity and natural infallibility of first judgments. We shall study this activity of reason first in its *mode* and then in its *nature*.

¶ *1. Discourse as a Mode of Rational Knowledge.* The mode of the first operation of the mind is passive and abstractive[13]; the mode of the second is concrete and compositive[14]; the mode of the third mental operation is characterized by the *discourse* that is called reasoning. To discourse is to go from the knowledge of one truth to that of another, to proceed from the known to the unknown. It is a kind of movement in which reason tries to draw from the immediate and certain truths it possesses other truths which escape it.

Discursion expresses movement of a kind. Now all movement is from something before to something after. Hence discursive knowledge comes about according as from something previously known, one attains to the knowledge of what is afterwards known but which was previously unknown.[15]

Precisely because of this typical mode of knowing, reason is distinguished from intellect, in the Thomistic vocabulary, not as a distinct faculty but as a complementary aspect of an intellect in whose shadow it works.[16]

To understand is to grasp intelligible truth absolutely, and *to reason* is to advance from one thing understood to another, so as to know another intelligible truth. . . . But man arrives at the knowledge of intelligible truth by advancing from one thing to another. And therefore he is called rational. Reasoning therefore is compared to understanding *as movement to rest*, or acquisition to possession.[17]

Since discourse implies a kind of movement from one evident truth to another, the latter being linked in some way to the former, we must have a look at the two terms of this movement, for on the nature of these terms depends the mode of the knowledge properly called discourse. Comparison with the modes and operations of apprehension and judgment, which we have already studied, will clarify this statement. In the activity of apprehension we saw that the intellect could reflect on its concepts, divide and compare them, and arrive, at least ideally, at a definition.[18] This division and comparison of concepts taken as absolute is not discourse but an orderly arranging of several concepts into a higher unity.

Also, in the judicative activity of composing and dividing concepts, comparison and division do not aim to discover a third concept possessing a higher unity, but aim rather to set up a sort of existential unity or multiplicity between concepts; here again there is no discourse properly so called. In order that discourse exist, this mental movement's point of departure must be an already known evident truth that serves as starting point for the discovery of another previously unknown evident truth, whose coming into existence is not the result of chance but of its linkage to the evident truth which was the starting point. Thus, discourse always starts from either a categorical or hypothetical statement,[19] to which it tries to link (or from which it tries to separate) one or more propositions in order to arrive at new evidence in which the discourse terminates.

This brief explanation has therefore shown that, as immanent activity, discourse cannot be an absolute starting point in the pursuit of truth, but that it always presupposes the existence of evidence already possessed and recognized as such. Still in this context of immanence, discourse has no value in itself; by nature it is destined to result in new vision and to disappear so that it may give way to vision. Essentially it is an intermediary between two judgments that it unifies or opposes, as the case may be. In the order of discovery and unification of mediate truths, it plays the role of composition and division in the conscious organization of our concepts, an organization that gives rise to immediate truth.

¶ 2. *The Nature of this Third Operation.* Whereas to know is to assimilate the real by being informed by it,[20] whereas to know truth is to see that what we have become by knowing is conformed to that is real[21]—to discourse is to *seek.* Since the act of seeking is naturally conditioned by the habits of the seekers and their preoccupations, that is, by what they are looking for, it is not surprising that this rational activity of the mind displays an extraordinary variety. This variety is revealed by the number of names Aquinas applied to this search, as well as by those added since the emancipation of modern science from the tyranny of philosophical methods of research. There is, first of all, the word *cogitare, cogitatio,* which means a sort of restlessness of mind in face of experienced ignorance, a restlessness that imposes on the mind an incessant activity until that ignorance is conquered.[22] *Inquirere, inquisitio, investigatio* more typically indicate the search itself, the movement of reason which, haunted by curiosity, the desire to know or to act, seeks to discover the bonds that exist between what it sees and what still remains obscure, by using every indication and mark that might orient it in a definite direction.[23] There are two other terms that express the gathering together of the diverse elements reason discovers in the course of its quest, as well as the comparison it sets up between them; these are *collatio*[24] and *conferre.*[25] There are also the words *deducere*[26] and *inducere,*[27] which more precisely indicate the manner in which the search is carried on and the nature of its starting point and destination; for induction takes a particular truth as the starting point of its search and terminates with universal evidence, whereas deduction or the syllogism proceeds in the opposite direction.[28] Finally, there are two other words used by St. Thomas to describe the activity of reason; these are *resolutio* and *compositio,* which are opposed as methods of research.[29] To these we shall return at length in the two remaining sections of this chapter.

Simply by analyzing the vocabulary, therefore, we can see that rational activity or discourse covers all the work man must do to arrive at truths that are not immediate. This activity is essentially labor, study.[30] It includes everything that is the object of discovery and teaching and excludes none of the possibilities at the disposition of man to increase his knowledge and to unify it into a powerful synthesis. The whole field of inquiry—whatever its particular domain, be it philosophical, scientific, artistic—belongs to the nature of this activity, which is truly the Cinderella of the mind. To it is consigned everything that is laborious, long, and unsatisfying in the order of knowledge, both speculative and practical. If we limit our consideration to the *exercise or immanence* of this rational activity—without bothering about its specifying aspect, that is, the mediate truth toward which it tends by nature—we can easily see how extraordinarily supple it is. It is also clear that to confine this activity within the rigid framework of the demonstrative syllogism, or within the mathematical framework of Cartesian deduction, or, again, within the inexorable laws of scientific induction—to do this is to deprive it of a great part of its methods of inquiry and thereby to diminish our rational life as such. The whole domain of the probable, and that is the most extensive and daily aspect of human life, belongs properly to the reason and is its object. Whether or not we are aware of the procedure used, it is impossible to be a philosopher, a scientist, an artist, technician, moralist, or simply a man, without continually having recourse to this activity of *linking*, which is reasoning. Indeed, it is impossible for us to live humanly without trying to bring unity into the different kinds of knowledge we possess. Instrument of synthesis, reasoning or discourse as immanent activity is, therefore, essentially a principle of organization of the world of knowledge, insofar as this knowledge is directed toward truth of any kind. In the context of the immanence of intellectual life and of the progressive perfection acquired by this life as we become more aware and more autonomous,[31] this discursive activity of our reason assumes its full meaning, for it belongs on the metaphysical plane that is typically assigned to epistemology by St. Thomas.

We have, indeed, seen that human knowledge takes on its full meaning in Thomism only in the context of the imitation of the divine, wherein man somehow breaks through his specific limitations to attain a sort of divine infinitude,[32] by participating in God's knowledge of things. In God, to know and to know perfectly are the same thing, whereas in man there is a distinction between his knowledge of things and the perfection of this knowledge, for there is a distinction between the being, of man and the perfection of his being, which is progressively acquired by means of accidents.[33] From this results the explanation of the act of judgment as the perfecting of the being of knowledge that is apprehension[34]; out of this also comes the conception of discourse as the complementary and perfective activity of the judgment. Just as substance is the source and end of the accidents perfecting it, so some accidents are the source and end of other accidents that perfect them.[35] Now, that is exactly what goes on in the order of the knowledge of truth. Judgment, in taking possession of immediate truth is the source and end of reasoning, which renders distinct and actual the truths existing in a confused and virtual state in immediate truths.

Hence it is that human reasoning in the order of inquiry and discovery, proceeds from certain truths absolutely understood, namely the first principles; and again in the order of judgment returns, by analysis to first principles, in the light of which it examines what it has found.[36]

The truth of first principles, despite its evidence and its certitude,[37] is essentially vague and virtual, therefore imperfect, for it is but initial truth reflecting the indistinction and universality in the elements of simple apprehension of which it is composed. It is modest truth precisely because it reflects the imperfection of our intellect.[38] And that is why, although reasoning has its source in the truth of these first principles, it is essentially the perfective instrument of such truth. For, thanks to reasoning, this first indetermination progressively disappears to be replaced by distinct vision enriched by the real, known no longer in its superficial appearances but in its nature and its existential opulence. This, in turn, brings us to the second aspect of discursive activity, that of its specification by exterior reality.

B. REASONING AS SPECIFIED BY AN EXTERIOR TERM

In studying this aspect of discursive activity, we no longer concentrate on the inner process of inquiry and the laws ruling it, but
rather on the exterior object that measures it and is its end. What is
this object? What do we know when we discover mediate truth? In
the study of human knowledge as such, i.e., apprehension of the real,
that which specifies sensory knowledge is external accidents,[39] whereas the specifier of intellection is being as grasped first in its moving
actuality, then in its quiddity, and finally in its existing as such.[40] In
analyzing knowledge of immediate truth, we find it is concrete unity
of the real thing in its accidental, substantial, and existential aspects
that terminates the judicative act of composition; this is what St.
Thomas called *ipsum esse rei*.[41]

Besides substance, accidents, and the act of existing, can there be
anything else in the real thing which is a genuine aspect of being
and serves as term or object of discursive activity? There is the whole
field of *real relations* that exist between real things, relations of cause
and effect, of concomitance and succession, of law and fact, of harmony between parts of a whole, between means and end, finally of
everything which, added to the absolute unity of the real, involves
the thing in a plurality of relations or orders. This is the precise
aspect of the real in which discursive knowledge should terminate.

¶ *1. Order Between Beings as Exterior Term of Reasoning.*
Order is a substitute for identity and is the soul of multiplicity. "In
creatures, however, one form does not exist in several except by
unity of order as the form of an ordered multitude. . . . For we say
that many men are a college, or an army, or a people."[42] A sort of
composition or synthesis exists between different things whose distinction does not preclude every bond of kinship or origin. And
wherever there exists a principle capable of unifying a multitude from
within, whatever the nature of this principle and the realities it groups
together,[43] there is order. "Order always has reference to some principle. Therefore, since there are many kinds of principles . . . so there
are many kinds of order."[44]

The ancients, in fact, discovered three categories of principles, of which the first unifies the multiplicity of local movements, the second unifies the becoming of things from within, and the third unifies this same becoming from without.[45] The latter categories include the four causes, which are unifying principles in the respective domains of matter, form, efficiency, and finality.[46] Furthermore, considered in relation to their effects, or to the diversity they unify, these four causes give rise to twelve different ways of being first principles, i.e., of being the unifying form of a multitude.[47] If to these twelve modes we add the principle that measures and orders the multiplicity of local movements, we have thirteen possible bonds between beings, thirteen different orders that unify the different aspects of reality, consequently becoming the term of this immanent inquiry called reasoning or discursive activity. Actually, the real does not consist in a complex of properties and appearances, scattered at random, but in certain bonds, in certain constant relationships. It is the constancy and necessity of these bonds that are the object of our reasonings, in whatever field they may be discerned. And that is why the fact of necessity is intimately bound to the notion of principle and cause[48] and is consequently part of order, which we have said is the specifying object of rational discourse.

Since there are as many different orders as there are unifying principles, and since, on the other hand, these diverse unifying principles are taken from the different levels of the real known by the intellect, the typical character of discursive knowledge varies according to the nature of the multiplicity whose unity of order we are trying to grasp. Thus, it is obvious that the order discerned by the mathematician in the multitude of his equations is completely different from that discovered by the physicist in the phenomena of matter-energy; and the latter order is also totally different from that perceived by the sociologist reasoning on the social behavior of human beings. The scientific law expressing the coherence and constancy of phenomena in these different fields evidently corresponds to an objective order observed and analyzed by reason, but this order has not the same nature in the case of the mathematician, the physicist, and the sociologist,[49] because the unifying principle around which the aspects of a frequently bewildering multiplicity and diversity are grouped does not have the same nature. And this unifying principle is often harder to perceive in human facts than in matter, as Lévy-Bruhl penetratingly remarks:

It is not facts that sociologists lack. In many cases they know enough of them to try to determine laws. What they frequently lack is the scientific apprehension of facts . . . the perception of the *planes of cleavage* which would make these laws apparent.[50]

These planes of cleavage are nothing but the organizing principle for sociological or other facts, a principle that transforms the multitude of facts into a whole obeying strict laws capable of explaining events and foreseeing them.

Now, after analyzing the nature of knowledge, we have to admit that not only do facts penetrate the human intellect, but also that natures, beings with their substantial and accidental, essential and existential aspects, come to lodge in this dwelling of infinite capacity that is our soul, and that if scientific facts, in the modern sense of the word, can dwell there, so too can the deeper levels of reality which are the objects of philosophical knowledge. Just as the scientist can, by his discursive activity, discover bonds, relationships between facts grouped around a hypothetical principle that sets order among them, so is it possible for the philosopher to discover, by means of the same discursive activity, bonds of coherence between the different aspects that reality offers to his reflection. And since the material dealt with by philosophical reflection is not uniquely phenomenal and factual, since it is not necessarily screened by an instrumentation which lets through only that part of reality capable of being numbered,[51] and since this material comprises, on the contrary, each and every aspect of the real—the aspects observed by science as well as those perceived by the senses and intellect—the principles of order are much more varied in the field of philosophy than they are in science. Consequently, the links perceived by philosophic discourse are not based only on statistical laws but are formulated and stated in terms of cause and effect, necessity and contingence, in the philosophical meaning of these words.[52] A *causal order*, such is the term or object of reasoning of philosophical knowledge.

¶ 2. *Causal Order as the Term of Philosophical Reasoning.* We must now elaborate a bit upon the nature of the causal order, which we have said is the object term of discursive activity in philosophy. To do this we will have to look back at some of the explanations already given during our analyses of the nature of human knowledge and of the knowledge of truth. We should not forget that, unlike the work of Descartes and Kant, our treatise on epistemology does not begin the study of human knowledge by identifying the latter with knowledge of infallible truth.[53] The study of *mediate* infallible truth, in which we are engaged, comes at the end of an epistemological treatise because it is the effect of the nature of truth, which is itself the effect of the nature of human knowledge as such.[54]

Now we have seen that, by nature, intellectual knowledge evolves progressively toward grasping the real as being by starting from the apprehension of the real as moving, and by proceeding successively to the intuition of its nature and to that of the perfective complexity which is the composition of substance and its accidents.[55] In analyzing judgment and its exterior term, the *ipsum esse rei,* we rediscovered the same links that, within a being, unite the substantial and accidental, the essential and existential aspects.[56] Finally, in analyzing those truths called primary and immediate, we saw that the perception of a causal link is natural to the human intellect as soon as it is confronted with contingent activity and an act of existing.[57] Therefore, we have all the elements necessary for understanding the nature of the causal order that is the object term of discursive activity in the service of philosophical reflection and whose proper function is to measure mediate truth, just as the *ipsum esse rei* serves as the measure of immediate truth.[58]

(a) *Causal order in a being.* To know is interiorly to live the exterior real, and this exterior real is first and foremost the whole material universe in which we live and of which we are a part. In order for us to be this exterior real, it must come into us, and this comes about by means of sensory knowledge, our only contact with the exterior world.[59] But this contact is fragmentary and superficial; each sense reports only the exterior appearances of things; the intellect uses these appearances as so many routes to the inner depth, of the real, that is, to the comprehension of its nature.[60] From this nature grasped in its distinction from accidents, grasped as substance with respect to its accidents, the intellect passes to unified knowledge of this substance and its accidents; this is the function of judgment, which knows accidents as inherent in substance. But beyond this factual inherence, the intellect wants to perceive the *causal* links that explain the *why* of this inherence, and this is the object of reason and the term of its discursive activity.

Judicative knowledge gives rise to a whole list of why's in the soul. Why does the substance of things have extension? Why are things discontinuous? Why is there local motion and why all the qualitative and quantitative alterations that we observe in the real? Why are material beings measured by time and space? Why do they have distinctive qualities? Why do some beings have certain real relations, while others do not? Why are some beings active and others passive? Insofar as reason can grasp the causal links binding these substances to these different accidents, insofar as these accidents depend directly or indirectly on substances as matter and form, as the source and end of everything issuing from it—to that same measure is the philosophical knowledge of these mediate truths possible. If these causal links cannot be perceived, then philosophical knowledge must give way to scientific knowledge in the modern sense of the word, be it physics, chemistry, biology, psychology, and/or their appendages, the historical and geographical sciences. Since the constancy of the links discerned by these sciences depends upon observations of fact—on recurrences, on coexistences that are always factually interlinked, but not upon a genuine causal bond—the truth derived therefrom is probable and not certain in the philosophical meaning of this word.[61]

(b) *Causal order between beings.* Modern science has accustomed us to a statistical order that acts like a sort of exemplary cause to which individuals submit, not as a particular being, but as helping to constitute a number within a multitude.[62] The individual as such has no meaning or interest in an order of this kind for the very simple reason that science can exist only by virtue of a great number, and not through natures, for although *nature* exists in physical science, *natures* do not exist there.[63] In the happy phrase of F.H. Bradley, the private nature of natures—of this whole world of substances and secondary qualities—is only a fiction; science has a hell from which it returns to interpret the world, but the inhabitants of that hell are only shadows.[64] The philosopher does not consign the real to hell in order to explain it; that is, he does not convert it to shadows so that he may then number it and thus predict what will happen when he brings statistical laws into play. He is content to contemplate it in its existential and actual reality, as actually present to his mind. He does not try to impose an order upon the real for the purpose of subjugating it but tries rather to know an order that exists prior to his perception, serving as object for that perception and making it true.[65] The hypothetical order, discerned by modern science in matter-energy, is part of this unified whole that is the physical world, but the philosopher discerns many others. He is particularly interested in discerning the whole causal aspect found in living beings that take their nourishment from the physical world and thus use it on a different level. There is also all the reproduction of living things, this sort of vital reversibility that runs counter to entropy. There is the causality exerted by man upon the physical world, where he lives, and upon other humans, his traveling companions. There is the causality of the astral world upon the organization of human life, upon the order of the seasons, upon the fertility and infertility of living things. And even though the philosopher cannot grasp the *how* of this causality, he can grasp its origin and its finality. Finally, there is the origin and end of this universe and of the beings composing it, as well as of the activities they initiate. In all that, the philosopher can perceive the principle and give a causal explanation. This brings us to the realm of metaphysics, a world into which the philosophy of nature introduces reason, in order that it may discover therein the *why* for the contingency of its existence and its activity, as well as the meaning of this act of existing and the activities flowing from it. In that domain we perceive the *principle* of all things and, consequently, *order* in the best sense, the order to which all others are reduced more or less directly—because this *Principle* is God, and God is the beginning and end of all that was, is, and shall be.

Such, very briefly, is the causal order that we have offered as the object term of reasoning in philosophical knowledge as contrasted to scientific and mathematical knowledge.[66] This order does not exist for science; it cannot be found by experimental methods; it is not instrumentally verifiable but has its own methods of research and its own verification. We shall now study its methods of research.

Section II: Method of Research Used by Mediate Truth

Every search for truth that is not immediately knowable has its own methods. Mathematics has its own, the experimental sciences have theirs; and it is the same with philosophical science and wisdom. What typifies the mediate truth discovered by the philosopher is its *necessary* and *causal* character.[67] It must be seen in a causal order and in a necessary and proper causal order; otherwise, it is probable truth and depends not on philosophy but on dialectics, rhetoric, or poetry.[68] Its method of research must therefore satisfy these requirements for necessity and causal properties, which means that the evidence serving as starting point for the perception of mediate philosophical truth must not only disclose the conclusion but reveal it to be a proper and necessary effect of the evidence that was the starting point. In order thoroughly to know the nature of the philosophical method of discovering mediate truth, we must, before analyzing the methods of discovery properly so called, seek out the nature of starting-point evidence. Hence, there are two subdivisions in this section: *a*) the nature of evidential principles, and *b*) the method of discovery that starts from such evidence.

A. THE NATURE OF THE EVIDENTIAL PRINCIPLES OF MEDIATE TRUTH

The proper context for the discovery of mediate or "concluded" truths is one of evident and infallible knowledge. The question involved here is: How can truths, whose evidence is not immediately visible to the intellect, be infallibly known by the intellect by means of a sort of participation in evidence and in the necessity of the immediate truths that we possess by a natural legacy that compels our intellectual consent?[69] In order to participate in the evidence of these natural infallible truths, mediate truths must necessarily be caused in some way by this evidence. Since all participation implies causality,[70] mediate truths must therefore be rooted in immediate truths.

Reasoning is compared to understanding as movement to rest, or acquisition to possession. . . . And since movement always proceeds from something immovable . . . hence it is that human reasoning, *in the order of discovery and inquiry*, proceeds from certain truths absolutely understood, namely the first principles.[71]

In the texts in which he explains the relations that must exist between evidential principles and the truths concluded therefrom, St. Thomas seems to maintain that mediate truth must spring from *common* principles or primary evidence,[72] and, on the other hand, that it must necessarily proceed from *proper* principles, or lose its causal character.[73] At first sight, it seems difficult to reconcile these two apparently opposed requirements; therefore, we shall have to examine more closely the nature of these common or first principles in their relationship with proper and immediate principles.

First of all, we must note that proper as well as common principles must be immediately evident and known in themselves, since, by nature, "concluded" truths must have an immediately evident principle as their starting point.[74] But there are two kinds of immediately evident truths that are intuitively known by the human intellect.

For a thing to be immediately evident *in itself*, all that is needed is that the predicate pertain to the nature of the subject. For then the subject cannot be considered without it appearing that the predicate is contained in it. But for something to be immediately evident *with reference to us* we have to know the meaning of the subject in which the predicate is included. Hence it is that some things are immediately evident to everybody, as for instance, when propositions of this sort have subjects which are such that their meaning is evident to everybody, as every whole is greater than its parts. For everyone knows what a whole is and what a part is. Some things, however, are immediately evident only to those with trained minds, who know the meaning of the terms, whereas ardinary people do not know them. It is in this sense that Boethius says: There are two types of *common notions.* One is common to everybody; for example, if you take equal parts from things that are equal what is left of each of them is also equal. The other common notion is found only in the more educated; for example, that non-bodily things are not in a place. . . . For the thought of ordinary people is unable to go beyond imagination to reach the nature of incorporal things.[75]

Of these two categories of evidence, one of which belongs to every man and the other only to the learned, the second can and must provide the necessary proximate principles for the discovery of mediate truth, since it contains the immediate cause of properties flowing from the nature of things. The first category could, at most, serve as a remote or first principle for a causal demonstration,[76] with the exception of certain sapiential demonstrations in which universal evidence can be utilized by the philosopher in order to come to these conclusions.[77] But we might ask ourselves this question: What bond is there between common principles and proper principles which justifies the statement that all sciences, in the philosophical sense of the word, are derived from first principles or from evidence that is indefectibly admitted by all? This is the bond that exists between a first principle and a proximate or second principle, and it belongs not so much to the order of efficient causality as to that of exemplar causality. For secondary principles share in the efficacy of first principles as the imperfect participates in the perfect,[78] because all their intelligible value is derived from their measurement by primary evidence, especially by the principle that has priority over all others —the principle of noncontradiction.

In the first operation there is a first thing conceived by the intellect, namely, what I call being: and nothing can become intelligible in this operation except under the aspect of being. Furthermore, since the principle, "it is impossible to be and to not be at the same time," depends upon the grasping of being as such, just as the principle, "the whole is greater than the part," depends upon grasping the whole and the part, we must admit that the principle in question also is naturally *first* in the second operation of the intellect, that is, the operation which composes and divides. And no one can know *by means of this second operation* unless he has perceived this principle. For just as the whole and the parts can only be grasped if we have grasped being, so the principle, "the whole is greater than its parts," can likewise only be grasped if we have perceived the above mentioned principle, which is the most certain of all principles.[79]

The point of interest in the teaching set forth by the above text lies in the statement of the hierarchy of principles within universally recognized principles; for if it is by a sort of inclusion in the evidence of noncontradiction that all these evident principles are perceivable by the mind, it is with all the more reason that the proper principles of mediate philosophical truths contain this wholly primary evidence. This evidence will therefore be found at the origin of this discovery of mediate truth, but contracted, proportioned according to the anology or the mode of being it applies to, coassumed, and applied within a more restricted vision of the real.[80]

It is therefore true to say that the evidential principles which are the points of departure in the search for mediate truth are the first evidence infallibly accepted by the human mind, and that it is by and in the light of these infallible truths that reason succeeds in arriving at previously unknown truth. Thus, the infallibility of this new truth is but a participation in the infallibility of the evident principles with which the human intellect is naturally endowed. Since the object term of philosophical reasoning is the real order that exists between effects and causes, between its starting point and its goal, causal links must exist, the conclusion must spring from the premises that cause it and explain its content. Such must be the nature of the evidential principles of mediate truths in Thomistic epistemology.

B. THE METHOD OF DISCOVERING MEDIATE TRUTHS

Now that we know that the specifying term of philosophical reasoning is the causal order which links beings to each other and that its starting point is evidence which is immediate and necessary and which causes the truth conclusion,[81] we must briefly examine the method the mind uses to make this ensemble of mediate truths (germinally contained in truth principles) pass from the virtual to the actual, without any possibility of error, so that, at the end of its work, the intellect may possess an immanent universe perfectly arranged in a hierarchy modeled after the various causal relations concealed in the extraordinary diversity presented to the mind by the exterior world. What we must now study, therefore, is the problem of philosophical logic considered as the art of discovering nonevidential truth, quickly, easily, and without danger of error.[82]

Now, everyone knows the profound contempt in which Descartes and modern thinkers hold Scholastic logic; to them, it is formal, vicious, and does violence to the mind without giving it evidence. And what is worse, it is absolutely sterile as an instrument for discovering truth.[83] According to Descartes, the source of these capital sins of the Scholastic method is in its essentially synthetic character, which completely excludes analysis, by which fact the only method of discovering truth is excluded.[84] These statements made by the putative father of philosophic method are owing to his total ignorance of the texts of ancient philosophers as well as to his identification of the method of discovery proper to mathematical truth with that of philosophical truth.[85] In order to dispel these misunderstandings, and the unjust and gratuitous prejudices that contemporary minds have inherited from the father of modern epistemological method, we shall first of all establish the *existence* of a method of discovery by a brief historical excursion into the texts of Scholastic thinkers, then we shall see this method at work in the acquisition of the truths of science and wisdom.

¶ *1. The Existence of a Method of Discovery in Scholastic Texts.* It is interesting to note in the philosophical texts of the ancients how extremely aware they were of the importance of method, as much in the field of discovering new truths as in that of a control for these new truths. They even have technical expressions to designate these two moments in the knowledge of truth. The method of discovery is called *via inventionis, via inquisitionis, scientia inveniendi,* whereas the method of control is called *via seu scientia judicandi.* These expressions, whose meaning is very general, cover two processes whose use is constantly and perfectly defined: analysis and synthesis. We shall take a brief lexicographical look at these two words in the vocabulary of Aquinas and his predecessors, in order to perceive their exact meaning. This will make it easier for us to understand their continual use as methodological instruments.

(a) *The etymological meaning of analysis and synthesis.* The words *analysis* and *synthesis* are obviously only modern transcriptions of the two Greek words *analusis* and *sunthesis,* which Latin writers translated by two typically Latin terms that have no verbal analogy with their Greek equivalents but nevertheless render their meaning perfectly. The Latin word *solutio* (alone or with a prefix, *re-solutio*), translates *analusis,* while *compositio* is a faithful rendering of *sunthesis.*[86] We must center our study of Latin texts on the pair of terms, *compositio-resolutio,* in order to discover the philosophical meaning given by medieval thinkers to these terms, as well as the more or less extensive use they made of these two methodological processes in discovering new truths. Let us sound out the predecessors of St. Thomas so that we may be more familiar with the materials from which he drew to elaborate his philosophical method.

(b) *What* compositio-resolutio *meant to St. Thomas' predecessors.* The correlated terms, analysis-synthesis, as defining the philosophical method of inquiry and discovery, are first found in a commentary of the Neo-Platonic Chalcidius on the *Timaeus* of Plato. Chalcidius explains this method in dealing with the already old problem of the number and nature of the principles of reality.[87] *Analysis* consists in a movement of inquiry whose starting point is the least real, the least knowable, and is posterior in itself, but which is most knowable and prior for us, i.e., the sensible world. The terminal objective of this movement is the principle of material properties of this same sensible world, *silva,* or first matter. This notion of analysis corresponds to what the moderns call regressive deduction.[88] *Synthesis,* which follows analysis, makes use of the elements left aside by analysis, i.e., all the formal elements separated from matter. In using these elements, reason perceives that there is order among them and, since order implies harmony, that there is an intelligent principle of this order. Thus, it concludes upon the existence of a divine activity that organizes the world of change.[89] In reading Chalcidius, we might get the impression of taking part in one of those "long chains of thought" of which Descartes speaks, but with the difference that what Descartes calls analysis, Chalcidius calls synthesis, and vice versa.[90]

The translations and commentaries of Boethius upon Aristotle are the second source from which medieval thought drew its doctrine on analysis and synthesis. In his translation of Aristotle's work on logic, Boethius uses the word *resolutoria* as equivalent to *analutika*. Since analytics are the very method that philosophical knowledge uses in its own construction, he gives analytical process first place as an instrument for acquiring knowledge. To analytical process, which is *judicativa veritatis*, Boethius opposes dialectical or topical procedure, which is *inventiva veritatis*.[91] It proceeds by way of composition or synthesis. These are the expressions and this the use of the analysis-synthesis terminology that entered into Scholastic logic and gave it its framework and vocabulary.

By his translations of pseudo-Dionysius, Scotus Erigena added further to the medieval explanation and usage of the method of analysis and synthesis. Erigena extended their field of application and made their usage more supple. Two points are to be noted in his explanations of them: first of all, contrary to Chalcidius, analysis is no longer restricted to the field of material principles of reality but can lead to the attainment of God; secondly, analysis and synthesis constitute not only an epistemological methodology but express the metaphysics of the real, as is shown by the title of Erigena's major work, *On the Division* [i.e., analysis] *of Nature*.[92]

Albert the Great, St. Thomas' teacher, is probably Aquinas' most important source, for in this contemporary's works there is a very searching study of these two notions, a study in which are integrated statements of Chalcidius, Boethius, and Scotus Erigena. Albert the Great first uses the correlative terms *analysis-synthesis* to describe the intellectual act of apprehension. In this activity, synthesis consists in that knowledge of the singular through the universality of our concepts by which we grasp the formal elements of the thing; whereas analysis is the inverse process, consisting in the formation of the universal starting from the singular, a process whose result is a more-known *quoad se* and less-known *quoad nos*.[93] He makes use of these two notions to explain the method of philosophical knowledge.

He divides this method into two sections: a method of inquiry or discovery that he identifies with the *Topics* or dialectics, and a method or science of judging that he identifies with the *Analytics*. The first part of the latter method corresponds to the analysis of conclusions into their formal principles, whereas the second part seeks the ontological principles of these same conclusions.[94]

What have we learned about analysis and synthesis, now that we have made this inquiry into the notions that the ancients held about them?

First of all, we know that these notions are as old as philosophical method itself, since they are an essential part of logic. Of these two, analysis is more important in the order of definition and reasoning because it provides an intuition of essences and of the mediate truths discovered by synthesis, whereas the latter plays a preponderant role in the discovery of new truths.

Furthermore, we know that the process of analysis goes from the complex to the simple, from what is less in being and less knowable in itself to what is greater in being and more intelligible, from the effect to the cause, from the divisible to the indivisible; whereas the process of synthesis proceeds inversely, going from the simple to the complex, from the one to the many, from cause to effect.

Finally, we know that although analysis precedes synthesis in the order of discovery of new truths, synthesis is prior in the order of explanation, i.e., not only as a teaching procedure but especially as a method of explaining the real and our knowledge of the real.[95]

(c) Resolutio-compositio *in St. Thomas.* St. Thomas utilized all the discoveries made by his predecessors. But through his talent for using other discoveries to add new perspectives to Truths, perspectives whose only limits are those of the human intellect, he applied these notions to previously unforeseen fields. Here is a brief account of the different meanings these two words have according to their context.

Compositio and its equivalents: Composition or synthesis is union and not unity, and consequently it implies diversity.[96] By virtue of its nature, synthesis has very diverse characteristics, depending on whether the parts to be united are homogeneous or heterogeneous.

Thus, a heap of stones is unified by place, the materials in a house are unified by the idea of the architect, a mixture by its form, the elements of a number by the order existing between them.[97] There is a synthesis of essence and existing, of matter and form, of substance and accidents, of parts in a whole. Synthesis enters into explanations not only in the field of the exterior real but also in epistemology; it is to be found in the formation of a definition, of judgment, and of reasoning.[98]

Compositio is not the only word used to mean synthesis; we also find, in its place, *inventio, inquisitio, collatio rationis, deducere, ordo, ordinare.*[99] This group of words, constantly used in the works of St. Thomas, shows the importance of synthesis as an essential factor in his philosophical method.

Resolutio and its equivalents: At times St. Thomas gives a metaphorical meaning to resolution, but most frequently he uses it in a very definite technical sense. It accounts for the decomposition of mixtures into their elements and of these elements into matter and form. It also describes the return of effects to causes, of means to the end, of particular notions to first notions, of judgments to simple apprehensions, of conclusions to principles.[100] Like synthesis, analysis is thus adapted to the field of existing as well as to that of knowing. The word *resolutio* is not alone in expressing these notions; very often the following words are found in its stead: *reductio, examen, abstractio, inducere, via judicii et divisio.*[101] This diversity of vocabulary makes a lexicographical study longer and more difficult, but at the same time it shows the functional scope which analysis has in the philosophical constitution of our knowing.

Thus, analysis and synthesis are two antinomic processes used by the mind to derive from the real the secret of its nature and of the order resulting from the different bonds that beings establish between each other. Never could analysis be transformed into synthesis, or vice versa, for they are irreducibly opposed procedures, one of which is always the opposite of the other.[102] Now we shall study analysis and synthesis as philosophical processes by means of which our reason, using first truths as a sort of springboard, rises to the pursuit of new truths more distinct but less evident than the first, in order to get a concrete and unified grasp of being according to its mode of existing,[103] thus giving rise to new adequations between our intellect and the real, and, therefore, to the discovery of hitherto unperceived truths.[104] This will show us the dynamism of analysis and synthesis in this work of inquiry and discovery that reason sets up in order to bring a variety of nutritive and fortifying foods to the banquet of truth to which its nature issues an invitation with no possibility of refusal.

¶ *2. Analysis and Synthesis as Methods of Philosophical Knowledge.* Philosophical knowledge has always been, and will always be, a knowledge of things through their causes, both intrinsic and extrinsic.[105] Because these causes can be explanatory at a double depth of being—that of the accidents of real things taken as particular and diverse (accidents whose existence is habitually given us by the senses), and that of substances and of being, taken as such (grasped only by the intellect)—there is a double exploration of the real. The first is concerned with the immediate causes of phenomena perceived by the senses, or by their scientific extensions that are technical instruments. The second looks for remote or first causes that are primarily the constitutive elements from which each being results as such, and then their origin and unique end, i.e., their last principle in the order of efficiency and finality.

A truth which is known through another [i.e., a mediate truth] is understood by the intellect, not at once, but by means of the reason's inquiry, is the term of this inquiry. This may happen in two ways: First, it so happens that it is the last in some particular genus; secondly, it so happens that it is the ultimate term of human knowledge. And since things that are knowable later in relation to us are knowable first in their nature, hence it is that which is last with respect to all man's knowledge is that which is knowable first and chiefly in its nature. And about these truths is wisdom, which considers the highest causes. . . .

But in regard to that which is last in this or that genus of knowable truths, it is science that perfects the intellect.[106]

Therefore, philosophical knowledge is made up of two categories of mediate truths, and it is the task of analysis and synthesis to discover them. These truths are measured by being in the process of becoming as such, and their object is being as being. The truths of the first category belong to the field of the philosophy of nature, while the second truths belong to the realm of metaphysics or wisdom. Although the truths in these two fields differ in nature, the method used by reason to discover them is the same, since it is always a question of mediate truths to be perceived as the result of a rational effort of either analysis or synthesis. Consequently, in our study of this method we shall not be unduly concerned with the duality of its fields of operation. This duality affects the content of the discovered truths more than the way to discover them. For analysis as a process of discovery always starts from a truth that is more known to us and has as a term a truth more knowable in itself; whereas synthesis proceeds exactly to the contrary.

In every inquiry (*inquisitio*) one must begin from principle; and if this principle *precedes both in knowledge and in being*, the process is not by way of resolution, but rather *by way of composition;* for to proceed from cause to effect is to proceed in a composite way, since causes are more simple than effects. But if that which precedes in knowledge *is later in the order of being, the process is one of resolution,* as when our judgment deals with known effects, which we reduce to their simple causes.[107]

Starting from this rather laconic description of analysis and synthesis, we shall try to get a view of their true nature as instruments for discovering new truths that proceed from evidence already possessed. To facilitate our understanding of these two activities of our reason, we shall deal with them separately, starting with analysis and then proceeding to synthesis.

(a) *Analysis as a method of discovering mediate truth.* For St. Thomas, as for all his predecessors, the analytic method of discovering truth is characterized by the fact that its point of departure is better known to the seeker but less knowable in itself.[108] This distinction between what is more evident or known in relation *to us*, and what is more evident or perceptible *in itself*, is fundamental in St. Thomas. It is, in fact, bound up with the very nature of the procedure man uses to acquire knowledge, a process by which he enters into contact with sensibles before arriving at the intelligible. This is one of the characteristics of the rational method in the vocabulary of St. Thomas.

In a third way *a method is called rational* from the rational power, that is, inasmuch as in our procedure we follow the manner proper to the rational soul in knowing; and in this sense a rational method is proper to natural science. . . . First in this respect that just as the rational soul receives from sensible things which are *more known relatively to us*, knowledge of intelligible things which are *more known in their nature*, so natural science proceeds from what is more known relatively to us and less known in its own nature.[109]

Discovery by means of analysis is therefore coextensive with demonstration *quia* or *a posteriori*, i.e., it enters into every argumentation that starts from a sign and an effect in order to get back to the existence of what is signified and of the cause when the sign and effect are more known relatively to us than is the signified and the cause, whose intelligibility is greater in itself. This is the normal situation for the great majority of truths belonging to the field of natural philosophy.

Secondly, natural science uses a rational method in this respect: that it is characteristic of reason to move from one thing to another; and this method is observed particularly in natural science, where we go from the knowledge of one thing to the knowledge of another, for example, *from the knowledge of an effect to the knowledge of its cause.* Nevertheless the procedure in natural science is not to go simply from one thing to that which is other according to reason and not other in reality, as when we go from the concept of animal to the concept of man. . . . But in the case of natural science in which demonstration takes place through extrinsic causes, something is proved of one thing through another thing *entirely external to it* . . . and on this account natural science among all the others is most in conformity with the human intellect.[110]

This method of finding truth does not enter into play merely in the philosophy of nature; on it depends that whole part of metaphysis or wisdom which, starting from contingent and created realities, rises to the existence of necessary causes and especially of the first cause of all things: God as the creator and end of the universe. Thus all the proofs of the existence of God, and of the existence of His attributes, belong to the realm of thought that is the analytic method, because they have as their starting point something better known to us, and as their goal that which is more knowable in itself but less known to us.

Some things are knowable to us through themselves; and in bringing such things to light the speculative sciences use their definitions to demonstrate their properties, as happens in the sciences *which demonstrate propter quid*. There are other things which are not knowable to us through themselves but *through their effects*. And if indeed the effect is adequate to the cause, we take the quiddity itself of the effect as our starting point to prove that the cause exists and to investigate its quiddity, from which in turn its properties are made evident. But if the effect is not adequate to the cause, then we take the effect only as the starting point to prove the existence of the cause and some of its conditions, although the quiddity of the cause is always unknown. And this is what happens in the case of the separate substances.[111]

This passage is capital for the understanding of the analytic method in philosophical science. Every time the human intellect cannot grasp the substance of things intuitively, or therefore the cause of their properties, it must proceed analytically, i.e., from the effects to their cause. Now this situation is natural to the human intellect, as soon as we admit its dependence on the senses; for being unable to grasp the substance of things intuitively, it has to pass through the intermediation of their accidents to their definition.[112] This is what happens in the field of material natures whose accidents, being adequate to the substance that is their source and end, permit of a more or less precise grasp of the very essence of reality. But when it is a question of realities other than material substances, and particularly when it comes to the sole cause of everything that is, then no effect can bring us to perceive the essence of this cause, and the analytic method terminates in *quia est*, the simple fact that the cause exists.

Now we cannot know the quiddity of separate substances from what we receive from the sense, although by means of sensible things we can come to know of the existence of these substances and some of their conditions. So we cannot know *what* a separate substance is through any speculative science, although through them we can know of their existence and some of their conditions; for instance, that they are intellectual, incorruptible and the like.[113]

All natural theology or theodicy comes under the sign of analytic method, since it is concerned with the existence of God as efficient, exemplary, and final cause of all the created perfections whose nature our intellect can know, although it cannot use this knowledge to help it grasp the nature of Him who causes these perfections. This is what the Angelic Doctor calls *sapientia de altissimis, ad altissima,* as opposed to wisdom *ex altissimis* which starts from the understanding of things divine to explain creatures.[114] The distinction between *ratio superior* and *ratio inferior* has the same meaning in his teaching, because it designates two distinct functions of human reason, one of which starts from the creator to explain creatures, whereas the other uses creatures in order to understand divine things.

Now these two, namely eternal and temporal, are related to our knowledge in this way, that one of them is the means of knowing the other. For in the order of discovery (*via inventionis*), we come through temporal things to the knowledge of things eternal. . . . But in the order of judgment (*via judicii*), from eternal things already known, we judge of temporal things, and according to the laws of eternal things we order temporal things.[115]

All these demonstrations that deal with the eternal or divine as the term of natural inquiry are based on *analysis* and demonstration *quia.*

Demonstration can be made in two ways: one is through the cause and is called *propter quid,* and this is to argue from what is *prior absolutely.* The other is through the effect and is called a demonstration *quia;* this is to argue from what is *prior relatively only to us.* When an effect is better known to us than its cause, from the effect we proceed to the knowledge of the cause. And from every effect the *existence* of its proper cause can be demonstrated, so long as its effects are better known to us; because, since every effect depends upon its cause, if the effect exist, the cause must pre-exist. Hence the existence of God, in so far as it is not self-evident to us, can be demonstrated from those of His effects which are known to us.[116]

Thus, the law of evidence plays a role that is as essential in Thomistic method as it is in Cartesian method; for where there is no evidence, demonstration is impossible, since reason has no starting point in truth to use as a springboard from which to arrive at a

truth as yet unknown to it. But, unlike Descartes, St. Thomas admits
two kinds of evidence, which are sometimes antipodal to each other.
For him, in the analytic order of discovery, reason never uses
truth that is evident *in itself* as its starting point, but always truth
that is evident *to us*. But what is most evident to man, in explaining
the concrete real, is sensible evidence, because the intellect progressively discovers its natural object by starting from the sense, and it is
at the heart of material things that it seeks the being most immediately able to measure its judicative activity, or, rather, the first
truths by which it is nourished.[117] The starting point for the mind's
inquiries is therefore immediate evidence concerning the being that
is least intelligible in itself—material being—and concerning what is
least intelligible in material being—material accidents.[118] Thus,
analytic method is, in some way, a substitute for Cartesian deduction,
but instead of having its point of departure in evidence absolute in
itself, it starts from that which is evident relative to the human
intellect, i.e., in evidence where sensory knowledge plays a primary
role. This conforms to the general principles of Thomistic epistemology, for which human knowledge cannot be explained without
the continual interplay of all our cognitive sensory powers.[119] And
the term of this process is the discovery of a new truth, known not in
its nature but in its existence.[120]

(b) *Synthesis as a method of discovering mediate truth.*   Like
all discursive activity, of which it is an aspect,[121] synthesis requires,
as starting point for its movement, an evidential truth from which
it draws a hitherto unknown truth, not merely the successive consideration of two truths.

In our knowledge there is a twofold discursion. One is according to succession only, as when we have actually understood anything, we turn
ourselves to understand something else; while the second mode of discursion is according to causality, as when through principles we arrive
at knowledge of conclusions. . . . This second mode of discursion presupposes the first, for whosoever proceeds from principles to conclusions
does not consider both at once . . . because to advance thus is to proceed
from the known to the unknown. Hence it is manifest that when the
first is known, the second is still unknown; and thus the second is known
not in the first but from the first.[122]

What then is the typical aspect by which synthesis differs from analysis, since both are rational or discursive methods for acquiring knowledge of the existence of a new truth starting from an anterior truth that is its source? The distinctive aspect by which synthesis differs from analysis as an order of discovering mediate truth is the very nature of the evidence the former uses as principle and point of departure.

In every inquiry one must begin from some principle. And, if this principle *precedes both in knowledge and in being,* the process is not by way of analysis but by way of synthesis; for to proceed from cause to effect is to proceed in a synthetic way, since causes are more simple than effects.[123]

The comprehension of a really existing causal order is therefore at the beginning of the discovery of the existence of a new truth, for this truth is nothing but the measuring of our mind by the *ipsum esse* of a known effect as such.[124] Setting aside the domain of local movement, thus setting aside all that characterizes modern science, we have seen that there are twelve different modes of catalyzing the multiplicity of the real, that is, of linking up the diversity of things to their principle. These twelve modes are reducible to four categories of principles: those which explain the complexity of the nature and of the thing existing as such, i.e., matter and form on the one hand, essence and existence on the other; and those which account for becoming and the existing of real things in becoming, and these are the efficient, exemplar, and final causes.[125]

This being the case, in its march toward truth the synthetic method can take as its starting point one or the other of these causes whose evidence will be the source of a new and previously unknown truth.

Reason sometimes advances from one thing to that which is other in reality, as when the demonstration is through *external causes* . . . by synthesis indeed when we go from causes to effects, for causes are simpler than effects and exist more unchangeably and uniformly. . . . Sometimes, however, reason advances from one concept to that which is other according to reason, as when we proceed according to *intrinsic causes*; by synthesis indeed when we go from most universal forms to more particular ones.[126]

To the reader familiar with the Scholastic categories, the meaning of this doctrinally massive text is not ambiguous, for he knows that the relations of material, formal, efficient, exemplar, and final causality are realities belonging properly to our universe and that, by means of these relations of diverse causality, this universe escapes the hurly-burly of chance and is a perfectly unified complex of its parts, just as the complexity in a being derives its unity from intrinsic causal bonds. But to a mind trained in scientific methods, this text is not so clear, for in this context the notion of *cause* has lost all its metaphysical meaning to become synonymous with *succession: cause has become identified with law*.[127] Such a mind interprets merely mathematical classifications of physical laws in terms of explanation, of *why*, that is, in a vocabulary of causality.[128] In other words, the expression *causal order* has become ambiguous for contemporary minds because it is called upon to signify two completely opposite realities, either the *image* of the world that science constructs by its laws, or the ontological universe itself with the real relations that exist between its different parts, a universe that philosophy tries to understand and to explain by reference not to its mathematicized image but to its existential mode.[129] True, an attempt is being made to remove this ambiguity. Every scientific endeavor that ceases to be "legal" in order to become explanatory is branded as vicious and parasitic,[130] but the confusion between legality and causality continues in the modern mind and makes incomprehensible any philosophical explanation that eschews legality to dedicate itself exclusively to causality. Yet St. Thomas well understood the difference between the two when he said that no hypothetical statement could serve as starting point for genuine knowledge, that is, for knowledge of the causal order.[131] But he recognized the legitimacy of legality for describing phenomena whenever it unified them into a harmonious whole. He himself cites an instance of opposition between causality and legality, in the case of Greek astronomical theory:

Reasoning may be brought forward for anything in a twofold way: firstly, for the purpose of furnishing sufficient proof of some principle; as in natural science sufficient proof can be brought to show that the movement of the heavens is always of a uniform velocity. . . . Reasoning is employed in another way, not as furnishing sufficient proof of a principle but as showing how the remaining effects are in harmony with an already posited principle; as in astronomy the theory of eccentrics and epicycles is considered *as established because* thereby the sensible appearances of the heavenly movements can be explained; not however as if this proof were sufficient, since some other theory might explain them.[132]

Thus, we must have an extremely precise notion of what is meant by causality in philosophy, as opposed to scientific legality. The latter rests entirely upon the principle of identity, upon a sort of identifying reduction between the law and its phenomena, whereas philosophical causality rests upon the otherness and even the diversity between an effect and its cause. The difference between legality and causality is vividly brought out by comparing their respective relations with phenomena and with effects. Thus, while physical phenomena remain identical, laws change with the progress of science; disappearance or change in a cause, however, necessarily entails disappearance or change in the effect.[133] Furthermore, legality is an invention of the mind, it is an order set up by the mind to bring unity into phenomena, whereas causality is an order that the mind contemplates but does not make.[134] It is constitutive of the most inward structures of the universe, whose reality is to be participation, that is, a total gift of Him who is Being by essence and therefore Cause by essence.[135]

Consequently, when we speak of causal order in philosophy, we are at the very heart of the object of philosophy, i.e., of being in all its modes. What we call intrinsic causes are none other than that which defines reality as composite, whether this composition is that of a nature from matter and form or that of a being from essence and *esse*. It is the principle of identity, in the philosophical sense of this word,[136] that simultaneously governs the distinction between compositive elements and their unity as nature and as being. As for extrinsic causes, they link accidents to substances and substances to

each other in a hierarchy of perfection according to nature and
existing; ultimately they blend into an absolute unity, when absolute
efficiency, exemplarity, and finality meet in Him who is Being.
This is the depth of the real that must be sounded if we are to grasp
what St. Thomas means by causal order, and what he means when he
says that synthesis starts from the evidence of causes in order to
come to the evidence of effects.[137]

It could be objected that if the synthetic order of discovery works
at this depth of the real, there are few opportunities to use it, for
when do we know beings by their causes? The objection is valid,
for we must admit that demonstrations concerned with the proper
causes of singular beings are very few and far between. Science,
however, is not much better suited to know the singular scientifically,
for it exists only by virtue of statistical laws, and the singular as
such has for science neither value nor existence.[138] But the synthetic
order of discovery has absolute efficacy when it comes, for example,
to defining mobile being as such, and to linking up all the properties
of this reality in its mutability, its mobility, its temporality, and its
localization—as can be seen in the *Physics* of Aristotle. The same is
true for living being and the specific properties of the different
modes of life as such. Finally, in questions dealing with man and
being as being, demonstration can really be an extraordinary instrument for the discovery of the nature of man and the properties flowing from this nature.

The synthetic order of discovery is, in short, the inverse of the
process used to know natures. Whereas we know the latter by starting from accidents that lead us to natures by a sort of *reditus*,[139] in
demonstration there is a kind of *exitus* of accidents of which substances are causes, or an *exitus* of creatures of which God is the
Creator. Such is the second procedure for discovering mediate truth.
Like the first, it is a consequence of the weakness of our intellect
that becomes reason—knowledge by mode of movement—only because it is ill equipped by nature to fulfill its function as intellect or
intuitive power. More perfect than the first order of discovering
truth, the synthetic order, because of its very perfection, has a more
restricted use, since it is closer to the intellectual processes than is

the analytic order. For synthesis begins with an intuition of causes in order that it may intuit effects, whereas analysis goes from the existence of effects to that of causes. And this is why the synthetic order belongs rather to wisdom than to natural philosophy, as we shall see in the following section and in the conclusion of our treatise on epistemology.

Section III: Value Judgment upon Mediate Truth, or Assent to Conclusions

Analysis and synthesis, as instruments for discovering new or mediate truth, are instruments for the enrichment of the human intellect, since truth is its good and its perfection, just as error is its evil and its corruption.

The good of our understanding is the knowledge of truth. Accordingly, those habits by which the understanding is perfected for the knowledge of truth are called virtues . . . because they make the act of understanding good. Falsity, on the other hand, is not only lack of truth, but also a corruption of it. . . . Consequently, just as truth is the good of the understanding, so that which is false is its evil.[140]

But it is not enough to possess riches; we must assess their value, for some riches can be destroyed as easily as wood by fire. The market place of truth is like the stock exchange: it includes more and less secure values, and bankruptcy is always possible if stocks are bought without full knowledge of their soundness or security. All truths do not, in fact, possess the same guarantees of stability, for the true can be either contingent or necessary,[141] and only necessary truth is sufficiently well guaranteed to allow the intellect to rest in it as in an immutable good.

Since the act of our understanding is good because it considers the true, it must be impossible for a habit existing in the understanding to be a virtue unless it is such that, by it, one *infallibly speaks the truth*. For this reason, opinion is not an intellectual virtue, whereas scientific knowledge and understanding of principles are.[142]

Therefore, once mediate truth is discovered, it must be evaluated, so as to arrange the hierarchy of its value as a good and to ascertain that the intellect's new treasure is safe from the gnawing worm of contingence or fallibility. We know that in Thomism the act by which we judge the value and infallibility of truths already possessed is called assent.[143] We also know that the intellect is compelled to assent only when faced with an infallible truth so evident that it cannot reasonably be denied.[144] In immediate truths, evidence presents no difficulty because the link between subject and predicate is the object of intuition and requires no proof or witness.

Yet those things are said to be present to the understanding which do not exceed its capacity, so that the gaze of the understanding may be fixed on them. For a person *gives assent* to such things because of the witness of his own understanding and not because of somebody else's testimony.[145]

But, by definition, mediate truths are not of themselves evident to the intellect; their very lack of evidence constrains the intellect to that process of inquiry which aims to discover them.[146] The question therefore is: How can a truth, possessing no claim to the immediate evidence that alone forces assent, become the object of assent? This is the last aspect of the discourse on Thomistic method, which, after having set up two critical approaches for the discovery of mediate truths, brings in a third to evaluate these discovered truths by projecting upon them the light of first evidential principles. In so doing, it gives them a share in the intelligibility of these first principles and thereby a share in their compulsive power upon the mind. We shall now make a brief study of this last phase of Thomistic epistemology, first considering the vocabulary that indicates its existence in the works of Aquinas, and then describing the nature of this critical method of mediate truth.

A. THE VOCABULARY OF ASSENT TO MEDIATE TRUTHS

St. Thomas always characterizes the act of assent by its opposition to the activity that grasps or discovers truth. Although he uses many words to signify the perception of the existence of truth,[147] he always uses the same terms for the act of evaluating discovered truth, expressing its infallibility by reference to its nature. These terms are as follows: *judicare, dijudicare, via judicii, via judicandi.* Here are two important texts on this subject:

Now the reason is speculative and practical, and in both we find *apprehension* of truth, which pertains to its discovery, and *judgment* on the discovered truth. Accordingly, for the apprehension of truth, the speculative reason is perfected by understanding. . . . In order to judge rightly, furthermore, the speculative reason is perfected by wisdom.[148]

Human reasoning, in the order of discovery or inquiry, proceeds from certain things absolutely understood, namely first principles; and again, in the order of *judgment* (*via judicii*), it returns, by analysis, to first principles, in the light of which it examines what it has found.[149]

But this *via judicii*, which is opposed to the *via inventionis* studied above and which terminates in assent, includes particular procedures of the mind, which Aquinas expresses by the words *examinare, examinatio.*

Similarly the movement of reason would not reach anything certain unless there were an *examination* of that which it came upon through discursive movement of the mind. This examination proceeds to first principles, the point to which reason pursues its analysis. . . .[150]

We do find a circle in the knowledge of the soul. . . . The circularity is observed in this, that reason reaches conclusions from principles by way of discovery, and *by way of judgment examines the conclusions* which have been found, analyzing them back to principles. . . .[151]

All speculative knowledge is derived from some most certain knowledge concerning which there can be no error. This is the knowledge of first general principles, *in reference to which* everything else which is known is *examined*, and *by reason of which* every truth is approved and every falsehood rejected.[152]

There is, finally, another term in this lexicography whose importance is the greater because it indicates the nature of this act by which the mind examines the mediate truths discerned by reason. This term is *resolutio, resolvendo,* which we meet again here, no longer in a context of the discovery of truths, but as the process of

evaluation used by the human mind to sift its harvest of truths and
to separate the pure wheat of necessary truth from the straw of
contingent and mutable truth. Now it remains for us to examine the
functioning of this evaluation of mediate truths that is analysis in
the order of judgment or assent.

B. ANALYSIS AS A MEANS OF ASSENT TO MEDIATE TRUTHS

To judge is not a property of reason through which it can be distinguished from understanding; for understanding, too, judges that this
is true and that false. But judgment is referred to reason and comprehension to understanding to this extent: that in us *judgment commonly
takes place through analysis (per resolutionem) into principles,* whereas
direct comprehension of truth takes place through understanding.[153]

We must not forget that this last chapter in our epistemology is
concerned with infallible knowledge of mediate truth, the only truth
whose infallibility is called into question, since it alone is produced
by the human reason, first or immediate truths being the spontaneous
fruit of the very nature of our mind.[154] Now, how can we know
that the result of long and delicate workings of reason contains truth
whose necessity is such that its negation would entail the negation of
first truths? For this is the result we must achieve if the value of
mediate truth is to be indisputable; the evidence of mediate truth
must be experienced by the mind, must be present to it with the
same cogency as that of first truths.

The whole certainty of scientific knowledge arises from the certainty of
principles. For conclusions are known with certainty when they are
reduced (resolvuntur) to principles. Therefore, that something is known
with certainty is due to the light of reason divinely implanted within us,
by which God speaks within us. . . . Nevertheless we would never attain
the certainty of scientific knowledge . . . unless there were within us the
certainty of the principles to which the conclusions are *reduced.*[155]

The role of analysis in the critique of the truth of conclusions
consists therefore in making the evidence of the conclusion to be

present to the intellect, by showing that this conclusion is essentially a participation in first evidence, a sort of attenuated luminosity of this same evidence.

Whatever things we know with scientific knowledge properly so called, we know by reducing them to first principles which are *naturally present* to the understanding. In this way, all scientific knowledge *terminates in the sight of a thing which is present.*[156]

How does analysis realize this kind of identification between the evidence of mediate truth and that of first principles? In other words, what is this activity of reduction or resolution to first principles? To understand its full epistemological value, as well as its essentially critical function, we must recall the definition of this activity of the mind as described in the preceding section. What characterizes it as a discursive movement is that it has as starting point the complex, the least being, the least knowable, the effect, the sign, and as goal the simple, the most being, the most knowable, the cause, the signified.[157] Every time the mind is confronted by a mediate or concluded truth, this latter is inevitably a particularized truth, for each science possesses a particular domain that is the object of its inquiry. Since its own proper principles are particularizations of first evidences,[158] its conclusions are necessarily still more determined than are their proper principles and, *a fortiori*, than first principles or evidences. This being so, who does not see that the typical task of analytical discourse is to reduce this particular evidence, which is an effect, a least knowable, a complex, to evidence that, on the contrary, has the most absolute simplicity, knowability, and causality, each and every one of which possesses the evidence of a principle, especially the evidence of noncontradiction?[159]

To avoid long explanations about this process of reduction of mediate truth to the evidence of first principles, a reduction that compels intellectual assent, we shall illustrate this process of identification by a simplified example that will show more clearly than pages of explanation how every concluded truth can be thoroughly criticized and how, by means of this criticism, the mind can be compelled to adhere to a conclusion under pressure of its only absolute good, infallible truth as such. Let us consider the following demonstration:

> Everything spiritual is immortal. (Major.)
> But the human soul is spiritual. (Minor.)
> Therefore the human soul is immortal. (Conclusion.)

The major is an absolute, although not a common, principle, for it presupposes the notion of spirituality that only metaphysical knowledge can provide. The minor is evident only after long and painful inquiry and reflection on the different activities of man, as St. Thomas admits, and as he himself shows in his treatises on man and the soul.[160] Once the evidence of the major and minor is seen, the conclusion necessarily flows therefrom, and we have a mediate truth. Can this mediate truth force the assent of the intellect? No, as long as it is not made present to the mind with the very evidence of first principles, which alone are cogent. Therefore, this particular truth must, by process of analysis, be identified with primary evidence, and then only will the mind judge this truth, i.e., give it its assent. Let us try to effect this identification by analyzing the notions included in the conclusion. There are two, the soul and immortality.

¶ *1. The Soul.* We define it in the minor as a spiritual substance, and we accept this definition since the inquiry preceding it was exhaustive and eliminated all possibility of error. To be spiritual is not to have matter, to be immaterial, and not to be material is the same as not having any quantity, for quantity is a consequence of matter. But everything that is not quantity is indivisible for divisibility presupposes the existence of parts, and the existence of parts implies the existence of quantity and, therefore, of matter. Thus, being immaterial is identical with being indivisible, and to define the soul as immaterial is to define it as an indivisible absolute.

¶ *2. Immortality.* What is immortality? It is the absence of mortality, and mortality is the separability of a body and its vivifying principle. In order that a living thing be mortal, it must be composed of two principles, and of two separable principles. Thus, the concept of mortality implies, from its very notion, the idea of divisibility, and death implies not only divisibility but division in fact. If therefore, a being is divisible but never divided, he will be mortal but will not die. But if a being is indivisible because he is simple or because he completely lacks compositive parts, then he not only will not die but will be immortal *by right*. Immortality *de jure* implies indivisibility of the living being, so that to say of a being that he is immortal, or to say that he is indivisible, is to say the same thing.

Let us reconsider our conclusion now, in replacing the original terms by their synonyms; let us replace the soul by absolute indivisibility and immortality by indivisibility, and we have the following: *The indivisible* (the soul) *is indivisible* (immortal). As anyone can see, this statement is nothing but a statement of the principle of identity, a sort of application of the primary evidence: being is being. Thus, by this analytical process, we have identified a particular conclusion with primary evidence; we have reduced mediate truth to an immediate truth possessing the same characteristics of simplicity, greater knowability, and causality that are possessed by the principle of identity. Just as assent is compelled by the evidence of the principle of identity, so also can it not resist this reduction of the conclusion to the principle of identity; the mind is compelled to adhere to the conclusion that the soul is immortal.

Also, were anyone to deny this evidence verbally, his denial could be reduced to the absurd by reducing the conclusion to the principle of noncontradiction: If the indivisible is not the indivisible, being is not being, therefore being is nonbeing, and if being is nonbeing, the principle of noncontradiction is false, which reduces the intellect to the realm of the absurd.

This example establishes the meaning of the *resolutio* of conclusions to principles and at the same time shows us that, for St. Thomas, to know does not consist in lining up arguments one after the other and producing conclusions. These conclusions must show their identification papers as necessary and infallible truth, and only on this condition do they enter into the realm of truths forming the imperishable treasure that our intellect seeks and whose possession constitutes our human happiness.

All science puts the intellect in possession of its good, for all truth is a good for the intellect. But not every science enriches the human soul with its *best good*, for only that which brings it to *first truth* can do that.[161]

Therefore, mediate truth must, somehow bathe in the light of first truth,[162] in order to possess this value as beatifying perfection which it has only as intellectual end. But it cannot bathe in this evidence of first truth unless, by a movement of return, it rejoins that of which it is only a participation; for the sapiential vision of being as such is the source of all discursive activity productive of truth, and also is its last measure, since it is by being confronted with this vision that every conclusion receives its letters of credit or has its unauthenticity unmasked.

In reference to the first general principles, everything else which is known is examined, every truth is *approved*, and every falsehood is *rejected*.[163]

There are two reasons that first truths have this function of testing, in relation to all other truths: first, because they are *natural* and, consequently, participate in the infallibility of the intellect considered as nature, i.e., as direct effect of divine wisdom.[164] Furthermore, these first truths have themselves been judged by wisdom, for it belongs to the latter to define the notions that make up first principles, because wisdom has ultimate causes as its domain, that is, all things divine, God and His proper effects.

Now to know the definition of being and non-being, of whole and part and of other things consequent to being, which are the terms of which indemonstrable principles are constituted, *is the function of wisdom*, since universal being is the proper effect of the highest cause, which is God. And so wisdom makes use of indemonstrable principles, which are the object of understanding, not only by drawing conclusions from them, as other sciences do, but also by *passing its judgments* on them, and by vindicating them against those who deny them.[165]

Now, in analyzing first principles, we have judged them[166]; we have shown the absolute necessity of the intellectual act in its adherence to truth.[167] Furthermore, we have just seen that the whole structure of

discursive thought and, particularly, the whole dynamism of philosophical science depend upon this sapiential vision of first principles,
which are their starting point and their end. This means that, in
Thomism, the whole epistemological edifice is the work of wisdom,
not science, and that to wish to construct a discourse on Thomistic
method by taking science as point of departure is to try to justify
intellect by reason, the end by the means, the cause by the effect
which amounts to seeking an absurd criterion by absurd means.

Therefore, we believe it right and opportune to conclude this
treatise on Thomistic epistemology by underlining its essentially
sapiential character, for by this character it stands in contrast to all
modern epistemologies, both idealist and realist. Thanks to this character, the thought of St. Thomas has been able to achieve the mighty
synthesis that surmounts both time and space, towering above science
and its evolution, to remain as presently true in the twentieth century
as it was at the moment of its creation.

CONCLUSION

The reader sufficiently courageous to follow our epistemological explanations to this conclusion is probably divided between two contrary impressions: one, that he has been witnessing an authentic exploration of St. Thomas' gnosiological theory; and the other, very different, that he has found nothing here that remotely resembles a treatise in critical philosophy as the subject has been conceived since Descartes and Kant. To understand the reason for the ambiguity that beclouds the notion of Critique and to divest it forever of the scientific mask behind which the putative fathers of philosophical method have hidden it—a mask that for three centuries has hidden the true face of Critique—we must paraphrase the Gospel maxim and, "give to science what belongs to science, and to wisdom what belongs to wisdom." Such justice has not been rendered since the fourteenth century.

During three centuries, from the fourteenth to the seventeenth, so-called wisdom denied science its liberty of method and autonomy of movement in the field of experimentation and mathematization of experimental facts. Since the seventeenth century it is philosophy that has been imprisoned by the mortal chains of scientific method. And just as philosophy gained nothing from persecuting science and its methods, so science has won nothing by its tyranny over philosophic thought. All humanity has suffered from this paralysis of the philosophic impulse, induced by repeated injections and massive doses of alleged scientific vaccine against error.

This treatise on epistemology has attempted merely to put the evangelical maxim into practice, and to distinguish the orders of knowledge so as to give philosophy what rightfully belongs to it:

its proper methods and its proper objects. Now, only the sapiential part of philosophy has this self-critical power, a power that it can exert over the other aspects of human knowledge.

But wisdom has something proper to itself above the other sciences, inasmuch as it *judges* of them all, not only as to their conclusions, but also as to their first principles. . . . So both understanding and science depend on wisdom . . . for it contains beneath itself both understanding and science, adjudging both the conclusions of sciences and their principles.[1]

Since philosophical epistemology has no purpose other than to explain and justify its own typical knowledge—knowledge of its possession of things through the ultimate causes that explain this immanent possession—it evidently cannot ask either Aristotelian science or *a fortiori* modern sicence to determine its method and objects. Only a wisdom whose proper object is precisely the final causes of all things, as well as the final causes of knowledge, since the latter is a reality possessing its own ontological value—only a wisdom has sufficiently broad vision simultaneously to explain the reality of knowing and of the real thing that is the object of knowledge. Therefore, by way of conclusion, we would like to underline the sapiential character of St. Thomas' epistemology, taking as basis the diverse methods that according to him, characterize the different aspects presented by human knowledge to the reflecting mind. A brief commentary on an essentially methodological text will terminate this work, which has, up to this point, been a long commentary on the epistemological thought and texts of Aquinas.

To the methodology of speculative sciences St. Thomas has devoted a whole question, divided into three sections: one on natural science, one on abstract science, that is, mathematics, and one on divine science or wisdom.[2] In the first article of this question he draws a comparison between these three types of knowing by emphasizing the characteristic method of each. Here is the question as he states it:

Must we proceed according to the mode of reason *(rationalibiliter)* in natural science, according to the mode of learning in mathematics, and according to the mode of intellect in divine science?[3]

To this threefold question there are three answers, each of which in substance contains all that is both common and contrary to the methodology of each of these modes of knowing. We shall comment briefly on the first two answers and linger a bit longer over the third, which with utmost clarity reveals the laws governing the structure of philosophical epistemology and its sapiential character.

A. THE RATIONAL CHARACTER OF THE METHOD USED IN NATURAL SCIENCE

St. Thomas begins by distinguishing three meanings of the word *rational* as applied to method:

The first meaning is identified with logic, which should be expected for logic, as its name implies, is identical with the rational. The word *ratio* translates the Greek word *logos*, from which logic draws its name. Logic moreover, is defined as *philosophia rationalis*.[4] Interpreted in this logical context, rational method cannot characterize natural science for that would run counter to its very nature as a particular science.

But this method of proceeding cannot belong properly to any particular science, which will fall into error unless it proceeds from its own proper principles.[5]

In its second meaning the word *rational* applies to dialectical method or probable reasoning, as an instrument of research directed to the discovery of truth but failing to discover it for lack of causal evidence.

Sometimes, however, the investigation of reason cannot arrive at the ultimate end, but stops in the investigation itself, that is to say, when two possible solutions still remain open to the investigator. And this happens when we proceed by means of probable arguments which are suited to produce opinion or belief but not science. In this sense, rational method is distinguished from demonstrative method. And we can proceed *rationally* in all the sciences this way, preparing the way for necessary proofs by probable arguments.[6]

In this context of dialectical argumentation, rational method cannot be characteristic of natural science since it is common to all the demonstrative sciences. In fact, this method is characteristic of experimental science in the modern sense of the word, in which hypothesis or law plays the same role in the explanation of phenomena that cause plays in philosophy.

Reasoning is employed in another way, not as furnishing a sufficient proof of a principle but, a principle being posited, as showing how harmoniously the effects follow this principle. As in astronomy the theory of eccentric and epicycles is considered *as established*, because thereby the sensible appearances of the heavenly movements can be explained; not however, as if this proof were sufficient, since some other theory might explain them.[7]

Finally, in its third sense the word *rational* describes the method proper to the philosophy of nature, because this aspect of our knowing corresponds to the very structure of the human mind, which is defined as reason and not as intellect or understanding. Now, what characterizes reason, as contrasted to understanding, is that it cannot intuit the substance of things without first grasping this substance's accidents and, secondly, that its primary object is something more knowable *to us* which leads it to something more knowable *in itself.* Thus, reason knows by mode of movement, by passing from what is more known to what is less knowable. That, actually, is the exact procedure of natural philosophy, whose proofs start from effects, from signs that are more knowable to us but less intelligible in themselves, in order to grasp causes of greater intelligibility, since they explain the existence and nature of effects and signs. In so doing, the philosophy of nature proceeds by mode of movement, which is typically rational, for physical proof does not travel from one concept to another, but from a real effect to a real cause, therefore, from one reality to another.

Natural science uses a rational method in this respect, that it is characteristic of reason to move from one thing to another . . . for example, from the knowledge of an effect to knowledge of its cause. Nevertheless the procedure . . . is not to go simply from one thing to that which is other according to reason and not other in reality. . . . But . . . demonstration takes place through extrinsic causes; something is proved from one thing through another thing *entirely external to it*. So the method of reason is particularly observed in natural science . . . and it is especially characteristic of it.[8]

Also, just as our mind is reason because it depends on sensory knowledge both to receive its proper object and to contemplate it, since it has to return to the senses as to its principle, so must the philosophy of nature terminate in the senses because the senses are the control on the accidents of material substance.[9] Such is the nature of the methodology to be used by the philosophy of nature, according to St. Thomas.

B. THE DISCIPLINARY CHARACTER OF MATHEMATICAL METHOD

In order to understand the exact meaning of the word *disciplinabiliter* and its technical character, we would have to go back to the beginnings of Christian speculation among the Fathers of the Church and observe the transformation that this word underwent at the hands of medieval thinkers.[10] For our purposes, however, it is enough to note that in the language of St. Thomas and his contemporaries, this term designates the most direct and surest method of acquiring absolutely certain knowledge. It possesses this clarity and this certainty because its object is less complex than that of the philosophy of nature and more intelligible for us than that of wisdom or metaphysics. St. Thomas adopts Ptolemy's statement as his own: "Mathematics alone will give the inquirer firm and unshaken certitude, namely, demonstrations carried out with unquestionable methods."[11]

Coming from St. Thomas, this praise of mathematical method might seem strange, for he seems to be talking like the mathematician Descartes, whereas nothing in his works justifies the high esteem he bestows upon this method in comparing it with the respective methods of natural philosophy and of wisdom. We might therefore ask ourselves this question: If mathematical method has such evidence and leads to such certitude, why did St. Thomas not use it to construct a "Discourse on Method" that would teach men how best to use reason in the sciences? First of all, for Aquinas, the method of each science is dictated by the object of this science; and, secondly, mathematical method is also drawn from reason as such, with this difference, that its data come from the imagination and that its term is also the imagination and not sense.[12] Now, neither the object of a *rational* science in the strict sense of the word *rational* nor consequently its method can explain being as such or knowing as such. For it is the intellectual or intuitive character of the human mind that accounts for reason and not reason that is the source of the intellect, whose weakness and deformity it reveals.

The *certitude* of reason comes from the intellect, but the *necessity* for reason is a defect of the intellect. For beings in whom intellect possesses its full strength do not need reason but grasp truth in a simple glance, as do God and the angels.[18]

Since everything certain, therefore everything perfect,[14] in rational demonstration—whether in natural philosophy or in mathematics—originates in the intellect and not in reason, and since the need for reason springs from a deficiency of intellect, we must ask the intellectual aspect of our knowing power to construct a method of knowledge, for the perfect explains the imperfect, and not vice versa. In order for a method to satisfy the requirements of our knowing power and to justify its defects, i.e., justify its need for recourse to reason and reason's method of inquiry, this method must be *intellectual* and not *rational;* that is, it must be the fruit of wisdom and not of a science. And that is the third problem Aquinas deals with in his brief treatise on the methodology of human knowledge.

C. THE INTELLECTUAL CHARACTER OF THE SAPIENTIAL METHOD

Since the distinction between science and wisdom is the characteristic note of Thomistic epistemology, being the reason for its power

as well as the cause of numerous misunderstandings and misinter-
pretations during the centuries—since this is true, the inner opposition that constitutes the pair of terms, *intellectus-ratio,* must be carefully pinpointed.

Reason is related to understanding as to its source and its term. It is
related to it as to its source because the human mind could not move
from one thing to another unless the movement started from some simple
perception of truth, and this perception is understanding of principles.
Similarly, the movement of reason would not reach anything certain
unless there were an examination of that which it came upon through
discursive movement of the mind. This examination proceeds to first
principles, the point to which reason pursues its analysis. As a result, we
find that understanding is the source of reasoning in the process of
discovery and its term in that of judging.[15]

Hence, St. Thomas describes science as *rationalis consideratio,*
whereas he calls wisdom *intellectualis consideratio.* Should we therefore conclude that wisdom is the source and term of all scientific
knowledge? If so, what becomes of the chronological order of our
acquisition of knowledge, which starts from what is best known to
us and proceeds to what is most knowable in itself, therefore, which
goes from the philosophy of nature to wisdom, and not the reverse?

In the beginning, the sensible effects from which the demonstrations of
natural science proceed are more evident to us. But when, through them,
we know the first causes, from these latter there will become evident
to us the reason for the effects on which the proof of the demonstration
of the fact *(quia)* rest. In this way natural science contributes something
to divine science and nevertheless *it is divine science which explains its
principles.* That is why Boethius places divine science last, because it is
last relatively to us.[16]

To understand this reasoning, which at first seems contradictory,
we must call to mind the two ways in which science proceeds: the
one that consists in discovering the truth, and the one by which truth
that has been discovered is judged.[17] Only the second phase is scientific knowledge in its perfect state, because it gives perfect truth to
the intellect.

In the *acquisition* of knowledge, principles and elements are not always
first; for sometimes from sensible effects we arrive at the knowledge of

principles and intelligible causes. But in *perfect knowledge*, the knowledge of effects always depends on the knowledge of principles and elements.[18]

This then is the context of *perfect knowledge* or knowledge by final causes in which St. Thomas' argumentation must be understood when he makes science depend on wisdom, i.e., *rationalis consideratio* on *consideratio intellectualis*, as on its source and term; for it is wisdom that judges the principles of science, and wisdom, too, that judges the conclusions of these same sciences. Here is the way Aquinas describes the intellectual method of wisdom:

Just as we attribute a rational method to natural philosophy because it adheres most closely to the method of reason, so we attribute an *intellectual method* to divine science because it adheres most closely to the method of intellect. Now reason differs from intellect as multitude from unity. For it is distinctive of reason to disperse itself in the consideration of many things and then to gather one simple truth from them. . . . Conversely, intellect first contemplates a truth, one and undivided, and that truth comprehends a whole multitude. . . . Now in its process of analysis (*via resolutionis*), the whole consideration of reason *in all the sciences terminates* in the consideration of divine science. For, as we have said, reason sometimes advances from one thing to that which is other in reality, as when the demonstration is through external causes or effects. . . . Consequently the ultimate end of analysis in this life is when we arrive at the highest and most simple causes which are the separate substances. Sometimes, however, reason advances from one concept to that which is other according to reason, as when we proceed according to intrinsic principles. . . . Now what is most universal is common to all beings; and so the ultimate end of analysis in this life is the consideration of being and the properties of being as being. And these are what divine science considers, namely the separate substances and what is common to all beings. It is clear therefore that its consideration is supremely intellectual.
It also follows from this that divine science gives *all the other sciences* their principles, inasmuch as intellectual consideration is the starting point of rational consideration; and for this reason it is called *first philosophy*.[19]

Thus, wisdom is the perfection of the human mind which, having the natural desire to know and to know through ultimate causes, can only satisfy this desire by acquiring a wisdom that gives the human intellect possession of ultimate intrinsic causes, that is, essence and existence, and of ultimate extrinsic causes—God as creator and as final term of every being and every activity of beings. But, as we have seen, the perfection of our mind lies in its participation in divine intelligence, therefore, in the simplicity of divine intuition that is supreme wisdom, because it is knowledge of all things through contemplation of supreme being. In its own way, the human mind imitates divine knowledge insofar as it needs *rationalis consideratio* to fill the gaps that the weakness of the intellect as such cannot fill. Human wisdom has this peculiarity, that it is a synthesis of *intellectus* and *ratio*, that is simultaneously possesses the essential perfection of the intellect and the relative perfection of rational activity; thus, wisdom holds a privileged place in the hierarchy of the human ways of knowing, because it contains them all through its power of judging the principles and conclusions of the sciences as well as its own objects.[20] Therefore, it comes naturally within its function to assign to each type of philosophical knowledge its proper method. To ask that it beg of the subjects it rules, not by election but by nature, both permission to govern its kingdom and information about the structure of this government, is nonsense and demagoguery. Yet, this is the absurd regime that Descartes and Kant imposed on philosophy when, in the name of the clarity and certitude of mathematical or physical sciences, they conceived a *rational* method of knowledge to which philosophy must submit or risk extinction. They were not aware that this forced submission of philosophical thought to scientific procedure was itself an abdication and negated every possibility for metaphysics to exist as such. And the conclusion Kant came to did not justify his critique but made it manifestly clear that when reason tries to be the basis of wisdom, wisdom is inevitably doomed to destruction and death.

This is the conclusion to which we must come after having studied the problem of human knowledge through both history and philosophical reflection. The first part of our treatise sought the ultimate causes of the successive failures suffered by the critical problem during the three last centuries; the conclusion of this historical study was that the problem had been incorrectly stated at the start, precisely because science had assumed the responsibility of stating and solving it within the framework of scientific or rational reflection. Knowing the cause of these failures, we tried to state and solve the epistemological problem in the name of wisdom, by means of a sapiential, an intellectual, not a rational, method. This enabled us to define knowledge by its proper causes of immanence and objectivity[21] without rejecting the least bit of objective reality, or discarding even the smallest of our cognitive activities. Having defined the nature of knowledge in terms of its constitutive principles, we were able to examine the specific accidents flowing from this nature, and we discovered, first, the existence of truth and the nature of the act that gives it birth.[22] Then we discovered the different modes of truth and their opposition to error, as well as the natural and spontaneous character of the act that contemplates truth as the perfection for which our intellect is made.[23] There remained a last problem, that of rational truth, i.e., the truth which escapes the intellect because of its native imperfection and which the intellect must seek in order to discover and evaluate its goodness and necessity. This study, too, was conducted in the light of the causes of this rational process, both that which gives it birth and that which judges its perfection. In both cases we found that the true cause was the intellect: the intellect as *habitus* of first principles giving rise to the rational process, and the intellect in its sapiential state being the supreme judge of rational procedures and the truths it gathers along the way.[24] Such is the atmosphere of an epistemological treatise according to Aquinas, and such are the progressive phases in a study of human knowledge and its properties.

Here and there in his works, St. Thomas likes to repeat that stability is the work of wisdom and is its sign, restating what Aristotle had said in a humorous vein: "We do not look upon the happy [wise] man as a kind of chameleon."[25] A discourse on method is not better because it is up-to-date, or because it evolves with the latest advances of contemporary science, for then it does resemble a chameleon—as the history of the past three centuries has amply proved. Epistemology receives its stability from being the product

of a sapiential vision of man and the universe, a vision that includes
science but of which science cannot even suspect the existence, for
Wisdom has Itself defined Its dwelling place: "I dwell in the highest
places, and my throne is in a pillar of a cloud."[26] Such was and such
remains the epistemology of St. Thomas. May he help us to understand it and to make it understood to those who have taken science
as their guide. For if the blind be led by the blind, they will both
fall into the pit. And in the realm of wisdom, science is blind.

NOTES TO THE TEXT

NOTES TO THE TEXT

Foreword

[1] M. Baldwin, *Dictionary of Philosophy and Psychology* (New York, Scribners, 1901), I, pp. 333, 414.
[2] G. Van Riet, *L'Epistémologie thomiste* (Louvain, Institut Supérieur, 1946), pp. 634–639.

Part One: Prologue

[1] Aristotle, *Politics*, I, 2; 1252a24.
[2] Cf. L.M. Régis, *St. Thomas and Epistemology*, Aquinas Lecture, 1946 (Milwaukee, Marquette U. Press, 1946), p. 61, note 2.
[3] Cf. A Lalande, *Vocabulaire technique de la philosophie* (Paris, Alcan, 1947), II, pp. 596–602, where we find L. Brunschvicg's definition of metaphysics in terms of epistemology.

Chapter I

[1] Sir Arthur Eddington, *New Pathways in Science* (New York, Macmillan; Cambridge, University Press, 1935), pp. 1–2.
[2] J. Dewey, *Logic: The Theory of Inquiry* (New York, Scribners, 1938), p. 68: "The separation and opposition of scientific subject-matter to that of common sense, when it is taken to be final, generates those controversial problems that still dog the course of Philosophy." Cf. Eddington, *New Pathways*, pp. 1–10; E. Meyerson, *Essais* (Paris, Alcan, 1932), pp. 24, 54, 60–61, 68; H. Bergson, *L'Evolution créatrice* (Paris, Alcan, 1932), p. 352.
[3] A. Rivaud, *Le problème du devenir* (Paris, Alcan, 1906), pp. 5–49.
[4] J. Burnet, *Early Greek Philosophy* (London, Macmillan, 1920), Chap. IV.
[5] E. Gilson, *God and Philosophy* (New Haven, Yale U. Press, 1941), pp. 1–37. Cf. V. Monod, *Dieu dans l'univers* (Paris, Fischbaker, 1933), pp. 26–78.

[6] E. Gilson, *Reason and Revelation in the Middle Ages* (New York, Scribners, 1938); *La philosophie au moyen âge* (Paris, Payot, 1944), pp. 125–138, 201–222, 413–502.

[7] Monod, *Dieu dans l'univers*, Chap. IV onward. Gilson, *God and Philosophy*, Chap. II onward.

[8] Sir James Jeans, *Physics and Philosophy* (Cambridge, University Press, 1942), pp. 105–125. Eddington, *The Philosophy of Physical Science* (New York, Macmillan; Cambridge, University Press, 1949), p. 47; *New Pathways*, pp. 74–75. P.S. Laplace, *Essai philosophique sur les probabilités* (Paris, Gauthier, 1921).

[9] Eddington, *New Pathways*, pp. 81–82, also Chap. V. Cf. G. Bachelard, *Le nouvel esprit scientifique* (Paris, Alcan, 1937), Chap. VI.

[10] Since the birth of contemporary science, there have been more volumes published on the subject matter of epistemology than in the preceding two hundred years. This proves that when there is no opposition between knowledges there is no problem. For bibliography on contemporary problems of science, see Bachelard, *La formation de l'esprit scientifique* (Paris, Presses Universitaires, 1938), *Essai sur la connaissance appliquée* (Paris, Vrin, 1928), *Le rationalisme appliqué* (Paris, Presses Universitaires, 1949); H. Weyl, *Philosophy of Mathematics and Natural Science* (Princeton, Princeton U. Press, 1949); A. D'Abro, *The Evolution of Scientific Thought* (New York, Dover Publications, 1949); F. Gonseth, *Les mathématiques et la réalité* (Paris, Alcan, 1936); E. Meyerson, *Le cheminement de la pensée* (Paris, Alcan, 1931); also the previously cited works of Jeans and Eddington.

[11] Cf. 155 D.

[12] *Metaph.* A, 2; 982b12–18, 983a12.

[13] *In 1 Metaph.*, lect. 3, nn. 54–56, 66–67; *In II Metaph.*, lect. 1, nn. 274–288; *Summa Theologiae*, I–II, 3, 8, c.; 32, 7, c.

[14] Cf. *Traité des passions de l'âme*, Part I, art. 53 (ed. Adam-Tannery, 12 vols., Paris, Cerf, 1897–1910, hereinafter cited as A-T, XI, p. 373, lines 5–17); *Meditationes*, III (A-T, IX, p. 45). See also Francis Bacon, *De Augmentis scientiarum* (London, Montagu, 1929), VIII, p. 81.

[15] G. Jugnet, *La structure des nouvelles théories physiques* (Paris, Alcan, 1933), p. 105. A statement that completely confirms the importance of wonder for the study of nature can be found in Bachelard, *Le rationalisme appliqué*, p. 24: "Thus God is a schoolmaster who likes to cause wonder (*étonner*) in his pupil. He keeps a reserve of wonders (*merveilles*) in order to confound a presumptuous student." See also F. Nietzsche, *Le gai savoir* (Paris, N.R.F., 1949), p. 59.

[16] O. Bloch, *Dictionnaire étymologique de la langue française* (Paris, Presses Universitaires, 1932), I, p. 275.

[17] Note that Descartes does not identify admiration and wonder; the latter is a kind of paralysis of the soul. Cf. *Les passions de l'âme*, Part I, art. 73 (A-T, XI, pp. 383–384).

[18] Ernout et Meillet, *Dictionnaire étymologique de la langue latine* (Paris, Klincksieck, 1939), p. 335.

[19] Aristotle, Metaph., A, 2; 982b18. St. Thomas, *De Potentia*, VI, 2, c.; *S.T.*, I, 105, 7, c. Descartes, *Météores*, Disc. VII (A-T, IV, pp. 312, 366); *Les passions de l'âme*, Part II, art. 53 (A-T, XI, p. 374).

[20] Gilson, *La philosophie au moyen âge*, pp. 561–565; *Dante et la Philosophie* (Paris, Vrin, 1939), pp. 316–325. See also F. Van Steenberghen, *Siger de Brabant* (Louvain, Institut Supérieur, 1942), II, pp. 375, 688.

[21] For Descartes, admiration is a passion of the order of knowledge, not emotivity; that is why admiration is prior to good and evil. *Les passions de l'âme*, Part I, art. 53–56 (A-T, XI, pp. 374–375). Although the same idea seems to be taught by Aquinas (cf. *S.T.*, III, 15, 8; *Summa contra Gentiles*, IV, 3) this interpretation is superficial and must be understood in the context of these two references, in which St. Thomas compares the sensibility of the brutes with that of humans. This will be seen in the texts of the next note.

[22] Cf. *S.T.*, I–II, 23, and following. Descartes does not admit any kind of division in the soul and consequently does not divide the passions into two groups. Cf. *Les passions de l'âme*, Part I, art. 68 (A-T, XI, p. 377).

[23] Cf. *In III Sent.*, 26, 1, 3, sol.; *De Veritate*, XXVI, 6, ad 6; *S.T.*, I–II, 41, 4, c.; II–II, 19, 7, c.

[24] Cf. *S.T.*, I–II, 41, 4, ad 5; 45, 4, ad 3; III, 180, 3, ad 3.

[25] Cf. *S.T.*, I–II, 27, 2; 76, 2.

[26] Cf. *S.T.*, I–II, 40, 4, c.; ad 3; 46, 1–8.

[27] Cf. *S.T.*, I–II, 42, 2, c.; 41, 4, ad 5.

[28] Cf. above, pp. 12–13 and notes 11 to 15.

[29] See above, p. 12.

[30] Rivaud, *Le problème du devenir*, pp. 108–140. Burnet, *Early Greek Philosophy*.

[31] For the doctrinal position of Léon Brunschvicg, see *La modalité du jugement* (Paris, Alcan, 1897). See also a long and objective study by Roger Vernaux in *Revue de philosophie*, XLI (1934), pp. 73–104, 176–210, 283–294, and a critique of Brunschvicg's position by Guérard des Lauriers in *Revue des sciences philosophiques et théologiques*, XXIV (1935), pp. 407–433; XXV (1936), pp. 76–103, 269–298.

[32] J.I. Beare, *Greek Theories of Elementary Cognition* (London, Oxford U. Press, 1906). Rivaud, *Le problème du devenir*, p. 127.

[33] The affirmation of the void and the atom by the atomists was the basis of their explanation of unity and multiplicity. Cf. Burnet, *Early Greek Philosophy*, Chap. IX; Rivaud, *Le problème du devenir*, pp. 144–178.

[34] Cf. *Cratylus*, 439C–440B; *Phaedo*, 65A–66D; *Republic*, 524 ff.; *Theaetetus*, 171D–201; *Parmenides*, 128A–135C; *Sophist*, 237B–257. See the study on this subject by A. Diès, *Autour de Platon* (Paris, Flammarion, 1930), pp. 107–154.

[35] The doctrine of unity and multiplicity is a key notion in Aristotelianism; the distinction of matter and form, substance and accidents, cause and effect, act and potency, is based on that doctrine. Cf. J. Owens, *The Doctrine of Being in the Aristotelian Metaphysics* (Toronto, Pontifical Institute, 1950), Chaps. I, II, V, VII.

[36] Modern scientists use it; thus, in French *choc* and *obstacle* denote a psychological necessity for the progress of science and for its evolution. Cf. Bachelard, *Le rationalisme appliqué*, p. 15; Brunschvicg, *La modalité du jugement*, pp. 102–103; Guérard des Lauriers, in RSPT, XXV (1936), pp. 100–103.

[37] Cf. Jeans, *Physics and Philosophy*, p. 16; Eddington, *New Pathways*, "Epilogue," p. 318.

[38] "Pure unity, which is the *raison d'être*, the principle of intelligible judgment, does not imply necessity imposed on it as an external bond, for this unity it not a law of the mind, it is the mind itself." Brunschvicg, *La modalité du jugement*, p. 106.

[39] G. Barbarin, *La géométrie non-euclidienne* (Paris, Alcan, 1935), pp. 7–9. E. Meyerson, *Le cheminement de la pensée*, II, sects. 285–289.

[40] Bachelard, *Le nouvel esprit scientifique*, p. 24.

[41] Cf. below, Chap. II, pp. 33–39; and Gilson, *The Unity of Philosophical Experience* (New York, Scribners, 1937), pp. 126–130.

[42] Cf. above, pp. 12–13.

[43] E. Boisacq, *Dictionnaire étymologique de la langue grecque* (Paris, Klincksieck, 1923), p. 737.

[44] F. Ast, *Lexicon Platonicum* (Leipzig, Weidmann, 1855), I, pp. 251–252; II, p. 4.

[45] *Metaph.*, A, 2; 982a15–17.

[46] *Metaph.*, a, 1; 993b8–10.

[47] *Metaph.*, B, 1; 995a23–25.

[48] Cf. Owens, *The Doctrine of Being*, pp. 113–146; P. Farrell, "The Portals of Doubt," *The Thomist*, VIII (1945), pp. 326–331.

[49] Ernout et Meillet, *Dictionnaire étymologique de la langue latine*, pp. 285, 290.

[50] *In III Sent.*, 26, 2, 4, ad 5; 17, 4, sol.; *S.T.*, III, 18, 4, ad 2; *De Potentia*, XXIV, 3, c.

[51] *In I Metaph.*, lect. 2, nn. 54–56, 66–67; *In II Metaph.*, lect. 1, nn. 274–288.

[52] Ast, *Lexicon Platonicum*, I, p. 253; II, p. 4.

[53] H. Bonitz, *Index aristotelicus* (Berlin, Reimer, 1870), pp. 309a69–b5, 85a16–39.

[54] For the relations between ignorance and wonder, see notes 50–52 above.

[55] Cf. above, pp. 13–14.

[56] J. Owens, *The Doctrine of Being*, pp. 115–116.

[57] Cf. below, pp. 82–89.

[58] This would be the Cartesian position, in which the will is the principle of judgment because it is a free act. Cf. E. Gilson, *Discours de la méthode, Texte et commentaire* (Paris, Vrin, 1928), pp. 171, 285–286.

[59] *Metaph.*, a, 1; 993a8–11.

[60] *Topics*, VI, 6; 145a37–b2; 145b17–20. Cf also Bonitz, *Index aristotelicus*, p. 85a50–55.

[61] *In III Sent.*, 17, 1, 4, sol.; *S.T.*, II-II, 1, 4, c. Cf. L. Schütz, *Thomas-Lexikon* (Paderborn, Schöningh, 1895), p. 261.

[62] The study of the relations among wonder, doubt, and ignorance will be found above, pp. 13–17, 23–28.

[63] See the analysis of wonder in the following texts of Aquinas: *In II Sent.*, 18, 1, 3, sol.; *De Potentia*, VI, 2, c.; *S.T.*, I, 105, 7; I–II, 3, 8, c.; II–II, 180, 3, ad 3.

[64] This word *ratio* possesses a technical meaning that can be seen in the texts printed in Schütz, *Thomas-Lexikon*, pp. 686–688.

[65] *Medium* and *sufficiens* are also technical terms in the vocabulary of Aquinas. Cf. Schütz, *Thomas-Lexikon*, p. 476; also M.D. Chenu, in *RSPT*, XXII (1933), pp. 250–259.

[66] *In III Sent.*, 17, 4, sol., and ad 2. *In III Sent.*, 26, 1, 3, sol.; 23, 2, 1, ad 6.

[67] *In I Post. Analyt.*, lect. 6, n. 7; *In IV Metaph.*, lect. 3, n. 567; lect. 4, n. 578; *In VII Metaph.*, lect. 6, n. 1405; *In lib. De sensu et sensato*, lect. 19, n. 292; *S.T.*, I, 14, 8, c.; *In lib. De divinis nominibus*, Chap. 1, lect. 1.

[68] *C.G.*, III, 39, *Amplius*.

[69] Eddington, *New Pathways*, "Epilogue," pp. 310–311.

[70] *S.T.*, I–II, qq. 2–3.

Chapter II

[1] Cf. above, Chap. I, pp. 27–31.

[2] For a historical sketch of this period see Gilson, *The Unity of Philosophical Experience*, pp. 102–121.

[3] Cf. Gilson, *Discours de la méthode*, pp. 137–139.

[4] Cf. Descartes, *Responsiones*, IIa (A-T, VII, p. 130, lines 17–29), IIIa (A-T, VII, p. 171, line 20, to p. 172, line 10).

[5] *Discours de la méthode*, (A-T, VI, p. 29:10), Gilson's *Commentary*, pp. 269, 291.

[6] Gilson, *Discours de la méthode*, pp. 180–196, 295–297, 354.

[7] *Ibid.*, pp. 217–219, 222, 272. Cf. Descartes, *Regulae*, I (A-T, X, p. 360, lines 3–15); *Principes* (A-T, IX, p. 14, lines 23–31).

[8] Gilson, *Discours de la méthode*, pp. 136–139, 201–202, 215–216.

[9] Cf. Régis, *St. Thomas and Epistemology*, p. 64, notes 9–10.

[10] Cf. Gilson, *Discours de la méthode*, pp. 135, 165, 167.

[11] *Ibid.*, pp. 134, 379–383. Régis, *St. Thomas and Epistemology*, pp. 64–65, notes 7–16.

[12] Cf. above, Chap. I, pp. 7–8, 11–12.

[13] Cf. Gilson, *Discours de la méthode*, pp. 373–384, 152, 157–160, 180, 201–202, 217, 219, 222, 272.

[14] Cf. L.W. Keeler, *The Problem of Error from Plato to Kant* (Rome, Gregorianium, 1950), Chap. VII.

[15] *Critique of Pure Reason*, "Preface to First Ed.," p. 8. (All references are to the edition by Norman Kemp Smith, London, Macmillan, 1902.)

[16] *Ibid.*, p. 8.

[17] *Ibid.* ("Preface to Second Ed."), p. 21.

[18] *Ibid.*, p. 22.

[19] *Ibid.*, p. 17.

[20] *Critique of Pure Reason*, "Introd. VI," p. 56.

[21] Cf. A. Koyré, *Descartes und die Scholastik* (Bonn, Hanfstein, 1923), pp. 44-48.

[22] Cf. above, pp. 11-31.

[23] Cf. above, pp. 16-18.

[24] Gilson, *Discours de la méthode*, pp. 159-160, 165-167, 249-250, 327.

[25] *Ibid.*, pp. 83-89, 177-178, 140.

[26] *Ibid.*, pp. 165-167, 176-178, 302-304. St. Thomas knows the meaning of prejudice. See *C.G.*, I, 11, *Praedicta;* III, 38, *Felicis.*

[27] Gilson, *Discours de la méthode*, pp. 176-178, 165-167, 61-67.

[28] *Ibid.*, pp. 170-171, 285-286.

[29] *Ibid.*, pp. 285-292.

[30] *Ibid.*, pp. 201-202, 292.

[31] *Ibid.*, pp. 295-297, 354.

[32] *Ibid.*, pp. 86, 166, 301, 307, where Descartes expresses his distrust of the word *soul.*

[33] *Ibid.*, pp. 86-89, 165-167, 302-304.

[34] *Lettre à X, août 1647*, (A-T, III, p. 423, line 11, to p. 424, line 18).

[35] *Regulae*, I (A-T, X, p. 360, lines 7-10). For the theory of innate ideas, see Gilson, *Discours de la méthode*, pp. 249-250, 327.

[36] *Principia philosophiae*, Pars Prima, sect. 71 (A-T, VIII, p. 35, lines 5-36). Cf. also Gilson, *Discours de la méthode*, p. 167.

[37] *Recherche de la vérité* (A-T, X, p. 507, line 2, to p. 509, line 9).

[38] Cf. above, pp. 33-39.

[39] This is the subtitle of Descartes' *Discourse on Method.*

[40] Cf. above, pp. 42-43.

[41] Cf. *Au P. Vattier* (A-T, I, p. 559, line 13, to p. 560, line 6).

[42] *Discours de la méthode* (A-T, VI, p. 1).

[43] Cf. *Principes* (A-T, IX, p. 12, lines 18-27).

[44] Cf. above, notes 8-9.

[45] Gilson, *Discours de la méthode*, pp. 157-160, 217, 219, 222, 272.

[46] *Ibid.*, pp. 180-196, 201-202. Cf. Régis, *St. Thomas and Epistemology,* note 19.

[47] *Ibid.*, pp. 136-139, 201-202, 215-216, 295-297.

[48] Cf. above, pp. 36-38.

[49] *Critique of Pure Reason*, "Preface to Second Ed.," p. 21.

[50] *Ibid.*, p. 22.

[51] *Ibid.*, p. 20.

[52] *Critique of Pure Reason*, "Preface to First Ed., p. 9. See also "Appendix to the Transcendental Dialectic," Sect. I.

[53] *Critique of Pure Reason*, "Introd. VI," pp. 55-58; "Transcendental Dialectic," pp. 152-155, 228-283.

[54] *Critique of Pure Reason*, pp. 56-57.

[55] *Ibid.*, "Transcendental Doctrine of Method," pp. 606-607.

[56] St. Thomas, *In II Post. Analyt.*, lect. 1-6.

[57] *Critique of Pure Reason,* "Introd.," pp. 61–62.

[58] *Critique of Pure Reason,* "Transcendental Doctrine of Elements," p. 93.

[59] *Critique of Pure Reason,* "Transcendental Dialectic," Bk. II, Chaps. I and III, especially pp. 270–275; Bk. I, Chap. II, pp. 161–162; "Preface to Second Ed.," pp. 27–28.

[60] *Critique of Pure Reason,* "Transcendental Aesthetic," Sect. I, pp. 65–67.

[61] *Critique of Pure Reason,* "Transcendental Ideas," Sect. I.

[62] *Ibid.*

[63] *Critique of Pure Reason,* "Transcendental Aesthetic," Sect. I, 2–3; Sect. II, 4–8.

[64] *Critique of Pure Reason,* "Transcendental Ideas," Sect. I.

[65] *Critique of Pure Reason,* "Transcendental Aesthetic," Sect. I, 1.

[66] *Ibid.,* Sect. I, 2, p. 68.

[67] For the definition of object as such, see *Critique of Pure Reason,* "Transcendental Dialectic," Bk. II, Chap. III, Appendix II, pp. 549–570.

[68] *Ibid.,* Bk. I, Chap. III, Appendix I; "Transcendental Aesthetic," Sect. I, 2–3; Sect. II, 4–8, pp. 82–91.

[69] Cf. above, note 58.

[70] *Critique of Pure Reason,* p. 270.

[71] The definition of this word may be found in *Critique of Pure Reason,* "Transcendental Dialectic," Bk. I, Sect. I.

[72] *Critique of Pure Reason,* "Transcendental Deduction," Sect. II, p. 130.

[73] *Ibid.,* Sect. II, n. 17.

[74] *Ibid.,* Sect. II, nn. 20–21.

[75] Cf. Régis, *St. Thomas and Epistemology,* note 27.

[76] See above, pp. 49–50.

[77] The distinction between *to think* and *to know* is elaborated at length in the following texts: *Critique of Pure Reason,* pp. 27–28, 161–162, 257–275, 606–607.

[78] *Ibid.,* "Transcendental Doctrine of Judgment," Chap. III.

[79] *Critique of Pure Reason,* "Transcendental Aesthetic," n. 8, 4.

[80] *Critique of Pure Reason,* "Introd.," n. 2.

[81] The whole content of the "Transcendental Dialectic" (*Critique of Pure Reason,* pp. 297–572) is nothing but a very careful analysis of this transcendental illusion which is metaphysics. For the meaning of the word *dialectic,* see *Critique of Pure Reason,* pp. 97–100; Régis, *St. Thomas and Epistemology,* note 29.

[82] *Critique of Pure Reason,* p. 570.

[83] Cf. above, pp. 33–39.

[84] Cf. above, p. 32.

[85] Cf. Eddington, *New Pathways,* pp. 12–13; Jeans, *Physics and Philosophy,* pp. 11, 13; B. Russell, *The Analysis of Matter* (New York, Macmillan, 1927), pp. 161–163; Meyerson, *Le cheminement de la pensée,* III, p. 823.

[86] Newton's work, *Philosophiae naturalis principia mathematicae* (published in 1687), has been the gospel of scientists for more than two hundred years. The title is very significant: who would, nowadays, entitle a book of science

the *Philosophy of Nature?* Newton was convinced that mathematical principles rule the whole of nature.

[87] Laplace, *Essai philosophique sur les probabilités.* (Paris, Gauthier-Villars, 1921), p. 87.

[88] Cf. Barbarin, *La géométrie non-euclidienne;* Jugnet, *La structure des nouvelles théories physiques.*

[89] Cf. Eddington, *The Philosophy of Physical Science,* pp. 172–175; Jeans, *Physics and Philosophy,* pp. 55–60.

[90] General bibliography on this problem has been given above, Chap. I, note 10.

[91] Cf. above, pp. 7–12.

[92] Cf. above, pp. 33–39.

[93] Jeans, *Physics and Philosophy,* pp. 142–143. Cf. also Eddington, *The Nature of the Physical World* (London, Cambridge U. Press, 1929), p. 194; Meyerson, *Le cheminement de la pensée,* III, pp. 759–764, notes 33–41. See also Eddington, *New Pathways,* Chap. V.

[94] Jeans, *Physics and Philosophy,* pp. 143–147.

[95] Eddington, *The Philosophy of Physical Science,* pp. 1–3. Cf. also Jeans, *Physics and Philosophy,* pp. 14–15; Bachelard, *Le nouvel esprit scientifique,* pp. 4–11; *Essai d'une connaissance approchée* (Paris, Alcan, 1923), pp. 272–282.

[96] Jeans, *Physics and Philosophy,* pp. 80–81.

[97] Bachelard, *Le nouvel esprit scientifique,* p. 5. Cf. also Boutry, *La vérité scientifique* (Paris, Alcan, 1908), p. 7; Guérard des Lauriers, *L'Activité du jugement,* in *RSPT,* XXIV (1935), pp. 407–433; XXV (1936), pp. 76–103, 269–298.

[98] Cf. above, pp. 39–40, 51–53.

[99] Descartes, *Le Monde* (A-T, XI, p. 47, lines 4–22). Cf. above, note 25. See also Kant, *Critique of Pure Reason,* p. 93 (cf. above, notes 58–75) and "Transcendental Analytic," pp. 125–141, 233–238.

[100] Jeans, *Physics and Philosophy,* pp. 183–190. Eddington, *New Pathways,* Chap. VI; Bachelard, *Essai,* pp. 224–225.

[101] Bachelard, *Le nouvel esprit scientifique,* pp. 141–142; *Le rationalisme appliqué,* pp. 31–32. Meyerson, *Le cheminement dela pensée,* II, pp. 427–428: *La foi agissante du mathématicien.*

[102] Guérard des Lauriers, *L'Activité du jugement,* in *RSPT,* XXIV (1935), pp. 423–424. Cf. Meyerson, *Le cheminement de la pensée,* II, p. 298; III, p. 865; Gilson, *Discours de la méthode,* pp. 318–323, 373–374.

[103] Descartes, *Le Monde* (A-T, XI, p. 47, lines 4–22). Cf. Kant, *Critique of Pure Reason,* p. 125; Meyerson, *Le cheminement de la pensée,* II, p. 577.

[104] Jeans, *Physics and Philosophy,* pp. 141–143, 168–171, 215. Eddington, *Philosophy of Physical Science,* pp. 29, 35, 90, 99. *New Pathways,* Chap. V. Bachelard, *Essai,* pp. 272–275; *Le nouvel esprit scientifique,* pp. 134–179.

[105] Cf. Eddington, *New Pathways,* Chap. V; *The Philosophy of Physical Science,* pp. 35, 29, 90–98. Meyerson, *Le cheminement de la pensée,* III, p. 768, note 49.

[106] Cf. Jeans, *Physics and Philosophy,* pp. 141–143; Bachelard, *Essai,* pp. 243–293; Eddington, *New Pathways,* Chap. V.

[107] Jeans, *Physics and Philosophy*, pp. 143-147. Bachelard, *Le rationalisme appliqué*, p. 33.

[108] Eddington, *New Pathways*, pp. 76, 78, 81.

[109] *Ibid.*

[110] *Ibid.*

[111] Jeans, *Physics and Philosophy*, p. 179.

[112] *Ibid.*, p. 178. Cf. also Eddington, *New Pathways*, Chap. VI, sect. 6.

[113] Cf. Eddington, *The Philosophy of Physical Science*, pp. 29-48; Jeans, *Physics and Philosophy*, pp. 9-12.

[114] Jeans, *Physics and Philosophy*, pp. 42-44, 183-190. Eddington, *New Pathways*, Chap. VI, 6. Bachelard, *Le nouvel esprit scientifique*, pp. 41-58; *Le rationalisme appliqué*, p. 36.

Chapter III

[1] Georges Van Riet, *L'Epistémologie thomiste* (Louivain, Institut Supérieur, 1946). The purpose of this work is to analyze neo-thomistic treatments of the problem of knowledge during the past one hundred years. It reveals much of the confusion associated with this problem. For the roots of this confusion, see the end of the present chapter, below, pp. 104-108.

[2] This is Etienne Gilson's rejoinder to Léon Brunschvicg's accusation that his epistemological position was borrowed from the Scholastics. See *Le réalisme méthodique* (Paris, Téqui, 1934), p. 101.

[3] Van Riet, *L'Epistémologie thomiste*, pp. 3-32. Cf. Régis, *La critique néo-thomiste est-elle thomiste?* in *Etudes et Recherches, Philosophie* (Ottawa, Université d'Ottawa, 1938), II, 120-138.

[4] Gilson, *The Unity of Philosophical Experience*, pp. 198-220.

[5] *Ibid.*, pp. 236-247.

[6] Léon Noël, *Notes d'épistémologie thomiste* (Louvain, Inst. Sup. de Philos., 1925), p. 23.

[7] M.D. Roland-Gosselin, *Essai d'une critique de la connaissance*, in *Bibliothèque Thomiste*, Le Saulchoir-Paris, Vrin, 1932), XVII, p. 12.

[8] Léon Noël, *Le réalisme immédiat* (Louvain, Inst. Sup. de. Philos., 1938), pp. 23-24.

[9] Cf. above, pp. 7-8.

[10] Cf. above, pp. 11-21.

[11] Cf. above, pp. 74-75.

[12] J. Maritain, *Les degrés du savoir* (Paris, Desclée de Brouwer, 1932), translated as *The Degrees of Knowledge* by B. Wall and M. Adamson (New York, Scribners, 1938). Cf. E. Gilson, *Réalisme thomiste et critique de la connaissance* (Paris, Vrin, 1939).

[13] H. Gouhier, *Introduction à la théorie thomiste de la connaissance*, in *Revue des cours et conférences*, XXXIII (1931-1932), Première série, pp. 481-493, 648-653, 707-713; Deuxième série, pp. 29-32, 248-263.

14 Cf. Van Riet, *L'Epistémologie thomiste*, pp. 645-647; Régis, *La critique néothomiste*, pp. 135-139.

15 Van Riet, *L'Epistémologie thomiste*, pp. 349-375, 495-520.

16 Roland-Gosselin's position cannot be compared with the other positions; he died before completing his work.

17 Cf. above, pp. 77-78.

18 *Le réalisme immédiat*, p. 28; see also pp. 45-46, 102.

19 *Notes d'épistémologie thomiste*, p. 23.

20 *Ibid.*, pp. 98, 101, 180, 271, 273, 281.

21 *Le réalisme immédiat*, pp. 90, 260, 270.

22 *Ibid.*, pp. 108, 151, 167; *Notes d'épistémologie thomiste*, p. 22.

23 *Le réalisme immédiat*, pp. 262, 270, 283.

24 *Ibid.*, pp. 144, 166, 170-171, 261, 273.

25 *Ibid.*, pp. 164-165, 283.

26 F. Van Steenberghen, *Epistémologie* (Louvain, Inst. Sup. de Philos., 1948), translated as *Epistemology* by J.W. Flynn (New York, Wagner, 1949).

27 Cf. *Principia philosophiae*, I, 39 (A-T, VIII, p. 19, line 25, to p. 20, line 5); Gilson, *Discours de la méthode*, pp. 170-171.

28 Cf. Gilson, *Discours de la méthode*, pp. 199-200, 237-238.

29 *Ibid.*, pp. 286-287, 295-297.

30 *Ibid.*, pp. 198-199.

31 Cf. above, pp. 41-45.

32 Cf. Gilson, *Discours de la méthode*, pp. 177-178, 287.

33 *Ibid.*, pp. 170-196.

34 Cf. above, pp. 29-31.

35 St. Thomas, *De Veritate*, XXII, 5, ad 3. Cf. Régis, *La critique néothomiste*, p. 164.

36 Cf. below, pp. 140-144, 225-248, on the interrelations of sensibility and intelligence.

37 *S.T.*, I, qq. 89-90.

38 Cf. Gilson, *Réalisme thomiste*, pp. 50-60.

39 Cf. above, Chap. I, notes 50-51.

40 Cf. Régis, *La critique néothomiste*, p. 165.

41 *C.G.*, I, 5, *Alia autem utilitas.*

42 Cf. Gilson, *Discours de la méthode*, pp. 137-139, 197.

43 Cf. above, pp. 42-45.

44 Cf. Gilson, *Discours de la méthode*, pp. 170-171, 284-297.

45 *Ibid.*, pp. 285-286.

46 *Ibid.*, pp. 286-287.

47 Cf. Descartes, *Discours de la méthode* (A-T, I, p. 31, line 27, to p. 32, line 16).

48 Noël, *Le réalisme immédiat*, pp. 114-117, 139-140, 145, 163-164, 167, 291.

49 *In III Metaph.*, lect. 1, nn. 343-344.

50 Cf. Régis, *La critique néothomiste*, p. 166, notes 5-7.

[51] *In II Metaph.*, lect. 1, n. 273; lect. 2, n. 274.

[52] *In II Metaph.*, lect. 2, n. 294.

[53] *In III Metaph.*, lect. 1, n. 338.

[54] Cf. above, pp. 26–30.

[55] Cf. above, Chap. III, note 47.

[56] Cf. below, pp. 126–137.

[57] *In I Post. Analyt.*, lect. 21, 22, 26.

[58] *In IV Phys.*, lect. 1, n. 4; *S.T.*, I, 1, 8, c.

[59] *In III Metaph.*, lect. 1, n. 343.

[60] Cf. Gilson, *Discours de la méthode*, pp. 137–139, 170–178, 197, 284–287, 290–292.

[61] Noël, *Le réalisme immédiat*, pp. 87, 135.

[62] Cf. Gilson, *Discours de la méthode*, pp. 177–178.

[63] *Ibid.*, pp. 285–286.

[64] Cf. above, pp. 39–47.

[65] Cf. below, Chap. X.

[66] *In IV Metaph.*, lect. 6, n. 607.

[67] *Ibid.*, n. 606. On the meaning of the word *supposition*, see Régis, *La critique néothomiste*, p. 170, note 2.

[68] *In II De caelo et mundo*, lect. 22, n. 10.

[69] *Le réalisme immédiat*, p. 108; *Notes d'épistémologie thomiste*, p. 22.

[70] Descartes, *Discours de la méthode*, (A-T, I, p. 32, lines 1 to 23); *Regulae*, I (A-T, X, p. 360, lines 3–15); *Principia* (A-T, IX, p. 14). Cf. Gilson, *Discours de la méthode*, pp. 327, 349–350, 160–167, 302–304.

[71] Gilson, *Discours de la méthode*, pp. 284–292.

[72] Cf. Régis, *La critique néothomiste*, pp. 171–174. See also below, pp. 349–355.

[73] Cf. Régis, *La critique néothomiste*, pp. 174–175.

[74] *In IV Metaph.*, lect. 17, n. 736.

[75] Cf. Régis, *La critique néothomiste*, p. 177, note 1.

[76] Cf. below, Chap. VIII, on the distinction between being, as first known, and the knowledge of being as being. See also Régis, *L'Odyssée de la métaphysique* (Paris, Vrin, 1949), pp. 18–36; *St. Thomas and Epistemology*, pp. 37–39.

[77] Cf. Régis, *L'Odyssée*, pp. 58–69; and below, Chap. XII.

[78] Cf. Gilson, *Discours de la méthode*.

[79] Cf. above, pp. 80–89.

[80] *Le réalisme immédiat*, pp. 19–22.

[81] *Ibid.*, pp. 23–24; *Notes d'épistémologie thomiste*, p. 23.

[82] *Le dynamisme intellectuel dans la connaissance objective*, XXIX (1927), pp. 137–165; *Au seuil de la Métaphysique: abstraction ou intuition*, XXXI (1929), pp. 27–52, 121–147, 309–342; *L'Aspect dynamique de la méthode transcendentale chez Kant*, XLII (1939), pp. 341–384.

[83] Cf. *Le point de départ de la métaphysique*, Cahier V (Louvain, Museum Lessianum, 1923), pp. 30–31.

[84] *Critique of Pure Reason*, "Introd.," p. 41.

[85] Cf. below, pp. 176–183. See also a typical text on the subject, *S.T.*, I, 16, 2, c.

[86] *Quodlibeta*, VIII, 19, c. *De Veritate*, X art. 8–9. See below, pp. 276–279.

[87] *In De Trinitate*, VI, 2, ad 5.

[88] *Critique of Pure Reason*, "Introd.," pp. 41–42.

[89] *Ibid.*, p. 43.

[90] *Ibid.*

[91] *Ibid.*, p. 44.

[92] *Ibid.*, p. 42.

[93] Cf. *In IV Metaph.*, lect. 6, n. 606.

[94] *Critique of Pure Reason*, "Transcendental Analytic," Bk. II, Chap. II, pp. 189–191.

[95] Cf. *In IV Metaph.*, lect. 6, n. 599; *In II Post. Analyt.*, lect. 20, 4–14; *In I Metaph.*, lect. 1, nn. 14–20; *In III Sent.*, 34, 1, 2, sol.; *C.G.*, II, 83, *Item necesse*; *S.T.*, I–II, 51, 1.

[96] *In IV Sent.*, 9, 1, 4, sol. 1.

[97] *De Veritate*, XII, 3, ad 3.

[98] Cf. above, pp. 52–57.

[99] Cf. the relations established by Kant between intellectual consciousness without intuition and empirical consciousness: *Critique of Pure Reason*, "Preface to Second Ed.," pp. 34–36.

[100] For the distinction between *to know* and *to believe*, see *Critique of Pure Reason*, "The Canon of Pure Reason," Sect. III, pp. 644–652.

[101] *Le point de départ*, Cahier V, p. 39.

[102] *Ibid.*, p. 5.

[103] Cf. *Critique of Pure Reason*, "Introd.," pp. 55–56.

[104] *Ibid.*, p. 56.

[105] *Ibid.*, pp. 56–57.

[106] *Ibid.*, "Transcendental Doctrine of Elements," pp. 92–93.

[107] *Le point de départ*, Cahier V, p. 39.

[108] *Ibid.*, pp. 39–43, 375–381.

[109] That this was not the case has been shown in our comparative study of Cartesian and Thomistic doubt; see above, pp. 82–92.

[110] *Critique of Pure Reason*, "Introd.," p. 92.

[111] *Ibid.*, p. 59.

[112] *Ibid.*, "Transcendental Logic," p. 92.

[113] *Ibid.*, p. 95.

[114] *Ibid.*, p. 103.

[115] *Ibid.*, pp. 297–300.

[116] *Ibid.*, p. 103.

[117] Cf. Maréchal, *Au seuil de la Métaphysique*, in *Revue néoscolastique de philos.*, XXXI (1929), pp. 31–33, 46.

[118] *Ibid.*, p. 29.

[119] Cf. below, pp. 284–306.

[120] Maréchal, *Le point de départ,* Cahier V, p. 96.

[121] *Ibid.,* pp. 97–108.

[122] *Critique of Pure Reason,* p. 300.

[123] For the critical study of this problem see Gilson, *Réalisme thomiste et critique de la connaissance,* (Paris, Vrin, 1939), Chap. I–V.

[124] Cf. Meyerson, *Le cheminement de la pensée,* pp. 674–713; *Essai,* pp. 55, 58.

[125] Cf. Régis, *St. Thomas and Epistemology,* p. 75, notes 56–61.

[126] Cf. above, pp. 32–39.

[127] *L'Epistémologie thomiste,* "Introd.," p. 5; "Concl.," pp. 634–639.

[128] For this study of the confusion among Neo-Scholastic thinkers, see Régis, *La critique néothomiste,* pp. 106–145.

[129] *L'Epistémologie thomiste,* pp. 635–637.

[130] *Ibid.,* p. 636.

[131] Cf. above, pp. 39–41, 47–50.

[132] Cf. above, pp. 50–56.

[133] Cf. *In VII Metaph.,* lect. 17, nn. 1651–1658; *In II Post. Analyt.,* lect. 3–6. See below, pp. 128–140.

[134] *Critique of Pure Reason,* p. 97.

Chapter IV

[1] *In II Post. Analyt.,* lect. 5, n. 4.

[2] Cf. above, pp. 41–45, 48–51, 57–61.

[3] Cf. M.D. Chenu, *Introduction à l'étude de saint Thomas d'Aquin* (Paris, Vrin, 1951), Chap. II; Gilson, *History of Christian Philosophy in the Middle Ages* (New York, Random House, 1955), pp. 139–153.

[4] One of the best studies of St. Bonaventure's thought will be found in Gilson, *La philosophie de saint Bonaventure* (Paris, Vrin, 1943).

[5] *Itinerarium,* V, 4 (in S. Bonaventurae, *Opera Omnia,* 10 vols. Quaracchi, Ex Typographia Collegii S. Bonaventurae, 1882–1902, tome V, p. 334; this edition is subsequently cited under the symbol AQ). See also *Itinerarium,* V, 3, 5; III, 3; *In Hexaemeron,* III, 3–4 (AQ, V, 343); I, 13–18; *De scientia Christi,* q. II, art. 5.

[6] *In II Sent.,* 3, 1, 1, 1, concl. 3 (AQ, II, 91).

[7] *In I Sent.,* 8, 2, 2, 2, concl. (AQ, I, 168); *In II Sent.* 3, 1, 1, 1, concl. (AQ, II, 90–91).

[8] *In I Sent.,* 8, 2, 2, sol. (AQ, I, 168); *In II Sent.,* 3, 1, 1, sol. (AQ, II, 90–92); see also *In II Sent.,* 12–17 (AQ, II, 293–424).

[9] *In II Sent.,* 1, 1, 1, 2 (AQ, II, 19–24); 1, 1, 3, 1–2 (AQ, II, 47–51); 17, 1, 1–3 (AQ, II, 410–419).

[10] *In Hexaemeron,* XII, 15 (AQ, V, 386); *In II Sent.,* 37, 1, 2, sol. (AQ, II, 641–644).

[11] *In II Sent.,* 16, 1, 2, ad 4 (AQ, II, 397); *Itinerarium,* II, 12 (AQ, V, 303).

[12] *In II Sent.*, 12 (AQ, II, 293–306).

[13] *In II Sent.*, 13 (AQ, II, 310–324).

[14] *In II Sent.*, 15, 2, 1, sol. (AQ, II, 372–385).

[15] Cf. G. Klubertanz, "*Esse* and *Existere* in St. Bonaventure," *Mediaeval Studies*, VIII (1946), pp. 169–188.

[16] *In II Sent.*, 7, 2, 2, 1, sol. et ad 6 (AQ, II, 198–199); *In II Sent.*, 18, 1, 3, sol. (AQ, II, 440); *Breviloquium*, IV, 2 (AQ, V, 221–222).

[17] *In I Sent.*, 8, 1, 1, 1 (AQ, I, 151–152); *In I Sent.*, 46, 1, 4 (AQ, I, 828–829); *Breviloquium*, V, 1, 22 (AQ, V, 354, 357).

[18] *De scientia Christi*, IV, (AQ, V, 23).

[19] *Ibid.* (AQ, V, 24–25).

[20] *Itinerarium*, II (AQ, V, 302–312).

[21] *In Hexaemeron*, I, 13–18 (AQ, V, 331–333); *Sermo* IV, 19 (AQ, V, 572); *De donis*, IV, 19–22 (AQ, V, 476–478).

[22] Cf. Gilson, *La philosophie de saint Bonaventure*, Chap. XV, translated into English as, *The Philosophy of St. Bonaventure* (New York, Sheed and Ward, 1938).

[23] *In Hexaemeron*, IV, 2 (AQ, V, 349); *De donis*, IV, 3–13 (AQ, V, 476); *Itinerarium*, III, 6–7 (AQ, V, 305–306); *De reductione artium*, 4–5 (AQ, V, 320–321).

[24] *Sermo*, IV, 18–19 (AQ, V, 572); *In III Sent.*, 35, 2, 3, concl. (AQ, III, 778).

[25] *Sermo*, IV (AQ, V, 572); *De donis*, IV, 19–22 (AQ, V, 477–478).

[26] He borrowed from Scotus Erigena the notion of *status* and of the universe theophany. Cf. Gilson, *La philosophie au moyen âge*, pp. 201–222.

[27] From Gilbert de la Porrée he borrowed the doctrine of the multiplicity of substantial forms. Cf. Gilson, *La philosophie au moyen âge*, pp. 264–268, 370–372.

[28] From Avicenna was derived the division of being into necessary and possible. Cf. *La philosophie au moyen âge*, pp. 353–355; *Being and Some Philosophers*, pp. 81–82.

[29] William of Auvergne had attenuated the Avicennian division of being into necessary and possible by giving back to God the freedom of His creative activity, which was an article of faith. Cf. Gilson, *La philosophie au moyen âge*, pp. 419–424; *Being and Some Philosophers*, pp. 83–84.

[30] Cf. Gilson, *Pourquoi saint Thomas a critiqué saint Augustin*, in *Archives d'histoire doctrinale et littéraire du moyen âge*, I (1926–1927), pp. 5–127. See also *La philosophie au moyen âge*, pp. 580–590; Chenu, *Introduction à l'étude de saint Thomas d'Aquin*, pp. 45–48.

[31] The condemnation by Robert Kilwardby (March 7 and 18, 1277) of seventeen propositions clearly revealed the Augustinian prejudices against the Aristotelian teachings: the pure passivity of matter, the unicity of substantial form, the simplicity of separate substances, the existence of a personal agent intellect, and the distinction of the soul from its powers. Cf. Gilson, *La philosophie au moyen âge*, pp. 485–487; *L'Esprit de la philosophie médiévale* (Paris, Vrin, 1943), pp. 95–124.

[32] Cf. above, Chap. IV, notes 15–16.

[33] Cf. Gilson, *La philosophie au moyen âge*, pp. 580-590.

[34] Cf. Gilson, *God and Philosophy;* Monod, *Dieu dans l'univers.*

[35] The Aristotle known after the middle of the thirteenth century was the Averroist Aristotle, irreligious and rationalistic, one who was an occasion of scandal for the religious-minded thinkers of this period. For a synopsis of the opposition, see Gilson, *La philosophie au moyen âge*, pp. 500-515.

[36] *In II De anima*, lect. 7, n. 314.

[37] See Aristotle, *De anima*, III, 5; 429a10-430a26. For continued discussion of this problem by thirteenth-century theologians, cf. St. Thomas, *S.T.*, I, 79, 4-6, and the parallel texts.

[38] Cf. A. Pegis, "Matter, Beatitude and Liberty," *The Thomist*, V (1943), pp. 265-280.

[39] Such are the affirmations of the creation of the universe in time, of the nature of God, of Providence, of human beatitude, and so on.

[40] Cf. *C.G.*, I, 7; *De unitate intellectus*, ed. Mandonnet, pp. 42, 69; Gilson, *Le thomisme* (Paris, Vrin, 1945), pp. 20, 186-189.

[41] Gilson, *Le thomisme*, pp. 18 ff.

[42] *Ibid.*, pp. 196, 251, note 2.

[43] Cf. Chenu, *Introduction à l'étude de saint Thomas*, pp. 44-52.

[44] Cf. Gilson, *La philosophie au moyen âge*, pp. 587-588.

[45] We must not forget that Aristotle, and not Plato, was the inventor of a philosophy of nature; Plato wrote a mythology of nature in his *Timaeus.*

[46] Cf. Bonaventure, *De donis*, IV, 3 (AQ, V, 476).

[47] See the numerous texts that affirm this creative aspect of Aristotle's doctrine: *S.T.*, I, 79; 83-89; *De spiritualibus creaturis*, 3, c.; 5, c.; 9, ad 6; 11, ad 8; *In II Post. Analyt.* lect. 4, nn. 4, 8; *In I Metaph.*, lect. 10; *In II Metaph.*, lect. 15.

[48] Cf. above, pp. 85-89. See also Gilson, *Le réalisme thomiste*, p. 68, with the footnote.

[49] *In III Metaph.*, lect. 1, n. 344.

[50] Cf. below, pp. 284-306, on the process of our knowledge from potency to act, which is identical with *per se notum quoad nos* as distinct from *per se notum quoad se*. See also *In V Metaph.*, lect. 13, nn. 947-949.

[51] *De spiritualibus creaturis*, 5, c. Cf. Gilson, *Le thomisme*, p. 391.

[52] Cf. above, Chap. IV, note 31, on the propositions condemned by Kilwardby; all propositions mentioned in that note were defended by Thomas Aquinas.

[53] Cf. L.B. Geiger, *La doctrine de la participation* (Paris, Vrin, 1943); this book in itself is a proof that Aquinas took the truth where he found it, irrespective of the person who taught it.

[54] Cf. Gilson, *Being and Some Philosophers*, (Toronto, Pontifical Institute, 1949), pp. 154-189.

[55] Such are the doctrines of creation, Providence, the unicity of God, and so on.

[56] Cf. Gilson, *Pourquoi, etc.* (see note 30 above).

[57] Cf. J. Durantel, *Saint Thomas et le Pseudo-Denys* (Paris, Alcan, 1919).

[58] *In I Metaph.*, lect. 15, n. 231; *In III Metaph.*, lect. 11, nn. 468, 471; *In I De*

Caelo, lect. 22, n. 10; *In I De anima*, lect. 8, n. 1; *In I Phys.*, lect. 15, n. 10; *In I Sent.*, Prolog. 1, 1, sol. et ad 3; *In II Sent.*, 8, 1, 3, ad 1; *De Veritate*, XXII, 11, ad 8; XXIII, 3, c.; *In II Post. Analyt.*, lect. 16, n. 8.

[59] *S.T.*, I, 1, 9, obj. 1 et ad 1, 2, 3; *In lib. De divinis nominibus*, IV, lect. 19.

[60] *In III Metaph.*, lect. 11, nn. 468–472; *In I Perih.*, lect. 7, nn. 2–6. See Chenu, *Introduction à l'étude de saint Thomas*, pp. 53, 99, 194.

[61] Cf. *Index Auctoritatum*, sub nom. Aristotelis, in S. Thomae, *Opera Omnia*, Ed. Leonina (Romae, 1949), vol. XVI, Pars, I, II A.

[62] Cf. Gilson, *Le thomisme*, pp. 8–14.

[63] Of the fourteen hundred pages of the text of Aristotle, not more than ten are devoted to the separate substances.

[64] *C.G.*, II, 2–3.

[65] *Ibid.*, 4; *S.T.*, I, 1, 1–6; *C.G.*, I, 9, *Modo ergo*.

[66] *In lib. De divinis nominibus*, Prolog.; *S.T.*, I, 79, 5–7; also pp. 84–87.

[67] Cf. Chenu, *Introduction à l'étude de saint Thomas*, pp. 173–192.

[68] Note the technical expressions by which Aquinas determines the value of the arguments given by Aristotle: *ostendit, manifestat, determinat, probat, concludit, rationem ponit, disputat, exemplificat, analytice vel logice procedit*, etc. His Aristotle commentaries are replete with such expressions.

[69] *De spiritualibus creaturis*, 3, c.; *In III Metaph.*, lect. 4, n. 371.

[70] *IN VIII Phys.*, lect. 1 et 21; *In II Metaph.*, lect. 1, n. 286; *In I Perih.*, lect. 8, nn. 15, 21; *De unitate intellectus*, ed. Mandonnet, pp. 37–38; *C.G.*, III, 9, *Potest etiam*.

[71] *De unitate intellectus*, ed. Mandonnet, pp. 50, 58. Cf. A Festugière, *Notes sur les sources du commentaire de saint Thomas*, in RSPT, XVIII (1929), pp. 282–290.

[72] Cf. Chenu, *Introduction à l'étude de saint Thomas*, pp. 122–125.

[73] *In III Metaph.*, lect. 4, n. 371; *In II Metaph.*, lect. 1, n. 284; *In IV Metaph.*, lect. 1, n. 529; *In VI Metaph.*, lect. 1, n. 1164; lect. 3, n. 1216; *In VII Metaph.*, lect. 17, n. 1661; *In I Phys.*, lect. 15, n. 11; *In III De caelo*, lect. 3, n. 7; lect. 6, nn. 4–5; *In I De anima*, lect. 6, n. 74; *In I Ethic.*, lect. 2, nn. 28, 31; *Quaest. de anima*, 5, ad 4; *De substantiis separatis*, 12–15; *C.G.*, III, 9, *Potest etiam*.

[74] *In lib. De divinis nominibus*, Prolog. On the superficial assimilation of Aristotelianism by the predecessors of St. Thomas, see Gilson, *La philosophie au moyen âge*, pp. 489, 497, 508–539.

[75] *C.G.*, I, 9, *Modo ergo*; *S.T.*, I, 1, 6–8; cf. Chenu, *La théologie comme science au XIII*ᵉ *siècle* (Paris, Vrin, 1942).

[76] Cf. above, pp. 115–116.

[77] *In XII Metaph.*, lect. 9, n. 2566; *in II Metaph.*, lect. 1, nn. 287–289; *In I De caelo*, lect. 22.

[78] *In I De caelo*, lect. 22, n. 5; *In I Metaph.*, lect. 11, n. 180. See the critique of the abuses of authority in philosophical argument, in *Quodlibeta*, IV, 18, c.; and Chenu, *Introduction à l'étude de saint Thomas*, pp. 25–27, 58.

[79] *Sermo* IV, PL 211, 37.

[80] John of Salisbury, *Metalogicon*, III, 4 (ed. Webb, Oxford, 1929) pp. 23, 136.

[81] *S.T.*, II–II, 49, 3, ad 2; *In I Metaph.*, lect. 10, n. 151; lect. 11, n. 180.

[82] The acquisition of truth has a social character for Aristotle and St. Thomas. Cf. *In II Metaph.*, lect. 1, nn. 276-288; *In XII Metaph.*, lect. 9, n. 2566. See also the preceding note.

[83] Cf. above, pp. 48-50.

[84] See Régis, *L'Opinion selon Aristote* (Paris, Vrin, 1935), pp. 133-162.

[85] *In II De Caelo*, lect. 22, n. 10; *In II Post. Analyt.*, lect. 20-21.

[86] *In II Post. Analyt.*, lect. 1-20.

[87] Aquinas' *Commentary* is more than four times as long as the commented text of Aristotle.

[88] Cf. above, pp. 7-14; also, *S.T.*, I, 105, 7, c.; I-II, 3, 7; *C.G.*, III, 50.

[89] *In VII Metaph.*, lect. 17, n. 1669.

[90] *In II Post. Analyt.*, lect. 1, n. 6; *C.G.*, III, 25, 41, 46, 50.

[91] *In II Post. Analyt.*, lect. 1, n. 2; *In V Metaph.*, lect. 9, n. 595.

[92] *In II Post. Analyt.*, lect. 1, n. 3. Cf. below, Chap. VIII.

[93] *In II Post. Analyt.*, lect. 1, n. 4; *In VII Metaph.*, lect. 17, nn. 1651-1671; *S.T.*, I, 105, 7, c.

[94] *In II Post. Analyt.*, lect. 1, n. 5; lect. 16, n. 7; *In I Post. Analyt.*, lect. 13, n. 11; lect. 21, 23.

[95] *Quodlibeta*, II, 3; *In V. Metaph.*, lect. 9. Cf. Schütz, *Thomas-Lexikon*, ad verb. *causa, actus, potentia*.

[96] *In I Perih.*, lect. 5, nn. 8-9; lect. 8, nn. 9-11. Cf. below pp. 317-327.

[97] See the study of the proper object of the judgment, below, pp. 327-333.

[98] See the treatise on God, *S.T.*, I, qq. 2-11.

[99] *In III Sent.*, 23, 1, 2, sol.; *In I Sent.*, 3, 1, 2, sol.; *In VII Metaph.*, lect 17, n. 1648; *In I Post. Analyt.*, lect. 19, nn. 3-5; *Quodlibeta*, VIII, 4, c.

[100] *In II Post. Analyt.*, lect. 2, n. 2; *De spirit. creaturis*, 8, ad 3; *In II Post. Analyt.*, lect. 6, n. 4; lect. 7, n. 3.

[101] *In II Post Analyt.*, lect. 7, in toto; lect. 8, nn. 6-7; *In VII Metaph.*, lect. 3, nn. 1328-1332.

[102] *In II Sent.*, 3, 1, 6, sol.; *In III Sent.*, 26, 1, 1, ad 3; *In IV Sent.*, 14, 1, 1, sol. 6, ad 1; *In IV Sent.*, 44, 2, 1, sol. 1, ad 1; *De ente et essentia*, 5; *C.G.*, I, 3; IV, 1; *De Veritate*, IV, 1, ad 8; X, 1, c. et ad 6; *De Potentia*, IX, 2, ad 5; *De spirit. creaturis*, 11, ad 3; *In Symbolo Apost.*, ed. Mandonnet, IV, 350; *In I De anima*, lect. 2, n. 15; *In VII Metaph.*, lect. 12, n. 1552; *In I De Gen. et corrup.*, lect. 8, n. 5; *In I Post. Analyt.*, lect. 4, n. 16; *In II Post. Analyt.*, lect. 13, n. 7; *S.T.*, I, 29, 1, ad 3; 77, 1, ad 7; I-II, 49, 2, ad 3.

[103] *Quodlibeta*, II, 4, c.; IX, 2, c.; *In VII Metaph.*, lect. 1-4.

[104] *Quodlibeta*, IX, 5, ad 1; cf. Schütz, *Thomas-Lexikon*, ad verb. *accidens, definitio*.

[105] On the correlation between unity and intelligibility, see below, pp. 316-317.

[106] *In VII Metaph.*, lect. 1-11.

[107] Cf. below, pp. 136-140.

[108] *In III Sent.*, 23, 1, 2, sol.; *Quodlibeta*, VIII, 4, c.; *In VII Metaph.*, lect. 17, n. 1658.

[109] *In V Metaph.*, lect. 9. Cf. below, p. 282.

[110] *In I Post. Analyt.*, lect. 5; *In II Post Analyt.*, lect. 1; *In V Metaph.*, lect. 6.

[111] *S.T.*, I, 78, 6, c. et ad 3; *In De Trinitate*, V, 4, ad 4; *In V Metaph.*, lect. 10, nn. 888–893.

[112] *S.T.*, I, qq. 3–11; *Quodlibeta*, IV, 18.

[113] Cf. Schütz, *Thomas-Lexikon*, p. 666, a.

[114] *In II Post. Analyt.*, lect. 7, n. 3; lect. 8, in toto; lect. 17, nn. 4–6; *In I Post. Analyt.*, lect. 25, n. 5; *In VII Metaph.*, lect. 17, nn. 1649–1655; *In V Metaph.*, lect. 6, n. 838; *S.T.*, I, 78, 6, c. et ad 2, ad 3; *In II Post. Analyt.*, lect. 1, nn. 6–9; lect. 17, nn. 4–6.

[115] *S.T.*, I, 84, 3, ad 3; *Quodlibeta*, IV, 18, c.

[116] *In II Post. Analyt.*, lect. 7, n. 5; *In VII Metaph.*, lect. 17, n. 1666; *S.T.*, I, 2, 2, ad 2; *C.G.*, I, 10, 12.

[117] The whole basis of Thomistic epistemology lies in the intelligible necessity of the reality of the natural object of the human intellect. For the relation of this natural object to being as the first object known by our intellect, see below, Chap. VII, pp. 276–278, 283–291. See also the discussions of the knowability of the soul and God: *S.T.*, I, 2, 84; *C.G.*, I, 10–11, 46.

[118] *In I Perih.*, lect. 1, nn. 5–12; *In II Post. Analyt.*, lect. 8, n. 5.

[119] *In II Post. Analyt.*, lect. 1, nn. 6, 8; lect. 2, n. 7.

[120] *Quodlibeta*, IX, 3, c.; *S.T.*, I, 2, 2, ad 3; 48, 2, ad 2; *In V Metaph.*, lect. 9, n. 996; *In II Post. Analyt.*, lect. 6, nn. 3–4; lect. 7, n. 3. Cf. below, pp. 317–327.

[121] Cf. R. Vernaux, *La philosophie de M. Brunschvicg*, in *Rev. de philos.* XLI (1934), pp. 178–180, 286–288.

[122] Cf. below, pp. 140–143.

[123] Careful study of Aquinas' two masterpieces, the *Summa Theologiae* and *Summa contra Gentiles*, reveals that these four questions constitute the structure of all the treatises in these two works.

[124] Cf. above, Chap. IV, note 111.

[125] Cf. below, Chap. X.

[126] Cf. above, pp. 33–47.

[127] *In V Metaph.*, lect. 2–5; Cf. Schütz, *Thomas-Lexikon*, ad verb. *causa, effectus.*

[128] Cf. Gilson, *Being and Some Philosophers*, Chap. I.

[129] Cf. above, pp. 115–117.

[130] See the treatise on divine government, *S.T.*, I, qq. 103–119.

[131] S. Kierkegaard, *Miettes philosophiques* (Paris, N.R.F., 1927), pp. 100–101; in English, *Philosophical Fragments*, translated by D.F. Swenson (Princeton, Princeton U. Press, 1936).

[132] *S.T.*, I, 93, and the parallel texts.

[133] *S.T.*, I, 16, and parallel texts, in which God is described as the Exemplar of all creatures; this relation constitutes the ontological truth of every created being. Cf. below, Chap. IX.

[134] *De veritate*, II, 2, c.; *In III Sent.*, 27, 1, 4, sol.; *In lib. De divinis nominibus*, 5, lect. 1; *In II De anima*, lect. 5, n. 283; *In III De anima*, lect. 13, n. 790; *S.T.*, I, 14, 1, c.; 80, 1, c.

[135] *De veritate*, I, 1, c. See also Régis, *L'Odyssée*, pp. 55, 77–78.

[136] Cf. Schütz, *Thomas-Lexikon,* ad verb. *operatio, esse.*
[137] *C.G.,* I, 22; *S.T.,* I, 4, 3.
[138] *C.G.,* III, 29–31.
[139] *C.G.,* III, 21–24, 147; *S.T.,* I. 3, 2.
[140] *C.G.,* III, 27–49.
[141] Cf. below, pp. 289–302.
[142] Cf. Régis, *La critique néothomiste,* pp. 186–191.
[143] *Ibid.,* pp. 188–189.
[144] *Ibid.,* pp. 183–186.
[145] *Ibid.,* pp. 185–186. Cf. below, pp. 248–252.
[146] *C.G.,* III, 129; *S.T.,* I, 92, 3. Cf. above, pp. 41–43, 83–86.
[147] *De Malo,* XVI, 7, ad 18. Cf. Schütz, *Thomas-Lexikon,* ad verb. *instinctus.*
[148] *De spiritualibus creaturis,* 6, in toto; 9, ad 3 to ad 14; *S.T.,* I, 76, and qq. 89–90; *C.G.,* IV, 1; *In lib. De Trinitate,* V, 2, ad 5. See below, pp. 229–252.
[149] *De spiritualibus creaturis,* 5, 10; *C.G.,* III, 91, *Similiter.*

Conclusion of Part One

[1] Cf. above, Chaps. II–III.
[2] C. Gibran, *The Prophet* (New York, Knopf, 1923).
[3] *C.G.,* III, 49.

Part Two: Prologue

[1] *In I De caelo,* lect. 22, n. 2.
[2] Cf. Vernaux, in *Rev. de philos.,* XLI (1934), pp. 189, 197, 287; Bachelard, *Le rationalisme appliqué,* p. 29.
[3] Eddington, *New Pathways,* pp. 12–13. Jeans, *Physics and Philosophy,* pp. 11, 13. B. Russell, *The Analysis of Matter* (New York, Macmillan, 1927), pp. 161–163.
[4] *De veritate,* V, 9, c. See also Maritain's work, *Distinguer pour unir* (Paris, Desclée De Brouwer, 1932) translated as, *The Degrees of Knowledge.*
[5] Cf. A. Von Weizäcker, *The History of Nature* (Chicago, Chicago U. Press, 1949), pp. 80–95. The organization of matter from which the natures of the different bodies result is a form of death compared to the pure energy of the atoms, which means that what is a form of perfection for the philosopher is a degradation of being for the physicist. Cf. Meyerson, *Le cheminement, de la pensée,* II, p. 693; and *De spiritualibus creaturis,* 3, ad 14.
[6] The law of probability has the same unifying function in the world of science that the laws of nature have in the world of philosophy; without probability, matter is not knowable, that is, not measurable; and without nature,

physical being is not intelligible. Cf. Meyerson, *Le cheminement de la pensée,* I, pp. 189–193; II, 426, 699; Eddington, *New Pathways,* Chaps. III–IV.

[7] In terms of science, *to know is to measure.* See Bachelard, *Essai,* pp. 52–54; *Le nouvel esprit scientifique,* pp. 4–11, 144; and the Brunschvicg quotations in Vernaux, *Rev. de philos.,* XLI (1934), p. 197; also Eddington, *Science and the Unseen World* (London, George Allen, 1925), p. 20.

[8] By definition, to know speculatively is *to be measured,* not to measure. See *In I Ethic.,* lect. 1, nn. 3–6; *In I Metaph.,* lect. 1, in toto; *S.T.,* I, 14, 6, c. et ad 1.

[9] *De spiritualibus creaturis,* 4, c.

[10] *C.G.,* II, 2; *S.T.,* I, 5, 4.

[11] *S.T.,* I, 83; *Quodlibeta,* III, 7, c.

[12] *In I De anima,* lect. 4, n. 43; *In II De anima,* lect. 12, n. 377; *In III De anima,* lect. 13, n. 789; *S.T.,* I, 84, 2, c., et 4, c.

[13] *De spirit. creaturis,* 2, c.; 10, ad 7; *De unitate intellectus,* ed. Keeler, pp. 58–59; *In VI Metaph.,* lect. 1; *S.T.,* I, 75, 2, c.

Chapter V

[1] *C.G.,* I, 46, *Amplius; S.T.,* I, 14; 54, 1–2; *De ente et essentia,* 6.

[2] Cf. *De ente et essentia,* 6; and above, Chap. IV, note 111.

[3] *In IX Metaph.,* lect. 3, n. 1805. Cf. below, p. 288.

[4] *S.T.,* I, 41, 1, ad 2.

[5] *S.T.,* I, 40, 2, c.

[6] *De veritate,* II, 5, ad 15. *De unitate intellectus,* ed. Keeler, pp. 71–72; *C.G.,* II, 45–47; *De veritate,* VIII, 6, c.

[7] *Quaest. de anima,* 13, c.

[8] Cf. Rivaud, *Le problème du devenir,* pp. 5–49.

[9] Cf. Jeans, *Physics and Philosophy,* pp. 2, 59, 190, 195–205: "It is more probable that reality is mental." See Eddington, *New Pathways,* "Epilogue," sect. 3.

[10] *In II De anima,* lect. 1, n. 219.

[11] Cf. Régis, *L'Opinion selon Aristote,* p. 250 note 6; p. 256, notes 1–3.

[12] *C.G.,* I, 97; *In III Sent.,* 35, 1, 1, sol.; *S.T.,* I, 18, 1, ad 3.

[13] *S.T.,* I, 18, 3, ad 1, in Pegis (ed.), *The Basic Writings of St. Thomas* (New York, Random House, 1948, 2 vols.), hereinafter cited as, *BW*), I, p. 192; *De spirit. creaturis,* 4, ad 6; *In IX Metaph.,* lect. 8, nn. 1861–1866.

[14] *In lib. De Trinitate,* V, 4, ad 2, ad 3; *S.T.,* I, 18, 1, ad 1; *In II De anima,* lect. 10, nn. 350–351; lect. 13, n. 381.

[15] *C.G.,* I, 14, *Est autem; In lib. De Trinitate,* V, 4, c.; *In II Post. Analyt.,* lect. 6–8.

[16] *In VIII Metaph.,* lect. 3, n. 1805. Cf. below, Chap. VII, note 144.

[17] *In III Phys.,* lect. 1, seq.; *In III De anima,* lect. 12, n. 766. Cf. Schütz, *Thomas-Lexikon,* ad verb. *motus.*

[18] See the first proof of the existence of God, *S.T.,* I, 2, 2; *C.G.,* I, 13.

[19] *Ibid.*

[20] *C.G.*, III, 69, *Non est; Quodlibeta*, IX, 6, c.

[21] *In lib. De Trinitate*, IV, 1–3; *In II De anima*, lect. 12, n. 377; *S.T.*, I, 7, 3, ad 3; III, 90, 2, c. Cf. Schütz, *Thomas-Lexikon*, ad verb. *quantitas, quantum.*

[22] *In III Phys.*, lect. 3–23.

[23] *In I Phys.*, lect. 9–14.

[24] *S.T.*, I, 18, 3, c. (*BW*, I, pp. 190–191).

[25] *C.G.*, I, 97, *Adhuc.*

[26] *C.G.*, I, 13; *S.T.* I–II, 51, 2, ad 2; I, 76, 4, ad 2; *C.G.*, II, 82, *Secundo quia.*

[27] *S.T.*, I, 18, 1, c.; 2, c. et ad 1.

[28] Cf. above, pp. 162–164.

[29] That it is metaphysically impossible for the same reality to move and to be moved at the same time and under the same aspect, see *C.G.*, I, 12.

[30] *C.G.*, IV, 11.

[31] *Ibid.*, *init.* For the meaning of the word *emanare*, see Schütz, *Thomas-Lexikon*, p. 271.

[32] Cf. above, p. 160.

[33] Cf. the text quoted above, Chap. V, note 24.

[34] *S.T.*, I, 18, 3, ad 1 (*BW*, I, p. 192).

[35] *C.G.*, I, 50, *Amplius;* III, 2, *Sunt autem;* 3, *Amplius;* 10, *Hoc autem;* 23, *Nam;* 25, *Item* 69, *Item.* Cf. Schütz, *Thomas-Lexikon*, ad verb. *agens, actus.*

[36] *De Potentia*, II, 1, c.

[37] *De ente et essentia*, 5; *S.T.*, I, 18, 1–4; *C.G.*, IV, 11.

[38] *De spirit. creaturis*, 4, c.; *S.T.*, I, qq. 76 et 78.

[39] *C.G.*, I, 45–47; *S. T.*, I, qq. 14–15; 18, 3–4.

[40] *In II De anima*, lect. 11, nn. 365–366; lect. 12, n. 382; *In I De anima*, lect. 11, nn. 157–161.

[41] Cf. above, pp. 140–144.

[42] Cf. above, pp. 162–167.

[43] *C.G.*, II, 58; *S.T.*, I, qq. 74–75. Cf. above, Chap. IV, note 31.

[44] *S.T.*, I, 76, and the parallel texts.

[45] *S.T.*, I, 77, 1, c., et ad 3, ad 4 (*BW*, I, p. 720). See also *S.T.*, I, 54, 1–4.

[46] *S.T.*, I, 77, 3, c. (*BW*, I, p. 724); *De spirit. creaturis*, 11, c. et ad 4.

[47] Cf. above, pp. 137–140.

[48] *S.T.*, I–II, qq, 1–5; *C.G.*, III, 25–63.

[49] *S.T.*, I, 77, 2, c. (*BW*, I, pp. 722–723). Also Pegis, *In Umbra Intelligentiae*, in *New Scholasticism*, XIV (1940), pp. 146–180.

[50] Various texts describing the soul as microcosm are found in *BW*, II, p. 1141.

[51] *Quaest. de anima*, 13; *De veritate*, XV, 2, c.; *S.T.*, I, qq. 77–79.

[52] *S.T.*, I, 77, 5–7; I–II, 17, 4, c. et ad 1.

[53] See the geometrical comparison used by Aquinas, *De unitate intellectus*, ed. Mandonnet, p. 47.

[54] *S.T.*, I, 77, 6, ad 3; *C.G.*, IV, 11.

[55] *S.T.*, I, 77, 6. c. (*BW*, I, p. 728).

⁵⁶ *S.T.*, I, 77, 6, ad 2 (*BW*, I, p. 728).
⁵⁷ *S.T.*, I, 77, 7, c. (*BW*, I, p. 728).
⁵⁸ *S.T.*, I, 77, 7, ad 1 (*BW*, I, p. 728).
⁵⁹ *S.T.*, I, 77, 7, ad 2 (Pegis, *BW*, I, p. 728).
⁶⁰ Cf. below, pp. 265–276.
⁶¹ Cf. below, pp. 228–252.
⁶² Cf. below, pp. 315–317.
⁶³ Cf. below, pp. 311–327.
⁶⁴ Cf. below, pp. 338–348.
⁶⁵ Cf. below, Chap. X.
⁶⁶ Cf. above, pp. 137–140, 154–155.
⁶⁷ *S.T.*, I, 77, 8, c.
⁶⁸ *S.T.*, I, 77, 5–7.

Chapter VI

¹ *C.G.*, III, 46.
² It was to eliminate this difficulty that Plato invented his theory of reminiscence, and Augustine developed his doctrine of memory. A sketch of the history of this chapter in the philosophy of ideas can be found in St. Thomas, *De veritate*, XIX, 1; and *De spirit. creaturis*, 9, c.
³ *De veritate*, XXII, 10, c. *C.G.*, II, 96, *Sensibilis*; *S.T.*, I, 78, 1, c. Cf. A. Hayen, *L'Intentionel dans la philosophie de saint Thomas* (Louvain, Nauwelaerts, 1945), pp. 122–124.
⁴ *In III Sent.*, 27, 2, 4, sol. 2. *De veritate*, XXII, 10, ad 1; *C.G.*, II, 14, 35, *Nam*; *S.T.*, I, 76, 3, ad 4; *De spirit. creaturis*, 3, ad 1, ad 15, ad 17; *Quaest. de anima*, 3, ad 8.
⁵ *In II Sent.*, 17, 1, 2, sol.; *In lib. De Trinitate*, V, 1, c. Cf. above, note 4.
⁶ *S.T.*, I, 77, 3, ad 4 (*BW*, I, p. 725). *C.G.*, I, 51, *Item. Quanto*; 31, *Hujus autem*; 65, *Praeterea. In omnibus.*
⁷ *S.T.*, I, 1, 3, ad 2 (*BW*, I, p. 8). *In III Sent.*, 33, 1, 1, sol. 1; *S.T.*, I, 59, 4; 81, 2, c.; 82, 5; II–II, 50, 3, c.; I–II, 9, 1, c.
⁸ Cf. above, pp. 162–170.
⁹ *De Potentia*, III, 4, c.; *C.G.*, IV, 42, *Habet etiam*. Cf. above pp. 137–140.
¹⁰ *The Philosophy of Physical Science*, p. 16.
¹¹ Cf. above pp. 167–173.
¹² *C.G.*, III, 46 (*BW*, II, p. 81). *De veritate*, X, 8, c.; *Quodlibeta*, VIII, 4, c.; *In II De anima*, lect. 6, n. 308; *In I Sent.*, 17, 1, 4, ad 4.
¹³ *S.T.*, I, 78, 1, c. (*BW*, I, pp. 734–735). *C.G.*, IV, 11, *Est autem.*
¹⁴ *In III Sent.*, 24, 1, 1, sol. *De caritate*, 4, c.
¹⁵ *S.T.*, II–II, 1, 1 (*BW*, II, p. 1056). *In I Sent.*, 45, 1, 2, ad 1; 48, 2, sol.; *In II Sent.*, 20, 2, 2, ad 2; *In III Sent.*, 23, 2, 4, sol. 2; *S.T.*, I–II, 57, 2, ad 2.
¹⁶ Cf. above, pp. 177–183.

[17] *In III Phys.*, lect. 1; *In I Sent.*, 8, 4, 3, obj. 4; 33, 1, 1, sol.; *De Potentia*, IX, 5, ad 2; VII, 10, c. et 9 c.; VIII, 1, ad 4; *C.G.*, IV, 14.

[18] *S.T.*, I, 28, 2, c. (*BW*, I, pp. 284–285). *De Potentia*, VIII, 2, c.; *Quodlibeta*, IX, 4, c.

[19] *Quodlibeta*, IX, 4, c. et ad 3. *Quodlibeta*, I, 2, c.; *In III Sent.*, 8, 1, 5, ad 3; *S.T.*, III, 35, 5, c.

[20] *S.T.*, I, 77, 3, c. (*BW*, I, p. 724). *In II De anima*, lect. 6, nn. 305–307.

[21] For the technical meaning of the word *sufficient*, see Chenu in *RSPT*, XXII (1933), pp. 250–259.

[22] *S.T.*, I–II, 10, 2, ad 1, ad 2. (*BW*, II, p. 262).

[23] *In I Sent.*, 45, 1, 2, ad 1. *In II Sent.*, 9, 1, 2, sol.; *In III Sent.*, 24, 1, 1, sol. 1; *S.T.*, II–II, 1, 1–3; 2, 2 et 5; I–II, 57, 2, ad 2; 66, 5, ad 4; I, 2, 2, ad 2.

[24] *In I Sent.*, 48, 1, 2, sol.; 17, 1, 1, sol. et ad 2; *In II Sent.*, 20, 2, 2, ad 2.

[25] *S.T.*, I–II, 52, 1, c. (*BW*, II, p. 393). *S.T.*, I, 67, 1, c. (*BW*, I, p. 629–630); *De virtutibus in communi*, 11, c.

[26] *In V Metaph.*, lect. 17, n. 1004. *S.T.*, I, 28, 4, c. (*BW*, I, p. 288); *De Potentia*, VIII, 2, c.; *C.G.*, IV, 14; *Quodlibeta*, VI, 1; IX, 4, c.; *In I Sent.*, 8, 4, 3, sol.; 26, 2, 1, sol.; *In III Sent.*, 8, 5, sol.

[27] Cf. above, pp. 162–167.

[28] Cf. Schütz, *Thomas-Lexikon*, ad verb. *modus, esse.*

[29] *In I De anima*, lect. 10 nn. 159–160. *De veritate*, IV, 1, ad 1; *De Potentia*, VII, 8, c.; *De veritate*, X, 8, ad 11; *Quodlibeta*, VIII, 3, c.; *In II De anima*, lect. 11, nn. 365–366.

[30] *In V Metaph.*, lect. 17, n. 1003, 1026–1029. *In X Metaph.*, lect, 8, nn. 2088, 2095; lect. 9, n. 2103; *De Potentia*, VII, 10, c.

[31] *In V Metaph.*, lect. 17, nn. 1026–1027.

[32] *In I Sent.*, 30, 1, 3, ad 3. *De Potentia*, VII, 9–11, c.; *S.T.*, I, 13, 7, c.; *C.G.*, II, 11–12.

[33] Cf. below, pp. 258–308.

[34] *De Potentia*, VII, 6, c. et 11, c.; *In V Phys.*, lect. 3, n. 8; *In I Sent.*, 25, 2, 1, sol.; *S.T.*, I, 28, 1.

[35] *S.T.*, I, 13, 7, c. (*BW*, I, pp. 123–124). *C.G.*, IV, 14, *Ex his etiam; Quamvis autem.*

[36] Cf. J. Legrand, *L'Univers et l'homme dans la philosophie de saint Thomas,* (Paris, Desclée, 1946), II, pp. 119–281.

[37] *S.T.*, I, 13, 7, c.; *In V Metaph.* lect., 17, n. 1027; lect. 9, n. 896.

[38] *S.T.*, I, 84, 2, c. (*BW*, I, p. 796).

[39] *Ibid.* (*BW*, I, pp. 796–797).

[40] *S.T.*, I, 84, 4, c. (*BW*, I, p. 801). *In III De anima*, lect. 7, nn. 677–683; *S.T.*, I, 55, 2, obj. 1.

[41] *S.T.*, I, 55, 2, c. (*BW*, I, p. 797).

[42] *S.T.*, I, 84, 4, c. (*BW*, I, p. 802).

[43] Cf. above, pp. 162–167.

[44] *S.T.*, I, 84, 3, c. (*BW*, I, pp. 799–800).

[45] Cf. above, pp. 183–192.

[46] Cf. above, pp. 52–57.

[47] *In III De anima*, lect. 13, n. 790. *S.T.*, I, 84, 2, ad 2.

[48] *S.T.*, I, 77, 7, c. (*BW*, I, p. 730).

[49] Cf. above, pp. 167-170.

[50] *De veritate*, XVI, 1, ad 13. *In II De anima*, lect. 6, n. 305; *S.T.*, I, 77, 3, c.

[51] *S.T.*, I, 56, 1, c. (*BW*, I, pp. 522-523). *S.T.*, I, 14, 2, c. (*BW*, I, pp. 137-138).

[52] *S.T.*, I, 56, 1, c. et ad 3; I, 12, 2, c., et 5, c., ad 1, ad 2; I, 54, 2.

[53] Cf. below, pp. 253-260.

[54] *S.T.*, I, 56, 1, c. (*BW*, I, p. 523). *S.T.*, I, 14, 2, c. (*BW*, I, pp. 137-138); I-II, 51, 2, ad 2.

[55] *In II De anima*, lect. 11, nn. 365-366; lect. 12, n. 382; *In I De anima*, lect. 10, nn. 157-161; *S.T.*, I, 79, 2, c.

[56] *S.T.*, I, 52, 2, c.; *De veritate*, I, 6, c.

[57] *S.T.*, I, 12, 5; *In IV Sent.*, 49, 2, 1, ad 2.

[58] *S.T.*, I, 78, 1, c. (*BW*, I, pp. 734-735). *In II De anima*, lect. 15, nn. 437-438.

[59] Cf. above, pp. 140-144; also J. de Finance, *Etre et agir* (Paris, Beauchesne, 1946).

[60] Cf. below, pp. 300-306.

[61] *De Potentia*, II, 1, c. Cf. Schütz, *Thomas-Lexikon*, ad verb. *actus, agens*.

[62] *In I Sent.*, 4, 1, 1, sol. Cf. Schütz, *Thomas-Lexikon*, ad verb, *forma, communicare*.

[63] De Finance, *Etre et agir*, pp. 69-70.

[64] *C.G.*, II, 54; *S.T.*, I, 3, 4, c. Cf. de Finance, *Etre et agir*, pp. 97-118.

[65] *De Potentia*, V, 8, c. *In II Sent.*, 19, 1, 3, ad 1.

[66] Cf. Hayen, *L'Intentionel*, p. 132; de Finance, *Etre et agir*, p. 271; B. Romeyer, *La connaissance de l'âme par elle-même* (Paris, Beauchesne, 1928).

[67] Cf. Jeans, *Physics and Philosophy*, pp. 2, 58, 190, 195-205; Eddington, *The Philosophy of Physical Science*, pp. 115-117, 146-152.

[68] Eddington, *The Philosophy of Physical Science*, pp. 117, 132-136.

[69] *Ibid.*, pp. 152-169.

[70] *S.T.*, I, 78, 3, c. (*BW*, I, p. 739). *In II De anima*, lect. 14, n. 418.

[71] *Ibid.* Cf. Hayen, *L'Intentionel*, pp. 121-141.

[72] *In V Metaph.*, lect. 2, nn. 766-773.

[73] *S.T.*, I, 78, 3 (*BW*, I, p. 739). Cf. Legrand, *L'homme dans l'univers*, II, pp. 19-28.

[74] Cf. Eddington, *The Philosophy of Physical Science*, p. 156; Jeans, *Physics and Philosophy*, pp. 13-16.

[75] *S.T.*, I, 54, 5, c. (*BW*, I, p. 515). *C.G.*, II, 83, *Item necesse est.*

[76] *S.T.*, I, 75, 6, c. (*BW*, I, pp. 691-692).

[77] *C.G.*, II, 56, *Corpora enim*; 57, *Sed hoc esse*; 83, *Item necesse*; *De spirit. Creaturis*, 2, c.; *De unitate intellectus*, ed. Keeler, Chap. 1, sect. 23.

[78] *S.T.*, I, 77, 1, ad 3 (*BW*, I, p. 721).

[79] *S.T.*, I, 77, 1, ad 4 (*BW*, I, p. 721). *S.T.*, I, 45, 8, ad 2; *C.G.*, III, 69.

[80] *C.G.*, II, 56, *Corpora enim*; *De veritate*, XXVI, 1, c.

[81] *S.T.*, I, 78, 3, ad 1 (*BW*, I, p. 739). *In VII Phys.*, lect. 4, nn. 2-3; lect. 5-6, nn. 6-9; *In I De anima*, lect. 5, nn. 159-163.

[82] *In II De anima*, lect. 14, n. 425; *In IV Metaph.*, lect. 1, nn. 5-9.

[83] *S.T.*, I, 78, 3, ad 4 (*BW*, I, p. 740). *S.T.*, I, 85, 4, ad 2; *In IV Metaph.*, lect. 14, nn. 694-697, 702; *De ente et essentia*, 7; *In lib. De Trinitate*, IV, 3, c.

[84] *In II De anima*, lect. 13, n. 394; *In lib. De sensu et sensato*, lect. 2, n. 29; *In IV Sent.*, 49, 2, 2, sol. Cf. Meyerson, *Le cheminement de la pensée*, III, p. 692. See also *De ente et essentia*, 7; *S.T.*, I, 85, 4, ad 2; I–II, 49, 2, c.

[85] *Dispositio* is a technical word in the vocabulary of St. Thomas; cf. below, pp. 241-242. See P. Hoenen, *La théorie du jugement selon saint Thomas* Rome, (Gregorianum, 1946), pp. 70-79 (in English: *Reality and Judgment*, translated by H.J. Tiblier, Chicago, Regnery, 1952).

[86] *In III De anima*, lect. 2, n. 592; *In II Phys.*, lect. 2.

[87] The sense of touch has a primary importance for the establishment of this relation: *In I Metaph.*, lect. 1, nn. 8-9; *In IV Metaph.*, lect. 14, nn. 695-703; *S.T.*, I, 70, 3-4. On the importance of touch and sight in the constitution of scientific notions, cf. Jeans, *Physics and Philosophy*, pp. 11-15; Eddington, *The Philosophy of Science*, p. 74.

[88] When reality is not strong and perfect enough to cause sensation, then comes the *instrument* which is built to help reality and not the senses. Thus, a pair of spectacles is made to correct a defect of the eyes, but a microscope is made to correct the lack of power of reality; the first is for the knowing subject, the second for the object. We should always compare the senses and instruments made by men, as different tools, the one made by nature to grasp reality in its perfection, the other built by men to compensate for the lack of perfection in physical being.

[89] *S.T.*, I, 78, 3, c. (*BW*, I, p. 739). *In III De anima*, lect. 1, n. 583; *Quaest. de anima*, 13, c.; *In IV Sent.*, 44, 2, 1, sol. 2 et 3; *In II De anima*, lect. 24, nn. 552-553.

[90] Cf. above pp. 162-167.

[91] Cf. above, pp. 198-204.

[92] *S.T.*, I, 14, 2, c. (*BW*, I, p. 136). *In lib. De sensu et sensato*, lect. 2, n. 20; lect. 4 and 15-19; *In II De anima*, lect. 5, nn. 282-285; *In III Sent.*, 23, 1, 4, sol.

[93] Cf. Paul Valéry, *Eupalinos: L'âme et la dance* (Paris, N.R.F., 1927), p. 67.

[94] *Quodlibeta*, VIII, 3, c.; *In II De anima*, lect. 14, n. 425; *In III De anima*, lect. 7; *In I Metaph.*, lect. 1, n. 6; *In IV Metaph.*, lect. 14, nn. 695-697.

[95] *S.T.*, I, 45, 2, ad 3 (*BW*, I, p. 436).

[96] *S.T.*, I, 45, 3, c. (*BW*, I, p. 436).

[97] *C.G.*, II, 18.

[98] Cf. above, pp. 188-192.

[99] *Quodlibeta*, VIII, 3, c.

[100] *S.T.*, I, 14, 1, c. (*BW*, I, p. 136). *In I Sent.*, 35, 1, 1, sol.; *De veritate*, II, 1, c.; *C.G.*, I, 44; *Compendium Theol.*, I, 28; *S.T.*, I, 85, 8, ad 3; 14, 12, c.; *In II De anima*, lect. 12, n. 377; lect. 13, n. 394; lect. 14, n. 425.

[101] Cf. above, Chap. V.

[102] Cf. above, pp. 196-204.

[103] *De veritate*, VIII, 7, ad 2 *in contrarium*; VIII, 6, c.

[104] *De veritate*, II, 5, ad 17. *S.T.*, I, 14, 13; 88, 1, ad 2; *In II De anima*, lect.

12, n. 377; lect. 13, n. 394; lect. 14, n. 425; lect. 24, nn. 551–552; *C.G.*, I, 72 *Adhuc; De veritate*, II, 6, c.; VIII, 9, ad 3; X, 4, c.; *Quodlibeta*, VIII, 4, c.

[105] *De ente et essentia*, 4.

[106] Hayen, *L'Intentionel*, p. 15.

[107] Cajetan, *Commentarium in S.T.*, I, 55, 3, sect. 12. Cf. de Finance, *Etre et agir*, p. 70.

[108] Cf. above, pp. 140–144.

[109] Cajetan, *Comm. in S.T.*, I, 55, 3, sect. 13.

[110] *Quodlibeta*, VIII, 4, c.; *S.T.*, I, 56, 2, ad 3; 80, 1, c.

[111] Hayen, *L'Intentionel*, pp. 56–59, 111–117.

[112] *S.T.*, I, 45, 7, c. (*BW*, I, p. 444); 93, 6, c.

[113] *S.T.*, I, 35, 1, c. (*BW*, I, p. 339); 93, 1. *De veritate*, X, 7, c.

[114] *S.T.*, I, 93, 1, ad 2; *In II Sent.*, 16, 1, 1, sol.; *In I Sent.*, 3, 3, 1, ad 5; *C.G.*, IV, 14 *Adhuc; In Epist. ad Coloss.*, I, lect. 4.

[115] Cf. below, pp. 235–237.

[116] *In I De anima*, lect. 2 et seqq.

[117] Cf. Schütz, *Thomas-Lexikon*, ad verb, *recipere*.

[118] *S.T.*, I, 78, 2, c. Cf. above, pp. 208–215.

[119] *Quodlibeta*, VIII, 3, c.; *In II De anima*, lect. 13.

[120] *S.T.*, I, 4, 3, c., and parallel texts.

[121] Cf. Geiger, *La participation chez saint Thomas* (Paris, Vrin, 1943).

[122] *S.T.*, I, 14, 12, c. (*BW*, I, p. 153). *In II De anima*, lect. 12, n. 377; lect. 13, n. 394; lect. 14, n. 425.

[123] *S.T.*, I, 88, 1, ad 2 (*BW*, I, p. 846). *In II De anima*, lect. 14, nn. 551–552; lect. 5, n. 284; *De veritate*, II, 6, c.; X, 4, c.; VIII, 11, c. et ad 3; *C.G.*, I, 72 *Adhuc; De veritate*, II, 5, ad 17.

[124] *S.T.*, I, 85, 8, ad 3 (*BW*, I, p. 829).

[125] *S.T.*, I, 14, 13, ad 2. Cf. above, Chap. VI, note 114.

[126] Cf. Ernout et Meillet, *Dictionnaire étymologique*, ad verb. *species*.

[127] *De veritate*, II, 2, c.; *In II De anima*, lect. 5; *C.G.*, II, 68; *S.T.*, I, 14, 1. Cf. above, pp. 140–144.

[128] *S.T.*, I, 15, 2–3; 16, 1 and 3–7; 17, 1–3, and parallel texts.

[129] Cf. below, pp. 260–275.

[130] Cf. below, pp. 263–264.

[131] *S.T.*, I, 55, 1, ad 2. Cf. the doctrine of the passivity of our cognitive powers, above, pp. 198–203.

[132] For the interrelation between the knowledge of the accidents and that of the substance, cf. below, pp. 294–298.

[133] *Quodlibeta*, VIII, 4; *De veritate*, I, 4–8; *S.T.*, I, 16, 4–7.

[134] It is in the light of such metaphysical doctrine on the nature of the human soul and its powers that we should re-examine the psychoanalytic theories of Freud and Jung on the collective and individual unconsciousness.

[135] The description of the physical causality on the sensitive organism is the part of St. Thomas' teaching that is a thing of the past; it must be replaced by the data of contemporary science and psychology. But the spiritual im-

mutation and the nature of the sensible species has nothing to do with science; it rests on metaphysical causality and must be studied in a metaphysical context.

[136] Cf. Eddington, *New Pathways*, "Epilogue"; *Science and the Unseen World* (London, George Allen, 1929), pp. 20–30, 34, 38–41, 56.

[137] Cf. above, pp. 176–197.

[138] Cf. above, pp. 198–204.

[139] *S.T.*, I, 57, 1, ad 2 (*BW*, I, p. 529). *S.T.*, I, 86, 1, ad 4; *De vertate*, X, 4, ad 2; 5, ad 3; 6, ad 2; 8, ad 2 *in contrarium; C.G.*, II, 66–67; *C.G.*, III, 56 *Amplius; C.G.*, IV, 11, *Est autem.*

[140] *S.T.*, I, 79, 3, c.; *C.G.*, II, 62, *Adhuc.*

[141] Cf. above, pp. 186–188.

[142] Cf. Gilson, *Being and Some Philosophers*, Chaps. III–IV.

[143] *S.T.*, I, 79, 3, c. (*BW*, I, p. 749). *Quaest. de anima*, 4.

[144] *S.T.*, I, 85, 1, ad 3 (*BW*, I, p. 815).

[145] S.T., I, qq. 84–87. Cf. below, pp. 284–306.

[146] Cf. above, pp. 176–180.

[147] Cf. above, pp. 39–61, 112–114.

[148] *De Potentia*, VI, 3, c. Cf. Durantel, *Le retour à Dieu* (Paris, Alcan, 1934), Chaps. IV–V.

[149] *C.G.*, II, 77, *Adhuc.* Cf. also *In II Metaph.*, lect. 1, nn. 282–285; *De veritate*, IX, 1, ad 18; *S.T.*, I, 14, 4, ad 2; 80, 1, c.

[150] *S.T.*, I, 79, 4–6; *C.G.*, III, 72–82.

[151] *De veritate*, II, 2, c.; *De Potentia*, VII, 10; *Quaest. de anima*, 5, ad 3; *De spirit. creaturis*, 8–9; *S.T.*, I, 13, 7.

[152] *C.G.*, II, 25, *Rursus;* 76, *Si autem; De spirit. creaturis*, 10, ad 15. Cf. above, pp. 198–203.

[153] *S.T.*, I, 54, 4, c. (*BW*, p. 174). *S.T.*, I, 79, 3–4; *C.G.*, II, 75–78; *De spirit. creaturis*, 10; *Quaest. de anima*, 4, c.

[154] For the axiom, "essences are like numbers," see Schütz, *Thomas-Lexikon*, ad verb. *essentia, numerus, species.*

[155] *C.G.*, II 77, and the *Commentary* of Sylvester of Ferrara, *C. G.*, II, sect. 8–12.

[156] *C.G.*, II, 25, *Primo quidem; In II Sent.*, 3, 1, 1, ad 3; *In I Sent.*, 17, 2, 1, ad 3; *De ente et essentia*, 4; *veritate*, III, 2, ad 5; *S.T.*, I, 50, 2, ad 2; 79, 2, c.

[157] *C.G.*, II, 25, *Rursus; De spirit. creaturis*, 11, ad 15; *S.T.*, I, 77, 3; *In II De anima*, lect. 6, n. 306. Cf. A. Krempel, *La doctrine de la relation* (Paris, Vrin, 1952).

[158] *Quaest. de anima*, 4 et 13; *S.T.*, I–II, 18, 2, ad 3.

[159] *S.T.*, I, 85, 1, ad 3, ad 4, ad 5 (*BW*, I, p. 815); *C.G.*, II, 77, *Differt.*

[160] Cf. above, pp. 212–217.

[161] *C.G.*, I, 53, *Haec autem. S.T.*, I, 56, 1, c.; *De unitate intellectus*, ed. Keeler, p. 171; *C.G.*, II, 75, *Secunda vero; Licet autem.*

[162] Cf. Schütz, *Thomas-Lexikon*, pp. 4–5, 455–456; J. Guillet, *La lumière intellectuelle d'après saint Thomas*, in *Archives d'histoire doctrinale et littéraire*

du moyen âge, II (1927), pp. 79–88; F.A. Blanche, *La théorie de l'abstraction*, in *Mélanges thomistes* (Paris, Vrin, 1935), pp. 237–251.

[163] *Quaest. de anima*, 18, ad 11; *In III Sent.*, 14, 3, 3, sol.; *Quodlibeta*, V, 1. Cf. above, pp. 225–227, and below, pp. 238–241.

[164] *S.T.*, I, 88, 1, c. (*BW*, I, p. 884). *S.T.*, I, 89, 1, c.; 84, 7, c.; *In III Sent.*, 31, 2, 4, sol. For an explanation of the expression, *natural relation*, see *Quaest. de anima*, 16, c.: *aspectum inclinatum ad phantasmata.*

[165] *S.T.*, I, 85, 1 (*BW*, I, p. 813). See the parallel texts.

[166] Cf. above, pp. 198–216.

[167] *In IV Sent.*, 45, 2, 1, ad 1; *Quaest, de anima*, 1, c. et ad 1; 15, ad 8; *De veritate*, XIII, 1, c.; *C.G.*, II, 45, *Quod est.* Cf. below, pp. 289–294.

[168] Cf. M. Congar, *Le rôle des images dans l'abstraction intellectuelle*, in *Revue thomiste* (1934–1935), pp. 224–245.

[169] *De veritate*, X, 6; *Quaest. de anima*, 4, ad 4; 18, ad 11; *S.T.*, I, 79, 3–4.

[170] *De veritate*, XVIII, 8, ad 3. Cf. Guillet, *op. cit.*, pp. 83–84; *De veritate*, X, 6, c.

[171] The word *formatio* technically expresses the vital production of the intelligible in act. See *De veritate*, X, 6. Cf. Guillet, *op. cit.*, pp. 83, 84, note 2; and Maréchal, *Le thomisme devant la philosophie critique*, Cahier V, pp. 275–285.

[172] *De veritate*, VIII, 7, ad 2 *in contrarium;* also art. 6. Cf. above, pp. 210–216.

[173] *De veritate*, XIX, 1, c.; VIII, 9; *De sensu et sensato*, lect. 2; *C.G.*, II, 96; *De veritate*, II, 2, c.

[174] *Compendium Theol.*, I, 33; *C.G.*, IV, 11, *Considerandum est; De veritate*, III, 2, c.; *De rationibus fidei*, 3.

[175] *S.T.*, I, 54, 4, *Sed contra*, c. et ad 2 (*BW*, I, p. 513). *S.T.*, I, 79, 3, ad 2; *Quaest. de anima*, 18, ad 11; *De veritate*, VIII, 11.

[176] *In IV Sent.*, 49, 2, 1, ad 15. Cf. Congar, *op. cit.*, pp. 230–234.

[177] Cf. above, pp. 226–229.

[178] *S.T.*, I, 85, 1, ad 3, and the parallel texts.

[179] *S.T.*, I, 85, 1, ad 4 (*BW*, I, p. 815). *De veritate*, X, 6, ad 1 et ad 8; *Quaest. de anima*, 4.

[180] Cf. above, pp. 142–144. See also *S.T.*, I, 88, 1.

[181] *S.T.*, I, 77, arts. 4, 6, 7; 89, 1, c.; 55, 2, c.; 94, 2, c.; *De spirit. creaturis*, 6, c.; *Quaest. de anima*, 1, ad 1, ad 12; 15, ad 6; 17, ad 17; *In II Metaph.*, lect. 1. Cf. Pegis, *In Umbra Intelligentiae*, in *New Scholasticism*, XIV (1940), pp. 146–180.

[182] *S.T.*, I, 89, 1, c. (*BW*, I, p. 852).

[183] *De veritate*, XVIII, 8, ad 3. *In II Sent.*, 20, 2, ad 2; *Compend. Theol.*, I, 104; *Quaest. de anima*, 16, c.; 18, ad 11.

[184] Cf. above, pp. 176–183.

[185] *S.T.*, I, 50, 2; *De veritate*, X, 5, ad 1, ad 5; 6, ad 2; *C.G.*, IV, 11.

[186] Cf. above, pp. 176–183.

[187] Cf. P. Garin, *La théorie de l'idée* (Paris, Desclée, 1932); Legrand, *L'Univers et l'homme*, Vol. II; F.X. Maquart, *L'Action de l'intellect agent*, in *Rev. de philosophie* (1929), pp. 380–416; Congar, *op. cit.*, pp. 225–245.

[188] Cf. above, pp. 223–231.

[189] *S.T.*, I, 77, 3, c. (*BW*, I, p. 724). *De veritate*, XVI, 1, ad 13; *In II De anima*, lect. 6, n. 305.

[190] *S.T.*, I, 104, 2, ad 3; 45, 2.

[191] Cf. Schütz, *Thomas-Lexikon*, ad verb. *materia circa quam*, p. 467, sect. b.

[192] Technically, *phantasmata* designates the result of the work of all the interior senses. Cf. below, pp. 236–241.

[193] Cf. above, p. 233.

[194] Cajetan taught that the phantasms were spiritualized by the illumination of the agent intellect; see Congar, *op. cit.*, pp. 230–234.

[195] This is the opinion of Sylvester of Ferrara; see Congar, *op. cit.*, pp. 235–237.

[196] This last position is that of John of St. Thomas; see Congar, *op. cit.*, pp. 238–244.

[197] The distinction between these two modes of causality—efficient causality producing the order of exercise and objective causality producing the order of specification—will be found again in the explanation of the object as term of the act of knowledge. See below, Chap. VII.

[198] *De veritate*, X, 6, ad 7. *In III Sent.*, 14, 1, 1, sol. 2, ad 2.

[199] Cf. above, Chap. VI, note 183.

[200] Cf. Hayen, *L'Intentionel*, pp. 108–117.

[201] *S.T.*, I, 79, 4, ad 3 (*BW*, I, p. 752). *S.T.*, I, 84, 5, c.; 88, 3, ad 1; *De spirit. creaturis*, 10, ad 8; *Quaest. de anima*, 5; *In IV Sent.*, 49, 2, 1, ad 15; *De veritate*, VIII, 11, ad 3; X, 6, ad 1.

[202] *Quaest. de anima*, 5, ad 6 et ad 9. *De spirit. creaturis*, 9, c.; 10, ad 15; *In II Sent.*, 14, 2, 3, c.

[203] *In III De anima*, lect. 10, nn. 738–739. *In II Sent.*, 3, 3, 4, sol.; *C.G.*, II, 77, *Si quis*; *De veritate*, VIII, 8, ad 3; 15, c.; X, 6, c.; *De spirit. creaturis*, 10, ad 4; *S.T.*, I, 85, 1, ad 3; *De malo*, XVI, 12, ad 2.

[204] *De veritate*, IX, 1, c. *Quodlibeta*, VII, 1, c.; *In IV Sent.*, 49, 2, 1, ad 15.

[205] *S.T.*, I, 54, 4, c.; 85, 1–3; 89, 1; *C.G.*, II, 59 et 80; *C.G.*, III, 41–42; *In III De anima*, lect. 10; *In II Sent.*, 20, 2, 2, ad 2; 3, 1, 6, sol.

[206] Cf. above, pp. 183–197.

[207] Cf. above, Chap. VI, note 183; *De veritate*, XIV, 5, c.; XII, 12, c.; *S.T.*, II–II, 9, 2, ad 3.

[208] *In II Sent.*, 20, 2, 2, ad 4. *De veritate*, XVIII, 7, c. et ad 5.

[209] *In II Sent.*, 20, 2, 2, sol. *De veritate*, XVIII, 7–8; *S.T.*, I, 101, 1–2; 8, 3, c.; *C.G.*, II, 60.

[210] *S.T.*, II–II, 173, 2, c. *De veritate*, XII, 7, c.

[211] *S.T.*, I, 77, 4, c.; 7, c.

[212] Recall the theory that substances are known only through their accidents; see above, Chap. IV, note 102.

[213] *S.T.*, I, 79, 4, ad 3 (*BW*, I, p. 752). *S.T.*, I, 75, 3, ad 2; 89, 5; I–II, 67, 2, c.

[214] *S.T.*, I, 84, 8, ad 2; I–II, 51, 3, c.

[215] *S.T.*, I, 89, 5, c.; II–II, 173, 2, c.; *C.G.*, II, 77, *Si autem*.

[216] *S.T.*, II–II, 173, 2, c.; *De veritate*, XI, 3, c.; *In II Sent.*, 11, 1, 5, ad 6.

[217] *In V Metaph.*, lect. 20, n. 1058. Cf. Schütz, *Thomas-Lexikon*, pp. 241–243.

[218] *De virtutibus in communi*, 1, ad 9.

[219] *S.T.*, I, 91, 3, c.; I–II, 50, 1–3; *Quaest. de anima*, 8.

[220] *S.T.*, I–II, 74, 5, ad 3 (*BW*, II, p. 606). *S.T.*, I–II, 88, 3, c.; *C.G.*, II, 72, *Videtur.*

[221] *S.T.*, I, 77, 7, c. (*BW*, I, p. 730).

[222] *S.T.*, I, 78, 4, c.; 84, 6, ad 2; *De veritate*, X, 6, ad 5; *Quodlibeta*, VIII, 3, c.

[223] *C.G.*, II, 53, *Amplius;* 81, *Sciendum;* 70, *Dicit enim;* 73, *Si autem.*

[224] *C.G.*, II, 81, *Sciendum;* 76, *Potest autem;* 72, *Adhuc; S.T.*, I, 89, 5.

[225] *S.T.*, I–II, 51, 1, c. (*BW*, II, p. 388). *S.T.*, I, 75, 3, ad 2; 76, 5.

[226] *S.T.*, I, 85, 7, c., and parallel texts.

[227] *Ibid.* See also *C.G.*, II, 84, *Sciendum est.*

[228] *S.T.*, I–II, 50, 3, c. (*BW*, II, pp. 381–382). *S.T.*, I–II, 50, 5, ad 3; 51, 3, c.; 17, 7, c. et ad 3; *S.T.*, I, 81, 3, c. et ad 3; *De veritate*, XXV, 4, c.; *De virtutibus in communi*, 4, ad 6.

[229] *S.T.*, I–II, 50, 3, ad 2.

[230] *De veritate*, XI, 2, c.; *S.T.*, I–II, 50, 3, ad 3. For the use of examples to facilitate the understanding of abstract truths in teaching, see *C.G.*, II, 75, *Sciendum tamen*, 98, *Non est, Exempla; De veritate*, IX, 5, c.; *S.T.*, I, 84, 7, c.

[231] *De veritate*, XI, 1, ad 11 et ad 14. *S.T.*, III, 7, 1, c.; 9, c.; I, 117, 1, c. et ad 3; II–II, 174, 3, c.

[232] *S.T.*, I, 94, 3, c., and parallel texts.

[233] *S.T.*, I, 84, 5, c. (*BW*, I, p. 804).

[234] *S.T.*, I–II, 109, 1, ad 2 (*BW*, II, p. 981).

[235] *In I Sent.*, 3, 4, 5, sol.; *De veritate*, X, 8, ad 10 *in contrarium; Quodlibeta*, X, 7, c.; *De spirit. creaturis*, 10, c.; *C.G.*, II, 77, *Differt; S.T.*, I, 79, 3, ad 2; 79, 4, c.; 85, 5, c. et ad 1.

[236] *S.T.*, II–II, 171, 2, c.

[237] *S.T.*, I, 84, 5, c.; *C.G.*, III, 49. Cf. Pegis, *In Umbra Intelligentiae*, in *New Scholasticism*, XIV (1940), pp. 157–180; and below, pp. 315–317.

[238] *S.T.*, I, 89, 1, c. (*BW*, I, p. 853).

[239] Cf. above, pp. 186–197.

[240] Cf. Hayen, *L'Intentionel*, pp. 117–119.

[241] Cf. above, pp. 183–187, on the hylemorphism of the object of knowledge. See also *S.T.*, I, 56, 1, c.; I–II, 67, 2, c.; *Supplementum*, 92, 1, c.; *C.G.*, I, 46.

[242] *S.T.*, I, 86, 1, ad 4; *De veritate*, X, 6, ad 2; 8, ad 2; XXV, 3, c.

[243] *S.T.*, *Supplementum*, 92, 1, c.; *Quodlibeta*, VII, 1; *De veritate*, IX, 1, c.; *In IV Sent.*, 49, 2, 1, ad 15. Cf. above, p. 177; and Schütz, *Thomas-Lexikon*, ad verb. *medium* and *lumen.*

[244] Cf. above, pp. 140–145.

Chapter VII

[1] *S.T.*, I, 54, 2; 56, 1, ad 3; 57, 1, ad 2; 12, 2, c.; 12, 5, c. et ad 3.

[2] Ernout et Meillet, *Dictionnaire étymologique*, p. 532. The word *elicere* comes from *lax* and means a magical apparition, a surprise, a cunning move.

[3] *De veritate*, II, 6, ad 15. *De spirit. creaturis*, 4, ad 6. Cf. above, pp. 162–167.

[4] *De veritate*, XIV, 8, ad 5.

[5] Cf. above, Chap. V.

[6] *S.T.*, I–II, 9, 1, c. (*BW*, II, p. 250–251). *De malo*, VI, 1. Cf. Hayen, *L'Intentionel*, p. 239, note 3, where a queer interpretation of this distinction is given.

[7] Cf. Ernout et Meillet, *Dictionnaire étymologique*, p. 67: *arceo*.

[8] Kierkegaard, *Le concept d'angoisse* (Paris, Gallimard, 1935), p. 202.

[9] Cf. above, pp. 198–199.

[10] See the etymology for *elicere* above, Chap. VII, note 2.

[11] *In III Sent.*, 27, 4, sol. 3. *S.T.*, I–II, 6, 4, c.; 1, 1, ad 2; III, 86, 2, ad 1.

[12] *S.T.*, I, 105, 5, c. (*BW*, I, pp. 976–977). *S.T.*, I–II, 49, 3, c.

[13] *S.T.*, I–II, 49, 3; 54, 1, c.; *In III Sent.*, 23, 1, 1, sol.

[14] Cf. above, Chap. V.

[15] *S.T.*, I, 85, 7, c. (*BW*, I, pp. 826–827). *S.T.*, I–II, 51, 1; 52, 1–3. The same principle applies for the degrees of beatitude in heaven, where the Light of Glory is diversely participated by the Blessed; see *S.T.*, I, 12, 5.

[16] Cf. above, Chap. VII, note 6.

[17] Cf. above, pp. 192–197.

[18] *S.T.*, I, 13, 7, c. (*BW*, I, p. 124). *C.G.*, IV, 14, *Ex his etiam; Quamvis autem; In X Metaph.*, lect. 2, nn. 1956–1958.

[19] *S.T.*, I, 28, 2, c. (*BW*, I, p. 285). *Quodlibeta*, VII, 4, c.; I, 2, c.; IX, 4; *De Potentia*, VIII, 2, c.; *In V Metaph.*, lect. 17, n. 1029.

[20] Cf. above, pp. 132, 137–138.

[21] *S.T.*, I, 84, 4, ad 6; *Quodlibeta*, VII, 4, c. Cf. above, pp. 154–155, 175–177.

[22] *C.G.*, IV, 11.

[23] Notice that the number of external senses is dependent on *objective necessity* but the number of interior senses depends on the *perfection of the knowing subject.*

[24] *S.T.*, I, 78, 4, c. et ad 2 (*BW*, I, pp. 742–743). *Quaest. de anima*, 13, c.; *Quodlibeta*, VIII, 3, c.; *C.G.*, II, 74, *Quod quidem.*

[25] *In II De anima*, lect. 13; *In III De anima*, lect. 6, n. 661; *S.T.*, I, 17, 1–2.

[26] *In III De anima*, lect. 2–3.

[27] *S.T.*, I, 87, 3, ad 3; *In III De anima*, lect. 2, nn. 584–591.

[28] *C.G.*, III, 104; *In III De anima*, lect. 6; *De veritate*, VIII, 5, c.; *Quodlibeta*, VIII, 3, c. Cf. below, pp. 265–266.

[29] *S.T.*, I–II, 17, 7, c.; 53, 3, c.

[30] *S.T.*, I, 78, 4, c.; 81, 2–3; *Quaest. de anima*, 13.

[31] *De veritate*, I, 9, c.; *In IV Metaph.*, lect. 6, n. 599; *In I Metaph.*, lect. 1, n. 15.

[32] Cf. above, pp. 197–210, 229–241.

[33] *S.T.*, I, 57, 1, ad 2 (*BW*, I, p. 529). *C.G.*, IV, 11, *Est autem*; *C.G.*, II, 76.

[34] Cf. *In V Metaph.*, lect. 9, where the relation between being and knowledge is indicated.

[35] *S.T.*, I, 67, 3, c. et ad 1; 77, 3, c.; 78, 3, c. et ad 2; I–II, 49, 2, c.; 50, 1, ad 3.

[36] *S.T.*, I, 85, 1, ad 2; *In VII Metaph.*, lect. 9, nn. 1469, 1473; lect. 2, n. 1304; *In VIII Metaph.*, lect. 5, n. 1760; *In III De anima*, lect. 8, n. 706; *In lib. De Trinitate*, V, 2, c.

[37] *S.T.*, I, 78, 3, ad 1 (*BW*, I, p. 739). *In II De anima*, lect. 13, nn. 384, 394.

[38] *In II Phys.*, lect. 3, n. 5; *In V Metaph.*, lect. 20, nn. 1065–1067; *In VII Phys.*, lect. 4.

[39] *S.T.*, I–II, 51, 1, ad 2. Cf. above, pp. 210–221.

[40] *In II De anima*, lect. 13, nn. 379, 394. *In lib. De sensu et sensato*, lect. 1, n. 29; *In lib. De memoria*, lect. 2, n. 319; *Quaest. de anima*, 13; *S.T.*, I, 78, 3, ad 2.

[41] Cf. above, pp. 64–65, and note 93 in Chap. II. In the man-sized world there are three dimensions grasped by human sensation; in the world of the *nebulae* and of the electron, geometrical representation is left behind—to be replaced by probabilities and mathematical symbols that describe not nature but certain observations about it.

[42] *In lib. De sensu et sensato*, lect. 1, n. 29.

[43] Cf. above, Chap. V.

[44] *S.T.*, I, 78, 4, ad 1 (*BW*, I, p. 743). *In III De anima*, lect. 12, nn. 773–774; lect. 3, nn. 609–612; *Quodlibeta*, VII, 2, ad 1; *In lib. De sensu et sensato*, lect. 19, n. 288.

[45] *De veritate*, XV, 1, ad 3, et 2, c.; *S.T.*, I, 1, 3, ad 1; 54, 2, c.

[46] *In II De anima*, lect. 13, nn. 390–391; *In III De anima*, lect. 3, n. 599.

[47] *S.T.*, I, 57, 2, c. (*BW*, I, p. 531). *In lib. De sensu et sensato*, lect. 14, nn. 280–287, 293.

[48] *In II De anima*, lect. 13, n. 390. *In III De anima*, lect. 3, nn. 599–612; *S.T.*, I, 78, 4, ad 2; *In lib. De sensu et sensato*, lect. 19, n. 287.

[49] *S.T.*, I, 78, 4, c.; *In III De anima*, lect. 12, nn. 767–769, 771.

[50] *S.T.*, I, 52, 2, c.

[51] *In III De anima*, lect. 6, n. 664; *C.G.*, III, 104; *S.T.*, II–II, 51, 3, c.

[52] *In I Sent.*, 19, 2, 1–2; *In V Phys.*, lect. 15–23; *S.T.*, I, 10, 2, ad 1; 4, ad 2; 6, c.

[53] *In lib. De memoria*, lect. 1, n. 310; lect. 2, nn. 314–326; lect. 3, n. 363; *In lib. De sensu et sensato*, lect. 8, n. 111; *In IV Phys.*, lect. 15, n. 6; lect. 17, nn. 2–8.

[54] *In lib. De memoria*, lect. 1, n. 310; lect. 2, n. 319; *S.T.*, I, 10, 1–6; *In I Sent.*, 19, 5.

[55] *In lib. De sensu et sensato*, lect. 18, n. 270.

[56] *In IX Metaph.*, lect. 3, nn. 1805–1806. *S.T.*, I, 10, 1, ad 1, ad 2; 75, 6; *In IV Sent.*, 49, 3, 2, sol.

[57] Cf. below, pp. 284–294.

[58] Cf. Legrand, *L'Homme dans l'univers*, II, pp. 30–40; Hayen, *L'Intentionel*, pp. 160–169, 174–181.

[59] *In lib. De memoria*, lect. 2, nn. 319–323.

[60] *S.T.*, I, 78, 4, c.; 85, 2, ad 3 (*BW*, I, p. 742). *In III De anima*, lect. 6; *Quaest. de anima*, 13; 4, ad 2; *Quodlibeta*, V, 9, ad 2; VIII, 3, c.; *In lib. De memoria*, lect. 2.

[61] *In lib. De memoria*, lect. 2, n. 319; lect. 3, n. 328. *S.T.*, I, 81, 3, ad 3.

[62] *De veritate*, I, 12, c.; *In III De anima*, lect. 4, n. 633; lect. 5, n. 645; *S.T.*, I, 17, 2, ad 2.

[63] *In III De anima*, lect. 6, nn. 664–665; *In II De anima*, lect. 13; *S.T.*, I, 17, 1–2.

[64] *In III De anima*, lect. 4, n. 624; lect. 6, nn. 660–670; *S.T.*, I, 81, 3, ad 3; *De veritate*, I, 12, c. Cf. Schütz, *Thomas-Lexikon*, ad verb. *imaginatio, phantasia.*

[65] *S.T.*, I, 8, 4, ad 6.

[66] *In lib. De memoria*, lect. 2, n. 322.

[67] *In II De anima*, lect. 13, nn. 395–396; *In III De anima*, lect. 1, n. 580; lect. 4, n. 635; *In III Eth. Nic.*, lect. 19, n. 605; *In III Sent.*, 26, 1, 1, ad 4; *In IV Sent.*, 49, 2, 2, sol.; *S.T.*, I, 85, 1, ad 4.

[68] *S.T.*, I, 78, 4, c.; *In III De anima*, lect. 4, n. 635. Cf. Simonin, *La notion d'intentio*, in *RSPT*, XX (1930), pp. 445–463.

[69] *S.T.*, I, 81, 1, c.; 80, 1, ad 3. For the analogy between the cogitative power and the practical intellect, see *In II Sent.*, 24, 2, 1, sol. et ad 2; *C.G.*, II, 72, *Quia. Cum, Adhuc. Scientia*; *S.T.*, I, 81, 2, ad 2; I–II, 30, 3 ad 3. Cf. Legrand, *L'Homme dans l'univers*, II, pp. 35–38, 82–94, 158–164.

[70] *In II De anima*, lect. 13, n. 398. *In II Post. Analyt.*, lect. 20, n. 14; *In VI Eth. Nic.*, lect. 7, nn. 1214–1215; *In I Sent.*, 26, 1, 1, ad 3; *S.T.*, I, 84, 7, c. For the definition of *particular*, see *S.T.*, I, 75, 2, ad 1; *In lib. De causis*, lect. 19.

[71] *In lib. De memoria*, lect. 1, n. 299; lect. 8, nn. 399, 407; *In lib. De divinis nominibus*, lect. 7; *In lib. De causis*, lect. 19.

[72] *In I Eth. Nic.*, lect. 1, nn. 1–2; *In II Post. Analyt.*, lect. 20, n. 14; *De veritate*, XIV, 1, ad 9. Cf. Schütz, *Thomas-Lexikon*, ad verb. *cogitativa.*

[73] *S.T.*, I, 81, 2, c. (*BW*, I, pp. 774–776). *De veritate*, X, 5. Cf. V.J. Bourke, *Ethics* (New York, Macmillan, 1952), p. 234 and Texts II–V, pp. 245–246.

[74] *In I Metaph.*, lect. 1, n. 14. *In III Eth. Nic.*, lect. 19, n. 611.

[75] The word *intuition* is synonymous here with the notion of experimental knowledge. Cf. *In II De anima*, lect. 13, n. 396; *In IV Sent.*, 49, 2, 2, sol.; *S.T.*, I, 12, 3, ad 2.

[76] Cf. G.P. Klubertanz, *The Discursive Power: Sources and Doctrine of the Vis Cogitativa*, (St. Louis, Modern Schoolman, 1952).

[77] Cf. above, pp. 241–244.

[78] *S.T.*, I, 78, 4, c.; *Quaest. de anima*, 13, c. Cf. Legrand, *L'Homme dans l'univers*, II, pp. 89–92.

[79] *In I Metaph.*, lect. 1, nn. 11–22; *In II Post. Analyt.*, lect. 20, nn. 8–14; *In IV Metaph.*, lect. 6, n. 599.

[80] *C.G.*, II, 33, *Adhuc. Si tempus*; *In IV Phys.*, lect. 15, nn. 3–7; lect. 16, n. 6; lect. 17, nn. 2, 6, 10–13; lect. 17; lect. 21, nn. 2–10; lect. 23, nn. 4–12; *In I Sent.*, 19, 2, 1, sol. et art. 2; 37, 4, 3, sol.; *In IV Sent.*, 49, 3, 1, sol. 4, et art. 2, sol.; *S.T.*, I, 10, 2, ad 1; 4, ad 2; 6, c.

[81] *In lib. De sensu et sensato*, lect. 1, n. 9; *In III Sent.*, 26, 1, 1, ad 9.

[82] *S.T.*, I, 10, 1, c. (*BW*, I, pp. 74–75). *In I Sent.*, 19, 2, 1, ad 4.

[83] *S.T.*, I, 75, 6, c.(*BW*, I, p. 692). *C.G.*, II, 96, *Palam est.*

[84] *C.G.*, II, 66, *Item.*

[85] *S.T.*, I, 87, 3, c. (*BW*, I, p. 841). Cf. *In II De anima*, lect. 6, nn. 304–306; *In III De anima*, lect. 9, nn. 724–727; *In III Sent.*, 23, 1, 2, ad 5; *De veritate*, X, 8, ad 2 *in contrarium; In lib. De Trinitate*, I, 3, c.

[86] *De veritate*, X, 8, c. *S.T.*, I, 79, 1, c.

[87] *S.T.*, I, 87, 3, ad 2; *In I Sent.*, 17, 1, 5, ad 4; *Declaratio*, q. 81 (ed. Mandonnet, III, 238).

[88] Cf. above, Chap. VII, notes 23–24.

[89] *S.T.*, I, 77, c.; *In lib. De causis*, lect. 17; *In lib. De Trinitate*, I, 3, c.

[90] Cf. above, pp. 142–144, 248–250.

[91] Cf. above, pp. 176–183, 222–226.

[92] Cf. above, pp. 226–248.

[93] *S.T.*, I, 79, 2–6; *C.G.*, I, 53, *Considerandum est.*

[94] *S.T.*, I, 87, 3, ad 3 (*BW*, I, p. 841). *S.T.*, I, 75, 2, ad 3.

[95] *S.T.*, I, 85, 2, c. (*BW*, I, p. 817). *De veritate*, I, 9, c.

[96] Cf. above, pp. 265–266.

[97] *C.G.*, I, 53, *Ulterius; C.G.*, IV, 11, *Dico autem; In I Sent.*, 27, 2, 1, sol.

[98] *Comp. Theol.*, I, 33. *C.G.*, IV, 11, *Considerandum est; De veritate*, III, 2, c.; *De rationibus fidei*, 3 (ed. Mandonnet, III, 254.

[99] *C.G.*, I, 53, *Ulterius autem. De potentia*, VIII, 1, c.; IX, 5, c.

[100] Cf. above, pp. 241–244.

[101] Cf. J. Peghaire, *Intellectus et ratio selon saint Thomas* (Paris, Vrin, 1936), pp. 15, 86–94.

[102] *S.T.*, I, 58, 4, c. (*BW*, I, p. 543). *C.G.*, III, 108, *Item est nobis; In II Sent.*, 3, 1, 6, sol. Cf. Pegis, *In Umbra Intelligentiae*, in *New Scholasticism*, XIV (1940), 165–170.

[103] These are the three essential aspects of Thomistic epistemology, as stated above, pp. 137–140.

[104] *Ratio* does not designate another intellectual power but a specific function of the intellect. See *S.T.*, I, 79, 8, and parallel texts.

[105] Cf. Chenu in *RSPT*, XVI (1927), pp. 445 ff.; Peghaire, *Intellectus et ratio*, pp. 90–92.

[106] See Blanche, *La théorie de l'abstraction*, in *Mélanges thomistes*, pp. 237–251.

[107] Cf. Régis, *Philosophie de la nature:abstraction et métaphysique*, in *Philosophie*, Cahier I (Ottawa, 1935), pp. 130–155.

[108] *S.T.*, I, 40, 3, c. (*BW*, I, p. 386). *S.T.*, I, 85, 1, ad 3; *In III Metaph.*, lect. 3, nn. 355–356; *De spirit. creaturis*, 9, ad 13; *In lib. De Trinitate*, V, 3, c. Cf. above, Chap. VII, note 107.

[109] Cf. Régis, *L'Opinion selon Aristote*, pp. 145–147.

[110] Cf. *S.T.*, I, 79, 6, c., ad 2, ad 3, and parallel texts.

[111] *S.T.*, I, 75, 2, ad 3 (*BW*, I, p. 686).

[112] *S.T.*, I, 57, 2, ad 1 (*BW*, I, p. 529). *C.G.*, IV, 11, *Est autem; Quodlibeta*, VIII, 4, c.; *In III Sent.*, 35, 2, 2, ad 3.

[113] Cf. Peghaire, *Intellectus et ratio*, pp. 85-89; Pegis, *In Umbra Intelligentiae*, in *New Scholasticism*, XIV (1940), pp. 163-167.

[114] *In IV Metaph.*, lect. 6, n. 605.

[115] *S.T.*, I, 5, 2, c. (*BW*, I, p. 44). *C.G.*, II, 83, *Adhuc. Cum naturam.*

[116] *S.T.*, I-II, 94, 2, c. (*BW*, II, pp. 772-773). *S.T.*, I-II, 55, 4, ad 1; *In I Post. Analyt.*, lect. 5, n. 7; *De veritate*, I, 1, c.; XXI, 4, ad 4; *In I Sent.*, 8, 1, 3, sol.

[117] *S.T.*, I, 87, 3, ad 1 (*BW*, I, p. 841).

[118] For an exposition of this intuitive character of the intellect, see Peghaire, *Intellectus et ratio*, pp. 35, 38-40, 47-52.

[119] *In II Sent.*, 23, 2, 1, ad 3; *De veritate*, VIII, 3, ad 3; *De potentia*, IV, 2 ad 4; *S.T.*, I, 12, 4, ad 2.

[120] *S.T.*, I, 85, 3, c. (*BW*, I, p. 819). *In I Phys.*, lect. 1, nn. 6-10; *In II Metaph.*, lect. 4, n. 233; *In I Sent.*, 3, 4, 2, ad 1; *In II Sent.*, 9, 1, 2, ad 1; *In IV Sent.*, 44, 1, 1, sol. 2; *In I Post. Analyt.*, lect. 4, nn. 15-16; *In lib. De Trinitate*, I, 3, c.; *In lib. De divinis nominibus*, 2; *In lib. De causis*, 1; *C.G.*, III, 37, *Non est autem; In VII Metaph.*, lect. 2, nn. 1300-1305; *De rationibus fidei*, 3 (ed Mandonnet, III, 225).

[121] *In I Metaph.*, lect. 2, n. 46; *Quodlibeta*, VII, 1, c. Cf. below, pp. 300-302 and notes.

[122] *In I Metaph.*, lect. 17, n. 272. *In I Metaph.*, lect. 11, n. 172; *In I Phys.*, lect. 10, n. 5; *C.G.*, I, 4, and 42, *Huic etiam; C.G.*, II, 37; *De spirit. creaturis*, 5, c.

[123] *In II Phys.*, lect. 1, n. 8; *In lib. De hebdomadibus*, 2.

[124] Cf. above, pp. 233-240.

[125] Cf. above, pp. 260-275.

[126] *In II Post. Analyt.*, lect. 20, n. 13.

[127] *In V Metaph.*, lect. 8, n. 865; *S.T.*, I, 85, 8, c.

[128] *S.T.*, I, 78, 3, ad 2 (*BW*, I, p. 740). *In II De anima*, lect. 13, n. 294; *In lib. De sensu et sensato*, lect. 2, n. 29; *In lib. De memoria*, lect. 1, nn. 318-319; *In V Metaph.* lect. 7 nn. 852-856.

[129] *In IX Metaph.*, lect. 3, nn. 1805-1806. *In IX Metaph.*, lect. 5, n. 1826; lect. 8, n. 1861; *S.T.*, I-II, 7, 2, c.

[130] *In I Perih.*, lect. 4, n. 7; lect. 5, n. 5.

[131] *In III Phys.*, lect. 5, nn. 16-17. This text is important in explaining the necessary link between movement and causality, and our knowledge of them.

[132] *In I Post. Analyt.*, lect. 5, nn. 8, 10.

[133] *In I Perih.*, lect. 5, n. 22. See the text quoted above, at note 129; *In V Metaph.*, lect. 9, n. 893.

[134] *S.T.*, I, 85, 3, c. See text quoted above at note 120.

[135] *S.T.*, I, 55, 3, ad 2 (*BW*, I, pp. 520-521). *In lib. De causis*, lect. 10. Cf. Pegis, *In Umbra Intelligentiae*, in *New Scholasticism*, XIV (1940), pp. 173, texts 4-7.

[136] *Quodlibeta*, VIII, 4, c. *In lib. De Trinitate*, VI, 4, c.; *De veritate*, I, 1, c.

[137] Cf. Régis, *L'Odyssée*, pp. 52-53, notes 60-63.

[138] *In II Sent.*, 20, 2, 2, sol. *De veritate*, XVIII, 7, c. Cf. above, pp. 237-241.

[139] In more than fifteen hundred places, Aquinas affirms the dependance of the intellect on the phantasm.

[140] *In III Sent.*, 35, 2, 1, sol. 1. *In Evang. Joan.*, 1, lect. 1, n. 1; *In lib De divinis nominibus*, 7, lect. 2; *In lib. De causis*, lect. 1.

[141] *S.T.*, I, 18, 2, c. (*BW*, I, p. 189). *S.T.*, I, 77, 1, ad 7; 85, 8, ad 1; *De spirit. creaturis*, 11. ad 3; *C.G.*, III. 69, *Amplius. Si effectus.*; 108, *Item. In nobis;* IV, 1, *Per has igitur; In II Post. Analyt.*, lect. 7, nn. 6–7; lect. 13, nn. 7–8; *In VIII Metaph.*, lect. 2, nn. 1694–1701; *In II De generatione*, lect. 2; *In I De anima*, lect. 1; *De veritate*, IV, 1, ad 8; X, 1, c.

[142] *In II Post. Analyt.*, lect. 8, n. 6; *De veritate*, X, 12, ad 4 *in contrarium; In VII Metaph.*, lect. 3, nn. 1325–1330; lect. 4, n. 1339.

[143] *S.T.*, II–II, 173, 2, c. Cf. above, pp. 237–241.

[144] Cf. above, pp. 233–237.

[145] *C.G.*, II, 73, *Si autem dicatur. In III Sent.*, 14, 1, 3, sol. 2, sol. 3; *In lib. De Trinitate*, VI, 2, ad 5; *S.T.*, I, 84, 7, c.; 85, 1, ad 4, ad 5.

[146] *S.T.*, I, 84, 7, c. (*BW*, I, p. 809).

[147] Cf. Ernout et Meillet, *Dictionnaire étymologique*, p. 822.

[148] *In II Sent.*, 37, 1, 2, sol.

[149] Cf. above, Chap. VII, note 140.

[150] *Genus* is sometimes used by St. Thomas as the synonym of *commune* or *indeterminate* or *potentiale*. See *In lib.*, *Metaph.*, prolog.; *In II Sent.*, 34, 1, 2, ad 1; *In lib. De hebdomadibus*, 2. Cf. Schütz, *Thomas-Lexikon*, ad verb. *genus*.

[151] Cf. above, Chap. VII, note 135.

[152] Cf. above, pp. 137–144; Pegis, *In Umbra Intelligentiae*, in *New Scholasticism*, XIV (1940), pp. 169–170.

[153] *S.T.*, I, 85, 5, ad 3; *In V Metaph.*, lect. 7, n. 862; *In IX Metaph.*, lect. 11, n. 1898; *C.G.*, II, 95, *Scire igitur.*

[154] Cf. above, pp. 151–153.

[155] *S.T.*, I, 77, 6, ad 2 (*BW*, I, p. 729). *In IV Metaph.*, lect. 1, n. 539; *De veritate*, XXI, 4, c.

[156] Cf. above, pp. 265–271.

[157] *S.T.*, I, 5, 1, ad 1 (*BW*, I, p. 43). *S.T.*, I–II, 18, 3, c.; I, 5, 5, c.; *De veritate*, XXI, 1–2; *C.G.*, III, 74, *Item. Quod non est.*; 20, *Est autem.*

[158] Cf. Schütz, *Thomas-Lexikon*, pp. 83–87, for the axiom: *bonum est in rebus.*

[159] *In VII Metaph.*, lect. 1, nn. 1252–1256; *In V Metaph.*, lect. 9; *In IV Metaph.*, lect. 1.

[160] *S.T.*, I, 77, 6, c.

[161] *In II Post. Analyt.*, lect. 5–6. Cf. above, pp. 135–137.

[162] *In IX Metaph.*, lect. 5, nn. 1826–1829.

[163] Cf. above, p. 288.

[164] *In IX Metaph.*, lect. 8, n. 1861. Cf. above, pp. 276–277.

[165] Cf. Gilson, *Being and Some Philosophers,* Chaps. IV–V.

[166] *C.G.*, II, 96, *Palam est.*

[167] *In II De anima*, lect. 1, nn. 220–223.

[168] *In I De anima*, lect. 4, n. 52.

[169] *In II De anima*, lect. 1, n. 224; *S.T.*, I, 79, 6, c.

[170] *C.G.*, I, 20, *Procedit ergo.*

[171] *S.T.*, I, 50, 2, ad 3 (*BW*, I, p. 484). *S.T.*, I, 75, 5, ad 4; 90, 2. ad 1; *C.G.*, II, 53, *In quocumque.*

[172] *S.T.*, III, 77, 1, ad 2.

[173] *S.T.*, I, 4, 1, ad 3. *S.T.*, I, 8, 1, c.; *C.G.*, I, 23.

[174] *S.T.*, I, 5, 2, ad 2; *De veritate*, XXI, 2, ad 2; *Quaest. de anima*, 6, ad 2.

[175] *De potentia*, III, 5, ad 2.

[176] *C.G.*, II, 26: Being is the working matter of the divine art, through which we can discover the Artist himself.

[177] Cf. above, pp. 284–289.

[178] Cf. above, pp. 290–294.

[179] *C.G.*, I, 26, *Item. Res;* II, 42; *De ente et essentia*, 5; *De potentia*, VII, 2, ad 5, et 4, c.; *S.T.*, I–II, 29, 1, ad 1, et 5, c.

[180] *S.T.*, I, 85, 3, c. Cf. above, pp. 284–285.

[181] *S.T.*, I, 3, 4, ad 1; 13, 11, c.; 79, 2, c. et ad 3; *C.G.*, II, 54, *Tertio; In lib. De divinis nominibus*, lect. 5; *In lib. De causis*, c. 2; *De ente et essentia*, 6; *De potentia*, VII, 2, ad 6, et 5, c.; *In lib. De Trinitate* V, 4, ad 4; *In lib. Metaph.*, Prolog.; *In IV Metaph.*, lect. 1, nn. 532, 534; *S.T.*, I, 66, 5, ad 4.

[182] *S.T.*, I, 14, 6, c.; 85, 3, c.; 89, 3, c.; *C.G.*, I, 50, *Item. Quidquid. Amplius;* 54; 65, *Amplius. Natura; C.G.*, III, 75, *Item. Cognitio;* 80, *Quum autem; In lib. divinis nominibus*, c. 7, lect. 3; *De veritate*, II, 4, c. et 5, c; VIII, 11.

[183] Cf. above, p. 289.

[184] *De veritate*, X, 4, ad 1; 5, ad 5; 6, ad 2; VIII, 10, ad 1; *C.G.*, IV, 11, *Est autem; Quodlibeta*, VIII, 4, c.; *In III Sent.*, 35, 2, 2, ad 3; *S.T.*, I, 57, 1, ad 1; 12, 4, ad 3.

[185] *De veritate*, VIII, 11, c.; *De malo*, XVI, 6, ad 16; *S.T.*, I, 57, 2.

[186] *S.T.*, I, 14, 6, c.; *C.G.*, I, 50 et 69; II, 98, *Hoc autem;* III, 75; *In lib. De causis*, lect. 10; *In lib. De divinis nominibus*, c. 7, lect. 3.

[187] See Chap. II (ed. Roland-Gosselin, p. 18, lines 6–23).

[188] *C.G.*, I, 26, *Quod est commune*, 42, *Esse abstractum; In lib. De hebdomadibus*, 2; *In VII Metaph.*, lect. 2, n. 1275; lect. 6, n. 1378. Cf. Geiger, *La doctrine de la participation*, pp. 338–340.

[189] Cf. Geiger, *op cit.*, pp. 53, 78–79, 138–142, 303–308, 399–408. See also *C.G.*, I, 30; *In lib. De causis*, lect. 22.

[190] *Quodlibeta*, VII, 1, ad 1.

[191] *In lib. De hebdomadibus*, c. 2; *C.G.*, I, 30, *Dico autem; De potentia*, VII, 2, ad 7. Cf. Geiger, *op. cit.*, pp. 131–138.

[192] *S.T.*, I, 12, 4, ad 3 (*BW*, I, p. 98). *S.T.*, I, 13, 11, c.; *C.G.*, I, 42, *Esse abstractum; In lib. De hebdomadibus*, c. 2; *De potentia*, VII, 2, ad 7.

[193] *In I Perih.*, lect. 5, n. 22. *C.G.*, I, 82, *Amplius esse; De potentia*, VII, 2, ad 9; *S.T.*, I–II, 67, 6, c.

[194] *Quodlibeta*, VII, 1, c.; *De veritate*, III, 5, c.; *De potentia*, III, 5, c.; VII, 1; *C.G.*, II, 37, *Communis; S.T.*, I, 13, 11; I, 3, 4; I, 44, 2; *C.G.*, I, 22.

[195] Cf.Gilson, *Le thomisme*, pp. 136–139.

Conclusion of Part Two

[1] Cf. above, Chap. V.

[2] Cf. above, Chap. VI.

[3] Cf. above, pp. 295–306.

[4] Cf. above, pp. 132, 137–144.

[5] *S.T.*, I, 3, 8, c. (*BW*, I, pp. 35–36.)

[6] *S.T.*, I, 75, 2, ad 2 (*BW*, I, p. 686). See also *In I Sent.*, 17, 1, 1, sol. 3; *In III Sent.*, 8, 1, 2, ad 3; 17, 1, 1, sol. 1, et ad 1; *In IV Sent.*, 44, 1, 1, sol. 3, et ad 3; *De veritate*, II, 6, ad 3; XXII, 13, ad 7; XXVII, 3, 2; *Quodlibeta*, VII, 11, ad 3; IX, 7, c.; *De spirit. creaturis*, 2, ad 2; 9, ad 15; 10, ad 15; *Quaest. de anima*, 19; *In I De anima*, lect. 10, n. 152; *S.T.*, III, 62, 3, c.; *In II Post. Analyt.*, lect. 1, n. 11; lect. 20, n. 14.

Part Three: Prologue

[1] *In VI Metaph.*, lect. 4, nn. 1239, 1234. Cf. *S.T.*, I, 82, 3, ad 1.

[2] Cf. above, pp. 167–173.

[3] Cf. above, pp. 197–221.

[4] Cf. above, pp. 307–308. Cf. *De veritate*, III, 7.

[5] Cf. above, pp. 140–142.

[6] *De veritate*, VIII, 1; *C.G.*, II, 98.

[7] *In I Metaph.*, lect. 10, n. 158; *S.T.*, I, 85, 3; *In lib. De Trinitate*, V, 3. Cf. Régis, *Abstraction et métaphysique*, pp. 123–156.

[8] *S.T.*, I, 14, 14, c. (*BW*, I, p. 158). *De rationibus fidei*, 3; *De veritate*, II, 7, c.; *C.G.*, I, 59, *Adhuc. Divina simplicitas*; *C.G.*, I, 58, *Adhuc. Ea quae*.

[9] *S.T.*, I, 58, 4, c. (*BW*, I, p. 543). Cf. above, pp. 236–241, 284–294.

[10] Cf. above, pp. 294–297.

[11] *In VI Metaph.*, lect. 4, nn. 1239–1240. *S.T.*, I, 16, 1, c.; *De veritate*, I, 3, 8, et 9; *In I Perih.*, lect. 3, nn. 6–9; *De veritate*, XV, 1, c.; XVIII, 6, c.

[12] *In VI Metaph.*, lect. 4, nn. 1228–1229; *In III De anima*, lect. 11, nn. 747–752; *In I Perih.*, lect. 6, nn. 6–9.

[13] *In VI metaph.*, lect. 4, n. 1241. *De veritate*, I, 8, ad 3; *Quodlibeta*, IX, 3, c.; *In III De anima*, lect. 11, n. 755; *S.T.*, I, 85, 2, ad 3.

[14] *In VI Metaph.*, lect. 4, n. 1243. *Quodlibeta*, II, 3, c.; IX, 3, c.; *De potentia*, VII, 2, ad 1; *S.T.*, I, 48, 2, ad 2; *In V Metaph.*, lect. 9, nn. 895–896; *In I Perih.*, lect. 15, n. 15.

[15] Cf. above, pp. 294–297.

Chapter VIII

[1] Cf. above, pp. 228–248.

[2] *S.T.*, I, 80, 2, ad 3; 82, 4, ad 1; 78, 1, ad 3; I–II, 10, 1, ad 3; *C.G.*, III, 48, *Omne quod est.*

[3] Cf. below, pp. 337–361.

[4] On the continual influence of the action of the agent intellect, see: *Quodlibeta*, VII, 1; X, 7; *De spirit. creaturis*, 10, c.; *De veritate*, VIII, 7, ad 13; X, 6, ad 6; 9, ad 11 of the second series; *Quaest. de anima*, 18, ad 11; *In III Sent.*, 14, 3, sol. et 1, sol.; *In I Sent.*, 3, 4, 5, sol.; *S.T.*, I, 79, 3, ad 2; et 4, c.; 84, 5, c.; *C.G.*, II, 76–77; III, 15, *Quia vero; S.T.*, II–II, 171, 2, c.

[5] Cf. above, Chap. V, and Chap. VI, pp. 228–248.

[6] *In III Sent.*, 14, 2, sol. 1; *Quaest. de anima*, 15, ad 9; 16, c.

[7] *Quodlibeta*, VII, 1, c., where St. Thomas elaborates the theory of the *lumen sub quo* as a moving cause always actually present.

[8] *De veritate*, IX, 1, c. *In II Sent.*, 3, 3, 4, sol.; *In III Sent.*, 14, 3, sol. 5; 2, sol. 1; 23, 1, 1, sol.; 24, 2, 2, sol. 2; *In IV Sent.*, 49, 2, 1, ad 15; *Quodlibeta*, VII, 1, c.; *De veritate*, X, 6, ad 2, et ad 7; XVIII, 1, ad 1, et ad 10; *Quaest. de anima*, 15, ad 9; *De spirit. creaturis*, 10, c. et ad 8; *S.T.*, I, 12, 5, ad 2; 88, 1, c.; *C.G.*, II, 60.

[9] On this problem and its doctrinal and historical aspects, cf. Meyerson, *Identité et réalité*, pp. 438–512; *Le cheminement de la pensée*, I, pp. 91 ff.; III, pp. 1001–1002. See also above, pp. 7–10 and *S.T.*, I, 12, 10; 58, 2; 85, 4; *C.G.*, I, 55, *Intellectus enim*, *Item. Vis cognoscitiva; Quaest. de anima*, 18, ad 5; *Quodlibeta*, VII, 2, c.; *De veritate*, VIII, 14; *In III Sent.*, 14, 2, sol. 4.

[10] *In I Perih.*, lect. 1, n. 5.

[11] *De veritate*, I, 10, c. *S.T.*, I, 85, 2, ad 3.

[12] *In III De anima*, lect. 11, n. 751 (trans. Foster and Humphries, p. 437). *De veritate*, I, 8, ad 3; *De potentia*, VIII, 2, ad 1; *Quodlibeta*, II, 3, c.; *In VI Metaph.*, lect. 6, n. 1241; *C.G.*, I, 58, *Amplius, Propositionis; S.T.*, I, 12, 9, ad 2; 14, 13, ad 2; *Quodlibeta*, VIII, 3, c.

[13] Cf. Schütz, *Thomas-Lexikon*, pp. 140–141.

[14] Cf. *Ibid.*, pp. 146–147. See also *In III Sent.*, 27, 1, 1, ad 5; *S.T.*, I, 60, 3, obj. 2.

[15] Cf. Schütz, *Thomas-Lexikon*, p. 826.

[16] *In I Perih.*, lect. 3, n. 4. *In I Perih.*, lect. 8, n. 4; *De veritate*, III, 1, ad 3; 2, ad 5; VIII, 11, ad 3 et ad 11.

[17] *In III De anima*, lect. 11, n. 747; *In VI Metaph.*, lect. 4, n. 1229; *De veritate*, VIII, 14, c.; *S.T.*, I, 14, 14; 58, 2.

[18] Cf. above, Chap. VIII, note 9.

[19] *In I Perih.*, lect. 1, n. 5; what is said here of *words* is also true of *concepts.*

[20] *In I Perih.*, lect. 4, n. 1; *De veritate*, II, 7, c.

[21] *De potentia*, VIII, 2, ad 7; cf. above, pp. 307–308.

[22] *In I Perih.*, lect. 5, nn. 5–11.

[23] Cf. above, pp. 288–294.

[24] *In I Perih.*, lect. 4, nn. 7–8; lect. 5, nn. 5, 15.

[25] *In I Perih.*, lect. 5, nn. 5, 8, 10, 12; *In V Metaph.*, lect. 9, n. 892; *De potentia*, VII, 2, ad 7.

[26] *In I Perih.*, lect. 5, n. 8.

[27] *Ibid.*, n. 9.

[28] *Ibid.*, n. 22; *De potentia*, VII, 2, ad 7; *In V Metaph.*, lect. 9, n. 893.

[29] *S.T.*, I, 13, 12, c. (*BW*, I, p. 133).

[30] *S.T.*, I, 13, 1, ad 2, et ad 3; 32, 2, c.; *C.G.*, I, 30, *Quia enim; S.T.*, I–II, 53, 2, ad 3.

[31] *S.T.*, II–II, 60, 1, ad 2, et ad 3.

[32] Cf. Ernout et Meillet, *Dictionnaire étymologique*, pp. 1056–1057.

[33] Cf. *Ibid.*, pp. 265–268.

[34] Cf. Hoenen, *La théorie du jugement*, pp. 157–191.

[35] Cf. above, pp. 248–252.

[36] Cf. above, pp. 311–314.

[37] *In I Eth. Nic.*, lect. 1, nn. 1–5, where St. Thomas defines philosophical knowledge by the notion of order.

[38] *In I Perih.*, lect. 3, n. 4.

[39] *S.T.*, I, 13, 12, c. (*BW*, I, p. 133).

[40] *In V Metaph.*, lect. 9, nn. 889, 895.

[41] *In V Metaph.*, lect. 9, n. 896. See also *In II Sent.*, 34, 1, 1, sol.; *S.T.*, I, 48, 2, ad 2; *Quodlibeta*, II, 3, c.; IX, 3; *In II Perih.*, lect. 2, n. 2; *In IV Metaph.*, lect. 2, n. 553; *In XI Metaph.*, lect. 8, n. 2283.

[42] Cf. above, pp. 318–320.

[43] *S.T.*, I, 3,4, ad 2 (*BW*, I, p. 31). *De potentia*, VII, 2, ad 1; *In III Sent.*, 24, 1, sol. 2; *Quodlibeta*, IX, 3, c. (contains a very pertinent synthesis of this problem). See also the *Commentary* of Cajetan on the quoted article of *S.T.*

[44] *S.T.*, I, 85, 5, ad 3 (*BW*, I, p. 824). *S.T.*, I, 13, 12, c.; *C.G.*, I, 36, *Quamvis namque; In I Sent.*, 4, 2, 1 ad 1.

[45] *In I Perih.*, lect. 8, nn. 11, 15.

[46] Cf. Ernout et Meillét, *Dictionnaire étymologique*, pp. 687–688, ad verb. *nuntius.* See also *S.T.*, I–II, 92, 2, c.

[47] *S.T.*, I–II, 90, 1, ad 2 (*BW*, II, p. 743). *S.T.*, I, 85, 2, ad 3;*De potentia*, VIII, 1, c.; IX, 5 c.; *De veritate*, III, 2, c.

[48] *In I Perih.*, lect. 3, n. 4; *De veritate*, III, 1, ad 3; 2, ad 5; VIII, 11, ad 3, et ad 11.

[49] *S.T.*, I, 85, 3, ad 1, ad 3; *In I Perih.*, lect. 10, nn. 3–6. The division of concepts into *predicables* and *predicaments* is an illustration of this law, cf. above, pp. 276–278.

[50] Cf. above, p. 311.

[51] *In I Perih.*, lect. 8.

[52] *Ibid.*, lect. 10, nn. 1–16.

[53] *Ibid.*, lect. 8, nn. 19–21; lect. 9, nn. 2–6.

[54] *Ibid.*, lect. 9, n. 5; lect. 3, n. 13; lect. 5, nn. 12–13; lect. 8, nn. 8–9; lect. 13, nn. 3–5; *In II Perih.*, lect. 1, n. 5. A study of the repercussions of these philosophical problems on theological thought is found in Chenu, *Grammaire et théologie aux XII et XIII siècles*, in *AHMA*, X (1935–1936), 5–28.

[55] *S.T.*, II–II, 173, 2, c.; *De veritate*, II, 7, c. et ad 2.

[56] Cf. above, pp. 315–328.

[57] Cf. Gilson, *Being and Some Philosophers*, pp. 202–212; Hoenen, *La théorie du jugement*, pp. 42–81.

[58] Cf. above, pp. 311–314.

[59] Cf. above, pp. 311–312.

[60] *C.G.*, I, 59, *Cum enim*.

[61] *In lib. De Trinitate*, V, 3, c. *In I Sent.*, 19, 5, 1, ad 7; 38, 1, 3, sol.

[62] Cf. above, pp. 282–288.

[63] Cf. above, pp. 291–297.

[64] Cf. above, pp. 278–282.

[65] Cf. above, pp. 296–299. See also Geiger, *Abstraction et séparation*, R.S.P.T., XXXI (1947), pp. 1–40; *De l'unité de l'être*, R.S.P.T., XXXIII (1949), pp. 5–10.

[66] *In I Sent.*, 38, 1, 3, sol. *In I Perih.*, lect. 9, n. 4; *In II Perih.*, lect. 2, n. 2.

[67] *S.T.*, I, 85, 5, ad 3 (*BW*, I, p. 824). *In IX Metaph.*, lect. 11, nn. 1898–1900; *Quodlibeta*, IX, 3, c.; *In IV Metaph.*, lect. 2, nn. 550–558; *S.T.*, I, 13, 12, c.; *C.G.*, I, 36, *Quamvis namque*.

[68] *In V Metaph.*, lect. 9, n. 896; *Quodlibeta*, IX 3, c.

[69] *In V Metaph*,. lect. 9, n. 890. *In II Sent.*, 37, 1, 2, ad 3.

[70] Cf. above, pp. 201–204, 221–226.

[71] Cf. above, Chap. VII.

[72] *C.G.*, I, 53, *Ulterius autem; De potentia*, IX, 5. Cf. above, pp. 270–271.

[73] Cf. below, pp. 340–342, where this aspect will be studied in relation to truth.

[74] Cf. above, pp. 199–200.

[75] *S.T.*, I, 85, 2, ad 3 (*BW*, I, p. 818); *Quodlibeta*, VIII, 3, c.; *De veritate*, VIII, 6, c.

[76] Cf. above, pp. 199–201.

[77] *In I Perih.*, lect. 3, n. 4.

[78] Cf. above, pp. 328–333.

[79] *In I Perih.*, lect. 13, n. 3; *S.T.*, III, 16, 1, ad 1.

[80] *In V Metaph.*, lect. 9, nn. 891–892; *In I Perih.*, lect. 13, nn. 5, 12; lect. 15, n. 4.

[81] *In I Perih.*, lect. 8, nn. 9, 11. *In I Perih.*, lect. 10, n. 23.

[82] *In IX Metaph.*, lect. 11, n. 1898. *In I Perih.*, lect. 5, n. 3; lect. 8, n. 9; *S.T.*, I, 13, 12, c.; III, 16, 7, ad 4; 9, ad 3; 10, c. et ad 2; *In III Sent.*, I, 5, 5, ad 5; 6, 1, 3 ad 3; 11, 1, 2, ad 3.

[83] *In I Perih.*, lect. 1, n. 8; lect. 8, n. 9; *C.G.*, I, 67, *Praeterea, si*.

[84] *In I Perih.*, lect. 1, n. 8.

[85] *C.G.*, I, 69, *Cum enim. De veritate*, I, 3, c.; *In III De anima*, lect. 11, n. 760; *S.T.*, I, 16, 7, c.; *In I Post. Analyt.*, lect. 44, n. 3; *In V Metaph.*, lect. 9, n. 895.

[86] *In I Perih.*, lect. 3, n. 4; lect. 9, n. 2.

[87] *De veritate*, XVIII, 6, c.; *De malo*, XVI, 6, c.

[88] *In I Perih.*, lect. 7, n. 2.

[89] *Ibid.*, n. 4; lect. 8, nn. 6, 21; lect. 1, n. 3.

Chapter IX

[1] *In I Sent.*, 19, 5, 2, ad 2.

[2] Cf. Schütz, *Thomas-Lexikon*, pp. 841–847, ad verb. *veritas, verus.* See the following texts: *In I Sent.*, 19, 5; 33, 1; *De veritate*, I, art. 1–9; *In VI Metaph.*, lect. 4; *S.T.*, I, 16–17.

[3] *De veritate*, I, 3, 9; *C.G.*, I, 59; *In III De anima*, lect. 11; *In I Perih.*, lect. 3, nn. 5–10; *S.T.*, I, 16, 2; 17, 3.

[4] Cf. Schütz, *op. cit.*, see note 2.

[5] On the technical language of analogy in the works of Aquinas, see F.A. Blanche, *La notion d'analogie dans la philosophie de s. Thomas*, in *RSPT*, X (1921), pp. 52–59, 169–193; *La théorie d'analogie*, in *Rev. de Philos.*, XXXIX (1932), pp. 37–78.

[6] *S.T.*, I, 31, 1, ad 1; 2, ad 2; 33, 1, ad 3; 67, 1, c.; II–II, 57, 1, ad 1; 92, 1, ad 2.

[7] Cf. Boisacq, *Dictionnaire étymologique*, ad verb.

[8] Cf. Ernout et Meillet, *Dictionnaire étymologique*, p. 1095, ad verb., *verus.*

[9] On the function of nominal definition in philosophical inquiry, cf. *De veritate*, IV, 2, c.; *C.G.*, I, 1, *Veritatem meditabitur; In I Post. Analyt.*, lect. 4, n. 6; *In II Post. Analyt.*, lect. 8, n. 6; *In VII Metaph.*, lect. 4, n. 1325; lect. 5, nn. 1339–1341.

[10] *In IX Metaph.*, lect. 11, n. 1897.

[11] *S.T.*, I, 16, 1, obj. 3 (*BW*, I, p. 168).

[12] *S.T.*, I, 16, 1, ad 3 (*BW*, I, p. 170). See also *In V Metaph.*, lect. 9, n. 896; *De veritate*, I, 8, ad 1; *In lib. De div. nom.*, chap. 7, lect. 2; *S.T.*, I–II, 29, 5, c.

[13] Cf. above, pp. 198–204, 222–224.

[14] Cf. above. pp. 253–260, 327–333.

[15] *In V Metaph.*, lect. 9, n. 896. See also the definition of an object as a being of reason, *above*, pp. 176–177.

[16] *In I Sent.*, 19, 5, 1, sol., 3, sol. et ad 4. *In I Sent.*, 33, 1, 1, ad 1; 2, 1, 3, sol.; De potentia, I, 1, ad 10; VII, 6, c.; 11, c.; *De veritate*, IV, 6, c.; *In V Phys.*, lect. 3, n. 8; *In IX Metaph.*, lect. 11, nn. 1895–1896; *In V Metaph.*, lect. 9, nn. 896–897; *In I Perih.*, lect. 14, n. 4.

[17] Cf. above, Chap. IX, note 12.

[18] *In IX Metaph.*, lect. 11, n. 1898. *In I Perih.*, lect. 8, n. 11; *In I Post. Analyt.*, lect. 44, n. 4; *S.T.*, I, 39, 3, c.; 85, 5, ad 3. Cf. above, pp. 327–333.

[19] Cf. above, pp. 188–192.

[20] *S.T.*, I, 16, 3, c.; *De veritate*, I, 1–2; XXI, 1.

[21] Cf. above, pp. 327–336.

[22] Cf. Schütz, *Thomas-Lexikon*, pp. 525–529, ad verb. *nomen.*

[23] *S.T.*, I, 39, 3, c. (*BW*, I, p. 368). *S.T.*, I, 11, 1, ad 2; 42, 3, c.; I–II, 17, 4; *In X Metaph.* lect. 4, nn. 1983–2022; *In I Sent.*, 20, 1, 3, sol. prima; *C.G.*, I, 34; II, 39; De potentia, IX 8, ad 2.

[24] Cf. above, Chap. VIII, note 9; also Bachelard, *Essai*, p. 257.

[25] *In I Sent.*, 19, 5, 2, ad 1; 22, 1, 2–3; 35, 4; *De veritate*, II, 11; IV, 1; XVIII, 5;

De ente et essentia, 6; *In lib. De Trinitate*, V, 4; *De potentia*, VII, 4–7; *In lib. De div. nom.*, chap. 1, lect. 3; *C.G.*, I, 15, 53; *Quaest. de anima*, 16; *comp. Theol.*, I, chap. 25–27.

[26] *In I Perih.*, lect. 2, n. 5; lect. 3, n. 1; lect. 10, n. 4.

[27] *In I Perih.*, lect. 7, n. 2; *De veritate*, II, 1, c.; IX, 4, c.; *De potentia*, VII, 6, c.; *S.T.*, I, 13, 1.

[28] *In I De caelo*, lect. 24, n. 2; *S.T.*, III, 60, 3, ad 1. Cf. Schütz, *Thomas-Lexikon*, pp. 25–27, ad verb., *aequivicatio*.

[29] *S.T.*, III, 60, 3, c. *S.T.*, III, 2, c. et ad 1.

[30] Cf. above, pp. 337–340.

[31] *In V Metaph.*, lect. 17, nn. 1003–1004, 1026–1029. Cf. above, pp. 188–192.

[32] *De veritate*, I, 1 and 9; *S.T.*, I, 16, 1–2; 17, 1–3; *C.G.*, I, 59.

[33] Cf. above, pp. 185–187.

[34] Cf. Schütz, *Thomas-Lexikon*, pp. 228–229, ad verb., *cognitio*.

[35] *De veritate*, I, 3, c. *S.T.*, I, 16, 2; *In VI Metaph.*, lect. 4, nn. 1231–1235; *In I Perih.*, lect. 3, nn. 5–9; *C.G.*, I, 59, *Cum enim*.

[36] Cf. above, pp. 311–327.

[37] Cf. above, pp. 327–332, 340–343.

[38] *C.G.*, I, 59, *Amplius, cum; In IX Metaph.*, lect. 9.

[39] See the text quoted above, p. 341, at note 18.

[40] Cf. above, pp. 340–343.

[41] Cf. above, pp. 333–336.

[42] *C.G.*, I, 59, *Cum enim. In V Metaph.*, lect. 9, n. 895; *In VI Metaph.*, lect. 4, nn. 1223–1224; *In IX Metaph.*, lect. 11, n. 1896. For *comparatio*, as used in this text, see Schütz, *Thomas-Lexikon*, p. 136; Chenu, *Pour l'histoire du traité de la foi*, in *Mélanges thomistes*, pp. 123–140; Hoenen, *La théorie du jugement*, pp. 174–176.

[43] *S.T.*, I, 16, 6, c. (*BW*, I, p. 175).

[44] *S.T.*, I, 16, 7, c. (*BW*, I, p. 176). *De veritate*, I, 3, c. and 8, c.

[45] Cf. above, pp. 335–337.

[46] *S.T.*, I, 16, 2, c. (*BW*, I, p. 171). *C.G.*, I, 59, *Amplius, cum; In III De anima*, lect. 11, n. 760; *In VI Metaph.*, lect. 4, nn. 1238–1239; *S.T.*, I, 17, 2–3.

[47] *In III De anima*, lect. 11, n. 761. *In VI Metaph.*, lect. 4, nn. 1223–1224; 1237–1238.

[48] *In VI Metaph.*, lect 4, n. 1240.

[49] *Quodlibeta*, VIII, 4, c. et ad 1; *De veritate*, X, 8–9; *C.G.*, III, 46; *S.T.*, I, 87, 1, c. Cf. B. Romeyer, *Saint Thomas et notre connaissance de l'esprit humain*, in *Arch. de Philos.*, VI, 2 (1928), pp. 49–106.

[50] For the distinction between the *quia est* and *quid est*, see *In II Post. Analyt.*, lect. 8, n. 6; *In VII Metaph.*, lect. 3, n. 1325; lect. 4, nn. 1335, 1339–1345; *De veritate*, X, 12, ad 4 *in contrarium*.

[51] Cf. above pp. 131–137; *In II Post. Analyt.*, lect. 7, n. 5; *In VII Metaph.*, lect. 17, n. 1666; *S.T.*, I, 2, 2, ad 2.

[52] Cf. above, pp. 36–38; E. Renouvier, *Traité de logique générale et de logique formelle* (Paris, Colin, 1912), I, p. 65 ff.

[53] Cf. above, pp. 78–80; and Van Riet, *L'Epistémologie thomiste*.

[54] Cf. J. Wébert, *Reflexio*, in *Mélanges Mandonnet* (Paris, le Saulchoir, Kain, 1930), pp. 285–325; Roland-Gosselin, *La théorie thomiste de la vérité*, in *RSPT*, X (1921), pp. 222–234; C. Boyer, *Le sens d'un texte de saint Thomas*, in *Gregorianum*, V (1925), pp. 424–443 (in English, in Hoenen, *Reality and Judgment*, Chicago, 1952, pp. 295–309). See also Hoenen, *op. cit.*, pp. 137–182.

[55] Cf. above, pp. 275–283.

[56] Cf. above, pp. 340–349.

[57] *De veritate*, I, 9, c. *In III Sent.*, 23, 1, 2, ad 3; *In VI Metaph.*, lect. 4, n. 1236; *In I Perh.*, lect. 3, n. 9; *S.T.*, I, 16, 2; 87, 2; *In lib. De Trinitate*, VI, 2, c.; *De veritate*, X, 9; *Quodlibeta*, VIII, 4.

[58] Cf. above, pp. 267–268.

[59] Cf. above, pp. 334–336, 349–351.

[60] *De veritate*, XIV, 8, ad 5. Cf. above, pp. 162–167.

[61] Cf. above, p. 351.

[62] Cf. above, pp. 327–332.

[63] Cf. above, pp. 343–351.

[64] Cf. above, pp. 311–315.

[65] Cf. above, Chap. VIII.

[66] Cf. above, pp. 248–250, 282 ff.

[67] Cf. above, pp. 229–246, 283–290.

[68] *De veritate*, X, 5, c. *S.T.*, I, 86, 1, c. Cf. above, pp. 170–73. See also *Quaest. de anima*, 20, ad 1; and H.D. Simonin, *La connaissance humaine des singuliers*, in *Mélanges Mandonnet*, II, 289–306.

[69] Cf. above, pp. 307–308.

[70] *De caritate*, 9, ad 1. *In IX Metaph.*, lect. 11, n. 1903; *In I Post. Analyt.*, lect. 4, n. 5; *In VIII Phys.*, lect. 3, 6; *In I Sent.*, 19, 5, 1; *S.T.*, I, 16, 3, *sed contra*; I–II, 3, 7; *C.G.*, I, 62, *Sicut enim*.

[71] Cf. above, Chap. VI, notes 218–227.

[72] Cf. above, pp. 236–240, 340–343.

[73] *S.T.*, I, 16, 3, *sed contra*.

[74] *In IX Metaph.*, lect. 11, n. 1898.

[75] Cf. above, Chap. IX, note 71.

[76] *In IX Metaph.*, lect. 11, n. 1900.

[77] *Quodlibeta*, VIII, 1, c. *De veritate*, XVIII, 4, ad 10; *In II De anima*, lect. 12, n. 378; *In I Sent.*, 33, 1, 1, ad 1; *S.T.*, I, 13, 9, c.

[78] *In VII Metaph.*, lect. 3, n. 1310.

[79] Cf. Blanche, *L'Abstraction*, in *Mélanges thomistes*, pp. 237–252; Geiger, *Abstraction et séparation*, in *RSPT*, XXXI (1947), pp. 1–40.

[80] Cf. above, pp. 327–335.

[81] Cf. above, pp. 294–303.

Conclusion of Part Three

[1] Cf. above, pp. 314–336.
[2] Cf. above, pp. 337–355.
[3] Cf. above, pp. 357–360.
[4] *S.T.*, I, 16, 6, ad 1.
[5] Cf. above, p. 258 and note 15.
[6] Cf. above, p. 337.

Part Four: Prologue

[1] Cf. above, pp. 260–306, 349–359.
[2] Cf. above, pp. 135–140.
[3] *S.T.*, I, 16, 6, ad 1; *C.G.*, III, 25 (*BW*, II, p. 45).
[4] *De veritate*, III, 1, c.; *S.T.*, I, 85, 2, c. Cf. Schütz, *Thomas-Lexikon*, ad verb., *reflexio*.
[5] Cf. above, pp. 351–361.

Chapter X

[1] Cf. above, pp. 335–336.
[2] *In IV Metaph.*, lect. 9, n. 658.
[3] *In III De anima*, lect. 4, n. 624. *Quaest. de anima*, 14, ad 16; *C.G.*, I, 4. On this question of the human capacity to err, see P. Synave, *La révélation des vérités divines naturelles*, in *Mélanges Mandonnet*, I, 327–365. For other references to Acquinas, see Pegis' *Index* in *BW*, II, 1158a.

[4] Cf. Keeler, *The Problem of Error from Plato to Kant*, p. 89; J.H. Nicolas, *Le problème de l'erreur*, in *Revue thomiste*, LII (1952), pp. 328–357, 528–566.

[5] Cf. Schütz, *Thomas-Lexikon*, ad verb., *contrarium*.

[6] Roland-Gosselin, *La théorie thomiste de l'erreur*, in *Mélanges thomistes*, pp. 253–274; *Erreur et péché*, in *Rev. de Philos.*, XXXV (1928), pp. 466–478.

[7] *In II Metaph.*, lect. 1, n. 275. *Quaest. de anima*, 15, ad 16; *In I Phys.*, lect. 10, n. 5.

[8] *De motu cordis* (ed. Mandonnet, p. 29). *De potentia*, II, 3, ad 3; *De veritate*, XVI, 2, ad 3; 3, c.; XXII, 12, ad 2; XXIV, 1, ad 29; *In IV Metaph.*, lect. 6, nn. 595, 606–610; lect. 15, n. 718; *In I Ethic.*, lect. 2, n. 27; *In I Post. Analyt.*, lect. 19–20; *S.T.*, I, 60, 2, c.; 82, 1, c.; 85, 6, c.

[9] *In lib. Job*, cap. 13, lect. 2.

[10] *C.G.*, I, 7 and 84; *De potentia*, I, 3, c.; *In lib. Job*, cap. 13, lect. 1; *De veritate*, XV, 7, c.

[11] Cf. above, pp. 24–31.

[12] *De spirit. creat.*, 9, ad 14. *C.G.*, III, 85, *Item, ex quae; S.T.*, I, 18, 3; 79, 5, ad 3.

[13] *S.T.*, I, 44, 1, 2, and 3, and the parallel passages.

[14] *De potentia*, III, 7, ad 9 et ad 7. *S.T.*, I, 60, 1, ad 3; 103, 8.

[15] *Compend. Theol.*, I, 103 and 148. *In lib. De causis*, lect. 1; *In VIII Phys.*, lect. 1, n. 2.

[16] *De substantiis separatis*, cap. 8, et 10; *Quaest. de anima*, 7; *C.G.*, II, 39, 42 et 44; *In XII Metaph.*, lect. 12, nn. 2628–2637; *S.T.*, I, 103–105.

[17] *S.T.*, I, 103, 8 (*BW*, I, p. 960). *S.T.*, 1, ad 3; 60, 1, obj. 2; *De potentia*, III, 7, ad 3; *In I Sent.*, 17, 1, 1, ad 3; *De subst. separat.*, cap. 23–24; *De rationibus fidei*, cap. 6; *De veritate*, XXII, 8; *De malo*, XVI, 6, ad 18; 12, ad 5; *In lib. De causis*, lect. 5; *Comp. Theol.*, I, 112 et 123; *C.G.*, III, 3, 67–70, 94, 97, 111– 114, 147; *S.T.*, I–II, 40, 3; 114, 1; *In II Phys.*, lect. 14, n. 8; *In XII Metaph.*, lect. 12, nn. 2632–2637.

[18] *S.T.*, I, 19, 10, c.; 83, 2; 41, 2 c. et ad 4, ad 4; 82, 1; 116, 1; I–II, 12, 5, ad 3; 13, 2, ad 3, c.; II–II, 18, 4, c.; *C.G.*, II, 83, *Amplius, si; Praeterea, si; Adhuc;* III, 129, *Praeterea.*

[19] Cf. above, pp. 176–183.

[20] Cf. above, pp. 265–267.

[21] *S.T.*, I, 80, 1, ad 3 (*BW*, I, p. 769). *S.T.*, 1, 77, 3; 78, 1, ad 3; I–II, 26, 1, ad 3; 30, 1, ad 3; *De veritate*, XIV, 2, ad 6; XV, 2; XXII, 3, ad 5; XXIII, 4; XXV, 1, et 2, ad 8; *De virtut. in communi*, 6.

[22] *In II De anima*, lect. 13; *In III De anima*, lect. 6, nn. 661–663.

[23] *S.T.*, I, 17, 3, c. (*BW*, I, p. 183) and the parallel passages.

[24] Cf. above, pp. 307–308.

[25] *S.T.*, I, 17, 3, ad 2 (*BW*, I, p. 184). Cf. Hoenen, *De Origine primorum principiorum*, in *Gregorianum*, XIV (1933), pp. 153–184.

[26] *C.G.*, I, 7, *Item, Illud autem. C.G.*, III, 47, *Quomodo autem; In II Sent.*, 28, 1, 5; *In III Sent.*, 30, 5; *In IV Sent.*, 49, 1, 3, sol. 2a; 33, 1, 1; *Comp. Theol.*, I, 119; *De malo*, XVI, 12, ad 5; *iDe spirit. creat.*, 10, c. et ad 1; 11, ad 8 et ad 9; *Quaest. de anima*, 5, c. et ad 6; *De veritate*, XI, 1, ad 3; XVIII, 1, ad 7, et ad 10; *S.T.*, I, 105, 3; I–II, 109, 1; II–II, 8, 1, ad 1; 49, 6, c.; *In VII Metaph.*, lect. 1, nn. 1257–1259.

[27] *In lib. Job*, cap. 38, lect. 3.

[28] Cf. above, pp. 248–250.

[29] *De veritate*, XVI, 1, c. (St. Thomas Aquinas, *Truth*, translated by R.W. Mulligan, J.V. McGlynn and R.W. Schmidt, Chicago, Regnery, 1952–1954, 3 vols., II, p. 304; hereafter identified as *Truth*, Regnery.) *De malo*, 5, c.; *De virtut. in comm.*, 8; 10, ad 3; *In II Sent.*, 24, 2, 3; *S.T.*, I, 79, 12; I–II, 57, 2. Cf. Pegis, *In Umbra Intelligentiae*, in *New Scholasticism*, XIV (1940), pp. 146–180.

[30] *De veritate*, XVII, 1, ad 6 *in contrarium;* I, 4, ad 5; XVIII, 1, ad 10.

[31] *S.T.*, I, 79, 5, ad 3; 84, 5, c.; 109, 1; *De veritate*, X, 6.

[32] *S.T.*, I, 117, 1, c. (*BW*, I, p. 1076). *S.T.*, I, 85, 5; 105, 1, c. et ad 1; 88, 3,

ad 1; I–II, 17, 6 c.; *De veritate*, X, 6, c.; XVI, 3; XX, 6, ad 2; XXII, 5, ad 8; *In III Sent.*, 27, 1, 1; *In III De anima*, lect. 10, nn. 729–730; *Quaest. de anima*, 5; *C.G.*, II, 78, *Amplius, Aristoteles.*

[33] *In IV Metaph.*, lect. 6, n. 599. *In III Sent.*, 34, 1, 2; 23, 3, 2, ad 1; *In II Post. Analyt.*, lect. 20, nn. 11–12, 15; *Quaest. de anima*, 4, ad 6; 18, ad 8; *S.T.*, I–II, 51, 1, c.; *C.G.*, II, 83, *Item, necesse est.*

[34] *In III Sent.*, 23, 1, 1–5. *In III Sent.*, 24, 1, 1–2; 2, 4, ad 4; *Quaest. de anima*, 5, c.; 4, ad 4; *In I Post, Analyt.*, lect. 44, n. 3; *S.T.*, I–II, 94, 1, c.

[35] Cf. Schütz, *Thomas-Lexikon*, pp. 779, 401, 518–520, for texts illustrating some of these terms. See also Peghaire, *Intellectus et Ratio*, p. 174.

[36] Cf. Ernout et Meillet, *Dictionnaire étymologique*, pp. 808–810.

[37] *In V Metaph.*, lect. 1, n. 761 (the whole *lectio* should be read). *In I Phys.*, lect. 10, n. 3; *In I Post. Analyt.*, lect. 42, nn. 11–13; lect. 4, n. 16; *In VII Phys.*, lect. 1, n. 6; *S.T.*, I, 33, 1, c. et ad 1.

[38] *S.T.*, I–II, 94, 2, c. (*BW*, II, p. 774). *S.T.*, I–II, 47, 6, c.; I, 17, 3, ad 2; 62, 8, ad 2; 84, 3, ad 3; *In lib. De Hebdomad.*, 1; *In I Sent.*, 3, 1, 2; *In I Post. Analyt.*, lect. 30, n. 5; lect. 42, nn. 11, 13; lect. 44, nn. 3, 8; lect. 19, nn. 2–3; and lect. 5–6, 19–20; *In I Ethic.*, lect. 11, n. 137; *De veritate*, X, 13; XIII, 2, c.; *In IV Metaph.*, lect. 5, n. 595; *In II Metaph.*, lect. 4, n. 2210; *C.G.*, I, 7 et 11.

[39] Cf. above, pp. 280–306, for the genesis of the concept of being.

[40] *Quodlibeta*, VIII, 5. *In IV Metaph.*, lect. 5, n. 595; *In XI Metaph.*, lect. 4, n. 2210; *In III Metaph.*, *lect.* 5, n. 389; *In lib. De Trin.*, VI, 4; *C.G.*, II, 83, *Adhuc., cum; S.T.*, I–II, 66, 5, and ad 4.

[41] *In I Post. Analyt.*, lect. 5, nn. 1–6; lect. 19, nn. 2–3; lect. 20, n. 5; lect. 36, n. 7; *In III Phys.*, lect. 11, n. 6; *In III Metaph.*, *lect.* 5, n. 390; *In IV Metaph.*, lect. 6, n. 605; *In lib. De Hebdomad.*, lect. 1; *C.G.*, II, 34, *Quod enim;* II, 37; *S.T.*, I–II, 94, 1, c., et 4, c.

[42] *C.G.*, II, 83, *Adhuc, cum. In IV Metaph.*, lect. 6, n. 605; *S.T.*, I–II, 94, 2, c.; *De veritate*, X, 12, c. et ad 7.

[43] On the historical evolution, number, and notion of the transcendentals, see Régis, *L'Odyssée.*

[44] *In I Post. Analyt.*, lect. 5, nn. 7–8; lect. 19, n. 1; *In IV Metaph.*, lect. 6, n. 606; *In XI Metaph.*, lect. 5, nn. 2211–2212; *In I Phys.*, lect. 6, nn. 7–8.

[45] *In III Metaph.*, lect. 5, nn. 387, 392; *In IV Metaph.*, lect. 6, nn. 600, 603, 605–606; *In I Perih.*, lect. 4, n. 2.

[46] *In VII Metaph.*, lect 17, nn. 1652–1657; *In IV Metaph.*, lect. 2, n. 566; *In X Metaph.*, lect. 4, nn. 1997–1998, 2006, 2014–2017.

[47] *In I Post. Analyt.*, lect. 20, nn. 1–2; *S.T.*, I–II, 94, 2, c.

[48] *In III Metaph.*, lect. 5, n. 387; *In IV Metaph.*, lect. 7, n. 626; lect. 16, n. 720; *In XI Metaph.*, lect. 5, nn. 2221–2223.

[49] *In I Post. Analyt.*, lect. 5, n. 6; lect. 20, nn. 1–2; *In IV Metaph.*, lect. 7–11; *In XI Metaph.*, lect. 5–6; *In I Perih.*, lect. 3, n. 7; lect. 12, n. 5; lect. 15, n. 3; *In III Sent.*, 37, 2, sol. 2, ad 2.

[50] *In I Perih.*, lect. 3, n. 7; lect. 11, n. 7; lect. 12, nn. 5–6; lect. 15, n. 4; *In I–V. Metaph.*, lect. 7–15; *In II Metaph.*, lect. 5–6. For the definition of contradiction, see *In I Perih.*, lect. 9, nn. 6–9; *In I Post. Analyt.*, lect. 5, n. 5; *C.G.*, II, 33, *Item, omne, Amplius, multae;* IV, 24, *In rebus; In VIII Phys.*, lect. 18, n. 5; *S.T.*, I–II, 67, 3, c.

[51] *In I Post. Analyt.*, lect. 5, n. 5; lect. 20, n. 3; *In I Perih.*, lect. 11, n. 5; *In IV Metaph.*, lect. 16–17; *In XI Metaph.*, lect. 5, nn. 2221–2224. For this principle, usually called the principle of excluded middle term in contradictory opposition, see *In X Metaph.*, lect. 6, n. 2041; *De potentia*, I, 3; *In IV Metaph.*, lect. 3, n. 566; *In I Perih.*, lect. 11, nn. 4–5; lect. 12, n. 6; lect. 13, n. 4.

[52] *In VII Metaph.*, lect. 7, nn. 1440–1446; *S.T.*, I, 2, 3; *C.G.*, I, 13–15. Causality is a self-known evidence contained in every movement: *In III Phys.*, lect. 5, n. 17. For the vocabulary of *participation*, a key notion for the understanding of the principle of causality and finalty, see Geiger, *La participation dans la philosophie de saint Thomas*, pp. 574 ff.

[53] *S.T.*, I, 5, 4; I–II, 1, 1–2; *De potentia*, V, 5; *De veritate*, QQ. XXI–XXII.

[54] Cf. above, pp. 343–350.

[55] *In IV Metaph.*, lect. 6.

[56] *In IV Metaph.*, lect. 3, n. 585; *S.T.*, I–II, 13, 3, c.

[57] *S.T.*, I–II, 66, 5, ad 4 (*BW*, II, p. 514). *De veritate*, X, 12, ad 10 *in contr.*

[58] *De malo*, VI, 1, ad 10; *In I Phys.*, lect. 10, n. 5; *In II Metaph.*, lect. 1, nn. 272, 276; *In lib. Job*, prolog; *In I De anima*, lect. 4, n. 93; *S.T.*, I, 44, 2; 88, 2; I–II, 10, 2, ad 2.

[59] Cf. above, pp. 311–313.

[60] *De veritate*, II, 7, ad 3; *De potentia*, VII, 1, ad 10; *C.G.*, I, 18, *Amplius, omnis*; *In VII Metaph.*, lect. 17, n. 1673.

[61] *C.G.*, I, 71, *Amplius, Deus.*

[62] Aristotle, *Categories*, cap. 10–20, 11b2–14a25. St. Thomas, *In V Metaph.*, lect. 12, nn. 913–935. Cf. Schütz, *Thomas-Lexikon*, ad verb., *oppositio.*

[63] Cf. Schütz, *op cit.*, ad verb., *relatio.*

[64] *In V Metaph.*, lect. 17; *De potentia*, VII, 9–10; *S.T.*, I, 28, 1–3.

[65] *In V Metaph.*, lect. 12, n. 922; *In X Metaph.*, lect. 6, nn. 2037–2058; *De potentia*, VII, 10, ad 4; IX, 7, ad 11; *In IV Metaph.*, lect. 3, nn. 565–566.

[66] Cf. above, pp. 280–306, on the concept of being *qua* being.

[67] *In IV Metaph.*, lect. 3, n. 566. *In IV Metaph.*, lect. 5, n. 595; *De potentia*, I, 3; IX, 7, c. et ad 6, ad 15; *In II Metaph.*, lect. 4, n. 2210; *In I Sent.*, 8, 1, 3; 19, 5, 1, ad 8; *In lib. De Trin.*, I, 3, c. et ad 3; IV, 1, c.; VI, 4, c.; *Quodlibeta*, VIII, 4, c.; X, 1, ad 3; *De veritate*, XXI, 1–3; *S.T.*, I, 16, 4, ad 2; I, 16, 8, c.; I–II, 94, 2 c.

[68] *De veritate*, I, 1. Cf. Régis, *L'Odyssée*, pp. 48–58.

[69] *In IV Metaph.*, lect. 2, n. 533; *S.T.*, I, 85, 5, ad 3.

[70] Cf. above, pp. 369–371.

[71] We will study the formulations numbered (1), (2), (4), and (8), as given above, pp. 379–380.

[72] Cf. above, pp. 283–306.

[73] Cf. above, pp. 283–289.

[74] *S.T.*, I, 16, 2, ad 2; *De veritate*, III, 4, ad 7; XXVII, 3, ad 9; *De potentia*, III, 4, c.

[75] Cf. I.M. Bochenski, *S. Thomae Aq. de modalibus opusculum et doctrinae*, in *Angelicum*, XVII (1940) pp. 180–218. See also *S.T.*, I, 14, 13, ad 3.

76 Burnet, *Early Greek Philosophy*, p. 83, frag. 5.

77 *S.T.*, I, 89, 7, ad 3 (*BW*, I, p. 862). *S.T.*, I, 16, 3, ad 2; 87, 1, c.; *C.G.*, I, 71, *Nec etiam;* II, 98, *Hoc autem sic; De veritate*, I, 1, ad 5; *In I Phys.*, lect. 1, n. 7; *In I Sent.*, 19, 5, 1, ad 2.

78 *In I Post. Analyt.*, lect. 20, n. 6.

79 *In IV Metaph.*, lect. 6–17; *In XI Metaph.*, lect. 5–7.

80 It is not accidental that the father of French Existentialism, Jean-Paul Sartre, has entitled his doctrine, *Being and Nothing*. This is nothing other than a justification of the absurd, resulting in total nausea.

81 *Absurdum* comes from *ab-surdus*, that which does not hear, or is not heard, because indistinct or discordant. Cf. Ernout et Meillet, *Dictionnaire étymologique.*, p. 1007.

82 We must remember that this general formulation of the principle of contradiction is not conceived explicitly, at first, under these universal terms but rather in more particular and concrete ideas. Cf. *In IV Metaph.*, lect. 6, nn. 591–593, 600; *In XI Metaph.*, lect. 5, nn. 2207–2208, 2212; *In I Perih.*, lect. 15, n. 2; *S.T.*, I, 87, 3, ad 1; *In I Post. Analyt.*, lect. 20, n. 8.

83 Cf. above, pp. 321–327.

84 On the significance of the word *foundation*, cf. above, pp. 340–342; and *In V Metaph.*, lect. 9, nn. 895–896, cited above, p. 340, at note 15.

85 *In IV Metaph.*, lect. 6, n. 601; *In XI Metaph.*, lect. 5, n. 2222; *In I Post. Analyt.*, lect. 5, n. 6; lect. 19, n. 3.

86 For this theory of the impossibility of two contraries coexisting in the same subject, see *In I Phys.*, lect. 10–11; *In VIII Phys.*, lect. 15, n. 2; *In I Perih.*, lect. 10, n. 20; lect. 11, n. 16; *De veritate*, XXVI, 10, ad 9; *S.T.*, I, 48, 3, ad 3.

87 *In V Metaph.*, lect. 9, n. 893; *In I Perih.*, lect. 5, nn. 12, 19–22.

88 *In IV Metaph.*, lect. 6, nn. 602–603, 606; lect. 15; *In I Perih.*, lect. 10, nn. 2–22; lect. 11, nn. 6–11.

89 Cf. above, pp. 384–386.

90 For the difference between the exercise and the specification of an act, cf. above, pp. 253–256.

91 Cf. above, note 56; also Lalande, *Vocabulaire technique de la philosophie*, I, p. 466, at *milieu*.

92 *In I Perih.*, lect. 11, n. 5; *In I Post. Analyt.*, lect. 5, n. 5; lect. 10, n. 8; *In IV Metaph.*, lect. 3, n. 566; lect. 14, n. 703; lect. 16; *In X Metaph.*, lect. 6, n. 2041; *De potentia*, I, 3, c.

93 Cf. above, pp. 342–349.

94 Cf. above, pp. 338–342, 357–361, 381–384.

95 Cf. above, pp. 385–388.

96 Cf. above, p. 387.

97 Cf. Hoenen, *La théorie du jugement*, pp. 229–231; Maritain, *Sept leçons sur l'être* (Paris, Téqui, 1933), pp. 109–116; Maréchal, *Au seuil de la métaphysique*, Cahier III, pp. 8, 15.

98 *In I Sent.*, 19, 5, 1; *In II Metaph.*, lect. 2, n. 298; *In IX Metaph.*, lect. 11, n. 1903; *In I Post. Analyt.*, lect. 4, n. 5; *In VIII Phys.*, lect. 3, n. 6; *C.G.*, I, 62,

Sicut enim; De caritate, 9, ad 1; *S.T.*, I–II, 3, 7, c. Cf. Hoenen, *La théorie du jugement*, pp. 72–79.

[99] For the different meanings of the word *ratio* in Aquinas, see Peghaire, *Intellectus et Ratio.*

[100] Cf. above, pp. 340–342.

[101] Cf. Maritain, *Sept leçons sur l'être*, pp. 102–103.

[102] Meyerson, *Le cheminement, De la pensée*, pp. 779–780.

[103] Cf. above, p. 379, note 46.

[104] Cf. Maritain, *Sept leçons sur l'être*, pp. 103–105.

[105] *S.T.*, I, 11, 1, and the parallel passages.

[106] *In V Metaph.*, lect. 11, nn. 906–912; *In X Metaph.*, lect. 4, nn. 1997–2013.

[107] *In V Metaph.*, lect. 11, n. 912. *In VII Metaph.*, lect. 17, n. 1652; *In I Sent.*, 19, 1, 1, ad 2.

[108] *S.T.*, I, 11, 1, c. (*BW*, I, 85).

[109] *De veritate*, I, 1; XXI, 1.

[110] *S.T.*, I, 39, 3, ad 3; *In I Sent.*, 25, 4; *In II Sent.*, 37, 1, 1; *De veritate*, XXII, 1.

[111] Cf. Ernout et Meillet, *Dictionnaire étymologique*, p. 822, ad verb., *res.*

[112] *In IV Metaph.*, lect. 2, nn. 553, 559–560; lect. 3, n. 566; *In VII Metaph.*, lect. 17, nn. 1652–1655; *In X Metaph.*, lect. 4, nn. 1990–1998; lect. 6, n. 2048; *Quodlibeta*, X, 1. Cf. Régis, *L'Odyssée*, pp. 54–55.

[113] *In II Post. Analyt.*, lect. 10; *In I Post. Analyt.*, lect. 25; *In V Metaph.*, lect. 19 and 22.

[114] Cf. above, pp. 334–335, note 80.

[115] *De veritate*, II, 2. Cf. above, p. 383, note 67.

[116] Cf. above, pp. 385–386.

[117] Cf. above, pp. 381–382.

[118] Cf. Ernout et Meillet, *op. cit.*, pp. 1016–1017, ad verb., *tangere.*

[119] *In VI Metaph.*, lect. 2, nn. 1182–1183. Cf. Schütz, *Thomas-Lexikon*, ad verb., *contingens.*

[120] Cf. Ernout et Meillet, *op. cit.*, p. 168, *cedo;* p. 661, *necesse.*

[121] *C.G.*, II, 30; *In V Metaph.*, lect. 6.

[122] Cf. Ernout et Meillet, *op. cit.*, p. 166, *causa.*

[123] *In V Metaph.*, lect. 2–4.

[124] Cf. above, notes 102–104.

[125] *S.T.*, I, 44, 1, ad 1. All theses notions are governed by the idea of *participation;* for the technical vocabulary see Geiger, *La participation*, Appendice I, pp. 457–472.

[126] Cf. above, pp. 340–348.

[127] Cf. above, pp. 140–144.

[128] *De potentia*, II, 1; VII, 11; *De veritate*, XX, 4; *C.G.*, III, 10. Cf. Schütz, *op. cit.*, pp. 31–36, *agens* and *agere.*

[129] Cf. above, Chap. V, on the immanence of the life of knowledge.

[130] *De potentia*, II, 1, c. *In II Sent.*, 34, 1, 3; *In II Sent.*, 37, 3, 2.

[131] Every created agent has to receive in order to be agent; see *S.T.*, I, 104,

5, and parallel texts. This passivity of the created agent is usually expressed by the formula, *physical premotion.*

[132] *In II Sent.,* 1, 2, 1. *In IV Sent.,* 46, 1, 1, sol. 2a; *De potentia,* V, 5, ad 3; *In Ephes.,* cap. 1, lect. 1.

[133] Cf. Schütz, *op. cit.,* pp. 86–87, *bonus.*

[134] Cf. Schütz, *op. cit.,* pp. 419–420; *intentio;* pp. 313–314, *finis.* On the notion of *intention* in the doctrine of St. Thomas, see M.D. Simonin, *La notion d'Intentio dans l'oeuvre de saint Thomas d'Aquin,* in *RSPT,* XIX (1930), pp. 445–463.

[135] Cf. above, pp. 287–288; Schütz, *op. cit.,* pp. 583–591, *perfectio.*

[136] Cf. Schütz, *op. cit.,* pp. 545–546, *operatio;* p. 284, *esse;* also de Finance, *Etre et agir.*

[137] Cf. above, pp. 377–381.

Chapter XI

[1] Cf. above, pp. 342–349.

[2] Cf. above, pp. 349–357.

[3] Cf. above, pp. 357–361.

[4] Cf. above, pp. 176–177.

[5] *In II De anima,* lect. 3.

[6] The word *assensus* is sometimes used by Aquinas in a wide and popular sense, meaning to accept, to agree to a request: *C.G.,* III, 93 and 95; *S.T.,* I–II, 15, 1, ad 3; 33, 1. However, its technical significance is the ordinary one, very often expressed also by such terms as: *accipere, acceptio: De veritate,* XIV, 1, c.; *adhaerere, adhaesio: De veritate,* XIV, 1, ad 3; X, 12, ad 6 *in contrarium; Quodlibeta,* VI, 6, c.; *S.T.,* I, 62, 8, ad 2; 63, 8, ad 2; *approbare, De veritate,* XXIV, 1, ad 20; *inclinare, inhaerere, determinare, determinatio, tenere: De veritate,* XI, 1, c.; XIV, 1, c.; *De div. nom.,* cap. 1, lect. 1; *In III Sent.,* 23, 2, 2, sol. 1. There are also several equivalents of *dissensus,* such as: *declinare, respuere: S.T.,* II–II, 2, 1, c.; *De veritate,* XI, 1, c. We also find the word *assensus* modified by a technical word determining its meaning in a particular way; for example: *praecisus assensus, assensus opinionis: In III Sent.,* 23, 2, 2, sol. 1; 25, 2, 2, sol. 1; *De veritate,* XIV, 1; XVIII, 6; *S.T.,* I, 94, 4; II–II, 2, 9, ad 2; *In IV Sent.,* 49, 1, 3, sol. 2; *In II Sent.,* 39, 1, 2, sol.

[7] *In II Sent.,* 25, 2, 2, sol. *In I Perih.,* lect. 14, n. 24; *In IV Sent.,* 44, 1, 3, sol. 2.

[8] Cf. above, pp. 342–349.

[9] *De veritate,* XIV, 1, c. (*Truth,* Regnery, II, p. 210). See also *In III Sent.,* 23, 2, 2, sol. 1; 24, 1, 1, sol. 2; *De veritate,* XIV, 12, c.; *De malo,* VI, 1, ad 16.

[10] Cf. above, pp. 335–337.

[11] For this distinction between the *exercise* and *object* of an act, see above, pp. 253–259.

[12] *S.T.,* I–II, 17, 6, c. (*BW,* II, pp. 310–311); II–II, 2, 9, ad 2; 9, 1, c.; *In Joan.,* cap. 8, lect. 4, n. 1.

[13] *In III Sent.*, 11, 4, ad 6. *S.T.*, II–II, 1, 5. Cf. above, pp. 333–336, the division of enunciations.

[14] *In I Perih.*, lect. 14, n. 24; *In II Sent.*, 7, 1, 1; *In IV Sent.*, 49, 1, 3, sol. 2; *In lib. De Trin.*, II, 2, ad 4; III, 1, ad 1; *De malo*, XVI, 7, ad 18; *In III Sent.*, 17, 2; 24, 2; *S.T.*, II–II, 2, 9; 1, 5, ad 4; 5, 3, c.

[15] *S.T.*, I–II, 17, 6, c. (*BW*, II, p. 311). *De malo*, XIV, 5, c.

[16] Cf. above, pp. 312.

[17] By opposition to the world of science in which the gold standard of truth has been replaced by probability; cf. above, p. 73.

[18] *In II Sent.*, 25, 1, 2, sol.

[19] *In III Sent.*, 23, 2, 2, sol. 1; *In I Perih.*, lect. 14, n. 24; *De veritate*, XIV, 1.

[20] *De veritate*, XIV, 1, c. (*Truth*, Regnery, II, p. 209).

[21] Cf. above, pp. 346–348.

[22] *De veritate*, XIV, 1, c.

[23] Cf. above, pp. 25–31. See also *In X Metaph.*, lect. 7, n. 2060, for the technical meaning of the word *utrum* in a context of contradictory opposition.

[24] *De veritate*, XIV, 1 (*Truth*, Regnery, II, p. 209). *In III Sent.*, 17, 2, sol. 1.

[25] Cf. above, pp. 373–377.

[26] On the technical meaning of *cogitatio*, see *S.T.*, II–II, 2, 1. Cf. Peghaire, *Intellectus et ratio*, pp. 85–103; Chenu, *Collatio, Collectio*, in *RSPT*, XIV (1927), pp. 435–446; G. Klubertanz, "St. Thomas and the Knowledge of the Singular," *New Scholasticism*, XXVI (1952), pp. 135–166.

[27] *De veritate*, XIV, 1, c. (*Truth*, Regnery, II, p. 210). XI, 1, c.

[28] *S.T.*, I–II, 17, 6, c. *ad fin.* and the parallel texts.

[29] *In IV Metaph.*, lect. 6, n. 605; *In I Sent.*, 3, 1, 2, c.

[30] *In VI Ethic.*, lect. 2, n. 1128. *In III Sent.*, 23, 2, 2, sol. 1; 24, 1, 2, sol. 2; *De veritate*, XIV, 1, c.; 12, c.

[31] Cf. F.M. Tyrrell, *The Role of Assent in Judgment* (Washington, Cath. U. Press, 1948), pp. 67 ff., 144 ff.; "The Nature and Function of Judgment," *New Scholasticism*, XXVI (1952), pp. 397–423.

[32] *S.T.*, I, 17, and parallel passages. Cf. Schütz, *Thomas-Lexikon*, ad verb., *ignorantia, error*.

[33] *In I Sent.*, 19, 5, 3, ad 3; *In III Sent.*, 11, 4, ad 6; 12, 1, 1; *De virtut. in comm.*, 12; *C.G.*, I, 76, *Item contingens*.

[34] *In II Sent.*, 25, 1, 2, sol. Cf. above, pp. 406–407.

[35] *De veritate*, XVIII, 6; *De malo*, XVI, 6; *In I Post. Analyt.*, lect. 44, n. 5. Cf. Roland-Gosselin, *Erreur et péché*, in *Rev. de Philos.*, XXXV (1928), pp. 466–478; *La théorie thomiste de l'erreur*, in *Mélanges thomistes*, pp. 253–274.

[36] *C.G.*, III, 50 (*BW*, II, p. 90); *De veritate*, 1, 5, ad 5.

[37] Etymologically, the word *sententia* means submission. Cf. Ernout et Meillet, *Dictionnaire étymologique*, pp. 276–278, *Do* and *Condo*.

[38] Cf. above, Chap. VIII, note 80.

[39] *In V Metaph.*, lect. 9, nn. 891–892. See also *Opusculum de propositionibus modalibus*, ed. Bochenski.

[40] *C.G.*, I, 67, *Item contingens, Adhuc.* Cf. A. Gardeil, *La certitude probable*,

in *RSPT*, V (1911), pp. 237–266; T. Deman, *Probabilis*, in *RSPT*, XXII (1933), pp. 260–290.

[41] Cf. above, pp. 409–411.

[42] *In IV Metaph.*, lect. 6, nn. 600–606.

[43] Cf. above, Chap. X, note 48.

[44] Cf. above, Chap. X, note 50.

[45] *In II Sent.*, 7, 1, 1; *In IV Metaph.*, lect. 6, n. 603; *In I Post. Analyt.*, lect. 19, nn. 2–3; lect. 20, n. 6. Cf. above, pp. 372–381.

[46] *S.T.*, II–II, 1, 5, ad 4 (*BW*, II, p. 1062). *In I Post. Analyt.*, lect. 2.

[47] Cf. above, pp. 334–335.

[48] *In III Sent.*, 10, 1, 1, sol.; 11, 4, ad 6. Cf. above, Chap. X, note 38, for references to texts on the *per se* predicate.

[49] Certitude was the great preoccupation of Descartes and Kant, as we have seen, above, pp. 33–38; it has also been the great worry of the Neo-Scholastics, above, pp. 75–78.

[50] For the importance of this notion in Thomism, see F.A. Cunningham, "*Certitudo* in St. Thomas Aquinas," *The Modern Schoolman*, XXX (1953), pp. 297–324.

[51] *C.G.*, III, 39, *Praeterea* (*BW*, II, p. 63). *De veritate*, II, 1, ad 4.

[52] Cf. above, pp. 405–415.

[53] *Quodlibeta*, VI, 6, c. *In Hebraeos*, cap. 11, lect. 1.

[54] Cf. Boisacq, *Dictionnaire étymologique*, p. 39; Ernout et Meillet, *Dictionnaire étymologique*, pp. 177–179.

[55] Cf. Régis, *L'Opinion selon Aristote*, pp. 185–200.

[56] *De ente et essentia*, cap. 1; *In VI Metaph.*, lect. 1, nn. 1145–1146.

[57] *In I Metaph.*, lect. 2, n. 47.

[58] *In X Metaph.*, lect. 2, n. 1945.

[59] *In XI Metaph.*, lect. 7, nn. 2249, 2256–2262; *In lib. De Trin.*, V, 1; *In I Post. Analyt.*, lect. 1, nn. 3–8.

[60] *S.T.*, II–II, 18, 4, c. *In III Sent.*, 26, 2, 4, sol. et ad 2; *De spe*, 2, ad 10; *S.T.*, I–II, 40, 2 ad 3.

[61] *In III Sent.*, 23, 2, 2, sol. 3. *In III Sent.*, 26, 2, 1; 14, 3, sol. 2 et 5. In this last text, one type of certitude is said to depend completely on the agent intellect.

[62] Cf. above, Chap. X, note 19.

[63] Cf. above, pp. 140–144.

[64] Cf. above, pp. 312–314.

[65] Cf. above, pp. 283–295.

[66] *In III Sent.*, 27, 1, 2, c.

[67] *In I Phys.*, lect. 10, n. 5. *In I Metaph.*, lect. 17, n. 272; *In II Metaph.*, lect. 1, nn. 276–288; *In II Sent.*, 39, 1, 2; *De veritate*, XV, 2, ad 3; *Quaest. de anima*, 13, ad 7; *C.G.*, III, 25, *Item, Amplius*; 26, *Quod autem*; *S.T.*, I–II, 56, 3, ad 2; 18, 6, c.

[68] *De veritate*, I, 5, obj. 5, et ad 5; Tyrrell, "Nature and Function of the Act of Judgment," *New Scholasticism*, XXVI (1952), pp. 403–409.

⁶⁹ *In I Post. Analyt.*, lect. 19, n. 3; *In IV Metaph.*, lect. 6, n. 599; *In III Sent.*, 23, 2, 2, sol. 1.

⁷⁰ *In I Post. Analyt.*, lect. 19, nn. 2–3; *C.G.*, III, 43, *Ostendit enim; In IV Metaph.*, lect. 6, nn. 597, 603; *In I Phys.*, lect. 10, n. 3.

⁷¹ *In III Sent.*, 27, 1, 2, ad 3.

⁷² *In III Sent.*, 27, 1, 3, ad 3. *S.T.*, I–II, 32, 3, c.; 33, 2.

⁷³ *In III Sent.*, 23, 2, 2, sol. 2; *De veritate*, XVIII, 6; XXIV, 1, ad 18; XXIII, 4, ad 11; *S.T.*, I–II, 10, 2, c. et ad 2; 14, 6, ad 1.

⁷⁴ For the relations between *limpiditas* and *certitudo veritatis*, see *In III Sent.*, 14, 3, sol. 2 et 5.

⁷⁵ Cf. above, p. 411.

⁷⁶ *De veritate*, XIV, 9, c.; *In III Sent.*, 27, 1, 3, ad 1; 23, 2, 3, sol. 2.

⁷⁷ *De veritate*, XIV, 1 et 9; *In III Sent.*, 23, 2, 2, sol. 1; *S.T.*, II–II, 2, 1.

⁷⁸ *De veritate*, XVIII, 6, c.; *S.T.*, I, 94, 4, c. Cf. Roland-Gosselin, *La théorie thomiste de l'erreur*, in *Mélanges thomistes*, pp. 253–274; *Erreur et péché*, in *Rev. de Philos.*, XXXV (1928), pp. 466–478; Nicholas, *Le problème de l'erreur*, *Revue thomiste*, LII (1952), pp. 328–357, 528–566.

⁷⁹ *In I Perih.*, lect. 14, n. 21; *In III Sent.*, 14, 3, sol. 5; *S.T.*, I, 14, 13, c.; II–II, 4, 8, ad 2; III, 30, 3, ad 2.

⁸⁰ *S.T.*, I–II, 17, 6, c. *S.T.*, II–II, 1, 4; *De veritate*, XI, 1, c.

Chapter XII

¹ Cf. above, pp. 283–306.

² *C.G.*, III, 37, *Non est autem* (*BW*, II, p. 60). *C.G.*, II, 83, *Item, si;* III, 38, *Amplius, cognitio; In I Perih.*, lect. 14, n. 24; *De veritate*, XVIII, 4, c.; *In Joan.*, XV, lect. 3, n. 3.

³ *De veritate*, XVIII, 4, c. (*Truth*, Regnery, II, p. 355). *De veritate*, XI, 1, ad 12; XI, 3, c.; *In II Sent.*, 7, 1, 1, sol.; *In lib. De Trin.*, VI, 4; *S.T.*, I, 94, 3, c.; I–II, 3, 6, c.

⁴ *S.T.*, I–II, 57, 2, c. (*BW*, II, pp. 431–432); *C.G.*, III, 47; *De veritate*, XIV, 4, c.; *In I Perih.*, lect. 14, n. 24.

⁵ Cf. above, pp. 337 ff.

⁶ Cf. above, pp. 162–167, 167–193.

⁷ Cf. above, pp. 311–314.

⁸ *S.T.*, I, 58, 4, c. (*BW*, I, p. 543). *S.T.*, I, 58, 3, c.; II–II, 47, 5, ad 2; *De veritate*, II, 1 ad 4.

⁹ *De veritate*, XV, 1, c. (*Truth*, Regnery, II, p. 272). *S.T.*, I, 60, 2, c.; II–II, 49, 5, ad 2.

¹⁰ Cf. above, pp. 253–260, 314.

¹¹ Cf. above, pp. 258–306.

¹² Cf. above, pp. 311–336.

¹³ Cf. above, pp. 229–232.

¹⁴ Cf. above, pp. 317–323.

[15] *S.T.*, I, 58, 3, ad 1 (*BW*, I, p. 542). *S.T.*, I, 14, 7, c.; *De veritate*, II, 1, ad 4.

[16] Cf. Pegis, *In Umbra Intelligentiae*, in *New Scholasticism*, XIV (1940), pp. 146–180.

[17] *S.T.*, I, 79, 8, c. (*BW*, I, p. 758–759). *S.T.*, I, 60, 2; I–II, 6, 2, c.; II–II, 88, 1, ad 2; 49, 5, ad 2; *De veritate*, X, 13, c.; XVIII, 4.

[18] Cf. above, pp. 277–281.

[19] Cf. above, pp. 334–336.

[20] Cf. above, Chaps. V–VI.

[21] Cf. above, Chap. VIII.

[22] *De veritate*, XIV, 1, c.; IV, 1, ad 1; 2, ad 2; *In I Sent.*, 27, 2, 1, ad 3; *S.T.*, I, 34, 1, ad 2; II–II, 2, 1. Cf. Schütz, *Thomas-Lexikon*, pp. 119–120.

[23] *S.T.*, II–II, 49, 5, ad 3; 53, 4; I–II, 14, 4–6; 57, 2; *In I Sent.*, 3, 4, 1, ad 4; *In II Sent.*, 3, 1, 2, et 6 sol., ad 2; 3, 1, 8, ad 2; cf. Schütz, *op. cit.*, p. 243, *disputatio*; p. 667, *quaestio*.

[24] *S.T.*, I–II, 32, 8; 45, 4; II–II, 47, 1; *In III Sent.*, 14, 1, 3, sol. 3. Cf. Chenu, *Note de lexicographie médiévale*, in *RSPT* (1927), pp. 445 ff.

[25] *In II Post. Analyt.*, lect. 20, n. 11; *In IV Phys.*, lect. 23, n. 4; *S.T.*, I–II, 14, 5; 32, 8; 46, 4; *In III Sent.*, 33, 1, 2, sol. Cf. Schütz, *op. cit.*, p. 129, and p. 234, *disciplina*.

[26] *S.T.*, I, 79, 10, ad 2; 82, 2. Cf. Schütz, *op. cit.*, p. 203.

[27] *S.T.*, I–II, 92, 2; *In I Post. Analyt.*, lect. 1, nn. 11–12. Cf. Schütz, *op. cit.*, pp. 389–390.

[28] *In I Post. Analyt.*, lect. 1, nn. 11–12; *De veritate*, VIII, 15.

[29] Cf. Régis, *Analyse et synthèse*, in *Studia Mediaevalia*, (Bruges, De Tempel, 1948), pp. 322–328.

[30] *Studium* technically implies an activity intermediate between two activities, of which one is effortless because given by nature, the other is also effortless because it is the culmination (*quies*) of the perfect: *C.G.*, III, 37, *Non est autem*; 41, *Adhuc, omnia*; *S.T.*, II–II, 24, 9.

[31] Cf. above, pp. 259–263, 275–282, 311–314.

[32] Cf. above, pp. 140–144.

[33] Cf. above, pp. 294–295.

[34] Cf. above, pp. 311–314.

[35] Cf. above, pp. 170–173.

[36] *S.T.*, I, 79, 8, c. (*BW*, I, p. 759). *De veritate*, XV, 1.

[37] Cf. above, pp. 371–379.

[38] *Quaest. de anima*, 4, ad 6. Cf. above, Chap. XII, note 2.

[39] Cf. above, pp. 264–266.

[40] Cf. above, pp. 284–303.

[41] Cf. above, pp. 329–335.

[42] *S.T.*, I, 39, 3, c. (*BW*, I, p. 368). *In V Metaph.*, lect. 5, n. 817.

[43] *In VII Metaph.*, lect. 17, n. 1674.

[44] *S.T.*, I, 42, 3, c. (*BW*, I, p. 407). Cf. Schütz, *op. cit.*, pp. 553–557.

[45] *In V Metaph.*, lect. 1–2, nn. 754–762.

[46] *In V Metaph.*, lect. 2, nn. 763–782.

[47] *In V Metaph.*, lect. 3, nn. 783–794.

[48] *In V Metaph.*, lect. 6, nn. 827–841. Cf. *C.G.*, II, 30.

[49] On the realistic character of scientific laws, see Meyerson, *Le cheminement de la pensée*, pp. 139–156.

[50] Lévy-Bruhl, L. *La morale et la science des moeurs* (Paris, Alcan, 1927), p. 189.

[51] Cf. above, pp. 151–153.

[52] Cf. above, pp. 375–377.

[53] Cf. above, pp. 59–61.

[54] Cf. above, pp. 135–140.

[55] Cf. above, pp. 284–296.

[56] Cf. above, pp. 333–336.

[57] Cf. above, pp. 371–403.

[58] Cf. above, pp. 340–349.

[59] Cf. above, Chap. V–VI, in toto.

[60] Cf. above, pp. 290–293; and Chap. IV, note 102, for a more complete set of texts.

[61] Cf. above, pp. 415–423. Plato had already discovered and described the opposition between these two kinds of truths: *Republic*, Bk. VII, 516C–517B.

[62] Cf. above, Part Two: Prologue, note 6.

[63] Cf. Eddington, *The Philosophy of Physical Science*, pp. 115–117, 152–169. Cf. also above, pp. 204–207.

[64] F.H. Bradley, *Appearance and Reality* (London, Macmillan, 1893), p. 493.

[65] Cf. above, Part Two: Prologue, notes 5, 6.

[66] For a complete bibliography on methods in mathematics and science, see Meyerson, *Le cheminement de la pensée*, pp. 297–459, 463–673.

[67] The word *causal* is equivocal for the modern mind because it has been emptied of its Scholastic signification of real and ontological dependence between two realities; this meaning has been replaced by that of pure chronological succession of phenomena. For an objective study of this development, see Meyerson, *Identité et réalité*, pp. 1–54.

[68] *In I Post. Analyt.*, lect. 1, nn. 5–6; lect. 4 and 17–25.

[69] Cf. above, pp. 372–381, 405–415.

[70] Cf. Geiger, *La participation*, pp. 364–398, 457–475.

[71] *S.T.*, I, 79, 8, c. (*BW*, I, p. 759). *De veritate*, X, 8, c.; *In III Sent.*, 34, 1, 2, sol.; 4, sol.; *S.T.*, II–II, 88, 1, ad 2. Cf. above, pp. 371–377.

[72] *S.T.*, I, 60, 2, c.; *In I Sent.*, 17, 1, 3, sol.; *In III Sent.*, 33, 1, 2, sol.; *De veritate*, XVIII, 4, c.; *In I Post. Analyt.*, lect. 15, nn. 3–4; lect. 5, n. 6; lect. 20, n. 4; lect. 43, n. 13; *S.T.*, I–II, 57, 2, c. Cf. above, pp. 371–377.

[73] *In I Post. Analyt.*, lect. 17, nn. 1–3; lect. 43, nn. 5, 9, 11; lect. 4, nn. 5–16; *In I Sent.*, 44, 1, 3, ad 5; *In II Sent.*, 39, 3, 2, sol.; *S.T.*, I–II, 57, 2; II–II, 9, 2.

[74] *In I Post. Analyt.*, lect. 5, nn. 6–7.

[75] *De veritate*, X, 12, c. (*Truth*, Regnery, II, p. 68). Cf. above, Chap. X, note 38.

[76] *In I Post. Analyt.*, lect. 43, nn. 6, 10, 11, 13; *In lib. De Trin.*, II, 2, ad 7.

[77] *In I Post. Analyt.*, lect. 17, nn. 4–6; lect. 20, nn. 4–6; *In IV Metaph.*, lect. 5, nn. 590–595; *In XI Metaph.*, lect. 4, n. 2210; *S.T.*, I–II, 57, 2; 66, 5, ad 4.

[78] *In II Metaph.*, lect. 2, nn. 292–294; *In X Metaph.*, lect. 2, nn. 1956–1960; C.G., I, 42; *Quaest. de anima*, 7. On the relation of dependence between the imperfect and the perfect, or a first and second principle in the doctrine of St. Thomas, cf. Geiger, *La participation*, pp. 469–472.

[79] *In IV Metaph.*, lect. 6, n. 605. *In XI Metaph.*, lect. 5, n. 2211; *De veritate*, I, 1, c.; C.G., II, 83, *Adhuc, cum.*

[80] *In I Post. Analyt.*, lect. 17, nn. 5–8; lect. 43, nn. 6, 10, 11, 16; *In III Metaph.*, lect. 5, nn. 391–392; *In IV Metaph.*, lect. 5, nn. 591–592; *In XI Metaph.*, lect. 4, nn. 2206–2208; *In II Sent.*, 39, 3, 2, sol.; *Quodlibeta*, III, 26, ad 1.

[81] Cf. above, pp. 432–441.

[82] *In I Post. Analyt.*, lect. 1, nn. 1–2.

[83] Cf. *Entretien avec Burman* (A-T, V, p. 175); *Discours de la méthode* (A-T, VI, p. 17); *Regulae*, XIV (A-T, X, pp. 430–440); *Secundae Responsiones* (A-T, VII, 155–156); *Regulae, II–II* (A-T, X, pp. 365–373); *Lettre à Mersenne*, (A-T, III, pp. 339–340).

[84] *Secundae Responsiones* (A-T, VII, p. 156); *Discours*, (A-T, VI, p. 17); *Regulae*, IV, (A-T, X, pp. 373–377).

[85] Cf. Régis, *Analyse et synthèse*, in *Studia mediaevalia* (Bruges, De Tempel, 1948), pp. 303–304, 313–329.

[86] Cf. Ernout et Meillet, *Dictionnaire étymologique*, pp. 567, 916, 954.

[87] F., Mullachius, *Fragmenta Philosophorum Graecorum* (Paris, 1867), II, p. 245.

[88] For the exact meaning of the expression in modern mathematical language, see Brunschwicq, *Les etapes de la philosophie mathématique* (Paris, Alcan, 1929), pp. 419–420.

[89] Mullachius, *op. cit.*, p. 246.

[90] *Discours de la méthode* (A-T, VI, p. 19); *Regulae*, III, (A-T, X, pp. 369–370).

[91] Cf. *In Top. Ciceronis*, I (PL, 64, 1047 B-C); *De Diff. Topicis*, I (PL, 64, 1174 C).

[92] Cf. *De divisione naturae*, II, 1 (PL, 122, 526).

[93] Cf. *In I Post.*, Tr. 2, cap. 3 (ed. Borgnet, I, 528b).

[94] *In lib. de Praedicabilibus*, Tr. 1, cap. 3 (ed. Borgnet, I, 3b); *In I Prior. Analyt.*, Tr. 1, cap. 1 (*ibid.*, 290a); cap. 2 (*ibid.*, 290b); *In I Post. Analyt.*, Tr. 1, cap. 1 (*ibid.*, 513b); *In I Top.*, Tr. 1, cap. 1 (*ibid.*, 658b); *In I Elench.*, Tr. 1, cap. 1 (*ibid.*, 840b).

[95] For Descartes' distinction of *explanation, demonstration*, and *proof*, see Gilson, *Discours de la méthode*, pp. 472–473.

[96] *De veritate*, II, 7, ad 3; *De potentia*, VII, 1, ad 10; C.G., II, 58, *Adhuc*; I, 18.

[97] *In VII Metaph.*, lect. 17, n. 1673.

[98] *In I Phys.*, lect. 1, nn. 7–11; *In I Post. Analyt.*, lect. 4, nn. 15–16; *In I Perih.*, lect. 6–8; *S.T.*, I, 16–17; 85, 3.

[99] For this vocabulary in the works of St. Thomas, see Régis, *Analyse et synthèse, loc. cit.*, p. 315, notes 1–4.

[100] Cf. *ibid.*, pp. 315–316, text and notes.

[101] *Ibid.*, p. 316, notes 1–4.

[102] *In II Sent.*, 22, 1, 1, ad 2; *In lib. De divin. nom.*, cap. 1, lect. 2; *In I Phys.*, lect. 13, n. 2; lect. 14, n. 11; *S.T.*, I, 79, 9; *In lib. De Trin.*, VI, 1, ad 3.

[103] Cf. above, pp. 328–335.

[104] Cf. above, pp. 341–357.

[105] Cf. above, pp. 128–134, 432–436.

[106] *S.T.*, I–II, 57, 2, c. (*BW*, II, pp. 431–432). *S.T.*, II–II, 9, 2, c.; *In lib. De Trin.*, VI, 4, c.

[107] *S.T.*, I–II 14, 5, c. (*BW*, II, p. 291). *In III Sent.*, 34, 1, 2, sol.; *In II Metaph.*, lect. 1, n. 278; *De veritate*, XVII, 1, c.

[108] *In I Metaph.*, lect. 2, n. 46; *In II Metaph.*, lect. 1, n. 278; *In I Phys.*, lect. 1, nn. 7–9; *In I Post. Analyt.*, lect. 35, n. 2; lect. 41, n. 8; *In lib. De divin. nom.*, 7, lect. 2; *S.T.*, I, 85, 3; 95, 8. Cf. above, pp. 443–445.

[109] *In Lib. De Trin.*, VI, 1, ad prim. quaest. (St. Thomas Aquinas, *The Division and Methods of the Sciences*, trans. by A. Maurer, Toronto, Pontifical Institute of Mediaeval Studies, 1953, p. 52; hereafter cited as *Division and Methods*, PIMS). This answer simply contradicts Descartes' position: see *Discours, de la méthode* (A-T, VI, pp. 8, 18); *Regulae*, II, (A-T, X, pp. 362–363); *Regulae*, III, (A-T, X, pp. 367–369).

[110] *In Lib. De Trin.*, loc. cit (*Division and Methods*, PIMS, pp. 52–53). *In I Post. Analyt.*, lect. 4, n. 16; lect. 13, n. 11; lect. 15, nn. 1–6; lect. 23–25; *S.T.*, I, 2, 2, et 7, ad 1. Cf. Schütz, *Thomas-Lexikon*, p. 217, *demonstratio;* p. 675, *quia.*

[111] *In lib. De Trin.*, VI, 4 (*Division and Methods*, PIMS, p. 77). *In lib. De Trin.*, II, 2; *C.G.*, III, 49 and 56.

[112] Cf. above, pp. 289–298.

[113] *In lib. De Trin.* VI, 4 (*Division and Methods*, PIMS, p. 76). *In lib. De Trin.*, V, 4; *In I Post. Analyt.*, lect. 41, n. 8; *C.G.*, III, 39, 42, 49 et 50; *De veritate*, XVIII, 2, et 5; *S.T.*, I, 2, 2; I–II, 3, 8.

[114] *In lib. De Trin.*, II, 2, ad 1; *In VI Ethic.*, lect. 5, nn. 1180–1183; *S.T.*, II–II, 9, 2, c. and ad 3; *In III Sent.*, 35, 2, 1, 1, ad 1; 35, 2, 1, 2; 35, 1, 3, 3, ad 1.

[115] *S.T.*, I, 79, 9, c. (*BW*, I, p. 760). *In II Sent.*, 2, 2, sol.

[116] *S.T.*, I, 2, 2, c. (*BW*, I, pp. 20–21). *C.G.*, III, 49. In Descartes' method, we find exactly the contradictory, the knowledge of the quiddity preceding that of existence. See Gilson, *Discours, de la méthode*, p. 342.

[117] Cf. above, pp. 328–335, 357–359.

[118] *S.T.*, I, 2, 3, c.; 85, 8; *C.G.*, III, 56, *Amplius, nulla; In lib. De Trin.*, I, 3; *In lib. De divin. nom.*, cap. 8, lect. 2; *In I Metaph.*, lect. 2, n. 46.

[119] Cf. above, pp. 193 ff.

[120] Cf. above, pp. 351–357; *In lib. De Trin.*, VI, 3.

[121] Cf. above, pp. 442–447.

[122] *S.T.*, I, 14, 7, c. (*BW*, I, p. 146). *S.T.*, I, 58, 3; *De veritate*, XVIII, 2, ad 1; XV, 1.

[123] *S.T.*, I–II, 14, 5, c. (*BW*, II, p. 291). *S.T.*, I, 79, 9; II–II, 9, 3; *In I Post. Analyt.*, lect. 23–25; *In lib. De Trin.*, VI, 1.

[124] Cf. above, pp. 327–334.

[125] Cf. above, pp. 213–220, 432–435.

[126] *In lib. De Trin.*, VI, 1, *ad tert. quaest.* (*Division and Methods*, PIMS, pp. 58–59). For the technical meaning of *universal*, as used in this context; cf. above, Chap. VII, notes 135, 184–186.

[127] Cf. Meyerson, *Identité et réalité*, pp. 1–54. This confusion regarding *cause* was denounced by Plato, *Phaedo*, 47A. Cf. H. Dolch, *Kausalität*, pp. 93–222.

[128] Cf. H. Poincaré, *Leçons sur la théorie mathématique* (Paris, Alcan, 1898), p. 1 ff.; P. Duhem, *La théorie physique* (Paris, Alcan, 1906), p. 26; Descartes, *Discours de la méthode*, IV (A–T, VI, p. 76); Gilson, *Commentaire sur le discours*, pp. 472–473.

[129] Cf. M. Planck, *Die Einheit des physikalischen Weltbildes* (Leipzig, 1909), p. 36.

[130] Duhem, *La théorie physique*, pp. 46–47; Meyerson, *Le cheminement, de la pensée*, pp. 297–409, 463–673.

[131] *In I Perih.*, lect. 1, n. 8; *In I De caelo*, lect. 3, nn. 7, 10; *In II De caelo*, lect. 17, n. 2.

[132] *S.T.*, I, 32, 1, ad 2 (*BW*, I, p. 318).

[133] *S.T.*, I, 2, 3; 96, 3, obj. 3; I–II, 75, 1; *C.G.*, I, 13.

[134] *In I Ethic.*, lect. 1, nn. 2–5.

[135] On this see Geiger, *La participation*, pp. 364–398.

[136] Cf. above, pp. 369–373.

[137] Cf. above, pp. 373–381.

[138] Cf. above, Part Two: Prologue, notes 3–5; Chap. VI, notes 67–69.

[139] Cf. above, pp. 284–306.

[140] *De veritate*, XVIII, 6 (*Truth*, Regnery, II, p. 370). *De veritate*, XIV, 8–9; *In III Sent.*, 23, 2, 3, sol. 3, et ad 3; *S.T.*, I, 16, 6, ad 1. Cf. above, pp. 311–314.

[141] *In III Sent.*, 17, 1, 1, sol. 3, et ad 3; *In III Sent.*, 23, 2, 3, sol. 2; *C.G.*, I, 67, *Item, contingens*; *S.T.*, I, 10, 3, ad 3; 79, 1, ad 3. Cf. above, Chap. XI, note 33.

[142] *De veritate*, XIV, 8 (*Truth*, Regnery, II, p. 244). *S.T.*, I–II, 52, 3; 57, 1–2, et 5, ad 3.

[143] Cf. above, pp. 404–426.

[144] Cf. above, pp. 406–415.

[145] *De veritate*, XIV, 9 (*Truth*, Regnery, II, p. 249). *In III Sent.*, 33, 1, 9, sol. 3.

[146] Cf. above, pp. 424–429.

[147] The most important of these terms are *apprehendere, percipere, capere, accipere, invenire.*

[148] *S.T.*, I–II, 68, 4 (*BW*, II, p. 534). *S.T.*, I–II, 57, 6; II–II, 9, 1; *In III Sent.*, 35, 2, 2, sol. 3; *De veritate*, XV, 8–9; *In VI Ethic.*, lect. 2, n. 1128.

[149] *S.T.*, I, 79, 8 (*BW*, I, p. 759). *In III sent.*, 34, 1, 2, sol., et 4, sol.; *De veritate*, X, 8–9.

[150] *De veritate*, XV, 1, c. (*Truth*, Regnery, II, p. 273).

[151] *De veritate*, X, 8, ad 10 (*Truth*, Regnery, II, p. 43).

[152] *De veritate*, XVI, 2, c. (*Truth*, Regnery, II, p. 309). *De veritate*, XVII, 1; *In lib. De divin. nom.*, cap. 4, lect. 7; *S.T.*, I, 79, 9, ad 4; 10, ad 3.

[153] *De veritate*, XV, 1, ad 4, et 3, c. (*Truth*, Regnery, II, p. 276). *In II Sent.*, 9, 1, 8, ad 1; *In III Sent.*, 35, 1, 2, sol. 2; 35, 2, 2, sol. 1.

[154] Cf. above, pp. 369–377.

[155] *De veritate*, XI, 1, ad 13 (*Truth*, Regnery, II, p. 86). *De spirit. creat.*, 9, ad 7.

[156] *De veritate*, XIV, 9, c. (*Truth*, Regnery, II, p. 250). *De veritate*, II, 2, c.; *In II Sent.*, 24, 2, 3, ad 4; *In IV Metaph.*, lect. 6, nn. 603, 607; *In I Post. Analyt.*, lect. 35, n. 2; *In II Post. Analyt.*, lect. 4, n. 2; *S.T.*, II–II, 51, 2, ad 3, et 4, ad 2; 53, 4; 57, 6, ad 3. Cf. above, Chap. XI, note 14.

[157] Cf. above, pp. 425–431, 443–447.

[158] Cf. above, pp. 438–441.

[159] Cf. above, pp. 376–383.

[160] *De veritate*, X, 8–9; *S.T.*, I, 75; and the whole *Quaestio De anima*.

[161] *Quodlibeta*, IV, 16, ad 1. *S.T.*, I–II, 3, 8.

[162] Cf. above, pp. 372–376.

[163] *De veritate*, XVI, 2, c.; *De veritate*, XI, 1, ad 13; *De spirit. creat.*, 9; *In lib. De divin. nom.*, cap. 6, lect. 7.

[164] Cf. above, pp. 370–375.

[165] *S.T.*, I–II, 66, 5, ad 4 (*BW*, II, p. 514). *De veritate*, X, 12, ad 10; *In lib. De Trin.*, VI, 1, *ad prim. quaest.*

[166] Cf. above, pp. 379–402.

[167] Cf. above, pp. 405–415.

Conclusion

[1] *S.T.*, I–II, 57, 2, ad 1, et ad 2. (*BW*, II, p. 432).

[2] *In lib. De Trin.*, VI, 1–4.

[3] *In lib. De Trin.*, VI, 1, statement of the question (*Division and Methods*, PIMS, p. 46).

[4] *In I Ethic.*, lect. 1, n. 2; *In III Phys.*, lect. 8, n. 2; *In I Post. Analyt.*, lect. 1.

[5] *In lib. De Trin.*, VI, 1, *ad prim. quaest.* (*Division and Methods*, PIMS, p. 51). *De veritate*, XII, 3, ad 2; XXVIII, 3, ad 6; *S.T.*, I, 84, 8.

[6] *In lib. De Trin.*, VI, 1, *ad prim. quaest.* (*Division and Methods*, PIMS, p. 51). *In I Post. Analyt.*, lect. 1, nn. 5–6; lect. 20, n. 5; *In IV Metaph.*, lect. 4, nn. 572–577; *S.T.*, I, 32, 1, ad 2; I–II, 57, 6, ad 3; 51, 2, ad 3.

[7] *S.T.*, I, 32, 1, ad 2 (*BW*, I, p. 318). *In I Perih.*, lect. 1, n. 8; lect. 8, n. 9; *In II De caelo*, lect. 17, n. 2; *C.G.*, I, 67, *Praeterea, si*.

[8] *In lib. De Trin.*, VI, 1, *ad prim. quaest.* (*Division and Methods*, PIMS, p. 52).

[9] *De veritate*, XII, 3, ad 2; XXVIII, 3, ad 6; *In lib. De Trin.*, VI, 2; *S.T.*, I, 84, 8. Cf. above, pp. 198–208, 259–275.

[10] For a study of the evolution of this term, see H.I. Marrou, *Doctrina et Disciplina dans la langue des Pères de l'Eglise*, in *Bulletin du Cange*, X (1934), pp. 5–25; Chenu, *Disciplina*, in *RSPT*, XXV (1936), pp. 685–692.

[11] *In lib. De Trin.*, VI, 1, *ad secund. quaest.*

[12] *In lib. De Trin.*, VI, 1, *ad secund. quaest.*, ad 4; et 2, c.

[13] *S.T.*, II–II, 49, 5, ad 2. *S.T.*, II–II, 180, 6, ad 2.

[14] Cf. above, pp. 416–423.

[15] *De veritate*, XV, 1, c. (*Truth*, Regnery, II, p. 273). Cf. above, pp. 460–465.

[16] *In lib. De Trin.*, V, 1, ad 9 (*Division and Methods*, PIMS, p. 16). *In I Perih.*, lect. 18; *C.G.*, I, 12; *S.T.*, I, 2, 2, c.

[17] Cf. above, pp. 450–465.

[18] *S.T.*, I, 85, 8, ad 1 (*BW*, I, p. 819).

[19] *In lib. De Trin.*, VI, 1, *ad tert. quaest. S.T.*, I–II, 57, 2; 66, 4.

[20] *S.T.*, I, 1, 6; I–II, 52, 2; II–II, 8, 8. Cf. Schütz, *Thomas-Lexikon*, pp. 719–722.

[21] Cf. above, Chap. V–VII.

[22] Cf. above, Chap. VIII–IX.

[23] Cf. above, Chap. X–XI.

[24] Cf. above, Chap. XII.

[25] *C.G.*, I, 4, *C.G.*, III, 25, 48, and 60.

[26] *C.G.*, III, 50, *Praeterea.*

INDEX